## Tractate VII

### On Elections According To The Sayings Of The Wise

**Chapter 1** – Page 1

**Chapter 2** – On Those Things Which Will Be Considered In This Tractate - Page 3

**Chapter 3** – On The Root Of Elections - Page 4

**Chapter 4** - On The Adapting Of Particulars – Page 5

**Chapter 5** - That An Election Ought To Agree With The Nature Of The Matter For Which It Is Chosen – Page 6

**Chapter 6** – That The Beginning Of A Matter Is Not Before The Matter Is Incepted – Page 8

**Chapter 7** - How Diverse Planets Are To Be Adapted For Diverse Persons – Page 9

**Chapter 8** - What Kind Of End Should Be Hoped For From The Matter Which We Begin – Page 10

**Chapter 9** - How A Sign Should Be Adapted – Page 11

**Chapter 10** - How A Planet Should Be Adapted – Page 12

**Chapter 11** - Again On The Same – Page 14

**Chapter 12** - On The Weakening Of The Planets – Page 22

**Chapter 13** - On The Particular Things Which Pertain To Elections – Page 23

**Chapter 14** - What Things Are To Be Considered In The Beginnings Of The Elections Of Those Whose Nativities We Know – Page 23

**Chapter 15** - If The Matter About Which A Question Were Proposed By Someone Ought To Be Perfected Or Not, When We Elect For It – Page 25

**Chapter 16** - When That Which Was Incepted Is To Be Believed To Be Perfected – Page 27

**Chapter 17** - From Which Planets The Signification Of Times Is Taken – Page 28

**Chapter 18** - On The Fixed, Common, And Mobile Signs – Page 30

**Chapter 19** - On The Common Signs – Page 30

**Chapter 20** - On The Mobile Signs – Page 31

### Second Part Of This Tractate

**Chapter 1** - On Those Things Which Seem To Pertain To Particular Elections – Page 33

### ON THE FIRST HOUSE

**Chapter 1** - On The Nursing Of Children – Page 34

**Chapter 2** - On Weaning Children From Milk – Page 34

**Chapter 3** - On The Cutting Of Fingernails And Toenails – Page 34

**Chapter 4** - On The Cutting Of Hair And The Shaving Of Beards – Page 34

**Chapter 5** - On The Circumcision Of Children – Page 35

### ON THE SECOND HOUSE

**Chapter 1** - On Lending And Borrowing – Page 36

**Chapter 2** - On Wealth, That It Always Remains In The Possession Of Him For Whom You Elect – Page 36

**Chapter 3** - When The Borrower Does Not Wish That The Loan Be Known – Page 37

**Chapter 4** - On Buying For The Purpose Of Making Money – Page 37

**Chapter 5** - In Other Common Purchases And Common Things – Page 37

**Chapter 6** - If Someone Wants To Sell Some Item To Make Money With Its Price – Page 38

**Chapter 7** - If Someone Wants To Practice Alchemy – Page 38

**Chapter 8** - On Another Manner Of Lending Money – Page 38

**Chapter 9** - On The Entrance Into A House Or Lodgings To Live In It – Page 38

## ON THE THIRD HOUSE

**Chapter 1** - On Short Journeys – Page 40

**Chapter 2** - On The Reconciliation Of Brothers And Other Relatives, And Neighbours And Fellow Citizens – Page 40

**Chapter 3** - On Those Things Which Pertain To A Divine Cult And Knowledge Of Them – Page 40

## ON THE FOURTH HOUSE

**Chapter I** - On The Buying Of Houses Or Inheritances And The Like – Page 41

**Chapter 2** - In The Reconciliation Of A Father With A Son – Page 42

**Chapter 3** - On The Construction Of Cities, Castles, Houses, And Similar Things, And On The Populations Of Lands Or The Fixing Of Fig Trees – Page 42

**Chapter 4** - On The Building Of Houses – Page 43

**Chapter 5** - On The Building Of Churches – Page 44

**Chapter 6** - On The Destruction Of Constructed Buildings – Page 44

**Chapter 7** - On The Renting Or Letting Of Houses, Or Of Lands Or Vineyards, Or Their Fruits, Or Of Any Other Things Which Are Rented Or Leased – Page 45

**Chapter 8** - On The Extension Of Rivers Or Canals And The Like – Page 46

**Chapter 9** - On The Planting Of Trees And Fig Trees – Page 46

**Chapter 10** - On The Sowing Of Seeds Which We Intend To Bear Fruit In The Same Year Or In The Following Year – Page 47

**Chapter 11** - On Beginning To Cultivate Inheritances – Page 47

**Chapter 12** - On The Putting Together Of Boats Or Galleys – Page 47

**Chapter 13** - On The Building Of Mills – Page 48

## ON THE FIFTH HOUSE

**Chapter 1** - On The Reconciliation Of A Son With His Father – Page 50;

**Chapter 2** - On The Sending Of Legates Or Messengers – Page 50

**Chapter 3** - On The Donning Of New Vestments Or Their Tailoring – Page 50

**Chapter 4** - On The Generation Or Conception Of A Son Or Daughter – Page 51

**Chapter 5** - On Taking Out Aborted Children From Women – Page 52

**Chapter 6** - On Handing Over A Son For Instruction – Page 52

**Chapter 7** - On Giving Or Receiving Gifts – Page 53

## ON THE SIXTH HOUSE

**Chapter 1** - On The Healing Of The Sick – Page 54

**Chapter 2** - On The Receiving Of Medical Treatment On The Occasion Of Some Illness – Page 54

**Chapter 3** - On Applying General Cures To The Head – Page 54

**Chapter 4** - If You Want To Apply A Cure To The Nostrils – Page 54

**Chapter 5** - If Someone Wishes To Heal The Eyes – Page 55

**Chapter 6** - On The Particular Cure Of Any Other Official Member – Page 55

**Chapter 7** - On Remedies Which Come About By Surgery – Page 56

**Chapter 8** - On Electing Of An Hour For Someone Wanting To Practice Bloodletting – Page 56

**Chapter 9** - In Giving Purgative (By Defecation) Medicines – Page 57

**Chapter 10** - On Giving Medicines Which Induce Vomiting – Page 57

**Chapter 11** - On Sneezing, Gargling, Vomiting, And Similar Things By Means Of Giving Potions – Page 58

**Chapter 12** - On Entering The Baths Or The Anointing Of Annora Or Psilotrum – Page 58

**Chapter 13** - On The Buying Of Captives, Slaves, And The Like – Page 58

**Chapter 14** - On The Freeing Of Prisoners, Or Captives, Or The Manumission Of Slaves – Page 59

**Chapter 15** - On The Buying Of Animals, Both Those Which Are Ridden, And Others – Page 59

**Chapter 16** - On The Buying Of Birds With Which We Hunt Other Birds – Page 60

**Chapter 17** - On The Approach Of A Doctor To A Patient – Page 60

## ON THE SEVENTH HOUSE

**Chapter 1** - On Marriage, And Those Things Which Pertain To It – Page 61

**Chapter 2** - On The Contracting Of Partnerships And Participations For The Reason Of Utility And Profit – Page 62

**Chapter 3** - On The Electing Of An Hour For Setting Out To War Or Conquering Enemies – Page 62

**Chapter 4** - On The Discovery Of The Combust Hours – Page 64

**Chapter 5** - On The Raising Of Flags, Or Great Banners, Or Pennants – Page 65

**Chapter 6** - On The Procuring Of Arms, War Horses, And Other Instruments Pertaining To War – Page 66

**Chapter 7** - On The Reconciliation Of Enemies Who Made War With Each Other – Page 66

**Chapter 8** - On The Election Of An Hour For The Expelling Or Ejecting Ghosts Or Some Malignant Spirit (Which Is Called The Devil By Some) Impeding Or Infesting Some Place, House, or Person; Or Destroying The Place Of An Oracle Of An Idol Or Similar Things – Page 67

**Chapter 9** - On The Purchasing Of All Things Generally, Both Mobile And Immobile, Under Which The Aforesaid Chapter On The Purchasing Of Animals Can Be Comprehended – Page 67

**Chapter 10** - On The Purchasing Of Seeds For Fields Or Gardens, etc., Such As Grain, Barley, Beans, Winter Wheat, Cabbage, And The Like – Page 68

**Chapter 11** - On The Borrowing And Loaning Of Money – Page 68

**Chapter 12** - On The Hunting Of Birds, Wild Animals, And Fish, By Land And Water – Page 68

**Chapter 13** - On Elections Of Games With Dice, Or Other Games Which Are For The Cause Of Profit – Page 71

**Chapter 14** - How Something Can Be Known About Something Which Is Said Or Handled Between People Speaking Secretly – Page 72

**Chapter 15** - If You Wish To Search For A Thief – Page 72

**Chapter 16** - When The Intention Of The Pursuer Is To Harm Him Who Flees – Page 73

**Chapter 17** - If Someone Wishes To Track Down Something From A Thief Or Detained Person, Or Someone Else Who Is Suspected Of Some Matter That Was Committed – Page 73

## ON THE EIGHTH HOUSE

**Chapter 1** - On The Election Of The Return Of An Absent Person – Page 74

**Chapter 2** - On The Adaptation Of An Election For Inheritances – Page 74

**Chapter 3** - On Making A Will Or Codicil – Page 75

# ON THE NINTH HOUSE

**Chapter 1** - On The Entrance Into Some City Or Some Other Place – Page 76

**Chapter 2** - On The Beginning Of General Journeys Not Pertaining To War – Page 77

**Chapter 9** - On Singing Lessons, As Much For Musicians, As For Others – Page 80

# ON THE TENTH HOUSE

**Chapter 1** - On The Election Of Kings And Noblemen, Or Of Magnates And The Wealthy – Page 81

**Chapter 2** - On Promotion To Kingship Or Dukedom Or Another Dignity Pertaining To Kingship Or Dukedom, Or Any Other Dignity – Page 81

**Chapter 3** - On The Enthronement Of The Kingship Or Dukedom, Or Another Dignity, Or Ascending To Its Seat – Page 81

**Chapter 4** - If Someone Wants To Go And Stay With A King, Or Duke, Or Powerful Person, Or With Another Such Person, Or To Travel With Them – Page 82

**Chapter 5** - If Someone Wants To Make An Enemy Of A King, Or A Duke, Or Someone Similar – Page 83

**Chapter 6** - On Reconciling With A King Or A Duke Or Similar Men – Page 83

**Chapter 7** - On The Taking Away Of Some Dignity – Page 83

**Chapter 8** - On Teaching Morals – Page 83

**Chapter 9** - On Lessons In Fighting, Doing Battle, Or Wrestling – Page 84

**Chapter 10** - On Swimming Lessons – Page 84

**Chapter 11** - On Lessons In All Things Generally – Page 84

# ON THE ELEVENTH HOUSE

**Chapter 1** - On Those Things In Which We Have Hope Or Trust Of Being Praised And Acquiring A Good Reputation – Page 86

**Chapter 2** -If Someone Wishes To Ask Some Person To Love Them – Page 86

**Chapter 3** - If Someone Wants To Seek Some Item From Some Person, Whether It Is Promised To Him Or Not – Page 87

# ON THE TWELFTH HOUSE

**Chapter 1** - On The Racing Of Horses Or Other Animals, Both Rational And Others Running For Prizes – Page 89

**Chapter 2** - On The Purchasing Of Large Animals, Both Of Horses And Others Of Those Which Are Ridden Or Tamed – Page 89

# Tractate VIII

## On The Revolutions Of The Years Of The World

Preface – Page 91

**Chapter 1** - How The Lord Of The Year Is Found – Page 92

**Chapter 2** - On Finding The Significator Of The King – Page 97

**Chapter 3** - When The Lord Of The Ascendant Is The Lord Of The Year, Whence Is Known The Condition Of The King, And His Assistants, And The Commoners, And Of Certain Men, Both Religious And Secular – Page 99

**Chapter 4** - What Is Signified By The Lord Of The Year Or Revolution, In The Places Which It Falls At The Hour Of The Revolution – Page 100

**Chapter 5** - On The Knowledge Of The Accidents Which Are Going To Happen In The Year, And In Which Parts They Ought To Happen – Page 101

**Chapter 6** - How The Earth Is Divided Into Two Primary Divisions – Page 102

**Chapter 7** - How The Second Of Three Other Secondary Divisions – Page 102

**Chapter 8** - How The Earth Is Divided Into Seven Other Divisions – Page 103

**Chapter 9** - How The Sun Is To Be Examined In The Revolution Of A Year, If It Is Diurnal – Page 106

**Chapter 10** - How The Moon Is To Be Examined If The Revolution Is Nocturnal – Page 107

General Delineation – Page 107

**Chapter 11** - On What Each One Of The Seven Planets Signifies In The Ascendant, In A Revolution Of The Year – Page 109

**Chapter 12** - On Saturn And Mars, If They Are Impeded In A Revolution, When They Are Above The Earth – Page 110

**Chapter 13** - On The Planets: When They Enter Into The Degree Of Their Exaltation – Page 111

On Eclipses – Page 112

**Chapter 14** - How The Condition Of The King, And Of The Nobility, And Of The Commoners Is To Be Considered, And What Will Their Condition Be Like – Page 114

**Chapter 15** - Why The King Will Travel, If He Is To Travel – Page 115

**Chapter 16** - Why The Person Of The King Should Be Feared For, If His Significator Is Under The Rays – Page 117

On The Mutual Reception Of The Planets – Page 117

Which Planets Are Friends Of The Lord Of The Ascendant In The Revolution – Page 117

**Chapter 17** - On Those Things Which Ought To Befall The King In The Revolution Of The Year – Page 118

**Chapter 18** - On The Conjunction Of Two Malefics, Saturn Namely And Mars, With Any Planet, In The Degree Of Their Exaltation: What Will Be Signified From It – Page 119

**Chapter 19** – When The Sun And The Moon Are Joined To One Of The Planets, Or Are Separating From One Of Them: What They Signify – Page 119

**Chapter 20** - On The Condition Of The King With Those Placed Under Him – Page 121

**Chapter 21** - On The Particular And Specific Condition Of The King – Page 121

**Chapter 22** - What The Significator Of The King Signifies In An Angular House – Page 121

**Chapter 23** - When The Significator Of The King, Or Any Other Planet, Is Free From Impediments And Moving To Its Exaltation – Page 121

**Chapter 24** - To Know When A Revolution Lasts For The Whole Year, And When For Half A Year, And When For A Quarter Of The Year – Page 122

What The Lord Of The Hour Signifies In A Revolution, And The Part Of Fortune – Page 122

**Chapter 25** - On The Knowledge Of The Accidents Which Are Going To Come In The Climes, From The Hour Of The Revolution – Page 123

**Chapter 26** - What The Lord Of The Year And The Significator Of The King Signify When They Are Well Disposited In The Revolution – Page 123

**Chapter 27** - What The Lord Of The Year And Other Planets Signify If They Are Impeded In The Revolution. – Page 124

**Chapter 28** - On The Knowledge Of The Planetary Significators In The Revolution Of The Year, As Much Of The Significator Of The King, As Of Certain Others – Page 125

**Chapter 29** - On The Condition Of The King And The Condition Of His Substance, And On The Condition Of His Soldiers Or Deputies – Page 125

If The Lord Of The Year Is The Significator Of The King – Page 125

On The Commoners And Their Substance – Page 126

Again On The Significator Of The King, When His Significator Is Mars Or Saturn – Page 126

When A Benefic Rules - 126

**Chapter 30** - On The Impediments Of Malefics, And On Their Aspects: What They Signify; And How Impediments And Impeding Things Can Be Known – Page 126

**Chapter 31** - What Is Signified By The Retrogradation Of The Significator Of The King, Or The Lord Of The Year, Or The Significator Of The Country Folk – Page 127

**Chapter 32** - What Mars And Saturn Signify In The Revolution Of The Year When They Are Badly Disposited – Page 127

**Chapter 33** - If The Lord Of The Ascendant, And The Moon And The Other Significators Are Impeded: What Will Follow From This – Page 128

**Chapter 34** - When War Is Signified In The Revolution Of The Year: Why Will It Be Made Or Incited – Page 128

**Chapter 35** - Which Of The Planets Signify Wars In The Revolution Of The Year, And Which Of Them Is The Dispositor – Page 129

**Chapter 36** - When War Is Signified In The Revolution Of The Year, And If It Is Signified, When Is Victory Signified, And When Flight, Or Total Defeat, And When Peace, Or The Extinction Of The War – Page 130

**Chapter 37** - How It Should Be Elected For Someone Wanting To Go To War – Page 131

**Chapter 38** - Through What Kind Of Men, Or People, Will The War Or Battle Come To Be – Page 131

**Chapter 39-** Whether The Captain Of The Adversary Is Young Or Old – Page 132

**Chapter 40** - If The Significator Of War Is Pacified With The Lord Of The Year: What Will Follow From This – Page 132

**Chapter 41** - What Malefic Planets Signify When They Are In Human Signs In The Revolution – Page 132

**Chapter 42** - On The Matter Which Introduces Fear In The Revolution Of The Year, And What The Malefics Signify In The Angles – Page 133

**Chapter 43** - What Is Signified If The Lord Of The Sign In Which The Lord Of The Year Is Placed Aspects Him, Or If It Does Not Aspect Him – Page 133

**Chapter 44** - On The Revolution Of The Year, When It Is At Sunset – Page 134

**Chapter 45** - If The Lord Of The Ascendant Is Impeded In The Revolution Of The Year: What Follows From It – Page 134

**Chapter 46** - What Follows From The Conjunction Of The Two Malefics With The Lord Of The Year, Or With The Significator Of The King – Page 135

**Chapter 47** - How The Bodies Of The King And The Commoners Are To Be Examined In The Revolution Of The Year – Page 136

**Chapter 48** - Which Of The Planets Signify Kings And Kingdoms, And On The Impediments Of The Four Angles – Page 136

**Chapter 49** - If The Moon Or Mercury Are The Lord Of The Year, Or The Significator Of The King, And Are Aspected By Malefics, What Follows From This; And On The Part Of Fortune And Its Lord – Page 137

**Chapter 50** - On The Lord Of The Year Committing Disposition To The Significator Of The King, What Will Follow From Thence – Page 137

**Chapter 51** - On The Conjunction Of The Caput Draconis With Saturn, And On The Conjunction Of The Cauda With Mars, And What Follows From These Things – Page 138

**Chapter 52** - On The Conjunction Of Mars And Saturn With The Cauda – Page 139

**Chapter 53** - On The Conjunction Of The Two Malefics (Namely, Saturn And Mars), With A Planet In The Degree Of Its Exaltation: What Follows From It – Page 139

**Chapter 54** - On The Lord Of The Fourth, If It Is In The House Of Pilgrimage At The Hour Of The Revolution: What It Signifies – Page 139

**Chapter 55** - What It Signifies When One Planet Commits Its Disposition To Another In The Revolution – Page 140

**Chapter 56** - When A Planet Is The Lord Of The Year, What It Signifies In Every Sign, And In Every Triplicity, And First, On Saturn – Page 140

**Chapter 57** - On The Corporeal Conjunction of Saturn and Jupiter – Page 141

**Chapter 58** - What Is Signified If Mars Is Joined To Saturn In The Revolution, And He Is In Good Condition – Page 142

**Chapter 59** - If The Sun Is Joined To Saturn In The Revolution, And Both Of Them Are In Good Condition – Page 143

**Chapter 60** - If Venus Is Joined To Saturn In The Revolution And They Are In Good Condition – Page 143

**Chapter 61** - On Mercury, If He Is Joined To Saturn In The Revolution, And They Are In Good Condition – Page 143

**Chapter 62** - On The Conjunction Of The Moon With Saturn In The Revolution, If They Are Both In Good Condition – Page 144

**Chapter 63** - What Saturn Signifies In Each Of The Signs, And In Each Of The Triplicities, And In Each Of The Houses, Whether He Is The Lord Of The Year Or Not – Page 144

**Chapter 64** - Saturn In Leo – Page 145

**Chapter 65** - Saturn In Sagittarius – Page 145

**Chapter 66** - Saturn In Taurus And Its Triplicity – Page 146

**Chapter 67** – If The Moon Suffers An Eclipse– Page 146

**Chapter 68** - Saturn In Virgo – Page 147

**Chapter 69** – Saturn In Capricorn – Page 147

**Chapter 70** – Saturn In Gemini And Its Triplicity – Page 147

**Chapter 71** – Saturn In Libra – Page 148

**Chapter 72** – Saturn In Aquarius – Page 148

**Chapter 73** -On Cancer And Its Triplicity, If Saturn Is The Lord Of The Revolution, And Is In It Or Its Triplicity – Page 149

**Chapter 74** – Saturn In Scorpio – Page 149

**Chapter 75** – Saturn In Pisces – Page 150

**Chapter 76** -What Saturn Signifies In Each House In The Revolution Of The Year, As Much Of The World, As Of Nativities, Or Questions, Whether He Is The Lord Of The Year, Or Not. – Page 150

**Chapter 77** -On The Conjunction Of Saturn And Mars In The Revolution: What It Signifies – Page 151

**Chapter 78** -What Jupiter Signifies In A Revolution, In Each Sign, And In Each Triplicity (If He Is The Lord Of The Year); And In Each House, Whether He Is The Lord Of The Year Or Not – Page 152

**Chapter 79** – Jupiter In Leo – Page 153

**Chapter 80** – Jupiter In Sagittarius – Page 153

**Chapter 81** – What Jupiter Signifies In Each And Every Revolution Of The Year, As Much Of The World, As Of A Nativity Or Question, Whether He Is The Lord Of The Year Or Not – Page 153

**Chapter 82** – What Mars Signifies When He Is The Lord Of The Year, In Each And Every Triplicity, And In Each And Every Sign, And In Each And Every House, Whether He Is The Lord Of The Year Or Not – Page 155

**Chapter 83** – Mars In Leo – Page 155

**Chapter 84** – Mars In Sagittarius – Page 156

**Chapter 85** – On Another Nefarious Signification Of Mars – Page 156

Mars In The Houses – Page 156

**Chapter 86** – Mars In Taurus And Its Triplicity – Page 158

**Chapter 87** – Mars In Virgo – Page 158

**Chapter 88** – Mars In Capricorn – Page 158

**Chapter 89** – Mars In Gemini And Its Triplicity – Page 159

**Chapter 90** – Mars In Libra – Page 159

**Chapter 91** – Mars In Aquarius – Page 159

**Chapter 92** – Mars In Cancer And Its Triplicity – Page 160

**Chapter 93** – Mars In Scorpio – Page 160

**Chapter 94** – Mars In Pisces – Page 160

**Chapter 95** – On The Sun, If He Is The Lord Of The Year: What He Signifies – Page 161

**Chapter 96** – What The Sun Signifies In Each And Every House In The Revolution Of The Years Of A Nativity, And In The Years Of The World, And In Nativities, Whether He Is The Lord Of The Year, Or Not – Page 162

**Chapter 97** – On Venus, If She Is The Lord Of The Year: What She Signifies – Page 163

**Chapter 98** – What Venus Signifies In Each And Every House In The Revolution Of The Year, Whether She Is The Lord Of The Year Or Not – Page 163

**Chapter 99** – What Venus Signifies In Each And Every Sign In A Revolution Of The Year – Page 164

**Chapter 100** – On Mercury, If He Is The Lord Of The Year: What He Signifies – Page 166

**Chapter 101** – What Mercury Signifies In Each And Every House, Whether A Revolution Of The World, Whether In Nativities, Or Whether In The Revolution Of A Nativity, Whether He Is The Lord Of The Year, Or Not – Page 168

**Chapter 102** – What The Moon Signifies If She Is Lord Of The Year – Page 169

**Chapter 103** – What The Moon Signifies In The Revolution Of The Year Of The World, In Each And Every House, Or In A Nativity, Or A Revolution Of A Nativity, Whether She Is The Lord Of The Year Or Not – Page 170

**Chapter 104** – What The Caput And Cauda, And Comets Signify In The Revolution Of The Year, Both Of The World And Of A Nativity – Page 172

**Chapter 105** – On Comets – Page 175

**Chapter 106** – What The Caput And Cauda Draconis Signify In Each And Every House, Both In Revolutions, And In Nativities Or Questions – Page 176

**Chapter 107** – What The Cauda Signifies In The Houses – Page 177

**Chapter 108** – What The Fixed Stars Signify In The Revolutions Of The Years, And Nativities, And What They Do In Them – Page 178

**Chapter 109** – On The Peculiar Nature Of The Aforementioned Stars In Each And Every House – Page 179

**Chapter 110** – What The Fortunate Fixed Stars Signify In Nativities, And Questions, And Revolutions Of The Years – Page 185

**Chapter 111** – On The Peculiar Nature Of The Fortunate Stars In The Twelve Houses – Page 186

**Chapter 112** – On The Varieties Of Customs – Page 190

**Chapter 113** – On The Impediments Which The Lord Of The Ascending Sign Of The Revolution Introduces When He Is Impeded (Whether He Is The Lord Of The Year Or Not) – Page 190

**Chapter 114** – On The Impediments Which The Lord Of The Midheaven Will Introduce, If It Is Impeded In The Revolution – Page 192

On The Significations Of Mars In The Revolution – Page 192

**Chapter 115** – How The Evil Or Horrible Accidents Which Are Going To Come In That Year Can Be Known From The Hour Of The Revolution – Page 192

On The Cazimi Of The Sun, According to Albumashar – Page 194

When A Planet Goes Out From Under The Rays Of The Sun, According To Albumashar – Page 194

On The Condition Of The Higher Planets In The Revolution Of The Year Of The World, And Particularly Of Saturn – Page 194

On The Other Planets – Page 195

**Chapter 116** – What The Planets Signify In A Revolution Of The Year In Which A Solar Or Lunar Eclipse Is Supposed To Take Place – Page 195

**Chapter 117** – How One Should Proceed Regarding The Significators Of The King And The Country Folk, According To Albumashar – Page 196

How The Condition Of The King Can Be Examined In That Year – Page 200

The Same On The Two Parts In A Revolution Of The Years Of The World – Page 201

Another Chapter On The Revolution Of The Years Of The World According To Albumashar – Page 201

## On The Projection Of The Parts And Their Significations

**Chapter 1** – What We Should Consider First In Particular Revolutions, And It Is A Chapter Related To The Entire Work – Page 204

**Chapter 2** – On The Parts Of The Seven Planets And On Their Particular Significations, And First On The Part Of The Moon, Which Is Called The Part Of Fortune – Page 205

On The Part Of Future Things, Which Is Called The Part Of The Sun – Page 206

On The Heavy Part, Which Is Called The Part Of Saturn – Page 207

On The Part Of Jupiter Which Is Called The Part Of Blessedness – Page 207

On The Part Of Mars, Which Is Called The Part Of Boldness – Page 208

On The Part Of Venus Which Is Called The Part Of Love And Of Concord. – Page 208

On The Part Of Mercury Which Is Called The Part Of Poverty And Middling Intellect – Page 208

**Chapter 3** – On The Significations Of The Parts Of The Twelve Houses – Page 208

**Chapter 4** – On The Parts Of The First House, That Is The Ascendant, And On Their Extraction And On Their Significations – Page 209

**Chapter 5** – On The Parts Of The Second House And On Their Extraction And On Their Significations – Page 211

**Chapter 6** – On The Parts Of The Three House And On Their Extraction And On Their Significations – Page 212

**Chapter 7** – On The Parts Of The Fourth House And On Their Extraction And On Their Significations – Page 212

**Chapter 8** – On The Parts Of The Five House And On Their Extraction And On Their Significations – Page 214

**Chapter 9** – On The Parts Of The Sixth House And On Their Extraction And On Their Significations – Page 215

**Chapter 10** – On The Parts Of The Seventh House And On Their Extraction And On Their Significations – Page 216

**Chapter 11** – On The Parts Of The Eighth House And On Their Extraction And On Their Significations – Page 218

**Chapter 12** – On The Parts Of The Ninth House And On Their Extraction And On Their Significations – Page 219

**Chapter 13** – On The Parts Of The Tenth House And On Their Extraction And On Their Significations – Page 220

**Chapter 14** – On The Parts Of The Eleventh House And On Their Extraction And On Their Significations – Page 224

**Chapter 15** – On The Parts Of The Twelfth House, And On Their Extraction, And On Their Significations – Page 226

**Chapter 16** – On The Recounting Of Certain Parts According To Albumashar, Of Which Mention Was Not Made Above, Which Are Called "The Fifth Category" – Page 227

**Chapter 17** – On The Knowledge Of Certain Extraordinary Parts, Of Which Mention Was Not Made Above – Page 229

**Chapter 14** – In Which There Is An Example Of The Method Of Extracting Some Of The Parts – Page 230

On The Extraction Of Parts – Page 233

On The Regions Where These Will Be – Page 233

On The Time When They Will Be – Page 233

On The Number Of Significators Of Any Part – Page 233 1

Parts Of Kings And Empires – Page 234

## Tractate IX

### On Nativities And Their Accidents, And Other Things Which Seem To Pertain To Nativities, In General And Particular

**Chapter 1** - Excusing Why This Tractate Has Been Delayed Until Now – Page 236

**Chapter 2** – That Two Things Are Principally Required For The Being Of Every Man – Page 236

On The First Beginning – Page 237

On The Second Beginning – Page 237

**Chapter 3** – How The Condition Of The Native Should Be Examined – Page 238

**Chapter 4** – On The Investigation Of An Unknown Ascending Degree – Page 239

**Chapter 5** – On The Narration Of The Divisions Of Nativities And Certain Accidents Of Theirs – Page 241

**Chapter 6** – On The Causation Of Natives' Stay In The Womb Of The Mother – Page 241

On The Narration Of The Four Species Or Varieties Of Nativities – Page 242

### Second Part

**Chapter 1** – How To Examine Regarding The Four Species Of Nativities, In Order – Page 243

On Finding The Ylem – Page 245

**Chapter 2** – On The Diversity Of Opinions Regarding The Ylem – Page 247

On The Knowledge Of The Alcocoden – Page 248

On The Knowledge Of The Years Of The Native – Page 249

When The Planets Increase The Years – Page 249

When The Planets Decrease Years – Page 249

On The Caput Draconis And Its Cauda – Page 249

On The Direction Of The Degrees To Planets, For Knowing The Accidents Of The Native – Page 250

**Chapter 3** – That All Planets Are Givers Of Years, But Not All Of Them Are Preservers Of Them Simply; But Rather Sometimes They Are Killers, Some Naturally, Some Accidentally, And Likewise The Caput And Cauda – Page 251

**Chapter 4** – On The Knowledge Of The Directions Of The Rays Of The Planets To The Ylem – Page 252

**Chapter 5** – On The Number Of Malefics And Benefics – Page 253

**Chapter 6** – On The Knowledge Of The Life Of The Native, And His Condition According To The Lords Of The Terms – Page 254

### The Third Part

### On The Form And Figure Of The Natives Body: And Likewise On Its Accidents, Generally And Particularly, And On The Qualities Of The Soul And On The Things Adjacent To These

**Chapter 1** – On The Form And Figure Of The Native – Page 256

**Chapter 2** – On Those Things Which Are Outside Of The Body Which Are Not Of Its Substance Nor Of The Substance Of The Soul – Page 257

**Chapter 3** – On The Form And Figure Of The Body Of The Native; And First On Those Which Saturn Bestows – Page 257

**Chapter 4** – On What The Quarters Of The Circle Of The Signs Operate In The Disposition Of The Form And Figure Of The Natives Body, And First On The First Quarter – Page 260

**Chapter 5** – On The Other Aids To The Forms And Figures Of Natives' Bodies, Besides The Aids Of The Quarters – Page 261

**Chapter 6** – On The Form And Figure Of The Native Which Jupiter Bestows – Page 261

**Chapter 7** – On The Form And Figure Of The Natives Body Which Mars Bestows – Page 262

**Chapter 8** – The Form And Figure Of The Natives Body Which The Sun Bestows – Page 263

**Chapter 9** – On The Form And Figure Of The Natives Body Which Venus Bestows – Page 264

**Chapter 10** – On The Form And Figure Of The Body Of The Native Which Mercury Bestows – Page 265

**Chapter 11** – On The Form And Figure Which The Moon Bestows Upon The Native – Page 266

## ON THE FIRST HOUSE

**Chapter 1** – On The Qualities Or Accidents Of The Natives Soul – Page 268

On The Three Superior Planets – Page 268

On The Signifying Stars – Page 268

On The Three Inferior Planets – Page 268

On Venus And Mercury – Page 269

On The Three Superiors – Page 269

On Fixed Signs – Page 269

On Common Signs – Page 269

On Mobile Signs – Page 269

On The Stars Dispositing The Soul Of The Native – Page 270

**Chapter 2** – On The Qualities Of The Natives' Soul Occurring Particularly, According To The Natures And Significations Of The Stars – Page 271

On The Signification Of Saturn If He Is The Sole Dispositor Of The Qualities Of The Native's Soul – Page 271

**Chapter 3** – On The Significations Of Jupiter If He Is The Sole Significator Or Dispositor Of The Qualities Of The Soul – Page 273

**Chapter 4** – The Qualities Of The Soul If Mars Is The Sole Significator – Page 274

**Chapter 5** – If Venus Is The Sole Significatrix Of The Qualities Of The Native' Soul – Page 276

**Chapter 6** – The Qualities Of The Natives Soul If Mercury Is The Sole Significator – Page 276

**Chapter 7** – On The Significations Of The Luminaries Concerning The Qualities Of The Soul Of The Native, And First On The Sun – Page 277

**Chapter 8** – On The Significations Of The Moon Concerning The Qualities Of The Natives' Soul – Page 277

## ON THE SECOND HOUSE

**Chapter 1** – On The Signification Of The Prosperity and Substance Of The Native, And On Its Acquisition – Page 279

**Chapter 2** – From Where The Native Will Acquire Substance, Or Money, And By What Means, And In What Part Of His Life – Page 284

**Chapter 3** – In Which Time Of His Life, And In What Part, The Native Will Acquire Substance – Page 284

**Chapter 4** – Why The Ancients Avoided Certain Of The Mentioned Significators – Page 285

**Chapter 5** – Whence And Because Of What The Native Will Acquire Substance – Page 285

**Chapter 6** – By What Means Will The Native Acquire Substance – Page 287

**Chapter 7** – At What Age Or In Which Part Of His Life The Native Is Going To Acquire Substance – Page 288

**Chapter 8** – When Other Significators Will Increase Or Diminish The Substance Of The Native, With The Triplicity Lords Of The House Of Substance – Page 289

**Chapter 9** – On What Is Signified By The Places Of The Circle – Page 291

The Part Of Fortune In The Dignities Of Different Planets – Page 292

**Chapter 10** – On The Same Topic, According To Aboali – Page 293

**Chapter 11** – On Another, Almost Extraordinary Thing Regarding The Condition Of The Nativity – Page 293

**Chapter 12** – On The Acquisition Of Substance, Again According To Aboali – Page 294

**Chapter 13** – On The Same – Page 296

## ON THE THIRD HOUSE

**Chapter 1** – On The Matter Of Siblings Of Either Sex And Of Their Multitude And Scarcity – Page 297

**Chapter 2** – On The Masculinity And Femininity Of Siblings – Page 297

**Chapter 3** – Who Will Die First Amongst The Siblings, Or Who Will Have A Longer Life – Page 298

**Chapter 4** – On The Matter Of Siblings – Page 299

**Chapter 5** – On The Masculinity Of Natives And Siblings, According To Ptolemy – Page 300

**Chapter 6** – On The Prosperity Of Siblings– Page 300

## ON THE FOURTH HOUSE

**Chapter 1** – On The Condition Of Fathers And Their Accidents, And From Which Place Of The Circle It Is Taken – Page 302

**Chapter 2** – On The Time Of The Things Mentioned Above – Page 302

**Chapter 3** – On The Kind Of Death Of The Father – Page 302

**Chapter 4** – On The Condition Of The Father And Mother – Page 303

**Chapter 5** – On The Condition Of The Father By Direction – Page 303

**Chapter 6** – On The Death Of The Father – Page 305

**Chapter 7** – On The Death Of The Mother – Page 305

**Chapter 8** – On The Knowledge Of The Years Of The Fathers Life – Page 305

**Chapter 9** – On The Length Or Brevity Of The Fathers Life – Page 306

## ON THE FIFTH HOUSE

**Chapter 1** – On The Matter Of Children And Their Condition – Page 307

**Chapter 2** – At What Age The Native Is Going To Have Children – Page 307

**Chapter 3** – On The Multitude Or Scarcity Of Children – Page 308

**Chapter 4** – On The Time Of Children According To Aboali – Page 310

## ON THE SIXTH HOUSE

**Chapter 1** – On The Natives' Slaves And Slavegirls, And Servants Or Assistants; And On Small Animals Which Are Neither Ridden Nor Yoked; And On His Infirmities, And Likewise Illnesses – Page 311

**Chapter 2** – On Domestic Animals And Other Animals Which Are Signified By The Sixth – Page 311

**Chapter 3** – On The Infirmity Of The Native And On His Illnesses – Page 312

**Chapter 4** – At What Age These Things Will Happen – Page 314

**Chapter 5** – In Which Body Part The Above Mentioned Things Will Occur – Page 315

**Chapter 6** – Again On The Above Mentioned Impediments - Where Will Be, And For What Reason Will They Will Occur, According To Ptolemy – Page 316

**Chapter 7** – On The Impediments Of The Soul, And Of Its Infirmities And Ways – Page 317

## ON THE SEVENTH HOUSE

**Chapter 1** – On The Native's Marriages, And His Associates, And His Enemies Openly Opposing Him – Page 320

**Chapter 2** – On The Manner Of The Natives Sexual Intercourse – Page 321

**Chapter 3** – What The Native's Wife Will Be Like – Page 321

**Chapter 4** – On The Time When The Wife Will Be Taken, And On The Number Of Wives, And On Their Durability In General – Page 323

On The Marriage Of Women – Page 323

What Will Her Husband Be Like – Page 323

**Chapter 5** – How The Marriage May Be Perceived By The Significations Of Venus, Mars, And Saturn – Page 325

**Chapter 6** – What Will Happen To The Native Because Of His Associates, And From His Associates, And Those Participating With Him – Page 327

**Chapter 7** – What Will Happen To The Native From Enemies Openly Opposing Him, Or Because Of Them, And Whether He Will Have Them Or Not – Page 328

## ON THE EIGHTH HOUSE

**Chapter 1** – On The Native's Death, And On The Accidents By Which Death Usually Occurs – Page 330

## ON THE NINTH HOUSE

**Chapter 1** – On The Religion And Faith Of The Native, And His Knowledge, And Likewise On His Pilgrimages Or Long Journeys – Page 334

**Chapter 2** – On The Natives' Faith And The Depth Of His Knowledge – Page 334

**Chapter 3** – On The Pilgrimages Of The Native, And On His Long Journeys – Page 337

**Chapter 4** – Which Of The Planets Assist Journeys And Which Don't – Page 338

## ON THE TENTH HOUSE

**Chapter 1** – On The Profession Of The Native, And On His Work, And His Duties, And On His Strength, Likewise On His Prosperity And Kingship And On The Condition Of The Mother – Page 341

**Chapter 2** – On The Natives' Strength And Prosperity Of, And On His Duties And His Kingship – Page 345

**Chapter 3** – How You Should Examine In The Matter Of The Mother – Page 348

## ON THE ELEVENTH HOUSE

**Chapter 1** – On The Natives Friends And Likewise On His Good Fortune And His Hope – Page 351

**Chapter 2** – On The Kinds Of Friends (Synastry) – Page 352

## ON THE TWELFTH HOUSE

**Chapter 1** – On Matters Of Hidden And Jealous Enemies, And On The Considerations Which You Ought To Have In The Significations Of The Twelve Houses, And Likewise In The Judgements Which Result From The Aforementioned Significations – Page 355

**Chapter 2** – On The Judgements Which Result From The Significations Of The Twelve Houses And Their Lords – Page 356

On Saturn In The Signs – Page 357

On Jupiter In The Signs – Page 358

On Mars In The Signs – Page 359

On The Sun In The Signs – Page 360

On Venus In The Signs – Page 361

On Mercury In The Signs – Page 362

On The Moon In The Signs – Page 363

**Chapter 3** – On The Years Of Fidaria And Their Dispositors – Page 364

**Chapter 4** – On The Eminence Of The Planets, Or The Transit Of One Over Another – Page 365

**Chapter 5** – On The "Opening Of The Gates" According to Alchabitius – Page 366

**Chapter 6** – On The Twelve Hours Of The Sun And The Moon Which Are Applied To The Sun – Page 366

**Chapter 7** – On The Profections Of The Years, Both Of The World, And Of Nativities – Page 367

**Chapter 8** – On The Order Of The Profection – Page 368

**Chapter 9** – On The Profection Of The Years Of The World – Page 369

**Chapter 10** – On The Direction Of The Significators To Be Directed In The Circle, And How Many Are The Significators Which We Must Direct, Which Were Directed By The Sages – Page 370

**Chapter 11** – On The Nature Of The Degrees Of The Signs, In Any Sign – Page 371

**Chapter 12** – On The Ninth-Parts Of The Signs And What They Will Signify – Page 372

**Chapter 13** – On The Lord Of The Circle Or Of The Orb Of Signs – Page 373

**Chapter 14** – On The Lord Of The Twelve Remaining Hours – Page 374

**Chapter 15** – On The Direction Of A Significator – Page 375

**Tractate X**

**On Rains And The Mutations Of The Air, And The Things Which Pertain To This**

What Be Set Out In This Work – Page 377

**Chapter 1** – On The Knowledge To Be Had Of The Benefics And Malefics, And Of All Temperate Or Changing Things – Page 378

**Chapter 2** – To Know When Coming Rains Will Be Signified, And When Not – Page 378

**Chapter 3** – On The Forecast Of Rains In General – Page 378

**Chapter 4** – Which Lunar Mansions Are Wet, Which Are Dry, And Which Are Common – Page 379

**Chapter 5** – On The Mutation And Variation Of The Air, And The Knowledge Of Future Rains – Page 381

**Chapter 6** - A Chapter On Rains, And The Mutations Of The Air – Page 383

**Chapter 7** – On The Hour Of Rains, Heavy Rains, And Winds – Page 383

**Chapter 8** – When Saturn Prohibits Rains – Page 384

**Chapter 9** – On The Application Of The Moon With Jupiter – Page 384

**Chapter 10** – On The Application Of The Moon With Mars – Page 384

**Chapter 11** – On The Application Of The Moon With The Sun – Page 385

**Chapter 12** – On The Application Of The Moon With Venus – Page 385

**Chapter 13** – On The Application Of The Moon With Mercury – Page 386

**Chapter 14** – On The Application Of The Moon With The Benefics Or Malefics – Page 386

**Chapter 15** – On The Four Tetragons, Or The Four Quarters, Or The Four Figures – Page 387

**Chapter 16** – To Know The Qualities Which Are Prolonged By More Than One Day– Page 388

**Chapter 17** – On What The Circles Which Are Around The Moon And The Sun, And Likewise Around The Other Stars, Both Wandering And Non-Wandering, Bring About – Page 389

**Chapter 18** – On Comets And Tailed Stars – Page 389

**Chapter 19** – On Shooting Stars – Page 389

**Chapter 20** – On The Significations Of Diurnal And Nocturnal Qualities – Page 390

**Chapter 21** – On The Rainbow, If It Were To Appear, And In What Times, And What It Would Signify – Page 390

**Chapter 22** – On The Investigation Of The Year, If There Ought To Be Much Rains – Page 390

**Chapter 23** – On The Application Of The Moon With Saturn And With The Rest Of The Planets – Page 391

**Chapter 24** – On Certain Extraordinary Things – Page 391

**Chapter 25** – On The Accidents Whose Durations Will Be Prolonged For A Little While – Page 392

**Chapter 26** – On The Consideration Of The Places Of Rains – Page 393

**Chapter 27** – On The Signs And Places Signifying Less Rain Than The Aforementioned Places And Signs – Page 393

**Chapter 28** – In The Conjunction Of Which Planets Rains Are Signified– Page 393

**Chapter 29** – If You Wish To Know Whether Some Month Will Be Rainy Or Not – Page 393

**Chapter 30** – On The Conjunction Of The Moon With Planets, And On The Conjunction Of The Other Planets Individually To Each Other – Page 394

# GUIDO BONATTI'S

## BOOK OF ASTRONOMY

## PART THREE

### On Elections According To The Sayings Of The Wise

#### I

ince after judgements, we are in need of elections before the other parts of Astrology, and they are matters which we meet with every day, nor without them can we perfectly attain the complete utility of many judgements, which is necessary for us to explain every day. It seems fitting to me to make a special Tractate on them, following in the footsteps of our sages.

However, an election is a pre-made plan made because of a desire for something favourable. However, to elect is a desire of the intellect resulting from an act of free will. And even if sometimes many fools and idiots in tunics rise up against me, saying that elections are worth nothing and are absolutely nothing, nevertheless elections and the other parts of astrology remain in their firmity, nor is their truth diminished from this. For through elections we can grasp many good things, and similarly we can avoid many evil things, which are set to happen according to the stars: yet I do not say that elections make the matter, but they do remove things prohibiting the matter from coming to be. For if victory were judged by an astrologer for someone about to move against his enemy (or for those things regarding which a question was made), unless the querent has a good election for the moving of his army against his enemies, he might succumb on account of the bad beginning of his journey; or it could at least diminish much of the good which was signified by the judgement. And if he were to have a good election under a good Ascendant (and it will be signified more strongly for him by a judgement), he will arrive at a good end of the matter, and overcome those enemies resisting him. For it is impossible that something which is done by the right plan, and by

law, to not have firmity and to arrive at a good end. For the most high and glorious Creator of all things made the heavens and incorruptible stars from the fifth incorruptible essence to rule and govern the inferior corruptibles made of the four corruptible essences (namely the elements); and He made the stars on account of men, so that from the stars, assistance would be provided to men and the other inferior things. For that which is made for man, ought to serve man; and if anyone says it is not so, these men are not to be argued with, since they understand nothing and believe nothing, but rather they are to be dismissed like a teacher dismisses errors and heretics dismiss the truth. For they are ignorant of the truth, since they are intent on monetary wealth, and it deprives them of knowledge, and makes their minds and hearts blind.

For the stars in the eight perceptible and mobile heavens are set down; for those which are in the primum mobile, which are called "fixed" by the philosophers, are almost like matter, and corruptible things are the forms. The planets are, and operate and exercise a certain medium through which the superiors operate in inferiors. Nevertheless they exercise their operations formally; and since matter is in a certain way unlimited, and forms come to be from matter; and this is the reason why no form of a rational thing is likened purely to that of another; and not only individuals, but also species are almost unlimited to us.

For why would God make the stars on account of men, who pursue utility from them; if they did not operate and imprint diverse things on the inferiors, now this, now that: which we see them do manifestly every day: for sometimes we see them operating for good in one place, and sometimes we see them operate in the same place to the contrary of what they first operated - which does not happen except from the diversity of their motions and positions. Wherefore on account of the diverse qualities of their motions, and the diverse positions of their bodies, diverse changes are made in the world. For we see that the planets moved by diverse motions, and according to these diverse motions they imprint in diverse ways in the inferior things: and these inferior things are changed and altered in diverse ways according to these diverse impressions. For they are made hot and made cold, dried and moistened. For when Mars and the Sun are joined together, and if it is summer, heat will rise. If it is winter, there will be a remission of the cold, and it will be restored to temperateness. If indeed, the Sun is joined with Saturn, and it is winter, the cold will increase. If however, it is summer, there will be a remission of heat.

Whence when an astrologer through his own investigation knows these diverse motions, and knows these impressions which they imprint in the inferior things on account of these motions, and that these motions are sometimes of a good quality, sometimes of a bad quality - then he can elect for good things when the qualities of these motions are good, and take it up. And he could elect something bad which is signified by the qualities of the motions when they are bad, and avoid it. Since just as is said elsewhere, a planet does not signify the same thing when it is retrograde, as it does when it is direct; nor does it signify the same thing when it is slow as when it is fast; nor the same thing when it is stationary as when it is progressing; nor the same thing when it is combust as when it has escaped; nor the same thing when it is void-of-course as when it is joined to another; nor the same when it is in another's dignities as when it is in its own; nor the same when it is in an angle as when it is in a cadent; nor the same when it is free as when it is impeded.

Whence, when it is known by someone experienced in this science when a planet is well disposed , it is then possible to make an election for the good; and when it is known by him when a planet is badly disposed, it is possible to make an election to avoid it, according to how the astrologer perceives it to be. And it is possible to elect a good hour from a bad, according to how Our Lord Jesus Christ elected when He said, "Let us go again to Judea etc.", and evil things which are set to occur according to the dispositions of the aforementioned motions, and bad things signified, can be avoided

in all beginnings of those things which we intend to do, as much in journeys, as in taking women as wives and celebrating marriage; as much as in the construction of things as their destruction; as much in planting things as in digging them up - and in exceptional things which we intend to do or which we intend to avoid. And so it is shown that the stars operate diverse things in the inferior things according to the diversity of their motions; and that astrologers can, through good elections, avoid much evils which follow from the motions of the stars; evils which unless precautions were taken, would have happened to him.

Whence they cannot diminish astrology, nor elections of some matters, in such a manner that they can easily adopt: yet they can in a certain way resist in those things which appear similar to the truth (even if everything can be defended): namely if they said that elections are not found for just any common person; and this is true in a certain sense, but not utterly. Since we cannot trust that any common person can himself do the quesited elected matter: but he can make a question on what can happen to him from a given matter, we will be well able to elect for him after that, having taken the significator of the election from the question made by him: for by his own question that which was considered lost by the significations of his root nativity, is now restored, since it is now about that which was quesited.

And in a certain way it appears that elections are common to everyone: since an election is not a voluntary matter, nor a certain one: nevertheless it still belongs to anyone who is advised by another, , or who consulted for another, and is a matter whose plan was produced first, and vouched for by reason and intellect. However, we can elect for magnates and noblemen (namely those who are fit to rule), and over nativities, and over questions, and always without them, and indifferently over all of their beginnings, as much for journeys as for other things. Indeed, when you elect for commoners without a question, and especially if there are several of them together, as sometimes happens when they wish to travel by land (provided that there are more than one of them, as there is on pilgrimages and similar things), you will not be able to elect for them as you do when you elect for one person only: since the fortunate and unfortunate planets differ in the roots of their nativities, so that the significator who is useful for one of them, can be the contrary for another; and so you will not be able to have such an election which will be useful for everyone in one hour. Since there is nothing which can carry out two natural and contrary operations at one and the same time, according to one and the same thing, and one and the same signification.

And that things are like this, is shown through this: since we sometimes see some people travel together at the same hour for some business, and it turns out well for some of them, and to the contrary for others. Whence if questions were had for all of them, it ought to be elected for those whose questions signified good; and it ought not to be elected for those whose questions signified the contrary. However, it is true that a good election either benefits or does no harm, provided that it is not contrary to the root of the nativity; however, elections are still not to be cast aside, but are to be observed according to the order which I said to you. For those whose significators are benefic planets will rejoice on good days, and be happy in them; in bad days they will sometimes be sorrowful. For those whose significators are malefics planets will rejoice on days which it does not appear that they ought to, and on good days they will be sorrowful and it will be bad for them: and this is not so unless for the reason that those malefics dominated in their root nativities. For malefics only benefit their own; and strive to harm others: while benefics always benefit their own, and strive to benefit others: and this is the reason why elections are better able to benefit than to harm. Therefore you ought not to disdain these things which I say to you: since if you consider them well, and you examine them well, you will be able to perceive the utility of elections; and from where they have an origin, and how, when, and for whom they have value.

For I want you to know that fortune rules in all matters, even if certain of the tunic clad idiots say that fortune does not exist, but only what God wills. The wise men of them secretly differ from this, even if in public they seem to assent to it, which is from fear of being condemned by their orders rather than that they believe they speak the truth. For if fortune doesn't exist, who would be so foolish as not to know from his own judgement how to acquire an abundance of all necessary things? But we clearly see the contrary every day - do you not see certain upstanding and intelligent wise men, who often do not have much to eat? And certain fools, who if a wolf carried off seven of their ten cattle, wouldn't know whether they were diminished or not, abounding in an overflow of necessities? For these men are rabid at their own Creator, saying that he is not just, and falling into abhorrent heresy.

## II

## On Those Things Which Will Be Considered In This Tractate

For in this tractate which is said to be about elections, it is fitting that you know these five things, which are as follows. If the elections which we make contain any utility in them. And similarly it is fitting that you consider the beginning of each matter which anyone intends to do or begin (why it is done). And whether the matters which they begin are going to arrive at completion or not. And if they are completed, whether the end of that which we began will be good or bad.

For to Ptolemy, who was the reconciler of this science before all others, it seemed that the judgements of elections were not to be excluded from the fruits of this science, in but rather they were to be counted as a fruit of this science: for it is necessary that a great part of the fruits of astronomy are elections. Since when we elect the beginning of any matter, through this election we can know what the beginning, middle, and end of this matter ought to be like. For if we elect for someone (of a suitable age) so that he can generate a child; or even if we do not elect for him, and know the hour of the conception (whether it is rational or irrational), we know what the child's future will be in the womb of the mother up to the day and hour of its nativity; and if we know the hour of the nativity, we will be able to tell him what will happen to the child from after its nativity up to the end of its life according to the natural order, and what ought to happen to him. For God gives to the native what the stars administer. And even if the matter is the same in them, nevertheless the operations are many and diverse; just as happens in the limbs, to which the First Cause gives each one its virtue in accordance with its operations; for it is not of its interest to prohibit some matter; even if certain men ignorant of astronomy do not acknowledge it.

Similarly when we elect for someone wishing to sow or plant, we will know what is going to happen concerning that planting or that sowing according to the administration and significations of the stars. Indeed, Sarcinator appeared to wish that we did not elect for low-class or mediocre people, unless over their nativity or question; however, he did not completely prevent us from electing for them; but it seemed safer to him to elect over nativities or questions than otherwise: since it is good to elect over nativities or questions. But if there is a situation where we cannot have any of these, elections are still not to be prohibited. And he said that we ought to elect even without these things, and he did not contradict himself in this. Sarcinator wanted to be certain, so that he could not be reprehended: and so he wanted to elect over nativities (which are rarely had), or over questions of their nature.

Indeed, Haly wanted to be more liberal in this, as he wished to benefit everyone, even if elections which are not made over nativities or questions are not as certain as those which are made over them, he was still confident that they would be effective, or at least that they would do no harm.

However, it appears to me that we can elect for everyone individually, provided that we do not elect for a plurality: and plurality is not to be understood as something communally shared, but rather a plurality of private concerns, such as people gathered together to go on a pilgrimage, and similar things. For I believe that mediocre people or commoners have their own nativities, in the same manner as magnates have their roots: since each one of them is born under an Ascendant. For if we adapt the Moon (who is a participator in all matters), then we have a part of a journey (or whatever other matter) adapted universally, which is of matters with roots, and which will not allow the traveller to be endangered easily, even if the Ascendant of the journey is contrary to the Ascendant of the nativity in which the Moon is a participator. And insofar as she is stronger in journeys, she destroys much of the contrary things which could be signified by other planets contradicting the journey: since her signification in journeys is twice as great as the significations of any of the other planets. Whence with her having so great a role in journeys, and all other matters, and being the participator of the nativities of travellers, and with us adapting her in journeys: it appears that the side of the root of the nativity of the traveller (or the one beginning something) is adapted, so that there will be prosperity for him in this journey, allowing possibly that everything may not turn out as prosperously as he wishes. Still, a good election will diminish and avert many evil things, which are due to happen according to the significations of the stars. And some good things will be obtained by him for whom it is elected, which would not have been without an election.

For those who avoid elections which are not made over nativities or over questions do not appear completely wise to me, since if they cannot have all of the good that they want, nevertheless they ought not to spurn whatever part of the good that they can get. For those men who do this, appear to do the same as that actor who went to a wedding at which there was said to be goose: and he went there and did not find any goose, but found partridge; and was able to eat as much of this as he liked; but this actor, since he didn't find any goose, did not want to eat partridge, but rather, led by stupidity, he left hungry.

Indeed, Trutannus said that

*"It is better to eat crickets than to eat nothing"*,

And even if it was spoken in a misapplied way, his intention was true, and so it is better to use elections than to dismiss them entirely.

### III

### On The Root Of Elections

For the root of our elections is adapting their foundations; and toward this, the Moon is to be adapted: since (as said elsewhere) she has participation and signification in all beginnings, in all journeys, in all places, in all times, in all matters, and in all hours. And it is similar with these, as Haly said: the Sun, who is chief the other planets, like a king; and the planet who signifies the matter which we want to begin - so that if we wish to begin a war, or anything else which is operated by fire and iron, we ought to adapt Mars, who naturally signifies this. If we wish to acquire money, we ought to adapt Jupiter, who naturally signifies this. If we wish to celebrate a wedding, or similar delightful things, we ought to adapt Venus. And understand thus for the significations of any planet. Moreover, we ought to adapt the sign which is of the nature of the matter which we wish to begin, and which signifies it: so that if we want to make a journey by land, we should adapt an earth sign; if by water, we should adapt a water sign. And to adapt them is to make it so that they are free from impediments, and from malefics and their aspects; and place this as the Ascendant of your election; or place the Lord of the Ascendant or the Moon in it - or both, if you can.

These are necessary in all common elections, as much in elections which are made over nativities or questions, as in others, if it can be done; and certain things are opportune, even if they are not necessary: namely to adapt a masculine sign for a man, and a feminine sign for a woman.

## IV

### On The Adapting Of Particulars

After you have adapted the aforementioned universal things, it is necessary that you adapt the particular ones, namely after you have adapted the luminaries, the Lord of the Ascendant, the planet signifying the matter which the inceptor intends to do, and the house which has signification over the matter about which your election and the intention of the inceptor is. And this is done in two ways: for in the case of those whose nativities or questions you have, you ought to adapt the house signifying the matter in the nativity or the question. And for those who you do not have a nativity or question for, adapt the house signifying the matter at the hour of the election or beginning. You also ought to adapt the first and the fourth house, and the Lords of each of them in every election: the first and its Lord to guard and keep safe the person of him for whom you elect: and the fourth and its Lord so that the matter is perfected and its end is good and praiseworthy.

And Haly said to adapt the house signifying the matter itself for this reason: since one and the same sign can make different houses, which will have diverse significations according to the diversity of regions: so that if Aries is the first house in Toledo, at the same hour the same sign will be the twelfth house in Forli: and in the same hour (that is, of the time then) it would be the eleventh house in Corinth or close to it, and so on up to the end of the habitable earth, the houses will diversify according to the diversity of longitudes, regions, and their distances from each other; giving each one 770 miliaria (according to how the ancient sages measured the earth; or perhaps according to the measurement as it is contained in their books). Whence I do not place much force in it, except for you to see the method of the diversity of the houses, in order for you to perceive their significations according to the diversity of regions, for the reason that what the one sign signifies in one land, can be signified by another sign in another land different from it. And so it appears that elections are not to be avoided in every respect, even if nativities or questions are not always at hand.

And if someone says "if we always make benefics strong, and malefics weak in elections, and one of the malefics was the significator of the nativity of him for whom we elected for, we will do the contrary of what we ought to for him, and thus will make ourselves contrary to him when we ought to be useful to him". To which we can respond that we ought to follow in the footsteps of nature, which is always directed toward what is better; and we ought to be directed toward what is better. For it is better that if we do not have nativities or questions, that we adapt the benefics and weaken the malefics: since the weakness of benefics is worse than the weakness of malefics. For if we weaken all of the benefics, it is possible that no good will remain in the election. However, if we weaken all of malefics, we will not be able to weaken them so that no good will remain in it: since none of the malefics (even if one of them signifies good in a nativity) signifies good universally and everywhere. However, for of the benefics, there are many who naturally and universally always and everywhere signify good, as Venus does, who always has the signification of bethroals and celebrating marriage, and other matters of women in all hours, and in all lands, and similar things: and the Moon who has signification in all matters of mothers, and in all of our actions, as said elsewhere; and likewise with the Sun over matters of dignities; and Jupiter, who naturally, and always and everywhere, in all hours, and in all lands is the significator of substance. And so, always when we strengthen the benefics, or the stars signifying what we intend, we preserve something of the good for him for whom we are electing - which does not happen with malefics.

Moreover there are only two naturally malefic planets, namely Saturn and Mars: while there are five naturally good planets, namely, the Sun, Venus, Mercury, and the Moon. Whence, since the benefics are greater in number than the malefics, it is fitting that they conquer them in strength: and so we ought to have consideration for much good, than to have fear for much evil And in this, those men who say that we ought not to use elections err: for just as it is said elsewhere: an election is not able to harm, but it is able to benefit. For it is impossible but that there is good in a good hour, and evil in a bad hour. For since we can discern good from bad, why should we not take a good hour and avoid a bad hour?

If someone wants to travel to battle, who perhaps is in a rush to go, sought advice from you to elect a good hour for him: or asked you to examine for him if this hour is good or not: and you see that the significator is badly disposed in that hour, so that if he went to battle at that time he would be killed: and you saw another hour in which he could travel without danger, and you did not advise him not to travel at this time, and to wait for the hour in which he would be able to travel safely; or if you said to him "go, since this hour will not harm you, if God wills it"; and if he travelled then and was killed, would you not have committed murder? You should know that just as I have said, if you refused to give him the advice, you would be culpable. That is if he wanted to compensate you for your services: but sometimes it is different, for you are not obliged to serve him for free, if he cannot pay you.

For an election can be strong, so that it does not avert the evil of him whose nativity is unknown, and who doesn't have a question: and it is also true that even if evil is signified for him by his nativity or question, it is possible for him to avert it by a strong election.

Similarly if any traveller enquires of you regarding which one of three roads would be better for him and more secure: one of which it is said publicly that bandits are never on; another where bandits are sometimes on it, sometimes not; and the third, where there are always bandits: and you say to him, "travel by this road" (namely in which there were always bandits) "since you will not meet bandits on the road, if God wills it so", if he travels by this road and is robbed, would you not be bound to him

for the restitution of those things of his which he lost, since you could have advised him to go by the road where there was said never to be bandits - through which, if he had travelled, even if he was robbed, you wouldn't be bound to recompose him for it?

For elections operate according to more and less: for if we elect for him whose nativity we know, or whose question we have, and his nativity or question signifies something good for him in its root, and the election concords with one of those good things, it signifies a good and perfect end of this matter and its effects; however, if one is discordant with the other, it will reduce the good. And if the nativity or the question signifies evil, and the election signifies good, the good of the election will reduce the evil that is signified by the nativity or question; or perhaps destroy it in whole, just as a good antidote will reduce or sometimes totally destroy the harm of poison; and we see sometimes doctors give medicines to certain people who are dying from an illness, and for whom there is no hope had for their escape; nevertheless it is possible, that sometimes the strength of the medicine is so great that the patients nature is strengthened from it, and thus he is freed from illness. And if the medicine does not free the ill person, at the least it does not harm him - and so a good hour always ought to be elected.

## V

### That An Election Ought To Agree With The Nature Of The Matter For Which It Is Chosen

However take care that your election agrees with the nature of the matter for which you elect: since the effects and impressions of the superior bodies are not naturally adapted, except by subjects suitable to accept them: nor can an election give anything to a subject, except what is his own, and what pertains to him according to the natural order of his kind. For it is not possible to elect for a man such an hour which could allow him to fly: nor one which could allow him to run like a hare, or a deer: nor even one which can allow him to travel 500 or 1000 miliaria in a day. But only what can be adapted to him according to the natural order should be elected for him. For the most high Architect of the world, assigned an order to every creature according to its own nature, and according to what was suitable for it; for every creature and every individual has as much power as their as their natural form permits; for virtue must respond to figure; for nothing can have something through its own nature, unless it can be given through its own nature, unless perhaps it is monstrous.

Therefore do not elect the impossible for anyone, since lay people, and also certain tunic-clad men, and almost all people indifferently, strive to deride astrologers, and fashion unheard of lies to deride them with. Do not elect an hour to conceive for 80 or 90 year old women, since old age prohibits it. Do not elect a year to generate for a 10 or 12 year old boy; since his age will neither allow it nor permit it. Do not elect for someone wanting to ride a two or three month old foal, since its tenderness will not allow it. Likewise, that which nature denies, nobody will readily dare. Do not elect for someone wanting to sow corn in planes of Italy in June or July, nor someone wanting to sow barley or millet in Hungary or Germany in the month of October or November, since the region, or the disposition of the air is not suitable for it. Neither should you elect for someone wanting to sow on the seashore, since the location is not suitable for this. For an agent will not produce anything besides what proceeds from his nature. Do not elect for someone who does not know how to swim, wanting to throw himself into deep water, since he will be drowned. Do not elect for someone wanting to throw himself into a burning furnace, since he will be burnt up. Do not elect for someone wanting to throw himself from a high tower to the ground, since he will break his neck. Do not elect for an unarmed man to battle with a lion, since he will be torn to pieces. Do not elect for a cripple wanting to battle with someone much stronger than him, or for few men wanting to battle with many: since they will succumb (for violence will make for virtue), but you should elect for equals or those slightly weaker. For natural reason does not incline to anything except to that which it naturally pertains to; yet it is sometimes elected well for few against many, and the few win: but still, what happens sometimes is not to be taken as a general rule. For it is sufficient for whom you elect, if you elect for him against a force that is one quarter or one third greater than his own. However, if it exceeds this, the election will not be very safe; since power often makes reason turn back.

For indeed, the super-celestial bodies do not operate on anything, except what is presented to them by nature. Indeed, they are of eight kinds: since each planet is of its own kind, and the fixed stars are likewise of their own kind. And it is also possible to say that any given fixed star is of its own kind, and since their kinds are diverse, so are their operations and significations (even though they are equally incorruptible).

However, is it true that I once elected for count Guido Novello of Tuscany against the Florentines, who expelled him from Florence and demolished all of his castles which he had in Tuscany, and pillaged him of all his goods - and Count Novello for his part had 3200 soldiers, almost 13000 foot-soldiers, and 300 ballista-men: and his adversaries had 5300 soldiers, almost 12,000 foot-soldiers, and 500 ballista-men or more. And we still completely defeated them and we conquered them entirely; and this was in the valley of Arbia in the open mountains. However, I first had it through a question that we had ought to win, and then we had the strongest election in setting out to battle; and I knew through private messengers sent to it, that their time of departure was bad, or rather, the worst. However, you ought to consider in all of your elections according to how the nature and being of each individual matter appears able to allow the thing signified by the election to happen; and if you do this, you won't err.

For it is necessary if your election is to perfect what you intend, and that he for whom you elect arrives at a good end to the matter, that you adapt all of the things which I said to you, if you can; namely, the first and its Lord; the fourth and its Lord; and also both the luminaries, and the Part of Fortune; and similarly the Lords of the houses in which they are placed; and the house signifying the matter for which you elected, and its Lord; and the planet to whom the Moon first joins after your election or beginning; and the Lord of the fourth sign from the sign in which the Moon is placed (since this has participation in signifying the end of matters): and also the Lord of the fourth sign from the sign in which the Part of Fortune was; and the Lord of the house in which the Lord of the sign in which the Moon is placed - as much in all of the things mentioned above, as in the construction of cities, castles, or houses, and similar things.

Therefore, when you want to adapt any election, insofar as you wanted to build a tower, or a castle, or whatever other thing that you wanted to begin, it is necessary for you to become intent regarding the matter and regarding the person of him for whom you elect: since the first and its Lord are to be adapted for his person; and you also ought to adapt the first and its Lord, the Moon, and the Part of Fortune, for the matter which is begun, so that its end will be good. Whence if some matter is begun, (whether it is a building, or a journey, or something else) and these significators are well disposed, it will be good for the matter or for him for whom you elect for. If indeed, all of them are impeded, it will be to the contrary. While if the Lord of the first and the Moon are impeded, and the Part of Fortune is safe, it will be good for the matter which is elected for: but not for him whose matter it is; but still the virtue of the Part of Fortune is not so great (even if it benefits) that it can defend business in this way, when the participants with it are impeded.

## On The Destruction Of A Building

If however, your election is for such a matter that you want to destroy some building (namely a house or castle, or something similar), its significators should be weakened, and especially the Lord of the fourth, and the planet to which the Moon is joined - on account that they signify what is going to happen concerning the matter. And above all other significators, Mars should be weakened: since he has the signification of the reconstruction of the destroyed building, and especially to the contrary of those who destroy the building, or cause it to be destroyed. If however, the intention of the one destroying it was to reconstruct it: or if his intention was to destroy it with ease and speed: or perhaps if it was not of his concern whether the destroyed building was rebuilt or not - make the Moon separated from a malefic, and joined to a benefic which is oriental and direct; or have her joined to the Lord of the house in which she is in by a trine or sextile aspect, descending in her circle.

## VI

## That The Beginning Of A Matter Is Not Before The Matter Is Incepted

Also know that the inception or the beginning of a matter cannot exist before the matter is begun; nor does it exist after it is begun, but it exists in the beginning of the matter itself (just as I will say to you): not when the beginning is made, not when it is not made, nor even when it is in progress; but only when it comes to be; just as when we construct a tower, or a house, or whatever other building when we seek durability and we set down the first stone, and place it in the required location: and these first setting downs, can be said to be the beginnings of any building or construction.

If someone says that digging or measuring the ground is the beginning of a building, they don't appear to be correct to me: since all beginnings fix the origin of a matter, or are the intrinsic aspect of the matter which we begin or intend to begin. But the extrinsic aspect is what is not of the beginning itself: since sometimes someone can build without digging, just as when we build on rocks or similar places: but without the first stone we can never build a thing which we want or intend to begin. It is clear then that the placing of the first stone and the first stone itself, and its required location is the intrinsic beginning of the matter, and of the building which we intend to make or begin, and of the act of construction. However, measuring and digging, even if they are preparations for construction, they are still not of the building, except in terms of gathering stones and scattering lime, and similar things. Yet you would not be reproached if you were able to adapt all of these things.

And if it is necessary that the buildings have a foundation of wood (as sometimes happens with bridges and similar things), where sometimes it is not possible to make the beginning of the construction with stones, the first piece of timber which is laid in this foundation is to be adapted, as this is the beginning of this building since it is of the building.

## *When It Is Constructed Without Walls*

And if it is a building without walls, take the beginning as being the placing of the first column in the pit that was made, this since it is the last and necessary placing, and the like. And since it appears almost impossible to adapt as many significators as I named to you, if you cannot adapt them all, adapt those which you can adapt, since even if you only adapt a few of them, it will benefit your election, even if it is not as much as you want. For if you could adapt them all, it would be a matter blessed in every way: however, it will be blessed according to the quantity of significators that you adapt.

Whence if you can adapt the first and its Lord, the Moon also and the Lord of the house in which she is in, and the planet to which the Moon or the Lord of the first is joined; and the Part of Fortune, and the Lord of the house in which you find it; and the planet signifying the matter which you intend to do, and also the Lord of the hour.

If you cannot adapt all of those, then adapt the Lord of the 1st, the Moon, the planet signifying the matter, and the Lord of the hour.

And if again you cannot adapt these, adapt the Moon, and the Lord of the hour.

Which if you cannot do this, consider over what matter your election is made: for if it is a journey or going out on a hunt, or similar things, then adapt the Lord of the hour more so than any of the others, and make the Moon cadent from the Ascendant so that she is neither in it, nor or aspecting it. If however, it is something other than a journey or a hunt, adapt the Moon as best you can, and it will benefit you in the matter which you intend to begin or do.

If however, anyone says, that we ought not to prolong elections like this, as I said, when almost everyone seems to appear to want to say something other than this, it is possible to respond to them like this: since the sages wished for their elections to be so blessed that they are perfect in every way; and they considered elections which someone can wait forever, until the significators can all be adapted as they said. But we often do not have much time to wait, whence it is necessary that we elect in the space of time which we have available, and mix whatever good we can into our elections.

## *On The Strengthening Of The Sun*

It should always be your concern to strengthen the Sun as best you can in durable matters, and especially for noblemen and magnates (of which, mention has been made elsewhere), also in other elections in which you are able to adapt him. For elections (just as I have touched on for you elsewhere) are diverse, namely according to nobility, according to time, according to age, according to place, according to office or magistracy, and according to the nature and kind of the elected matter. However, for those whose nativities we know, or for whom we have questions, we ought not to weaken any of the planets who have strength in the root of their nativities or questions.

And Haly said, that these agree in all beginnings, except that for certain men we ought to put certain of the following things which are not to be placed universally in the others, since they are singled out for these men, and are practically necessary in their actions, just as I will tell you now.

# VII

## How Diverse Planets Are To Be Adapted For Diverse Persons

In elections for kings the Sun is to be adapted, and the tenth and its Lord. They are not to be adapted for those who accompany them: but they are of the necessities and roots. Since you ought to know that it is necessary for you to adapt these things in matters of kings, powerful people, and the like: that is, matters pertaining to kingship and other lay dignities; and the Sun is even to be adapted for Babylonians and Eastern Romans.

Mercury is to be adapted for scribes and merchants, for he naturally signifies writings and minds, and such things on account of his convertibility, and Indians, since his strength is in that land.

Mars is to be adapted for boxers, butchers, bakers, craftsmen, and similar people: since he naturally signifies contentions and those things which are operated through fire and iron; and Western Romans, since his strength is in those parts.

Jupiter is to be adapted for the secular religious, and merchants wishing to do business justly: since he signifies substance, and especially that which is acquired in a good way; and also for Iraqis, since his strength is in the lands of Iraq.

Venus is to be adapted for women, since she naturally signifies matters of women; and Arabs, since she naturally signifies this people, and her strength is in the Arab lands.

Saturn is to be adapted for Jews, farmers, old people, the religious wearing black vestments, and similar people, on account of the heaviness of his motion; and for Aethiopians, since he signifies this people.

Whence, as I have said to you many times now, adapt those significators which you can, even if you can't adapt all of them that you wish for this, so that our election can increase whatever good and reduce whatever evil that we can, even if we cannot do everything that we want.

Indeed, Haly said that in all of our elections we ought to consider the Lord of the Ascendant and the Moon, and make the stronger one of them the significator of our matter: and he praised this, since it signifies what would follow from the beginning. And he said that when the Lord of the Ascendant is fortunate (namely joined with benefics), and is weak (namely cadent from an angle or from the Ascendant); and the Moon is strong (namely in an angle of the Ascendant, or in a succedent in the eleventh or the fifth, aspecting the Ascendant), and is unfortunate (namely, joined to malefics): we ought not to judge evil, but rather, we ought to judge good. Since the Moon is then said to have little participation in that matter. But if the Lord of the Ascendant is then strong and fortunate, not much force is to be placed in the Moon; but rather he said that sometimes it is fitting for us to make her unfortunate, that is to weaken her, and to make the Lord of the Ascendant fortunate, as is the case with hunting.

However, Zael and Aomar appeared to say that the Moon should be made fortunate in hunting: but Haly said that the Moon is to be made unfortunate in hunts; but what Haly said was unique to him. For he said that he understood "unfortunate", as meaning weakened, since every planet can be strong and unfortunate, or weak and fortunate, just as is said elsewhere. And he said to place her with malefics - she can even be placed with malefics without being made unfortunate; and there are certain malefics with whom it is appropriate for us

to place her with in hunting; sometimes it is even appropriate for us to weaken her and make her unfortunate, such as in the investigation of fugitives, as will be said elsewhere. When the others said that she is to be made fortunate, they did not understand that she was to be strengthened.

## VIII

## What Kind Of End Should Be Hoped For From The Matter Which We Begin

Indeed Albumashar said that for us to know the end of an election, it is necessary for us to consider five things. And he made the Lord of the fourth the first of these, not as a preface, but as the most deserving - since he signifies the end, and the end is more deserving than the beginning. He made the second one the Lord of the sign where the Moon is placed. And if the Moon is then in Cancer, then she herself will be considered (namely after the Lord of the fourth). And made the third one the planet to which the Moon joins in her first conjunction after the matter is begun. He made the fourth one the Lord of the house or sign in which the Part of Fortune is in. He made the fifth one the fourth sign from the sign in which the Moon is in. And (as Haly said) certain men wanted to add on the Lord of the fourth from the place of the Part of Fortune. But since all of these cannot be easily adapted at one and the same time, I told you these five. And even if the Lord of the fourth signifies the end of a matter which someone wishes to begin (whether it is a journey or something else) it sometimes happens that it does not signify the end, whence it is necessary for you to look for another.

To give an example: the Lord of the first signifies the matter as the one preceding all other significators; and (as I said) the Lord of the fourth, namely if it aspects the fourth, has signification before all others in respect of the end of the matter. Whence, if at the beginning of any journey, or any construction etc., the Lord of the fourth aspects the fourth, the end of the matter should be sought from it alone. If it does not aspect the fourth, the end should be sought from the Lord of the house in which the Moon is in: which if it aspects the Moon, signifies the end of the matter; if not, then it doesn't. Wherefore, you will then seek the end of the matter from the planet to whom the Moon first joins after the beginning of the matter (I say if she is joined to, or seeks a conjunction with, any planet). If however, she is solitary, so that she joins nobody, nor seeks a conjunction with anyone, then seek the end from the planet in whose domicile the Part of Fortune is placed: for if it aspects the Part of Fortune, it will be the significator of the end of the matter, if not, the signification will remain over the Moon and over the Lord of the house in which she is in; and he will be stronger than her in participation, and all the aforementioned significators and the Lord of the first will even participate with them. But he (namely the Lord of the house in which the Moon is) will be more authoritative than them all.

And Haly said that if you give the signification to the Lord of the fourth sign from the place of the Part of Fortune, it will be considered as being less than all the others. And he said that if the Moon is corporeally joined degree for degree with some planet in the sign in which she is in, that this planet will be the significator of the end of the matter, whether it has dignity there or not; and he will be preferred to the Lord of the sign in which the Moon is in; wherefore, if you find him so, then consider the participation of the aforementioned significators with the planet to whom the Moon is corporeally joined in the sign which she is in degree for degree; and then it returns to the Lord of the first (as it appeared to Alchindi), since he signifies the querent or inceptor, and what happens to him from the beginning of that matter. And the Lord of the sign in which he is placed has the signification of what happens to him in the middle of the matter. And if he is in his own domicile, he will signify the middle and the beginning. And the Lord of the sign in which the planet who is the Lord of the house where the Lord of the first is placed has the signification of what kind of end the matter will have, and what will happen to the inceptor from this. Whence, see what the condition of these three planets is like, and judge on the condition of the matter in each of the aforementioned times accordingly.

However, our sages (if what they said was possible) wanted to adapt so many significators that we could perfect all of our business to our liking. However, we cannot adapt them all as we say they are to be adapted; nor do we always have the opportunity to wait until we can adapt them in this way: since perhaps for the entire time of our lives we shall not be able to make one election so perfect, that it does not lack one of the aforementioned things. Therefore it is necessary that we adapt our elections just as best we can; and if we cannot have everything that we want: we can have something good enough for our labour not to be in vain. Since as said by our most revered predecessor Albumashar (who was better in this art than any Latin ever was, and who studied in Athens, when study thrived there) in a certain book of his, and as he confessed, it is impossible for us to adapt twelve houses: since the malefics cannot be removed from the heavens; whence it is necessary that we adapt what we can adapt, and make whatever good we can. And observe the method which I told you above in adapting the significators which you can adapt: and by doing this you will obtain whatever utility that can be obtained from elections.

And Hali said that the adaption of the house of the end of the matter (namely the fourth) is very necessary, after you have adapted the other root matters; namely, the Lord of the first, the Moon, the Lord of the tenth, and the Part of Fortune. And he said that these are the body of the inceptor. And the planet signifying the matter which someone intends to begin, and the house of the same matter and the Lord of this house signify the perfection of the matter: and therefore he said they are to be adapted.

## IX

### How A Sign Should Be Adapted

Hali said that we ought to adapt the sign signifying the matter which we intend to do or begin: and that it is adapted when it is remote from all impediments. That is, so it is free from malefics and their square aspects and oppositions; and that it is not besieged by two malefics or by their rays, but is clean of them; and this way the sign will signify good. And it will signify greater good if there is some benefic or its rays in it; and this will be better if it aspects it from a trine or sextile aspect. And if many benefics are in it, or aspect it: the more there are, the more its signification for good will be increased.

And he said that if a sign is made fortunate, as was said, that even if it is cadent from an angle, or besieged by malefics, it will not be impeded for that reason; and if it were slightly impeded, this impediment will be such that it will only do the slightest harm, or none at all. But if benefics aspect this sign from square aspect or from opposition, he said that it would not benefit as much (and this is true).

And he said that if benefics and malefics aspect the sign, or are in it together at the same time, the virtue of each of them will be mixed; and the goodness or badness of that sign will be judged according to the multitude of the fortitudes of the benefics or malefics.

However, if it is aspected by, or contains, benefics and malefics in equal measure, it should be spoken of as if there were no benefics or malefics in it. And if the planets who aspect it, or who are in it, have any dignity there, it will be good: since if they are benefics it will increase the good, and if they are malefics it will reduce the evil.

And he said that the Lord of the sign is to be adapted, so that it has two significations there, one from the rulership that it has in it: the other from the good place it is in.

## X

### How A Planet Should Be Adapted

Haly said that to adapt a planet is to make it so that no evil can be said of it, and that it is removed from all impediments, and so that it is clean from all malefics (namely from their conjunctions and aspects), and that it is direct, and not retrograde, combust, nor cadent: nor in a sign that is cadent or impeded in any other way; nor weakened in any other way. Which if it is so disposed, it will strengthen and make fortunate the matter which we want to do or begin, and the place signifying the matter and its end (if it were its significator, whether it is a benefic or not); and in whatever place it is and in whatever sign, the beginning, middle, and end of this matter will always be blessed. And if it is clean from malefics, and disposed as was said, and strong, and in a good place: it is said to be in the perfection of goodness. Still, if one of the benefics were to support it, it is said to increase its perfection. And if the aspect of this benefic is in front, it is even better: if it is behind, it will not increase it as much, even if it will increase it. If however, one of the malefics were to aspect him, it will reduce some of its goodness, and will reduce more if it aspects from the front rather than from behind.

And if we adapt the sign and planets which signify the matter which we want to begin (as was said), our election and its hour will be good and perfect, according to how the sign and planets were adapted. And it is also fitting, if you can, to make the sign and planet (or at least one of them) from which we take the signification agree in nature with the matter which we want to begin. That is, if we want to elect for a matter which is done in water, or through water, or next to water (such as going fishing, sailing, building a boat, building a mill, digging wells, and similar things), we ought to adapt a water sign and a moist planet, or signifying moistness. And if it is an election for a matter on land or by land, (such as is going out to hunt by land, digging ditches, extracting minerals from rocks or stones, or building walls which are not desired to be greatly elevated from the earth, and similar things) we ought to adapt an earth sign, and a planet who is more suitable for it. And if it is an election for matters which pertain to the air, or which are done in the air - such as hunting birds with birds (such as hawks, falcons, ziri, kestrels, and the like); or if we want to build a windmill, or other buildings greatly elevated, which pertain to the air, and similar things; we ought to adapt an air sign and a planet more suited to it. And if our election is for matters which pertain to fire, we ought to adapt a fire sign, and a planet suited to it, as we would do in elections for craftsmen, bakers, and similar people.

And if we elect for matters which we want to be perfected quickly, and those we do not wish to prolong, we should adapt a sign that agrees with quickness, namely a mobile sign, as is the case with taking women as wives (since we want to celebrate the wedding quickly); and in works which we wish to write so that action which is begun will be quickly perfected; and in the sowing and planting of vines; and in the selling of wine to the minute; and in all of those things from which we desire swiftness, and which we want to be perfected quickly.

And if it is an election for something that we wanted to carry out related to quadrupeds, it is fitting that a quadrupedal sign is adapted, according to the species of the animal, and that we place this as the house signifying the animal: so that if we want to buy cows, or other large animals which are cloven hoofed, or if we wanted to do something with them, such as breaking them or castrating them, or something else which pertains to them, we should then adapt the 12th house and make it a sign signifying the aforementioned animals, such as Taurus, or the last half of Sagittarius. And if we wish to carry out a matter related to small animals, we ought to use the sixth, and make it a quadrupedal sign signifying these animals, as are dogs, birds with which we hunt, and also other birds, and similar creatures: such as Aries, and Capricorn, who have the signification of animals (especially small ones) with cloven hooves, as are pigs, sheep, rams, deer, and goats. And we can even attribute these same small cloven hoofed creatures to the 12th house, when we carry out their matters; especially in the selling of them, since they are then signified by the sixth; just as the small animals of others are signified by the twelfth; and also horses, mules, and donkeys as said elsewhere.

And if you wish to head out to hunt cloven hoofed animals, such as stags, deer, and similar creatures: one of those cloven-hooved signs should be placed as the house signifying hunting. And if you are setting out to hunt other animals, who strike with their claws or teeth, such as lions, bears, wolves, and similar beasts: one of the signs which signify these animals should be placed as the house of hunting, if you can do it. But their Lord is not to be strengthened in a hunt, but rather he should be weakened, just as will be explained in its own place below.

Haly also said that we ought to adapt Aries, Leo, and Sagittarius in matters of kings, and magnates: since these signs are suited to them, and this is true: since this triplicity is more noble than the other triplicities by reason of actions, just as fire is the most noble element among the elements, on account of its action. And since the lion is the strongest out of these three animals, it merits being preferred in matters of kings, on account of their excellence among other men. Aries is to be placed second after him, since it is first among the fire signs. And Sagittarius is to be placed last, since it is the last sign in the triplicity, and less strong in heat on account of its dual form. Whence one of these signs are always to be placed as the Ascendant in matters of kings (if we can do it), where it is fitting for them to be the Ascendant; or in the tenth, when it is fitting for them to be the tenth. Similarly we ought to place the significators of the elected matters in the aforementioned signs if we can (provided that they are not weakened from this for

some reason): such as the Lord of the first, and the Moon, and the place signifying the matter, and similarly the planet signifying it.

And Haly said that the domiciles of the planets signify the same things that their Lords do - just as the domiciles of Saturn, which signify darkness and profundity, just as Saturn; and the domiciles of Jupiter, which signify goodness and honesty like Jupiter; similarly the domiciles of Mars, which signify wars and contentions, just as Mars does; the domiciles of Venus, which signify games and joy, just as Venus does; similarly the domiciles of Mercury, which signify writings and philosophy, like Mercury does; and the domiciles of the luminaries, which signify sublimity and clarity, just like the luminaries. For these, when they can be, belong to those things which increase good and fortune, namely when it is the Lord of the house signifying the matter, signifying the same things as its domicile does - or at least the planet should be of the same nature as the sign. So that if it is not possible that the planet is of the same nature as the house signifying the matter, it should be of the nature of the Ascendant or its Lord, or it should signify the same thing as either of them, or at least aspect them by a praiseworthy aspect.

And also take the greatest caution in every election and every beginning (if you can do so), that the nature of the Ascendant and its Lord are not contrary to the nature of the house signifying the matter, or its Lord. And it is even good to make the Lord of the hour of the ayz of the Ascendant, or at least its Lord, it you can, and the more of the significators are the ayz of the Ascendant or its Lord, or the ayz of the house signifying the matter, or its Lord, the better it will be.

Similarly, it should be strived for that a masculine significator of a matter is in a masculine sign, and that a feminine significator is in a feminine sign.

And if it is a durable thing whose end is not expected, or one that the inceptor does not want to end quickly: make the Ascendant Taurus, Leo, Scorpio, or Aquarius; and place the Lord of the Ascendant, the Moon, the Lord of the house signifying the matter, ,the Lord of the hour, and the Part of Fortune and the Lord of its house, all in fixed signs. And if they all cannot be in fixed signs, place as many of them as you can in fixed signs:

since all of these things act toward the good condition of the matter.

If however, it is a matter which someone did not want to last long, make the Ascendant Aries, Cancer, Libra, or Capricorn, and also place its Lord, and the Moon, in such a sign, and make the house signifying the matter a mobile sign, and its Lord in a mobile sign, if you can.

If it is a matter which someone wishes to alter, change, or repeat, as are business partnerships, participations, buying things which we wish to sell, as businessmen do, and similar things, make the Ascendant Gemini, Virgo, Sagittarius, or Pisces.

And it is also good if (along with the other adaptations) we can make the Ascendant one of the signs of direct ascension: since they help the matter, and especially in the pursuit of truth when we want to investigate it.

And if you can place the Moon or the other significators in those signs which I named for you, it will be good.

And similarly, make it so that the Lord of the domicile (or exaltation, or two of the lesser dignities) in which the Moon is placed, aspects the Moon (or any of the significators you can make it aspect) by a trine or sextile aspect, or at least by a square with reception; or at least have the term Lord aspect her, or any of the other significators. And if it does not aspect the Moon, it is better that it aspects the Sun, rather than one of the aforementioned significators. And if the planet who aspects the Moon (or the Sun, or one of the other aforementioned significators) is in a place that is aspected by the Lord of the domicile or exaltation in which it is, it will be better, and then its aspect to the Sun, or to the Moon will be more beneficial.

And place the Part of Fortune or its Lord in the house signifying the matter which we want to do. Or place one of them in the first, the 10th, or the 11th; and make the angles fixed (especially in matters which we want to last for a long time), and not remote, since this will hinder its durability. But if it happens that the angles are remote, make the Lord of one sign aspect that of the other: so if the Ascendant is 28 degrees Pisces, and 3 degrees Taurus is the second house, this angle is of two planets - namely Jupiter and Mars: Jupiter through the direct circle by equal degrees; and Mars by the oblique circle and degrees of ascension. Whence if Jupiter and Mars aspect each other, the remoteness of the angles will not harm, but the aspect will be good and perfecting; and this will be stronger and better if they aspect the first house, or at least one of them. And if they aspect each other, or if they aspect the first house from an angle, and it is an election for some magistracy, dignity, or office from which fame or glory is expected, it will signify, exaltation, glory, a great name, and sublimity. If however, the Lords of these signs do not aspect each other, then you will consider the virtues of both signs, and you will say that Mars and Jupiter are participators of this election which you made.

Also consider the fixed stars (namely those which signify fortune and good, which I will name to you in the Tractate on revolutions), and see if you can place any of them in the degree of the first house, or in the tenth or eleventh, or in the degree of the house signifying the matter for which you wish to elect: for they will increase the good beyond all other significators, and this will be stronger and better if they are of the nature of the planet signifying the mater.

## XI

### Again On The Same.

Again we take up the reigns from Albumashar, who of all astrologers, besides Ptolemy and Hermes, was most perspicuous in judgements, and also the most eloquent of them all: and he said that when we want to elect something (whether it is a pilgrimage or something else), and we find the Lord or exaltation Lord in the sign signifying the matter being elected for, and it is strong (that is, free from impediments), we ought not to have any suspicion of the matter. Or if one of the luminaries is there, and if it is received, it will be better than it could be otherwise. And if one of the benefic planets are in it, it will be good and useful (nor is it a concern whether it has dignity there or not); likewise if there is a malefic there, who is free from the above mentioned impediments, and who has dignity there. And he said that the Sun and Moon should be received, provided that the sign of the Ascendant is not the detriment of either of them.

And Alchindi said that the Moon is not to be placed in the Ascendant, since she is contrary to it; but he allowed the Sun to be placed in it, since he is not contrary to it, since he is of its nature, and he uncovers hidden matters and reveals them, just as the Ascendant uncovers and makes manifest to us what was covered and hidden under the horizon: and the Sun divides things joined together, and reveals secrets. And he said that in the case of the Moon, the opinions of Albumashar are more fitting and more in harmony to the saying of Ptolemy than the opinions of Alchindi; and he said that according to Albumahsar, the Moon is hot and wet, like Venus. And Albumashar testified to this when he spoke about pilgrimages. And he said that Messala and his associates prohibited the Moon being placed on the Ascendant in pilgrimages. And he said that Albumashar did not assent to the sayings of Messala on this. And he said that they judged the Moon to be cold and wet, and the Ascendant to be hot, therefore they were not agreeable together. And he said (and it is true, just as is said elsewhere) that she has signification over beginnings, and especially over the beginnings of pilgrimages: and therefore they said that she ought to be put in a place agreeable to her - which I believe to be the 10th, 11th, 3rd, or 5th; even if they did not specify a place. And he said that they said that the Sun was not to be placed in the Ascendant - because the Sun is a malefic in the conjunction and prevention. And he said that many disagreed with their opinions.

And Haly said that when a benefic is on the Ascendant, and it is unimpeded and favourable, it will be very good. And he said that it was more greatly commended by Aomar Tiberiadis if a benefic was in the first one-third of the house of the Ascendant, since he said that this hastens the matter. However, he said that it seemed to him that if a benefic was in the first degree of the Ascendant, or a little bit after the ascending degree, that it is better, and a more fortunate Ascendant. However, that which Aomar said, was not said for any reason other than that it most rarely occurs that a planet is found on the degree of the Ascendant, and therefore he made more of its strength being greater in the first third of the Ascendant, than in either of the other two thirds; however, he did not deny that the degree of the Ascendant is stronger than the others. What Haly spoke about the degree of the Ascendant itself, he spoke for greater certitude and caution. Regarding those who said that the Sun is not to be placed on the Ascendant,

their intention was regarding when he was malefic - and this is whenever he corporeally joined to any planet, or when he is in the opposition of any planet by five degrees before the degree of the opposition or two after. Whence to avoid all of these impediments, they placed him anywhere except the Ascendant.

Regarding what Alchindi said (that the Moon is not to be placed on the Ascendant) and what Messala likewise said: their intention was on journeys or pilgrimages, since the Moon is naturally impeded from the full moon onwards up to the conjunction, and even before the full Moon by 15 degrees. For in these 15 degrees she is impeded on account of the opposition. From the opposition up to the third dichotomy she is impeded on account of dryness which thrives in her at that time. And from the third dichotomy up to her conjunction with the Sun she is impeded on account of coldness, and at this time she is not to be placed in the Ascendant of a journey, since she will afflict the body of the traveller. Whence, for these reasons they avoid placing her in the Ascendant, and so they would avoid all of her impediments, lest any election might be mistaken in this.

Regarding this, Hali and Albumashar praised the saying of Ptolemy - namely, that the Moon is to be placed in the Ascendant: since she is hot like Venus; it is true, even if Venus herself is judged to be cold and moist, nevertheless she has a certain hidden heat, which appears in the fact that Venus signifies delights, elation, and games: and these are not without an admixture of heat. And similarly the Moon has a certain hidden heat, and also she has a manifest heat, since when she is in the first dichotomy she is moist in nature, and in the second dichotomy she is hot in nature, by the testimony of the Philosopher, and therefore those who placed her in the Ascendant acknowledged it, by the considerations that heat and moistness are more noble than coldness and dryness, and more consistent with the operations of nature, they wanted it to be able to bring more benefit than the cold and dryness could bring in harm. Whence they did not put much force in this impediment, but rather they placed her in the Ascendant.

Allowing that I have said this elsewhere to you, nevertheless I will remind you again, that if you can adapt all the things that the sages told you to, the ultimate good will be in your elections (which appears practically impossible to me). But when you cannot adapt all that you wish at the same time, adapt those which you can; however, make sure to at least adapt the Moon: and if you cannot adapt her, make her cadent from the Ascendant, and adapt the Lord of the hour at the very least, and it will be of some assistance to you in your matter.

There are also certain other things which increase fortune and prosperity and good: namely the degree of the conjunction and the degree of the prevention which are before your inception or election which you intend to make: namely when it (and its Lord) is fortunate and clean from malefics and their aspects, if you can do this. The place of the conjunction is the degree in which the Sun and Moon were joined together. Indeed, the place of the prevention is the degree and minute of the luminary which was above the earth at the hour of the prevention. And if one luminary was in the oriental degree and the other in the occidental degree: the degree of the prevention is that which was in the east.

For Alchindi said that the conjunction has signification over all things which come to be between the conjunction and the prevention; and the prevention has signification over everything which comes to be between the prevention and the conjunction; therefore it is necessary in every beginning, nativity, and election, that (if possible) you adapt the place of the conjunction or prevention, and consider it, so that we know whether it is in an angle, a succeedent, or a cadent, and which of the planets might be in the degree of the conjunction or prevention; and which of the benefics or malefics (or their aspects) are in its sign; and who are the planets that aspect this degree by whatever aspect. And likewise consider the Lord of the degree of the conjunction or prevention, that is, if it is under the beams of the Sun, or in its own light. These are the things which signify what is going to be regarding those things which come to be between the conjunction and prevention, and between the prevention and the conjunction: which if they are safe, signify the perfection of matters and their goodness. If they are impeded, they will signify their weakness and instability.

And it should also to be considered that the Moon is not joined to malefics when she is separating from the degree of the conjunction or prevention; but rather than she is joined to benefics, and that the degree of the conjunction or prevention is with benefics in any of the angles. And also that the Moon is moving towards a conjunction with a benefic in the hour of the conjunction or prevention, if it can be done: since these things will signify the exaltation and goodness of matters, their perfection, and a praiseworthy end.

If however, the place of the conjunction or prevention is impeded, and the Moon is joined to a malefic after separating from any of these two places, it signifies that even if the beginnings of matters made within these times were laudable, nevertheless their end will be bad; and the conjunction of the Moon with the planets is stronger than the degree of the conjunction or prevention. Whence if she was joined to benefics after her separation from these places, even though one of those places might be in an angle with malefics, even if the beginning of these matters were not praiseworthy, nevertheless their end will be praiseworthy and good. If however, the place of the conjunction or prevention were with malefics, as was said, and when the Moon was joined to malefics when she separated from these places, it signifies the beginning, middle, and end of these matters to be evil, and not praiseworthy; unless the Lord of the sign in which the conjunction or prevention was were oriental in an angle, and in its own domicile, exaltation, triplicity, terms; or aspects that house where the conjunction or prevention was - since if this is so, it shatters the malice of the others: since it has greater virtue than any of the above-mentioned significators in matters which come to be in the aforementioned times. If indeed, it is in a succedent from an angle, even if the beginning of the matter might be weak, nevertheless its end will flourish and be good. However, if it is occidental or outside of its dignities mentioned above, or cadent from an angle, or not aspecting that house, it will increase the malice of the others, and will make matters worse. And if the place of the conjunction is cadent from an angle, the things which were begun between that conjunction or prevention will be evil and of no utility. All of this is referred back to the intention of Alchindi, but his intention was not absolute, but was so that we made a good election; and that those things which he said were all well disposed; for he said that elections will be assisted from this, and that incepted matters will arrive to a better and faster end; and if they are not well disposed, that it will subtract something from the good, but will not be able to destroy the beginning of a well elected matter. And if the election is bad, and these are badly disposed, the evil will be increased and come to pass quicker.

And Haly said that what clearly increases the good, is if we adapt the place of the Lord of the quarter or the year in all elections, just as was said regarding the place of conjunction or prevention. However, he said that the adaptation of the place of the conjunction or prevention is more appropriate in this work than the adaptation of the Lord of the quarter of the year; and that of the Lord of the quarter of year is more appropriate than the adaptation of the Lord of the year of the world: nevertheless he said that we can adapt all of them that are not evil.

Indeed, Albumashar said that when the Lord of an election is the Lord of the sign of the Moon in the revolution of the year, or the Lord of the Ascendant of the year is made fortunate in the hour of an election and the hour of the revolution, it signifies the increase of the inceptors' honour, and a praiseworthy end of the matter. And he said when the Lord of the Ascendant of the year does not testify in either of the places of the luminaries, nor the place of the Midheaven, the matters begun will be worthless, middling, and meagre .

Indeed, Atabari said (just as Haly recites) that when the place of the conjunction or prevention, and its Lord are in a praiseworthy place, that matter (namely was begun at that time) will be durable and firm. And likewise if someone is born in the same hour, or appointed (whether placed in command of a position of command, or an office or a dignity), the matter will be firm and durable. And he said, that these places are laudable in the hour of the beginning of matters.

And the ancients took testimony (in adapting matters to be done) from the Lords of the triplicities of the sign in which the Moon was at the hour of the conjunction or prevention, saying that they are guardians of matters, as much of the person beginning or doing a matter, as of the matter itself, as of journeys, and as of other things: which if they are received in the hour of the inception or election, will signify good; if however, they are to the contrary, they will signify evil. And they said that what increases the good is when the Ascendant of an election is a fortunate sign in the revolution of

the year; and that the benefic which makes this sign fortunate is in the first or the tenth; or the eleventh or fifth, or at least in the second; or is in the house which signifies the matter which we elected for; so that it will work out well for him wanting to do it. And the significators of the matter which we begin should be in places agreeing with the aforementioned significators (namely a domicile of the aforementioned triplicity); and that the significators are strong in the hour of the election or beginning.

And Haly said regarding the strengths of the planets, such as when they are ascending in the north: that it is sometimes necessary that a planet is ascending in the south, and it is a strength for it: such as the Moon when she is increasing in light and number is stronger ascending in the south, than if she is then ascending in the north; and that the Moon should be in angles increasing in light and number in matters which we want to be increased; in matters to the contrary, she should be to the contrary. And he said that the significators should be going under the benefics and over the malefics, indeed, the Moon and the significator of the quesited matter, or the matter about to be begun or done, should be above the earth in every matter that we want to make manifest. And in all matters which we want to hide, the Moon and the significators should be below the earth; and the Lord of the Ascendant and whatever other significators we can make so, should be oriental; and the planet to whose conjunction the Moon moves, should be benefic - this planet signifies the end of the incepted matter, and what will come to be regarding it.

And Alchindi said that when the Sun and the Moon aspect each other by a friendly aspect, it signifies the strength and goodness of any incepted matter; and more strongly so if the Moon is in the third degree of Taurus, since then it signifies the ultimate goodness of the matter which we wish to begin or do, even if the other significators are not well disposed - provided that they are not besieged by two malefics without reception.

And Messala said, that planets are said to be strong when they are occidental from the Moon, just as they are when they are oriental from the Sun: since the Moon rules at night just as the Sun rules in the day.

However, Atabari said that if we cannot adapt both the Moon and the Ascendant, let us adapt one of them. For it is a diurnal election, we should adapt the Ascendant, especially if the Moon is under the earth: however, if it is a nocturnal election, we should adapt the Moon, and especially if she is above the earth. And he said, that if we are able to defer our election from the day to the night, or from the night to the day, it should be considered which of them is better adapted) namely the Moon or the Ascendant, and we ought to do with them what appears better to us.

And Haly said that the condition of the Moon under the earth in the day, and above the earth at night is good, and increases the strength of the Ascendant. And if it is necessary for us to elect for anyone, and we cannot adapt the Moon, we should place Jupiter or Venus in the first, or in the tenth - for they will adapt the matter with a great adaption. And he said that they make it last a long time.

Nevertheless Haly said that the adaptation of the Moon is to be preferred in all matters which we wish to last for a long time, such as constructions, as much of cities as of houses; and the celebration of marriages and similar things. And when the Moon is weak, she is to be removed from the angles; and if we cannot remove her from the angles, she is not to aspect the Ascendant or its Lord; nor the house of the elected matter or its Lord; nor even the planet which signifies the matter elected for. And if we cannot remove her from all the aspects mentioned above, she should at least be removed from those which she can be removed from

And Alchindi said that if we were unable to adapt all of the significators, but we were able to adapt the Moon, it will be good. However, he did not promise us that the matter wouldn't be destroyed. Whence, if the Lord of the house signifying the matter which we want to do or incept can be adapted, it is better on account of the matter, so that it can last, or come to the end which we desire from it; and the burden will be considered less by the astrologer, than if he had adapted the Moon and the Lord of the first, which signify the person of the querent or inceptor: but for the preservation of the person of the querent or inceptor, the Moon and Lord of the first should be adapted. However, men only consider what happens concerning the matter itself, and they look to its occurrence, not caring about the state of the person.

If however, the Moon is slow-of-course (namely similar to the course of Saturn), that is, she moves less than 12 degrees in a single day, it signifies difficulty and slowness; however, if that which we intend to make or begin is a building, or something which the inceptor intends to raise above the earth, and the Moon is slow-of-course, and the other significators are below the earth, that building will never be raised; and if it is raised, it will happen extremely slowly; nor will it be raised in the whole age in which it was begun.

And if you cannot make the Moon fortunate like you wished to do in your matter, and there is a planet who makes her unfortunate, and you cannot avoid this impediment, place the planet who impedes her as the Lord of the first: since the first does not impede itself nor the Moon to its own detriment. And if you can place him in the first, and make him free from the impediments which are spoken of elsewhere, it will be better. And if you cannot place him in the first, place him in one of the other laudable places (such as the tenth, eleventh, or fifth): and if it were possible that he could receive the Moon, it will shatter all of his malice completely; for the praiseworthy condition of the Moon and the other significators increases the good and diminishes the evil: and their bad condition increases the evil and diminishes the good.

And beware of the conjunction of malefics, and their square aspect or opposition without reception, with the Moon or with the other significators, and that they are not impeded. For it does not harm from a trine or sextile aspect, provided that they are otherwise free; in fact, when they are received from a trine or sextile aspect, and they are free, they are made benefics.

And always place the significators as strongly as you can, and guard them and the Moon from the impediments of malefics as best as you know how; and make it so that there are not malefics in the places by which the matters which we intend to do or begin are signified; nor aspecting these places from a square aspect or from opposition.

And Haly said to beware of eclipses, and especially if the eclipse is in a sign in which a luminary was in the nativity of him for whom we elect. And he said not to have the Moon under the rays, and that she is to be completely removed from all impediments; and do not have the significator joined to the Sun, nor him to the significator; and the square aspect and opposition of the Sun are to be guarded against; but nevertheless if there is reception between them, it will be somewhat easier. And he said that the opposition always gives disputes and contrarieties.

And also make it so that malefics are not in the angles, and especially not in the Ascendant or the tenth; and maximally if malefics are the Lords of the houses signifying evil (these are the sixth, the eighth, and the twelfth): since then they will signify that which is signified by their houses. And he said the Ascendant should not be a sign whose Lord is about to enter into combustion in that year; nor should the Ascendant should be a sign which is impeded in the revolution of the same year; nor should the Moon be slow-of-course in any matter which we want to come to pass quickly, since she postpones it and slows it down, unless there are many significators.

And he said that mobile signs are to be removed in all matters which we want stability and durability from: and in the same way fixed signs are to be removed in all matters which we want to transpire quickly. Common signs are to be removed from all matters which we want to come to be just as the matter occurs: for these return whatever is difficult in them.

And he said to beware lest any of the fixed stars which are of the nature of malefics are in the degree of the Ascendant, the Midheaven, or the house of the matter elected for; and I found all of the sages who make mention of these things in agreement on this topic - since these stars are malicious.

One of which is in the fourteenth degree of Aries, and another in the fifteenth degree of the same.

One is in the tenth degree of Taurus, and another in the twentieth.

One is in the eighteenth degree of Gemini.

One of them is in the eighth degree of Cancer, another in the eighteenth degree.

One is in the sixteenth degree of Leo.

One is in the eighth degree of Virgo, another in the sixteenth degree.

One is in the sixteenth degree of Libra.

One is in the seventh degree of Scorpio; and there are two in the ninth degree of the same sign.

One is in the twentieth degree of Sagittarius, another is in the twenty-second degree of the same.

One is in the twenty-eighth degree of Capricorn, another in the next.

One is in the tenth degree of Aquarius.

Another is in the fifth degree of Pisces.

I strongly recommend that you do all of the things which he said that you should do; and that you avoid all that he said that you should avoid, if you can do it. However, it seems to me that it is hardly or ever possible to do so. Nevertheless you, as I have said to you elsewhere, should do whatever good things you can do, and avoid whatever bad things you can avoid; since it will hardly be but that it will be beneficial, even if it is not as much as the person undertaking the matter wishes.

And Alchindi said that it is bad for the angles to be remote. Indeed, Haly praised the angles being remote, but the intention of Alchindi was that the angles were remote by receding from the angles: that is, that if one sign was the ninth house, or the twelfth, or the third, or the sixth; and this same sign which was the ninth house was the tenth house; or that sign which was the twelfth house was the first; or that sign which was the third house was the fourth; or that sign which was the sixth house was the seventh: the angles being remote in this way is bad, since they are removed toward the cadents.

Indeed, others understood by this remoteness that it is made toward the angles: that is, if one sign is the tenth house, and the same sign is the eleventh; or it one the first house, and is also the second; or if one is the fourth and also the fifth; or if one is the seventh and also the eighth - this remoteness is not bad, since it is toward the angles moving towards them; and this is the remoteness which Haly praised in matters whose durability we desire.

And Haly said that it should be guarded against that the Lord of the Ascendant, or the Lord of the house signifying the matter for which we elect, or even the planet signifying the matter itself, or the Lord of the sign in which the Moon is, or the planet to which she joins (if she joins anyone), are not in the second from the Sun. Namely, that when they are occidental, they are not so close to him that they fall in the second domicile from him; unless it is Venus or Mercury, since they do not have so great a prerogative or being greatly elongated from him. Since this signifies the worthlessness, delay, and impurity of the matter. Indeed, the three superiors, when they are distant from the Sun by two whole signs, and occidental up to the completion of the third sign, are said to be in decline, which is a certain impediment for them in elections: and especially in things which we intend to perfect quickly: since it delays the matter; but does not prohibit it so that it does not happen: even if it will not happen as fast.

And Haly said, that if it is necessary for us to elect something, and we were to have one of the laudable hours: then it will not harm by a great harm if the Moon is joined to Mars or Saturn at that time, provided that the matter for which we want to elect is one of the matters which are signified by the benefics; such as a lay dignity, or a magistracy, or similar things which are signified by the Sun; or is for substance or the accumulation of money, which are both signified by Jupiter; or they are matters of women, or games, or other things which are signified by Venus; or writings, trade, or commodities, which are signified by Mercury, and similar things; since the malefics cannot impede these matters so that they do not come to be, or that they are not perfected - even if they can mix in some of their malice (which they naturally signify). And especially when they are received they will only impede a small amount, or not at all: since then the malice will be made a small fraction of whatever malice there is from it. Indeed, when wild and horrible malefics are not received, they will impede more; nevertheless they cannot avert the matter so that it does not come to be.

However, if there is a matter which we want to elect for which is one of those things which we wish to hide, and the Sun aspects the Ascendant or its Lord, and the Sun is in good condition; and the Moon aspects Mercury, and they both aspect the Sun by a laudable aspect - the matter will not be hidden or kept secret, but will be made public. And if the flight of someone is begun at this time, he will be captured. And if the Sun aspects the Ascendant or its Lord, or the Moon by an evil aspect (namely a square or opposition), the matter will be revealed by a vile and reprehensible revelation. And if the significators of the matter are above the earth, the matter will also be revealed; and this more strongly so if they are in the Midheaven. If the Ascendant or the Moon are under the rays of the Sun; or if the Sun and Moon are cadent from the Ascendant, and do not aspect each other; or if the Moon and the significators of the matter for which we are electing are under the earth, and especially in the fourth - it signifies that the matter will be hidden and will not be revealed. And if the Lord of the Ascendant is Mars or Saturn, or some other unfortunate planet, evil and contrary things will follow for the concealer from the concealment of matter; and this more strongly so if the luminaries are impeded; however, if the luminaries are free, the evil will not harm him.

And Haly also said that all of the things which are praiseworthy, and which are not praiseworthy, were not to be considered until after the adaptation of the roots of those things named above. And he said, that when the benefics are strong and rule in these roots, we ought not to examine those things which were arranged beforehand, even if they were evil. And he said when benefics are strong, and ruling in the election, we only ought to examine those things which we saw that ought to be praised. And he said that if the roots are praiseworthy, the good fortune and good is multiplied. If indeed, the roots are evil, that which follows, even if it is laudable, will neither change nor remove that malice, but will increase it according to its own malignity.

And he said that if it is necessary for us to begin anything, and malefics preside over the inception, the things that follow should be adapted: since they will subtract something from the evil, even if they will not destroy it in whole.

And he said that it should be guarded against, lest these things that follow are evil: such as if someone enquires from an astrologer to elect a good hour for him to do something; or if it is a matter which he does not want to disclose to the astrologer, now the astrologer is in doubt as to what he wants to incept, since he has not revealed his intention to him; nor is the astrologer certain as to which planet or sign signifies the intended matter. Whence he ought to then adapt the Ascendant and its Lord, both of the luminaries, and the fourth and its Lord, to guard the body and mind of the inceptor, and the end of the matter (whether the matter which he intended to do is perfected or not).

And he said that in all such matters, they should be incepted in hours in which Jupiter, Venus, or the Sun rule: since by observing this, you will adapt all matters, whatever kind they are.

And he said that if we know the nativity of the querent or inceptor, or if we have his question, and if it is necessary for us to weaken one of the significators: we ought to weaken the seventh of the nativity or the question, or its Lord; just as we do when we want to depart for war or hunting, in which cases we weaken the Lord of the seventh, and the like. If however, we do not know the nativity, and we do not have a question, we should adapt what was said to be adapted (namely the Ascendant of the election and its Lord, and the Moon, etc.); and we should weaken the seventh of the election and its Lord, etc., as was said elsewhere. And we ought to adapt a planet, a sign, and an hour, signifying the sex of the person for whom we are electing: like Venus for women in their affairs, as was said above; and we ought to adapt them a feminine sign if we can, and make the hour of their affairs one of the feminine and nocturnal hours. In the affairs of men we ought to adapt masculine signs, and likewise make their affairs in masculine and diurnal hours, if we can. And a sign and planet signifying the inceptors' people is also to be adapted.

And you also ought to adapt the planet which signifies the region, province, or city of him for whom you elect; but it is a very difficult matter to know which planet rules a city or land; not will you be able to know this otherwise than through conjecture, unless perhaps you have the hour of the founding of the land, which is very rarely possible to obtain: however, you could get its signification more easily through a question. But if you do not have the hour of its founding, or a question: consider the character and customs of the men of this land, and their life; and consider what tend to happen to them in great and difficult businesses of victories and defeats. And you will be able to judge its significator according to what planets you see ruling in these accidents (whether they are good or bad). Also consider the character and customs of their citizens, of what kind they are: for if they are good and honest, and they are men of a good way

of life, and freely making money from honest profit, or at least from things that are not shameful; and who freely spend and live honourably, even if they may over abound in luxury: nevertheless the sign is that Jupiter is their significator: whence you can adapt him in their elections which you do not have a question for.

Nevertheless a question is a trivial matter, and you will easily get the significator of the city, and its citizens through one: provided that it is asked by someone whose business it is - such as through a leader or administrator established over it, and other such people.

However, if they are avaricious men, thieves, miserable men, those whose customs are different to others, striving to make profit in any way they can, not considering whether it is by licit or illicit means - the sign is that Saturn is their significator.

If however, they are stately men, striving to rule, and desirous of praise, yet of a good and praiseworthy life, and appropriate expenses - the sign is that the Sun is their significator.

However, if they are bellicose, criminal, contentious, spirited, evil doers, furious, arrogant, making money from anywhere they can, and by lawful and unlawful means, pilfering, stingy, avoiding spending, and having disgraceful habits and vices - the sign is that Mars is their significator.

If they are ingenious, wise, literary, profound in the sciences, of good expenses, of good character, not jealous, not avaricious, merchants of average dealings, spurning money, not intent on acquiring wealth - the sign is that Mercury is their significator.

However, if they are men of comfort, games, feasts, foods and drinks, musical instruments, and whatever kind of amusements, spurning avarice - the sign is that Venus is their significatrix.

However, if they are unfaithful, changeable, wandering, unstable, sometimes wanting this, sometimes wanting that, and engaging in small business deals - the sign is that the Moon is their significator.

We can even adapt any planet we want to diverse matters: for we can adapt Saturn to the aforementioned, and we also can adapt him for those wishing to dye things in the colour black, since he naturally signifies blackness; and he is to be placed so that he aspects the first and is Lord by a praiseworthy aspect; and also place the Moon (or at least the Lord of the house she is placed in) in a friendly aspect with him; or have her in a domicile of Saturn, not cadent from the Ascendant or from the tent (however, it is better that she aspects Saturn from a good aspect).

Likewise, we can adapt Jupiter to the aforementioned, and many other things, and especially those which we wish to dye in the colour citrine: since he naturally signifies this, and he should be placed as was said of Saturn.

We can also adapt Mars to the aforementioned, and many other things, and especially those which we want to dye in the colour red: since he naturally signifies this colour, and he is to be adapted as was said of Jupiter. Mars can also be adapted for slaves on account of his falsity, since slaves often act by it.

Furthermore we can adapt the Sun to the aforementioned things, and certain others, and especially those things which we want to dye in a mixed colour, which participates in a mixture of many and diverse colours.

Similarly we can adapt Venus to all of the mentioned things, and to many others, and especially those which we wish to make white: since she naturally signifies white.

We can also adapt Mercury for all of the things named above, and similarly to certain other things, and especially those things which we want to dye in a colour that is almost indigo, or purple, or semi-purple, and all other mixed and variously composed colours.

Similarly we can adapt the Moon to everything said above, and many other things besides; and especially those which we wish to dye in a pale yellow colour; likewise for all colours of little durability.

And just as one planet can be adapted to many and diverse things, so can one house be adapted to many and diverse things: and many houses can be adapted to one and the same matter, just as the second house is adapted to substance, and the sixth similarly is adapted to substance - since it signifies slaves which are substance, and small animals which are also substance; and similarly the twelfth signifies large animals, which are substance. And understand this for all of the houses, just as was said in the Tractate on the twelve houses.

And many planets can also be adapted to one thing, such as if we wanted to elect for a slave or purchased Slav: since he is also to be counted among slaves: we can adapt Mars or Saturn for any of them, since each of them speak falsely. Likewise we can adapt Venus to all things, and also for the adaptation of clothing and other women's ornaments. However, if it is a war banner or other garments which pertain to war: as is a sack for supplies and equipment, and similar things: Mars, the Lord of the first, the Moon, and her Lord should be adapted. And if it is another item of clothing, we will adapt the first and its Lord, the Moon also, and as many of the other planets as we can; and we will put the Sun in the tenth, just as will be said in its own special chapter, when the donning of new vestments is dealt with.

## XII

## On The Weakening Of The Planets

For just as sometimes the planets are to be adapted, at other times some of them are to be weakened (as I remember touching on above), in proportion to the necessity of weakening a matter which we want to do. For if we wanted to set out against an army, it is fitting that we weaken the 7th and its Lord as much as we can, and that we strengthen the Lord of the first, etc. However, if we wish to go out hunting, it is fitting for us to weaken the seventh and its Lord; and it is fitting for us to debilitate the Moon, but not make her unfortunate, unless perhaps she is made unfortunate by the Lord of the first or the Lord of the sixth (since they have signification of the aforementioned things or the animals with which we hunt). Still, there are certain men who say she is to be made unfortunate. If we want to follow a robber or another fugitive, it is fitting for us to weaken the Moon, and even make her unfortunate - and especially if we can make it so that the Lord of the first is the planet who makes her unfortunate: since then it signifies that the fugitive will not escape from the clutches of those who follow him.

Sometimes the Moon is to be weakened, but she is not to be made unfortunate, such as when we administer drugs: since she is then to be placed in Scorpio, so that the humours flow through all parts in which the medicine is apt to exercise is power and what pertains to it. And it is fitting that we then guard against malefics, namely from Mars and Saturn: for Saturn can bind medicine together, while Mars can incite it so much that it leads to the loss of blood; and perhaps that it injures the intestines, and it is possible that dysentery could arise from this, which could cause the death of him who took the drug. And so we ought not to make the Moon unfortunate in these matters, but only to weaken her; and to strengthen the Lord of the first and make him fortunate: and on this, our ancient sages appear to agree

## XIII

## On The Particular Things Which Pertain To Elections

After having a general discussion in the preceding chapters concerning the steps pertaining to general elections, it appears fitting to descend to particulars: for those things which are universally called particulars, are best known through experience. Nor is it necessary for us when dealing with the particulars to recall to memory those things which were said about universal things: for that would overly prolong the work and generate boredom in the reader: but only to subjoin those regarding the matter or each chapter. Yet it is not possible to pass over this without getting our feet wet, and occasionally touching on some of the aforementioned things. Nevertheless I will proceed down as easy a path as I can: nor will I involve myself in saying everything which could be understood from the sages regarding elections: even if certain men said that the Indians always avoid the combust hours in every matter. Nevertheless I would give praise if someone could adapt every contingency; but just as I remember having said to you elsewhere, it seems almost impossible to be able to adapt everything, and if we wished to inspect everything to a point, the hours would grow to a frightening number, so that we would only make the rarest and fewest election. Nevertheless you should follow what I have told you.

*On The Diminishing Hours*

And the Egyptians avoided certain hours of certain days of every month, which they called diminishing days and hours; which if someone could observe, it would be good: but if they cannot be observed, it is not a dangerous thing, like some people believed. And I will make you out a table, so that if you wish to avoid them, you can know when they are. Nor should you be surprised if mention is not made here of many things which appear appropriate for this work (namely the work of elections) namely about the sex of a figure, of their regulating, of their ascending and setting, and similar things: since all of these, if you remember well, are discussed elsewhere. For here they are not discussed, with the sole exception of the useful ones, just as the remedies of the philosophers are excepted as being the useful things from their books.

## XIV

## What Things Are To Be Considered In The Beginnings Of The Elections Of Those Whose Nativities We Know

In the elections mentioned above, the things which ought to be universally considered were discussed; what is to be examined next are those things in particular cases which are to be examined first and principally. And the ancients said that there are three principle things in elections:

They said the first of which is to consider which planets are stronger in the root of the nativity or question, and that (if possible) he is to be placed in an angle or their succedents; and that he should be free from malefics and other impediments, and should be strong and fortunate, and above the earth joined to benefics; and if he is a benefic, it will be better; but if he is a malefic, he should be removed from the angle, since he will be exasperated in his operations, so that he might impede the matter so it is not done, (and it appears that he will be the cause of a faster destruction). Nor is he to be placed in a cadent, since then his virtue will not be strong enough to perfect the matter; and so he is to be placed in a succedent, and thus his virtue and power will be suitable for our matter. And the Lord of the sign in which the Part of Fortune was at the hour of the nativity or question should be adapted;

and likewise the Lord of the revolution of the nativity or the question, if it is possible; and the Part of Fortune of the revolution of the year and its Lord; and the Lord of the second sign from the Ascendant of this revolution, and the Lord of the hour of the election, which certain men call the "*Lord of the Orb*".

The second is to make the Ascendant of the election and its tenth free from malefics and their prohibited aspects; and it is recommended that there is any benefic in it, or that a benefic aspects it from a trine or sextile aspect, and it is also recommended to make the Ascendant of the election the first sign of the root nativity or question (or its tenth, or at least its eleventh), if it is free at that time, and is free in the nativity or question. And it is a greater impediment if it is not free in the election than if it is so in the nativity. If this cannot be done, the Ascendant of the election is to be placed as the sign in which the Part of Fortune was placed in the nativity or question; or the second from the Ascendant of the nativity or question provided that it is free. If it cannot be one of these, as often happens, adapt the Ascendant of the election as best you can, and the others as I said to you. And if you cannot adapt what you want, adapt what you can: so that your election is of value to him who you elected for.

And you can elect in another manner, which is not to be condemned, namely that you place the Ascendant of the election as the sign in the nativity or question which signifies the matter for which you elect, provided that it is free from malefics and their aspects - unless this impeding malefic is the Lord of the sign of the Ascendant of the nativity or question, since then it will not impede itself.

And before all other avoidable things, it is to be guarded against that the Ascendant of the election is not the sixth, eighth, or twelfth, of the nativity or question. And if you can make the Ascendant of the election one of the good places which were in the nativity or question, it will be good; and if possible, even adapt the place of the Part of Fortune of the nativity or question (and its Lord) in your election: and the sign of the profection, and its Lord; which if you cannot adapt them all, remember what I have told you many times: adapt those of them which of them you can. And regardless of what happens with the others, adapt the Ascendant and its Lord, the Moon, the Lord of the Ascendant of the election,

and the planet signifying the matter for which you elect; and make them as strong as you can, and place them in the aspect of benefics. And if you cannot place them all in the aspect of benefics, at least place the Lord of the Ascendant, the Moon and the planet signifying the matter in the aspect of benefics: since these will remove all of the malice from your election. And if you can place the planet signifying the matter for which you elect in the Ascendant of the nativity, your matter will come to be more easily, and without great labour.

And if the benefics which aspect the aforementioned significators are strong and free from malefics and from other impediments, the matter for which you elected will arrive to any end you wish. If however, the Lord of the nativity, election, or question, is in a house signifying the matter for which you elect, and is free, or aspects the house from a trine or sextile aspect, the matter will come to be, but with difficulty, obstacles, and labour. If however, it is impeded, it will impede the matter and will hardly or never permit it to be perfected. And if the Lord of the matter for which was elected aspects with the Lord of the Ascendant of the election (or the nativity, question, or revolution) by a trine or sextile aspect, and they are free and not impeded, it signifies that the matter will arrive at a praiseworthy end.

Indeed, the third is to examine whether the person whose nativity is at hand, or for whom we have a question, wants to incept something from which he hopes for good, such as great journeys, great businesses, or even great buildings, or any other such works, that are reputed as great: for then it is to be examined through his own nativity or general question, or the question made on the occasion, as to whether something unlucky, or something horrible that is to be feared is signified in that year which he intends to do the thing: for then he is to be prohibited from beginning that work until the disposition passes from that planet who appears to threaten evil for him at that time. If it cannot be deferred, make the Lord of the Ascendant of the election fortunate and strong; and also the Moon and the Lord of the house signifying the matter; and make the planet who is threatening the horrible thing weak, and not aspecting the Ascendant, nor the signifying houses, nor their Lords, nor the Moon. And if you cannot avoid all of this, at least make it so that it doesn't aspect the Ascendant, or is Lord, or the Part of Fortune (or at least its Lord);

and make it (if you ever can) that some benefic, or its rays from a trine or sextile aspect, fall in the place in which that impeding planet was in at the hour of the nativity or question. And if you cannot do this, then remove the malefic who threatens that horrible thing from the Ascendant, and from the place of the matter, as was said. Also remove as many of the other malefics as you can from these places. And whenever you see a planet in your election who signifies the impediment of the matter for which you elect, in the nativity of him for whom you elect; weaken it as much as you can, and strive in every way to strengthen the planet signifying the matter, and the sign in which it was placed in the nativity or question; and if you cannot strengthen them both, at least strengthen the sign. And strive to strengthen everything which I said to you; and if you cannot do what you wish, again I say to you: do what you can in the relief of the things said above: namely, that you ought to guard against the planet signifying fear in a nativity. If it is signified in the nativity that the matter which you (or another) wishes to begin is useful, you will hardly ever be able to make an election so weak, that its effecting won't be good; nevertheless, your election is still to be adapted as best you can, so that it turns out better for you from it.

You should also take precautions that you make no election about any matter in the hour of the eclipse of one of the luminaries, unless perhaps it were about a matter which is to be hidden: and elections are more greatly to be avoided at this time, if the eclipse is in the sign that was the Ascendant at the hour of the nativity or question; and it is good if you can avoid the whole of that triplicity; however, it is not as much of a concern as the Ascendant.

If possible, you should also take care that if Venus is impeded in the nativity, you do not place the Moon in sextile aspect to Mars or Saturn, whether they receive her or not. And if Jupiter was impeded, do not place her in their trine aspect. And if Mars was impeded, don't place her in the square aspect of Saturn. And if Saturn is impeded, do not place her in opposition to Mars. And if Mercury was impeded, do not place her less than 31 degrees away from any of them, if you can.

## XV

### If The Matter About Which A Question Were Proposed By Someone Ought To Be Perfected Or Not, When We Elect For It

As was said elsewhere, many wise men (one of whom was Alchaiat), when they wished to elect for someone, and they did not have his nativity for the purpose of knowing whether he quesited matter could be perfected or not, they took the question of whatever matter was going to be incepted, and if they saw that it ought to be perfected, they examined whether it would be useful or not; and they elected according to that question just as they would elect over a nativity. Nor did they elect otherwise for anyone, and it appeared that their opinion was sound for this purpose, as their elections were secure, and perfected.

But it did not appear useful to elect thus for someone wanting to have an election over a matter which he wanted to begin: however, it was good to elect over a nativity or a question. But sometimes agreeable elections occur, about which we cannot judge questions, nor see their end according to judgements: and nevertheless it is necessary for the astrologer to elect for him who consults him; and I have already told you above that you can elect for anyone wishing to begin something, and your election will be useful to him, just as I have shown to you elsewhere, if you remember well.

It is even true that by a nativity or question we can know the end of an incepted or about to be incepted matter, which does not happen through any election; still, we ought to hope that they will be useful, wherefore we elect what seems better to us; since as I have told you already, a good election can benefit, indeed, it can do little harm; nor did I ever find Ptolemy (who was the best astrologer) prohibit the astrologer from electing without the aforementioned nativities or questions. And it was the intention of the philosophers that the evils which were signified through a nativity or a question could be destroyed by a good election, and if they were not destroyed in whole, they could be greatly diminished and alleviated.

Likewise, there were certain others who wished that we only elected for those whose nativities we knew; and there are few of these, and few would benefit from elections if this was so. For they said that a nativity is a natural thing, a question is not so, in fact it is an unnatural thing. But still, even if a question is not a natural matter, nevertheless it is very close to one; just as the reason for appealing a judgement, is that close to the principle reason, that he who wins the appeal is made stronger in the judgement of the matter being judged.

And there is another way of electing, and it can be known through it whether a matter will be perfected after a question is posed: that if the Ascendant of the question was made fortunate, or the Ascendant of the conjunction or prevention which was made before the question, was made fortunate: the sign is that the matter will be perfected. If indeed, it is made unfortunate, it signifies an impediment so that the matter will not be perfected. If however, a nativity or question is had, the Ascendant or tenth of the nativity or question, is to be placed as the Ascendant of the election, or the sign signifying the matter which we want to begin, if it is fortunate. If indeed, one of these are not fortunate, it is to be considered what the Ascendant was at the hour of the Sun's entry into Aries that year (or the hour of his entry into any other quarter of the year, if the year revolves according to quarters): and if it is fortunate; or its tenth; or the sign signifying the matter in that hour: and whichever one of these you find more fortune - make that the Ascendant of the election for the matter for which you elect; and do this for both those whose nativities are known, or for whom questions are had, and for others. And this likewise signifies the effecting of the matter.

It can also be elected in another way for those whose nativities are unknown, and whose questions are not had: but this way is difficult, since we do not know everything which happens to someone. But if some big accident of someone's is made plain to you, you can know how you ought to elect for him in the inceptions of his matters; and this will be stronger, better, and more secure, if that accident is the first thing that happens to him, whether this accident is good, or bad - good as in dignities or some great magistracy, or similar things which do not usually happen to him; and the greater these dignities are, the greater will be the similarly between Ascendant of the election and that of the nativity of him for whom you wanted to elect; and likewise, the greater the evil is, the more

its Ascendant and his Ascendant will be in harmony.

But if that accident is evil, that Ascendant is to be avoided in his election, just as it will be something to be taken up if the accident is good; and its contrary (namely the seventh) should be rejected, and you could elect for him through the seventh from the Ascendant of the evil accident, if you do not have his nativity or question. Indeed, accidents are said to be evil when something greatly disagreeable befalls him: like adversities which do not usually happen to him, such as the loss of his greatest, or great matters, or infirmities, shipwrecks, a long captivity, and similar things. Whence the Ascendant of these accidents is to be known, and is to be observed, just as the Ascendant of the nativity or question, if you can know it; and if you can't, do it as I said to you elsewhere - adapt what you can adapt, so that your election can benefit him for whom you elect.

And according to this same method we can consider that when some planet is fortunate and strong, or some sign is fortunate, and pleasing and useful will happen to someone, that this has virtue in his root nativity; and when some sign is unfortunate or some planet is unfortunate, and things turn out adversely for him - that this sign or planet has virtue in the root of his nativity. Similarly if one of the aforementioned accidents happens to some magnate (namely one of those who are fit for kingship): that planet or that sign has virtue in his nativity. You can say the same for some clime or region, when some great and horrible thing befalls it; and also when such a thing happens to some city or camp, or some building of great duration - that by some sign or planet placed in an impeded way, the sign is that it has power in the beginning of that building. Whence you can place this as your Ascendant in your elections; or when some great good befalls him, you can do the same for this sign and this planet which appear strong and fortunate; and likewise in all the customs of the citizens of some city or kingdom, regarding what sign or what planet they are likened. And you can give them this as their significator: and it can also have a place in private and individual matters.

## XVI

### When That Which Was Incepted Is To Be Believed To Be Perfected

When we begin anything and the Lord of the first, the Moon, and the Lord of the matter which we begun are in angles, or in succedents free from impediments, and fortunate (or at least the planet signifying the matter which we began; and it is a durable matter, such as the construction of a city or a castle, or even the construction of a house, or the planting of trees, and similar things: and they are in the trine or sextile aspect of the Sun in the day (or even his square aspect with reception); or those of the Moon at night, or the aspect of those planets which are the Lords of the houses in which they are in - the sign is that the matter will be perfected, and will arrive at a good end, and will last for a long time. Whence in such cases you ought to always place the significators in fixed signs, and in angles or in succeedents, strong and fortunate, just as well as you can.

However, in matters which we want to be finished quickly, and which we do not want to last for a long time (as are banquets, declarations of women, and bethroals, of which we desire a quick end and swift durability) the significators can be placed in the cadents from the angles, provided that they are not otherwise impeded. And if the Ascendant is a mobile sign, it will be better, provided that its Lord is not impeded: for the speed and slowness of matters is to be considered according to what the nature of the matter (such as its magnitude or smallness) requires. For if one matter ought to be perfected in one hour, and its nature requires this, and it lasts for four or five hours before it is perfected, it returns a certain slowness to this matter, which ought to be perfected quickly, but instead is perfected slowly: such as with someone who invites people to lunch, and was supposed to prepare the food for them in the third hour, and delayed preparing up until the fifth hour; and in this manner the matter is delayed, since it is not prepared at the time that it ought to have been. Similarly with someone going to some place on that day, who postponed the journey to the following day, and thus his journey was delayed, since he did not travel on the appointed day. For this is just like magnitude.

For smallness should be considered, just as it refers to its signification, such as "big ants" and "small horses".

Likewise regarding speed, so that when someone was supposed to travel to someone who promised that he would give him a horse after one year, and he travelled to him before the middle of the year, or indeed, before the year: in this way he hastened to go to the place where he was supposed to travel, since he arrives before the ordained and required time. And understand the same for every hastening and quickness, whether this swiftness or delay lasts a year, or a moment. And so it can be said regarding diverse matters according to diverse considerations, and according to diverse considerations: since according to the same year, according to the same month, according to the same day, according to the same hour, according to any identical times, it is possible to say slowness or swiftness. And the significations of all the times are taken from the signs and the planets, from the places in which they are, and from their natures. Because the slow planets signify slowness, and chiefly retrograde, or even stationary planets, and especially in their first station and when they are slow-of-course. Indeed, the light planets signify swiftness according to the condition of their motion, and especially when direct: and more strongly so when they are increasing in number.

From the signs we take the signification of time - since fixed signs signify the slowness and delaying of time; common ones the average speed of time; the mobile signs signify swiftness and ease. And even signs of direct ascension assist in slowness; and signs of crooked ascension assist in swiftness, and planets constituted in them assist in similar ways.

Likewise air signs assist in swiftness, and fire signs more than air. Water signs increase slowness, and earth signs increase it more than water.

Similarly angles assist in swiftness; cadents in slowness; indeed, suceedents appear to moderately assist in swiftness.

Whence if one of these signs are ascending, or were the house signifying the matter to be incepted, or one of the aforementioned planets are in one of these places, whichever one of them it is will assist or impede in swiftness or slowness according to the nature of the sign or place in which it is: so that if a fast planet is in a place, sign, or house signifying swiftness, it will assist this swiftness and the matter will be come to be more quickly. However, if it is in a sign or house signifying slowness, it will reduce something of the slowness. And if there were a planet signifying slowness in a house or sign signifying slowness, it will assist this slowness, and the matter will come to be more slowly. And if it is in a house or sign signifying swiftness, it will reduce something of its swiftness. And if the significators are oriental from the Sun, it will assist in swiftness, and reduce something of the slowness. And if they are occidental from him, it will assist in slowness and reduce the swiftness.

And Hali said that the signification should be taken from the places of the signs, according to how they are from the houses. For he said that the Ascendant and the tenth signify swiftness, days namely, and hours; the seventh slowness, that is, less swiftness, as in months or weeks; the fourth even less swiftness, since in the place of months it can signify years. Indeed, succeedents signify that which their angles do, but delay the matter somewhat more. Cadents signify slowness. However, he also said that those which are above the earth, universally signify more certain swiftness than those placed below the earth. And he said that the oriental quarter, which is from the Midheaven to the Ascendant, signifies swiftness; the southern quarter, which is from the tenth to the seventh signifies moderate swiftness; the occidental quarter, which is from the seventh to the fourth, signifies moderate slowness; the northern quarter, which is from the fourth to the first, signifies slowness. And he said that if it happens that a sign signifying swiftness is in a quarter signifying swiftness, and a mobile sign is in the Ascendant or the tenth, this will be the swiftest swiftness that we can have from the signs.

## XVII

## From Which Planets The Signification Of Times Is Taken

Indeed the planets from which we take the faster significations are the Lords of the matter, and the planet who is joined to one of them, or who transfers the disposition of one of them to another, and the luminaries, and the planet to which the Moon is joined. And whichever of the aforementioned planets has more dignities or fortitudes in the Ascendant and in the tenth of the matter, or at least in the house of the matter - from him we take the signification of the time of the occurrence of the matter which we want to know.

And Hali said that the swifter swiftness and the slower slowness of any matter in its own kind, and in its own condition, is signified by the planets according to their speed. And he said that the planets signifying the time in which the incepted matter ought to be perfected (whether the thing signified is good, or not) will give their own signification when their condition changes from strong to weak, or vice versa. And he said, that the weakest change which a planet can make, is when it is in some quarter or the circle, and moves from this quarter to another: such as from the rising one to the setting one; or if it was below the earth and moved above the earth, or descends from the superiors to the inferiors. And he said that their change is strong, if they are oriental and become occidental, or vice versa; or if they change from one sign to another: and especially if they move from a sign in which they have dignity to another in which they don't have dignity, and vice versa.

Moreover, in order to know the time of an incepted, or soon to be incepted matter, when it will be come to be or when it will be ended, it is necessary that you take the number of degrees which are between the planetary Almutem over the place signifying the matter, and another who likewise has signification over the same matter: and if the planet is one of those signifying hours, however, many degrees there are between them will be the number of hours to the end or perfection of that matter, or of its duration; and if the planet signifies days, it will be that many days; and if it signifies months, it will be that many months; and if it signifies years, it will be that many years - all according to the nature of the place, and according to the nature of the significator, and according to the nature of the matter, just as it is capable of coming to be, or being ended, in hours, months, or years.

To give an example: posit that Mercury is the significator of time, and is in the ninth degree of Pisces, and that Jupiter (to whose conjunction Mercury travels) is in the sixteenth degree of Cancer; and there are 7 degrees between them and the completion of their own conjunction. And so, since Mercury is one of the lighter planets, which signify the hastening of matters, he now signifies hours, (or days, in a matter which is not very fast). Whence if it is one of the faster things (namely if it ought to come to be in the same day), the matter will come to be in up to 7 hours; if it is of the things which are less fast (which transpire over a week), it will come to be in up to 7 days, or up to the hour in which Mercury is in 16 degrees Pisces, so that he directly aspects the degree in which Jupiter was at the time when the matter was incepted (or of the question proposed about it), if his arrival to that the degree were after 7 days. And if it is a matter which is expected to take months, it will come to be in as many months. And if it is a matter which is expected to take years, it will come to be in as many years.

Understand the same about everything according to the quantity of the distance in degrees existing between the significators: and that will be the hour of the perfection or the occurrence of the quesited or incepted matter. And if there were a greater quantity of degrees between the significators, it will likewise come to be according to as many hours, days, months, or years, according to its own nature, and its relation to the matter. And if it is such a quantity of degrees that a sign can be made out of them, the matter will come to be in as many hours, days, months, or years, as there are signs resulting from these degrees, and fractions of these time periods according to the quantity of degrees of an incomplete sign.

To give an example: between a planetary significator (of whatever sort he was) and a heavier planet to which he joined, there were 180 degrees: from which 6 signs result - signifying the effect, or duration, or completion of this matter would be six hours, if it was one of those things which come to be in hours, as their nature requires. And if it was one of those things which come to be in days, it would come to be in up to six days. And if it was one of those things which are done in fortnights, it would be done in up to six fortnights. And if it was one of those things which come to be in months, it would come to be in up to six months. And if it was one of those things which come to be in years, it would come to be in six years; and perhaps some fraction may fall between them, but nothing that could lead it in error.

And understand the same about all distances of the number of degrees or signs, by comparing all proportions just as you meet with them. Moreover if the planetary significator of a matter is joined to another planet, or another planet is joined to him, and there is mutual reception between them, their years are to be considered: so that if they were in angles, and if the significator had authority (namely that he had more virtue or power in the matter), you will consider the greater years of the significator from the heavy planet who signifies years: and say that the matter will last up to as many years. And if the beginning of his inception is at this time, and the significators are below the earth, the matter will be completed up to as many years as are the greater years of the planet signifying it. And if the significator is in a succeedent, put the number of years according to the medium years of the planet. And if it is in a cadent, place the number as his lesser years. And if the significator is one of the planets signifying months, days, or hours, make their number according to the number of the aforementioned years, and the aforementioned method, in proportion to how strong or weak the significators are, and how light or heavy they are.

And Haly said that the Moon signifies hours in every matter, and especially swift ones; and likewise the Sun. However, the Sun can signify days where the Moon signifies hours, and months where she can signify days. And he said that when some planet arrives who carries disposition (whether by body or rays) between the significators and the planet to which it carries disposition - the degrees between them should be taken, and days or months are to be placed for every degree.

And he said that if the Lord of the Ascendant and the Lord of the house of the matter are conjoined, it will signify the swift effecting of the matter, if it is testified to; and especially if the Lord of the Ascendant is heavier.

And he said, that when the Moon descends in the Ascendant, or in the house of the matter, or aspects any of them from a square aspect or opposition, that will be the hour. And he said that the Sun signifies the same thing as the Moon in the same places. And he said that the Sun is stronger than the Moon in this work. And he said that when the Moon reaches the place of the significator, that will be the hour. He said the same of the Almutem regarding the beginning of the matter.

And he said that he found certain men who extracted the ylem of the matter, just as is done in nativities, and directed the degree of the ylem to the places of benefics and malefics; and for each degree by ascensions they placed a year, or a month, or a day, according to the nature of the matter. If the direction reaches at a benefic first, before a malefic, they said that the matter would be perfected with success. If however, it reaches a malefic first, before a benefic, they said that the matter would be perfected with adversity.

And he said that Mars signifies swiftness, but mixed with something of martial matters. And they did the same with the degree of the Ascendant and the degree of the house of the matter as they did with the degree of the ylem.

However, it appears to me that even if it is possible to be so, that it would be greatly complicated, and that the above opinion should suffice for you. And since it would take a very long time to explain everything that we meet with to a fine point, and the sayings of the philosophers, and would be something almost abominable, and boring for the reader: you should understand the aforementioned from your own industry, and you should see and perceive what ought to be perceived - namely, whether the significators are of the light or heavy planets; or are in angles, succeedents, or cadents; or are in fixed signs or mobile signs; or direct or crooked signs; or in places signifying years, months, or days: if you consider and perceive all of these things well, you will be able to perceive what you intended from the aforementioned.

## XVIII

### On The Fixed, Common, And Mobile Signs

Indeed Zael put great force in signs, and put great significations in them, and not without reason. And they are to be referred to the significators when they are in them, and to the Moon; and to her before the rest of the significators, since she is the significatrix of all matters, just as is said elsewhere. Even if all of the other significators are abandoned, she should always be considered, except that the Lord of the hour should be observed beforehand in the place which I told you.

For the same wise man stated that fixed signs are congruent with all works where stability and prolongation of time is sought, and those that their author wishes to be durable, good, and useful: and among these are buildings, celebrating marriage (with the betrothal having been made in mobile signs). And if a wife is sent away from her husband in a fixed sign, she will not return to him in a short space of time; understand this unless many benefics gave testimony to them. And he who is bound in them, will have his imprisonment prolonged; and he who becomes angry in them, will not be able to be assuaged quickly; indeed, farming and renting are useful in them; and construction and laying foundations will be good. And he said that Scorpio is the lightest of all the fixed signs; and Leo is more fixed; Aquarius is slower and worse: Taurus is more easy.

## XIX

### On The Common Signs

And he said that the common signs are useful in partnerships and participations, and that whatever is done in them will often be repeated; and indeed, buying, (understood as things which we want to remain in the possession of the buyer) and celebrating marriage are not useful in them; and there is ingenuity and deception in them. And whoever has an accusation levelled at him in these signs will escape and be relieved of that which he is accused of; and he who is imprisoned under them, will not be stuck in there, but he will have fear on account of the littleness of his own servants, and his exit; and he who exits from prison will return home; and if he is captured under these signs, he will make a second flight; and he who goes before a judge under them, will not have his sentence made firm, nor his judgement; nor should someone travel by boat under them, for they will have to change from one boat to another for no good reason. And when anything is permitted under them, it will be dissolved, and it will not be completed; and a sick person will be cured in them, and then suffer a relapse of his illness. Therefore everything that happens to men under these signs, both good and bad, will be duplicated over them; and if someone dies under them, then someone nearby in that place will die after him; and exchanges, and the washing of the head and beard; and the purification of gold and silver, and sending boys to school, are agreeable under them.

And the same author said that if, however, you wished to begin one of the things which he said to you under these signs, then place the Moon in the domicile signifying the matter which you intend to do, and conjoin her with a benefic receiving her in that sign. And he said that diurnal signs are stronger in operations during the day; and to make the Ascendant a diurnal sign, or a sign signifying your matter. And he said that air signs (which are Gemini, Libra, and Aquarius) are suitable for hunting by land and sea; and the signs of kings (Aries and Leo) are suited to kings; and the signs having voices are suited to singers and those wishing to play musical instruments; and fire signs are fitting for all matters which we wish to do by fire; and the equinoctial signs are suitable for all equality and all measuring, and all matters where truth is valued, and pole-bars (which are balances), and measures, and the weighing of justice. And mobile signs (and these are those in which night and day begin to change) are suitable for those who wish to change from thing to thing, or from place to place. And he said to consider what is the nature of that sign in the circles for every work which you wish to begin; and conjoin the Moon and the Lord of the Ascendant with that substance; and the root of that nature and its virtue in that hour (namely the hour of the inception).

And consider the Sun in the affairs of Lords, magnates, princes, and chief administrators of cities, and officials, as is said elsewhere. And in the affairs of those making generous and great expenses, consider Jupiter. And in the affairs of farmers and commoners, consider Saturn. And in the affairs of generals and masters of armies, and fighters, consider Mars. And in the affairs of writers, painters, money changers, or accountants, salesmen, and also merchants, consider Mercury. And in the affairs of queens and other women of excellence, and even mothers and stepmothers, consider the Moon. And in the affairs of other women, consider Venus, and chiefly for young girls and those who eagerly decorate their faces to please men. And in all of these things, strive to consider those things you ought to consider, just as you were told to consider them.

## XX

## On The Mobile Signs

And he said that mobile signs signify the hasty mobility of matters, and nothing durable comes to be under them; nor is the time of deeds done prolonged while the Moon and the significators are in them. However, they are convenient for those who wish to sow, and secure a woman and get betrothed, for all of these things are successful under them; similarly buying and selling merchandise, and those things which quickly change from the hands of one to the hands of another; and if someone falls ill at this time, he will be liberated of his illness, and it will be terminated quickly, and if a lawsuit is begun at this time, it will not be prolonged; and if someone flees at this time, he will be returned quickly; and if someone promises anything to anyone, he will not keep his promise; but it will be good and useful to go on a pilgrimage under them; rumours which are heard at that time are false; and dreams in these hours do not have signification; nor is it good to begin to cure a sick person at this time, if it is such an illness that treatment can be put off while the Moon is placed in a mobile sign; nor are trees whose durability we desire to be planted at these times; nor are fig trees to be planted; nor are any buildings to be started, or foundations to be laid; and nothing of which we desire durability or prolongation is to be done or begun. But for whatever matter you desire swiftness, it should be begun under these signs; and those are swifter, which are of greater crookedness and greater mobility, such as Aries and Cancer: while Libra, and Capricorn are stronger and more temperate.

And Zael said to adapt the Moon according to your ability. And the Moon is never to be placed in the Ascendant of any beginning, and especially in that of a journey: since this signifies that some infirmity (or something equivalent to an infirmity) will befall the traveller in his body, unless the Lord of the Ascendant or a benefic aspects the degree of the Ascendant: since when a planet aspects the Ascendant or its Lord, it is similar to a man who guards his own house: since whoever is in it, fears him, and whoever is outside of it, is afraid to go in there. If indeed, it does not aspect it, it will be to the contrary. And if the Lord of the first is a malefic, make him aspect it from a trine or sextile aspect; and beware that you do not place the Moon or the Lord of the Ascendant in an angle with a malefic aspecting it, unless possibly it is received from a trine or sextile aspect. Nor should you even place the Moon in an angle, unless she is free. But place benefics and the Part of Fortune in angles; and in every way, if you ever can, make it so that the Moon aspects the Part of Fortune or is corporeally joined to it, (allowing this rarely happens). And if you cannot make it so that the Part of Fortune is not cadent from the Ascendant, make it so that the Lord of the Ascendant aspects it, or is joined to it, as I said to you of the Moon. And strive, if you can, to place the Lord of the Ascendant with the Part of Fortune; since this signifies greater wealth on a journey, and greater utility. And take care that you do not place the Moon in the second, the sixth, the eighth, or the twelfth: since this is horrible and is something to be feared.

Zael said that if you can do it, strive to place the Ascendant and its Lord, and the Moon, in signs of direct ascension (namely since they signify ease and progress), and that you should not place them in crooked signs; for he said that they signify complications, duress, and delay - and the Ascendant and the fourth signify what will happen from this election. Therefore, examine the benefics and malefics with regard to their places, and their strength and weakness, and speak according to what you were to find with regards to the strength or weakness of the beginning or end of the matter.

And Dorotheus said that when you find the Moon impeded, and it is a matter which you cannot defer, do not give the Moon a part in the Ascendant; and make her cadent from it; and place a benefic in the Ascendant; and strengthen the Ascendant it and its Lord. And by no means are you to place the Moon in the Ascendant on journeys, whether she is impeded or not.

## SECOND PART OF THIS TRACTATE

## On Those Things Which Seem To Pertain To Particular Elections

### I

### Preface To Particular Elections Of The Houses

Even if enough has been said above on those things which generally pertain to elections; nevertheless it does not appear that what has been said is perfectly sufficient for those who wish to use elections, unless we arrive at those things which pertain to particular elections. And these are those which will be stated in the manner of a standard or collection of the aforementioned. Nor does it appear possible to descend to particular elections, without touching on some of those things that we set out in what preceded; and it was said above that we ought to adapt certain things which are in the roots of the elections, as much as it seems possible, even if it is impossible for us to always be able to adapt everything that we want.

And these are the first sign and its Lord; similarly the fourth and its Lord; the Moon and the Lord of the sign in which she is then in: the Sun and the Lord of the sign in which he is in; and also the Part of Fortune and the Lord of the domicile in which it falls in the election; and also the house signifying the matter for which it is elected, and its Lord; and the planet which naturally signifies that matter; and the Lord of the sign in which this planet is in. All of these are to be adapted according to the sayings of the wise in the beginning of every election, so that the election is made secure in every way. But, as I have said to you, this will hardly or never be possible. And I have said to you many times already: if you cannot adapt whatever you wish, adapt that which you can adapt.

And Haly said, that none of the significators which we ought to weaken are to be placed in the beginning of any matter which we want to begin, and especially if they are strong in the nativity or question (if the nativity or question of him for whom you elect is available), or in the revolution of the year. And perhaps it will sometimes be necessary for us to weaken one of the aforementioned significators in some matters, just as the Moon is to be weakened in setting out for hunting, or in the investigation of a thief or another fugitive; and also to weaken the planet to which she is joined, and to strengthen that planet from which she separates.

And 12 sections will be included in this tractate, following from the number of the 12 houses, to which the chapters will be subordinated. And it should not be surprising if some of the things listed above will be listed in them: since there are certain things of a univocal meaning, which are of equivocal signification; and also sometimes put in one place for one signification, and put in another for another signification.

The first chapter is on the first house and its significations; the second is on the second and its significations; the third is on the third and its significations; the fourth is on the fourth and its significations; the fifth is on the fifth and its significations; the sixth is on the sixth and its significations; the seventh is on the seventh and its significations; the eighth is on the eighth and its significations; the ninth is on the ninth and its significations; the tenth is on the tenth and its significations; the eleventh is on the eleventh and its significations; and the twelfth is on the twelfth and its significations.

## ON THE FIRST HOUSE

### I

### On The Nursing Of Children

If someone wishes to hand over a child to a wet nurse to be nursed: it is fitting that when the nurse begins feeding him, that firstly the Moon be corporeally joined with Venus; which if this cannot be, make her joined to her by a trine or sextile aspect with reception (namely from Taurus or Libra); and if Venus is descending in her eccentric or epicycle, it will be better.

And Haly said that it is necessary for you to first adapt the root matters; however, you should adapt what you can adapt from the rooted matters, and if you cannot adapt all of them, still adapt what I told you above (namely Venus and the Moon).

### II

### On Weaning Children From Milk

When you want to wean a child from milk, place the Moon as far away from the Sun as you can, namely from 90 degrees up to 167 degrees. And Haly said that it appeared to certain men that the Moon was not to be placed in one of the domiciles of Venus in this work: since they feared that the mother would not remove the child from the breast. And a certain man said that if we separate the child from the wet-nurse when the Moon is in Azarfa, which is the twelfth lunar mansion (and is in Libra), the child would not care for milk afterwards. And certain others said that the Moon and the Lord of the Ascendant should be in the signs of seeds (namely Taurus, Virgo, and Capricorn): since this signifies that the child will incline to eat seeds and plants. And if she was in Leo he would incline to eat meat. And if she was in Cancer, Scorpio, or Pisces, he would incline to eat fish. And if she was in other signs, he would eat whatever was given to him to eat.

### III

### On The Cutting Of Fingernails And Toenails

If you wish to cut fingernails or toenails, make the Moon in a succedent of an angle; and if she cannot be placed in a succedent, place her in an angle - for cadents are to be avoided. And make the Moon increasing in light and number; and not in Gemini, and especially if one of the malefics (namely Mars or Saturn) were to aspect her from a square aspect or from opposition. For if Saturn aspects her, it should be feared that they will not grow back; and that if they did grow back, that they did not become ingrown. However, if Mars aspects her from one of these aspects, it will be feared that he may cut the inner flesh of his finger, from which discomfort and pain will follow; and perhaps that the pain can be so greatly increased that abscess or something similar results from it.

And Haly said that she should not be in Gemini or Sagittarius, nor joined to their Lords; but should be in Aries, Taurus, Cancer, Leo, or in Libra (outside of the via combusta), and she should not be impeded in these signs.

However, in the cutting of toenails, beware of Gemini and Pisces, and the via combusta, and the impediments of malefics.

### IV

### On The Cutting Of Hair And The Shaving Of Beards

If you want to cut hair or shave a beard, place the Moon in any common sign apart from Gemini. And Haly said that there was a certain man who did not recommend Virgo, and who did not condemn Libra, Aries, Taurus, or Capricorn; and he did not give a reason for this. I however, do not condemn Aries for trimming hair or beards, but I do condemn it for shaving heads or beards. And he said that when the Moon and the Ascendant are in the signs of seeds and safe, that the hair will grow back and increase quickly. And he said that one should guard against the impediment of Saturn and Mars, lest an infection should arise there and then in the hair.

## V

## On The Circumcision Of Children

It appeared to certain men that this chapter should be comprehended under the sixth house, since it seemed to them that it was a certain infirmity. However, it seems to me that it should be comprehended under the first house, since it is practically one of the first accidents of the body: for it is usually performed on the body of the native on the seventh day after the nativity; nevertheless, under whatever place it is comprehended, you do not want to be there at the hour of the election! Whence if you wanted to elect for someone to circumcise a boy, make the Moon joined to Jupiter by a trine or sextile aspect, or by square with reception; and make her north from Venus; and beware lest Saturn aspects the Lord of the first, the Moon, or Venus, by a square aspect or from opposition; or even the Ascendant itself: since this signifies the putrification of the incision. And, if possible, make the Lord of the sign in which the Moon is in northern, and have the Moon moving toward an angle. And beware of Mars, lest he be in one of the angles; but let him be in a cadent. If you do not wish to place him in a cadent, beware that the Ascendant is not Scorpio; and do not let the Moon or the Lord of the Ascendant be in it.

## ON THE SECOND HOUSE

### I

### On Lending And Borrowing

In the significations of the second house we cannot descend to particulars in the beginning, without some things which seem to be universal being set out in advance - namely what pertains to substance or wealth, or anything from which wealth is expected. For instance, it is necessary for us in this matter to adapt the Lord of the second house, and the planet in whose domicile he is placed; and even Jupiter is always to be adapted in all elections which naturally pertain to substance, as was said elsewhere.

And Zael said that if you wish to elect an hour for the borrowing and lending of money, place the Moon in Leo (outside of its first terms), or Scorpio, or Sagittarius; and do not put the Moon in the first degree of any of them. Nor should you place her in Gemini, nor should you place the Ascendant in the first terms of any of them: since these signify the good of the borrower, and the contrary for the lender.

However, for repayment, place the Moon in Aquarius or Pisces; and have the Moon decreasing in light. Also have Jupiter and Venus (or either of them) ascending to a longer longitude; and have them (or at least one of them) aspecting the Ascendant or the Moon, or its Lord; and do not have any of them impeded, if you can. However, at least save one of them.

And make Mercury (who naturally signifies coins) clean from the impediments of malefics; and likewise the Moon, and especially from the impediments of Mars: since when the Moon is impeded by Mars in such a matter, it signifies contentions, disputes, difficulties, and denials in the recovery or restitution of the money or commodities. However, if she is impeded by Saturn, it signifies complications, prolongation, fatigue, and much destruction in its recovery or restitution.

### II

### On Wealth, That It Always Remains In The Possession Of Him For Whom You Elect

If indeed, the intention of the person for whom you elect is to make money which will always remain in his possession, so that it is not handed over to another person in the end, place a fixed sign as the Ascendant at the hour of the election; and place the Lord of the Ascendant, the Moon, and the Lord of the second, in fixed signs, free from impediments; and make it so that the angles are not remote.

If indeed, it is an election to profit from a matter which is to be sold, or given away in another way, or to be repeated, make the Ascendant a mobile sign or a common one (yet mobile signs are more efficacious in this); and make it so that the Lord of the Ascendant and the Moon are in mobile or common signs; and that they are free from impediments; and that the angles are remote, if you can do so: and in any of these cases, always adapt whatever you can from the root matters. If indeed, the intention of him who profited was the store the acquired thing (that he wanted to use it); adapt the first and its Lord, and Jupiter, in its taking and storing; and make Mars cadent from the aspect of the Moon, and the Ascendant, and the part of fortune, and the part of substance, and from its house, and from all the Lords off their houses, or at least from the Moon and from the Ascendant and its Lord. They also praised common signs in the taking of money whatever way it is acquired.

If indeed, the item which someone wants to store is of those which are chewed, as are grains, meats, and similar things which men commonly use, we should take care that the Ascendant is not one of the signs of much eating (which are Aries, Taurus, Leo, the last part of Sagittarius, Capricorn, and Pisces); and that the Lord of the first, or the Moon, are not in these signs; and that Saturn is not aspecting the Ascendant, or its Lord, or the Moon; and that none of them are in his corporeal conjunction. For these things signify that it will be eaten beyond measure; and under the guise of eating, the matter will be devastated more than it ought to be.

## III

## When The Borrower Does Not Wish That The Loan Be Known

If you were to accept a loan, and you did not want anyone to know this, but you wished to make it hidden so that it is not perceived by anyone: when you accept it or ask for it have the Moon under the rays of the Sun moving toward a conjunction with some benefic, so that she joins an unimpeded benefic by aspect immediately when she exits out from under the rays: for this is easy for the person elected for, and will keep him safe in such a way that the matter will in no way be made public: even if it is a deposit or some other matter, whatever it may be, which someone wants to be hidden. And take care that the Moon is not joining to malefics at that time: since if she moves towards Mars when she has separated from the Sun, the matter (of whatever sort it was) will be made public, and will be divulged, and fall into the mouths of men who eagerly speak evil. Also beware lest the Moon be with the Caput Draconis, or the Cauda; or in the Via Combusta, since this is evil and horrible.

And Dorotheus said that you should neither lend nor borrow while the Moon is in the first degree of Leo, Gemini, or Sagittarius; nor while any of these signs are ascending: since this is horrible for loans.

## IV

## On Buying For The Purpose Of Making Money

If someone wants to buy something for the purpose of making money, as many men are in the habit of doing, and his intention is only to make money from it; adapt the Moon in all of these things (since she participates above all others in these things which men do); and also adapt Mercury, who naturally signifies this type of thing; and adapt the Lord of the second house; and also adapt the Lord of the Ascendant if you can adapt him (do not put much emphasis on him); and make the Moon joined to Mercury; and make it so that both of them are free from the impediments of Mars, to the best of your ability. However, if you cannot adapt Mercury, adapt the Moon and the eleventh and its Lord; nevertheless do not neglect to make it so that Mercury is free from Mars and

his rays: however, if you can, have him joined to Venus (or the Lord of the eleventh) by body or by rays. And always let this be your concern, since the better you adapt Mercury in these matters (after the adaptation of the Moon), the greater confidence you will be able to have of gaining wealth from the matter which someone enquired about: since Mercury, the Moon, the second, and the eleventh dominate in these matters, and wealth is sought from them. And always have them clean from Mars and his rays to the best of your ability.

## V

## In Other Common Purchases And Common Things

However in other purchases which are commonly made by everyone indifferently on a daily basis, adapt the Part of Fortune as best you can; and make it fall in a domicile of Jupiter, and make it so that Jupiter of some other benefic aspects it - since this will be better for the buyer than the seller. Similarly if the Moon is in a crooked sign reducing in light, it could not get any better for the buyer.

However, if the Moon were in a sign of direct ascension, increasing in light and number, and joined to benefics, it will be better for the seller than the buyer. And it will hardly ever happen that the buyer profits from the purchase which is made at this time, or that he does not lose from it. And in all of these cases, always make Mars cadent from the Moon, and from Mercury: since Mars is always contrary to buying and selling, and always introduces labour and contention. And beware lest the Cauda Draconis is with the Moon, or Mercury, or the Part of Fortune: since Mars is not much worse than her.

And there is also another method in buying and selling: since Atabari seems to say that the Ascendant and its Lord belong to the seller, and the seventh and its Lord belong to the buyer - which appears contrary to the sayings of the wise, when in fact it is not so. For Atabari considered when the sale takes its motion or beginning from the seller: that is, when the seller incites the buyer; while others understood it as being when the buyer incites the seller); whence he said the Ascendant and its Lord are the sellers; the seventh and its Lord being the buyers; the Midheaven and its Lord the price;

and the fourth and its Lord the thing to be sold. The planet from which the Moon is separating is the sellers, and the Moon herself is the thing to be sold, and the planet to which she is joined is the buyers.

Alchaiat said that it is not bad if the Moon is in the Ascendant in buying and in selling, even though she is to be hated there in journeys.

## VI

### If Someone Wants To Sell Some Item To Make Money With Its Price

When someone wants to sell an item, and his intention is to make money on the price that he accepted for the item, place the Moon in Taurus, Cancer, Virgo, or Pisces, not impeded, and make it so that she is separating from benefics (or at least from one), whether by body or by aspect; and that she is joined to malefics by aspect (not by body): for these things signify good for him from whom the item is separated from, and who sells it.

## VII

### If Someone Wants To Practice Alchemy

At one time men applied themselves, and even today certain men (who often condemn others for avarice) apply themselves to the art of alchemy; and they often waste their work, time, and expenses; nor does this happen to them only from one error, but from many: for it sometimes happens since they don't know how to arrive at the conclusion of that which they practice: sometimes since they don't know the proportions of the bodies with the spirits; other times since they do not know to elect an hour, nor an Ascendant, nor how to place the Moon where she ought to be placed in order to perfect the work; and this is one of the greater errors which an alchemist can make. Nor do they know to also adapt the planet signifying the matter which they intend to work on.

Whence if someone wishes to practice something related to these matters, and he wants you to elect the hour of its inception for him, place the Moon in common signs, clean of all impediments, and from all defects, and every bad condition; and make the Ascendant a common sign, and make its Lord adapted and free from impediments. And adapt and

strengthen the planet signifying the kind of material which he intends to work on: so that if it is lead, adapt Saturn; if it is bronze or brass adapt Jupiter; if it is copper, adapt Mars; if it is gold, adapt the Sun; if it is tin, adapt Venus; if it is electrum, adapt Mercury; if it is silver, adapt the Moon; and strengthen each one of them in the beginning of his work, according to the kind and according to the condition of each. However, if it is a matter which ought to be repeated, you will do the same.

## VIII

### On Another Manner Of Lending Money

Moreover, here is another chapter on lending according to Haly: for he said that the Ascendant and its Lord belong to the debtor; while the seventh and its Lord belong to the creditor (namely the lender). Mercury and the Moon signify the debt itself. Therefore if there is concord between the Lord of the Ascendant and the Lord of the seventh, and Mercury is in the Ascendant or with its Lord, and fortunate, it will be perfected with ease. If indeed, the Moon is under the rays of the Sun, the Sun will signify the substance in place of the Moon. And he said, if she is in the via combusta, or descending in the south, or is in the first degrees of Leo or Gemini or Sagittarius, or if these are the degree of the Ascendant itself, it does not signify good for giving, but does confer utility to the one borrowing. And he said that certain men said that there is no utility in lending in the hours of Saturn or the Sun.

## IX

### On The Entrance Into A House Or Lodgings To Live In It

If you want to elect for someone about this matter, see whether it is their own house or a rented one: for if it is his own house, make the Ascendant a fixed sign, and place the Moon in a fixed sign. And if it is a rented house make the Ascendant a common sign, and similarly place the Moon in a common sign. Whence the Ascendant and its Lord, and the Moon and the Lord of the sign she is in are to be adapted; and the second and its Lord; and the fourth and its Lord; and the Part of Fortune and its Lord are also to be adapted. For the Ascendant and its Lord, and the Moon and her Lord are or the person of the lodger; the second and its

Lord, and the Part of Fortune are for gaining wealth and conserving the substance already acquired; and this will happen if you can place Jupiter, fortunate, in the second house in that hour; and whatever condition he is in, Jupiter will still be effective in this case. And you will adapt the fourth for the end of the whole matter.

And Haly said to make Taurus or Leo the fourth house: for these signify that the place will be good, and the house will be clean, and will have few impeding or poisonous animals staying in it (for Scorpio signifies venomous reptiles, and more strongly if it is aspected by Saturn). You should protect the aforementioned places from malefics and their aspects, just as best as you can; and make them blessed with benefics and their aspects as much as possible. And if you cannot make them all blessed; at least make the first and the second blessed, or at the very least one of them: for after men have made money, they do not care much about other things.

## ON THE THIRD HOUSE

### I

### On Short Journeys

If someone wanted to make a short journey (which is a journey of one day or less) which did not pertain to war, and you want to elect him an hour for making this journey, adapt the Ascendant and its Lord; also the Moon and the Lord of the sign in which she is in; and the Part of Fortune and its Lord; also the third and its Lord; likewise the planet to which the Moon is joined; and likewise the Lord of the hour; and the house signifying the matter for which the he travels (if he specified it to you),and its Lord. And again I tell you, if you cannot adapt everything that you ought to and want to, adapt those which you can, among which have the Moon and the Lord of the hour at least. If you cannot adapt the Moon, and you cannot defer the journey, at least adapt the Lord of the hour, and make the Moon cadent from the Ascendant: and also from its Lord if you can; and your election will not be wasted, even if it is weakened. Nevertheless, these things will be discussed more widely below in the treatment of the ninth house.

### II

### On The Reconciliation Of Brothers And Other Relatives, And Neighbours And Fellow Citizens

Sometimes brothers disagree with each other, and also some disagree with their younger or lesser relatives, or even those who are equal to them, as much in wealth or power, as in age; and they sometimes want to be reconciled together. And they want you to elect them an hour for doing this, so that their reconciliation can be long lasting and strong. Whence if one of these people come to you, for you to elect an appropriate hour for them to do this - adapt the Ascendant and its Lord, the Moon also and the Lord of the sign in which she is; likewise the third and its Lord (which signify brothers and relatives). And make the Lord of the third in conjunction with the Lord of the first, or in its trine or sextile aspect, and this with perfect reception (namely from domicile, exaltation, or two of the lesser dignities): and make it so that the Lord of the third aspects the Ascendant from a praiseworthy aspect; and that the Lord of the first aspects the third in the same way, if you can do it; or place the Lord of the first in the tenth or eleventh, and the Moon aspecting both significators, or at least one of them. And it is also necessary for you to consider whether this reconciliation is made with older brothers, middle brothers, or younger brothers. For if it is with older brothers it is necessary for you to adapt Saturn after the adaptation of the aforementioned. However, if it is with middle brothers it is necessary for you to adapt Mars. If indeed, it is with younger brothers if it is necessary for you to adapt Mercury - and all of these should be understood for males. However, if it is with sisters it will be necessary for you to adapt Venus, just as was said for Saturn with older brothers. Understand the same of relatives, neighbours, and fellow citizens, according to the condition of each one of them in their own kind.

### III

### On Those Things Which Pertain To A Divine Cult And Knowledge Of Them

Certain ancients said that the third house signifies religion, just as the ninth house - which is true in lesser religions, not in great ones, which are called clerical or famous dignities, as are the Papacy, cardinalships, archbishoprics, bishoprics, abbacies, abbots, and religions of great voices or great fame, as are those which are below the above-written in name and fame, and who are of strict lives and labour in divine worship.

Whence if you want to elect for someone wishing to adhere to one of these religions, or to study those things which pertain to the worship of God: adapt the Ascendant and its Lord, the Moon also and the Lord of the sign in which she is in; and adapt the third house and its Lord; and even adapt Jupiter who naturally signifies this; and adapt the Sun. Also make it so that the Ascendant is Sagittarius or Pisces, if you ever can. And if you wish to give more exact attention to those things which pertain to religion, adapt Mercury, and make it so that the aforementioned significators aspect each other by a praiseworthy aspect, and that each one aspects the house of the other, or the planet in whose house each of them are in themselves: and if you cannot adapt all of these, adapt those which you can adapt.

## ON THE FOURTH HOUSE

### I

### On The Buying Of Houses Or Inheritances And The Like

To certain sages it seemed that the chapter on construction should be placed before this one, since building a house or castle, and similar things is more noble and celebrated than buying land or other possessions - with whom I can agree with well enough: nevertheless to me it appears to be more fitting to first have the land upon which we build, than that we first begin construction: allowing there is not great importance in this.

Whence if you want to elect an hour for someone wishing to buy some inheritance, or a house or land, or some other estate, adapt the first and its Lord,; also the Moon and the Lord of the sign in which she is in; the fourth also, and its Lord; also adapt the Part of Fortune and its Lord. And if you cannot adapt all of these, adapt the Moon and the fourth, and add the Part of Fortune to these if you can: and if not, at least do not let the adaptation of these two be lacking. Examine also if the place is adapted, or needs to be adapted so that it can be inhabited: make the Moon in Cancer or in Taurus, or in the tenth, or at least the eleventh, and aspecting the Lord of the first by a praiseworthy aspect. And take care that she does not aspect Mars from any aspect, and if you cannot free her from his aspect, make it so that he receives her from a trine or sextile aspect, and that he is not impeded at that time. And make the fourth house (as was said) Taurus or Leo, or at least Aquarius; and make it so that the Lords of the angles are oriental in the world, and from the Sun (or from one of them) and are ascending northern.

And Hali said that in the buying of any inheritance that the benefics should have dignity in the angles; and if they cannot have dignity in all of the angles, they should have it in the first and the fourth, or at least in one of them; and the luminaries should also be aspecting the Ascendant and the fourth (or at least one of them) by a loving aspect; and the Lords of the angles should not to be retrograde; nor should retrograde planets be in the angles.

And Alchindi said that malefics are not to be in the ninth, or the first, or the eleventh; and that the fourth house is not to be a fire sign, nor have a fiery planet in it, and especially if it is cadent from the benefics. And if the fourth house is a water sign, take care that Saturn does not aspect it. And the Lord of the tenth should not be a malefic.

For the Ascendant and its Lord signify the land itself which someone buys, and his possession of it and the utility of it. The tenth and eleventh and its Lord signify whatever is elevated from it above the earth, and from its surface, as are trees and other things born of the earth which grow old in it. Indeed, the seventh and its Lord signify its cultivators.

And Hali said that it appeared to certain men that the seventh signified plants. The fourth indeed, and its Lord are said to signify the goodness of the matter and whatever is gotten from it in terms of seeds. And he said that whichever of these you find good, judge good for those things which it signifies. If you find benefics in the first, judge the goodness of the trees and of those things which are elevated from the surface of the earth. However, you find them in the 7th judge the goodness of the farmers. If however, you find a benefic in the 4th judge the goodness of the matter and the goodness of the seeds placed in it. And if you find one of the malefics in one of these places, judge evil according to the significations of the house, and especially in the 7th, which signifies the deceit and malice of the farmers according to the nature of the malefic which signifies them. Saturn signifies their deceit and dishonesty. Mars signifies their inconstancy and thievery.

And Atabari said that Jupiter and the planet from which the Moon separates belong to the buyer; and the planet to which the Moon is joined, signifies the end of the matter and to what it will arrive to.

However, if you intend to buy land or a vineyard, or some other similar thing without building, not with a consideration of building on it, but only to utilise it and have it, and keep the fruits of it, and the returns from the labourers or tenants, or even others, adapt the aforementioned: namely the Ascendant and its Lord, the Moon and her Lord; and also the Part of Fortune and its Lord; and also adapt Saturn, since he signifies this on account of his severity: and since these things are acquired from severe work put into the land. Therefore place him in Libra; or if the purchase is made in the day, place him in Capricorn or Aquarius; and if it is made at night, place him in Aries, Leo, or Sagittarius: (however, Aries is less useful); and you can even place him in these signs in diurnal purchases: but he will not be as strong in them as he is at night. Or place him in one of his own terms; and make him fortunate and strong; also make Jupiter aspect him by a trine or sextile aspect or a square from an angle; and make Mars cadent from the angles; and make the Moon in the beginning of the increase of her light (namely in the first dichotomy), increasing in number, aspecting Saturn (or a planet which aspects him) from a friendly aspect. And if Jupiter aspects her, it will be good: since he signifies the population of this land, and that it will be planted with many fruitful trees, and also other small ones; and that it can give good and useful returns.

And Zahel said that if you cannot have the aspect of Jupiter with Saturn, make it so that you have the aspect of Venus with him instead of the aspect of Jupiter; and you will make water signs fortunate, since when they are made fortunate with benefics, they will be better than air signs. And he said to place the Moon in her exaltation, or the Midheaven, and with the Lord of the Ascendant aspecting her. And he said that the Moon and the Ascendant are to be clean of malefics and defects.

## II

### In The Reconciliation Of A Father With A Son

Just as there are sometimes disagreements between brothers, so too it happens that a father disagrees with his son, and vice versa. And if they want to reconcile together, and the son comes to you to elect an hour for him that is suitable for this: adapt the Ascendant and its Lord, and the Moon and the Lord of the sign in which she is in; also adapt the fourth and its Lord, which signify the father, the grandfather, the father in law, and all older relatives (natural ancestors): yet even if any one of them could be signified by their own house. And have the Lord of the fourth joined to the Lord of the first by a trine or sextile aspect, and with reception if you can do it; and aspecting the Ascendant by the same aspect; and place the Lord of the first in the first, or the 10th or 11th. Make the Moon aspect the Lord of the first, and the Lord of

the fourth, or at least one of them: for these things signify a useful, good, and durable reconciliation.

## III

### On The Construction Of Cities, Castles, Houses, And Similar Things, And On The Populations Of Lands Or The Fixing Of Fig Trees

Men tend to build according to diverse methods of construction, and according to diverse conditions of men, and also to plant trees and fix fig frees, and to populate lands, in diverse ways, all according to the diverse customs of men. For, even though all of these ways appear to tend toward the same end, nevertheless it is necessary to elect in diverse ways for people wishing to use diverse methods of construction to build diverse kinds of buildings. For there is one way of electing for those wanting to build cities or castles; another for those wanting to build other buildings, such as sacred buildings and profane buildings (which will be discussed in their own proper place and time): another for those wanting to plant trees or fix fig trees; another for those wanting to sow seed.

Whence if you wish to elect an hour for someone to construct a city or castle, adapt the Ascendant and its Lord; also the Moon and the Lord of the sign in which she is in; and likewise the Part of Fortune and its Lord; and in the Ascendant of the construction of a city or camp place one of the fixed stars which are of the nature of Jupiter, or the Sun, or Venus, or Mercury or Saturn (if Saturn is in good condition), or the Moon, or at least one of the nature of the Lord of the Ascendant of that hour. For these signify the prolongation of the city or castle and its perpetual durability, on account of their extremely slow motion, and their extremely slow mutability. For cities and castles ought to be things of perpetual durability; and this must, by necessity, happen through the succession of their individual parts, which are houses, which, even though they last a long time, are not perpetuated unless by succession.

And it appeared to Hali that Saturn was to be adapted in the building of cities. Indeed, Zael appeared to not want us to give Saturn a part in construction - yet they did not contradict each other: since Hali understood this in terms of the building of cities; Zael in terms of the building of houses.

And Hali said that the Ascendant should be a fixed earth sign in constructions, and likewise that the Lord of the Ascendant, and the Moon should be in fixed earth signs. And he said that the Moon should be increasing in light and number, moving toward her exaltation: and that she should be joined to a benefic which is in its own exaltation, or in the exaltation of the Moon, and that she should be received. And Hali also said that it did not appear fitting to him to place the Moon in a water sign, and that it is useful if she is otherwise ascending, and if she is in more than half of her light.

And Zael (with whom it seems fitting enough to agree with) said to make Mars cadent from all the significators of the building, and to never give him any role in building. And he said that if you cannot make it so that he is not given any role in it, put Venus strong in her own place; and give her strength over Mars, and join her to him by a trine or sextile aspect: since Mars does not impede Venus, if received, or even if a benefic aspect (namely a trine or sextile) intervenes, on account of the greatness of their friendship. And he said to make Saturn cadent from Venus to the best of your ability, on account of her enmity with him.

## IV

### On The Building Of Houses

However, in the construction of houses you are not to consider the fixed stars, but only the planets, whence you should adapt the Ascendant and its Lord; the Moon also, and the Lord of the house in which she in, and the planet to which she is joined; also the fourth and its Lord; the second and is Lord; the tenth and its Lord - and this more strongly so if it is a building which ought to be greatly elevated above the earth. And take care that you don't place the significators of the building under the earth, since they will not permit the building to be elevated, unless perhaps after a great length of time, as happened with the tower of Viviani which is at St Gugliemos' in Forli. Yet still, if the Moon is below the earth (namely in the 5th or the 3rd) joined to an unimpeded planet above the earth, it will not be horrible. And Atabari said to place the Moon in crooked signs (which signify increase). Indeed, Alchindi said to place the Part of Fortune in

an angle, and make it so that the angles are not remote; and place the Cauda in the 12th; and the Lord of the conjunction in any of its own dignities, fast-of-course, whose opinion Haly praised; and similarly he recommended that Saturn should aspect the significators from a trine aspect with reception - and he strongly recommended this. But since it seems, nay, since it is almost impossible, that we can adapt everything which is necessary for us in buildings, and since we meet with elections for buildings every day, we must adapt what can be adapted in each individual case. That is, if someone wants to build a city or a castle, adapt the Ascendant and the rest of the things which were said above; and if you cannot adapt them all, adapt the Lord of the exaltation of the Ascendant, and use him more in this than the Lord of the domicile or of the other dignities. And if again you cannot do this, adapt the Ascendant with one of the aforementioned fixed stars. And beware lest one of the fixed stars of the nature of malefics fall on the degree of the Ascendant, or close to it by two degrees. I say the same for the fourth house (namely about the stars named in an appropriate place in the tractate). And when you have this done, you have already adapted the beginning of the building of the city or castle, even if you could not adapt anything else.

Indeed, in the construction of houses, if you cannot adapt all of the aforementioned things, adapt the Ascendant and its Lord; likewise the Moon; and the second and the fourth, and their Lords (or at least the second); and make the Moon joined to Jupiter from any aspect besides the opposition; and if you can, place Jupiter in the second: then you will have adapted the greater part of the construction of the house, and so too in guest houses. You should even adapt the Lord of the exaltation of the sign in which the Moon is in, more strongly so than the Lord of the domicile, if it can be done. For the Lord of the exaltation should be preferred to the Lord of the domicile in all buildings and plantings: and adapt whatever you can from the aforementioned; but those which I have just told you are to be preferred - for the conjunction of Jupiter with the Moon, signifies the comeliness, beauty and goodness of the house.

And take care in the construction of houses that you do not give Saturn or Mars any role in them: even even if Saturn is given a role in the construction of cities, Mars should never be given a role in any building. And take care that you do not place the Cauda in the first, the 2nd, or the 4th (and especially in the second), since she diminishes substance: However, the Caput can be placed in these houses with confidence, since he increases it. And beware of the conjunction of the Moon with Saturn, Mars, or with the Cauda; or any of them placed in the first, or even the 2nd or 4th (unless perhaps Mars, if you cannot avoid him, however, this should be with the adaptation of Venus, as was said). For Saturn in the first or in the fourth signifies the deformity and slowness of the building, and that the house will hardly or never be built up. And if it is built up, it will hardly or never be inhabited (and especially by its builder). And if it is inhabited, its inhabitants will suffer many disturbances, such as fears, horrible dreams, and diverse tribulations; and it signifies that the building will be shaken and broken, and perhaps that it will collapse from this shaking. Indeed, in the second he signifies the diminution of substance. However, when Mars is in one of these places, he signifies the burning of the house or of the building; and its collapse and destruction; and the loss of substance by fire and robbery; and this more strongly if he is ascending to his auge, or to a further longitude, or were otherwise ascending.

And Zael said to make the Moon increasing in light and number, since it signifies utility for the master of the house; and make it so that the Lord of her domicile is aspecting her. And he said to make the Lord of the Ascendant aspecting the Ascendant, and clean from malefics. And he said if the Lord of the Ascendant is not aspecting the Ascendant, the master of the house will not stay long in it. If however, the building belongs to a low class, ignoble, or humble person, adapt all that you of the above mentioned things; since that if you adapt many significators, they will make up for the weakness of the root of his nativity.

V

**On The Building Of Churches**

However, if it is a religious building, you will consider it in two ways. For if it is a humble building, not very expensive, as are common churches, small hermitages (such as those of the Order of St. Augustine and of Brother Zanniboni), and abbeys similar to hermitages, and parish churches, and chapels, and monasteries, and similar things which are not of great fame: in such cases you will adapt the Ascendant and its Lord; similarly the Moon and her Lord; and the ninth and its Lord.

However, if it is a famous or stately building, as are great monasteries, such as Claraevalentia, the church of St. Mark in Venice, the Cathedral of Pisa, St Vitalis of Ravenna, and many other churches, such as those of the Minor Brothers of Bologna, the Campanile in Forli, thee Baptistry of Florence, and similar buildings exceeding the norms of religion - you will not elect for these as you would for spiritual buildings, but as you would for temporal ones. Whence for these buildings you will adapt the Ascendant and its Lord, and the Ascendant's exaltation Lord; and chiefly the Moon and her Lord; and similarly the 10th instead of the ninth. And if it is the construction of a house of study, adapt Mercury, and make him of good condition, fortunate and strong; and put him in a good place, in such a way that he aspects the Ascendant by trine or sextile aspect.

However, if it is a building of delights, such as those of drinking, games, and the like, adapt Venus, and make her fortunate, strong, and in good condition, and have her aspect the Ascendant by an aspect of friendship. However, if it is a building where foodstuffs ought to be stored (such as grains, wine, olives, honey, and other foods and drinks): adapt Jupiter, make him fortunate and strong, and make it so that he aspects the Ascendant by a praiseworthy aspect. However, if it is a building in which people will be imprisoned, adapt Saturn, and make him strong in his own place, and make it so that he aspects the Ascendant from any aspect except for the opposition.

VI

**On The Destruction Of Constructed Buildings**

It seemed that this chapter ought to be placed amongst the chapters on the 7th, but it seemed to Haly that it ought to be placed before this, amongst the chapters on the fourth house. For he said that since destruction is the contrary of construction, its chapter ought to be placed next to the chapter on construction (however, there is little significance in this).

He also said that if you wish to destroy any building, place one of the fire signs, or one of the air signs as the Ascendant. And Atabari said to make the Ascendant a sign of direct ascension, and to have the Lord of the Ascendant occidental, reducing in number, moving towards a sign in which it is in fall; yet it is not to be made retrograde, but it is to be made cadent from an angle. And also the Moon should be reducing in light and number, cadent from an angle; and also joined to a planet cadent from an angle going toward its fall; or place her in Scorpio or Capricorn; and she should be below the earth; or joined to a planet placed below the earth; and have her descending southern, or joined to a retrograde planet; and also have her in the final dichotomy of the lunation, and make it so that the Moon is cadent from the Sun, and that she is not received; and make the Lord of the fourth house weak, and the planet to which the Moon is joined, and even the other significators of the building. And above all else you should weaken Mars; even if you are not able to weaken all of the others, do not forget to weaken him - since just as he is contrary to construction, so too is he contrary to destruction, since he strives to rebuild the building. For those things which I said to you above do not permit a destroyed building to be restored, nor rebuilt. However, if the inceptor does not care whether the building is rebuilt or not, make the Moon separated from a malefic and joined to an oriental benefic, or make her received, and this building will be destroyed more easily.

## VII

### On The Renting Or Letting Of Houses, Or Of Lands Or Vineyards, Or Their Fruits, Or Of Any Other Things Which Are Rented Or Leased

If you want to elect an hour for someone to rent something, or lease it out for a certain price, and certain returns, or to receive or recover a certain portion of the fruits of the thing, adapt the Ascendant and its Lord; also the Moon and the Lord of the sign in which she is in. For the Ascendant and its Lord signify him who rents the thing, the seventh and its Lord signify him who leases it out. The tenth signifies that which is offered for rental. However, the fourth signifies the end of the matter, and to what end the rental arrives at, and what follows from it for both parties.

Therefore, examine which of the aforementioned places are fortunate, and which are unfortunate. For if the Ascendant and its Lord are fortunate, it signifies good for the renter, and that he will be truthful and lawful, and that he will keep his promise to the leaser. However, if it is unfortunate and evil it will be to the contrary. If the seventh and its Lord are fortunate, it signifies that the leaser will keep his promise to the renter, and he will be lawful and of good faith. However, if it is evil and unfortunate, he will lie to his associate, and will not keep his promise, and will be fraudulent to him. If both of the significators are fortunate and good, both will keep the faith of the other, and both will be lawful. If both are evil and unfortunate, each of them will strive to deceive the other, and they will be fraudulent to each other.

And Haly said that planet to whom the Moon is joined signifies him who leases, and the planet from which she is separated signifies him who rents: yet I think he considered it as being when the lease was put into motion by the leaser: but if the renter put it into motion first, it will be to the contrary. The Lord of the sign in which the Moon is in signifies the end of the matter.

And Athabari said that we should adapt Jupiter and Saturn, and place them aspecting each other by a praiseworthy aspect. And he said this for the purpose of ensuring that the promises of the leaser and renter would be kept, and be firm.

And Hali said that in leasing, the Ascendant and its Lord are to be adapted, and it should be going toward an angle in an earth sign, and likewise the Moon; or put in the angle of the earth. Indeed, the planet from whom the Moon separates should be free and in one of its own dignities, since it signifies the land. And he said to make the Lord of the seventh house fortunate, and in harmony with the Lord of the Ascendant; and do this to the best of your ability. Indeed, the planet whose conjunction the Moon seeks, should be in harmony with the planet from which she separates. And he said that the seventh and its Lord, and the planet to whom the Moon is joined, signify the leaser; and the Ascendant and its Lord, and the planet from which the Moon separates signify the renter; and it signifies the Lord of each of them. And the fourth and its Lord signify the land. And he said that in the inception of an election about land, use the same election.

## VIII

### On The Extension Of Rivers Or Canals And The Like

If someone wishes to extend a river or canal (or other waters), and you wish to elect an hour for them which is suitable for this, adapt the Ascendant and its Lord; the Moon also and the sign in which she is in; also adapt Saturn so that he is oriental; and also make the Lord of the Ascendant oriental, free from impediments, in an angle, and in any of its own dignities; and place the Moon under the earth in the third or the fifth, in an earth sign. And if she is above the earth, place her in the tenth or eleventh.

And Hali said that it is good for Saturn to be in the eleventh, provided that the Moon is not joined to him by body. Also adapt Jupiter, and do not allow any malefic to be in the tenth.

And Alchindi said to place the Moon in the first square from the Sun, fortunate, increasing in light and number; and place her in an angle (namely the first, tenth, or fourth); and make it so that the angles are not remote; and place a water sign as the Ascendant, made fortunate with a strong benefic.

Even the Part of Fortune is to be adapted, and the Lord of the conjunction or prevention which was before the election, and the rest of the things which were said in the renting of land. If you cannot adapt all of these things, adapt those of them which you can - the most important of which to adapt is the Moon; even adapt the Lord of the Ascendant and the Part of Fortune.

## IX

### On The Planting Of Trees And Fig Trees

The methods of planting trees or shrubs are many: for either they are planted or fixed. And again, of trees, some are planted with roots or stakes, as are figs, olives, apples, almonds, nuts and similar things. Others are planted without roots, and are called "fixed", as are poplars, willows, and the like. Others are called shrubs, as are vines, wild olive trees, and similar things. And of those that are planted, certain ones are sometimes fixed; and out of those that are fixed, certain ones are sometimes planted: and every one of these methods can be called planting.

Whence if you want to elect an hour for someone to plant trees or shrubs, or fixing fig trees; begin from the Moon and place her in Taurus joined to Venus by whatever means, if you can. And if you can't place the Moon in Taurus, place her in Aquarius (but Aquarius is below Taurus). If you cannot do this, place her in Leo (yet Leo is below Aquarius). If again you cannot do this, place her in Pisces or Virgo (but these are below Leo); provided that she is aspected from some planet from a water sign when she is in Leo. But Taurus is to be preferred before all others.

And place Saturn in the first, and make him direct; or in the eleventh, fifth, or second, in any of his own dignities or fortitudes, or have him occupy one of the aforementioned signs there. And if you cannot place him in the first, place Jupiter there aspecting Saturn; or wherever Jupiter is, have him aspecting Saturn by a friendly aspect; and have Jupiter in a place where he has some testimony. And if neither of them can be placed in the first, place the Moon there; or place her in the tenth or in the eleventh, or at least in the fifth or the third. And never have her impeded in planting or sowing. And take care that you do not give Mars a role in planting or sowing, except if it is in buildings; and make the Moon (and the Lord of the sign which she is in) cadent from him, and likewise the Part of Fortune; and adapt the Lord of the exaltation of the Ascendant if you can, since it is not bad if it is preferred to the Lord of the domicile in this.

And Alchaiat said to have the Lord of the house of the Moon aspect her from a water sign. And if the Ascendant is not a fixed sign, make the Lord of the Ascendant and the Moon (or at least one of them) oriental, and ascending. For if the Lord of the Ascendant is oriental, and is ascending towards its auge, or to a further longitude: it signifies that the tree which is planted at that time will grow quickly. If indeed, it is ascending and is not oriental, it signifies that the tree will grow quickly, but it will delay the bearing of its fruit: and this does not harm in trees without fruit. And if it is oriental and descending from its auge, or to a closer longitude, it will grow slowly, but bear fruit more quickly. And if it is occidental and descending, it will be slow in growing and bearing fruit.

And if you cannot make the Ascendant as a fixed sign, make it a common sign, and place the significators in common signs. But since it is difficult to adapt everything that is considered in elections, as I have already told you many times, if you cannot adapt everything that you want, adapt those things which you can. For in the planting of trees, if you cannot adapt anything else, at least adapt the Moon, and place her in Taurus, free and unimpeded; or in the last half of Sagittarius joined to Jupiter by any aspect, except for opposition. And do not allow Jupiter to be impeded: and if possible, place him in the Ascendant, free; or in the tenth, eleventh, fifth, or fourth. And I say the same about the Part of Fortune, if it can be done.

## X

### On The Sowing Of Seeds Which We Intend To Bear Fruit In The Same Year Or In The Following Year

If you want to elect an hour for someone to sow seeds, it is fitting in all sowing that the Ascendant is a mobile or common sign, and that the Lord of the Ascendant is in a mobile sign, if you can do it. However, as I told you in plantings, begin from the Moon, and operate through her: since in sowing her virtue is to be preferred to the virtues of all the other planets.

And Haly said to place the Moon in mobile signs: whence she should be placed in a mobile or common sign, and an earth sign, or a sign of seeds. But if she is in Aries, it is necessary that a planet aspects her from a water sign, lest a portion of these seeds dry out. And Hali praised Cancer and Capricorn; indeed, he praised Virgo before the rest of the earth signs, or the signs of seeds, as much in seeds which bear fruit in the same year, as those which bear fruit in the following year (as are those which are seeded when they are planted, as are leeks and cabbage, and similar things); and sometimes they bear fruit in the same year that they are planted.

Indeed, Zael said, to make the Ascendant a common sign; and to place its Lord in a mobile sign, aspecting the Lord of its house; also make the Lord of the Ascendant free from malefics: since if malefics aspect it, the seed will be found impeded. And have the Moon increasing in light and number: since if she were under the rays, or decreasing in number, it would signify that the seeds will be reduced, and nothing will emerge from them, only a small amount.

And out of the fixed signs, Taurus is recommended, but the seeds will be thinned according to the quantity of them which are sown. Whence it is necessary that somewhat more of the seed be cast out than usual, yet not an excessive amount. And the last half of Sagittarius is also of value in sowing, and even Pisces is recommended. If it were the seed of trees (just as sometimes some men do in the propagation of trees), place the Moon in Taurus. However, if you cannot adapt all of the aforementioned things, place the Moon in Virgo free from impediments and you will have adapted the hour of sowing.

## XI

### On Beginning To Cultivate Inheritances

If you want to elect an hour for someone wanting to begin to cultivate an inheritance which they had obtained, or that another person left to them: adapt the Ascendant and its Lord, and the Moon, and the planet whose house she is in, so that all of them are received; and make it so that each planet who receives one of them is in an angle or a succedent, free from impediments; and if you cannot do all of this, at least make the Moon received by a fortunate and strong planet, and place the Moon herself in a good place. And, if you ever can, make it so that a benefic free from impediments is in the second.

And Alchindi said to place the Lord of the Part of Fortune and the Lord of the conjunction or prevention in any of the angles, or have them moving towards an angle; and place the Moon in a domicile of a benefic; which if all of these were lacking, at the least make it so that the Moon is in the Ascendant, or received in a good place from it.

## XII

### On The Putting Together Of Boats Or Galleys

The methods of putting together boats are three, to which all others are subordinated. For either it is the putting together of a galley or an equivalent boat used to overcome enemies; or it is the putting together of a great ship for transport; or it is a boat for other common navigations, as are small trading voyages, and similar things.

Whence if someone wishes to put together a galley, or another fast boat, whether to overcome enemies, or to sail the sea in another fast way, adapt the Ascendant and its Lord; the Moon also and the planet in whose domicile she is in; and place them in the Ascendant or in the 10th or 11th; and make the Ascendant a fixed sign; and likewise make the other angles fixed signs if you can; and adapt the 4th and its Lord, since it naturally signifies boats; and if you can, make so that the 4th is a water sign; or at least place his Lord in a water sign, free from impediments and joined to one of the benefics. And make the planet from which the Moon separates strong and fast. And if you cannot place the Lord of the Ascendant or the Moon in the 10th, place a strong and fortunate benefic there, having strong testimony there, and make it oriental and fast-of-course; however, make the Lord of the seventh weak and slow-of-course.

However, if it is a boat for sea-crossings, make the Moon be in her average course, (with the other things mentioned above being adapted just as was said), so that she does not run more than her average course in one day; and if she travels less than that by three or four minutes in one day, it will not be bad on account of fear that the boat would be harmed by excessive speed.

Indeed, if it is one of the other aforementioned boats, you will adapt the aforementioned things, but it will not matter whether the Moon is fast-of-course or not, provided that she is not very slow (so that in one day she doesn't travel less than her own course by more than 31 minutes). And strive to adapt the Lord of the conjunction or prevention to the best of your ability, since this is good; and if the Moon is separated from another planet, make it so that she is joined to one of the benefics; and if the Lord of the Ascendant is not in an angle, make it so that he is moving towards one.

And Hali said that certain men affirmed that it is good for the Moon to be in Taurus or Gemini. And he said that we should guard against the aspect of Mars with the Moon, the Lord of the Ascendant, or the Lord of the fourth in the putting together of boats.

And Hali said that it is useful if the Moon is above the earth. And he said that these same things are to be adapted in the launching of boats into the water, and in their purchasing. However, you should adapt all that you can adapt; but always make it your concern to adapt the Moon. And when the mast is raised on a great ship, then the tenth and its Lord are to be adapted; and similarly the Moon is to be placed in it.

## XIII

## On The Building Of Mills

Mills are constructed in many ways: for some are built in boats, others are constructed on a balance, so that it is raised up and pressed down as its manager wishes - and this is called a hanging mill. Another is constructed immovably, so that it is neither raised up nor pressed down, but rather it remains firm - and this is called a transverse mill. Another is constructed in an inhabited house, and is turned by some animal or by some crafted instruments - and this is called a posternum mill. Another is built in a high place, and is turned by wind - and this is called a windmill. And according to their diverse methods of construction, their elections are diversified. Whence if someone wants to build one of the mills mentioned above, and comes to you to elect them an hour suitable for this; and it is a mill on a ship, make the Ascendant the last half of Pisces, or the last half of Virgo. However, if it is a mill suspended on a balance or a boat (which is called a hanging mill), make the Ascendant the first half of Aries or the first half of Libra: since these signify equality.

If it is a fixed mill which is neither raised up nor pressed down (which is called transverse), or a mill in a house, which is turned by animals or crafted instruments (which is called a posternum), make the Ascendant a fixed sign, and either a water sign or an earth sign. If it is a mill which is turned by wind (as tend to be made in some places), make the Ascendant an air sign, and place the Moon in the aforementioned signs or in the Ascendant, or the tenth, or the eleventh.

And Haly said to beware lest the Moon is in Cancer or Capricorn; likewise to be avoided are Gemini and Sagittarius, on account of the great inequality of the days and nights when the Sun is in them; and always, in the construction of any mill, have the Moon in her average course, or slightly faster, if you can. However, if you cannot place the Moon in the aforementioned signs, and you cannot place the

Ascendant in them, but the Moon and the Ascendant are in other signs, Haly said that if it is with the aspect of a malefic it will be good; however, if it is with the aspect of a benefic it will be better.

The beginning of a boat-mill is when her builder begins constructing the first-boat. Indeed, the beginning of other mills is when they begin to be built by those professionals who are of the substance of mills. And if it is a mill which requires a watermill, make the beginning of the digging of the watermill, when the other aforementioned beginnings come to be.

Lest you believe or fear some contradiction, superfluity, or broken thing in the judgements or elections of astronomy, it shall always be found in any chapter according to how it is found in the sayings of the wise. Judge thusly, and you will not care for what is stated elsewhere, nor will you be able to err, but you will always judge and elect correctly.

## ON THE FIFTH HOUSE

### I

### On The Reconciliation Of A Son With His Father

Just as a father disagrees with his son, so too does a son sometimes of his own impetus disagree with his father. Whence if a father comes to you wanting to reconcile with his son, and for you to elect an hour for him that is suitable for this, adapt the Ascendant and its Lord; the Moon also and the Lord of the sign in which she is in; also adapt the fifth and its Lord (which signify the son); and make it so that the Lord of the fifth is joined with the Lord of the first by an aspect of friendship; and if this is with reception, it will be better. Also place the Lord of the first in the first, or in the tenth or the eleventh; and have the Moon aspecting the Lord of the first and the Lord of the fifth (or either of them) - for the purpose of making their reconciliation long lasting.

### II

### On The Sending Of Legates Or Messengers

If someone wishes to send a messenger or legate to some person, you will consider the Moon in this matter before the rest of the significators, and have her joined to a planet signifying the person to whom the messenger is sent to, by a trine or sextile aspect; and if you can, make it so that this planet receives the Moon, or at least the Lord of the first. If he is sent to a king, make it so that she is joined to the Sun, or the Lord of the tenth; and place the Sun or the Lord of the tenth (whichever the Moon joins) in the first, or the tenth, or the eleventh. And if you cannot place it in any of these places, place it in the ninth, the fifth, or the third, but this will be of little utility.

And beware when you send someone (or travel) to a king, that the Moon is not in Aquarius or Pisces.

And if he is sent to some noblemen, magnates, judges, or to the Pope, or cardinals, or bishops, or any other religious figures, have the Moon joined to Jupiter by one of the aforementioned aspects, in an angle, or in a good place from the Ascendant. And if he is sent to bellicose men, have her joined to Mars, and do not make this conjunction from an angle, nor place Mars in an angle, but place him in

a succeedent. And if he is sent to old men, or Jews, or famers, or similar people, have her joined to Saturn from the aforementioned aspects, and make Saturn in good condition, and placed in a succeedent. And if he is sent to women, have her joined to Venus. And if he is sent to wise men, or writers, or merchants, or to young men from 14 to 20 years of age, have her joined to Mercury - and beware lest Mercury (or any one of the planets to whom the Moon is joined) is then impeded.

### III

### On The Donning Of New Vestments Or Their Tailoring

To certain sages it seemed that this chapter should pertain to the first house, since it appears to be of the matters which pertain to the first: yet to me it seems fitting (even if there is not great significance in this) that it can pertain to the fifth house, since the fifth house signifies delights and joys, and men delight in new vestments, and rejoice in them, just as in other delightful things. Whence, if you wish to elect an hour for someone to buy, tailor, make, or wear new vestments, adapt the Ascendant and its Lord, and the Moon; and place the planets in mobile signs; and make the Ascendant a mobile sign: therefore place the Moon in Aries, with the exception of the seven degrees with are after the eighth up to the end of the fifteenth degree of the same sign; and with the exception of the twenty-third and twenty-fourth degree of the same; or place her in Cancer, with the exception of the first six degrees, and the last three; or place her in the first half of Libra; or in the first eighteen degrees of Virgo; or in the first nineteen degrees of Sagittarius; or in the first ten degrees of Pisces.

And the sages said that fixed signs are not to be recommended, except for vestments pertaining to war; yet I did not usually avoid the first 20 degrees of Taurus, since it is the domicile of Venus, who signifies delights; and since the Moon is exalted in it. And they all unanimously condemned Leo. Whence Ptolemy, in his Centioloqui said *"It is dangerous to make or deal with new vestments when the Moon is in Leo"*. And I do not dissent from him, unless perhaps the Sun were to aspect the Moon by a trine or sextile aspect. And wherever you find her received by perfect reception, you will not condemn her. However, if you can adapt her as was said, it is good; and if you can't, place her outside of Leo and outside of Capricorn and outside of the Via Combusta; and never place her impeded anywhere, but rather have her free.

And Haly said to adapt the second and its Lord, and especially in the buying of vestments: and that the Moon should be increasing in light. If you cannot adapt all of these, adapt the Moon in the donning of new vestments, and in the making of them; and place the Sun in the Midheaven. For these things signify that the vestments will be eye-catching and beautiful. And if you can adapt nothing else, make it so that the Moon is not impeded, nor in Leo without reception, as was said; and that the Sun is in the Midheaven.

Certain fools are sometimes in the habit of sophistically asking why does food not harm, or why is it not prohibited for the Moon to be in Leo considering that food enters the body, and why are vestments prohibited, when they don't enter the body. The response to which is that food is potentially of the nature of the body - having been received through the mouth and transmitted into the stomach, its power arrives into action by the mediation of the motions of the supercelestial bodies and the directing virtue of the body, and it is effected by the substance of the body. For from nutrition and what nourishes, become one thing - just like food and eating.

Whence it must defend it, and guard it, and maintain it naturally by the aforementioned virtue, not contradict it, nor can it impede it. Indeed, clothes are accidents, and they do not defend the body, nor even its nature: for that which they have, they have accidentally: and so anyone can live without clothes, while they can't without food. And even if clothes make for the good condition of the body, they do not make for the being of the body, nor are they of its substance. Indeed, the superior bodies operate in the donning of new vestments solely by their own motions; however, in food it is not so, since even if they operate in the taking up of food from their own motions, they do not operate without the agency of the internal nature of the person acting by the transmutation the food into the nature of the body by nourishing it. Whence it does not impede on account of this reason - for it is not in the interest of nature to impede itself. And also since nature is first in the generation and corruption of something growing, and in the destruction of perishing bodies, by means of the motions of a regulating planet; and since it is the intention of nature to preserve, it does not impede it.

## IV

## On The Generation Or Conception Of A Son Or Daughter

Zael said that if you wish to elect an hour to conjoin with your wife to generate a son, make the Ascendant and its Lord, and the Moon, and the Lord of the house of children, all in masculine signs, or in the masculine half of the circle (which is the dexter half), at the house of the conjoining; and do not place anything except masculine planets in the Ascendant, or in the sign of children, in the same hour. And if you want a daughter, place these significators in feminine signs, and in the feminine half of the circle (which is the sinister half). And if you cannot do this, and the significators are diverse (namely, that some of them are in masculine signs: and some of them are in feminine signs), the Lord of the hour will participate with the planet who receives the disposition of the Moon. And judge from those which have more testimonies in masculine signs or in feminine signs, and the conceived child will be according to this.

Hali had a longer discussion on this than Zael. For he said that in this election it is necessary that the Ascendant should be a masculine sign, and one of direct ascension; the angles should be fixed and not remote; and that the Lord of the Ascendant should be in the Ascendant or in the Midheaven, or the eleventh; and that the first planet that comes to the degree of the Ascendant by its own motion should be a benefic. And he said, it is known necessarily through those things which were set out in advance, that both luminaries should be adapted in a like manner in these matters; and especially that it is very necessary to adapt the Lord of the time; and make it so that no malefics are in angles, but free and strong benefics. And he said that it is also fitting that we turn our attention to the Lord of the Ascendant; and that we strive from the beginning to prevent the Lord of the Ascendant from being a planet which is impeded in the ninth month; for we often see births happen in that month. It is even recommended that we guard against the same in the seventh and tenth month: for births sometimes tend to happen in these months. And the Lord of the

Ascendant ought to be fortunate and strong in these places; and the luminaries also. And beware lest the Lord of the sixth or the eight house (if it is a malefic) is mixed with any significator in any way. And those things are to be universally avoided which are said to be blameworthy in the book of nativities; and we should observe those things which are recommended in the roots of elections.

And Alchaiat said that what we said is best if the Moon is placed in the Ascendant in the trine aspect of the Sun. He also said to beware of the via combusta, and that we ought to adapt Venus: if indeed, Venus is impeded, the binding will be corrupted (that is, the woman or womb): if the Moon is impeded, the semen will be corrupted. Also adapt the fifth house and its Lord. Certain men also approve the odd-numbered hours in this, that is, the first, third, fifth, and the like. If it happens that the Ascendant and the Moon are in Libra (which is a rational sign) it will be good, provided that Libra and its Lord are free: for then Cancer (which is a sign of many children) will be in the Midheaven; and the remaining significators should be in masculine signs, for then she will be impregnated and will conceive a son. And we should apply our work in matters which pertain to this, that is, we should judge that the binding or womb is not distorted or in any natural infirmity. For the circular significators perfect according to how the material subjects can receive them. This is the opinion of Haly on generation and corruption.

But since it is difficult to adapt so precisely, and to observe the sayings of the philosophers just as they professed them; it seems to me, namely that you should adapt the Ascendant, the Moon, and its Lord in the conjoining of the husband and wife; and that you should place Jupiter in the degree of the tenth house, if you can do it: since this signifies that the woman will conceive in the first cotius which is had at that time, unless it is Virgo, in which case she would not conceive in the first cotius, yet she could conceive in the second. And if you cannot place Jupiter in the degree of the tenth house, place him in the tenth or the eleventh in such a degree that he aspects the Ascendant degree for degree; or place him in the fifth, in such a way that he aspects the Ascendant, or the Moon, or the Lord of the fifth by a praiseworthy aspect; or place the Lord of the first and the Moon (or one of them) in the fifth; so that they are above the line of the fifth house by two degrees, or at most three, or fifteen degrees at

the most below. For these signify that the woman will conceive at that time. If the greater part of the significators are masculine or in masculine places, it signifies a son; and in feminine, a daughter. And if there are as many masculine significators as there are feminine (namely one or more masculine, and the same feminine) either of the two can be signified, or a hermaphrodite.

## V

### On Taking Out Aborted Children From Women

As it often happens, if a baby dies in the mother's womb, and you wish to elect an hour for removing it (whether by means of surgery, or by means of drugs, or by means of *industricum*, or by whatever means it is), make the Ascendant a feminine sign of direct ascension, and similarly make the Moon defective in light, it you can, and place her beyond the line of the tenth house by six degrees or more, descending towards the seventh house; also have a benefic aspecting the Moon by a trine or sextile aspect, or a square (whether it receives the Moon or not). And if Mars aspects her at that time by the aforementioned aspects with reception, it will be good; however, if it is without reception, it will not be evil, provided that the Moon is in a feminine sign, and that the Ascendant is a feminine sign of direct ascension, as was said. And beware lest the Ascendant is a crooked sign, or lest the Lord of the Ascendant of the Moon is in any of them.

## VI

### On Handing Over A Son For Instruction

It seems that this chapter ought to be contained under the house of professions: but since nothing is mentioned there regarding the instruction of children, it is more suitable to be placed under the fifth house, which signifies children. Whence when you wish to elect an hour for anyone to hand over his son to an instructor, or to learn some lesson, or skill, or profession (whether it is numbers, or measuring, or singing, or astronomy, or some craft), make the Ascendant one of the domiciles of Mercury (the better of which is Gemini); and make the Moon free from impediments, and joined to Mercury by a trine or sextile aspect; and make Mercury safe and free from impediments, and make him oriental, ascending, direct, fortunate, and strong; and make the Lord of the house in which Mercury is placed free and safe; also make the Moon increasing in light and number - since this signifies swiftness of learning; whereas if she is slow or decreasing in light, it signifies slowness of learning.

And Zael said to make the Lords of their houses aspect them. If you are not able to do all of these things, adapt the Moon to the best of your ability; and adapt Mercury so that he is not retrograde or under the rays of the Sun, nor in his first station, and make him occidental from the Sun, or even oriental (provided that he is direct).

# VII

## On Giving Or Receiving Gifts

In this matter (namely, giving gifts to guests), two things are to be considered, namely giving and receiving: just as men receive gifts, so too do they sometimes give them -and the whole of this is called gifting, just as in Latin, he who takes in guests is called a "hospes", and he who is taken in is likewise called a "hospes". Whence if someone wants to accept a gift from another, then the first and its Lord are to be adapted; and the Moon and the Lord of the sign in which she is in; also to be adapted are the second and its Lord, to turn the gift for the utility of the receiver. Also to be adapted are the Part of Fortune and its Lord, to amplify this utility. Jupiter is likewise to be adapted (who naturally signifies substance acquired by moral means), to conserve the amplified utility, and that it may be transferred to the substance of him who receives the gift, and that it may happen regularly.

However, if someone is going to give a gift that was already acquired, or already sent to someone, the fifth and its Lord should be adapted; and Jupiter; and (in either case) make Mars cadent from the Ascendant and its Lord, and from the Moon also, and from the planet in whose domicile she is; likewise from the second and its Lord; and also from the Part of Fortune, the Part of Substance, from the fifth, and from their Lords. And if you can do it, make the second and fifth house common signs: the better of which are Sagittarius and Pisces; and Virgo is below these, and Gemini is below Virgo. Also beware lest Saturn aspects the Moon, or the Ascendant or its Lord, or the Part of Fortune or the Part of Substance, without reception. And make the Lord of the Ascendant elevated above the Lord of the seventh. If you cannot do all of this, adapt the Moon and the Lord of the second house, and Jupiter, in the receiving of gifts; indeed, in the giving of gifts, adapt the Moon, the Lord of the fifth house, and Jupiter and/or the Part of Fortune.

## ON THE SIXTH HOUSE

### I

### On The Healing Of The Sick

If you wish to elect an hour for someone wanting to heal a sick person, examine if it is a general illness in the whole body: or is it a particular illness, namely in some particular body part, such as in the eye, or the ear, or any other official member, as are arms, hands, and similar things.

For if it is an illness in the whole body, make the Ascendant one of the human signs (of which Libra is recommended): for the Ascendant signifies the whole body, unless a body part is specified. If indeed, it is an illness in a certain one of the twelve parts of man listed above, which are the head, neck, arms, shoulders, chest, back, stomach, privates, hips, upper thighs, knees, legs, and feet - Arthephius said to make the Ascendant the sign assigned to the diseased body part; also make the Lord of the first free from impediments, and make the planet signifying that body part safe and free; the Moon should also be adapted.

And Hali said to beware lest the Moon is in opposition to the Lord of the sixth or the eighth house at that time, even if it is a benefic. However, if it is a benefic and the aspect is a trine or sextile, then it is not to be feared. However, if a malefic is the Lord of the sixth or the eighth, the Moon is not to be in any aspect with it. If you cannot avoid that she is in aspect with it, make it a trine or sextile, and not from any other aspect; nor from the corporeal conjunction; nor have the Moon descending.

And Messala said that the Moon should be in the sign assigned to the diseased body part when someone heals it. Understand this by means of drugs, or by an ointment, or plasters; but not by means of surgery (so that the body part is touched by fire or iron or the like). According to Ptolemy in Centioloqui

*"To touch a body part with iron when the Moon is placed in the sign assigned to this member is dangerous".*

### II

### On The Receiving Of Medical Treatment On The Occasion Of Some Illness

If you want to elect an hour for some sick person to accept medical treatment for the purpose of expelling an illness (such as a headache, toothache, cramp, stomach ache, and similar things), which is performed via ointments, plasters, or through the application of cupping glasses, or sponges, and similar things - Zael said to make the Ascendant Libra or Scorpio; and to place the Moon in it, joined to a benefic. And none of the malefics should be in an angle of the Moon; and if you cannot prohibit the aspects of malefics, make them be from a trine or sextile. And do not have her besieged nor impeded from the rays of two malefics: nor have her combust or moving towards combustion; but rather make her free and unimpeded - since if she is not free, the treatment will cause pain and impediment for the sick person.

### III

### On Applying General Cures To The Head

If someone wanted to elect an hour to apply some general cure to the head, or to get some humour down from the head (as is vomiting and gargling, and similar things), make the Ascendant Aries and place the Moon in it, or in Taurus; and have her joined to one of the benefics, and little in light.

And Zael said to beware of the square aspect of the Sun, and of his opposition in Aries, on account of the particular heat of the Sun.

### IV

### If You Want To Apply A Cure To The Nostrils

When you wish to elect an hour for someone wanting to heal via the nostrils (with some ointment or other things, such as sneezing and inhaling fumes, and similar things), make the Ascendant Cancer, Leo, or Virgo; and place the Moon in the Ascendant joined to one of the benefics. And guard against the conjunction of any malefics with her; and do not have her joined to any planet impeded by retrogradation or combustion or fall, or by any other means.

## V

### If Someone Wishes To Heal The Eyes

If you wish to elect an hour for someone wanting to heal the eyes, if there is a blot in them, or a stye, or something stuck in them, or a pterygium, or inflammation, or something which should be removed by surgical means, or by any other means, whether by instruments or medical arts - do this when the Moon is increasing in number and light and joined to a benefic.

And Zael said, guard against her conjunction with Mars when she is increasing in light and number; and place Jupiter above the earth, namely in the Ascendant, the eleventh, or the ninth: and if you cannot put him in these places, have him aspecting the Ascendant from a trine or sextile aspect, or at least by square, provided that he is not impeded.

And guard against the Moon or the Ascendant being in earth signs. And if you can avoid the conjunction of the Moon with Mars, defer your work until she has separated from him; and dismiss him in every curing of the eyes; however, in the end of the month he harms less.

However, Zael said that the sages agreed on the impediments of Mars in the head, and they said that in anything which is cured by fire or iron, the Moon is not to be placed in the sign signifying the body part which is being cured; also that she is not to be in a mobile or common sign. And they said that when she is badly disposed with Mars or Saturn, that if any part of the body is cut or punctured, it will putrefy. They also said that in all of these matters we should beware of the conjunction of the Moon with the Sun, and her prevention, while she transits the Sun by 12 degrees or less.

## VI

### On The Particular Cure Of Any Other Official Member

If you wish to elect an hour for someone wanting to cure some other part of the body, and if the illness is in the neck, make the Ascendant Taurus, and place the Moon there.

If it is in the shoulders, arms, or hands, make the Ascendant Gemini and place the Moon there

If it is in the chest, make the Ascendant Cancer and place the Moon in it.

If it is in the back or the spine of the back, make the Ascendant Leo and place the Moon in it.

If it is in the stomach, the navel, or the adjacent parts, make the Ascendant Virgo, and place the Moon in it.

If it is in the hips, make the Ascendant Libra, and place the Moon in it.

If it is in the privates, make the Ascendant Scorpio, and place the Moon in it.

If it is in the upper thighs, make the Ascendant Sagittarius, and place the Moon in it.

If it is in the knees, make the Ascendant Capricorn, and place the Moon in it.

If it is in the legs, make the Ascendant Aquarius, and place the Moon in it.

If it is in the feet make the Ascendant Pisces, and place the Moon in it.

And always understand the Lord of Ascendant is to be safe and free from impediments, if at all possible; and if you cannot do so, always place Jupiter in the sixth, and this will not be less than if you adapted the aforementioned.

And Messala said that in every curing you should examine the place of the infirmity in the body, for if it is in the head. the gullet, the shoulders, the arms, or the hands, cure it when the Moon is in Aries, Taurus, or Gemini, which are the superior parts. And if it is in the chest, back, stomach, or navel, cure it when the Moon is in Cancer, Leo, or Virgo, which are the parts in the middle. And if it is in the hips, privates, or thighs, cure it when the Moon is in Libra, Scorpio, or Sagittarius, which are the parts sloping downwards. And if it is in the knees, legs, or feet, cure it when the Moon is in Capricorn, Aquarius, or Pisces.

And in every one of these cases, make the Moon increasing in light and number, joined to a benefic, if possible; and if you cannot do this, at least adapt Jupiter as I told you. And he said that all pains and illnesses which are from the head to the pubis, ought to be cured when the Moon is between the angle of the earth up to the Midheaven, since this part of the circle is ascending (which is called the high part of the circle). And if it is from the pubis down to the inferior part of the feet, it ought to be cured when the Moon is between the angle of the Midheaven up to the angle of the earth, which is the submerging half, or the low part of the circle. And place a benefic in the Ascendant.

For these things signify that the medical art will be beneficial, and that the sick person will be cured. And you should know that the places to be adapted for speed are from the first up to the tenth, and from the seventh up to fourth; the remaining places make for slowness. However, you should always keep this in mind - do not touch a body part with iron or fire while the Moon is placed in the sign assigned to that body part; but with other remedies and other cures, such as drugs, ointments, poultices, and similar things, you can cure with confidence.

## VII

## On Remedies Which Come About By Surgery

If you want to elect an hour for someone wanting to cure by means of surgery, place the Moon increasing in light and number, and also make her fortunate by Jupiter or Venus.

And Alchaiat said to beware of all impediments of Mars; for he said that the Moon is more greatly impeded by Mars when she is increasing in her light, and less so when she is decreasing in light. And when she is decreasing in light she is more greatly impeded by Saturn; and she is less impeded by him when she is increasing in light. And he said to place the Moon in a fixed sign; and that she is not to aspect the sign signifying the body part to which is being healed by iron by any aspect; nor should the Lord of the Ascendant be in this sign; nor should this sign be the Ascendant; nor should the Lord of the Ascendant or the Moon be cadent. It is also good if the Lord of the Ascendant in the Ascendant or the Midheaven: and have things the same way in the curing of eyes, on account of an abscess, blemish, or whiteness. And adapt the sign and planet signifying the body part. And I commend this opinion, if it can be observed; but if you cannot observe it in whole, observe what you can of it, and especially adapt the Moon and the Lord of the Ascendant, or at least the Moon, in such a way that she is not in the sign assigned to that body part: nor in the conjunction or aspect of one of the malefics.

## VIII

## On Electing Of An Hour For Someone Wanting To Practice Bloodletting

If you wish to elect an hour for someone wanting to practice bloodletting, adapt the Ascendant and its Lord; and do not make the Ascendant Gemini, or have the Moon in it. And beware lest Mars or Saturn are in the Ascendant; and the Moon should not be in the opposition of either of them; however, make her joined to Mars by a trine or sextile aspect in this work, provided that her aspect to him is not from Taurus (so that she is not in one of them); nor should Mars be ascending in the north or in the circle of his auge.

And Ali said to make the Lord of the house of the Moon aspecting it from a praiseworthy aspect. And he said that a certain man said to beware of Taurus and Leo in this work: and testified that the two of these signs are not to be feared, and especially if a benefic is in them; however, I have found that the corporeal conjunction of the Moon with Jupiter ought to be prohibited in the draining of blood by bloodletting; and I found the rest of the sages who spoke about the bloodletting of the arm to agree with me on this. And certain men said that if it is necessary to drain a small amount of blood, place the Moon in Libra or Scorpio; however, I recommend the first half of Libra; and if Mars aspects the Moon by a praiseworthy aspect, I recommend the last half of Scorpio. And the sages hated mobile signs, and prohibited the conjunction of the Moon with Mercury or with Saturn; and they hated Virgo, Capricorn, and even Pisces; and they placed the Moon in the defect of her light. And the same sages said that the second house from the house of the Moon was not to be made unfortunate; they said that all of these things were to be avoided, unless they were aspected by benefics. However, it seems to me that all of Aries and the first half of Libra, as I said, are to be praised, even though they are mobile signs.

And Albumashar said, Mars is unfortunate in work, except in those things which pertain to blood and the opening of veins and the draining of blood by cupping glasses or in medicating the sick by veins - this is true when the Moon is in the defect of her light, and joined to him by a friendly aspect.

And Alchindi said that it is necessary for the Moon to be in air signs or fire signs, and their Lords. Nor is any body part to be touched while the Moon or Lord of the Ascendant are in the sign which the body part belongs to. They also recommended that the Lord of the Midheaven should be a benefic aspecting the Moon or the Lord of the Ascendant; and that the Lord of the Ascendant and the Moon were in the fourth house (and air signs are better after the prevention).

And they said that draining is more greatly recommended in the beginning of the month - which I say has a place in those who are in need of bloodletting from the 45th year onwards. Even beware of the conjunction of the Lord of the eighth house with the Moon. And beware lest the Moon be under the rays of the Sun, or in the combust degrees.

## IX

### In Giving Purgative (By Defecation) Medicines

When you wish to elect an hour for anyone wishing to receive through the mouth any medicines which induce defecation, adapt the Ascendant and its Lord, if you can adapt them; and whether you can adapt them or not, place the Moon in the last half of Libra, or in the first half of Scorpio; and also make the planet whose domicile she is in (whether it is Venus or Mars), free from impediments, fortunate, and strong. And if you can make the Ascendant either of these two signs, it will be good. However, if you can't, place the Ascendant in one of the southern signs, and make its Lord safe. Similarly, if the Moon cannot be placed in Libra or Scorpio as I said, at least place her in one of the southern signs.

And if the purgation is because of an illness of some specific body part, place the Moon in a sign signifying that body part.

And if your intention is to heat up the body with this medicine, place the Moon or the Ascendant in a fire sign. And if you want to cool it down, place the Moon or the Ascendant in a water sign. And if you want to dry it out, place the Moon or the Ascendant in an earth sign. And if you want to moisten it, place the Moon or the Ascendant in an air sign.

And beware lest the Moon or the Ascendant (and particularly the Moon) are in one of the cud-chewing signs, which are Aries, Taurus, the last half of Sagittarius, and Capricorn: since they signify nausea and vomiting. And Capricorn is worse than the others; Aries is below him; Taurus is below Aries; and the last half of Sagittarius is below Taurus.

Even have the Moon ascending southern.

And Alli said that a certain person said that out of the cud-chewing signs only Capricorn is hateful. And the ancient sages prohibited the Moon from every aspect of Mars and Saturn: for Saturn presses together and constricts the medicine; Mars excites it and makes it lead to the emission of blood. Understand the same about any laxative medicine, whether it is one that melts in the mouth, or a decoction, provided that it does not harm, whatever kind of Ascendant it was, and provided that its Lord and the place of the Moon are fortunate. And beware lest the Lord of the Ascendant or the Moon are not in the eighth house or joined to its Lord.

## X

### On Giving Medicines Which Induce Vomiting

And if you wish to elect an hour for someone wishing to take medicine that induces vomiting, you should then use the cud-chewing. Whence, the Moon and the Ascendant are to be placed in one of them, if it can be done; and Taurus is the better one of signs, on account of the dignity of the Moon in it; more strongly so if she is in the first three degrees of it, where the degree of her exaltation is. And if the vomiting is necessary for a particular illness of some body part, place the Moon in the sign assigned to that body part, namely fortunate and strong; and adapt that sign to the best of your ability.

And Hali said that if the Lord of the Ascendant is going towards its exaltation, it will be good.

## XI

### On Sneezing, Gargling, Vomiting, And Similar Things By Means Of Giving Potions

If you wish to elect an hour for someone wanting to induce sneezing, gargling, or vomiting, or anything similar, Hali said that it is necessary for him who wishes to use any of these to place the Ascendant and the Moon, and the place of the significators (from one of the cud-chewing signs), with everything what was said in the purging medications.

And Athabari said that the Moon should be in diminished light and course, ascending in the circle of her auge.

Indeed, Alchaiat said to place the Moon and the Lord of the Ascendant in Cancer, Leo, or Virgo.

## XII

### On Entering The Baths Or The Anointing Of Annora Or Psilotrum

When you wish to elect an hour for the entry to the baths, or anointing *annora* (which is a certain ointment for removing hair, which by some is called *psilotrum*, and certain others call it *sconapilos*), place the Moon in Aries or Scorpio joined to Jupiter, the Sun, or Venus by a trine, sextile, or square aspect, but not by a corporeal conjunction; nor should you place her joined to any of them by body; nor should you place her in the aspect of Saturn; and if she is not in these signs, place her in Cancer or Leo. However, do not place her in Taurus, Gemini, Virgo, Libra, Capricorn, or Aquarius. Indeed, if he not he will anoint himself with annora when he enters the baths or the steam-room, let her be in any sign at all; nor even should it be condemned if the Moon is under the rays of the Sun in the use of baths or anointing of annora.

And Zael said that in the anointing of annora, the Moon is not to be placed in hairy signs, which are Aries, Taurus, Leo, the last half of Sagittarius, and Capricorn.

## XIII

### On The Buying Of Captives, Slaves, And The Like

If someone wants to buy a captive, slave, or a Slav, just as often happens in certain places, and they wish for you to elect an hour for them that is suitable for this, you should adapt the Ascendant and its Lord, and also the Moon, and place her in fixed signs (except Scorpio) of direct ascension, or domestic ones: since this will signify that the slave or other purchased person, will be submitting, supportive, and honouring toward his master. And adapt the sixth and its Lord, and make him joined to the Lord of the Ascendant by a trine or sextile aspect if you can, with reception, or with the Moon, or with the Lord of the domicile in which she is in. And if you can make it so that he is joined with all of the aforementioned, or with two of them, it is better than if it were only with one.

For indeed, the sages recommended to place the Moon in Taurus, or in the last half of Sagittarius. And they likewise recommended to place the Moon and the Ascendant in signs formed in the image of man, or even in others (except for Aries, Leo, Scorpio, Capricorn, and Pisces), but not without the conjunction of benefics. And beware lest the Lord of the Ascendant, or the Moon, or the Lord of the sixth house are placed in one of the aforementioned signs which are prohibited.

For Aries signifies that the slave or purchased person will be negligent, and that he will not care for the utility of his master, but will rejoice from his harm. Leo signifies that the slave or purchased person will be proud, gluttonous, a thief, desirous, and greedy, but not in the utility of his master. Scorpio signifies that he will be wrathful, an evildoer, and an accuser. Capricorn signifies that he will be a destroyer and injurer of his master. Pisces signifies that the slave or purchased person will be impetuous, and that he will reproach his master, and plot to betray him; and that he will disparage him in every way he can, and he will speak evil of him. Nor will this slave be obedient to his master. And if there is one of the malefics in the sixth, or elsewhere under the earth in such a way that it aspects the sixth, it signifies that the purchased person or slave will be unfaithful and malevolent.

If indeed, the Lord of the sixth is in Sagittarius, it signifies that he who is sold is not a slave, nor of servile condition, but free.

## XIV

## On The Freeing Of Prisoners, Or Captives, Or The Manumission Of Slaves

If it is your intention to elect an hour for the freeing of captives or prisoners, or the manumission of slaves, adapt the Ascendant and its Lord and the Moon: since the Ascendant and its Lord, and the planet from which the Moon separates, signify the one who frees or manumits. The seventh and its Lord, and the planet to which the Moon is joined, signify the person who is freed or manumitted. The 10th and its Lord signify him who makes the freeing or manumission happen, or through whose intermission it happens. The fourth signifies what results for any of them from the freeing or manumission.

For you will then consider whether the Moon is fortunate or unfortunate. For if she is fortunate, see in which house she is placed: since if she is in the first, it signifies good for the manumitter from this liberation. However, if she is in the tenth it will be good for the person interposing himself to make it happen. If she is in the seventh it will be good for the person liberated or manumitted. If she is in the 4th the end of the matter will be good for all of them.

But if she is unfortunate and is in the first, it signifies that it will be bad for the person manumitting. If she is in the 10th it signifies that it will be bad for him who interposes himself to make it happen. If she is in the seventh it signifies that it will be bad for the person liberated or manumitted - for it signifies his return to prison or servitude. If she is in the fourth, it signifies that it will be bad from the liberation or manumission for all of those mentioned above.

And Zael said to make the Moon increasing in light and number joined to benefics; and similarly make the benefic to which she joins oriental, and increasing. If this is so, it signifies that good things will happen to him and he will be safe.

Indeed, in the decrease of her light it signifies that evil things will befall him and pains, whence it will not cease to be so as long as he remains. And he said that in the increasing of her number she signifies the discovery of substance. And he said to make the Sun and the 10th clean from malefics: since if they are impeded, he who liberates and manumits will be somewhat impeded. And he said to beware lest the Moon be in the 12th (following Dorotheus). And he said to make the hour of liberation be when the luminaries are aspecting each other by a trine or sextile aspect, so that there will be love between the slave and the master, and so that one will find good from the other; while the square aspect is middling; indeed, the opposition signifies that if the Moon is impeded, servitude will be better for the slave than freedom. Therefore, place the Moon in fixed signs (understand, her being placed as was said above).

## XV

## On The Buying Of Animals, Both Those Which Are Ridden, And Others

If you wish to elect an hour for someone wanting to purchase some animal, place the Ascendant and the Moon in a sign signifying this animal, or one that is closer to his species than the others; and make the Moon fortunate by one of the planets; and if you can make it so that she is made fortunate by the Lord of that sign, it will be better. And if she is not received, it will still be good, provided that she is in the praiseworthy aspect of an unimpeded benefic. And if she is received, it does not make a difference whether the planet who receives her is a benefic or malefic; nor even will anything to be feared then. Whence if it is a cow or a horse or another large animal, whether it can be ridden or not, place the Moon in Taurus, or the last half of Sagittarius. If indeed, it is a sheep, a pig, a goat, or similar animal, place her in Aries, or Capricorn (or Taurus itself if you cannot do otherwise).

And Haly said that if the animal is male, place more of the significators in masculine places and signs. However, if it is a female animal, place them in feminine signs and places. And he said that if it is necessary to adapt some body part of this animal, make the Moon fortunate, and place her in a sign signifying that body part: and if it is a dog with which men hunt wild animals (such as hares, foxes, boars, deers, and similar beasts), place the Ascendant in the last half of Leo, and the Moon in it, or in Sagittarius; and by no mean should you forget to adapt the 6th and its Lord.

And Athabari said that the best thing is for the Moon to be in the last part of Gemini, or in Leo or Sagittarius, since Lepus is there, and this will make the dog daring, impetuous and snappish.

And Hali said that a certain man called for the Moon to be placed in Cancer, since Cancer is the domicile of the Moon; and the Moon has a faster motion than the rest of the planets, which signifies the speed of the dog. He appeared to say the same in their training and their instruction for hunting.

## XVI

### On The Buying Of Birds With Which We Hunt Other Birds

And if you wish to elect an hour for someone wanting to purchase a falcon, or an Asturian hawk, or a common hawk, or similar birds with which men hunt other birds, adapt the Ascendant and its Lord, and place the Moon in Gemini, Libra, or Aquarius, or the first half of Capricorn (since the philosophers said that the Hawk is there). Also to be adapted are the sixth and its Lord in all purchases of every hunting bird, and also other birds, as much domestic as wild. You will adapt the same when instructing or training these birds to hunt, and in the training of dogs that hunt birds, as are pointers, *sensei,* and similar dogs.

## XVII

### On The Approach Of A Doctor To A Patient

If a doctor is called to some ill person, you will consider whether it is possible to delay him or not. If a delay cannot be interposed on his part, so that you cannot wait for an election, make the beginning of his journey in the name of God Most High. However, if it is possible to wait for an election, place the Ascendant and the tenth one of the rational signs if possible; and if you cannot do this, at least make the Ascendant a rational sign, and place one of the benefics in it, and another in the 10th, and another in the 7th, and another in the 4th if you can; or at least have the mentioned angles aspected by benefics; which if you cannot do, make the angles free from malefics and their

aspects - except Mars in the business of wounds, the opening of veins, or any other useful shedding of blood.

For a benefic in the first signifies that the doctor will be useful for the sick person. In the tenth it signifies that the sick person will be obedient to the doctor. In the seventh it signifies that the illness will be alleviated, not only by the medicine, but also from the presence of the doctor. In the 4th it signifies that the medicine will be beneficial to him. And say the contrary about the malefics in the aforementioned places. Also place a benefic, especially Jupiter, if you can do it, or the Part of Fortune, unimpeded in the second, since this signifies the doctors profit, or joined to the Lord of the eighth or the eleventh, and this likewise signifies the doctors profit. And if the Lord of the second or the Lord of the first does not receive any of them, beware lest they are joined by opposition or square aspect; and beware lest one of the malefics who does not have testimony in the 9th be impeded there - since this signifies that the doctor will not acquire honour from this infirm person, but rather he will acquire infamy or disgrace from him (both with reason and without reason). However, if a benefic is there, it signifies that he will acquire praise from it, both with reason and without reason; and this more strongly so if the benefic has testimony there, provided that it is not impeded.

However, in surgical treatments Mars is less of an impediment. And in any treatment which you do, strive to place Jupiter in the 6th, or at least in the 7th - but the sixth is more efficacious, since he who then provides treatment to the sick person will benefit him.

## ON THE SEVENTH HOUSE

### I

### On Marriage, And Those Things Which Pertain To It

When someone wishes to perfect a marriage union, wedding, or celebrate nuptials, and you wish to elect an hour suitable for them to do this: the sages said to adapt the Ascendant and its Lord, the Moon also and the Lord of the sign in which she is in; and to make the Ascendant a fixed sign, and likewise place the Moon in a fixed sign (the sages said that Taurus and Leo are the better of these). It is also true that Zael did not recommend Leo absolutely: for he said that the marriage would be favourable, and that there will be firm love and harmony between them, but they will not care for the increase of substance, but rather they will, on the contrary, care to destroy it - unless when the Moon is in Leo she is joined to the Sun from a trine or sextile aspect, since this will shatter all malice; indeed, a square aspect will greatly reduce it. Scorpio and Aquarius are to be avoided, and especially for men - since they are malicious, and the domiciles of malefics, whence they harm men. Indeed, for women they are not so malicious.

If a man inquires, the Ascendant and its Lord, and the Sun and the planet from which the Moon separates, signify the condition of the man. The seventh and its Lord, and Venus, and the planet to which the Moon joins, signify the condition of the woman. The tenth and its Lord signify what is going to happen between them. The fourth and its Lord signify the end for both of them (namely the man and the woman).

And Zael said that it appeared to certain men that the fourth signified dowries. Another assuredly affirmed this.

And Hali said that if the significators of the man and woman are in masculine signs, it will be better for the man from the woman than it will be for her from him. And if they are in feminine signs, it will be better for the woman from the man than it will be for him from her. And if the significator of the man is in a masculine sign, and that of the woman is in a feminine sign, it will be good for both of them. However, if the significator of the man is in a feminine sign and that of the woman is in a masculine sign, it signifies that it will not be a harmonious union, nor will they rejoice well together, and they will be harsh and hateful to each other.

Hali (from whom it does not appear to me that one should dissent) said that certain men took the significator of the inceptor from the planet from which the Moon separates, and others from the planet to which she joined. And they gave the Moon as the significator of both, and they gave Mercury to children. And they said that the Moon was not to be placed in a rational sign - for this signifies the loquaciousness of the woman.

And Hali said that if someone wishes to purchase a female captive, it will be the same election; and likewise if he wished to carry on with her. And Hali said in the purchasing of other female captives, this is not to be considered, but rather what was said in the first chapter of slaves.

And Zael said that Scorpio and Aquarius are useful for women, and less malicious than for men; and that the first half of Taurus is better than the last; and that the first half of Gemini is worse than the last; and that Aries and Cancer are bad. And he said that Virgo is not useful for virgins, but for corrupted women it is. Libra is bad, and the end of Scorpio, for it signifies that their partnership will be of little duration (indeed, the beginning of it is less bad for the woman). Sagittarius is bad, and the first half of Capricorn, the last half less so. And he said that Aquarius and Pisces are bad; nor is there any utility in them; nor when Venus is aspected by malefics. However, if you wish to improve an election for marriage, place Venus in one of the domiciles of a received benefic (or at least in their terms), joined to them. And if she is in the domicile of a malefic, make her separated from it, and make Jupiter elevated above her, or make Venus joined to him by trine or sextile aspect (but the trine is better), and especially if it is from the water triplicity. Also make the Moon free from the impediments of malefics, and increasing in light and number; also always place Venus in one of her own dignities, or in a place where she rejoices, or at least in her own hayz, or make her joined to Jupiter or Mercury, and make Mercury fortunate and strong.

And always beware of the conjunction of malefics with the Moon by body or aspect, unless perhaps there is reception there. And if the woman is corrupted, place the Moon in a common sign, and make the Ascendant one of the signs discussed above in marriage, and place the Moon in it. And do not place a malefic in the Ascendant, nor have one aspecting it from a square aspect or from opposition.

If you can observe all of these things, it is good; however, if you can't, observe those which you can, and at least make it so that the Moon is safe, by making her free from the impediments of malefics, so that she is not joined to them. And if you cannot make it so that she is not joined to them, make it so they receive her from a trine or sextile aspect ;namely from domicile or exaltation, or at least two of the lesser dignities. And if you cannot adapt her like so, at the least place her in Taurus unimpeded; or in Leo received by the Sun, as said, and especially if it was set in motion by a man. However, it was set in motion by a woman, place the Moon in the aforementioned signs, or in the first half of Scorpio with reception.

And if you can place a benefic in the degree of the 10th house, it signifies that the woman will conceive in the first copulation, if she were corrupted. If she were a virgin, she will conceive in the same night. Whence women are sometimes accused (since they conceive in the first night), when they are free of blame; and are often accused by women who ought to defend them - for the accusers do not consider that there is a copulation on those nights.

## II

## On The Contracting Of Partnerships And Participations For The Reason Of Utility And Profit

If some people wish to contract a partnership or participation between them for the reason of their utility, and to profit from it, and they wish that you elect them an hour suited to this - adapt the Ascendant and its Lord; the Moon also and the Lord of the domicile in which she is in, if possible; or at least make it so that the Ascendant a common sign, and the Moon in a common sign (besides Gemini); even place the Lord of the sign where the Moon is in a common sign, or place it in Leo (Leo on account of the goodness of the Sun, and the Sun himself being agreeable with partnerships; and for

them, since their intention is to profit because of this); and make the Moon clean from all the impediments of malefics, and especially from their conjunction, opposition, and square aspect; and make her joined to benefics.

And if she is in Virgo, Sagittarius, or Pisces, with reception, it will be good. If indeed, it is without reception, Sagittarius or Pisces are not recommended: but with reception it signifies their profit. And if you cannot place her in the aforementioned signs, place her in Taurus, and beware of the southern signs, except for the aforementioned ones; and have her received in them. And Libra is judged to be the worst of them all, on account of the *via combusta* placed in it. And Aquarius is judged to be bad in these things. And make the Moon increasing in light and number; and received from a trine or sextile aspect: for this signifies that their separation will be good, and with benevolence. For the square aspect and the opposition signify litigation and disputes in their separation. However, if you cannot adapt all of these things, adapt those which you can. For after adapting the Lord of the Ascendant and the Moon, adapt the second, the fourth, the eleventh and their Lords, and the Part of Fortune (even if the sages did not mention these). If you cannot adapt all of these, adapt the Moon and the Part of Fortune, which are both necessary in this matter, or at least adapt the Moon.

## III

## On The Electing Of An Hour For Setting Out To War Or Conquering Enemies

If you wish to elect an hour for someone wanting to travel to war or to conquer enemies, adapt the Ascendant and its Lord, the second also and its Lord, and weaken the seventh and its Lord; the eighth also, and its Lord; and make it so that the Ascendant is one of the domiciles of Mars, Jupiter, or Saturn, the strongest of which are the domiciles of Mars, and Scorpio is stronger than Aries. Whence if you can place and adapt Scorpio as the Ascendant, make Mars strong and fortunate. And even though certain people seem to dissent from this, place him in the Ascendant if he is the Lord of the Ascendant; however, it will be very good if you can place some benefic with him in the Ascendant. And you will adapt Jupiter by placing him in the second, the first, or the eleventh - for the soldiers or assistants of the inceptor. And weaken Venus (the Lord of the seventh) for the enemy; and Mercury for his assistants. Place them in the first or the second, or have them retrograde, combust, or cadent from the angles, and away from a friendly aspect of the 7th or the 8th. If the Ascendant is Aries, make Mars (the Lord of the Ascendant) strong and fortunate. And weaken Venus (the Lord of the seventh), as was said.

However, if you cannot place one of the domiciles of Mars as the Ascendant, place one of the domiciles of Jupiter or Saturn: and place the Lord of this Ascendant fortunate and strong, namely in the Ascendant, or the 10th, or 11th. And strengthen the Lord of the second for his assistants, likewise by placing him in the Ascendant, or in the 10th, or the 11th, or in the 12th, fortunate and strong; and weaken the 7th and its Lord; and also the 8th also and its Lord, in every way that you can, and make them unfortunate to the best of your ability, and make it so that the planet who makes them (or at least one of them) unfortunate is the Lord of the Ascendant or at least the Lord of the second, since it will be good (and it is better if he who makes the Lord of the seventh unfortunate is the Lord of the Ascendant)

And beware lest you place Mars in the Ascendant, if he is not the Lord of the Ascendant, but make it so that he aspects the Ascendant or its Lord by a trine or sextile aspect, since it will be good; and do not make him impeded; and it he is impeded, place a benefic against him who prohibit the Ascendant. And beware lest you ever make the Lord of the Ascendant or the Lord of the second impeded, or place one of them in the 7th or 8th - since this is the worst thing you could do, since it signifies that they will be conquered. And likewise you should beware of the 4th, and make it so that the Lord of the Ascendant is not joined to a cadent planet or one placed in its own fall, unless perhaps that cadent planet were to receive it. And if you cannot place the Lord of the seventh in the Ascendant or in the second, make him joined to the Lord of the Ascendant, and moving towards him, and the Lord of the Ascendant towards the Lord of the seventh; and make their conjunction be such that the Lord of the seventh does not receive the Lord of the Ascendant, whether the Lord of the Ascendant receives him or not.

And Hali said to place Mars aspecting the Ascendant by a trine aspect after you have adapted him, and make it so that he has the greatest dignity in it; and it is better to make him its Lord, or that he aspects the Lord of the Ascendant by a praiseworthy aspect; and make the Lord of the 7th unfortunate, weak, and cadent; and it is better if you can make the planet by whom he is made unfortunate the Lord of the Ascendant, if possible; and make the Lord of the Ascendant moving toward an angle in one of his own dignities, elevated above the Lord of the 7th and the 10th. And it is also good when the Lord of the Ascendant is transiting over the Lord of the 7th (whether he is a benefic or a malefic);and that the Lord of the Ascendant is above the earth: and the Lord of the seventh is below the earth. Since if the Lord of the Ascendant makes the Lord of the 7th unfortunate, it signifies that the king or captain of the enemies will be captured. And make the Lord of the 10th aspecting the Ascendant, or at least its Lord, by a praiseworthy aspect, and having dignity there, if possible. And he said to not make him aspecting the 7th, nor its Lord, nor having any dignity there. If this cannot be done, make it so that he has greater dignity in the Ascendant than he does in the 7th. And he said that the Moon should be handled in the same way as the Lord of the Ascendant.

And Zael said that if you were to make them joined in angles, there will be war between them. And he said that you should not go to war unless Mars is the Lord of the Ascendant, or aspects the Lord of the Ascendant from a friendly aspect; and to make him fortunate and in a good place, not impeded. And he said to place him in signs of direct ascension, and in ayz of the Ascendant, so that there is assistance for him who goes to war. And place the Part of Fortune and its Lord in the Ascendant, or in the second, joined to their Lords, or at least with one of them. And never place them in the 7th or in the 8th, nor joined to their Lords. And he said make sure not to place the Ascendant or its Lord impeded in the inception of war (namely for him who wishes to begin war): and to observe the duodena of the Moon, since it is necessary in matters of war.

And Alchindi said that it is necessary that the prince against whom the enemy set out never begins to do battle with them, until the Moon is fortunate: but if battle is required, to do so when the Moon is not fortunate.

And Hali said that it is also hateful for the fighters to begin fighting in the hours which are called combust, about which I made mention to you; and that it is necessary for you to adapt the stars of war: namely, Mars and Mercury; and also the Moon and the Lord of her house; therefore examine these things in the adaptation of the hour, and do not be negligent in this, nor be given to forgetfulness. And he said to know that when either army is wisely led out to war, as was made known to you, victory will be obtained by him who was born at night, and in whose nativity Mars has a role - since Mars is the master of wars, and wars are committed to him. And he said that they might make peace or set the war aside, namely if the setting out to war of both of them were good.

### On The Revolution Of The Year Of The Captain Of The Army To Be Considered

And if the nativity of the king or of the captain of the army is known, it is fitting to examine his revolution: which if it signifies his victory over the enemy in that year, without a doubt his side will win. However, if it signifies the contrary for him, he should be removed in that year, and another substituted in his place.

## IV

### On The Discovery Of The Combust Hours

However you will be able to find the combust hours in this way: consider the hour of the most recent past conjunction of the Sun and Moon passed over and its minute, and begin from this minute and count up to 12 complete hours - since these 12 hours are combust, in which it is to be feared, according to what Haly said. Since if a war is incepted at this time, and especially in the first four of these hours, defeat should be feared for him, and the loss of body and spirit, even if he has an otherwise good election for setting out to war. And in this many ignorant men are sometimes deceived; deception coming to them since they do not consider the combust hours. The remaining eight hours border on danger, but not on the ultimate danger.

And after these 12 combust hours are 72 incombust hours, in which men can do their business. And after these 72 incombust hours are 12 combust. And after these 12 combust, there are 72 incombust. Whence if you calculate from the minute of the conjunction up to the hour and minute in which you are in, you will be able to know whether that hour in which you wish to begin the war is combust or incombust.

And if the adversaries begin to battle in these combust hours, the same misfortune will befall them, nor will they be contrary for those against whom the battle was begun. But since the adaptation of all of the aforementioned things is always impossible, and since men cannot ever wait so long that all of their elections are, as it was said, pruned: it is necessary that the astrologer does what he can, when he cannot do whatever he wants.

Therefore when you elect for the aforementioned make it so that you place the Ascendant as one of the domiciles of the superior planets; which, if they are not so disposed or so adapted that the domicile of one of them should be placed as the Ascendant: make Leo the Ascendant, and make the Sun fortunate and strong; and weaken Saturn if you can, namely by making him retrograde or combust, or in Leo, Cancer, or Aries; and he should not aspect his own domicile, nor a planet which renders light to it: and weaken Jupiter - who is the significator of the helpers on the side of the enemies; and strengthen Mercury - who is the significator of the helpers of the side for whom you elected. And if you can, adapt Mars so that you have him well on your side; and if you can't make it so that the enemy does not have him on their side; and do not place him in the 7th or the 8th, nor aspecting either of them, nor either of their Lords. Understand the same of Saturn and Jupiter.

And always make it your concern to strengthen the Ascendant and the 2nd, and their Lords; since as the Philosopher testifies, a multitude cannot be killed, and so there is no victory against a multitude; whence an election is weak against a multitude, nor is its assistance clearly perceived. If the side for whom you elect is equal to the other, or slightly lesser, you should elect for this equal or slightly lesser side. If the side is less, let it be by one-fifth, one-fourth, or for one-third, since from this point onwards it is superfluous, and will cast doubt on the side which you support.

And beware lest you place the Moon on the side of the enemies; and if she is their significatrix (namely that the Ascendant is Capricorn), weaken her to the best of your ability, and strengthen Saturn as much as you can, so that your side will win.

And it seemed to some of the ancients that retrograde superiors are stronger than direct inferiors - however, this is not purely and simply so. But rather, if the superiors are retrograde and close to their second station, they will be stronger than direct inferiors which are close to their first station.

However, if you cannot adapt the aforementioned in the way that I told you, defer your election until you can adapt them. If he who consults you does not want to defer, do not elect for him lest you fall into ignominy and not from your own fault. But make it so that it will seem possible to him - perhaps his root nativity is so strong that he will win, or perhaps the contrary will happen to him, which seems more likely, and would not be surprising.

## V

## On The Raising Of Flags, Or Great Banners, Or Pennants

It seemed to some men that this chapter should be placed before the last, since the raising of flags is one of the matters leading up to battle. To others is seemed that the previous chapter ought to precede, and that this chapter ought to follow, since even though the raising of flags is a sign that leads to battle, it still does not initiate the battle: for men can carry flags and do battle, and they carry them and not do battle; however, there cannot be a battle unless there is a battle. However, I place no significance in this issue.

The raising of flags or other signs for battle is threefold: for it is either the giving or confirmation of the kings' standard, or that of another magnate below the king; or it is the flag of a city; or the flag of another group of people. And if more ways are found, they will be subordinate to these. If a kind wishes to raise or establish his own flag, it is necessary that he raises it with his own hands, or that he commits it to another person who raises it in his name. And raising and confirmation differ from one another. For raising is when the standard is newly given to him who does not usually have it. Confirmation is when it is confirmed for him who then has it, or to whom it has already been given.

Whence if someone wants you to elect an hour for them that is suitable for this, adapt the tenth and its Lord, and place the Moon in Scorpio joined to Mars by a friendly aspect, with the conjunction or aspect of a benefic; and make Mars free (namely. fortunate and strong, and not impeded). And if you cannot place the Moon in Scorpio, place her in Aries (but Scorpio is more greatly praised), and make it around the end of the lunar month, if possible - however, always make the Moon safe. And if it is possible for Scorpio to be the tenth house, with the Moon in it; and for the Sun to be in Aquarius in a region in which Aquarius is then the first house, and for Saturn to be safe - it would be good. However, if Capricorn is the first house it will not be as secure. If it is the flag of some magnate below the king, and this person is the master of the war, it will be good to place the Moon in Scorpio when you elect for him, on account of the strength of Mars in it; and make the Ascendant Scorpio, as was said, and make the Moon free, and joined to Mars by a praiseworthy aspect.

However, it is the flag of some city, or some group of people, or of some magnate who is not the master of the war (namely that it is not his own war, but he wages it for someone else), place the Moon in a domicile of Jupiter, and make her clean (namely fortunate, strong, and free from impediments); and make Jupiter fortunate, strong, and free from all impediments. And do not place the Moon in Cancer at this time, nor in the domicile of a malefic, and this has a role when a specific battle is expected after the raising of their flag, even if afterwards the flag of a city or of the aforementioned people followed after this raising, as often happens. And if all of this cannot be done, whatever way the flag is raised, place the Moon in a domicile of Mars, as was said, and she should always be safe, and free from impediments; or place her in Leo joined to the Sun from a praiseworthy aspect. Understand the same regarding the purchasing of the aforementioned flags, and regarding their cutting, conjoining, and adaptation. Understand the same for vestments pertaining to war (when the Moon is in Leo), those which men use for this purpose alone, and not another purpose - taking into consideration that the making of or dealing with any common new vestments is prohibited by the wise men when the Moon is in Leo.

But if you cannot adapt all of these things, adapt those of them which you can; at least adapt the Moon and the Lord of the Ascendant. And if you can give the Ascendant the Part of Fortune, it will be good for the side of him for whom you elect. And you should weaken the seventh and its Lord as much as you can, and the planet to which the Moon is joined, if you can; and strengthen that planet from which she is separated, if you can do so. And never give the Part of Fortune to the adversary, if you can take it away from him.

## VI

## On The Procuring Of Arms, War Horses, And Other Instruments Pertaining To War

Just as it seemed to certain men that the raising of flags ought to precede setting out to war, so it seems to them that the procuring of arms ought to precede the raising of flags - but since battling is the most powerful part of war, it seemed to others that it should precede the two preceding things, and this third subsequent one also. Whence if you wish to adapt an hour suitable for this for someone wishing to procure arms, both for offensive arms, and also for defensive arms -as are cuirasses, shields, helmets and similar things; or to procure horses solely with the intention of, and for the purpose of battling with them; or for someone wanting to make the aforementioned arms, or paint them or adapt them in any other way: you will adapt the Ascendant and its Lord, the Moon also and the Lord of the house she is in. And place Mars free in any of his own dignities; and have the Moon joined to him by a friendly aspect; and do not make the Moon increasing in light at this time, but decreasing in light in the final dichotomy, or close to it, (provided that she is not under the beams, or moving towards combustion). And if you cannot make it but that the Moon is increasing in light, prohibit her from the aspect of Mars and from his corporeal conjunction: and make her otherwise free from impediments. And if you cannot adapt all of these, at least adapt Mars, as was said; and make him free (namely, fortunate and strong).

### On The Purchasing Of Horses

However, in the purchasing of horses you can make the Ascendant a common sign, and place the Moon in Taurus or Leo, and make the planet to which she joins direct, and ascending: for this indeed, signifies that the horse will increase in body and price. However, if the planet is retrograde, and ascending, his body will reduce, even if it were to increase in price. However, it is direct, and descending the horse will decrease in price, even if it might increase in body. But if it is retrograde and descending, both its body and price will decrease. Understand the same about all other horses.

## VII

## On The Reconciliation Of Enemies Who Made War With Each Other

Since in the preceding chapters mention was made of war and of those things which pertain to war, it appeared to the master Hali that a discussion on harmony or enmity reconciliation ought to follow immediately after what was said about war and fighting enemies. Whence, if you want to elect an hour suitable for someone wishing to be reconciled with his enemies, you will adapt the Ascendant and its Lord; make it fortunate and strong; and the Moon also, if you can, and the Lord of the house in which she is in; and weaken the seventh and its Lord; yet place a benefic in the first; and even though you weaken the Lord of the seventh, make it so that it is joined to the Lord of the Ascendant from a trine or sextile aspect, or at least aspecting the Ascendant from the same aspect.

And Hali said to also make the Lord of the twelfth weak and cadent. And he said that if the 12th house itself is impeded it will be good; and that it is to be done with the 12th and its Lord just as with the 7th and its Lord; and that the Lord of the eleventh and his Lord are to be adapted. And he said to place the Lord of the Ascendant in the Midheaven or moving towards it; and it should be in as strong a condition as it can; and likewise the planet in whose domicile it is; and make this planet in the greatest strength and fortune as possible. It is better if the Lord of the 12th were one of those planets which are friendly to the Lord of the Ascendant. And he said that if the degree of the Ascendant and the degree of the 12th are of the same strength, this will be better than could be in the adaption of houses. And he said that if he who makes peace is a king, that those things which were recalled in the introduction of this chapter are to be adapted; and have the Lord of the Ascendant be transiting over the Lord of the 12th. And if the signs from which the significators are taken are fixed or of direct ascension, it will be better. If they are harmonised through the hands of legates, or through charters, Mercury is to be adapted. However, if it is by actions and words of those present, Jupiter and the Lord of the Ascendant are to be adapted, and placed in signs of direct ascension, and the Lord of the seventh and the 12th should be placed in signs of crooked ascension.

And Atabari said that if the intention of him for whom you elect is to deceive his adversary by cunningly advancing on him, place the Moon in Aries, Taurus, Gemini, Scorpio, Sagittarius, Capricorn, or Pisces; and make the Moon joined to one of the benefics; or place one of them in the Ascendant; and do not place the Lord of the Ascendant cadent from an angle; but rather have him aspecting the Ascendant from a friendly aspect, and place him in the aspect of benefics; and it is necessary that you make the Lord of the twelfth weak.

## VIII

### On The Election Of An Hour For The Expelling Or Ejecting Ghosts Or Some Malignant Spirit (Which Is Called The Devil By Some) Impeding Or Infesting Some Place, House, or Person; Or Destroying The Place Of An Oracle Of An Idol Or Similar Things

And if someone wishes to eject or expel a ghost or some harmful spirit (which is called "the Devil" by some people), from some place or house, or some harmful things either terrifying or infesting the inhabitants of this place, or if there are violent movements or distress in some person which is called demonic, and you wish to administer some medicine or perform some exorcism, or something similar, and you wish to elect an hour suitable for him that is suitable for this, adapt the Ascendant and its Lord, and beware lest the Ascendant is Cancer, Leo, Scorpio, or Aquarius; and do not place the Moon in any of these signs. Make the Ascendant wherever other sign you want, and make its Lord free; and place the Moon in any other sign joined to one of the benefics, and unimpeded. However, in the destruction of a house in which idols are worshipped, or in which there is some prayer which is not divine, it is sufficient for you to weaken Venus and make her unfortunate.

## IX

### On The Purchasing Of All Things Generally, Both Mobile And Immobile, Under Which The Aforesaid Chapter On The Purchasing Of Animals Can Be Comprehended

The other chapters on purchasing can be comprehended under this one and subordinated to it. Whence if someone wishes to purchase something, and wants you to elect them an hour suitable for doing this, adapt the Ascendant and its Lord; the Moon also, and place her in the first or the tenth; also, if possible, make the first and the tenth feminine signs: however, in this case the tenth is more recommended than the first: or place her in the eleventh; also make the Lord of the house in which the Moon is in safe and free from impediments; and make the Lord of the Ascendant reducing in number, so that it moves less in one day than it does in its average-course; and also make Mercury and the Lord of the tenth safe and free from impediments.

And Hali said that the Moon is with Mercury it will be useful; and if Mercury is also decreasing in his course it will be good.

And Tiberiadis said that crooked signs are good for buyers and they also appear to help sellers. However, if the Lord of the Ascendant is increasing in number, and in signs of direct ascension, it is bad for buyers. Likewise, if the Moon is in signs of direct ascension, and is increasing in course, it will be worse: since this makes anything that one buys at this time dear; and makes it decrease in value so that loss can follow from it. However, when she is in crooked signs, and is decreasing in course, she makes anything one buys at this time cheap, and makes it more valuable so that profit can follow from it; and I maintain what I said above in the chapter on the procuring of arms and horses (both for war and for other purposes).

And Hali said that a certain man said that buying and selling in the first quarter of the lunar month is useful for both (namely for the buyer and the seller); in the second quarter it is more useful for the seller than the buyer; in the third quarter it is more useful for the buyer than the seller; in the final quarter it is very agreeable for the buyer. And he said that certain people did not disprove of the Moon being joined to Saturn, which seems commendable to me in the purchasing of heavy things, such as land and other estates, as much rural as urban, and those things which are hoped to remain with the buyer for a long time. However, in the purchasing of mobile things, and those of which are expected to be quickly transferred to others, it does not appear commendable to me.

However, if you cannot adapt all of the aforementioned things, adapt what you can. At least adapt the Moon, and use the quarters of the month as was said, if you can, and crooked signs. However, if it is the purchase of an animal which the buyer intends to fatten, as are pigs, chicks, and the like, make the Ascendant a common sign, and place the Moon in Taurus or Leo, or at least in a common sign; and make the planet to which she is joined (or which she will join first) direct, and ascending; and this will be if he is buying this animal to resell; however, if he buys it not to sell it again, but only to fatten it up for his own use, make the planet to which the Moon is joined direct; and you will not care whether it is ascending or descending.

## X

## On The Purchasing Of Seeds For Fields Or Gardens, etc., Such As Grain, Barley, Beans, Winter Wheat, Cabbage, And The Like

If someone wants to purchase some sowable seed whose utility and fruitfulness is expected, and you wish to elect them an hour suitable for this, adapt the Ascendant and its Lord; and make such an election be in the first quarter of the lunar month; and make the Moon increasing in number, if possible; also place her in crooked signs (which are said to be increasing ones), and in one of the masculine quarters (since these also increase), which are from the tenth to the Ascendant, and from the fourth to the seventh; and also place the Lord of the first in one of these places; and make

the tenth and its Lord free from the impediments of malefics.

And Hali said that the Moon should also be with Mercury, and that Mercury should be oriental, fast in his motion, and free; which opinion I approve strongly if it can be observed in whole; but if you cannot observe it entirely, at least observe it to the extent of adapting the Moon.

## XI

## On The Borrowing And Loaning Of Money

This chapter appears to be contrary to the chapter on the loaning of money; whence it is necessary that he who elects employs certain things contrary to those which are used in that chapter. Wherefore, if someone wishes to take out a loan, and they request you to elect them an hour adapted for this, adapt the Ascendant and its Lord; and place the Moon in Leo, Libra, Scorpio, Sagittarius, or Aquarius; and make her decreasing in light, and in the aspect of Jupiter, Venus, or Mercury; and make the Ascendant one of the aforementioned signs; and make the Lord of the first and the Lord of the seventh free from impediments; and if possible, make them in harmony, or receiving one another, from some of their dignities, whether they are great or small.

And Hali said that certain men hated the hour of Mars and the hour of the Sun in this.

## XII

## On The Hunting Of Birds, Wild Animals, And Fish, By Land And Water

Just as was said elsewhere, there are two ways of hunting, one on land and by land, the other in water and by water. That which is on land is divided, for it is either in mountains and by mountains, or it is on flat land and by flat land. Likewise, that which is in water and by water is divided: for it is in the sea, or it is in rivers, lakes, hollows, or brooks.

And again, hunting which is done on land, is either for wild animals, or for birds. And again, hunting which is for wild animals is either for wild animals which harm by their bite or claws, as are bears, wolves, foxes and the like; or it is for other wild animals having something in common with domestic ones, by chewing cud, or by having cloven hooves, as are hares, roebucks, deer, boars, and similar beasts. Similarly, that which is for birds is either for aerial birds (as are eagles, hawks, sparrowhawks, kites, and similar birds that snatch birds up); or for pigeons, agatias, cranes, great partridge, starlings, blackbirds, sparrows, ravens, and similar birds); or is for land fowl (as are pheasants, partridge, terns, quail, curnew, and similar birds); or it is for swamp birds, or those living on and near water (as are ducks, swans, geese, diving-birds, and the like). That which is done in water, is either done with a hook or a net, or with other ingenious instruments placed in the water, as are wicker traps, coverings, *nermelli,* and similar things.

Whence, if you wish to go out on a hunt, or you if you wish to elect an hour suitable for someone wanting to go, adapt the Ascendant and its Lord, and make the sign of the seventh, or at least of the Ascendant, of the nature of the kind of hunting which the hunter intends to do: however, it is better for the seventh to be of this nature than the first his than the first.

For if it is a hunt by mountains and for injurious wild animals, make the Ascendant a fire sign, the better of which are the last half of Leo, and also Sagittarius, but Sagittarius is below Leo; and Aries is below Sagittarius. And make the Lord of the Ascendant fortunate and strong, and likewise the Lord of the sixth. However, if it is a hunt for other cud-chewing or cloven-hoofed animals, make the Ascendant one of the quadrupedal signs, or one of the other earth signs. And if you cannot have this, make it so that you have one of the other quadrupedal signs (but the aforementioned ones have more power than the others), if you can get them. If it is a hunt for wild animals on flat land, whatever kind they are, make the Ascendant an earth sign or a quadrupedal sign; and make the Lord of the Ascendant fortunate and strong; likewise the Lord of the sixth.

However, if it is a hunt for aerial birds, whether it is in mountains or on flat land, make the Ascendant one of the air signs; and make the Lord of the Ascendant fortunate and strong, and in a common sign or an air sign, and likewise for the Lord of the sixth (or at least do so for one of them). If it is for landfowl, make the Ascendant an air sign, and place the Lord of the Ascendant in an earth sign, and the Lord of the sixth in an air sign, or make the both of them in an air sign if you can't do better. If it is a hunt for marsh-birds, make the Ascendant an air sign, and place the Lord of the Ascendant in a water sign; or make the Ascendant a water sign, and place the Lord of the Ascendant in an air sign or an earth sign, and likewise with the Lord of the sixth, if possible. However, if you cannot do this, place the Ascendant and its Lord, or one of them, in an air sign.

And you should never forget to adapt the sixth and its Lord to the best of your ability. For the sixth signifies dogs, birds, spears, and the other instruments with which men hunt every kind of quarry, as much terrestrial as aquatic. And it likewise signifies every place assigned over hunting, as are weels, coverings, snares, baskets, fowlers-nets, and similar things. And if someone wants to set up one of these instruments, namely a net, or any other one of them; or if he wants to teach a dog or a bird to hunt; or to prepare one of these places, and you wish to elect them an hour suitable for this, adapt the Ascendant and its Lord; also the sixth, and adapt its Lord no less than the first, if you can; and weaken the seventh and its Lord and make them unfortunate; and likewise, weaken the Moon as much as you can, and make her slow-of-course. And make it so that the Lord of the first or the Lord of the sixth is the planet who makes the Lord of the 7th or the Moon unfortunate: however, if you cannot make it so the Lord of the first or sixth makes them unfortunate, it is better that Mars makes them unfortunate, and that he himself is strong and fortunate (and Mars also has a role in every hunt by land, as much on flat land as in mountains); and make it so that they are joined together if you can: for the conjunction of the Lord of the seventh with the Lord of the first signifies the catching of the quarry with the hunters labour and pursuit. However, if the Lord of the seventh is joined to the Lord of the first, it signifies getting the quarry with ease and little fatigue; and this more strongly if the Moon is joined to it.

In water hunting (or fishing), if it is a hunt with a hook, adapt the Ascendant and its Lord, and make the Ascendant a common sign or a water sign; and make the Lord of the seventh and the Moon unfortunate and weak; and make them unfortunate by the Lord of the first, or the Lord of the sixth, or Saturn or Mars - even though Mars is prohibited from water hunting, nevertheless in water hunting or fishing using hooks or *floximae*, one can use him on account of the wound which follows from the hook and *floxima*. However, if it is fishing or hunting in the sea, make the Ascendant a common sign, but not a fire sign; place its Lord in a water sign; and make the Moon joined to the Lord of the house in which she is in, provided that she is otherwise made unfortunate and weak by the aforementioned method. If it is a hunt in other waters outside of the sea, (whether it is in a river, a brook, a lake, or a hollow), and if it is with hidden instruments placed in the water, make the Lord of the Ascendant strong and joined with Mercury; and make the Lord of the seventh and the Moon weak, as was said for the others.

And in each and every one of the cases mentioned above always understand that the Ascendant, the sixth, and their Lords are to be placed fortunately and strong; and that if you can adapt the fourth and its Lord, it will be good; and to make the seventh and its Lord, and the Moon unfortunate and weak. And even if the Moon is put on the side of the quarry, nevertheless, the hunter always has something to do with her - whence, she is never to be made void-of-course: for then she would signify the labour of the hunter to be in vain and empty, and the hiding of the quarry from his eyes. Also beware lest she is cadent from an angle, since this signifies the loss of the quarry after it is caught; likewise for the Lord of the seventh. Still it is better that the Lord of the Ascendant makes the Moon unfortunate than if the Lord of the sixth does: since even though the Moon does not signify the quarry, nevertheless, she always has something to do with the quarry. Whence if the Lord of the sixth makes the Moon unfortunate, there is a chance that the dog or bird with which he hunts (or one of the hunting instruments) might harm the hunter.

And always make it your concern to adapt the Lord of the hour in the hour of going out to hunt (and on all journeys). And in making the Moon unfortunate you must make it so that she is made unfortunate by the Lord of the first, the Lord of the sixth, the Lord of the second, the Lord of the eleventh, or the Lord of the Part of Fortune. And if she is made unfortunate by the Lord of the fourth, the utility could be preserved; however, she should not be made unfortunate by any of the others; but have her weakened by whatever means she can be weakened. I say this for the safety of the hunter, since she always has something to do with this, as I said. Her weakening always works for the hunter; making her unfortunate does not always work, unless she is made unfortunate by the aforementioned significators, or by any one of them. However, making the Lord of the seventh unfortunate always works for the hunter, and it is in his favour and utility.

And beware lest the Moon is made unfortunate by the Lord of the eighth; but have her made unfortunate by the Lord of the seventh, the twelfth, the third, the fifth, the ninth, or the tenth, for then you need not worry about the loss of the quarry after you get it (likewise with the Lord of the seventh). And beware of Mars in hunting by water, since he is evil; just like Saturn in hunting by land. For Saturn, if he impedes the Moon in fishing, or is joined to her by an inimical aspect, is as effective as when she is impeded by the Lord of the first or the Lord of the sixth, and increases the catch of the hunt or fishing. Likewise in the putting together of fishing instruments, provided that Mars does not aspect her then.

And adapt the Part of Fortune in every fishing or hunting trip, placing it in the first, or the sixth, or the fourth, or joined to their Lords. Likewise for the Part of Hunting, which is taken from the Caput Draconis to Saturn, and projected from the Ascendant. And also adapt the Lord of the hour in every hunt, and in every preparation of hunting instruments. However, if you cannot adapt all of the aforementioned things in the manner which I told you (since it seems almost impossible), adapt the Ascendant and the sixth and their Lords, and the house of hunting (which is the seventh): and make it a sign of the nature of the quarry which the hunter intends to hunt; so that if it were his intention to hunt quadrupeds, make the house of hunting an earth sign; if it were his intention to hunt birds, make it an air sign. And if his intention is to fish, or to hunt quadrupeds naturally spending time in water (as are beavers, otters, and the like), whatever kind of water it is, make it a water sign. And if possible, also place the Lord of the seventh in a sign congruent with the quarry; and make him weak and unfortunate; and make the Moon like this by the aforementioned method, and do not place her in an angle; however, the cadents, are worse than angles; so place them in succedents, the most useful of which is the second, then the fifth, and the eleventh is below the fifth, and the eighth is below the eleventh.

Also make the Lord of the first fortunate and strong, and have him, or the Lord of the sixth, or Mars (if it is on land), or Saturn (if it is in water), make the Lord of the seventh unfortunate. And if possible, make the planet from which the Moon is separating aspect the planet to which she joins. And adapt the Sun, since he has power in hunting. Also place the Lord of the seventh in the first, or the second, or the sixth; or make him retrograde, or stationary in his first station; and make it so that he is not in the seventh, nor aspecting it by a friendly aspect; also make the Lord of the seventh reducing in number, and aspecting the Lord of the first. And if it is a hunt on the sea, or in any other waters, make the Ascendant a common sign, the better of which is Pisces.

And Alchaiat said to place the Lord of the seventh in a succedent of an angle, and do not make it cadent: since this signifies the escape of the quarry from the hands of the hunter. And he said that if the Lord of the seventh does not aspect the Lord of the first, it is to be feared that we will not catch the quarry; and to make the planet which the Moon is joined cadent, or in its fall, with the Lord of the first elevated above him. If you cannot adapt all of these, adapt the Ascendant and the sixth and their Lords, and make them fortunate and strong, and weaken the Moon and the Lord of the seventh to the best of your ability. And place the Part of Fortune in the first or the sixth, or with their Lords; and likewise with the Part of Hunting if you can; and adapt the Lord of the hour. And again, if you cannot do this, adapt the Lord of the first for the protection of the body, and the sixth for the animals and instruments of hunting. If again you cannot adapt these, since sometimes they cannot wait very long, and hunts often happen in the day, and seldom at night (unless perhaps hunts on water, and snares for injurious quadrupeds, and similar things), at least adapt the Lord of the hour and weaken the Moon for him wanting to go hunting, as was said, and it will be effective, even if it is not as effective not as effective as the hunter wants.

## XIII

## On Elections Of Games With Dice, Or Other Games Which Are For The Cause Of Profit

When anyone wishes to go out for a game of dice, or another game which they intend to profit from, it seemed to certain ancient sages that the Ascendant ought to be a mobile sign, and that the fixed signs are not useful.

And Hali said that it is evident through their words that common signs are between the two of these, that is, they are neither very useful, nor are they useless: so that if the Ascendant is a common sign, and its Lord is in good condition, it signifies good; however, if its Lord is in bad condition, it signifies evil. And it is necessary that the Lord of the Ascendant is well disposed and in good condition; and that the Lord of the seventh is weak and impeded; and if possible, place the Lord of the eighth in the second or the first, received by the Lord of the second or the first, and not receiving the Lord of the second himself. And maximally when he approaches the game to begin to play, even make the Moon separating herself from a free benefic, joining herself to another benefic, and make her above the earth, and facing him who intends to play; and make her fortunate and strong. However, if she is unfortunate, it is to be feared lest she be contrary to him who has his face against her; and have her on the oriental side, if the inceptor seeks another to play. If he himself is the one sought, have her in the occidental side, and him facing her. And for whomever you elect for so that he can play to profit, always have his face and breast toward the Moon.

And if all of these things cannot be done, at least make the Ascendant a mobile sign when he goes out to the game, and have the Moon facing him when he plays. And again, if all of these things cannot be done, have the face and breast of the player be toward the Moon, and it will be effective.

## XIV

### How Something Can Be Known About Something Which Is Said Or Handled Between People Speaking Secretly

If you see some people speaking secretly amongst themselves, and you are suspicious of their deliberations, lest it might be harmful to you or another, and you wish to know something from it, consider the first and the seventh and their Lords: since the first and its Lord, and the planet from which the Moon separates, belong to him who first began to speak over the matter at hand. The seventh and its Lord and the planet to which the Moon joined, belong to him who he began to speak with. And the one of them who had his face toward the south or toward the west will be the one beginning, and he who had his face toward the east or toward the north will be the other. The tenth and its Lord signify that person, or those people who speak amongst themselves or between others, to whom that which is then adapted more greatly pertains.

And if it is a lawsuit or a contention that they are dealing with, the tenth and its Lord will signify victory, and the victor will be the one who the Lord of the tenth aspects more; the fourth and its Lord, and the planet in whose domicile the Moon is in, will signify the end of what is dealt with; but the planet in whose domicile the Moon is in will be stronger in signification than the Lord of the fourth house. Whence, then examine the Lord of the tenth, and see how he relates with the significators (namely with the Lord of the first and the Lord of the seventh): since if he is more favourable to the Lord of the first than the Lord of the seventh, he who undertakes the action will win. However, if he is more favourable to the Lord of the seventh than the Lord of the first, the person against whom the action is undertaken will win (which significators you will know from the aforementioned).

After this you will examine if the Lord of the first is one of the truth speaking planets: if so, then he who undertakes the matter, or he for whom it is undertaken, will act with truth and legality. If it is one of the false-speaking planets, he will act with lies and falsity; the same thing will be said about the Lord of the seventh. However, , if the Lord of the tenth is one of the truth speaking planets, the person discussing or managing the business will act

with truth and legality toward the person he is favourable to; and vice versa if he is one of the false-speaking planets. And if the Lord of the fourth or the planet to which the Moon is joined is a truth telling planet, then the matter at hand will be ended with truth and legality; and if it is a false-speaking planet then it will then be ended with lies, fraud, and falsity.

Likewise, examine the planet who signifies the completion of the matter, and see to whom it is joined after the perfection of the matter. For if it is joined to a good planet, or even a malefic who is not impeded and who receives him, utility and good will follow from the completion or perfection of the matter for him who wins. If it is joined to a malefic not receiving him, or an impeded benefic, the contrary will follow. You will be able to consider the same thing regarding the other matters whose end you desire to know.

## XV

### If You Wish To Search For A Thief

If someone wants to pursue or track down a thief, or some low-class person, or even their own attendant, it is necessary to make the Moon impeded, namely placing her in the same degree with the Sun, in such a way that there is more than 16 minutes between them (nor should this be in Aries or Leo): or place her in the last half of Libra; or in the first half of Scorpio; or with the Caput Draconis, or with the Cauda (namely by 12 degrees before or 7 after); and if you cannot place her like this, place her in the Ascendant (according to Athabari); or place her in the conjunction, or the opposition or square aspect; or in trine or sextile aspect without reception; and make her impeded by them; or make it three days before the hour of a lunar eclipse, or one day after. And if her eclipse were on those days, make the Sun free and clean of defects and the impediments of malefics, and of other impediments; and make one of the benefics in the 10th and especially in front of the line of the tenth by five degrees or beyond it by 3 degrees; and the more greatly the Moon is impeded, the greater the fugitive, or anyone who you desire to impede, will be impeded, and especially the above mentioned people, since she naturally signifies them, and all common people.

## XVI

### When The Intention Of The Pursuer Is To Harm Him Who Flees

This chapter can be subordinated to the other one mentioned above, since the things treated in it (namely, the fugitive) are comprehended under the other. But in this they differ from each other, since in the previous chapter the tracking down of the fugitive was treated; while in this one how someone can harm the fugitive is treated.

Whence Hali said that if the intention of the pursuer is to harm the fugitive (namely, to injure his person), make it so that the Moon in her fall, and in her weakness (just as was said in the preceding chapter), and likewise the 12th and its Lord. However, if the pursuers intention is not to harm his person, but only to capture or detain him, have the Moon joined to a malefic and impeded; but she should not be in the fourth (nor should the planet to which she is joined). And have the Lord of the first joined with the Lord of the seventh. And beware lest the Moon be joined to some planet which is in the 12th, since this signifies that the fugitive will not be captured; and if he is captured, he will escape from the hands of his pursuers, or from the hands of the person who catches him.

## XVII

### If Someone Wishes To Track Down Something From A Thief Or Detained Person, Or Someone Else Who Is Suspected Of Some Matter That Was Committed

If someone wants to track down something from a thief, or from someone else that is made public, which is enquired about, or whether they are guilty of that which they are suspected of, then place the Moon in Libra, and likewise the planet to which she is joined. And Hali said that Albumashar praised this opinion.

And he said that everything he said is to be done after the adaptation of the roots of the elections, and the roots of those things which follow from them. And he said to beware of everything which he said is to be avoided; and to work with those things which are discussed above. And he said that just as the 7th signifies all those things said before about thieves and fugitives, so the 12th signifies about animals, namely large ones. And he said that thus we ought to adapt the 7th and its Lord to the contrary of the aforementioned, in consequence of its significations, just as we adapt the 12th and its Lord in the purchasing of animals in consequence of its significations.

## ON THE EIGHTH HOUSE

### I

### On The Election Of The Return Of An Absent Person

In this chapter we must make remembrance of returning. And it seems to certain men that this chapter should be comprehended under the 10th house, since it immediately follows the ninth (which signifies journeys), and not under the 8th house, since this precedes the ninth, while a return does not precede a journey. But since the eighth is given to the absent person, and since there cannot be a return without an absent person, it is deservedly considered and taken from the 8th, and not from the 10th. And so, the 2nd (which precedes the 3rd) is adapted and examined in making a return.

Whence if you wish to elect an hour suitable for the return of some absent person, you ought to adapt the 2nd and its Lord, just like Ptolemy said in Centioloqui, "beware of malefics placed in the 8th in a journey, and in the 2nd returning". However, returning diversifies in an entrance in accordance with the diversity of persons. For if it is the return of a citizen or inhabitant of some place, who is ruled over by the master of this land, his entry is signified when he enters the threshold of the gate of his house, or of another place in which he lives, or in which he is revered by those subject to him. The entrance of a king, prince, or other magnate who rules over and is master of that city or land is when he enters the gates of the city, castle, or other land which he rules over as if a Lord. However, if after he travelled outside of that land, and is returning to it, Hali said that we need not worry about his return - namely, to know the things which ought to happen him from the hour of his return until he travelled outside of the land again, as men often do, both magnates as others. For this return is just like the revolutions of the years of nativities, since if the nativity is good, and the revolution is good, it will increase the good. However, if the revolution is bad, it will reduce the good which is signified by the nativity, even if it is not by much. And if the nativity is bad, and the revolution is bad, it will increase the evil. And if the revolution is good, it will reduce the evil, even if it is only a slight reduction. It happens similarly in the returns from the aforementioned journeys: if the first entrance is good, and the return is good, it will increase the good. And if it is bad, it will reduce something of the good. And if the entrance is bad and the return is bad, it will increase the evil; and if it is good, it will reduce something of the evil: and this will endure until the next time he travels outside of the land, since then the signification will expire, just as the signification of the revolution of the year expires when the next year of the revolution is revolved. It seemed to certain men that we should not consider the travellers entrances into the cities he passes through: since the traveller does not have anything to do in the cities he enters, except in the sense that he does in other parts of the road by which he travels.

### II

### On The Adaptation Of An Election For Inheritances

If you wish to elect an hour for the adaptation of any inheritance, Haly said, that it is fitting to make the 8th one of the domiciles of Jupiter or Venus, free and fortunate; and likewise to make its Lord free and fortunate, and in the succeedent of an angle (the best of which is the second). And to make it so that the second and its Lord are free from the presence of malefics and their opposition and square aspect, unless that malefic which impedes it is the Lord of the 8th house, or the Lord of its exaltation, or has two of the lesser dignities in it; and make him free from impediments.

It will even be good if the degree of the eighth house falls in the terms of the benefics (either Jupiter or Venus); and also make the Moon free, fortunate, and aspecting the 8th or its Lord by a trine or sextile aspect. You will also adapt the first and its Lord, and everything else which you can of those things which are considered in elections. And if you cannot adapt all of these, adapt the first and the eighth, and their Lords; the Moon also and the Lord of the domicile in which she is in; or at least adapt the 8th and its Lord, and the Moon; and you should not forget this.

## III

### On Making A Will Or Codicil

If someone wants to make a will or codicil, or to arrange any other final wish, and he wishes for you to elect him an hour suitable for doing this, place the Moon decreasing in number and increasing in light: since this signifies that the will shall be perfected and changed, but will remain firm just as it was arranged the testator. Is also recommended that the Moon and the Lord of the Ascendant (or either one of them) are joined to Saturn from a friendly aspect, since this signifies the perfect completion of the matter, and that it will not be changed after it is perfected once, not while the testator is alive, nor after his death. And Zael said that it signifies the prolongation of the life of the testator, even after the will is made. You will say the same as was said about Saturn if the Moon is joined to Jupiter or Venus.

And make the Ascendant a fixed sign, and likewise place the Moon in a fixed sign: since if the Ascendant is a mobile sign, or if the Moon is in a mobile sign, it signifies that the will shall be changed, and will not remain firm. Also beware lest the Moon be joined to a planet under the rays; and make it so that she is not joined to Mars by body or by opposition or square aspect; and that Mars himself is not in the Ascendant, nor aspecting it, or its Lord, by an inimical aspect: since this signifies that the will shall be changed and will not remain firm, and that the life of the testator will be shortened, and that he will not escape from his illness, and that the wishes of the testator will not be fulfilled, in fact the heirs and commissars will strive to pilfer what was adjudicated, and each of them will strive to extort things in his own utility, whatever kind of survivors there are, even if they are religious.

## ON THE NINTH HOUSE

### I

### On The Entrance Into Some City Or Some Other Place

Allowing that the ninth house is not mentioned in this chapter, nevertheless the chapter is comprehended under it, since it has the signification of local motion, as much of those who move from far away, as of others. Whence, if you wish to elect an hour adapted for this for someone, whatever kind of entrance it may be, whether into a city or into another land, or whether it is an entrance to inhabit some house in which he is not used to living in for a long time, adapt the Ascendant and its Lord; the Moon also and the Lord of the house in which she is, and make her increasing in light. Also adapt the 2nd and its Lord - whose adaptation is to place it in the Ascendant, free from impediments, fortunate and strong.

And Zael said to therefore make it a benefic, and make it above the earth (namely in the 9th, the 10th, or the 11th); and to never place him under the earth (namely in the 4th, the 5th, or the 6th): for he said that it is horrible in pilgrimages, and for the work which you seek in this region, regardless of whether it is a benefic or a malefic. And make it so that the Lord of the Moon is with the Lord of the 2nd above the earth: it is not recommended to place it below the earth, unless that which you seek in this region is something which someone wants to hide until it is perfected. And he said to place the Moon with the Sun, so that there are between 12 and 15 degrees between them; and it will be better if she is moving away from the Sun, close to exiting from the rays by 3 degrees, than if she were made fortunate. And this is recommended in all occultations, yet the Ascendant is more useful than the 10th or 11th; and if the Moon is fortunate, and is joined to the Ascendant, it will be better.

And beware lest you place him below the earth, or joined to a planet placed below the earth, and who is a malefic, unfortunate, or impeded. And make the Ascendant a fixed sign. And make the Lord of the tenth free from impediments and from malefics, and do not have him aspecting the 11th by an inimical aspect. Also make the fourth a fixed sign, if possible.

And if the Moon cannot be adapted, make her cadent from the Ascendant. Also have one of the benefics aspecting the 4th and the 10th, (or either of them, yet the 4th is better than the 10th). And if in addition to this you can place Jupiter in the second it will be the ultimate, since he naturally signifies profit and the acquisition of substance.

And if it is the intention of him who enters the land or place to withdraw from it later with prosperity and profit, place the Lord of the 7th oriental, increasing in number, and if in addition to this the Moon is also increasing in number, and the planet to which she joins, it will be better.

And Hali said to beware lest the Lord of the second commits disposition to the Lord of the 4th, 6th, 8th, or the 12th. And he said that it is detestable if he commits his own disposition to one of their Lords from one of those places; and more strongly so, if this is in one of those aforementioned places in the revolution of the year of the world, or in the nativity of the person for whom you elect - since this would be very detestable.

If you cannot adapt all of these things, adapt the Ascendant and the second and their Lords, and the Moon, and the planet to which she is joined. And if again you cannot adapt these, make it your concern to at least adapt the second and its Lord; especially when someone enters into the district of any city or any region.

And Zael said that if you wish to enter into a region or a city, or if you wish to enter any kind of land, it is necessary that you adapt the 2nd. And he said that when you have this done, you have already adapted the region; and that you make the Lord of the second fortunate, if you can; and place it in the 9th, 10th, or 11th. And he said that you should never place him below the earth (namely in the 4th, the 5th, or the 6th): since this is horrible in pilgrimages and in the work which you seek in this region. Always place it above the earth, whether it is a benefic or not. And he said to strive to place the Lord of the house of the Moon with the Lord of the second above the earth, and if you cannot adapt its Lord (namely the Lord of the second), at least place Jupiter in the second unimpeded; and this will be effective, at least for profit and the conservation of substance.

## II

## On The Beginning Of General Journeys Not Pertaining To War

In this chapter we will deal with the journeys which men meet with every day, except for those journeys pertaining to war. And even if journeys differ from each other, nevertheless they all are made either by land or by water.

Whence if it is a journey by land, make the Ascendant an earth sign. If it is by water, make the Ascendant a water sign. And place the Moon in the 11th, moving towards the 10th. And never place her below the earth. But if you cannot avoid this, place her in the 3rd or in the 5th, clean from malefics, and free from impediments. And if it is a journey by land, beware lest the Moon is joined to Mars by body, or from any aspect, unless perhaps by a trine or sextile aspect with perfect reception. Nor should Mars himself be in one of the houses of the journey; nor should Mars be aspecting the Ascendant or its Lord; unless he himself be the Lord of the Ascendant, or the 3rd, or the 5th, or the 9th -since then he will not impede his own house, if he aspects it from a praiseworthy aspect.

If it is a journey by water, make the Ascendant a water sign; and beware of Saturn in water, unless Jupiter (who can shatter his malice) aspects him by all of the stated methods and conditions, just as I told you about Mars on land.

And Zael said to beware lest Saturn be in a water sign; and he said that he should not be fixed in the Ascendant of the departure; nor should he be with the Moon. Which if you cannot avoid this, have the Moon joined with a strong benefic, or in its trine or sextile aspect from an angle - to take away the malignance of Saturn from shipwrecks or impediments and heavy storms.

In all journeys, both by land and water, you also ought to adapt the Moon and the Lord of the domicile she is in; since she has signification in them above all others, except perhaps the Lord of the hour in the matter of business, as much in short and medium journeys, as in long journeys, longer journeys, and the longest journeys. You will also adapt the Lord of the hour in the beginning of any journey from which utility or profit is hoped for.

In all significations of journeys, you should adapt the Ascendant to the place from which the traveller leaves; and adapt the second to guard his things. Whence, Messala said that if a malefic is in the second house who does not have testimony there, it signifies that impediment will befall those things which he leaves behind him. If it is Mars, it signifies contentions, or wars, or fires, or bloodshed: since he is disposed to do this. If it is Saturn, it signifies impediment by thieves or flooding, and similar things (just as was said above).

You will adapt the seventh for the place to which he travels. The eighth for the profit which he intends to make there. The tenth and its Lord for the accidents which ought to happen to him on the journey. You will adapt the fourth and its Lord for the end of the journey. And it is necessary for you to adapt all of the angles, if you can, and chiefly the seventh. And place the Moon increasing in light and number, and do not make her cadent; also make the Lord of the first, and the Lord of the domicile in which the Moon is placed, exiting from combustion; and place them in angles or in their succeedents.

And Haly said that the increase of the Moons light signifies that the traveller will quickly arrive at the place where he intends to go. He also recommended to make it so that Mercury has exited from combustion, and is joined to some benefic, and especially in the journeys of those wanting to travel for cause of buying or selling - since Mercury, as was said elsewhere, signifies commodities and merchandise, and especially the goods and dealings of merchants. However, if the journey is made for a different purpose, place the Moon joined to a planet signifying the matter, or place her in the house of the matter. So if it is a journey to a king, have her joined to the Sun (or at least the Lord of the 10th) by a trine or sextile aspect, and if it is with reception it will be better; and put the Sun in a good place, namely in the first, the tenth, or the eleventh: since if this is so, his journey will be useful and fruitful; in other places it will be worse. For if it is in the 3rd, the 5th, or the 9th, it signifies that the journey will be of little utility and great labour. If it is in the 7th or the 4th it signifies little utility and labour, namely with greater slowness. However, take care that you do not place the Moon in Aquarius for the journey of someone wishing to travel to a king, since the king will not care about him on account of Aquarius being opposite to Leo, which is the domicile of the Sun (who naturally signifies kings). Nor should you place her in Pisces, since the king will not want to see him, but rather he will avert his face from him: since Aries is one of the signs which have the signification over kings, and Pisces is the 12th sign from Aries, which signifies detriment and sorrow.

And if the traveller for whom you elect is going to warriors, or to bellicose soldiers, place the Moon joined to Mars by a trine or sextile aspect; and make both of them in good condition. And Zael said to beware of her conjunction with Mars from angles, and from the square aspect, and from opposition; and to place Mars in the succeedents of the angles.

If his journey is to bishops, or other religious people (of whatever sect they are), or to noblemen, or soldiers who are peaceful and not bellicose, nor using arms in the manner of warriors, or to judges, or doctors of law or decrees, and similar people, place the Moon joined to Jupiter by body or by trine or sextile aspect, or at least square with reception from an angle or another good place from the Ascendant.

And if his journey is to old men, men of a great age, or Jews, or to ignoble or low class persons, or to some rigid person that doesn't acquiesce in the sayings of anyone else, and wishes that whatever he says or does, will be considered as authoritative, whether it is good or bad (as was that tyrant Ezzelino da Romano), who is at least 45 years of age, place the Moon joined to Saturn by a trine or sextile aspect; and make Saturn in good condition, free from impediments, and in a succeedents of an angle (and especially in the 5th or 11th).

And make whatever planet to which the Moon is joined free from impediments: since her impediment signifies the impediment of the matter for which the journey was made.

And if his journey is to women (of whatever condition they are), have the Moon joined to Venus by a trine or sextile aspect; and place Venus in a masculine sign; and if you can place her in an angle or a succedent (and especially in the fifth), it will be good.

And if his journey is to genuine literary men, apart from the aforementioned, or to writers or merchants, have the Moon joined to Mercury by a trine or sextile aspect, and have Mercury in good condition, free and clean from impediments.

Zael said that whenever the planet to which the Moon is joined, or the planet which is in opposition to the Ascendant or the 7th, is slow or retrograde or impeded, it signifies complication and harshness in those ways.

And Hali said that if the Lord of the seventh is in the Ascendant, or if the Moon is joined to a retrograde planet receiving her, that he will meet that which he travelled for on the road.

And Alchabitius said that the journey is to be deferred whenever the Moon is in the 2nd or 3rd face of Libra.

And Alchaiat said to beware of the aspects of malefics to the Moon on journeys, for it is more serious than if they aspect the Ascendant, and especially in pilgrimages. And he said that the signification of a journey is given to the Moon, and she has her own signification over all beginnings, and therefore she is stronger.

And Hali said that if the nativity of the traveller is known, or his question is had, make the Ascendant of his journey be that of the house of his nativity or question, and make the Moon increasing in light or number, and make her joined to benefics from the 9th or the 3rd. And if the Moon is impeded, and we cannot defer the journey, make the Moon cadent from the Ascendant, and likewise the planet who impedes her; and we should adapt the entrance and be painstaking in that.

And Athabari said that whoever desires a swift and prosperous return should place both Venus and Jupiter in the square aspect of the Sun and the Moon; that is, so that one of them is in the 10th from the Sun and in the 4th from the Moon, or vice versa. And place the Moon between two benefics, separated from one and joined to another. And he said to make the Moon increasing in light and number. And he said that if the Sun is in opposition to benefics, it likewise signifies the swiftness of his return; and malefics make the return slower, and impede it by the greatest impediment. And he said if there is a benefic with them, prosperity will follow. And he said that when the Moon is in the 4th, she signifies a long stay; and this will be according to the nature and quality of the journey.

And Zael said that you are not to place the Ascendant of the nativity and its Lord cadent from the Ascendant of his departure. And he said to make the Ascendant of the return the 10th from the Ascendant of the nativity or question, if you are seeking kingship. And if you seek business, make the Ascendant its 11th; similarly in every matter which you seek. And he to make that sign the Ascendant, and to place the Moon in an angle or the succeedent of an angle; and if she is fortunate, have her aspecting the Ascendant. If she is impeded, make her cadent from the Ascendant. And he said to place the Lord of the Ascendant and the Lord of the house of the Moon in angles; and the Moon aspected by the Lord of her house. And beware lest you place the Moon with malefics, or in their square aspect or opposition. And he said that you should never place her in the fourth; but if you do place her below the earth, place her in the 5th, and make her fortunate: for this will shorten the labour of the journey, and increase its benefit, and act more for the salvation of the body of the traveller. And he said that you are not to place her in the Ascendant, since she is inimical to the Ascendant, and inimical to the traveller, just as was said elsewhere. Nor should you place her in the second, for this signifies the loss of substance and its diminution. And the Sun is friendly to the Ascendant. Whence if the Moon is in the Ascendant, it will be feared that there will be sickness in the travellers body, or some hardship similar or equal to illness. And never place her in the sixth, since illness will be feared for him; nor in the 8th, since death will be feared for him, unless God averts it; and this more strongly so if she is received by the Lord of these houses.

And Zael said that in sailing the sea you should not make the luminaries impeded: since if they are free and fortunate, it signifies safety and prosperity; however, if they are impeded, it signifies the death or loss of the traveller. And he said not to sail the sea on a New Moon, since this is horrible. And he said that if you sail the sea on account of business, adapt Mercury and the Moon; and have one of them aspecting Jupiter from Cancer or Pisces. And he said that Scorpio is horrible in sailing the sea, on account of the role of Mars and his enmity. And always fear the terms of malefics in sailing, and in travelling by land. And it is to be feared as much for journeys by land as by water, when the Moon is in the last half of Libra, unless Venus aspects her by a praiseworthy aspect, and she is in good condition, or if Saturn aspects her by a praiseworthy aspect in journeys by land, and he is oriental, direct, in his own domicile or exaltation, or two of his lesser dignities.

And Zael said that if you are seeking kingship in this region, adapt the Midheaven and its Lord, with the Lord of the second from the Ascendant, and the Moon. Understand the same about a position of power, and any office or lay dignity. And if the powerful person, when he travels to any land because of the position, power, or other office, were to adapt the aforementioned, it will be useful for him.

And Dorotheus said to examine the place of the Moon in the signs in pilgrimages by water: which if she is in the first face of Aries, it signifies the ease of the matter for which the journey is made, whether planets aspect her or not. If she were in Taurus, there will be less impediment on the sea. However, if she is aspected by Saturn, he will be impeded and a shipwreck will befall him. And in the second face of Gemini it signifies delay, after which it will be resolved. However, in Cancer it signifies the safety from every impediment. In Leo he said that it signifies impediment, and more strongly so if it is aspected by a malefic. In Virgo he said that it signifies prosperity, delay, and turning back. In Libra, when she has transited the tenth degree, you should not go on pilgrimages by land or sea. In Scorpio, say sorrow. In Sagittarius, say that before the journey is finished, he will return. In Capricorn, say that there will be some good in the beginning. In Aquarius, say slowness and safety, however, do not make a journey to a king. In Pisces, say impediment and hindrance. And he said that if it is aspected by a malefic, it will increase the impediment. If it is aspected by a benefic, it will reduce the impediment and increase the good.

## III

## On Singing Lessons, As Much For Musicians, As For Others

This chapter can be comprehended under either house, namely the ninth or the tenth, but to me it appears more fitting for it to be under the ninth than under the tenth, since the ninth house signifies ecclesiastical singing (which singers employ in temples and other religious places), more so than the tenth. For the tenth signifies melodies which are made by the laity and those rejoicing, and those who delight in secular and lay songs and games. Whence, if someone wants to teach singing, and you wish to elect an hour for them that is suitable for this, make the Ascendant or the 10th one of the rational signs, and adapt Mercury first and principally in ecclesiastical singing, and Venus secondarily. In secular and lay songs, adapt Venus principally, and Mercury secondarily. However, in musical instruments, adapt whichever of them you can. And make the Ascendant Libra or Taurus, or at least Pisces in delightful singing; or either Gemini or Virgo in ecclesiastical singing. In whatever type of singing, place the Moon in Cancer, Taurus, or Pisces, separating from Mercury and moving toward a conjunction with Venus, if possible. Also place Venus in one of her own dignities. Say the same of Mercury: also have Mercury joined to Venus by body or sextile aspect ,if you can do it; unless any of these three (namely Venus, Mercury, or the Moon) are cadent, unless perhaps they are in the ninth, since this is not condemned, provided that the planet in the ninth is otherwise fortunate and strong, since this signifies the goodness of the matter which he for whom you elect wishes to begin. And if you wish for the singer to be perfect, and one who nobody will surpass in singing, make Mercury direct, joined to a retrograde Venus in the house, exaltation, or two of the lesser dignities of either of them. However, if their conjunction is outside of these places, your work will be below this. Say the same in nativities with regards to singing and the composition of melodies.

And whatever the Ascendant is, if its Lord is in the 9th or the 10th it will be praiseworthy, provided that it is fortunate and strong.

And a certain one of the ancients said that if it is an election for the playing of musical instruments, as are lyres, hurdy-gurdys, or similar things, place the Moon in Capricorn. However, if it is an election for the playing of lay musical instruments, as are citharas, rottas and similar things, solely pertaining to lay players, place the Moon in the last face of Leo, or in Scorpio or Pisces, since these signs lack voices. And for the aforementioned instruments only having sound, such as the trumpet and similar things, the aforementioned signs are to be adapted, namely Cancer, Scorpio, and Pisces. In read-off and rhythmic songs, Virgo and Gemini are more useful, on account of their formation in the images of men, and since they have more beautiful voices than the rest of the signs; and likewise since they are said to be winged.

And Hali said that we should adapt the 9th and its Lord in this matter; but if our intention in this is for something that pertains to the work of kings, magnates, or the wealthy fit for kingship, then the 10th and its Lord are to be adapted, which can even be recommended in the beginning of any matter.

## ON THE TENTH HOUSE

### I

### On The Election Of Kings And Noblemen, Or Of Magnates And The Wealthy

Those things which pertain to elections of the ninth house were discussed in the preceding chapters. However, now we must discuss those things which seem to pertain to the tenth house. Whence, if you wish to elect for some king or duke, or similar people, regarding those things which pertain to kingship or dukedom, or to their affairs, or what is done for them, adapt the 10th and its Lord, the Sun also, and the Moon; and do not have the Sun, or the Moon, joined to any malefic; nor should you have the Sun moving towards a conjunction of Mars or Saturn, or towards their square aspect or opposition, even if there is reception; nor to their trine or sextile aspect without reception; but place him in an angle or a succeedent from an angle, or in Leo, not cadent, nor otherwise impeded. And if he is not in Leo, make it so that he is joined to the planet in whose domicile or exaltation he is in by a trine or sextile aspect. And if you cannot avoid the square aspect, make it with reception; however, you will avoid the opposition in every way, as much with reception as without reception; just as you should avoid his trine or sextile aspect with malefics without reception. And place the Sun in a masculine sign and a masculine quarter, if you can. Also place him in a sign where he has some dignity if it is possible.

Even consider if there was, or will be, an eclipse of one of the luminaries in that year, and avoid that sign in which it was, or ought to be. Also place both luminaries in the terms of benefics, aspecting each other by trine or sextile, if possible; and make it so that the Lords of their terms are in their own dignities, aspecting the luminaries (or at least one of them), and the better you adapt the luminaries, or the stronger or more fortunate you make them, the greater the good will be for the matter which you elected; and the less you adapt them, the more the matter will be below what you wished.

You should also beware lest the conjunction or prevention before the election is unfortunate: since if it is, you should not elect for the aforementioned people (unless it is after the aforementioned conjunction or prevention by fifteen days or more),

if you can avoid it, even if the election otherwise appears fortunate. If indeed, you can avoid this, your election will be more secure, better, and more fortunate.

### II

### On Promotion To Kingship Or Dukedom Or Another Dignity Pertaining To Kingship Or Dukedom, Or Any Other Dignity

If someone wanting to be promoted to kingship or dukedom, or anything similar consults you to elect an hour for them that is suited to this, make Leo the Ascendant, and place the Sun in Taurus in the tenth from the Ascendant, and place the Moon in the first joined to Venus, Jupiter, or Mercury, with these planets being fortunate and strong, both in the election and in the receiving of the dignity.

### III

### On The Enthronement Of The Kingship Or Dukedom, Or Another Dignity, Or Ascending To Its Seat

If you wish to elect an hour for the enthronement of a kingship, to ascend to the throne, or position, or dukedom, or whatever other dignity, make the angles fixed signs, and especially the first and fourth. And make the Lord of the tenth free from impediments; also place the Lord of the Ascendant in the Ascendant, or the tenth, or the eleventh, or the fifth, received. And make it so that the Lord of the tenth is received by the Lord of the house in which he is in, by a trine or sextile aspect. Also make the Lord of the fourth free, in the aspect of a benefic. If you cannot do this, make it so that the Moon is received. And if you cannot place the Lord of the fourth free and strong, prohibit him from aspecting the Ascendant or its Lord, and make it so that one of the benefics aspect the 4th and the 10th, or at least one of them, if you are ever able to do it.

## *On A Dignity Pertaining To War*

However, if it is a dignity which pertains to war, like the command of an army and similar things, make the Ascendant Aries or Scorpio: and make Mars fortunate and strong; and make it so that he aspects the Ascendant by a praiseworthy aspect (and a trine is better than the rest).

And if the Ascendant is one of the domiciles of the other planets, have Mars aspecting the Lord of the Ascendant by a trine aspect, and have Mars himself free from impediments. and make the Ascendant a fixed sign or at least a common sign.

In elections lasting a long time, fixed signs are better; common signs are beneath fixed signs; mobile signs are beneath common ones.

And in any election for any dignity, make the Moon with reception, or at least joined to the Sun from a trine or sextile aspect, or at least from square with reception. Also have the Sun joined to Jupiter from Sagittarius, Pisces, Aries, Cancer, or Leo, from a trine or sextile aspect, if possible. And if you cannot adapt all of these (as often happens), adapt those which you can, but your work will not be as perfect. For all of these are to be observed in the elections of kings, and all of their sons, and those of other dukes, in all stable matters.

If it is a dignity or office on account of which someone is given others money to distribute, as are chamberlains, administrators of some community, namely of a city or a castle, or the like, or retainers of magnates, and similar offices, you will adapt the second and its Lord in addition to the adaptation of the first and its Lord, and also the Moon. And if your election is for some scribe, you will adapt Mercury after the adaptation of the aforementioned things, namely making it so that Mercury aspects the Ascendant by a praiseworthy aspect: for this signifies that he will be faithful and lawful in the matter committed to him, and that it will be useful for him.

## IV

## If Someone Wants To Go And Stay With A King, Or Duke, Or Powerful Person, Or With Another Such Person, Or To Travel With Them

If someone wants to travel to a king, duke, prince, powerful person, or another magnate, to stay or travel with them, and they consult you to elect them an hour suitable for this, whatever way you make the Ascendant, place Jupiter in it, and have him joined to the Lord of the tenth, if you can: since this signifies that the king will be agreeable and affable, and that things will go well for your client from him. And if you make them joined from a trine or sextile aspect, or even from a square with reception, it will be good. And if you cannot do this, place him in the ninth: for this signifies that the traveller will come upon good and useful things in this journey, and things from which he will rejoice, and he will see things pleasing to him. And this will be better, if Jupiter is safe and free from impediments. And avoid placing him in the fourth: since even though the fourth signifies the end of the matter, nevertheless in this case you should avoid placing him in it. And make it so that the Moon aspects him from the 10th, if Jupiter himself is in the first; or from the seventh, if he is in the ninth. However, beware of the sixth and the twelfth. But if you cannot avoid this, it is less horrible in a case like this than it is in others. And if you cannot do this, have Venus testify to him from the first, the seventh, the tenth, or the fourth, whether with reception or not, or from the sixth or the third with reception.

And beware of Saturn and Mars, lest one of them be in the first or in one of the other angles. And likewise beware lest the Moon be impeded, and especially by the misfortune of combustion, or by being with the Cauda Draconis, or another one of the malefic or impeding planets - since this signifies that there will be no utility in the journey, but rather it is to be feared that the traveller will not return. Even if it is another journey, the same will be feared. And if the traveller falls ill, his death will be feared; and if he goes to battle, then he will succumb, or perhaps he will be killed; and to tell you the truth briefly, it will be great and almost miraculous if he were to escape the aforesaid danger.

## V

### If Someone Wants To Make An Enemy Of A King, Or A Duke, Or Someone Similar

Sometimes it happens that someone wants to have enmity with the king, or a duke, or some magnate who is fit for kingship, or their sons who will succeed them in their dignity or inheritance. Make the Ascendant one of the domiciles of Jupiter or Mars; and make the Lord of the Ascendant strong, fortunate, and free from impediments; and make the Lord of the seventh impeded and unfortunate, and weak in a malignant place from the Ascendant (the worst of which are the sixth and the twelfth), and not aspecting any of the benefics, nor the luminaries, nor have any of them aspecting him.

## VI

### On Reconciling With A King Or A Duke Or Similar Men

Sometimes someone is inimical to a king or a duke or similar people, and wishes to reconcile themselves with the king, and asks you to elect an hour for them that is suitable for this. Whence, if you wish to elect it for them, place any sign as the Ascendant, and make it impeded, and its Lord; and make its Lord unfortunate and weak; and make the Moon decreasing in light and number. And make the seventh fortunate and strong, and likewise make its Lord fortunate and strong, and the planet to which the Moon joins; and put the Lord of the seventh in a good place from the Ascendant, free from malefics and impediments - for this signifies the strength of the matter which you seek.

## VII

### On The Taking Away Of Some Dignity

Sometimes it happens that he who promotes someone to dignity, on account of certain things which are wont to happen, strives and wants to remove him from the dignity, and sometimes others also strive to do the same. However, whether it is he who promoted him or whether it is someone else, and he enquires of you to elect an hour for him that is suitable for doing this, you will consider if his intention is to remove him from the dignity in his hatred or in his favour.

Since if it is in his hatred, the Moon is to be made unfortunate and weakened by combustion, and given another great impediment. And make her reducing in light and number; and place her in the sixth or twelfth, and in a fixed sign in the domicile or exaltation of Jupiter or Venus or the Sun or Mercury, with these planets made unfortunate and weak; yet with the Ascendant and its Lord made fortunate and strong.

If it was his intention to remove him in his favour, namely that he might be re-established in order to obtain a greater position, or to be promoted to a greater dignity, place the Moon in Virgo, Sagittarius, Pisces, or at least in Gemini (but this will be beneath the others); and make her and the Lord of the Ascendant increasing in light and number; and make them ascending in the north: and place the Moon in the domicile or exaltation of some benefic, and make it so that this benefic is fortunate and strong; and make this benefic the Lord of the tenth if it is a lay dignity, or the Lord of the ninth if it is a clerical dignity. Nor is this contrary to what was said elsewhere (that the Moon is the significatrix of the business with the weakened Lord of the Ascendant), since here the Ascendant is understood to be free, and similarly its Lord is understood to be safe, and fortunate, and since the Lord of the Ascendant will be the significator, just as the signification pertains to the Ascendant and its Lord. Indeed, the Moon will be the significatrix of the matter which you intend to adapt; and she will have her own signification separate from the significations of the Lord of the Ascendant. And understand the same in similar cases.

## VIII

### On Teaching Morals

If anyone wants to be taught moral doctrine, and consults you so that you might elect him a time suitable for this, make it so the Ascendant is Gemini, Virgo, Libra, the first half of Sagittarius, or Aquarius; and make this sign free and fortunate; and adapt the Moon in one of these signs; and place the Lord of the tenth in the tenth, and make its Lord of the nature of the Lord of the Ascendant, or at least of its friendship. Also have the Moon joined to Mercury by body, or by a trine or sextile aspect; and make Mercury safe, free from impediments, fortunate, and strong. And if you can make it so that he aspects the Lord of the Ascendant by a friendly aspect, it will be good. Even have the Moon in her Auge, or going toward it, and don't have her descending from it. And by all means adapt the ninth and its Lord, if you can do so.

And Hali said that in the instruction of writing the Lord of the tenth is to be adapted with all of these: since it signifies what will be written. And he said that writing is science and work: and he said that we should comprehend the methods in this chapter.

## IX

### On Lessons In Fighting, Doing Battle, Or Wrestling

If you wish to elect an hour for someone wanting to be taught fighting, battling, or wrestling, make the Ascendant Aries, Leo, or Sagittarius for him; and make Mars strong and fortunate; and make the Moon fortunate and strong (and it will be better if she is in Taurus, provided that she is otherwise fortunate). And beware lest you place her in Scorpio or Capricorn, and especially in lessons of military combat. Also place the Lord of the Ascendant in its own exaltation, and in a strong place. And do not have him or the Moon cadent from an angle or from the Ascendant. And if you cannot do this, place the Moon and the Lord of the Ascendant (or either of them) in the tenth, or moving towards it.

And Hali said that certain men advised placing the Moon in Gemini.

## X

### On Swimming Lessons

If someone wants to be taught how to swim, and consults you so that you might elect them an hour suitable for this, make the Ascendant Cancer, Scorpio, or Pisces; also make it so that the Lord of the Ascendant is in the angle of the tenth or moving toward it, not more than 15 degrees away from it; and make him fortunate and strong. Also place the Moon in one of her own dignities, among which Cancer holds the principal position, and Taurus is beneath Cancer, and her other dignities are beneath Taurus. Even make her ascending in the north, and if possible, have her in her auge moving to a longitude closer to the contact of the line of the epicycle with the line of the eccentric.

## XI

### On Lessons In All Things Generally

If your election is general for all works which men are generally in the habit engaging in, as are those of craftsmen and similar works, however, you place the Ascendant, adapt the tenth and its Lord; and likewise the Moon; and make the planet naturally signifying the work which someone intends to begin fortunate and strong.

So if the work is difficult and laborious, or long drawn-out work, such as the cultivation of land or works of waters, or those which are done close to water, as are bridges, mills, and similar things, adapt Saturn.

And if it is a work that pertains to judges arbitrators wishing to judge justly, and the like, you will adapt Jupiter.

And if it is the work of a blacksmith, or a butcher, you will adapt Mars.

And if it is the work of a goldsmith or money-changers, and the like, you will adapt the Sun.

And if it is a work of the ornamenting of women, adapt Venus, and make Mercury joined with her (and likewise with the others) by body or by a fortunate and strong aspect: since he has participation in all of these things.

And if it is the work of painters or writers or the minting of coins, and similar things which are operated through keenness of art, as are the astrolabe and the quadrant, and similar things, adapt Mercury, and make it so that he is joined with the Moon; and make him fortunate, strong, and well disposed.

And if it is a work with pertains to sailors, (and chiefly to younger ones), such as navigation and similar things, you will adapt the Moon, and make her increasing in light and number, and not descending from her auge

And in all of the aforementioned cases, make it so that the Moon is joined to a planet signifying the matter which you intend to begin by a friendly aspect, and that she is received by this planet, or even by another, and especially in the house signifying this matter, and place her in one of her own dignities. Also make the sign of the

Ascendant, and the sign in which the Moon is, be suitable for the matter which is begun; such as an earth sign in terrestrial matters, and a water sign in aquatic matters, and a fire sign in fiery matters, and air signs in airy matters, if you can ever do this. If you do not do this, your work will be beneath what you intended, according to the diminution of those things which I said to you.

## ON THE ELEVENTH HOUSE

### I

### On Those Things In Which We Have Hope Or Trust Of Being Praised And Acquiring A Good Reputation

It seems possible that this chapter could be comprehended under the tenth house, since it is of those things from which good fame is acquired, which is acquired, and follows from hope which was had first. But it seems more suitable to be comprehended under the eleventh.

Whence, if you wish to do this, make the Ascendant Sagittarius or Pisces, or at least Cancer (but Cancer will be beneath Sagittarius and Pisces); and you should adapt Jupiter just as best as you can; and you should also adapt the eleventh and its Lord, to the best of your ability. And if you can place Jupiter in the 11th, it will be very useful for your matter. And if you cannot place him in the eleventh, place him in the first. If again you cannot do this, make it so that he aspects one of them by a praiseworthy aspect: and make him fortunate and strong and free from impediments. And if you can place the Lord of the first in the eleventh: or the Lord of the eleventh in the first, it will be praiseworthy.

And place the Sun in the 10th free from impediments, if possible, or in the first, provided that he does not impede Jupiter, or the Lord of the first, or the Lord of the eleventh; also make the Moon joined to them by a trine or sextile aspect, or perhaps a square with reception; and she should be free, fortunate, and strong; and also have her separating from Jupiter when she joins to the Sun, or to the Lord of the first or eleventh, if possible; and if so, it will be better, and the fame and renown will become more widely known and fall in the ears of men, and into their praises; and whichever of the significators you can adapt, it will be better: and especially if you can make it so that the luminaries aspect each other; or the Lord of the first with the Lord of the eleventh, by a trine or sextile aspect, or at least a square with reception. And if you can make it so that they regard each other, it will be better.

### II

### If Someone Wishes To Ask Some Person To Love Them

If someone wishes to ask some person to love them, just as one person loves another by way of friendship, not in a lewd manner: and he consults you to elect an hour for him that is suitable for this, make the Ascendant whatever sign you want, and place the Moon in the eleventh house; and if you could place the Lord of the Ascendant there, it will be better; and make it so that all of them are joined with Venus, if you can. And if you cannot do this, make it so that Venus is joined with the Moon, and with the Lord of the eleventh. Which if again you cannot do this, make it so that the Moon or the Lord of the Ascendant is joined with the Lord of the eleventh (or with Venus) from a trine or sextile aspect, with reception; or that he receives either of them from Taurus, Libra, or Pisces, and make him free, fortunate, strong, and well disposed. And if again you cannot do this, make it so that Venus is received by the Moon in Taurus or Cancer, and that the Moon is received by Jupiter (or even the Lord of the second) by perfect reception. And if again you cannot do this, place the Moon in Taurus, or the first half of Libra, or in Pisces, or in two of the lesser dignities of Venus, free, fortunate and strong.

However, if someone asks someone to love them for the reason of profit, and to acquire utility from it: place the Moon in the first, or at least in its triplicity, free, fortunate, strong, and received by the Lord of the domicile or exaltation of the sign which she is then in, and likewise put the Part of Fortune there.

However, if it is his intention to acquire some inheritance or estate, namely a house or land, or something similar, place the Moon in the eighth, with the Part of Fortune, and received. And if it is for the reason of small animals, place her in the sixth house: if it is for the reason of horses or other large animals, place her in the twelfth. And understand similarly regarding any house according to its own substance, and according to its significations, and always place the Moon with the Part of Fortune, and received.

However, if you cannot do these things which were said, then you will observe another method, namely, that if someone wants to ask some person to give something to him, or do something for him, make the Ascendant (whatever way it is) fortunate, and make it a fixed sign, or at least a common sign; and place its Lord in it, or in its triplicity, aspecting it by a praiseworthy aspect, namely a trine or a sextile. And beware lest the Moon be joined to malefics or impeded in another way; and make it so that she is aspected by the Lord of the domicile which she is in: since if she is not aspected by him, the matter at hand will not be perfected. And in such beginnings, make the Moon increasing in light and number, and joined to benefics. Also make the Lord of the Ascendant fortunate, strong, and free from impediments. Indeed, if the benefic to which the Moon is joined is direct, and increasing in number, it will be useful: for it signifies that what is sought by the seeker will be increased.

And always beware lest Mercury be impeded, or in bad condition: for this signifies its impediment or prohibition, unless perhaps he is received along with this impediment. For if he is received it signifies the perfection of the matter, but with striving, inconveniences, anxiety, labour, and complications, and still, it will hardly be perfected, if it is perfected; and that they will separate from each other by a vile and foul separation. And always make the significatrix (which is the Moon) joined to a planet signifying the matter at hand, just as I said to you above: as is the Sun in matters of magnates, and likewise Mars in matters of war: and understand the same about all the significators.

If you wish to elect for someone wanting to forge a friendship with someone, make the Moon clean from malefics, and especially from their square and opposition; and make her joined to a planet who signifies the matter which someone wants or intends to do, as was said: such as Venus in the affairs of women of women, and Mercury in the affairs of writers; and understand the same about the rest of the significators. And have the Lord of the eleventh aspecting this planet by a praiseworthy aspect; and if he aspects his Lord or the Moon, it will be better.

## III

## If Someone Wants To Seek Some Item From Some Person, Whether It Is Promised To Him Or Not

If someone proposes to seek some item from someone (whether that item is promised to him or not), and he consults you so that you might elect an hour for him that is suitable for this, you should adapt the Ascendant (whatever it is) and its Lord; also the Moon and the Lord of the domicile which she is in; and you will also adapt the second and its Lord; the eleventh also, and its Lord. The Lord of the Ascendant should also aspect the Moon, or at least one of them, by a praiseworthy aspect; and should receive them, or at least one of them; and the Lord of the house signifying the person from whom the item is sought should receive the Lord of the first and the Moon (or at least one of them): so that if someone seeks the item from his brother, make the Lord of the third receive the Lord of the first or the Moon; if from the father, make the Lord of the fourth receive the Lord of the first or the Moon; if from a child, make the Lord of the fifth receive either of them; if from a slave, make the Lord the sixth receive either of them; if from the wife or an associate, make the Lord of the seventh receive the Lord of the first and the Moon (or either of them); if from a bishop or similar person, make the Lord of the ninth receive them, or one of them; if from a king, make the Lord of the tenth receive one of them; if from a friend, make the Lord of the eleventh receive one of them, as was said.

However, if it is a petition to those people signified by Saturn (as are old men, Jews, and low class people) make the cusp of the eleventh house in Capricorn, Aquarius, or Libra, or at least in one of Saturn's dignities. If the petition is made to a scribe or a boy, make the cusp of the eleventh be in one of the dignities of Mercury, the weakest of which is face.

And Athabari said to make Mercury joined to Jupiter or Venus; and to make him moving towards the Lord of the Ascendant; and that you should adapt the aforementioned significators signifying the items which are sought. And if there are none of the aforementioned between him who seeks and him from whom it is sought, then the first signifies him who seeks, and the seventh is him from whom it is sought. And always make the Ascendant clean of malefics and their aspects, and likewise the seventh; or at least the seventh. And if you do not avoid this, it signifies that the matter will be destroyed, in vain, and annihilated, even after it appears arranged.

And if the matter sought is money, or things similar to it, then you will adapt the second and its Lord in addition to adapting those which you can of the aforementioned. And have the Lord of the Ascendant aspecting the Lord of the second; and do not have any malefics or their rays between them. Also make the Lord of the eleventh and the Lord of the house in which the Part of Fortune is placed (or one of them) aspect the second by a praiseworthy aspect, if you can.

And Hali said that if a woman's item, or one pertaining to weddings is sought, make the seventh and its Lord just as was said of the second and its Lord.

## ON THE TWELFTH HOUSE

### I

#### On The Racing Of Horses Or Other Animals, Both Rational And Others Running For Prizes

If someone wishes to make a horse or another animal run for a prize, or in another matter for the reason of acquiring or winning it, and you wish to elect an hour for him that is suitable for this, adapt the Ascendant and its Lord for him; and also the Moon and the Lord of the house in which she is placed; and likewise the planet to which she is joined, if you can; and likewise the Part of Fortune and its Lord; and make it so that the Lord of the first and the Moon (or one of them) aspect the Part of Fortune. And after you have adapted these, place the Lord of the hour in the Ascendant, when he steps out of the door of his house. You will also see how many animals are running, from the second up to the twelfth, so that you can see how that animal for which you elect will be disposed. For if you place the Lord of the hour in the first, as I said, he will come first; if in the tenth, second; if in the eleventh, third; if in the seventh, fourth; if in the fifth, fifth; if in the ninth, sixth; if in the third, seventh; if in the second, eighth; if in the eighth, ninth; if in the sixth, tenth; if in the twelfth, or the 4th, he will come last, or equal to last.

However, if there are more than twelve animals, the others will finish in an intermingled way, you will give watch the first signified ones you observed. And if you cannot adapt all of these, adapt the Lord of the hour, and the Ascendant and the Moon. And if you cannot do this, always make it your concern to adapt the Lord of the hour by placing him in the first; and likewise adapt the Moon.

And Alchindi said that the adaptation of the Moon is to place her in Sagittarius, or in the first half of Libra.

And beware lest the Lord of the Ascendant, or the Lord of the hour, or the Moon are in their fall: since it will be feared that the horse or rider may fall.

### II

#### On The Purchasing Of Large Animals, Both Of Horses And Others Of Those Which Are Ridden Or Tamed

If you want to elect an hour for someone for the purchase of an animal, whether for riding or taming, adapt the Ascendant and its Lord, and the Moon; and make her joined to some benefic which is direct, oriental, and ascending in the circle of its auge, if possible, or at least make it direct. And beware lest the benefic, or the Moon, be joined to a malefic by body or by aspect: since it will introduce fear in the animal, so that if it is a purchase, it will threaten harm, and that a good market price will not be gotten from him; if he is being ridden or tamed, what was intended will not follow from him, and the animal will be avoided: and all the more so if the impeding malefic is in the 12th. However, if this horse is already ridden, or if the other animal is already tamed, make the Ascendant of the purchase a common sign; and place the Moon in Taurus or Leo; also make her joined to direct planet who is ascending in the north, or at least in the south, provided that he is ascending: for this signifies that the animal will increase in price and body. If it is retrograde, it signifies that the animal will increase in price, but not as much, and will decrease in body. And if he is direct and descending, whether northern or southern, it signifies that he will increase in body, but decrease in price. Similarly, if it is southern and descending, it signifies that he will decrease in price and body: and this more greatly so if it is southern.

If it is an untamed animal, make the Ascendant a common sign, and place the Moon in a mobile sign joined to one of the benefics, having considered the aforesaid conditions according to ascent and descent, and direct and retrograde motion, as was said.

However, if someone wants to buy any animal (namely a horse, a bull, a donkey, or a camel) for reason of profit, or making improvements, it should be considered if the Moon is placed between the beginning of Cancer and the end of Sagittarius: for he will not profit from it easily, for he will buy it dear and sell it cheap. However, if he buys with the

Moon placed between the beginning of Capricorn and the end of Gemini, it will happen to the contrary: for he will buy it cheap and sell it dear. And not only will this happen from the aforementioned animals, but also from anything which someone buys at that time. However, this should not be overlooked: that benefics always bestow and increase good, and decrease evil; and malefics, on the contrary, increase evil and decrease good - each one according to its own nature, and according to whether it interests him to harm or help, increase or decrease.

# GUIDO BONATTI'S

## BOOK OF ASTRONOMY

## PART FOUR

### On The Revolutions Of The Years Of The World

#### *Preface*

After dealing with elections nothing seems more appropriate than to subsequently handle the revolutions of the years of the world, deservedly setting them apart and setting forth a special tractate on them. But first, we must briefly examine what a revolution is. A revolution of the year is the circular course of the Sun from one minute of any degree of any sign, up to his return to the same point; even if it can be defined otherwise, just as it seemed to certain men. And it is considered according to two methods: namely, according to the Revolution of the years of a nativity or other inceptions; and according to the Revolution of the year of the world - which is from the entry of the Sun in the first minute of Aries, up until he is revolved, and transits circularly through the whole Zodiac, and returns to the same point. However, a Revolution of the year of a nativity or of other beginnings, or of some inception, is from the minute in which the Sun was in the nativity of some native, up until he is revolved, and circularly transits the whole Zodiac, and returns to the same point - and the same is said about all other Revolutions.

A revolution is, among the rest, a very useful thing; and its significations are higher than the rest, just as to discover in its certainty is a strenuous and intricate thing. For through a revolution of the year of the world it is known what is going to be in that year, regarding the good and the bad; namely whether the year will be peaceful or troublesome; and whether or not there will be battles in the year which you are revolving. The same can be said about peace. And what will be the status of kings, princes, the wealthy, and magnates. And likewise that of the people, that of the commoners, and of the religious; even every individual in his own condition, of every kind according to the customs of men. It is likewise known what is going to be regarding those things born of the earth, whether there will an abundance or a scarcity of them expected; and what will come from them in the future, whether their prices will be low, mediocre, or high, just as will be said in its own place with regard to the Parts.

For through the Revolution of nativities the accidents of a native in his own year are known. Whence, if you wish to know the significations of the Revolutions of the years, as much of the world as of nativities, you will maintain this arrangement, according to what I hand down to you now; nor should you neglect this book, but it is necessary for you to know it, and to have it in your mind before all of the other books: since to know and understand it well takes great industry, so that by distinguishing the times you may harmonise the writings - lest you might believe there are contradictions in it, since there are not, if you consider those things well which present themselves to be considered. Since even if you were to find a statement (if there was such a statement), that "X signifies such-and-such an event", or "X signifies the multitude of such-and-such a thing"; and in this same chapter you find "X signifies the scarcity of the same thing", do not take this as a contradiction, but rather you should distinguish them to harmonise them. Since one will be general; the other will be particular - and the special restricts the general. However, it sometimes happens that the person modifying the matter speaks according to latitude, according to orientality, or according to occidentality, or according to direct motion, or according to retrogradation, and similar things. For these accidents vary the significations, and therefore the chapters do not contradict one another.

Should you want to know the Revolution of the year of the world, know at which hour the Sun enters the first minute of the sign of Aries: namely from the first second of the same minute, up to the 4th, at most the 5th, second of this minute. And when you find this by the most certain investigation, calculate the planets and houses to this hour, and to the minute of the same hour. And find the Ascendant as exactly as you can, and construct 12 houses by their degrees and minutes, to the minute of this hour, just as well and exactly as you can. Likewise you will calculate all the planets to the same minute of this hour; and you will discover their places as exactly as possible, by degrees and minutes, and likewise seconds, of each one of them, lest you fall into any error. And you will consider their condition (namely how they are disposed), and in which houses, and in which signs they are in. And which of them are direct, and which are retrograde, and which are stationary, and which are fast-of-course, and which slow: and whether any of them are northern, or if any of them are southern among themselves, or from the path of the Sun. For when a planet is northern from another, the planet which is northern from the other is said to go above the other, whether it is one the superiors, or of the inferiors. And likewise if they are southern, he who is less southern is said to go above the one who is more southern. And consider how one planet aspects another, or how it is aspected by another; and how one projects his rays upon the body or rays of another; and how they aspect the angles: since a good aspect signifies good; an evil aspect signifies the contrary. And when you do this, you will likewise see what sign is ascending - since then you can take the Lord of the year, and the signification of the commoners in general, from the Lord of the sign of the Ascendant (unless another impedes which deprives the Lord of the Ascendant of the rulership of the year). However, you shouldn't believe that the Lord of the Ascendant of the revolution will always be the Lord of the year absolutely (as some seem to want to say, in order to make things easier for themselves). But rather you will take the Lord of the year just as I tell you to below.

## I

### How The Lord Of The Year Is Found

After you are certain to a point regarding the time of the Sun's entrance into Aries (as was said); and of the Ascendant of his entrance; and of all other houses and of the places of the planets; see which planet is the Lord of the Ascendant, and how he is disposed, and where he is. For if he is direct, and free from combustion, and in the Ascendant three degrees in front of the line, or four after it, you should not seek another planet, since he will be the Lord of the year or revolution; and the significator of the condition of the commoners, and nothing else will be able to deprive him of that rulership. If he is retrograde, or combust, then he will not be able to be the Lord of the year or revolution, since a retrograde or combust planet cannot be the Lord of the year: for its virtue is annihilated, barring a great reason (which can only happen most rarely). Then seek the rulership from the exaltation. For if the sign of the Ascendant is the exaltation of any planet, seek the ruler from him: since if he is in the degree of the Ascendant, or three degrees in front of the line, or 4 behind, he will be the Lord of the year or revolution, and the significator of the condition of the commoners - if he is free from the impediments mentioned above. If indeed, he is impeded, as I said regarding the Lord of the Ascendant, he will not be the Lord of the year or revolution.

If the sign is not the exaltation of any planet (or if it is, and the exaltation Lord cannot be the Lord of the year), then seek the ruler from the Sun (if the revolution is in the day), or from the Moon, (if it is at night: since the luminary who has authority will be the Lord of the year or revolution - if it has any dignity in the Ascendant.

If again the luminary who has authority cannot be the Lord of the year, then seek the significator from the Lord of the terms; who will be the Lord of the year if he is in the Ascendant, three degrees in front of the line or 4 behind, and is free.

And again, if the term Lord cannot be the Lord of the year, then seek the ruler from the triplicity Lord, by the aforementioned method which I told to use for the others.

And if it is none of those which I said to you (the Lord of the domicile, exaltation, terms, triplicity, or the luminary who has authority, namely the Sun in the day, and the Moon at night, then seek the Lord of the year or revolution from the Lord of the tenth. And see if the Lord of the tenth house is in the tenth, three degrees in front of the line, or 4 degrees behind, and is not retrograde, or combust: if so, he will be the Lord of the year or revolution, and the significator of the condition of the commoners and the country folk. However, if the Lord of the tenth house is retrograde, combust, or otherwise impeded in such a way that he cannot be the significator, then seek the ruler from the Lord of the exaltation of the 10th house, if it is the exaltation of some planet. And if this planet is in the tenth and free from the aforementioned impediments, and is only three degrees in front of the line of the 10th house, or only 4 behind - he will be the Lord of the year and the significator of the condition of the commoners. However, if it is not the exaltation of any planet, or if it is, and the exaltation Lord cannot be the Lord of the year, then seek it from the luminary who has authority: since if it is in the tenth, and has any dignity there, he will be the Lord of the year. If again the luminary who has authority cannot be the Lord of the year, then seek the ruler from the term Lord of the degree of the tenth house; which, if it is in the degree of the tenth house, or three degrees in front of the line, or 4 behind, and is free from impediments, will be the Lord of the year, and the significator of the condition of the common people. If again the term Lord cannot be the Lord of the year, then seek the ruler from the triplicity Lord of the tenth house, which, if it is on the line of the tenth house, or three degrees in front, or 4 behind, will be the Lord of the year, and the significator of the commoners and/or the country folk.

However, if you cannot get the significator from the Ascendant, or from the tenth, seek him from the seventh through the same method, which I told you to use for the first and the tenth. And if then you cannot get him from the seventh, seek him from the fourth by the same method. And if again you cannot get him from the fourth, seek him from the eleventh by the same method. And if again you cannot get him from the eleventh, seek him from the 9th by the same method. And if again you cannot get him from the 9th, seek him from the fifth by the same method. And if again you cannot get him from the fifth, finally seek him from the third - always beginning from the Lord of the domicile; then from the Lord of exaltation; after

that from the luminary who has authority; then from the term Lord; and finally from the triplicity Lord. And it seemed to some of the ancients that you could do the same with the Lord of the face.

And whichever planet you find in any of the aforementioned places (after the falling away of the aforementioned significators from the rulership of the year), if it has any dignity there (even if it only has face there), and is free from impediments (as said of the others), will be the Lord of the year or revolution. And if there are several planets in any of the aforementioned places, the one who is more authoritative (or the Almutem) by number of fortitudes in that place will be the Lord of the year or revolution. And if they are equal in strength, the one who is closer to the line will be preferred. And if they are oriental, the one who is closer to the Sun will surpass the others. And if they are equidistant from the Moon, or from the Sun, then the one who moves more quickly from the degree he is in will be preferred. And if one of the aforementioned planets aspects one of the listed houses by a trine or sextile aspect, by two degrees in front (earlier degree) or three after (later degree), and if this planet has any dignity there, he will be the Lord of the year, after you found the aforementioned ones not to be the Lord.

And if the Ascendant is the domicile or exaltation of some luminary, and this luminary aspects the Ascendant from a trine or sextile aspect, namely two degrees in front, or three degrees after, or if the luminary is in the second from the Ascendant, it will be the Lord of the year. However, if this is not so, examine the Lord of the Ascendant, and the exaltation Lord of the Ascendant; and see if the luminary who has authority is in the domicile of either of them, and if it aspects the ruler of this domicile from a trine or sextile aspect, and is not cadent from the Ascendant, and is in a strong place: for this planet will be the Lord of the year.

And certain men prefer the luminary who has authority over the planetary Almutem. However, I do not see a reason why this is so, as I always place the Ascendant before the tenth and the tenth before the rest of the other houses; the 10th before the 7th, the 7th before the 4th, the 4th before the 11th, the 11th before the 9th, the 9th before the 5th, and the 5th before the 3rd, as was said.

And if one of the luminaries is not in any of the aforementioned places, see if the planet in whose domicile the luminary with authority is in, is in any of these places: for he will be the Lord of the year or revolution, whether he has dignity there or not. If this is not so, examine the Lord of the hour of the revolution: which if he is in any of the aforementioned places, will be the Lord of the year or revolution: and will be the significator of the commoners or the country folk.

And always understand this with regards to any significator, if it is on the line of the house in which it is in. or three degrees in front, or 4 behind- always preferring the Lord of the domicile, to the Lord of the exaltation, and the Lord of the exaltation to the Lord of the terms, and the Lord of the terms to the triplicity Lord. For the domicile Lord has 5 fortitudes, the exaltation Lord has 4 fortitudes, the term Lord has 5 fortitudes, and the triplicity Lord has 3 fortitudes. And even if the term Lord has as many fortitudes as the domicile Lord, and more than the exaltation Lord, nevertheless they are preferred on account of their excellence.

Again, if this is not so, know the places of the Lords of the signs in which the luminaries are; and the place of the Lord of the sign in which the luminary who has authority is placed, and consider him with the other significators.

And if all of the significators fail to be the Lord of the revolution, the one of them who is more authoritative by number of fortitudes will take command as the Lord of the year, or at least until the Lord of the Ascendant, or the 10th goes direct (if it is retrograde), or escapes (if he is combust). If again it were not one of these, the disposition will revert to the luminary who has authority. And if the revolution is at night, and the Moon is under the rays of the Sun, then the Sun will rule instead of her.

Albumashar (with whom it appears fitting for me to agree) said that the significations of the term Lord, the triplicity Lord, and the Lord of the hour are only to be considered in two places: namely, in the 1st and the 10th house. And some might believe that he is contradicting himself, for he said elsewhere that their significations are to be considered in all of the aforementioned places - but this is not contradictory. When he said they are to be considered in the 1st and the 10th, he understood by their own nature. And when he said, in all other places, he understood accidentally. And there are five testimonies of good or evil; and thus both statements should be followed. Moreover, if the Lord of the terms, triplicity, or hour, is in the Ascendant, or in the 10th, and the Lord of the Ascendant, or the 10th are in the degree of their own exaltation, or in one degree in front, or one behind (and if he could not be the significator), and one of them were to have the rulership of the year, he (namely the triplicity Lord) will acquire for himself the signification of the Lord of the first for one-third; the term Lord will have one fifth; and the Lord of the hour will have one seventh - in accordance with how strong they are. In the other places this does not happen to them, but rather their strength is decreased in them.

And however, many places and houses I name to you, from which the Lord of the year or revolution may be known, I want you to know that they are not equal in strength. For the Ascendant and the 10th exceed the other houses in strength; the seventh is below the tenth; the fourth is below the seventh; the eleventh is below the fourth; the ninth is below the eleventh; the fifth below the ninth; and the third is below the fifth. Whence, according to the house from which the Lord of the year is taken, so will the significations be stronger or weaker in that year, or half year, or quarter year, in the regions over which that revolution is. Wherefore it will be necessary for you to consider according to the part of the clime in which you are, or which the revolution is for. For it could be a revolution which is not a year, just as when the year is revolved according to halves or according to quarters.

Therefore, what remains are the testimonies by which the significations are known in these places: of which there are four. The first of which is the Lord of the domicile; the second is the Lord of the exaltation; the third is the luminary who has authority; the fourth is the planetary Almutem in the place from which the revolution is taken by nature, and the place in the circle in the hour which the year is revolved. After you could not operate by the Lord of the Ascendant, or by the Lord of its exaltation, or by the luminary who has authority, see if one of them is in one of the angles (after the failure of the aforementioned), and is in the degree of the cusp, or 2 degrees in front, or 3 after, and is not impeded: if so, he will be the Lord of the year.

And if the planetary Almutem is impeded, so that he cannot be the significator, then take the significator as being the planet in whose domicile the luminary who has authority is placed, if he is fit to receive the signification. And if he is not fit to receive the signification, or the rulership of the year, then the disposition and rulership of the year will return to the luminary who has authority, after the failure of all of the aforementioned. And if one of the luminaries commits its disposition to the Lord of the Ascendant, the Lord of the Ascendant will be the Lord of the year or revolution, and it will not be necessary for you to look for another.

After it appears that you have found the Lord of the year, you will also see if he is in the domicile of some other planet, and is joined to this planet by a praiseworthy aspect: since he will give it his virtue, and make it the Lord of the year if it is in an optimal place from the Ascendant; and this more strongly so if one of the luminaries, or either of them (or the Lord of the domicile that the luminary is in) were to aspect them (or either of them).

And it is also possible for the Sun to be the Lord of the year if he were receiving and collecting the light or fortitudes of the planets - such as if the revolution is at night, and the planet who ought to be the Lord of the year is nocturnal, and is under the rays of the Sun.

And if all of the aforementioned conditions are lacking, the disposition or rulership of the year will revert to the Lord of the Ascendant, whatever his condition is, and in whatever place he is in.

And since it would be difficult for you to always consider everything which has been said, I will shorten the rule somewhat for you, and recount for you the methods and considerations by which you ought to find the significator or Lord of the year or revolution. And there are 12 methods and fifty-four considerations.

The first of the methods is to examine the Lords of the houses from which the Lord of the year is sought.

The second is to examine the Lords of their exaltations.

The third is to examine the luminary who has authority.

The fourth is to examine the Lords of their terms.

The fifth is to examine the Lords of their triplicities.

The sixth is to examine the Almutem over the places.

The seventh is to examine the Lord of the hour of the revolution.

The eighth is to examine the planet in whose domicile the luminary who has authority is in.

The ninth is to examine if any planet aspects the Ascendant.

The tenth is to examine whether the Ascendant of the revolution is the domicile or exaltation of one of the luminaries, and if the luminary aspects it.

The eleventh is to examine if the luminary who has authority is in the domicile of the Lord of the Ascendant, or in the domicile of its exaltation Lord.

The twelfth is to examine the Lord of the domicile of the planet in whose house the luminary who has authority is placed, and what its condition is like.

In the end, it is possible to have certain other methods, but these are primary and more principal.

## Epilogue

As was said, there are fifty-four considerations.

The first of which is the Lord of the degree of the Ascendant.

The second is the Lord of the exaltation of the Ascendant.

The third is the luminary who has authority.

The fourth is the term Lord of the degree of the Ascendant.

The fifth is the triplicity Lord of the degree of the Ascendant.

The sixth is the Lord of the degree of the 10th house.

The seventh is the exaltation Lord of the degree of the 10th house.

The eighth is the luminary who has authority over the degree of the 10th house.

The ninth is the term Lord of the degree of the 10th house.

The tenth is the triplicity Lord of the degree of the 10th house.

The eleventh is the Lord of the degree of the 7th house.

The twelfth is the exaltation Lord of the degree of the 7th house.

The thirteenth is the luminary who has authority over the degree of the 7th house.

The fourteenth is the term Lord of the degree of the seventh house.

The fifteenth is the triplicity Lord of the 7th house.

The sixteenth is the Lord of the degree of the 4th house.

The seventeenth is the exaltation Lord of the 4th house.

The eighteenth is the luminary who has authority over the degree of the 4th house.

The nineteenth is the term Lord of the degree of the 4th house.

The twentieth is the triplicity Lord of the 4th house.

The twenty-first is the degree of the eleventh house.

The twenty-second is the exaltation Lord of the degree of the 11th house.

The twenty-third is the luminary who has authority over the degree of the 11th house.

The twenty-fourth is the term Lord of the same.

The twenty-fifth is its triplicity Lord.

The twenty-sixth is the Lord of the degree of the ninth house.

The twenty-seventh is its exaltation Lord.

The twenty-eighth is the luminary who has authority over the degree of the 9th house.

The twenty-ninth is the term Lord of the degree of the 9th house.

The thirtieth is its triplicity Lord.

The thirty-first is the Lord of the degree of the fifth house.

The thirty-second is its exaltation Lord.

The thirty-third is the luminary who has authority over it.

The thirty-fourth is the term Lord of its degree.

The thirty-fifth is the triplicity Lord of its degree.

The thirty-sixth is the Lord of the degree of the 3rd house.

The thirty-seventh is its exaltation Lord.

The thirty-eighth is the luminary who has authority over it.

The thirty-ninth is its term Lord.

The fortieth is the triplicity Lord of its degree.

The forty-first is the planetary Almutem in the degree of the house in which the Lord of the year or revolution is taken from.

The forty-second is the planet who is closer to the line of the house, if the planets are equal in strength.

The forty-third is the oriental planet who is closer to the Sun.

The forty-fourth is the planet who changes degree quicker, if more than one planet is oriental.

The forty-fifth is the planet who more greatly aspects the degree of the house signifying the rulership of the year.

The forty-sixth is when the Ascendant is the domicile or exaltation of a luminary, and this luminary aspects the Ascendant by a trine or sextile aspect, or is in the 2nd.

The forty-seventh is the planet in whose domicile the luminary who has authority is placed.

The forty-eighth is when one of the luminaries commits disposition to the Lord of the Ascendant.

The forty-ninth is when the Lord of the year commits disposition to one of the planets.

The fiftieth is the Lord of the hour of the revolution.

The fifty-first is the Lords of the signs in which the luminaries are placed.

The fifty second is the Lord of the sign containing the planet in whose domicile the luminary is in.

The fifty-third is when the planet who ought to be the significator is under the rays of the Sun.

The fifty-fourth is the planet changing figure: and this is the planet who is more quickly moved from one sign to another in the revolution of the year of the world; or who is oriental, and is more quickly made occidental; or who more quickly goes to the degree in which the Moon was at that time, or to the degree of the Ascendant (apart from the Moon).

## II

### On Finding The Significator Of The King

After you have found the Lord of the year or revolution, who is called the significator of the commoners or the country folk; it remains for you to find the significator of the king, since it is very useful to consider him in the Revolutions of the years of the world - which you can find in this way:

Examine the Lord of the tenth house of the figure of the Revolution of the year which you are revolving, as to whether it is free from combustion, retrogradation, fall, and the other impediments mentioned above: if this is so, and he is on the cusp of the tenth house, or three degrees in front, or five after, he will be the significator of the king without a doubt - operate through him and do not seek another. However, if you find him impeded by any of the aforementioned impediments, already we can say that he will not be the significator.

Then seek the significator from the Lord of the exaltation of the sign of the tenth house (if it is the exaltation of some planet); which, if it is free, as I said regarding the Lord of the domicile, and is on the cusp of the tenth house, or three degrees in front, or four behind, he will be the significator of the king. However, if he is impeded, he will not be the king's significator.

Then seek the significator from the Sun; which, if he is free and safe, as I said regarding the others, and is on the cusp of the tenth house, or three degrees in front, or five behind, he will be the significator of the king. However, if this is not so, already we can say that he will not be the significator.

Then seek him from the planet which is the Almutem in the sign of the tenth house by having a greater multitude of dignities. Which, if he is on the cusp of the tenth house, or three degrees in front, or five degrees behind, free and safe, he will be the significator of the king. However, if he is impeded, he will not be able to be the significator.

Indeed, Albumashar preferred the Sun to the Lord of the exaltation.

If you do not find any of these, then seek the significator from the planet who is on the cusp of the tenth house, or 3 degrees ahead, or 4 behind, and is otherwise free, and has some dignity there: since he will be the significator of the king. If indeed, he is impeded, he will not be the significator of the king. However, if he does not have dignity there, and is on the cusp, or two degrees ahead, or three after, or is the Lord of the house in which the Part of Kingship falls, and is free and safe from the aforementioned impediments, he will be the significator of the king.

If again this is not so, Albumashar said that if the Midheaven is the domicile of the Sun; and the Sun is on its cusp, not remote from it, or cadent, he will be the significator of the king; and likewise if he is in the Ascendant received by Mars, and Leo is in the Midheaven - since then the Ascendant will be Scorpio. And he said if the Midheaven is Aries, and the Sun is on the cusp according to what I said, and Mars is cadent from him, he will be the significator of the king; and if he aspects Mars, Mars will be the participating significator.

And he said that if Mars is strong in his own place, and in good condition, with the Sun joined to him, Mars will be the significator of the king; and this more deservedly if he is in Capricorn, and the Sun is joined to him from the Midheaven. And he said that if this Mars fell in the Midheaven, or in an angle from the Ascendant, and the Sun projects his rays to him, Mars will be more deserving of signification. And likewise if the Sun is in the angle of the Midheaven, or in one of the places aspecting the Midheaven (understand this as being by friendly aspects), and is the Lord of the Midheaven, the Sun will be more deserving of signification.

## When The Lord Of The Year Is Made The Significator Of The King

If you do not find things as I said to you, see if the 10th is the domicile or exaltation of the Lord of the year, and if he aspects it from any aspect, apart from opposition: if so, the Lord of the year or significator of the commoners will be the significator of the king.

If again this is not so, examine if the Lord of the year joins with the Lord of the 10th house, or with its exaltation Lord, from such a place that the Lord of the 10th receives him; wherefore he commits his disposition to him: if so, the Lord of the year will be made the significator of the king. Even if the Lord of the 10th house is in the domicile or the exaltation of the Lord of the year, so that the Lord of the year receives him; and the Lord of the 10th commits his disposition to the Lord of the year: for the Lord of the year will not be made the significator of the king, unless the Lord of the tenth commits his disposition to him.

If again this is not so, see if the Sun is the Lord of the year, and whether he has any dignity in the 10th; or if the Lord of the 10th is under the rays of the Sun (whether he has escaped from combustion or not, provided that he does not appear from under the rays): for if so, the Sun will be the significator of the king, and especially in the region in which this is.

And Albumashar said that if the Sun commits disposition to the Lord of the Ascendant, and he has some testimony in the Midheaven, the Lord of the Ascendant will be the significator of the king.

And he said that if the Midheaven is one of the domiciles of Saturn, or the sign of his exaltation, and he is on its cusp, free from combustion, Saturn will be the significator of the king.

And he said that if the Sun does not have testimony in the Midheaven, examine the Lord of the Midheaven, and the Lord of its exaltation, and whichever one of them is stronger; and has more testimony; and is in better condition; and collects and receives more light from the planets; and falls

in a better place from the Midheaven - he will be the significator of the king.

And if the Lord of the Midheaven, the Lord of its exaltation, and the Sun, are cadent from aspects to the tenth, and are in bad condition, and you do not find any of the aforementioned scenarios, see if any of the planets aspect one of the aforementioned significators not aspecting the tenth, and if he himself aspects the tenth, so that he lifts up the light of the other planet: since this will strengthen him regarding the disposition of the king, and will make that planet whose light is so carried to the tenth of the revolution, the significator of the king.

However, if you find none of them, then revert to the Lord of the year, and to the Lord of the tenth, and to the Sun, and whichever of them you find stronger, or less weak, or better disposed, or less bad, or in a better place from the tenth, or in a less bad place from the tenth, make this planet the significator of the king.

And Albumashar said that when the Sun is the Lord of the Ascendant, the Midheaven will be Taurus. And if Venus is under his rays, the Sun will be the significator of the king, since the Lord of the Midheaven is under the rays. However, if Venus had gone out from under the rays in her own light, she will be more deserving of signification, for she will be in the Ascendant, or in the domicile from which she aspects the tenth; and this will be better if she is in her own domicile or exaltation. And he said that if Venus is in the end of an angle, and pushes her strength to the Sun (which could not happen unless she is corporeally joined to him), then if Venus is the Lord of the Midheaven, and she has pushed her strength to the Sun - the Sun will be the significator of the king. And he said the angles of the planets are the aggregate of their equation, truth, or certainty: and this is taken by the diameters of their short circles.

## III

## When The Lord Of The Ascendant Is The Lord Of The Year, Whence Is Known The Condition Of The King, And His Assistants, And The Commoners, And Of Certain Men, Both Religious And Secular

With the significator of the year or revolution having been found, and the significator of the king, it remains to find the significator of other diverse persons, and also whence the significators of the king are examined. Which you can know, as Albumashar said, from Saturn, the Sun, the tenth, and the king's significator. Whence if you see these four well disposed, announce the good condition of the king, in whole, and in all respects. However, if you find them impeded, announce to the contrary in whole. If you find one of them free and another impeded, judge according to what you see of the impediment or liberation: but Saturn is of greater signification than any of them (except for the significator of the king), as much for good as for bad; and the significations of the Sun are beneath the significations of Saturn; and the significations of the Lord of the tenth are beneath the significations of the Sun in this case.

### How The Soldiers Of The King Are Examined

And he said that you ought to examine the soldiers of the king from the 11th and its Lord, whence if you see that the 11th is fit, and its Lord well disposed, and Mars well disposed, announce the condition of the kings soldiers to be good. However, if you see the 11th unfit, and its Lord impeded, and Mars similarly, announce the contrary of that which I said. However, if the Lord of the 11th or Mars is impeded, and the other is free, announce their condition to be middling.

### How The Wealthy And Great Men Who Are Below The King Are Examined

You will take the condition of the wealthy and great men who are below the king from Jupiter, and make the Lord of the domicile in which Jupiter is placed a participator: which, if you find them strong and well disposed, announce their condition to be good. However, if you find them badly disposed, announce the contrary.

### How Bishops, And Other Secular Clerics Are Examined

You will examine bishops, and other secular clerics; and the Pope and cardinals; and also legists, canonists, and counsellors, from Jupiter, and the Lord of his house, and from the ninth and its Lord: which if you find free, and well disposed, announce their good condition. However, if you find one strong, and the other weak, announce their middling condition according to the weakness or according to the strength which you find.

### How The Soldiers Of The King, And His Assistants, And Bearers Of Arms Are Examined

For soldiers and assistants of the king, and those bearing arms for the purpose of profiting from war, you will examine Mars; which if you find him well disposed, announce their good condition. However, if you find him badly disposed, announce the contrary.

### How The Religious Living Under A Rule Are Examined

For the religious living under a rule, serving God, and who are thus placed so that they may serve God (and you should not trust just any caped religious person, but only those who have dedicated themselves to their God, among whom monks are counted, and especially those wearing black vestments); and for old men, the decrepit, and low class people doing heavy work, as are ditch-diggers, and similar people; you will examine from Saturn, and if you find him free, fortunate, and strong, announce the good condition of those mentioned above; if however, you find him to the contrary, announce the contrary.

### How Women Are Examined

You will take the condition of women from Venus, and from her place: and if you find her well disposed, announce the good condition of women, and especially young women; if however, you find her badly disposed, you will announce the contrary.

## How Merchants And Traders Are Examined

As for the condition of merchants, traders, painters, scribes, and judges, wise men, the learned (and especially those learned in the quadrivium), and boys and adolescents, and similar people, you will take it from Mercury, which if you find him free and well disposed, announce their good condition; if however, you find him impeded, judge the contrary. However, the condition of merchants varies from the condition of others: since they are examined from the Lord of the year, and from the Ascendant and its Lord, and from the Moon, and from Jupiter, just as from Mercury, but Mercury and Jupiter prevail over the others in the signification of merchants.

## How Low-Class And Common People Are Examined

You will examine the lower class, commonners, and sailors of small boats from the Moon; and if you find her free and well disposed, announce their condition to be good. However, if she is impeded, announce the contrary.

And in all of the things mentioned above, make the Lord of the year a participator, and the Lord of the house in which you find the significator whose signification you seek: and mix them together, and see how they fare, and how they are conjoined. For if they are all free, fortunate, and strong ("they" being the planet naturally signifying the matter, the planet in whose house he is in, and the Lord of the year), judge good in all respects regarding the signification which you seek. However, if all are safe, except for one which is impeded, judge more good than bad. If two are impeded and one is safe, judge more bad than good: and you will judge the increase or decrease of the good or bad to be according to their liberation or their impediment being more or less, and according to the Ascendant at that time - such as if the Ascendant, or the tenth are one of the domiciles of a planet naturally signifying the sought significations. So that if you seek something signified by Saturn, and the Ascendant or the tenth is Capricorn, or Aquarius. Or if you seek something signified by Jupiter, and the Ascendant or the tenth is Sagittarius or Pisces. Or if you seek something signified by Mercury, and the Ascendant or the tenth is Gemini or Virgo. However, with Venus and the Moon, it is different: for if you seek something signified by Venus, neither the Ascendant, nor the tenth is considered; but rather the seventh and the fourth. So if the seventh or the fourth are Taurus or Libra, it will harm or benefit just as the Ascendant or tenth harm or benefit with Saturn, Jupiter, and Mercury; and if the seventh or the fourth is Cancer, on account of the femininity of the houses and the planet's places. For Mars the Ascendant and the tenth are considered, on account of their masculinity; the seventh and the fourth on account of their nocturnality.

## IV

## What Is Signified By The Lord Of The Year Or Revolution, In The Places Which It Falls At The Hour Of The Revolution

And now that you have found the Lord of the year or revolution and the significator of the king, and of those others of whose significators are to be considered in revolutions, in this chapter we will consider those things which seem possible to occur in the revolution. But first regarding the general accidents of the year, asides from those concerning things born of the earth and the like, which will be spoken of elsewhere in their own time and place.

Therefore, see in what place the Lord of the year or revolution falls in the figure which you erect for the hour at which the year is revolved: since if it falls in the Ascendant, or in a place friendly to the Ascendant, it signifies goodness, joy, and tranquillity for the persons of that clime, and of that region according to the nature of the house in which it falls, just as is said elsewhere. However, if it falls in a place inimical to the Ascendant, it signifies impediment, anger and contrariety; and this more strongly so if the Lord of the year is the Lord of the Ascendant. For if it falls in the sixth (which is one of the houses inimical to the Ascendant), infirmities in their bodies and damage to their small animals which are not ridden will befall the men of that region; and this more strongly so is the house was a sign signifying such a subject. However, if it falls in the seventh, contrarieties, whisperings, and war will befall them. If it falls in the twelfth, enmity and betrayals will befall them. And all of these things will happen according to the nature and substance of the sign in which the significator is placed. And not only does this have a place with the Lord of the

Ascendant, but it also has a place with the Lord of the exaltation, and of the terms, and the triplicity, and with the rest of the significators of the revolution. But the significations of the others are below those of the Lord of the Ascendant, according to the condition of each of them, whether their significations are good or bad.

And the evil of their significations will be stronger, if it happens that the Lord of the year or revolution is retrograde, allowing this very rarely happens: nevertheless, the disposition of the planets could be so bad, that of necessity it would be necessary for the Lord of the year to be retrograde, and then he would need of the support of another planet, who would lift him up and render his light to the Ascendant, or it would need to be rendered from planet to planet up until it were found by a planet who would render his light to the Ascendant (or the tenth, if it is the significator of the king).

## V

## On The Knowledge Of The Accidents Which Are Going To Happen In The Year, And In Which Parts They Ought To Happen

And even if it can be most difficult to see in which directions, and in which regions, and in which climates the accidents which are going to happen in the revolution, or the year which you revolve, ought to occur; nevertheless, to me it seems fitting to know, and not to omit, what can be known of it. And I will tell you certain things, through which you will be able to know something of these things, God willing. For I cannot tell you everything in full, on account of the great confusion cities and regions given to understand. For since the coming of Our Lord there are 18,345 ancient cities (or villas and castles, and other habitations equal to cities) in the climes, without the newly constructed ones, just as I have found stated by certain ancient sages.

Of which, Messala of India said that there are twelve exceeding the others in magnitude, of which in the first climate there are two assigned to Saturn. In the second there are two assigned to Jupiter. In the third there are two assigned to Mars. In the fourth there are two assigned to the Sun. In the fifth there is one assigned to Venus. In the sixth there are two assigned to Mercury. In the seventh there is one assigned to the Moon.

Whence, if you wish to know the accidents which are going to happen in the region in which you are, from the revolution or the year which you are revolving, you will note the Ascendant according to the ascensions of the city or region in which you are, and see how far up to the west: since that is how much the signification will extend, as long as the Ascendant does not undergo alteration (that it passes away by crossing five degrees), giving each degree 53 miliaria (and certain thing analogous to a miliaria, by which the ancient sages measured, which is 4,000 cubits according to equal cubits). And the signification will only extend by as much as there is of the nature of the Ascendant. So that if the Ascendant is the fifth degree of some sign, its signification will last toward the east up to five degrees after those five which have already crossed the line of the Ascendant; and toward the west up to three degrees of those five which have already gone beyond the line of the Ascendant. And thus, that signification will extend from the place in which you are, toward the east by 265 milaria; and toward the west by 159 milaria; and thus there will be 424 miliaria in all. And the significations will extend that far: allowing perhaps that sometimes this will be found to be more or less, according to the planets aspecting the place, or the Part, or the planet signifying the matter.

However, you will consider this from your own industry, and according to longitude and according to latitude: since it can sometimes happen that the signification extends 90 degrees in front and 90 degrees to the back; and the same to the right, and the same to the left. However, it is for you to judge, lest the region be so disposed, that this will impede the result of some direction, whether for good or evil. Since if the particular site of the region is good, it will increase the good and decrease the evil, such as mountains, valleys, lakes, marshes, and similar places which alter a region. You will observe the same in all climes, countries, and regions, according to their Ascendants, and according to their divisions, and according to their horizons.

## VI

### How The Earth Is Divided Into Two Primary Divisions

For the earth is divided into two primary divisions: one of which is from the oriental quarter and from the southern quarter: since they are united by the heat in which they agree, and which makes the nature of one resemble the nature of the other. The second is from the occidental quarter, and from the northern quarter: because they are united by the coldness in which they agree, and which makes the nature of one resemble the nature of the other.

## VII

### How The Second Of Three Other Secondary Divisions

Moreover, the earth is subdivided into three other secondary divisions, namely into the superior, middle, and inferior. And these three divisions are adapted to the three superior planets, namely Saturn, Jupiter and Mars; and therefore these are more powerful than the others: since from them descend greater significations than from the others. For even though the others participate with them, the virtue of the superiors is still far greater and stronger than the virtue of the inferiors.

For the first division, namely the superior one, which is northern, which is the seventh clime, and whatever is inhabited of the earth outside of the climes determined by the ancients, toward the arctic pole, is attributed to Saturn, whose participator is the Moon - which is shown through these things: since on account of the slowness of Saturn, and his darkness, and the thickness of the air of those parts, and the smokiness of t earthy and thick. The mass of men inhabiting these regions are of little knowledge, and little intellect, and are forgetful, but nonetheless lustful; nor does piety reign in them. Nevertheless, if it ever happens that one of them adheres to science, he will greatly exceed others, just like our most reverend predecessor Albumashar Tricas, who, even if he studied at Athens, was still a Latin, just as he himself confessed in the treatise "Agiget". And even certain others, even if they are rarely found, such as Michael Scot in my time; and a certain other young man by the name of Albert Teutonicus, of the Order of the Preachers.

That the Moon participates with Saturn is shown on account of their urgency and fury: which happens to them on account of the urgency of the Moon, and her instability and fast mutation, and alterations: and on account of their saffron, white, and often red colours; and account of the opposition the domiciles of Saturn and the Moon.

The second division, namely the middle part, which is the sixth, fifth, and fourth climes, is attributed to Jupiter, whose participator is Mercury (whose domiciles are opposed); and the Sun also participates with them in the fifth and fourth clime, and in the southern part of the sixth. And this is shown through these things: since those living in these regions are more often wiser, and more good-natured than the rest, and especially those living in Italy (if they are not much intent on pecuniary profit). For the citizens of these climes are good, and of a more certain intellect, and a more profound and sharper intelligence; and piety thrives in them; and truth in certain of them; and religion more so than in any others; and a prophetic manner. And this happens more in the northern part of the fourth clime, and in all of the fifth, and in the southern part of the sixth - but in Italy more so than in the other regions,

,even if Avicenna seemed to want to say otherwise. For he placed greater temperateness under the circle of equality than elsewhere. However, he did not speak as an astrologer, but as a doctor: and therefore he was deceived in his opinion.

That Mercury is a participant with Jupiter, is apparent on account of the sharpness of their intelligence, which is fit for learning and exercising every mystery, and to learn and comprehend every form of wisdom and science, as much mathematical as natural as theological; and even for learning all of the mechanical arts: even if certain of the inhabitants of the seventh clime are fit for certain mechanical arts. And it is also shown on account of the diverse mixtures of their colours, from white, red, black, and the like; and since their houses are mixed and compound; and on account of the temperate heat, and the fitting thinness of the air of their climes, and the moderate smokiness of the earth.

And that the Sun participates with him in the above mentioned climes, is shown through this: since they know above all others about how to rule by means of governance; they also know rhetoric, ethics, and politics above all others. And this division surpasses all the other divisions, and is better and more deserving than the rest.

Indeed, the third division, namely the inferior one, which is south from the others, which is the third, second, and first climes, is attributed to Mars, whose participator is Venus, (whose domiciles are opposed). And this appears through these things: since the inhabitants of these climes are pillagers, highwaymen, and thieves: indeed, they use a disgraceful form of sex; abusing men and brutes; they are drinkers and gamblers, maintaining an unfit way of drinking and gambling; and often are beast-like in all of their actions, disobedient, of a disgraceful life; disgraceful and tasteless in all of their actions; impudent; with a disordered and reprehensible way of life.

That Venus participates with him is shown on account of their desire of sex, drinking, and games; but Mars reduces all of this to shamelessness and ineptitude. Their colours are often burnt and horrible, and often are black and swarthy, on account of the deep heat and dryness in their flesh, even though this happens in one region more so than the others; which happens on account of the excessive heat of the Sun's rays, heating and destroying the disposition of these places, and on account of the intense heat of the air, and its overly destructive thinness: even though Alfraganus seemed to want to say that the winter makes this place of equal complexion. However, this is true with respect to our winter and our summer: for the Sun is as far from the equator when it is in Cancer, as when it is in Capricorn.

## VIII

### How The Earth Is Divided Into Seven Other Divisions

Again, these two and three divisions are subdivided into another seven divisions, according to the number of the seven planets, which are called climes, and which are adapted to the seven planets in this way.

The first clime is adapted to Saturn, who is higher, superior, and slower than the rest of the planets.

Indeed, the second clime is adapted to Jupiter, who immediately follows Saturn in slowness, and succeeds him in the order of circles.

The third is adapted to Mars, who follows immediately after Jupiter, and succeeds him as much in slowness, as in the order of the circles. The fourth is adapted to the Sun, who immediately follows Mars in the order of the circles.

The fifth is adapted to Venus, who immediately follows Mars in the order of circles.

The sixth is adapted to Mercury, who immediately follows Venus in the order of circles.

Indeed, the seventh and final clime is adapted to the Moon, who immediately follows Mercury in the

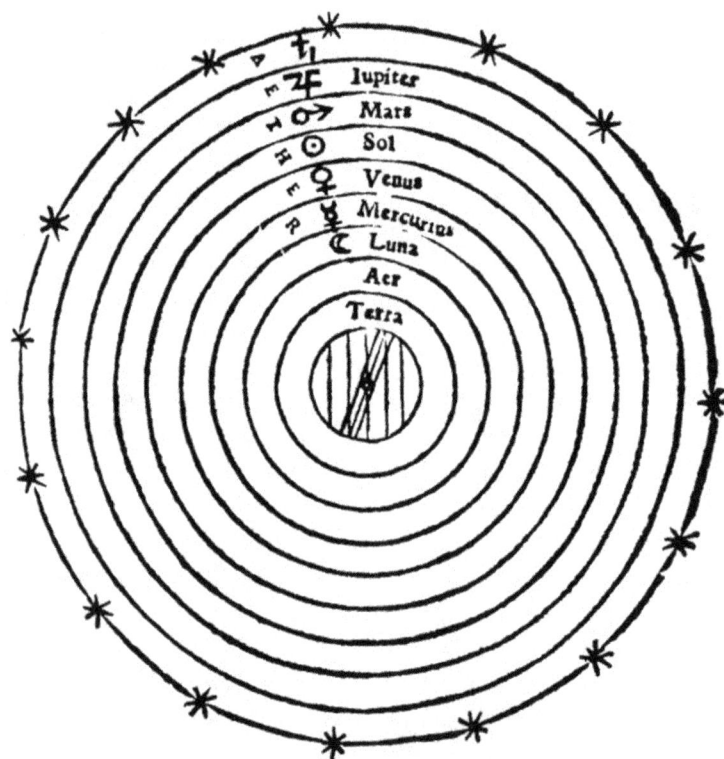

order of circles: since she is inferior to the rest of the planets, and faster than the rest.

Whence, each planet disposes more over the clime assigned to it than it does over the others: even if each one of them has something to do over every clime; sometimes according to more, sometimes according to less. And the signs likewise rule over

regions, and imprint in them according to their own nature. Wherefore the fire signs imprint more over hot regions; earth signs over dry regions; air signs over moist regions; water signs over cold regions: since the signs do not signify over the parts of the world by places, or by their position, but by their nature. Whence if a region which a fire sign rules is hot, this signification will occur more strongly than in a cold region. For it tempers the cold in a cold region; because a moist sign moistens in a wet region it tempers the dryness in a dry region, and vice versa.

Just as Aries, Leo, and Sagittarius (which are the first triplicity), heat in the eastern parts; they temper the coldness in northern parts: since they are fiery, and they are eastern signs. Whence if the Ascendant is one of these signs, it will strengthen and increase the signification; and the eastern wind is hot and dry.

And just as Taurus, Virgo, and Capricorn (which are the second triplicity), dry out in the southern parts, in western parts they temper the humidity: since they are earth signs, and southern signs. Whence if the angle of the tenth is one of these signs, it will strengthen the signification, and increase it; and the southern wind is hot and moist.

And in like manner Gemini, Libra, and Aquarius (which are the third triplicity), moisten in the western parts; and temper the dryness in southern parts: since they are air signs, and western signs. Whence if the angle of the seventh house is one of these signs, it will strengthen the signification and increase it; and the western wind is cold and moist.

And in like manner, Cancer, Scorpio, and Pisces (which are the fourth triplicity), make cold in northern parts, and temper the heat in eastern parts: since they are water signs, and they are northern signs. Whence if the angle of the fourth house is any one of these signs, it will strengthen the signification, and increase it; and the northern wind is cold and dry.

And the planets also assist this, for if the signification is in the north, and Saturn rules over it, he will assist the signification, and make it appear to a greater degree; and more strongly so if Mercury assists him, and if it is a cold signification.

And if it is in the west, and Jupiter rules over it, this signification will be increased; and he will make it appear to a greater degree; and this more strongly so if the Moon assists him, and if it is a moist signification.

And if it is in the southern parts, and Mars rules over it, and if it is a dry signification it will be increased, and he will make it appear to a greater degree.

And if it is in the eastern parts, and the Sun rules over it, and it is a hot signification, the Sun will assist it, and will make it appear to a greater degree. However, if Venus is a participant, she will temper something of this heat.

### Another Division Of The Earth

And after these two, and these three, and these seven divisions, the earth is subdivided again into another twelve divisions, according to the number of the twelve signs, and according to the degrees transited from east to west. For Aries is adapted to the first clime; whence Mars, who is the Lord of Aries, rules over the significations of this clime from the east to the west; but the term Lords participate with him, and the virtue of the term Lord prevails over the virtue of the domicile Lord in the particular significations of revolutions. For Jupiter, who has the first terms of Aries, disposes over the significations of the revolution of the first clime, from the beginning of the habitable earth from the direction of the east toward the west for 318 miliaria. And after him, Venus for 424 miliaria. And after her, Mercury for 371 miliaria. And after him, Mars for 265 miliaria: and his signification is stronger then, since he has the virtue of term and the virtue of domicile: and it happens in this way for the others. And after him, Saturn for 212 miliaria. Then the disposition reverts to Jupiter, and to the rest of the others, until it arrives at the end of the habitable region toward the west.

Taurus is adapted to the southern half of the second clime, and Venus, who is the Lord of Taurus, rules over its significations from the east to the west. And Venus, who has the first terms of Taurus, rules over these significations, and disposes over them from the beginning of the habitable earth from the east toward the west for 424 miliaria; and the significations will then be without the participation of anyone: since she is the Lord of the domicile and the Lord of the terms; and therefore they appear to a greater degree. And after her, Mercury for 371 miliaria. After him, Jupiter for 371 miliaria. And after him, Saturn for 106 miliaria. And after him, Mars for 318 miliaria. After him the disposition will revert to Venus, and she will rule over the significations for 424 miliaria, and so on for the rest of the term Lords.

Gemini is adapted to the northern half of the second clime; and Mercury, who is its Lord, rules over the signification of this half from the east to west, but with participation in the terms. For Mercury himself rules the first terms, and his significations appear stronger then (since he is the Lord of the domicile and the Lord of the terms) for 371 miliaria. And after him, Jupiter for 318 miliaria. And after him, Venus for 371 miliaria. And after her, Mars for 318 miliaria. After him, Saturn for 212 miliaria. Then the disposition reverts to Mercury, and so on for the rest, up until the end of the habitable earth to the west.

Cancer is adapted to the southern half of the third clime, from the east to the west; and her Lord, the Moon, rules over the significations of this clime from the east to the west, and the term Lords participate with her. For Mars, who has the first terms of Cancer, rules over the significations of the revolution which ought to be from the beginning of the habitable earth from the direction of the east toward the west for 318 miliaria. And after him, Jupiter for 371 miliaria. And after him, Mercury for 371 miliaria. And after him, Venus for 371 miliaria. And after her, Saturn for 157 miliaria. Then the disposition reverts to Mars, and to the rest of the other planets, up until it reaches the end of the habitable earth toward the west.

Leo is adapted to the northern half of the third clime, from the east to the west; and the Sun, who is his Lord, rules over the significations of this half generally, but the term Lords participate with him particularly. For Saturn, who is the Lord of the first terms of Leo, rules over the signification of the revolution from the beginning of the habitable earth from the direction of the east toward the west for 318 miliaria. And after him, Mercury for 372 millaria. After him, Mars for 265 millaria. After him, Venus for 318 millaria. After her, Jupiter for 318 millaria. Then the disposition reverts to Saturn, and the rest of the planets in succession, until it reaches the end of the habitable earth.

Virgo is adapted to the southern half of the fourth clime, from the east to the west; and Mercury, who is its Lord, rules over the signification of this half from the east to the west generally, but the term Lords participate with him; and Mercury himself, who is the Lord of the first terms of Virgo, rules over the significations of the revolution which ought to be from the beginning of the habitable earth toward the west for 371 miliaria. And after him, Venus for 318 miliaria. And after her, Jupiter for 265 miliaria. After him, Saturn for 318 miliaria. After him, Mars for 318 miliaria. Then the disposition reverts to Mercury, etc., as was said of the others.

Libra is adapted to the northern half of the fourth clime, from the east to the west; and Venus, who is its Lord, rules over the significations of this half from the east to the west generally, but the term Lords participate with her. For Saturn, who is the Lord of the first terms of Libra, rules over the significations of the revolution which ought to be from the beginning of the habitable earth, from the direction of the east toward the west for 318 miliaria. And after him, Venus for 265 miliaria. And after her, Mercury for 265 miliaria. After him, Jupiter for 414 miliaria. And after him, Mars for 318 miliaria. Then the disposition reverts to Saturn, and the rest, as was said of the others.

Scorpio is adapted to the southern half of the fifth clime; and Mars, who is its Lord, rules over the significations of this half generally, from the east to the west, but the Lords of the terms participate with him. For Mars himself, who is the Lord of the first terms of Scorpio, rules over the significations of the revolution which ought to be from the beginning of the habitable earth from the direction of the east toward the west for 318 miliaria. And after him, Venus for 371 miliaria. After her, Jupiter for 414 miliaria. And after him, Mercury for 318 miliaria. After him, Saturn for 159 miliaria. Then the disposition reverts to Mars, etc., as was said of the others.

Sagittarius is adapted to the northern half of the fifth clime, from the east to the west; and Jupiter, who is its Lord, rules over the significations from the east to the west generally, but the Lords of the terms participate with him. For Saturn, who is the Lord of the first terms of Sagittarius, rules over the significations of the revolution which ought to be from the beginning of the habitable earth from the beginning of the east toward the west for 424 miliaria. And after him, Venus for 318 miliaria. After her, Mercury for 165 miliaria. After him Saturn, for 318 miliaria. After him, Mars for 265 miliaria. Then the disposition reverts to Jupiter, etc., as was said for the others.

Capricorn is adapted to the southern half of the sixth clime, from the east to the west, and Saturn, who is its Lord, rules over the significations of this half from the east to the west generally, but the Lords of the terms participate with him. For Venus, who is the Lord of the first terms of Capricorn, rules over the significations of the revolution which ought to be from the beginning of the habitable lands, from the eastern part facing west, for 318 miliaria. And after her, Mercury for 318 miliaria. And after him, Jupiter for 371 miliaria. After him, Saturn for 318 milaria. After him Mars, for 265 miliaria. Then the disposition reverts to Venus, as said of the others.

Aquarius is adapted to the northern half of the sixth clime, from the east to the west; and Saturn, who is its Lord, rules over the significations from the east to the west generally, but the term Lords participate with him. For Saturn himself, who is the Lord of the first terms of Aquarius, rules over the significations of the revolution which ought to be from the beginning of the habitable earth from the direction of the east toward the west for 318 miliaria. And after him, Mercury for 318 miliaria. And after him Venus for 414 miliaria. And after her, Jupiter for 265 miliaria. And after him, Mars for 265 miliaria. Then the disposition reverts to Saturn, as was said for the others.

Pisces is adapted to the seventh clime, from the east to the west; and Jupiter, who is its Lord, rules over the general significations of this clime from the east to the west, but the Lords of the terms participate with him. For Venus, who is the Lord of the first terms of Pisces, rules over the significations of the revolution which ought to be from the beginning of the habitable earth from the direction of the east toward the west for 424 miliaria. And after her, Jupiter for 318 miliaria, And after him, Mercury for 318 miliaria. After him, Mars for 265 miliaria. After him, Saturn for 265 miliaria. Then the disposition reverts to Venus, as was said for the others.

However, if the clime is not of such a longitude that the significations of the planets can extend far enough for the number of miliaria to be completed, as was said, it does not matter. For when there is a lack of land, the significations of the terms of the planets expire.

Whence, you ought to examine the disposition, and condition of the planets in the revolutions of the years, both of nativities or questions, and of the world, and see if the condition of the Lord of the sign is good, since this signifies the good condition of the clime generally, according to the part which it rules. And likewise examine the condition of the planets ruling the terms. For if they agree in one condition, it signifies that the significations of the revolution will appear to a greater degree, as much for good as for bad: so that if the condition of the Lord of the sign and the condition of the Lord of the terms is good, it signifies complete good in the region which the Lord of the terms rules. However, if the condition of both of them is bad, it signifies that complete evil will appear in the region which is ruled over by the Lord of the terms. However, if they disagree, their significations will appear less, but the significations of the Lord of the sign will appear less than those of the Lord of the terms, as much for good as for evil.

## IX

### How The Sun Is To Be Examined In The Revolution Of A Year, If It Is Diurnal

Also examine the condition of the Sun and his disposition in a revolution of the year of the world (if the revolution is diurnal), and see whether he is going to be eclipsed in that year or not.

Likewise, examine the aspects of the planets to him, namely those of the benefics and malefics, since the benefics signify good, the malefic, to the contrary, signify evil. For if the Sun is fortunate and strong, it signifies exaltation and the occurrence of a great event (in diurnal revolutions).

Also examine the condition of the Lord of the Ascendant, and whether he is free from the mentioned impediments, or not: since if he is free, it signifies the goodness and tranquillity of the land ruled over by the sign on the Ascendant at that time; and also for the citizens of this region, and the peoples which are signified by that planet.

However, if it is impeded it signifies that impediment, damage, and evil will befall the inhabitants of this region, and those who are signified by the planet who is the Lord of the Ascendant of the revolution; and their condition will be disposed according to the substance of the sign ruling over the region which is signified by that sign. So that if the Ascendant is Libra, and Venus (its Lord) is cadent from the Ascendant, or from the angles, impeded (either retrograde, combust, or besieged by two malefics), or made unfortunate in another way, it signifies that destruction, infirmities, and sorrows will happen in Arabia, and to the inhabitants of this land, and to all who are signified by Libra or Venus. And if the Ascendant is Leo, and the Sun is impeded, it signifies that the aforementioned impediments will befall the Babylonians, and all who are signified by Leo and the Sun. However, if the Ascendant is Cancer, and the Moon is impeded by the aforementioned impediments, it signifies that the aforementioned impediments will befall the Romans, and all who are signified by Cancer and the Moon. And understand this with every sign, and with every planet, and according to the significations of each of them.

## X

### How The Moon Is To Be Examined If The Revolution Is Nocturnal

However, if it is a nocturnal revolution, then examine the Moon, just as you examine the Sun in a diurnal revolution: so that if she is the Lord of the revolution or the dispositor, and is in Cancer, then examine her alone. If indeed, she is outside of Cancer, then examine the Lord of the domicile in which she is in: who, if you find him strong and fortunate, from being in one of the strong places, or by the aspect of the benefics to him, it signifies good for the citizens of that region. However, if you find him weak, made unfortunate by the aforementioned things, it signifies the bad condition, and bad disposition of the citizens or inhabitants of this region, and their detriment.

*General Delineation Of The Revolution*

You can say the same thing regarding the Lord of the Ascendant of the revolution: since if he is in good condition, it signifies good things for the aforementioned citizens. However, if he is in bad condition, he signifies their detriment.

And know that in a nocturnal revolution, when the Moon is fortunate and strong, increasing in light and number, she signifies exaltation and is a signal for a great matter, and for the good.

Likewise examine if the luminary who has authority (especially in nocturnal revolutions), is joined to Saturn by body, or by aspect: since if it is joined to him by body or by any aspect, without perfect reception, the malice will be increased; and this more strongly so if the Moon is joined to him while she is decreasing in light. If she is separating from him at the time, and especially while increasing in her light, the malice will be reduced, and it will not produce as much detriment.

You will also see where the impeding malefic is placed, and of which house it is the Lord: since the harm will come from a matter which is signified by that house. So that if it is the second, it will happen because of substance, or one of those things which are signified by the second house. Indeed, if it is in the third, it will occur because of brothers, or because of short journeys, or because of those other things which are signified by the third house. However, if it is in the fourth, it will occur because of parents, or inheritances, or other things which are signified by the fourth house. If indeed, it is in the fifth, it will occur because of children, or women who are not wives or girlfriends, or those other things which are signified by the fifth house. And if it is in the sixth, it will occur because of infirmities, or slaves, or slavegirls, or those other things which are signified by the sixth house. However, if it is in the seventh, it will occur because of wives, or associates, or enemies, or because of one of those things signified by the seventh house. If it is in the eighth, it will occur because of death, or because of those things which are inherited from the dead, or because of one of the other things which are signified by the eighth house. And if it is in the ninth, it will occur because of religion, or religious people, or long journeys, or because of the seeking of those things which pertain to future eternal life, or one of the other things which are signified by the ninth house. However, if it is in the tenth it will occur because of a king, a kingdom, or a magistrate, or any of the other things which are signified by the tenth house. If indeed, it is in the eleventh, it will occur because of hope, or friends, or because of one of those other things which are signified by the eleventh house. But if it is in the twelfth, it will occur because of hidden enemies or large animals, or one of the other things signified by the twelfth house.

After you have examined the Lord of the Ascendant and judged concerning his condition, then examine the Lord of the second, and judge concerning him, just as you judged concerning the Lord of the Ascendant. So that if he is free from impediments and is fortunate and strong, judge the goodness and the increase of the substance, and likewise the profits of the citizens and the inhabitants of the region which is signified by the Ascendant and its Lord; and of those things which are signified by the second house in that region. However, if you find him impeded, say the contrary.

Then examine the Lord of the third, and if you find him free, fortunate, and strong, say that their short journeys will be fortunate, useful, and profitable: and that the brothers of this region will get along well with each other, and the rest of the things signified by the third house will be well disposed. However, if you find him impeded, say the contrary.

Next examine the Lord of the fourth, who if you find fortunate and strong, signifies that the fathers of this region will be good to their children, and their land will bear good fruit, and the rest of the things which are signified by the fourth house will be well disposed. However, if you find him impeded, say the contrary.

Then examine the Lord of the fifth, who if you find fortunate and strong, signifies that the children of this region will be good to their parents, and that there will be games and joyful things in this region, and that all things signified by the fifth house will be well disposed. However, if you find him impeded, say the contrary.

Next examine the Lord of the sixth, who if you find fortunate and strong, signifies the health of the bodies of the citizens of this region, and that their slaves, slavegirls, servants and maids will be good

to them; and so too will their small animals; and all of those things which are signified by the sixth house will be well disposed. However, if he is badly disposed, say the contrary.

Next examine the Lord of the seventh, who if you find strong, signifies that their wives will be good to their husbands more often, and that associates will cooperate well with each other, and there will be few enemies (unless perhaps the Lord of the seventh and the Lord of the first aspect each other by an inimical aspect), and all the things which are signified by the seventh house will be well disposed. However, if he is badly disposed, say the contrary.

Then examine the Lord of the eighth, who if you find fortunate and strong, signifies that there will be little mortality in that region, and that apart from a few, the people will not die bad deaths: but will pass away in their beds (unless perhaps malefics impedes the Lord of the Ascendant or the Moon by a great impediment). However, if you find him impeded, say the contrary.

Next examine the Lord of the ninth, who if you find fortunate and strong, signifies that their long journeys will be useful and praiseworthy, and that the religious people of that region will be increased, and that the rest of the things signified by the ninth house will be well disposed in that region. However, if you find to the contrary, judge to the contrary.

Then examine the Lord of the tenth, who if you find fortunate and strong, signifies that the king or ruler of this region will be well disposed, and that he will treat his subjects well, and that the rest of the things signified by the tenth house will also be well disposed. However, if you find him impeded, say the contrary.

Then examine the Lord of the eleventh, who if you find fortunate and strong, signifies that the hopes of the citizens of this region, and their trust, will reach a good end; and that their fortune will increase in the good, and there will be no enmity between them (save for a few); and that all the things signified by the eleventh house will be well disposed. However, if you find him impeded, say the contrary.

Then examine the Lord of the twelfth, who if you find fortunate and strong, signifies that the large animals of the citizens of this region will be well disposed, and will be increased in the good; and that there will be little reproach, and little slander between the citizens; and that the rest of the things signified by the 12th house will be well disposed. However, if you find him impeded, say the contrary.

Whence if you examine all the significators of the twelve houses well, you will be able to see how the accidents of that region will be disposed in the revolution. For according to how you find the Lords of the houses disposed, thus will the accidents of the significators of each house occur - namely, according to the strength or weakness of each one of them, and according to the place of the Lord of that sign from the sign itself. And the adaptation of the Lord of each house, will be according to the aspect of one to another; and according to how the malefics aspect the planet who is the Lord (namely, the Lord of that house).

Also examine the angles and their Lords more diligently and precisely than the rest: since their virtue exceeds the virtue of the others.

## XI

## On What Each One Of The Seven Planets Signifies In The Ascendant, In A Revolution Of The Year

### On Saturn In The Ascendant At The Hour Of The Revolution.

Also examine which planet is in the Ascendant at the hour of the revolution: since if Saturn is there, and he is not the Lord of the Ascendant, it signifies the detriment of the region which is subject to this revolution, in accordance with what is said elsewhere; and it signifies pestilences, such as infirmities, death, famine; and if he is direct, and especially in air signs, he signifies many harmful winds. If indeed, he is retrograde, it will speak against winds, and he will not permit them to strengthen; however, those which do occur will be harmful. However, if he is the Lord of the Ascendant, it will mitigate the aforementioned things, and they will not be as harmful.

### On Jupiter In The Ascendant At The Hour Of The Revolution: What He Signifies

However, if Jupiter is in the Ascendant at the hour of the revolution it signifies the general goodness of the disposition of the year or revolution, and that there will be peace and security, and good will between the men of this region more so than usual; and it will be good for the wealthy people and magnates of the region; and goods and profits will increase; and their business matters will improve. And if he is joined to the Lord of the Ascendant (or the Lord of its exaltation), or this planet to him, from any aspect (especially from trine, or sextile, or corporeal conjunction), and it is in good condition, there will be love between the king of that region and his subjects; and the country folk will come upon good from him, and he will please them.

### On Mars In The Ascendant: What He Signifies

If indeed, Mars is in the Ascendant at the hour of the revolution, namely if he is free, fortunate, and strong, he signifies that an earthquake will happen in this region. And if he is in an eastern sign, he signifies that it will be in the first quarter of this revolution. If indeed, he is in a southern sign, it signifies that it will be in the second quarter of this revolution. If indeed, he is in a western sign, it signifies it will be in the third quarter of this revolution. And if he is in a northern sign, it signifies it will be in the final quarter of this revolution. It also signifies little rain and little war. If he is impeded and in bad condition, say the contrary; namely instead of good, say bad, and instead of bad, say worse, except for rains (since he will not extinguish their power as much in it).

However, if he is on the line of the tenth house, or beyond it by 15 minutes or less, or after it by one degree or less, it signifies that the king or ruler of this region will capture or imprison more of his subjects. And if he is beyond the line by between 15 and 30 minutes, or after the line by between 1 and 3 degrees, he will capture a smaller quantity of them. And if he is beyond the line by between 30 minutes and the end of 1 degree, or after it from 3 degrees up to the end of 5 degrees, he will capture even less of them. And if he is beyond the line by 1 degree up to the end of 2 degrees, or after it from 5 to the end of 10, he will capture less of them again. However, if he is beyond the line by 2 degrees up to 5, or behind it by 10 degrees up to the end of 25 degrees, and the house is not remote, he will imprison almost none (even if he does imprison a few). And even if he imprisons them, nevertheless he will not kill them, and (apart from a few) he won't maim them; yet he will torture them.

However, if Mars is on the line of the fourth house at the hour of the revolution, or in the other degrees or places opposite to the aforementioned, he will kill those who he captures, according to the quantity, proportion, and way by which he captured them when Mars is in the 10th, and according to the places and degree opposite these.

If indeed, he is in the first or seventh in similar places and degrees, he will maim some of them according to the aforementioned quantities and proportions.

## On The Sun In The Ascendant: What He Signifies.

However, if the Sun is in the Ascendant at the hour of the revolution, free from malefics and other impediments, and the Lord of the year or revolution is with him, it signifies the good condition of the wealthy, and the magnates or nobles, and their joy, and the increase of the good, and the success or progress of matters. And if he is received, the removal of evil. However, if he is not in the Ascendant at the hour of the revolution, but is outside of it in a good place from it, free from impediments, he signifies the same, but below what was said above. If indeed, he is impeded, he signifies their detriment, and the contrary of that which I said to you.

## On Venus In The Ascendant: What She Signifies.

If Venus is in the Ascendant at the hour of a revolution, namely free, fortunate, and strong, it signifies joy, gladness, dancing, the and the diminution of battles, and especially signifies young women and young men engaging in sexual activities; and it signifies the good disposition of the Arabs and their goods; and this will all be better if she is with the Lord of the house, or the Lord of the exaltation of the sign in which she is in. And if she is impeded, it signifies the contrary of the aforementioned.

## On Mercury In The Ascendant: What He Signifies

If indeed, Mercury is in the Ascendant at the hour of a revolution, in the aspect of benefics, and is free from impediments (namely fortunate and strong), and he himself is the Lord of the year, he signifies the good condition, good disposition, and utility of the wise (namely, judges, and medical doctors), and of merchants, writers, and boys: and this will be better if he is joined with the Lord of the domicile or exaltation of the sign which he is in. However, if he is impeded, it signifies the contrary of those things which I said to you.

## On The Moon In The Ascendant: What She Signifies

If the Moon is in the Ascendant at the hour of a revolution, or is in the house of the Lord of the year or revolution, joined to him by body, or by aspect (but not by opposition), and is otherwise free from impediments, it signifies an abundance of waters or rain, and the increase of rivers and streams, and their flooding; the increase of cold, and the goodness of the disposition of men, and that they will rejoice in the good. However, if she is impeded, the aforementioned will be decreased, or possibly annihilated.

# XII

# On Saturn And Mars, If They Are Impeded In A Revolution, When They Are Above The Earth

Likewise, you will examine in the hour of a revolution if Mars and Saturn are impeded above the earth, since this signifies the severity of the year or revolution. And this more strongly so if Mars receives Saturn, and commits disposition to him: since this signifies serious and lasting accidents, and that these significations or detriments will appear and manifest: for they will signify the detriment and weakness of the king or ruler, and of the wealthy, and of the nobles, or magnates (namely those who are fit for kingship); and that faith and religion will be reduced (in fact they will be annihilated), and their religious men will suffer detriment; and that there will be many thieves, and highwaymen, or mercenaries; and wars and contentions will be multiplied; and there will be more disputes between men than usual, and even between the religious; and they will be envious of one another; and especially those to whom pride and vainglory is fitting; and this more seriously so if Saturn is in the tenth.

And the more the malefics are elevated above the earth: the more serious the accidents will be. And it will be worse still if the Moon is under the earth and commits her disposition to Saturn while he is placed above the earth, or is joined to him by opposition or square aspect: since then it signifies severe detriments, and great tribulations, and horrible and fearful things, such as the death of the king, and of magnates and the wealthy, or nobles, or a change of those in charge of the kingdom for the worse; and this more strongly so if the malefics themselves are retrograde, occidental, or otherwise impeded. However, if they are direct, or oriental, and not impeded, their significations will be more remitted.

And if Mars does not commit his disposition to Saturn, the significations of Saturn will not be so intense, and the significations of Mars will be stronger, and especially in contentions and battles. And if Saturn commits his disposition to Mars, the significations of Mars will be more intense, and the significations of Saturn will be decreased. And if benefics are above the earth, namely direct, fortunate, and strong, it signifies the removal of evil and the increase of the good; and this more strongly so if Jupiter is so disposed in one of his own dignities and is oriental. And Venus is stronger when she is occidental, provided that she is otherwise fortunate. Whence, if a planet goes out from under the rays of the Sun, it is like a man who had fallen ill, and is now freed, and begins to resume his powers, and is increased bit by bit, until he returns to his original strength, provided that the malefics do not aspect the planet: since then it is like a sick man who the crisis has come over, and who appears to have escaped, only to relapse afterwards. And when a planet enters under the rays, it is like a man who had been healthy, and begins to fall ill; or who was young, and begins to grow old, until his natural heat is gone.

## XIII

## On The Planets: When They Enter Into The Degree Of Their Exaltation

Again, examine if Saturn is entering into Libra, or is in Libra, and especially in the twenty-first degree of it: since his virtue will be greatly increased, and his significations will be made greater; and this more strongly so if he receives the disposition of other planets, and especially of the malefics. For then it signifies changes, and great, wondrous, and stupendous things; which was touched on in the recounting of the conjunction which Mars and Saturn make in the beginning of Cancer.

Also examine whether Jupiter is entering into Cancer, or is in Cancer, especially in the fifteenth degree of it: since then his virtue will be increased, and his significations will be made greater; and this more strongly so if he receives the disposition of one of the benefics. For it signifies great things, and wondrous, famous, and long lasting changes, nevertheless, they will be for the better.

Likewise, examine if Mars is entering into Capricorn, or is in it, and especially in the twenty-eighth degree of it: since then his significations will be increased and made greater; and this more strongly so if he receives disposition from the other planets, and especially from a malefic: for this signifies great and terrible things, of those things which seem to pertain to Mars.

And it is like this for all the other planets: that if they are found to be entering into their exaltation in the hour of a revolution, their significations will be increased and made greater (namely benefics for the good, and malefics for the contrary of good). But the significations of the superiors are considered more, since they are more vehement, and stronger, and loftier, and more notable

And Messala said that when the year is revolved, examine the benefics and malefics to see if they aspect from a fixed sign: for if so, what they signify will be prolonged, for good or evil. And if they aspect from a mobile sign, this will only be slight. If indeed, they aspect from a common sign, it will moderate.

# Tractate VIII

## *On Eclipses*

After this, if you know that an eclipse was going to happen in the same year, or in the same revolution, examine the Lord of the sign in which you saw it was going to happen; and see what his condition is, and how he interacts with the Lord of the sign of the Ascendant of the eclipse that is going to happen, and whether they aspect each other or not. And likewise, how he interacts with the Lord of the year or revolution, if they aspect each other or not; and whether benefics or malefics aspect him or not: since if the benefics aspect him, and also the Lord of the Ascendant of the eclipse (or the Lord of the revolution, or other benefic planets), it signifies good. However, if malefics aspect him, unless perhaps they receive him from a trine or sextile aspect (since reception reduces their malice, even if it does not completely destroy it): but if the aforementioned planets (or one of them), do not aspect him from a praiseworthy aspect, it signifies evil. If they aspect him together with the malefics, and are not impeded, they will neither signify this nor that. However, if they are impeded it signifies evil, yet slightly remitted. If they aspect without benefics, or the benefics aspect without them, it signifies good, yet slightly remitted.

Likewise examine the significator of the king, and see whether the aforementioned planets (namely the Lord of the sign where there ought to be an eclipse, and the Lord of the Ascendant of the eclipse) aspect him or not; and whether the benefics or the malefics aspect him: since the benefics signify the good condition of the king; the malefics, to the contrary, signify his bad condition. And the significations which the aforementioned planets signify will be greatly aggravated if they are impeded from the aspects of malefics. And the condition of the king will be more strongly aggravated if his significator is the Lord of the sign in which the eclipse is going to happen: since if this is so, it signifies his undoing. And this will happen when the Sun reaches the degree which is the tenth house at the hour of this eclipse. And if the Lord of the sign in which the eclipse is going to be, is also the Lord of the year (the significator of the commoners), it signifies that detriment is going to come over them. And the time of this effect will be when the Sun reaches the degree which is the Ascendant at the hour of the eclipse to come. And these effects will be in both the king and the commoners, either in their persons or their affairs.

For if the Ascendant of the eclipse is Gemini, Virgo, Libra, the first half of Sagittarius, or in Aquarius, these detriments will happen in their persons. But in Gemini, Libra, and Aquarius, they will likewise happen in birds. And this will more strongly befall them if Saturn is in one of those signs, whether he is direct or whether he is retrograde (but if he is retrograde it will be worse).

However, if the Ascendant is Aries or Capricorn, they will happen to sheep, or goats, or other small animals, according to the substance of the sign.

If indeed, the Ascendant is Taurus, or the last half of Sagittarius, they will happen in cows and in other large animals according to the substance of the sign; but in cows more severely than the others.

However, if the Ascendant is Cancer, or Pisces, they will happen in fish, and other animals living in water, which are useful to men. If it is Scorpio, they will happen in venomous animals, and those stinging with their tails, or other body parts; and more strongly to those living in water.

And always understand the increase of detriment when Saturn is in the sign assigned to that matter.

To know the duration of the detriments from the hour of the eclipse, you will consider how many hours, and how many minutes of the hour, the eclipse lasts. Since if it is a solar eclipse, they will last for one year for every hour of the eclipse, and one month for every five minutes. And if it is a lunar eclipse, they will last one month for every hour, and one day for every two minutes.

And examine to see where the impeding malefics are: since if they are in the tenth, the eleventh, or the ninth, the significations will occur in the seventh clime, and in those inhabited parts of the earth outside of the clime toward the arctic circle.

And if they are in the first, the second, or the twelfth, they will occur in the sixth, fifth, and fourth climes.

And if they are in the seventh, or eighth, or sixth, they will occur in the third, second, and first climes.

And if they are in the fourth, the fifth, or the third, they will occur in the northern parts of the regions in which they occur.

Nevertheless, if the impeding malefics are received, they will impede somewhat less.

And he who God willed to be a master said that if the Sun is the Lord of the Ascendant in the revolution, and Venus is under the rays (since she is the Lord of the Midheaven), the Sun will be the significator of the king. Then you will examine to see what the condition of the king will be like in that year or revolution: which you will be able to know by the place of his significator in the figure of that revolution. Therefore, see where he is, and how he is aspected by the planets, namely whether he is aspected by benefics or malefics; and whether he is in an angle, or a succeedent, or in a cadent (even if this rarely happens), and whether he the Lord of the domicile or exaltation of the sign he in aspects him or not. Since benefics signify good; malefics, to the contrary, signify evil, just as I said to you elsewhere.

You will also examine the significators of all the houses, and whichever of them you find fortunate and strong, judge good for the significations of the house of which that planet is Lord; and whichever of them you find unfortunate and weak (namely retrograde, combust, or cadent from an angle, or from the Ascendant, or from its own house), judge the badness of the house of which this planet is the Lord. And when you examine all of the houses, see in which of them benefics are found: since they increase the significations of these houses according to how fortunate and strong they are (the stronger they are, the more they will increase the significations). However, if they are weak, they will more weakly increase what they increase..

You will also examine the Part of Fortune, which if you find it alone in whatever house it is in, it signifies greater fortune for its significations. However, if some good planet aspects it, it will signify greater fortune. And if it is received by this planet, it signifies even greater fortune. However, if the malefics aspect it by a trine or sextile aspect with reception, it will be as if it is aspected by nobody; if this is without reception, it will reduce the good by one-fourth If indeed, one of the malefics is joined to it by square aspect, or from opposition, or corporeal conjunction, it will take away all of its good, and it will be of no benefit.

You will also examine the house in which the Caput Draconis is in: since it signifies the increase of the house in which he is, as much for good as for evil. For in the sixth he signifies the increase of infirmities, and of the other significations of this house; in the eighth he signifies the increase of mortality, and of the other significations. And with the rest of the houses, you should understand according to the significations of each one of them.

You will likewise examine the Cauda: since she signifies the decrease of the significations of the house in which she is in, as much for good as for evil. For in the sixth she signifies the decrease of infirmities; and in the eighth the decrease of mortality; and of the other significations of these houses. And understand this for the rest of the houses.

And if the Lord of a sign in which there is a benefic promises good, namely that it is free, fortunate and strong, the good will be multiplied: and if it is impeded, the good will be reduced, according to the quantity of the impediment. And if the Lord of the domicile in which there is a malefic who threatens evil, is impeded, this evil will be increased according to the quantity of the impediment; and this more strongly so, if the malefic is northern, or commits its disposition to another malefics who is northern; and if the Lord is free, the evil will be reduced according to the quantity of his strength.

And if the malefic (who is in the house of the impeding planet) commits his disposition to another malefic placed in the sixth, it signifies a multitude of infirmities: and this more strongly so, if he commits disposition from opposition or square aspect; however, if it is from trine or sextile, it will be something below this. If it commits to a benefic, it will reduce the significations even more greatly. And if it commits to a malefic placed in the eighth, it signifies mortality; and if it commits from opposition or square aspect, it will be severe; however, if it is from trine or sextile, it will be below this. If indeed, he commits to a benefic, it will be reduced even more. And if it commits to a planet in the ninth, the long journeys of the citizens of this region will be impeded. And if it commits to a planet in the tenth, it signifies the impediment of their officials and leaders. However, if it commits to a planet in the eleventh, it signifies the impediment of men's trust, and of their hope. If it commits to a planet in the twelfth, it signifies the impediment of large animals, and difficulties, enmity, contentions, battles, and captures. And understand similarly for the rest of the houses, for each one according to its significations, as I have touched on elsewhere.

If Venus is not under the rays of the Sun, and not otherwise impeded by a strong impediment, she will not be prohibited from being the significatrix of the king, and especially if she is in Taurus, or Libra.

## XIV

### How The Condition Of The King, And Of The Nobility, And Of The Commoners Is To Be Considered, And What Will Their Condition Be Like

After you have perceived the condition of the aforementioned persons (namely the king, the nobility, the magnates, and the commoners or the country folk), you will consider what will their condition be like in that revolution, and regarding their accidents, and what it will be like between them, namely how the king will be treated by his subjects, and what will follow for them from him, and how the citizens of this region will obey and follow the authorities and their administrators, or those placed over them. And you will examine the condition of each one of the aforementioned according to the condition of the king, which you can examine in the following way. You will see in which house his significator is, since his accidents will take their root or strength from the house he is in, according to its fortune or misfortune; and you will see his impediments, or his escape or liberation from impediments, according to this. And if you see that contrarieties are set to befall him, such as battles, litigation and similar things, you will be able to see what ought to happen to him from these things; and you will be able to know this through his significator, and the strength or weakness of his enemies. Likewise, you will see if he is going to make any journeys (long or short) in that revolution, which you will be able to perceive through the Lord of the ninth, and the Lord of the third. For through the Lord of the ninth you will perceive pilgrimages or long journeys; and through the Lord of the third you will perceive short or nearby journeys. Whence you ought to examine the Lord of the house of journeys in the hour of the revolution and his place: who, if he is well disposed, and in a fortunate and strong place, and is received from the house in which he is in,

signifies that he will travel, or go on a pilgrimage of his own devices, for the purpose of relaxing, or wandering, or for a stroll. And if the Lord is in his first station, or close to it by 5 degrees or less, it signifies slowness and laziness in the pilgrimage, or in travelling. And if it is retrograde, or stationary in its first station, and is received, it signifies that he will travel, but will return in a short space of time. However, if it is like this, but without reception, it signifies that he will not complete his journey, but rather he will suffer detriment in it, and anger or anguish.

Then examine the Lord of the house of the journey and see if the Lord of the domicile he is placed in is retrograde, and aspects his own domicile by a trine or sextile aspect: since this signifies that he will make a journey for the purpose of ordering and arranging his business; and for his subjects. However, if he aspects his domicile from a square aspect, or from opposition, it signifies that he will leave for the purpose of battling with rebels and enemies.

Then examine the significator of the king to see if he is free from impediments, and even if one of the planets who is naturally inimical to him is free; and that the Lord of the journey or pilgrimage is not in the house of infirmity, or in the house of death: since this signifies the guarding, and salvation of his person on that pilgrimage, or on that journey, in accordance with his significator being safe and free from impediments. And even if the significator of the king is found free from these things that were mentioned, if the Lord of the house of journeys or pilgrimages is impeded, it signifies impediment and sorrow, according to the significations of the house in which it is, as much for the house of infirmity as for the house of death, as for all the rest. And if the Lord of the house of the journey or pilgrimage is free from impediments, and the significator of the king is impeded, impediments which will be suspected, and which he feared, will befall him according to the signification of the house in which the significator is impeded, unless perhaps Jupiter aspects and receives him, and Jupiter himself is safe and free: since then all of the malice of whatever one it was, whatever kind of malice it is, will be shattered.

## XV

## Why The King Will Travel, If He Is To Travel

However to know the reason why he travels (if he is set to travel), you will examine the Lord of the house of the pilgrimage or journey, and you will see which house he is in: since one of the significations of that house will be the reason for his journey or pilgrimage.

For if the significator of the king, is in the first, or joined to the Lord of the first, the reason his departure will be the preservation of his own person: and it will seem more likely that he will not be on a pilgrimage, but will be in tranquillity and peace. But if there is another planet between him and the degree of the Ascendant, whether it is lighter or heavier than him, see of what nature it is: since if it is one of those inimical to the significator of the king, someone will come upon him, who will seek to deprive him of his kingdom or his dignity; and who will contend with him to take his dignity or kingdom away. If this was of his accidents, he who arrives will be such a person, that the king himself or the powerful person, will hand over the kingdom or dignity to him of his own free will, and the king himself will place this person in command. And see which house this planet is the Lord of: since from this it will be known who it will be that comes to do this - so that if it is the Lord of the second, it will be one of those people who are signified by the second house. If it is the Lord of the third, it will be one of those people who are signified by the third house. And understand the same for the rest of the significations of the houses; and perhaps that he will build in the land to which he travels.

If indeed, the Lord of the ninth is in the second, or joined to its Lord, it signifies that the journey will be because of profit, namely, to acquire money.

However, if it is in the third, since it will be in the house of his (namely the ninths) enemies, it signifies that his departure will be because of waging war or battling. And he will desire travelling and horse riding, and it will multiply his journeys (even if he will not desire these things with great desire if it is a pilgrimage).

And if it is in the fourth, or joined to its Lord, it signifies that his journey will be horrible and fearful, if it is a pilgrimage. And since it will be in the eighth from its own house (namely the ninth), his death will be feared. And if one of the malefics were to then aspect him by square aspect, or from the opposition, or were corporeally conjunct with him, or were to commit its disposition to him, he will hardly or never evade the danger. However, he will not have much desire for horse riding or travelling, but rather he will desire to be in peace and tranquillity.

And if it is in the fifth, or joined to the Lord of the fifth, it signifies his condition to be praiseworthy: and that he will be joyous, dancing and delighting; and he will desire to have a child, and will produce one according to sex of the sign in which Mars is, and the greater part of the significators (which are the Lord of the first; the Lord of the fifth; the Moon, and the Lord of the house in which she is; and Jupiter). And it also signifies that he will build in the land he is going to set out for, and that he will consider spending time there; but he will hardly or never spend time there.

And if he is in the sixth, or joined to its Lord, (namely so that he commits disposition to it), it signifies that he will become ill in that revolution.

And if it is in the seventh, or joined to its Lord, it signifies some strength of his enemies who are inimical to him, not because of the kingdom or a dignity, but for some other reason: and he will be more intent on sex than he ought to be.

And if it is in the eighth, or joined to its Lord from any aspect without reception, his death will be feared in that revolution. And if the Lord of the eighth receives him, and he does not receive the Lord of the eighth, it will be feared even more. And if he receives the Lord of the eighth, and the Lord of the eighth does not receive him it will be feared even more again, so that hardly or never will it happen that he doesn't die. However, if both of them receive each other, only God will be able to make it so that he doesn't die: since otherwise it will not be possible for him to escape death.

And if it is in the ninth, or is joined to the Lord of the ninth, or some planet in the ninth, he will be on journeys and pilgrimages, both long and short ones.. But if the Lord of the ninth were then cadent, or combust; death or the greatest troubles will be feared for him on his pilgrimage or journey. However, if it is not impeded like this, it signifies that the journey will be good and prosperous, and that he will strive at matters which pertain to religion and mercy, provided that one of the malefics do not aspect him from an inimical aspect: since this signifies that mourning and sorrow will come upon him, from the part of his own household members. And if it is a first square aspect, this will occur from the part of his enemies. However, if it is from a second square aspect, it will happen from the part of slaves, or on account of slaves, or from low-class persons. And it is necessary for you to examine the sign in which the second aspect of the Lord of the house of pilgrimages is, to see if one of the malefics is there; and to see of what substance that sign is: since if it is in the image of men, the misfortune of beasts will be feared with regards to him. However, if it is in the image of other animals, a blow, bite, or venomous puncturing will be feared, according to the substance of this sign.

And if he is in the tenth, or joined to the Lord of the tenth, it signifies goodness, and his strengthening in his kingship, and that his journey will be prolonged, and that he will want to make the matters of the kingdom fit.

And if it is in the eleventh, or joined to the Lord of the eleventh, it signifies the fitness of his own person, and of his followers, whether soldiers or household members, just as he is a king or a chief: and is also signifies the goodness of his mind: and that he will cruelly and eagerly strive to harm his subjects, and what's more, he will send away some guilty people unpunished; and that he will expend substance in the affairs of the kingdom, and also for other reasons, in a good way, and sometimes he will scatter it.

And if it is in the twelfth, or joined to its Lord, he will apply himself to searching for and investigating enemies, both his own, and those of the kingdom; from which you should fear that his enemies are not believed, and he will be occupied with this. And if it aspects the Lord of the twelfth without reception, he will catch them and hurt them. If indeed, it aspects from a trine or sextile aspect without reception, he will hurt them less: if this is with reception, he will hurt them very little or not at all.

And he who God willed to be a Master said that whenever you find the significator of the king joined to the Lord of some house, it signifies the same as if he was in that house, provided that he commits disposition to the Lord of this house.

And Albumashar said that you ought to examine marriages, just as you examine pilgrimages: since the union may be on account of seeking substance. And he said, then examine the Lord of the eighth, and the Lord of the second, to see if the Lord of the eighth commits disposition to the Lord of the second: for if so, he will come upon substance from the marriage. However, if the Lord of the second commits disposition to the Lord of the eighth, the woman will come upon substance from him. And he said that if the Lord of the house of marriage is in the eleventh, he will marry her on account of love and affection: and this more strongly so if the significator of the king and the Lord of the seventh aspect each other. And if it is in the tenth, his kingdom will be increased from this. And if it is in the fifth, he will seek a son from it.

And Ptolemy said to examine the significator of the king, and the Lord of the seventh, and judge according to what was said before in the chapter on pilgrimages. And examine the aspects of benefics and malefics in their places. And he said to examine the nativities of children in addition to this, and see how their condition towards each other will be.

## XVI

### Why The Person Of The King Should Be Feared For, If His Significator Is Under The Rays

And if the significator of the king is under the rays of the Sun, his death will be feared in that revolution. And if it is not under the rays, but is close to them by 12 degrees in front of them (if it is of the superiors), or behind them (if it is one of the inferiors), it will be feared for him when the significator enters under the rays, according to the conjunction of which of the two planets he will be joined: namely the Lord of the house of infirmity, and the Lord of the house of death. If it is neither of them, his death will be feared at the hour when the significator joins the Sun by body, or degree for degree. Also, if the 10th house is Leo, you will also examine whether Mars aspects the Sun at that time, or if they are corporeally conjunct: since if this is so, the killing of the king will be feared in that revolution.

However, to see from where this will come to him, examine in which house Mars is then placed: since the cause of this crime will be born from the significations of this house. And if Saturn aspects him, it will befall the king from a similar signification of difficulty; it will also be feared that the king may be poisoned in that revolution or year.

And he who God willed to be a master said that if the Lord of the year is combust in the Midheaven, it will be feared for the king in the same ways: and these things will happen to him in the region where he is at that time. And if it is combust in the angle of the earth, or the seventh, these things will befall him from someone who comes from outside the country. And he said that in this case, the opposition of malefics, and their square aspect is more serious than the corporeal conjunction. And he said that if the Sun is the significator of the king, and aspects Jupiter from opposition, the king will be inimical to the members of his households, and be suspicious of them, and oppressed by them. And likewise if he is opposite to the Lord of the Ascendant, he will be inimical to the country-folk, and will be suspicious of them, and will impede them.

### On The Mutual Reception of the Planets

After this you should know which planets receive each other, and to which places of the figure they project their rays: since in the regions subject to the signs to which they project their rays, the significations of these planets will have greater efficacy, and will imprint more greatly in these places than in other places.

### Which Planets Are Friends Of The Lord Of The Ascendant In The Revolution.

You should also know which planets are friends of the Lord of the Ascendant of the revolution, or which are his enemies, and which of them aspect more, or to which he commits disposition; and which aspect the Ascendant by a praiseworthy or inimical aspect: since according to how benefics of malefics aspect him or the Ascendant, so you will judge regarding their significations that are going to come in that revolution.

He who God willed to be a master said to know in regards to both malefics (namely Saturn and Mars), that if one of them is in an angle in the revolution of the year, and is direct, and in an earth sign, it signifies the destruction of trees, and the death of animals. And if Mars aspects the significator of the king, and he (namely Mars) is mixed with the light of Saturn, it signifies contention and the spilling of blood.

And Messala said that if he is in an air sign it signifies injuries and enmity. If indeed, he is not in an angle, and aspects the Ascendant, it signifies infirmities and blood; and more severely in every land in whose sign his light is, or his opposition, or square aspect. And he said that if he is retrograde he signifies pestilences. And if he is in a sign that does not aspect the Ascendant, and he is direct, it signifies the infirmity and detriment of seeds. If indeed, he is retrograde, it signifies death, infirmity, and blood.

## XVII

### On Those Things Which Ought To Befall The King In The Revolution Of The Year

After you have seen that the king is to go on a pilgrimage in that year, see what the condition of the Lord of the house of the pilgrimage is like, namely whether it is direct, or free from impediments; and whether it is in its own domicile, or that of another; or moving from the sign in which it is in, to one of its own domiciles; or if it is joined to the Lord of the domicile, or exaltation which it is in. And see in what hour it is going to enter into its own domicile, or in which hour it is going to come to the place in which the Lord of the domicile, or exaltation in which it was when it was joined to him. And see if the Lord of the ninth is retrograde, since if this is so, and it is received, it signifies that he will stroll along in his journey or his pilgrimage, and that he will return quicker than usual with respect to a journey. However, if it is retrograde and is not received it signifies that his journey will be difficult and tiring: and that impediments will befall him because of his journey or pilgrimage. However, if it is slower in course than its own first slowness, it signifies a long delay on his journey or pilgrimage; and that for various reasons he will be detained in it, in the regions to which he travels, or goes on a pilgrimage to; and it will be feared for him in that pilgrimage.

And Albumashar said that if the planet is in its second slowness he will return when the planet is direct, and his pilgrimage will not be completed. However, if it is retrograde, and aspected by the Lord of its house from a square aspect or from opposition, it signifies that his departure will be to war, against enemies who are publicly adversarial to him: and it appears that the war will be outside of his own region. However, if he aspects it by a trine, or sextile aspect, it appears that he will be going against some of his own subjects, who are being made, or have been made, rebels against him. However, if they are joined corporeally, it appears that he will arrive at the place of the contention. And when you have investigated this, examine the significator of the king: who, if you find free from the impediments of malefics, and not joined to any of the planets who are naturally inimical to him; and if the Lord of the pilgrimage is free, in an optimal place from the Ascendant, and is not in a place inimical to the Ascendant, and it is not found

in the 6th or the 8th, it signifies the safety and preservation of his body. However, if his significator is free from the aforementioned impediments, or is the Lord of the sign in which the Lord of the house in which the Lord of pilgrimages is found, and the Lord of the pilgrimage is impeded, it signifies that impediment will happen to him, and it signifies his destruction on that pilgrimage; and perhaps that some illness will befall him which is not of the nature of his usual illnesses, according to the substance of the sign which the Lord of the house of pilgrimages is in. If indeed, his significator is impeded, and the Lord of the house of pilgrimages is free, what was feared will befall him in the pilgrimage, from an illness which he usually suffers from.

You will also see whether the significator of the king is aspected by any of the planets, and whether that planet which aspects him is a benefic or a malefic. For if it is a malefic, it signifies enmity which will happen to the king in that year or revolution. Then you will see whether that malefic has any dignity in the sign in which it aspects the significator of the king: since if it has any dignity there, this enemy will be from the land of the king, according to the person which is signified by that dignity. Wherefore, if it is domicile, he will be one of the greater inhabitants of his land, and one of his household members. However, if it is exaltation, he will be of the more noble men of his kingdom, or of those who came from somewhere else and are in command of some dignities in that kingdom, or perhaps those who acquired some fortune there (signified by the aspect), and great riches, and they are not of powerful people (those who are fit for kingship and royal dignities), and they will of better stock if the aspect is a second square. Indeed, a corporeal conjunction signifies a relationship by marriage on the part of women. If it does not have dignity there, it will be one of the king's own relatives. And if it is triplicity, or term, he will be of the great citizens who are subject to the king. If this aspect is a first square, it signifies that the enemy will be a son of illegitimate birth. But if the aspect is from opposition, the enemy will be an open adversary of the king. If it is a sextile aspect, or a trine, it signifies that it will be someone close to, or from those close to the king.

## XVIII

## On The Conjunction Of Two Malefics, Namely Saturn And Mars, With Any Planet, In The Degree Of Their Exaltation: What Will Be Signified From It

Albumashar said to examine the conjunction of the malefics (namely Saturn and Mars) in a revolution of the year, to see whether they are joined by aspect with any planet who is in the degree of its exaltation (and this is worse if it is by square, or by opposition). For if it is Saturn, it signifies evil and destruction in the region assigned to that planet. And if the aspect of Saturn is from a fixed sign, this signification will be prolonged according to the quantity of degrees which are between their bodies, for years, months, weeks, or days. For if it is a signification which ought to be perfected within the year which you revolve, it will signify months according to the number of degrees. However, if it ought to go past the year or revolution, it will be prolonged for years. However, if it is from a mobile sign, it will signify days according to the number of degrees. And if it is not perfected in that many days, it will signify weeks. And if it is from a common sign, it will be weeks. And if it is not completed in that many weeks, it signifies months. However, if Saturn does not aspect him, but a planet transfers light between them, it signifies the occurrence of displeasing matters over the men of the region of this planet, or destruction and detriment will come over them in the form of peoples who are not of that region. However, if some planet did not transfer light between them, and the rays of Saturn touch the rays of a planet placed in its own exaltation, or a planet who is fit to be able to transfer their light between them, sorrow and grief will enter upon the men of this region, which they need not fear; for the fear will be dissolved, and it will not arrive into act, by the will of God.

### On The Aspect Of Mars To A Planet In Its Own Exaltation.

However, if the aspect of Mars is just as I said to you regarding the aspect of Saturn (and this will be worse if it is a square or opposition), the aforementioned things will occur as said of Saturn, in a similar way and for similar reasons. And this more so, since Mars will perfect accidents which are signified by fire and iron and shedding of blood.

You will also examine the Lord of the ninth, for if he is in the third he signifies that the king is going to make a pilgrimage for the religious reasons, and because of the pilgrimage of eternal life, and the future world of the Creator: since this place in this matter signifies the same as the ninth, even though it is its nadir.

And Albumashar said that if you see him in one of the houses of the 12 houses, do not dismiss his aspects from the places: and the significators of the opposites will be stronger: as is his signification and the significations of the sign that is the nadir of one planet; or if it is his domicile or exaltation, since then it signifies what I said.

## XIX

## When The Sun And Moon Are Joined To One Of The Planets, Or Are Separating From One Of Them: What They Signify

You will consider the Sun and the Moon, and see how they are disposed, namely whether they are joined to one of the planets, or separated from one of them: since the significations will be according to how you see them joined with planets or separating from them, as much by body as by aspect.

And Albumashar said that the square aspect is strong, the sextile is weak, and the conjunction is harsh.

### Again On The Accidents Of The King.

To know the accidents of the king, and how they will occur in the revolution which you seek, you will examine whether the Moon is found in the seventh house or not: since if she is in it, and is increased in light, fast-of-course, and joined to the Lord of the seventh, or the Lord of the exaltation of the seventh, or a planet having two other dignities in it, or a benefic planet, it signifies that the country people will venerate their king, obey him, and eagerly listen to him, and revere him, and none of them will be contrary to him, nor will an army be made by anyone over him, nor against him, nor will anything contrary to him be set in motion; in fact, he will see things which please him, and that which he loves, and which he rejoices about. But if the Moon is then impeded, and is diminished in light and course, and is not received, it signifies the contrary of those things which I said to you: since battles, contentions and wars will happen to him, and he will not be obeyed by his subjects. And this will not only happen to him when she is impeded in the seventh: but it will even be feared that these things will happen to him if she is impeded in other places by terrible impediments, or if she is cadent.

## *The Same on the Good or Bad Condition of the King*

In a revolution of the year, you will also examine the condition of the king (how things will come to him in that revolution) by the condition of the Lord of the Midheaven; and you will be able to weigh this carefully by the condition of Saturn, and the Lord of the year: also by certain other planets, just as I will explain to you. If the Lord of the 10th house is the significator of the king in the revolution of the year, and Saturn is combust (and this more strongly so if he is in front of the Sun), or is the significator of the king, joined to the Lord of the year, and commits disposition to him; and the Lord of the year is joined to a planet placed in the eighth from the Ascendant of the revolution of the year (which is the house signifying death in general), or to a planet placed in the fifth from the Ascendant of the revolution, from opposition or square aspect, it signifies the death of the king in that year or revolution. Or if the significator of the king is joined with the same Lord of the year, and the Lord of the year is corporeally joined to the Lord of the 5th or the 8th in one of the other houses (or from opposition or square aspect), it signifies his death. And this more certainly so, if a malefic is the Lord of the house in which this conjunction is. Likewise if the significator of the king is entering into combustion, it signifies the death of the king; and he will hardly or never be able to evade this. However, if Saturn is oriental, exiting from under the rays of the Sun, the king will not be impeded, but his condition will be improved.

If indeed, this conjunction is with a planet in the 3rd or the 6th, or with the Lord of the 3rd or the 6th, it signifies that an infirmity will befall him in that revolution. And according to the significations, and through the significations of the house in which the conjunction is, and on their occasion, the contrary things which are going to happen to him, will happen to him.

However, if the significator of the king does not commit disposition to the Lord of the year or revolution, it will not cause that much danger, but rather it will cause that much fear. And this is to be understood for every king, or those similar to a king, according to their clime, and according to their region. But if he has already passed over combustion, by as many degrees as are the degrees of his orb, until he touches the tenth minute of the last degree of his combustion, it signifies that anger, sorrow, contention, and likewise, fear, will befall the king in that revolution; and this more strongly so if a malefic aspects him. Since if a malefic does aspect him, it will cast doubt over the king, and it will be feared regarding him, and over him, according to the substance and significations of the house and the sign in which the malefic is placed. So that if it is in the second house, it will be because of substance. And if it is in the third, it will be because of brothers of journeys. And if it is in the fourth it will be because of fathers or inheritances. And if it is in the fifth it will be because of children. And if it is in the sixth it will be because of illness. And if it is in the seventh it will be because of wives. And if it is in the eighth it will be because of death. And if it is in the ninth it will be because of long journeys. And if it is in the tenth it will be because of the kingdom. And if it is in the 11th it will be because of deputies. And if it is in the 12th it will be because of hidden enemies. However, if a benefic aspects him, all of these things will turn around and it will be turned away from him.

And in order for you to know when these things ought to happen, see when the significator of the king will be joined with that malefic: since that will be the time of the arrival of those significations (whether the malefic who impedes him joins to him by body, or by opposition, or by square aspect). You will judge according to whichever one of them arrives first; or when the impeding malefic comes to the 10th from the Ascendant of the revolution, or at least to its Ascendant, unless a benefic then aspects the significator of the king, or the malefic itself, so that it shatters his malice. However, if this conjunction is in an angle, the time of their accidents will be when the significator is combust; or when the malefic reaches the place in which the significator of the king is at the time of the revolution.

## XX

### On The Condition Of The King With Those Placed Under Him

You will be able to know the condition of the king with his subjects, and the conditions of his subjects with him, by the conjoining of their significators to each other, or by their aspect with reception: since the significator who receives the other will commit disposition to him. Whence if the significator of the king commits its disposition to the significator of his subjects, the king will be benevolent and peaceful to his country folk, more so than they are towards him. If the significator of the commoners commits its disposition to the significator of the king, they will be obedient to him, and more benevolent to their king than he is to them. If indeed, both of the significators receive each other, the king will commit his disposition to his subjects and them to him; and one will want what the other wants, and each of them will be peaceful to the other.

## XXI

### On The Particular And Specific Condition Of The King

You will be able to know the particular and specific condition of the king according to the daily accidents which are supposed to befall him in that revolution, by his significator, namely according that you see him daily disposed to the good, or to its contrary. Since according to what will happen to him from day to day up until the end of the revolution, and according to whether he is joined to benefics or malefics, or according to him arriving at a places in which the malefics were at the hour of the revolution, or to other places which were then impeded: for according to this, good or bad things will happen to him (or his liberation from them).

## XXII

### What The Significator Of The King Signifies In An Angular House

Albumashar said that when the significator of the king is in the angle of the Midheaven, it signifies battle for the king; when it is in the Ascendant, the condition of men will be diminished. If it is in the occidental angle, or in the angle of the earth, the country folk will be destroyed. And he said that if the Lord of the year or the significator of the king goes away toward a malefic planet, or to the light of a slow and malefic planet in an angle, destruction and death are to be feared regarding him whose significator it was.

## XXIII

### When The Significator Of The King, Or Any Other Planet, Is Free From Impediments And Moving To Its Exaltation

If the significator of the king stands impeded before his own exaltation, and has already escaped from impediment, and is then joined to some benefic (and this will be better if that benefic receives him), and when he is separated from it, before he arrives to the degree in which he is exalted, if he goes to it immediately, and is not then impeded by any of the malefics - then there will be greater strength and stronger testimony than there ever could be otherwise.

Then see where the Part of the Kingdom falls, since if it falls in a place in which it is impeded, it will signify that contrarieties and impediments will befall the king, in his kingdom in that revolution. However, if it falls in the place of the significator's exaltation (toward which it then moves), it signifies the increase and goodness of his kingdom, without contrarieties, and without any impediments. For those wishing to resist the king, you will examine from the opposite places (however, you will not count them among the natural enemies of the king): since if these places are impeded, they will be impeded, and things will go badly for them. If they are not impeded, they will not be weakened at all in these things which they want against the king.

And if the significator of the king is the significator of one of the signified things, and was the Almutem over them, or if the Part of the Kingdom falls on him, and the Sun commits his own disposition to the significator of the king, in that revolution the king will rule over all of those things which are signified by Saturn, Jupiter, the Sun, and Mercury (if he is masculine). And if the Moon commits her disposition to him, the king will rule over all of those things signified by Mars, Venus, Moon, and Mercury (if he is feminine). It will add to his subjects in his kingdom according to how you see the Lord of the domicile in which its significator is placed, and the Lord of the year, and the Lord of the domicile in which the Lord of the year is placed.

## XXIV

### To Know When A Revolution Lasts For The Whole Year, And When For Half A Year, And When For A Quarter Of The Year

The revolution of the years, and the Lord of the year were discussed above. And I have often named the Lord of the revolution to you when I made mention to you of the Lord of the year, and not by chance: since every Lord of the year is called the Lord of the revolution, but this does not work conversely. For the Lord of the year is when the year you are revolting only requires one revolution: and this is when a fixed sign is ascending at the time of the Sun's entrance into Aries. For that revolution will contain all the quarters of that year in itself: and so the planet who is then the Lord of the year, will be the Lord of the whole year, and of the whole revolution. But if the Ascendant is a common sign, the revolution will only last for half of the year, namely, up until the entrance of the Sun into Libra: then it will be necessary for you to repeat the revolution, and the planet who is ruling at that time will be the Lord of the revolution up until the end of the second half of the year. If the Ascendant is a mobile sign, the revolution will only last until the Sun enters Cancer, and then it will be necessary for you to do the same for the other quarters of the year. And the Lord of the first quarter will be the planet who has rulership in the Sun's entrance into Aries. And the planet who has rulership in the Sun's entrance into Cancer will be the Lord of the second quarter of the year. And the planet who rules over the Sun's entrance into Libra will be the Lord of the third quarter. And the planet who rules over the Sun's entrance into Capricorn will be the Lord of the last quarter.

And in each one of the aforementioned entrances you will always renew your judgement, just as you did for the entrance of the Sun into Aries. And always make the Lord of the first revolution participate with the Lord of the second; and the Lord of the second with the Lord of the third; and the Lord of the third with the Lord of the fourth; until you have finished them all. Since each Lord will have one fourth of the rulership, according to what the Philosopher said. And so, whoever is the Lord of the whole year, will be the Lord of a revolution; whoever is the Lord of a half will be the Lord of a revolution; whoever is the Lord of a quarter will be the Lord of a revolution. However, it is not like this with the Lord of the year, even though he is likewise called the Lord of the year.

### What The Lord Of The Hour Signifies In A Revolution, And The Part Of Fortune

After you have carried out all of the things mentioned above in the order which it was described, and you have examined all the things which were to be examined, just as I said to you, then you will consider the Lord of the hour, and the Part of Fortune, and the Lord of the domicile in which the Part falls. Which, if they are well disposed, will assist the Lord of the year and the significator of the king; which, if you find well disposed, they will increase their good. If however, you find them impeded, they will reduce their impediment. If however, the Part of Fortune and Lord of the hour are impeded, and you find the Lord of the year and the significator of the king impeded, they will increase their impediment; however, you find the Lord of the year and the significator well disposed, they will reduce their good.

And Albumashar said to know the conjunction of the planets with the Lord of the year, and with the significator of the king, and their conjunction with the planets, and their separation and application in respect to one another, in the houses and aspects, and attach the rarer lesser things of their substances (understand this as their works in the circumstances of others) and mix these with the substances of the signs; and know that it might conquer over reception by nature; and learn the condition of the significators; and know their situation to one another, through diversity and binding, and with reception and return of light.*

## XXV

### On The Knowledge Of The Accidents Which Are Going To Come In The Climes, From The Hour Of The Revolution

The climes are divided by planets, just as was said elsewhere. Whence it is necessary for you to consider in the revolution of the year, which clime each planet rules, and to know its condition, if you wish to know the accidents which are going to come in that clime which the planet rules. Since the general accidents of that clime will be according to the condition of the planet who rules over it; and the Lord of the year, and the Lord of the Ascendant of the revolution, and the Lord of the hour, will participate with him. Whence, each of them will provide help or harm to the Lord of the clime, according to what its condition is like, as much in good as in bad. But you are always to remember those things which I said to you in the chapter above, about what the Lord of the year signifies in the places in which he falls, and how far the significations of every significator will be extended. And you will consider the Ascendant of the revolution according to the diversity of the ascensions of any region. And if it ever happens that one planet has signification over two climes, or rules one and participates in another, always place his signification over every region which he rules; and in this way you will be able to know the accidents which are going to come in that region, both general and particular, both for the king and the commoners. Because if the significator of the king and of the region whose year you revolve, is stronger in the tenth house than any of the planets, and is in its own domicile, and is otherwise safe and free, it signifies that the king will rule over all the magnates of that region and be their master. And if there is not a king in that region, these things will happen to him who is greater in that region. And you should not err in the consideration of the significators of the king: since you ought to consider them according to the regions and according to the climes over which their significations are extended.

## XXVI

### What The Lord Of The Year And The Significator Of The King Signify When They Are Well Disposited In The Revolution

Examine the Lord of the year and the significator of the king in the revolution of the year which you revolve, and see how they are disposed, and what is their condition like. If you find them well disposed and in good condition, and free from impediments, and in a place friendly to the Ascendant and the 10th, and in the noted aspect of planets received by them; and those planets receive them; and if the Sun (if it is a revolution in the day), or the Moon (if it is at night); or if one of the luminaries are one of the aforementioned significators (namely, that of the king or of the year); and the luminaries (or one of them) aspect the Ascendant or its Lord, and the luminary is free and in a good place from the Ascendant, it signifies that those people who inhabit that clime or that region (according to the extension of significations of the Lord of the year), will be of good condition, and prosperity, good things, achievement, and strength will happen to them.

And Albumashar said that this will be better if the luminary who has authority commits disposition to the Lord of the Ascendant: for nobles, magnates, and the wealthy, both those who are fit for kingship and others, will be subjected to the king of the same clime, or of the same region; and the citizens or inhabitants of this region will be in peace and tranquillity, and good will be rendered to them.

And if any of the planets commit disposition to the Lord of the year, from the conjunction or some good aspect, and he receives them, joy and happiness will befall them on all sides, according to the substance of the signs which the planets are in, in whose domiciles the luminaries are in; and especially if they aspect the luminaries (or at least if one of them) from a strong and good place. Since then it signifies that in this clime or region there will be security, peace, and health in everything, as much in their things as in their persons; and that they will avert their wills from doing evil, and they will strive to do good, and to maintain faith and justice, without detriment or diminution.

*Again On The Disposition Of The Lord Of The Year, According To The Place In Which He Is In The Revolution Of The Year*

Also examine the Lord of the year in the revolution, and the sign in which he is in, who if he is in good condition, and similarly the sign in which he is placed is well disposed: and the planet himself is fortunate and strong in the terms of a benefic, received by any of the benefics, and himself receiving any of them, it signifies that the king or Lord of the same clime will be in good condition, and will obtain much more than the other kings or magnates of this clime or region: and similarly for the Lord of the region assigned to the sign in which the Lord of the year is placed, and all the inhabitants of the region, and prosperity and good things will befall them.

*Again On The Same.*

And if you find the Lord of any city free, fortunate, and strong, and in good condition received by benefics, and you know the sign of that city or region, announce joy and happiness for its citizens, and the fitness of their things and persons. Therefore you may know to which sign and which planet a city or region belongs to. However, if you find the contrary, you will judge the contrary.

## XXVII

### What The Lord Of The Year And Other Planets Signify If They Are Impeded In The Revolution.

Just as you examined the Lord of the year or revolution, so too is it necessary for you to examine him and also others, in the significations contrary to these. Therefore examine in the revolution of the year, the virtue and power of the Lord of the year and of the other planets: since the effecting of their operations will be according to the places in which they are found at the hour of the revolution.

For if the Lord is impeded, and is in the Ascendant, men will be impeded in their own persons. If however, he is elsewhere outside of the Ascendant, they will be impeded according to the substance of the sign and house, in which he is impeded: so that if he is in the second, substance will be impeded, and so on with the rest of the houses according to their substances; and you will judge according to the significations of each house. If however, another one of the planets is impeded besides the Lord of the year, the significations of the sign will be impeded, and the domicile of which he is the Lord, namely, the domicile whose Lord he is after the Ascendant: so that if the Ascendant is Aries, Taurus will be impeded before Libra; and if the Ascendant is Taurus, Gemini will be impeded before Virgo, and so on for the others. And the condition of the citizens or inhabitants of the region or clime assigned to that planet will be weakened; and they themselves will say that they are impeded, and will be openly aware of their impediment, and they will say they are being deposed, and suppressed, and deprived of their status. And this more strongly so if the Lord of the year or revolution is in one of the angles (and especially in the 4th), and Mars or Saturn aspect him; and when he is in the terms of a malefic (and this more seriously if he is in the end of a sign), unless they are the terms of the malefic which aspects him: since then the impediment will be lessened somewhat, even if it is only slightly. And the impediment will be stronger again if he is besieged by two malefics: since then the evil, and the impediment of the citizens will be doubled, and more strongly so if he is besieged by corporeal conjunction, since this will remove the advantage from them, and bring harm to them. And if it is by opposition, the detriment will be less by one-quarter. If however, it is by square aspect, it will be less by a one-third.

And Albumashar said that if it is a corporeal conjunction if Saturn impedes in front, and Mars behind (understand for one malefic or the other), many of the citizens will be captured, but few of them will be killed. If however, Mars impedes the significator in front, and Saturn behind, many of the captives will be killed. And if the significator is combust, it signifies the destruction of the things and the persons, of the citizens of that region which it rules over. And exiling from that region on account of the intolerable impediment which will befall them.

## *Again On The Same*

Also know in the revolution of the year, which sign and which planet might rule in the revolution of the year over any city: since if the sign is badly disposed and the planet impeded, it signifies detriment and evil, and the destruction of the things and persons of the citizens of that city or region.

And Albumashar said that for every clime you should establish a planet from which the signification of the condition of the king might be taken, so that you might know what will happen to the kings, God willing..

## XXVIII

## On The Knowledge Of The Planetary Significators In The Revolution Of The Year, As Much Of The Significator Of The King, As Of Certain Others

If the Sun is in the 10th in the revolution of the year, not remote from the cusp of the 10th house by more than 4 degrees before, or 10 after, and the Lord of the terms of the degree of the 10th house is in those terms, or aspects its own terms from a good place from the Ascendant, and from a friendly aspect, these two so disposed signify kings and their affairs. For if the Sun (and likewise the Lord of the 10th house) is then free from the impediments of malefics, and in a good place from the Ascendant (and this will be better if the Lord of the terms is in an angle other than the fourth house), the king, and the magnates fit for kingship, and their affairs, will be saved. If however, the Sun and the Lord of the terms of the tenth house are impeded, and the places in which they are, were impeded by the presence of malefics, or their aspects (and this more strongly so if the impediment is from an angle, both of the figure of the revolution and of the significators), kings and the aforementioned magnates, and their affairs, will be impeded and their condition will be made worse.

If however, the 11th and its Lord are safe and free from the impediments of malefics, the soldiers and assistants of the king will be saved. But if they are impeded, these people will be impeded and will suffer detriment.

And Albumashar said that Mercury signifies scribes, businessmen, astronomers, doctors and sages. And he said that if Mercury and his place were adapted and durable, the aforementioned people will be fit. And Jupiter signifies counsellors and leaders, and if he is adapted and safe, these people will be safe. And likewise with Venus and women.

## XXIX

## On The Condition Of The King And The Condition Of His Substance, And On The Condition Of His Soldiers Or Deputies

You will also examine in the revolution of the year to see whether the significator of the king aspects the Part of Fortune: since if he aspects it from a friendly aspect, or is corporeally joined to it, it signifies that his condition will be good and fortunate (and this will be better if his significator is the Lord of the 10th house). You will then examine his substance, and his soldiers and deputies from the 11th house and its Lord: which, if you find well disposed, and in good condition, say that the condition of the king's soldiers and substance will be good and fortunate.

## *If The Lord Of The Year Is The Significator Of The King*

If however, the Lord of the year is the significator of the king, then examine his substance from the second and its Lord, just as you examine the substance of the plebs.

Albumashar sad that you will examine his soldiers and assistants from the triplicity Lords of the sign in which the significator of the king is placed, and you will judge regarding them in that revolution according to how you find them disposed. For if all of them are well disposed, judge their condition to be good throughout the whole year or revolution. If however, you find them badly disposed, judge the contrary. If however, one is well disposed and another is badly disposed, judge according to that. For if the first is well disposed, judge good in the first third of the revolution. If the second, in the second; if the third, in the third. And if you find the contrary, you will judge the contrary. And always make the Lord of the terms in which the significator of the king is placed a participator.

## On The Commoners And Their Substance

You will judge likewise concerning the condition of the common people through the Lord of the year, and of the condition of their substance through the second and its Lord; and the condition of each of them by the Part of Fortune: which if it is well disposed, signifies good: if however, it is badly disposed, it signifies the contrary.

## Again On The Significator Of The King, When His Significator Is Mars Or Saturn

If the significator of the king is Mars or Saturn, and it is not the Lord of the Ascendant or the tenth, or the exaltation of either of them, any one of them will impede by its presence, or opposition, or square aspect; and it will introduce destruction which will come to men from the direction of their own king; and its impediment will be stronger if the planet is in an angle. And if it is in the Ascendant, or in the eastern part, it will come from the direction of the east, and its arrival will be hastened. If it is in the seventh, or in the western part, it will come from the direction of the west, and will be slowed down somewhat. If however, it is in the fourth, or in the northern part, it will come from the direction of the north, and will be slowed down more. If indeed, it is in the 10th, it will come from everywhere, and will happen generally to all men: but it will occur more strongly in the northerly parts and the south, than it will in the east or the west, and the harshness over them will be slowed down, and especially in Germany and the parts adjacent to it.

## When A Benefic Rules

And if the significator of the king is a benefic, and is so placed as I said to you regarding the malefic, it signifies goodness, joy, and the gladness of the citizens or inhabitants of the aforementioned regions, according to where the benefic is in any of them, unless it is impeded from retrogradation, or fall, or descension: since if this is so, it signifies no good.

And Albumashar said, that if there is an evil aspect to the Lord of the Ascendant, or to the significator of substance, there will be unwholesomeness in the body: and if it is from the second, in substance; if from the third, in brothers; if from the fourth from parents, and older kin; if from the fifth, from journeys, and from those things which are from his own hands; if from the sixth, from infirmity; if from the seventh, from women and war; if from the eighth, from the things left behind by the dead, and contention. And if the sign (namely the eighth) is a mobile or a common sign, the king's death will be feared, if it is the significator of the king that is aspected by the malefic Lord. And if this aspect is from the eighth to the significator of the country folk, it is to be feared regarding the country folk. And if the significator of the king and of the country folk is the same planet, it is to be feared regarding everyone: for death will invade them. And if it is from the ninth, it will be from pilgrimages and religious men who seek justice. And if it is from the tenth, it will come from the king and his dominion. And if it is from the eleventh, it will come from friends. And if from the twelfth, from enemies. And he said to say the same for the good if the aspect is from a strong benefic, and the malefic is cadent. And he said to say the same in the revolution of the years of nativities.

## XXX

## On The Impediments Of Malefics, And On Their Aspects: What They Signify; And How Impediments And Impeding Things Can Be Known

Examine the significators in the revolution, namely those of the king and the commoners or country folk, and see whether they are aspected by malefics or not. If malefics aspect them from opposition, and these malefics are impeded, on account of the enmity of the aspect it signifies that impediments will arrive to the king and the country folk from enemies.

And Albumashar said that if the aspect is a square, the impediment will be from men who are not known to be enemies. And he said that since this aspect is moderate, and does not publicise enmity And if they aspect them from sextile, the impediments will come from certain people who are thought to be friends, yet it is not certain whether they are friends or not. If however, they aspect them from a trine aspect, the impediment will be from friends.

And Albumashar said that if the aspects of the malefics were such a figure from their own places, this is just as was said for the significator of the country folk. And if it is to the significator of the king, it will enter over the king. And he said that it is necessary to examine whether the country folk will assist the king: or whether the king will assist the country folk. And this is known through the complexion which there is between each of the significators, and the impeding or aspecting malefic; and this in accordance with their aspect, namely whether it is a trine, or a sextile, or a square, or opposition; and from what places or houses or dignities. If the malefic impeding the significator of the king, or that of the commoners or country folk, is in its own domicile, he from whom the impediment comes, will be from that clime, or that kingdom, or region (namely of those which are signified by those testimonies).So if he was in his domicile, he will be well known in the region, and will be of the household members of the king. And if he is in exaltation, he will be noble and powerful, namely one of those who are fit for kingship. And if he is in triplicity, they will not be one of those who are fit for kingship, but will be close to them. And if it is in term, he will be one of those people below the aforementioned, who are fit to be counts, or marquises, and the like. And if it is in face, he will be one of the more noble people. And if it is of the nobles, it will be of those who are below marquises, but are still magnanimous. If however, it is not in any of the aforementioned dignities, he will not be of good stock, nor known in the region: and men will say they don't know where he came from: and possibly that they will say he was born from an unknown father, or from fornication, or that the people are his father.

And Albumashar said that if the significator of the king is in charge, it will be an enemy from the same clime, and the king will be weak in prohibiting and repelling him. And he said that if the significator of the commoners is in charge, the enemy will not be from that clime, nor from his own rulership. And he said that the significator is the Lord of the year, and the significator of the country folk. And he said that the Moon is the significator of the country folk, and the common people, and she is not in charge: for all who are in charge are significators, but not conversely - since all significators are not in charge.

## XXXI

### What Is Signified By The Retrogradation Of The Significator Of The King, Or The Lord Of The Year, Or The Significator Of The Country Folk

If it ever happens that the significator of the common people is retrograde in the revolution of the year (even if this rarely happens, it still can happen) as is said elsewhere, it threatens truly horrible evil. For the retrogradation of the significator of the king signifies his weakness and his depression; and it will be a great thing if he avoids being deposed from his kingship, and if his kingdom escapes destruction in that year. Similarly, the retrogradation of the Lord of the year signifies the destruction and bad condition of the commoners, and the citizens of this region.

You will examine in whose terms each one of them are. For if they are retrograde in the terms of a malefics (and this more strongly so if those terms are in the domicile of any malefic), this will be a far greater danger, than if it was in the domicile or terms of a benefic; and likewise if the Lord of these terms is impeded, since this will increase the malice again, and multiply it. If however, it is free, it will reduce some of the malice, even if it is not much. If however, the significator is retrograde in the terms of a benefic, it will reduce the impediment; and all the more so, if in addition to this it were in the domicile of a benefic; and more so again if this benefic is well disposed.

## XXXII

### What Mars And Saturn Signify In The Revolution Of The Year When They Are Badly Disposited

When you revolve the year, examine to see if Mars is stationary in his first station, wanting to go retrograde, and is joined with Saturn, or if Saturn is so disposed that he moves toward Mars while he is stationary, or if Mars is moving toward Saturn while retrograde: for this signifies the austerity and hatefulness of men, so that there will not be anyone who wishes to obey his elders, it he can avoid it; and piety will be cut off; and there won't be anyone who zealously feels pity for another, but there will be an abundance of evil-doers, highwaymen, and mercenaries; and slaves will not revere their masters, nor will the religious fear the one ruling them; and this will be worse if Saturn is in Libra, and worse again if he is retrograde, and even worse than this again if the Sun aspects him by opposition, and Mars aspects the Sun, and the Sun Mars; and it will be even worse still if Mars is peregrine joining himself to Saturn. And it will be the ultimate evil beyond all others if the revolution is in the setting of the Sun, or close to it, namely a little bit before or after.

And Albumashar said, and war and disputes will fall between the citizens of the east and the west, and there will be battles in diverse places: therefore strive to understand all of these precise investigations.

## XXXIII

### If The Lord Of The Ascendant, And The Moon And The Other Significators Are Impeded: What Will Follow From This

The Lord of the Ascendant and the Moon signify the matters of the common people in the revolution of the year; which, if they are impeded, and are found in places inimical to the Ascendant, signify impediment that is going to come over men in their persons and in their things, according to the quantity of enmity, and according to the inimical place in which they fall. For if they fall in the sixth, they signify that infirmities and pains are going to come to men in that revolution. If however, they fall in the eighth, they signify death, and this more seriously so if the eighth is a human sign. And if they fall in the 12th, they signify enmity and betrayals according to the substance of the sign in which they are in: so that if they are in Gemini, it will be because of young men and adolescents. If they are in Virgo, it will be because of young women. If they are in Libra, it will be because of men of collected age. If they are in the first half of Sagittarius, or in Aquarius, it will be because of the general mass of men. If they are in Aries or Capricorn, it will be because of small animals. If they are in Taurus, or in the last half of Sagittarius, it will be because of large animals, and those that are ridden. And if they are in Leo, it will be because of wild, hardy, and feral animals. And if they are in Cancer, Scorpio, or Pisces, it will be because of animals spending time in water.

And if the Lord of the exaltation (if the Ascendant is the exaltation of any planet) and the Moon are not impeded in the aforementioned places, it signifies the same as the Lord of the Ascendant does; but it will be below the signification of the Lord of the Ascendant. And the significations or impediment of the Lord of the terms, will be below those of the Lord of the exaltation. And the significations of the triplicity Lord will be below those of the term Lord, if one of them are impeded. And the impediment of the Lord of the face, will be below the impediment of the triplicity Lord.

However, examine to see how the aforementioned planets are aspected by benefics or by malefics: since I say benefics will reduce the impediment, unless they are impeded by combustion or retrogradation; malefics will increase it, unless they are direct and well disposed, and receive the impeded planets inimical to the Ascendant.

And Albumashar said that if the impediment is from Mars, there will be a choleric fever, and sudden death. And if the impediments are from Saturn, there will be a fever from black bile, and death.

## XXXIV

### When War Is Signified In The Revolution Of The Year: Why Will It Be Made Or Incited

If you wished to know whether there will be battles or conflicts in the year which you revolved, and from whence they will be incited, and by whom; examine this matter according to the method which the ancients have handed down to us, and especially that most reverend predecessor of ours Albumashar, who was proficient, and very astute and audacious, in the science of the revolutions of years, and also in all the other areas of astronomy. For then you will erect a figure for the revolution of the year, and establish the Ascendant and the other houses, and all the planets in the domiciles which they were in; and examine Mars, and see from which planet he is being separated from, or from who he has already separated.

For Albumashar said that since the planet from whom Mars is separated is the one who sent him, and who incites war (even if it is a benefic from whom Mars is separated, and even if this benefic is Jupiter): nevertheless the inciter of war will be one of the persons who are signified by Jupiter (if it is Jupiter), and of the more powerful people; and it will be possible that he will be of the class of bishops and similar people. And if he is separated from Saturn (since Saturn in such cases signifies kings), it appears that it will be a king who incites war, or it will be from the advice of old and ignoble men.

And Albumashar said that there will be war if Mars commits his disposition to Saturn, and Saturn is joined with him and receives him. And he said that when Mars is separating from Jupiter and joined to Saturn, without reception, know that he who provokes war, and provokes it for justice, is one of the household members of the king. If however, he is not separating from Jupiter, and is joined to Saturn, the person who incites war, will be one of the ignoble men who are not fit for kingship, and are not of great dignity. And if you see Mars separated from Saturn, and joined to Jupiter, there will not be war, and if there is, it will not be between honourable men, nor Catholics, nor distinguished men, nor bishops, nor any similar people.

Therefore, after you see planet from whom Mars separates, and from whom it seems that the war ought to be incited, and the planet to which he is joined, and you do not see reception; see if their conjunction is in one latitude (and if it is a conjunction of Mars and Saturn, examine which of them is stronger in their own place) - and whoever rises above is stronger, that is, whoever moves over the other. The one who "moves over the other" is who is northern of the other in latitude, as is said above. And if Saturn moves over the other, it signifies the weakness of the war. If however, Mars moves over Saturn, it signifies its strength. You can say the same, if one of them receives the other.

And Albumashar said that the first thing that it is necessary for you to know in this chapter is what the kingdom's strength is like, and how great it is: for then you can know the time of the duration of the kingdom. And when you have seen what will happen for the kingdom, and you have seen the time of its duration, then examine the hour of the destruction of those rising up from the impediment of Saturn, Jupiter, and Mars; or of that planet from whom Mars is being separated.

And Albumashar said to know its destruction from the destruction of those three planets, since these are the ones who incite war. And if Mars is retrograde, and the others are direct, war will appear, but its appearance will not come to an end until Mars goes direct, for only then will its appearance come to an end. And he said that if a war is incited, and Mars is cadent from the Ascendant of the year, or peregrine, it will be weak.

And Albumashar said, if you see the first side received by his enemies, and it is opposite to the first side, or in its square aspect, there will be "strength of the sword". If however, the first side receives the second side, there will not be war. If the second is not received, and you see war, and the first side is received, there will not be strength in the insurgents; and there will be a stability of men with the first king, and their inclination will be towards him. And he said to likewise examine the second side: since reception is an aid and an appeasement, and a strength of the received. Therefore, if it does not receive, it will be peregrine, and there will not be trust in it, nor strength. And he said that the first side in the condition of the king; and their secrets, and the intention is the degree of Saturn. The second side is the degree of Jupiter. And he said that I have already made this clear to you in the book of conjunctions.

## XXXV

## Which Of The Planets Signify Wars In The Revolution Of The Year, And Which Of Them Is The Dispositor

Albumashar said that Mars arranges wars, and signifies the masters of the armies: and the captains of soldiers; which, if he is strong in an angle, signifies war; and if he is cadent, he doesn't signify it. And he said that the Moon is the key to these: and if she is adapted, they will be fit; and if she is impeded, they will be impeded.

## Again On The Same, According To Albumashar

Albumashar said that in the revolution of the year, if Mars is in one of the angles of the Ascendant, whichever one it is, he will incite war, according to the quantity of his own strength, and therefore he will incite war when he is in the square aspect of Saturn and Jupiter. And if you see that Mars is going to incite war, examine in what place he falls from the Ascendant, and also see where the Part of War falls, and which of the houses the Part rules: and see if any of the malefics (namely, one or more) aspect the house of Mars or the Part of War, from opposition, or square aspect, or if they are in them; or if they aspect the sign which rules over that city or region for which you revolve the year; or if the ones who rule over that clime or region aspect the significator of the king, or another magnate, from opposition or square aspect, or is corporeally joined with him: this signifies that if the king or nobleman will have a war with someone or some people in that revolution, his enemies will obtain victory over him; or at least grief and sorrow will enter over him, and tribulations and difficulties. And if the planet who is his significator is combust, it will signify the same and it will be feared regarding him; and if it is retrograde it signifies his flight, and the strength of his enemies, and his fall and dejection: likewise if he is first in a good place from the Ascendant, and then goes to a weak place.

## Again On The Same, If One Of The Malefics Rules, What Follows From It

Albumashar said that when Mars rules over the signification of the year, and is strong, there will be a war with ingenuity, worries, plundering and strong killing. And if Saturn rules over the year, or the quarter, there will be war by seduction and slyness, and by discipline and ingenuity. And he said when one malefic presides over the year, and another malefic is the Lord of a quarter: there will be war in the same quarter without a doubt. And likewise if a malefic aspects the Lord of the year, or the quarter, from opposition, or square aspect; or if the Lord of the quarter is in the seventh, or retrograde. And he said that if a malefic is inimical to the Lord of the quarter, it will be in the same quarter; and likewise if he is inimical to the Lord of the month, in the same month.

## XXXVI

## When War Is Signified In The Revolution Of The Year, And If It Is Signified, When Is Victory Signified, And When Flight, Or Total Defeat, And When Peace, Or The Extinction Of The War

After you have seen in the revolution of the year, that war is signified in the future, examine the planet who signifies it: since if it is direct and in good condition, it will not permit the war to end. And it will endure, and will be annulled from the side of the king or ruler of the region in which you are, or for which you revolve the year which you seek; and it signifies peace and the extinction of the war. Also examine how the significator is aspected by the planets, and by how many of them: since a multitude of planets aspecting him (and this more strongly so if they have dignity in the place where he is) will signify his strength and victory, and that he will be assisted more than his adversary, as much by his own people as from outsiders. And if it is stationary in its second station, it signifies him to be strong and powerful in that war, and likewise for his followers. If however, it is stationary in its first station, it signifies his strength in the beginning of the war; however, in the end he will not perfect it well, nor will he persevere. If however, it is retrograde, it signifies his flight and fracture.

And if the significator of the enemy, or the one wanting to wage war with him, is as I said to you of the significator of your kingdom by the aforementioned conditions, you will judge the contrary of what you judged. If however, the significator is direct, as I said, and not impeded, either it signifies peace, or if there is war or a battle, it signifies victory. And if you wish to know from the side of whose peoples, or whose assistants, his victory will be, and what will be the reason for his conquest of his enemies, examine which planet better aspect him, and from greater dignity: since this planet will be the significator of those who are the cause of his victory. So that if it was the Sun or Saturn, it will be a king or another great nobleman (but the Sun signifies younger people than Saturn). If however, it were Mars, they would be bellicose soldiers. And if it were Jupiter, they would be magnates, nobles, and wise men. And if it were Mercury, they would be learned men, both noble and common. And if it were the

Moon, they will be men who carry out trading, navigation, and similar things.

And Albumashar said that if it is Venus, they will be Arabs.

## XXXVII

### How It Should Be Elected For Someone Wanting To Go To War

If however, someone wishes to go to war, after which you see it is going to happen in that revolution, and you wish to elect them an hour for doing this, examine the three superior planets, to see whether they are retrograde or direct. If they are retrograde, Albumashar said to make the beginning of your hour for going to war, when they go direct. And if they are direct, when they begin going retrograde, and likewise when they begin burning up. And if they are combust, when they begin to emerge. And if they are occidental, when they become oriental. And if they are oriental, when they become occidental. Or when they are changed from the signs in which they were (namely at the hour in which the planets signify war), since then the planet is said to change figure; and likewise when it substance or significations are changed.

If however, Mars is received in the hour of the revolution (and this will be better if he is received by one of the benefics from domicile or exaltation), he will extinguish the war in that year, or that revolution. And if he is received from the tenth, it not only signifies that the war will be extinguished, but it also signifies peace in that year.

## XXXVIII

### Through What Kind Of Men, Or People, Will The War Or Battle Come To Be

When you examine the erected figure of the revolution of the year, and you find that there will be war or a battle, examine which side Mars appears to assist: for he will assist that side with whose significator he is friendlier with, and which he aspects more; and from which side of the east or west he is; and from which side is the planet, from which he separates - since that will be on the side of the Ascendant, and the one to whom Mars joins will be on the side of the opposition. For from whatever side Mars is, if

he is direct, the war will come to be from that side, by bellicose and virtuous men, who will confidently show their face to the enemy, and will not turn their backs to them. If he is retrograde, it will come to be through various men, who wish to be praised for what they don't do, and sometimes attribute to themselves something that others are doing, and they say more than they do, and threaten more than they strike, and who call for war with great urgency, but do not remain steadfast in war, but abandon it over the shoulders of others, and boast that they did great things, and are similar to pillaging thieves and highwaymen. And if Mars is stationary, it will be a stronger war, as I said to you above in another chapter where the station of the significator was discussed.

Likewise examine Saturn, who, even if he leads men to war ponderously, nevertheless he brings strong and terrible things before all the others, and more pestilences; wherefore he should be examined in this matter, since he signifies this from the side on which he is.

And Albumashar said that Saturn signifies a harsh condition for the citizens of the same side in which he is in, according to the quantity of the substance of the sign he is in, and the terms of his place, after you follow him, by succession; and the Ascendant, and the house of substance, and brothers, and the rest, up to the end of the twelve signs. And he said that when Saturn is retrograde, it will be as I said to you regarding Mars, but more severe. And someone could use these same chapters in questions of war, and in the hours of setting out to war, and in the taking out of war chariots and banners. And do not believe this chapter, or any other, to contradict the others, but distinguish the times, and harmonise the writings.

And Albumashar said that a retrograde planet signifies mixture in matters, and reversal and diversity, also war, and the victory of the Lord of the same clime that belongs to that planet. And a stationary planet signifies the desire for evil, and the reiteration of that which has now ceased, and killing. And its aspect signifies evil, disputes, seduction, and slyness.

## XXXIX

### Whether The Captain Of The Adversary Is Young Or Old

However if you wish to know the age of the captain or leader of the other side, examine the impeding malefic; if he does not impede, examine his place; and examine the place of the significator of the enemy. If both of them are oriental from the Sun, the captain, or leader will be young, and he will be younger still, if the Moon is oriental with them. If they are occidental, he will be old. If however, one is oriental, and the other occidental, he will be of middle age, not very young, nor very old: but a malefic signifies one younger than the Lord of the seventh, if it is oriental; and one older, if it is occidental.

## XL

### If The Significator Of War Is Pacified With The Lord Of The Year: What Will Follow From This

Albumashar said that if the significator of war is pacified with the Lord of the year, it will be good in that year. And if he is pacified with the Lord of the half year, or with the Lord of the quarter, it will be good in the same half, or in the same quarter. And if he is pacified with the Lord of the month, it will be good in the same month. And if with the Lord of the day, in the same day.

I say "pacified", which means "joined to him by body or aspect, with reception".

And he said that if the significator is pacified with the Lord of the profection, it will be good in the last half of the month. Understand the same regarding the Lord of the day and Lord of the hour.

And if the pacification is from the beginning of the sign up to seven and a half degrees, it will be good in the first six months. And if it is from seven and a half degrees up to the end of the fifteenth degree, it will be good from three months up to the halfway point of the year. And if it is from fifteen degrees, up to twenty-two and a half degrees, it will be in the last six months of the year. And if it is from twenty-two and a half degrees up to the end of the

sign, it will be from the ninth month up until the end of the year.

Understand the same regarding the month, the day, and the hour, and in those times there will be security and peace, and men will not suffer damage, but they will be free from danger, and it won't be necessary for them to fear.

## XLI

### What Malefic Planets Signify When They Are In Human Signs In The Revolution

Examine in the revolution, when you revolve the year, and see if one of the malefic planets are in human signs, namely in Gemini, Virgo, Libra, the first half of Sagittarius, or in Aquarius, and see whether it is slow-of-course. Likewise, examine if he is joined to the other malefic by body, or by opposition or square aspect (whether that planet to whom he is joined is retrograde, or direct): since this signifies that detriment is going to come to men. And if he is retrograde this will happen faster, and with greater injury. And if the conjunction is from angles, it will be more severe and crafty.

If the malefic who aspects the other (and the other is the retrograde one who is joined to him) is in the tenth, there will be impediment, whether harshness or evil, which will then be signified for all men generally, and in every region, unless the planet who is the Lord of the sign which rules over some region operates to the contrary; and this will be stronger and more severe, if the malefic who is impeding is in the Midheaven, and the Lord of the Ascendant is the Lord of the year, since then an obstacle will be found for him, and the detriment will begin from the eastern parts, and extend up to the west.

If however, the malefic who aspects the other in the tenth, and the retrograde one who is joined to him, are in the fourth, the impediment will begin from the western parts, and will extend up until the uttermost ends of south Aethiopia, and these regions will be oppressed because of this.

If however, the aspecting malefic is in the 7th, and the retrograde planet joined to him is in the 4th, the beginning of the impediment will be everywhere, and will be extended up to the west from the north.

And if the two malefics are being joined, the impediment will be more severe, and will appear more quickly; and there will be severe mortality in men, and this more strongly so, if it is Saturn who impedes, since he naturally impedes the significations of the sign in which he is placed.

Therefore you will examine in which place the malefic falls from the place of the other malefic (namely the slow one): since if they are joined in a common sign, or if he who is joined to the other joins him from a common sign, the evil will be determined by death. If however, it is in a fixed sign, or a mobile sign, the end of the signification will be according to the nature of whichever of the two malefics is then stronger by the place in which it is found. For if Mars is stronger, it will be determined by killing, or by pestilent and hot infirmities, according to whether he is more prepared to be joined with the Lord of the 8th or the Lord of the 6th, or with a planet who transfers light between him and one of them. If however, Saturn is stronger, they will either be determined by melancholic illnesses or pestilences, according to how he is joined (or prepared to join) with one of those planets, as I said regarding Mars.

And Albumashar said that you will mix the strength of death with him. And these things will happen more strongly if their conjunction is from the angles. If however, it is outside of the angles, their significations will be reduced, and they will not impede as much, and will be improved.

And Albumashar said that there will be greater destruction in the side in which the impeding malefic is placed. And he said to know therefore what cities and provinces the sign has, in which the two malefics are placed: since the aforementioned evil will occur in these places.

## XLII

### On The Matter Which Introduces Fear In The Revolution Of The Year, And What The Malefics Signify In The Angles

Sometimes horrible things tend to appear in the revolution of the year, which introduce fear. Whence if you see one of these things when you revolve the year, see whether the planet who introduces the fear is joined to, or aspects, Saturn or Jupiter (since these two are heavier than the rest): since the fear will be aggravated, and there will be fear regarding it. And this more strongly so if the aforementioned planets are impeded, and especially Saturn, since he will signify that long lasting pains will follow from that fear, and death.

If however, the planet doesn't aspect Saturn or Jupiter, and is not joined to one of them, it will harm very little. If however, the significator of the evil is in an angle, it signifies a multitude of evil, and its durability.

And Albumashar said that if it is before an angle it will be a small amount and of a brief duration. And he said that it will be helped by dignity in this time, and it will be help with both good and evil.

## XLIII

### What Is Signified If The Lord Of The Sign In Which The Lord Of The Year Is Placed Aspects Him, Or If It Does Not Aspect Him

In revolutions, look to see which planet is the Lord of the domicile in which the Lord of the year is placed: and see whether this planet aspects the Lord of the year by a trine or sextile aspect, and is not impeded. Since if this is so, men will be in a good state, namely in peace, tranquillity, and happiness. If it is not impeded, and is not aspected, or if it is aspected, and is impeded, judge between the two. If however, he is not aspected, and is impeded, it signifies sorrow, worry, fear, litigation or contentions, and the complete contrary to what it signified for the good.

And Albumashar said that this is according to the quantity of the complexion of the substance of the sign in which the significator is placed: since if he is in the first, it will be in their persons; if in the second, it will be in substance, and understand the same for the rest of the houses.

## XLIV

### On The Revolution Of The Year, When It Is At Sunset

You will consider whether the revolution of the year is at sunset. For Albumashar said that if this is so, the Sun will commit his disposition to the Moon, who is the luminary of the night. Therefore examine her, and where her place is from the Ascendant: and if she is fit to take up the disposition of the revolution, examine the Lord of the sign in which she is then placed; and see how it is aspected by the planets, and judge according to what you see. For if he is aspected by benefics, it signifies good; malefics will signify evil.

Also examine how she is placed with Saturn, that is, in what aspect, namely a trine or a sextile; and whether Saturn receives her from domicile, or exaltation, or from two other dignities: since then Saturn will commit his disposition to her. For if Saturn commits his disposition to her, she will be made stronger and will dispose the matters of that revolution better. If indeed, she commits her disposition to him, she will not disposit the revolution afterwards, and if she does disposit it, its disposition will be wicked.

And Albumashar said to examine the increase of her light, and its diminution, and whether an eclipse is going to happen in that year. And he said that in an eclipse it will be necessary for you to examine its place, and the degree of its fulfilment; and in a solar eclipse, its degree, and the place of the conjunction, and the Almutem over these places, and how the aspecting planets aspect them. The Almutem is the planet who is in charge of the degree of the conjunction, or prevention, by the multitude of its dignity or fortitudes.

## XLV

### If The Lord Of The Ascendant Is Impeded In The Revolution Of The Year: What Follows From It

Examine the Lord of the Ascendant in the revolution of the year. If you find him impeded, announce that there will be impediment over men in that year, according to the substance of the sign of the Ascendant: so that if the Ascendant is a sign formed in the image of men, it will befall them in their persons. If however, the Ascendant is a sign formed in the image of another animal, it will happen to animals formed in that image. And this will happen more severely in the land which is ruled by this sign, and the land which is ruled by that planet.

And Albumashar said that it will be more from the region of the east, and in the regions assigned to the planet who is the Lord of the ascending sign, than it will be in other regions: so that if the Ascendant is Libra, and Venus is impeded, the lands of Libra will suffer impediment from winds, and infirmities, and headaches, and similar things.

And if the Ascendant is Taurus, the lands of Taurus will suffer impediment, and detriment from cold, snow, and dryness; the destruction of the fruits of the trees; and the impediment of cattle, large pigs, and the like, according to the nature and disposition of each region, unless Mars operates to the contrary.

And if the Ascendant is Gemini, and Mercury is impeded, the lands of Gemini will suffer from the blowing of winds, and from the corruption of the air, and from pains in the head, the intestines, the tongue, the lungs, and in the breathing places of the body.

And if the Ascendant is Virgo, the lands of Virgo will suffer from coldness, dryness, moderate sterility, and from pains in the chest and the area of the heart, unless Jupiter operates to the contrary.

And if the Ascendant is Cancer, and the Moon is impeded, the lands of Cancer will suffer from rain, and pains in the eyes and the entire head, unless Saturn operates to the contrary.

And if the Ascendant is Leo, and the Sun is impeded, the lands of Leo will suffer from the heat of the air, and from the flowing down of rheum, and illnesses of the head and similar things, unless Saturn operates to the contrary in coldness and binding together.

And if the Ascendant is Scorpio, and Mars is impeded, the lands of Scorpio will be impeded by water and venomous reptiles, and from pains in the head, arms, and private parts, and similar things.

And if the Ascendant is Aries, and Mars is impeded, the lands of Aries will be impeded by the heat of the air, and the flowing down of rheum, and pains in the head, and similar things, unless Venus operates to the contrary.

And if the Ascendant is Sagittarius, and Jupiter is impeded, the lands of Sagittarius will be impeded by persons in the first part of the year, and by animals which are ridden in the latter half of the year; from illnesses of the head, and legs, and similar things.

If however, the Ascendant is Pisces, the lands of Pisces will be impeded by the flooding of waters, and from illnesses of the feet, such as gout, and similar things, unless Mercury operates to the contrary.

And if the Ascendant is Capricorn, and Saturn is impeded, then the lands of Capricorn will be impeded by coldness, dryness, sterility, and from pains in the knees, the joints, the head, and the feet, and similar things, unless the Moon operates to the contrary.

And if the Ascendant is Aquarius, and Saturn is impeded, the lands of Aquarius will be impeded by moist winds, and illnesses of the legs, the neck, and the head, unless the Sun operates to the contrary.

And if the Lord of the Ascendant of the revolution rules over other lands besides those ruled by the ascending sign, they will participate with the lands of the ascending sign in being impeded, even if they will not be impeded as much as those which are assigned to the ascending sign. And if the ascending signs are safe, and the planets free, the lands subject to them will be saved, joined to the condition of each of them.

And Albumashar said that after you have examined the Ascendant, examine the second, the third, the fourth, the fifth, and the rest of the houses, and their Lords, just as you examined the first, up until the end of the signs.

And he said to make the angles and their Lords more dignified, since there is work and strength for them above the rest of the signs which have the signification of the affairs of kings.

## XLVI

### What Follows From The Conjunction Of The Two Malefics With The Lord Of The Year, Or With The Significator Of The King

In the revolution of the year, examine the conjunction of the Lord of the year and the significator of the king, with the malefics. For if two malefics are joined with the Lord of the year (whether they join him, or he joins them), it signifies that severity will come over the country people or the commoners; and this will occur in the land or region of the sign in which the malefics are placed. If however, they are in diverse signs, it will happen in diverse regions, according to which ones are assigned to these signs. If however, the conjunction is with the significator of the king, it signifies that severity will come over the king from the regions mentioned above.

And Albumashar said that for victory the loftiness of the strength of malefics in his journey is examined. And he said that the testimony of Saturn and Jupiter is sought in this, according to how it is revealed to you in chapter of conjunctions.

### Again On The Same

Albumashar said that if one of the two malefics is joined to the other, and they are in human signs, whether by body, or by opposition, or by square, provided that they are joined together; and if one of the malefics is Saturn, and he is stronger than Mars, it will signify many, and serious infirmities, and very many will die from them. If however, it is Mars, and he is stronger than Saturn, it will signify killings, in the place of Saturn's infirmities. If however, one is in a human sign, and the other is in another kind of sign, each will introduce an impediment according to whatever sign it is in; however, this will be less, and it won't matter whether one or two are diurnal or nocturnal, or masculine or feminine. If however, they are received, their impediments will be reduced according to the reception.

And Albumashar said regarding those who are ill in the same year, health and safety will be hoped for them, besides the few who will die. If however, these malefic are received, there will be less death, and less killing.

And Albumashar said that they will be mixed with each other.

## XLVII

## How The Bodies Of The King And The Commoners Are To Be Examined In The Revolution Of The Year

After you have examined what will follow from the conjunction of malefics with the Lord of the year, and with the significator of the king. What now remains to be said in this chapter is how the condition of the persons of the commoners or country folk, and the king, are to be examined. Indeed, you will examine the condition of the persons of the commoners or country folk, and the king, from the Lord of the year, and from the Lord of the Ascendant; and see what aspects are in the Ascendant of the revolution (whether benefics or malefics aspect it). Since if benefics aspect the Ascendant and the Lord of the year, they signify the good condition of their bodies in that revolution; and this will be better, if they aspect the Lord of the Ascendant in addition to this; and better again if they aspect the Moon in addition to this; and even more perfect, if the Part of Fortune is there aspected by benefics.

If however, malefics aspect the Ascendant, and the other significators (and the Part of Fortune) are not safe, nor well placed, judge the contrary of those things which I said to you, namely, in the place of good, announce evil. So that if malefics impede the Lord of the year, you will judge impediments according to the substance of the impeding malefic. For Saturn signifies impediment from long lasting pains, and death. Mars indeed, signifies impediment by fire and iron and murder, as much in fleeing, as otherwise.

However, you will examine the condition of the king from the Sun, and from the 10th and its Lord; and also from the Part of Fortune and its Lord: which, if you find well disposed in the trine or sextile aspect of benefics, or in their square aspect with reception, or in their corporeal conjunction, and benefics aspect the tenth, judge the soundness of the kings body, everywhere and in whole. If however, you find the contrary, you will judge the contrary. And if you find the conditions to be less good than what I said to you, then you will judge less good things. And understand that the same is to be said about the bad condition of his body. And if you wish to make Saturn a participator in the aforementioned, you will not err.

## XLVIII

## Which Of The Planets Signify Kings And Kingdoms, And On The Impediments Of The Four Angles

Albumashar said that the Sun and Saturn signify kings and kingdoms. And he said that whatever kind of planet you find impeded out of the 4 angles, say that there will be evil from its substance. Whence, you should see where the Sun and the Moon fall in the figure of the revolution. For if they fall in good and strong places from the 10th, or in the 10th itself, they signify the general good condition of the king, and the good disposition of the kingdom.

Likewise the angles are to be examined, and their Lords. For if you find the angles and their Lords fortunate; and make the Moon and the Part of Fortune participators, which if you find well disposed, (namely fortunate and strong), announce good generally. If however, you find them badly disposed, announce the contrary. If however, you find some of them well disposed, and others badly disposed, announce according to what you find. For according to the significations of the well disposed ones, announce good; according to the significations of the badly disposed ones, announce evil.

## Again On The Same, According To Albumashar

Albumashar said that the stronger of the kings, will be the king whose clime and city are ruled by the Lord of the year. After this, it follows by the succession of the strengths of the signs; and all nativities which are under that sign, or under the sign of the Lord of the year, will be more trustworthy for the good, and of a better rank and dignity among men, unless their nativity is impeded in the root. Whence you ought to examine in the hour of a revolution, if the Lord of the year is the significator of the nativity, or of a region or clime over which a king rules, since that king whose kingdom is under the rulership of the Lord of the year, will be stronger than other kings, and his kingdom will be better, longer lasting, and in better condition than other kingdoms.

And those who are born in those cities, or regions, or that kingdom in this revolution (and the Moon should be made fortunate and strong) will be more fortunate and famous; and better reputed than those who are born in other kingdoms, provided that the planet who is the significator of whichever one of them, is not impeded in their root nativity. Even if the Part of Fortune is impeded, it will complete that which I said regarding the Part of Fortune. If however, the significator of the nativity of one of them is impeded, that native will not be as fortunate; nevertheless, he will be less unfortunate than other unfortunate people in other kingdoms.

## XLIX

### If The Moon Or Mercury Are The Lord Of The Year, Or The Significator Of The King, And Are Aspected By Malefics, What Follows From This; And On The Part Of Fortune And Its Lord

If it ever happens that the Moon or Mercury is the Lord of the year, or the significator of the king, and one of the malefics are joined with it, and impede it by an aspect or conjunction, it the condition of the year, and the mob or the common people, will be weakened and made worse - if it is the Lord of the year. If indeed, it is the significator of the king, his condition will be weakened and made worse, and this will not be possible to avoid or prohibit: and this will be on account of the planet who is the significator, since it will not be of such

virtue, that it will be able to expel the impediment introduced to it by the malefic with whom it is joined; unless the Part of Fortune (and its Lord operates to the contrary, by doing good on account of its disposition. If indeed, they are impeded, they will not signify good, but the contrary of it, according to the substance of the sign in which they are in: since the impediment will fall according to the significations of this sign, and over the significations of this sign; and then it will be then said to be inimical to the significator.

Then examine and see whether the significator of the king commits its disposition or strength to the significator of the commoners: since the disposition of the year or of the king, will be worse, if the significator will be impeded by a malefic, and is joined to a planet which is inimical to the Ascendant; and vice versa.

## L

### On The Lord Of The Year Committing Disposition To The Significator Of The King, What Will Follow From Thence

Albumashar said that if the Lord of the year commits his disposition to the significator of the king from a square aspect, the king will bear down upon the country folk in pursuit of substance; and for this reason difficulties will enter over them. And if it is from a trine or sextile aspect, they will surrender the wealth, without the entry of difficulties on the country folk. And he said that if it commits disposition without an aspect, this will be without the work of the king, and the king will think that he will not see it. And he said that if the significator of the king commits disposition to the Lord of the year, the king will withdraw substance in the same year. And he said that if however, the Lord of the 11th aspects the significator of the king, this will be done with his own good mind.

## LI

### On The Conjunction Of The Caput Draconis With Saturn, And On The Conjunction Of The Cauda With Mars, And What Follows From These Things

Albumashar said that the conjunction of the Caput Draconis with Saturn, signifies the impediment of the substance of the sign in which they are joined, just as an eclipse of the Sun and Moon does, unless their malice is shattered by the aspect of benefics.

Whence if the conjunction of Saturn with the Caput Draconis is in Aries, it signifies that impediment is going to come in that revolution in sheep and the like, unless Mars aspects them by a trine or sextile aspect, and Mars himself is fortunate: there will also be harm in the matters of kings, unless the significator of the king, or the Lord of the tenth house operates to the contrary.

If their conjunction is in Leo, the impediment will be in wild animals living by seizure of prey, and it will harm kings somewhat, even if it is not much.

And if their conjunction is in the first half of Sagittarius, the impediments will be in men. If however, they are in its final half, the impediments will be in large animals, but more strongly so in those which are ridden.

And if their conjunction is in Taurus, the impediments will be in cows and the like, and trees and plants; and it will also harm sheep and boys somewhat, and there will be little rain, and the yearly produce will be reduced, unless Venus and the Moon operate to the contrary.

And if it is in Virgo, the impediments will be in women, and especially in young women, and it will touch young men to some extent, and the seeds will be reduced, and those things which are born of the earth which turn into seeds.

And if it is in Capricorn, the impediments will be in goats and the like, and it will harm those things born of the earth to some extent (even though it will not be as much as in Virgo); and the coldness will be increased, unless Mars operates to the contrary.

If however, it is in Gemini, the impediments will be in humans, and more so in youths and adolescents, less so in those who are of mature age, and even less again in old people; and there will be impediments in birds, and harmful winds will blow.

And if it is in Libra, the impediments will be in humans, and more so in those of mature age, or complete age, and middle aged; less in old men and adolescents, and those who are 45 or under; and many winds will blow.

And if it is in Aquarius, the impediments will be in humans, and more so in old men and the lower-class, however, it will be less so in those who are of collected age, and even less again in youths and adolescents.

And indeed, if the Caput's conjunction is with Mars in the aforementioned signs, the impediments signified by Mars will be much below those of Saturn, but they will be through heat and dryness, unless Jupiter or Saturn operate to the contrary.

If however, their conjunction is in Cancer, the impediments will be from impeding and devastating locusts, in the regions in which they are in, and especially in the eastern and hot regions; and there will be more rain than usual in the regions fit for this.

And Albumashar said that the things born of the earth will be increased, and the things creeping upon the earth, as much the harmful ones as the non-harmful.

And if it is in Scorpio, the impediments will be in venomous animals, as much terrestrial as aquatic, and especially in scorpions.

And if it is in Pisces in animals spending time in water, and especially those which are of utility to men.

## LII

### On The Conjunction Of Mars And Saturn With The Cauda

If Mars is joined with the Cauda, it signifies destruction, killings, famine, and a multitude of evils.

If however, the Cauda is with Saturn, it signifies famine, and little good in whatever sign it is placed, and severe destructions, and cold, and the greatest fears, and the destruction of the harvest, and an overabundance of evil, and this will be in the region in which they are in.

## LIII

### On The Conjunction Of The Two Malefics (Namely, Saturn And Mars), With A Planet In The Degree Of Its Exaltation: What Follows From It

Albumashar said to examine the conjunction of the malefics (namely Saturn and Mars) in the revolution of the year, to see whether they are joined by aspect with some other planet who is in the degree of its exaltation (and this will be worse if it is by square or opposition). For if the aspecting malefic is Saturn, it signifies evil and destruction in the region assigned to that planet. And if the aspect of Saturn is from a fixed sign, the significations will be prolonged according to the quantity of degrees which are between their bodies; for years, months, weeks, or days. For if the signification is one which ought to be perfected within the year which you revolve, months will be signified according to the number of degrees. If however, the signification crosses over that year or revolution, it will be prolonged for years.

If however, it is a mobile sign, it signifies days according to the number of degrees. And if it is not perfected in that many days, it signifies weeks.

And if it is one of the common signs, it signifies weeks. And if it is not completed in that many weeks, it signifies months.

If however, Saturn does not aspect him, but another planet transfers light between them, it signifies the coming of the displeasing things over the men of the region of that planet; or destruction and detriment will come over them from peoples which are not from that region. If however, there is no planet which transfers light between them, and the rays of Saturn touch the rays of a planet placed in its own exaltation, or a planet which is fit to be able to transfer light between them, sorrow and grief will enter upon the men of this region, which they ought not to fear: for the fear will be dissolved, and will not arrive into act, by the will of God.

If however, the aspect of Mars is as I said regarding the aspect of Saturn (and this will be worse if it is a square or an opposition) the aforementioned things will happen just as I said regarding Saturn, in a similar way and for similar reasons, and more, since Mars perfects the accidents which he signifies by fire and iron and bloodshed.

## LIV

### On The Lord Of The Fourth, If It Is In The House Of Pilgrimage At The Hour Of The Revolution: What It Signifies

If there are prisoners at the hour of the revolution in the city or region in which you are, just as is sometimes tends to happen, and you wish to know what will happen from this in the that revolution, examine the Lord of the fourth from the Ascendant, and see whether he is in the ninth. Since if he is in there, it signifies the pilgrimage of those who are in prison in that city or region in which you revolve, and their exit from prison in that revolution: and this will happen to them without the permission and will of the king, or powerful person, or others who preside over this region. I say this will happen, unless the significator of the king aspects the Lord of the fourth from a trine or sextile aspect: since in this case it will be from his will. If however, it is from square aspect, or opposition, then not only will they exit without his permission, but also against his wishes and orders. And if the significator of the king or ruler is in the ninth, and the Lord of the fourth commits his disposition to this significator, it signifies that the king or ruler himself will lead the conquered men from the prisons by his own will. And if the Lord of the ninth does not receive disposition from the Lord of the fourth in the ninth, it signifies that an enemy of the king or ruler, will lead the prisoners away from the prisons.

And Albumashar said to mix the conjunction of the planets with each other, and judge according to their mixture.

## LV

### What It Signifies When One Planet Commits Its Disposition To Another In The Revolution

You will also see whether any of the planets commits its disposition to another in the revolution. For if the significator of the king commits his disposition to Saturn, the religious men (serving their religion), and old and decrepit men, and those doing heavy works, will find good from the king: and the king will spend on buildings of the religious, and also on his own private ones.

And if Saturn is then above the earth he will build royal buildings. And if he is below the earth he will build canals, ditches, and aqueducts, and will clear land, and this more so if it is in Ascendant, near the end of it; and more strongly in the third or the ninth; and he will be occupied with heavy works.

And if he commits to Jupiter, noble citizens, magnates, skilled men, the famous, bishops and similar people will obtain good from the king.

And if he commits to Mars, bellicose soldiers and carriers of arms, and leaders of armies, and the wagers of war, will obtain good from the king, and will be honoured by him, and he will hear them, and bring them closer to himself.

And if he commits to the Sun, those kindred to the king will find from him, and especially those who are fit for kingship.

And if he commits to Venus, women and all those people for whom Venus is the significator will obtain good from the king, and he will bring them into his household.

And if he commits to Mercury, then it signifies that wise men, or counsellors of the affairs of the king, scribes, sculptors, and artists, will find good , utility, and favour from the king in the same year, and he will hear them and bring them into his household.

If however, he commits to the Moon, it signifies that those who are signified by that planet to which she is joined, and to whom the Moon herself commits disposition, will find good from the king, and sailors likewise.

You will say the same of the Lord of the ninth: that if he commits his disposition to the aforementioned planets in a revolution, the aforementioned persons will find good from the Pope, or from other bishops, and similar people, according to what was said regarding the significator of the king and from the king.

## LVI

### When A Planet Is The Lord Of The Year, What It Signifies In Every Sign, And In Every Triplicity, And First, On Saturn

Allowing that Saturn is naturally malefic, he can still sometimes signify good things and fortune accidentally, and so can any malefic: just as benefics, allowing they naturally have the signify good, can still sometimes signify evil accidentally. Therefore, a malefic signifies evil and impediments through its own nature; and if he is joined with another malefic, or aspects it from any aspect, and if he himself is impeded, he will impede the other. If however, he is free from impediments, and well disposed, and joined with him by a trine or sextile aspect, he will not impede the other malefic, but will signify an adaption to good. Similarly, if a benefic is impeded and weak, its significations will be weakened. Whence if he is then aspected by an impeded malefic, or another planet who is in bad condition, he will take up its malice, and will signify evil, and impediment, and the impediment will be according to the nature of the malefic impeding that benefic.

Therefore, after you have found the Lord of the year, and the significator of the commoners or the country folk, and it is in Aries, or Leo, or Sagittarius, it signifies the appearance of things which will amaze the men in the cities, regions, or lands, which are ruled by that sign, and especially in the eastern parts; and this will be more concerning the wealthy, magnates, and powerful people surpassing the common magnates or nobles: and these things will come to be through shrewd and ingenious men, and those hiding their matters, and the like, and remaining silent about them. And

140

signs and wondrous portents will be shown, and this under the appearance of beautiful apparitions and imitations.

Then you will see whether he who rules the revolution is a benefic or malefic.

If indeed, it is a malefic, and it is Saturn, and he is free from impediments (namely fortunate and strong), it signifies the good condition and good disposition of his significations. If however, he is impeded and in bad condition at the hour of the revolution, it signifies impediment, and the bad disposition of all of his significations, and those which are in his division, which significations are the wealthy, old things, the religious, the religious living under a rule, Jews, farmers, the elderly and decrepit, and the like. Discord will arise between men; and they will abound in lies, and they will condemn each other.

And if Saturn is in good condition, and well disposed in the place in which he is in at the time, he signifies patience, exactness, and the investigation into all matters, as much of nobles as of the commoners, in that year. And he signifies that the country folk will obey their masters or kings, and they will be humble to them, and the empire or kingdom, or the rulership of the region in which you revolve the year will be exalted; and its name and fame will be increased.

And if Saturn is in bad condition, and is threatening evil or impediments in that revolution, and Jupiter aspects him from a trine or sextile aspect, and is himself free (namely fortunate and strong), he will shatter the malice of Saturn, and destroy it, and will not allow it to harm or impede.

If however, the Sun aspects him from a trine or sextile aspect, and is not cadent from the Ascendant, or from an angle (except for the tenth), and is not otherwise unfortunate, he will shatter one third of Saturn's malice.

If however, another benefic aspects him, and this benefic is fortunate and strong, and aspects him from the mentioned aspects (or if Jupiter aspects from a square aspect), it will shatter and destroy half of Saturn's malice. However, from other aspects, the benefic will reduce the malice of Saturn according to its condition.

If however, he is not aspected by a benefic who destroys or reduces his malice, it signifies the death of the wealthy, and of magnates; and their jealousy towards each other, and accusations, and negligence, and the hatred of the commoners (and those subject to them) towards them; it also signifies death because of waters, and impediments and fear, and death in the land or region which is signified by the sign in which he then is.

But if he is oriental, in his own lightdirect, fast-of-course, or in any of his own dignities, or in the dignity of some planet who is friendly to him (as are Jupiter, and both luminaries), and this planet is joined to him, and receives him, and he is in a good place from the Ascendant, and in his own ayz, he signifies that in that year men will apply themselves to the disposition of heavy and laborious works, as are works of water, planting of trees, the gathering together and raising up of groves, and the clearing of lands, and their care, the building of cities, castles, houses, and palaces, and things similar to these.

## LVII

## On The Corporeal Conjunction of Saturn and Jupiter

If Jupiter is corporeally joined to Saturn, the works which men do will be in silence, and they will work by religious means, and with the appearance of faith, and the observance of the precepts of justice.

If however, he aspects him by a trine or sextile aspect (and this will be better if it is with reception) it signifies that dominion will come over of the kings and magnates, which are in the regions which are ruled by the sign in which Jupiter is then placed, and it signifies matters which they will rejoice over.

If however, he aspects Saturn from opposition, it signifies that the contrary of what I said will happen: since it signifies that contentions of war will come to the kings, the wealthy, or the magnates from those regions which are in the division of the sign in which Saturn is placed - from the kings, magnates, or wealthy men of the regions which are in the division of the sign in which Jupiter is placed.

And Albumashar said that this will be according to the quantity of the degrees which are between Saturn and Jupiter, and the place of their conjunction, up to the hour in which the war and contrariety is.

And he said that if the aspect of Jupiter to Saturn is a square aspect, there will be differences between them in the place of wars, and these will be of the matters which are in the division of Saturn.

And if Saturn is in Taurus, Leo, Sagittarius, or Pisces, or even in Aries, and Jupiter aspects him, it signifies the increase of the goods of the wealthy, the magnates, and the nobility in that year.

And if the aspect is a trine or sextile, and he is in a good place from the Ascendant, it signifies that good, joy, and pleasing things will come to the commoners or country folk from the nobles or magnates.

## LVIII

### What Is Signified If Mars Is Joined To Saturn In The Revolution, And He Is In Good Condition

And if Saturn is the Lord of the year or revolution: and is in good condition, and likewise Mars, and Mars aspects him from a trine or sextile aspect, and each receives the other from domicile, exaltation, or two other dignities, or if both are received by one planet, it signifies that in the same year the substance of the commoners, the mob, or the country folk, will increase, and their honour and reputation will be mixed with magnates and the wealthy. If however, Mars aspects him, or is corporeally joined to him, and Mars is in bad condition, it signifies the diminution of the status of the wealthy and the magnates in that revolution, who are in the division of Aries or Leo or Sagittarius (in a short space of time without a great delay); and of those who are in the division of the sign in which each of the malefics are, the citizens of these regions will be evil towards each other, and there will be little piety between them, and no mercy.

But if their aspect is a trine or sextile, it signifies that gifts and similar things from which they will rejoice and be happy, will come to the nobles, the wealthy, or the magnates, who are in the division of Aries, Leo, and Sagittarius, from the citizens who

are in the division of the sign in which Mars is placed. The other inhabitants of these regions will also be in good condition, and pleasing things will come to them from the regions which are in the division of the sign in which Mars is placed.

If however, it is an opposition or a square aspect without reception, it signifies the contrary of what was said. For in the place of gifts, and other pleasing things, evil, injuries, disputes, contentions, and contrarieties will come between the wealthy or nobles and magnates of the regions which are in the division of the sign in which Mars is placed, and the wealthy and magnates of the aforementioned regions. For they will arise in them due to battles wars will arise in them, and they will strive against them, to expel them from their cities and regions, nor will this continue through them; and the roads between them will be cut off, and they will not allow things to be carried from these region to the others; and the entirety of the citizens in the regions which are in the division of the sign in which Mars is placed, will strive to injure and strike the citizens of the other aforementioned cities.

And if Mars is corporeally joined with Saturn, it signifies war and bloodshed, and a multitude of fevers: and it even signifies quartan fevers, and pestilences in the eastern parts, and it signifies youths, and that war and much killing by iron will fall between the wealthy and magnates.

And Albumashar said that the grain and wine will be oppressed, and butter will be multiplied. And he said that if Mars is close to the Ascendant of the year, there will be many battles; and there will be eye pains, inseparable infirmities; and thunder will be multiplied, and there will be detriment in the earth of every kind, unless Jupiter and Venus operate to the contrary; who, if they aspect Saturn and Mars, will shatter their malice: and only Jupiter can shatter the malice of each of them and lead them back to good.

## LIX

## If The Sun Is Joined To Saturn In The Revolution, And Both Of Them Are In Good Condition

If however, Saturn is the Lord of the year or revolution, and the Sun is joined to him, and both of them are in good condition, it signifies that the wealthy or the magnates of this region will exercise their works in seeking kingship, and sublime and splendid magistracies which pertain to nobles or magnates: and this will also be in part inclining towards the side of the honouring and pleasing of the Most High. If indeed, the aspect is a trine or sextile, gifts will come to those who are in the division of the sign in which the Sun is in.

And Albumashar said that goods and things for sale will be taken away from these parts; and the things will be taken from those who are signified by the Sun; and the merriment and dignities of men will be increased. If however, the aspect is an opposition, disputes, war, and contrarieties will arrive instead of the gifts, and things for sale will not be transferred from one of these regions to the other; and it will be to the contrary of what was said. And wicked and terrible rumours will come in the place of the prior happy things. If it is a square aspect, Albumashar said that there will not be war, nor will battles be multiplied; but there will be dispute and discord between wealthy men and magnates.

## LX

## If Venus Is Joined To Saturn In The Revolution And They Are In Good Condition

And if Saturn is the Lord of the year or revolution, and Venus is joined to him, it signifies the seeking of Venusian things, as are games, delights, songs, relaxation, sex, and similar things in which men delight; and that the country folk will mix with the wealthy from the beginning of the revolution, but their familiarity will not last. If however, Venus aspects him from a trine or sextile aspect, gifts and friendship will arrive to the wealthy who are in the division of the sign in which Saturn is placed, from the citizens who are in the cities which are in the division of the sign in which Venus is placed; and pleasing things will come to them, and that which is brought to them will be of the nature of Venus.

And Albumashar said that if however, she aspects him from opposition, there will be war and contrarieties instead of gifts and pleasing things, and these wealthy people will proceed to war with those wealthy people; and what was brought will be cut off from those cities; and the substance from those parts will be reduced. And he said that the wealth will be shattered, and evil rumours will come, and the good condition will be changed to bad, and disputes, mourning, and sorrow. And the root of all of these things will be from women, and because of women, and Venusian matters; and men will be more honourable than usual, and this more greatly so, if Saturn receives her, and the revolution is at night.

If however, she aspects him by square aspect, Albumashar said, that battles will not appear; but there will be diversities in the matters between the wealthy and commoners; and there will be the most ferocious dissension and discord between the citizens of those cities or regions - such that if a father was a citizen of one of the cities which was in the division of the sign in which Saturn is placed, and his son was a citizen of one of those cities which are in the division of the sign in which Venus is placed, they would not agree in the things which they ought to do. And likewise they would quarrel and contend with each other in their own business, and discuss their business openly with others and between themselves.

## LXI

## On Mercury, If He Is Joined To Saturn In The Revolution, And They Are In Good Condition

If however, Saturn is the Lord of the year or revolution, and Mercury is joined to him, it signifies that men, and especially the wealthy and magnates, shall be of a will to acquire pretences, and eloquence of speech, and of philosophy, astronomy, medicine, and dialectic. And likewise, one who is born under such a figure will study in these and be made fruitful in them and will advance in them.

And Albumashar said that the appearance of these things in this time, will be in the wealthy and the citizens of the regions which are in his division. And if Mercury aspects him from a trine or sextile aspect, good things will come to the wealthy from all of these; and merchandise for sale will be transferred to them; and substance and wealth will be multiplied from these things; and this will be praised in the cities which are in the division of Saturn and the sign in which he is placed: and the merchandise will often be of the aforementioned mercurial sort; and they will be firm and stable in their plans.

If however, he aspects Saturn from opposition, there will be contrarieties and war instead of gifts and familiarity; and the wealthy people will proceed contrary to them, in order to overcome them, and completely defeat them, and expel them from their own homes; and whatever good things were transferred from them to the magnates will be cut off; and substance will be deceased from the same parts; and wealth will be destroyed; and bad rumours will be heard, and the good will be hidden; and evil will appear from these cities, and this more strongly so if Mercury is impeded by malefics, or if he has any mixture with them. If however, he is made fortunate by benefics, then he will impede less, but it will not destroy the impediment of opposition.

If indeed, it is a square aspect, it will be below this, and war will not appear; nevertheless, there will be diversities between those wealthy men or magnates, and between the wealthy and the country folk.

And Albumashar said that the cause of these matters will be Mercurial things, just as he expounded this in his greater book, according to how he himself testified. Understand this, and keep it in your mind.

## LXII

### On The Conjunction Of The Moon With Saturn In The Revolution, If They Are Both In Good Condition

Indeed if Saturn is the Lord of the year or revolution, and the Moon is joined to him, there will be an appearance of legates and rumours, and scouts, and constitution of the affairs of braggarts; and this will be amongst the wealthy and the magnates, and even in the commoners, and they will want to become equal to magnates in that revolution.

And if the Moon aspects Saturn at that time from a trine or sextile aspect, it signifies that gifts, and things from which they will rejoice will come to the magnates or nobles who are in the division of the sign in which the Moon is placed; and merchandise and substance will be conveyed from those cities, and their wealth will be multiplied from this. And Albumashar said that their things will be transferred to the wealthy who are in the division of the sign in which Saturn is placed, and much of the things will be lunar things; and men will profit from planting.

And he said that if the Moon is aspecting Saturn from opposition, things will be to the contrary of what was said: for in the place of gifts and good things there will be contrarieties and wars; and those wealthy men who are in the division of the sign in which the Moon is placed, will go into their own harm and weakness; and those things which were transferred to them from those parts will be destroyed; and the wealth will be shattered and the trade routes will be cut off; and evil rumours will arise and appear; and the good will be destroyed and changed into evil.

And if the aspect of the Moon to Saturn is a square, it signifies that war will not appear; nevertheless, there will be contraries between the wealthy and magnates, and the country folk or commoners, because of lunar things.

## LXIII

### What Saturn Signifies In Each Of The Signs, And In Each Of The Triplicities, And In Each Of The Houses, Whether He Is The Lord Of The Year Or Not

### ♄ ♈

If Saturn is the Lord of the year, and he is in Aries or its triplicity, he signifies the severity of the matters of magnates and noblemen who are in the eastern parts; but chiefly in Aries.

Whence, if he is in Aries, he signifies many winds, and the death of women of prayer, or of those pertaining to religion, and this in the regions of Thoracey and Aiaroc; and a scarcity of grain, wine, and butter, and also oils and fats. If indeed, he is impeded, he signifies a multitude of thieves and highwaymen, and many tribulations in that revolution. And if he is the sole significator, and is cadent from the Ascendant and not aspecting it, and he is direct, he signifies that difficulties and tribulations will enter over the nobles.

And Albumashar said that if he is retrograde he will destroy the houses of substance, and their coffers; and this more severely so, if he receives the disposition of Mars: since then he signifies severe coldness, and the death of animals, in addition to what was said about battles and wars. If however, he is not aspected by Mars, the cold and winter will be severe, according to the disposition of that region, and animals will die in it. And he said, if he is not retrograde, he signifies that there will be contentions between businessmen, and pillaging and evil, and this more strongly so if Mars aspects him from an angle. If however, he aspects Saturn from a cadent, it will reduce the impediment, in fact it will almost be completely destroyed.

And Messala said that if he is direct in an angle, he signifies much rain; and contentions of the wealthy, and this more strongly so if he receives the rulership of Mars, and his strength - for then it signifies that the country folk or commoners will contend with the king. And if he is retrograde, the condition of men will be burdened. And he said that if Saturn receives disposition from Mars and the Moon at the same time, it signifies severe coldness, and the death of animals, and wars and battles.

Pay attention in the revolutions of the years of the world to see if Saturn is in a fixed sign: since then he has the signification of mortality, and the scarcity and decrease of things born from the earth. However, in Leo it is stronger, harsher, and longer-lasting than in the others. Indeed, in Scorpio it is less than in Leo. In Taurus, less than Scorpio. In Aquarius, less than Taurus. And by however, much worse he is disposed, by that much more will his malice be increased. And this more strongly so if Mars assists him, unless Jupiter (who diminishes Saturn's malice according to his own disposition) operates to the contrary.

If Saturn's latitude is northern, it signifies the corruption of the air, and its thickness and darkness in the usual and required seasons, more than usual. If his latitude is southern, it signifies severe coldness, and a multitude of frost, in its own seasons.

And if he is oriental he signifies the mournings and sorrows of the wealthy or magnates, and of their thoughts; and it seems that this will happen to them because of the frost. If however, he is occidental, he signifies that an earthquake is going to occur in that year: and you will know this from the quantity of degrees which there are; and he especially signifies this in the eastern parts; however, it is to be feared wherever you revolve the year and you find it so. But if he is oriental, this will be less; and less again if he is fortunate and strong. If however, he happens to be retrograde, it will be much worse.

## LXIV

ħ ♌

Know that if he is in Leo, and his latitude is northern, it signifies a multitude of rains, and the corruption of the matters of magnates and commoners, and the destruction of the acquisitions of businesses men.

And if he is oriental, it signifies that infirmities are going to come to the country folk and low-class persons.

If however, he is occidental, it signifies pestilences which will arrive in the earth, and mortality.

If indeed, he is retrograde, it signifies harsh things are going to come from the accidents which will happen to men, and that they will be prolonged and long lasting. If however, he is direct, it signifies their levity.

## LXV

ħ ♐

And if he is in Sagittarius, and his latitude is northern, it signifies a multitude of strong waters, and a cold winter.

And Albumashar said that if he is oriental, it signifies the nearness of the wealthy from their regions.

And if he is occidental, it signifies battles between men (namely nobles and magnates), and discords will fall between them.

And if he is retrograde, it signifies severity in the matters and goods of men, and wars and battles between them.

And if he is direct he signifies the prosperity of those journeying by land and by sea.

## LXVI

### ♄ ♉

If however, he is in Taurus, and its triplicity, it signifies the impediment of the wealthy and magnates: and this will be in the southern parts of the division of the sign in which Saturn is placed; but chiefly in Taurus.

Whence, if he is in Taurus, and he is direct, and in an angle, he signifies contentions and wars, and likewise the impediment of quadrupeds, and especially of cows and bulls, and especially in the lands assigned to the sign he is in.

And Albumashar said that if he is in an earth sign, it signifies the destruction of those things which are from its seeds, namely the scarcity of trees, and detriment from vermin which fall in them, and locusts. And he said, there will be tribulations, injuries, tremors, and earthquakes; and the destruction of cities, villages, and houses.

Moreover, if Saturn is in Taurus at the hour of the revolution, or if he is in Leo, Scorpio, or Aquarius, regardless of what the Ascendant is, he signifies battles, famine, and the scarcity of things born of the earth. And if he is impeded he signifies mortality in addition to this, and it will be feared concerning magnates in that revolution: and this will be worse and stronger in Leo than in Taurus; stronger in Taurus than in Scorpio; stronger in Scorpio than Aquarius; and in Aquarius these things will happen less so than in any of the others.

And if Mars is joined to him, and the Moon joins to them, and especially with Saturn in latitude, in whatever sign this is in, or from whatever sign, or whatever the Ascendant is, it signifies famine and mortality. If indeed, she is joined to Mars, it signifies the detriment of the kings, and their changes, and battles in the parts of that sign, in which the conjunction is assigned; and much bloodshed, changes, and battles. And if he is retrograde, it signifies the destruction of the harvest in addition to this; and it signifies war in many regions, lands, and parts (especially those of the east, and the south, more so than in other parts); and this will be more severe if he is then in the tenth, since the evil will be more universal, and there will be impediments in boys and youths.

And Albumashar said that if he is remote from the angles in these signs, and he aspects the Ascendant, and he is direct, it will happen as he said in the chapter below. Saturn in the third from it signifies death of the king, by the testimony of the matter of the years.

And Messala said that it will destroy seeds, and the harvests will be little. If however, he does not aspect the Ascendant, the evil will be less. And if he is retrograde, he signifies the destruction of seeds, and the harvest will be very slight; and it will be feared for young men in that year. And if he is cadent from the Ascendant, and not aspecting it, and he is direct, and Mars does not aspect him or the Ascendant, it signifies the diminution of the aforementioned evils, since then he will not be able to harm much, unless Mars operates to the contrary. And if he were retrograde, and Mars impeded him, it would signify the destruction of the harvests, and mortality in the lands which are ruled over by the sign in which he is then placed.

### If The Moon Suffers an Eclipse

And if the Moon is suffering an eclipse at that time, it signifies killing in the parts of the east, west, and south. And it signifies snow and rain in countries where it is accustomed to rain. In others it signifies the alteration of the air. And it signifies an abundance of seeds or harvests, and creeping things; and the death of bulls and cows, and there will be little wine and butter in western parts.

And if Saturn's latitude is northern, it signifies the goodness of the air, and its beauty, and the goodness of its complexion. It also signifies useful and beneficial rains, not harming seeds and similar things, but helping them. And the market price of things born of the earth will be middling; and also of other things, allowing not completely. If however, his latitude is southern, it signifies pestilences, mortalities, tremors and mixtures with the corruption of the air, and its deterioration, and the scarcity of its goodness.

And if he is oriental it signifies a multitude of rain, or infirmities, for this reason. But if he is occidental it signifies the fear of the wealthy and the magnates or nobles, because of the country folk or the commoners; and the mixture of their affairs.

If however, Saturn is retrograde, it signifies the death of magnates and noblemen, and a multitude of tremblings and difficulties amongst men. If he is direct, it signifies long lasting infirmities happening in the superior parts of men.

## LXVIII

### ♄ ♍

If indeed, Saturn is in Virgo, and his latitude is northern, it signifies the goodness of the winds, and their sweetness, and their strengthening in the times of harvest and sowing. And if his latitude is southern, it signifies little rain, and the wasting of waters of springs.

If however, he is oriental, it signifies that the women who are pregnant in that year will have abortions because of the winds; and even from the cause of having intercourse after becoming pregnant. But if he is occidental it signifies hastening fevers in that year, and terrible tremblings.

And if he is retrograde it signifies the fear of the king of that region from his enemies, lest they come in to his contrary over him. If indeed, he is direct it signifies that king obtaining over his enemies, and it signifies his strength against them.

## LXIX

### ♄ ♑

If he is in Capricorn, and his latitude is northern, it signifies the good disposition of the air, and the moderation of the rains. If however, his latitude is southern, it signifies the darkness of the air in winter, and its cloudiness, and coldness.

And if he is oriental, it signifies the bad condition of magnates and nobles in that revolution, and their terror, and that they will not act well with the country folk or commoners: and that they will act together badly. If indeed, he is occidental, it signifies a multitude of locusts in the usual regions, and great heat, harming and destroying the harvest.

If he is retrograde, it signifies that the country folk or the commoners will mix together and be irritable with each other. If however, he is direct, it signifies the good disposition of the wealthy, and the magnates or nobles; and that they will behave well toward everyone, and amongst themselves; and that they will esteem justice, rectitude, and mildness, and they will practice these things.

## LXX

### ♄ ♊

If indeed, Saturn is in Gemini or its triplicity, it signifies that whatever he signifies, whether it is good or bad, will mostly appear in the west. But if he is in Gemini, and is direct and in an angle, it signifies the severity of northerly winds, and a cold winter in that year.

And Albumashar said that there will be detriment and diminution in birds, and infirmities will befall men from the cold, and dryness, in whatever mixture of the hot and wet; and there will be contentious and untruthful men; and bloodshed will also be signified from this. And he said that if Saturn is in an air sign, he signifies the serenity of the cold, and the multitude of frost and clouds; and the corruption of the complexion of the air, and thunders, flashes, and lightning bolts, and impediment from the multitude of rains (and especially if he is from the 5th degree of the sign up to the 26th), and there will be impediments from these lightning bolts, and glowing sparks running through the air, under the spear shafts.

And if he is retrograde, it signifies contrarieties of the king and the nobles, and of the magnates or wealthy; and death will be feared in that year or in that revolution, for the reason that it signifies an earthquakes to happen in the same year.

And if he is remote from the angles, the winds (both eastern and western) will be multiplied.

And Albumashar said that it also signifies the severity of the cold; and that men will likewise be in motion. But if in addition to this he is retrograde, men will likewise be in motion; and there will be infirmities from winds, rains, dew, and hoar frost. If however, he is cadent, and not aspecting the

Ascendant, and is direct, these things will happen in the regions which are in the division of the sign in which Saturn is then placed; and the winds will be multiplied from the southern division. However, if he is direct, these things will happen for good fortune, without weakness; and infirmities, dissolutions, ruptures, and pillaging will befall the citizens who are in the aforementioned division of the sign; and they will happen more so, and more strongly, in the country folk, commoners, and low class persons.

However, Albumashar said that if Saturn is in the angle of the earth, and he were the Lord of the year, and in the mentioned triplicity; or if he is not the Lord of the year, but receives the disposition of the Lord of the Ascendant of that revolution, it signifies that in the same year, in the aforementioned places, many men will die from an earthquake. If he receives disposition from the Lord of the Midheaven, it signifies battles and contrarieties in the seeking of kingship or another dignity, or the diminution of the jurisdiction of some cities, or lands of a magnate, which another wishes to take away from him by force. And he said that it signifies a multitude of waters, and flooding of rivers, and drownings; also a multitude of snow, and detriment in grain; and there will be a multitude of winds, and it signifies death in men.

And if his latitude is northern, it signifies the vehement blowing of winds, and the darkness and corruption of the air, and the changing of its colour to the side of blackness; and it even signifies earthquakes, and especially in the regions of the sign which he is in. If however, his latitude is southern, it signifies the heat of the air, and its dryness; and the scarcity of rains; and a multitude of pestilences, of noxious and fatal things.

If however, he is oriental, it signifies that infirmities will come to the magnates of the Babylonian lands, and their king. If he is occidental. It signifies the dryness of the air, and the scarcity of rains - and this will be if he is direct: since if he is retrograde he will harm excessively.

## LXXI

### ♄ ♎

Albumashar said that if Saturn is in Libra, and his latitude is northern, it signifies the heat of the air and its dryness; and it signifies little rain in that revolution, and the using up of waters. And if his latitude is southern, it signifies the goodness of the air, and its sweetness, and there will not be harmful winds..

And if he is oriental, it signifies the desire of shameful, criminal men. And if he is occidental, it signifies infamy falling upon fornicators, and those abusing shameful sexual intercourse.

If however, he is retrograde, it signifies infirmities of slaves and slave-girls, and of low-class persons.

And if he is direct, it signifies the mediocrity of the yearly produce, and especially barley.

And Albumashar said that it signifies the breaking of the wealth over the king.

## LXXII

### ♄ ♒

If Saturn is in Aquarius and his latitude is northern, it signifies the multitude of rains, and the severity of the cold and frost. And if his latitude is southern, it signifies the scarcity of waters, springs, and rivers.

If he is oriental, he signifies the scarcity of the acquisition of inheritances, and the scarcity of the substance of the country people. And if he is occidental it signifies the multitude and strength of burning fires.

And if he is retrograde he signifies the severity of the same things.

And if he is direct, he signifies the death of animals which men use for their own utility.

## LXXIII

### On Cancer And Its Triplicity, If Saturn Is The Lord Of The Revolution, And Is In It Or Its Triplicity

♄ ♋

If however, Saturn is the Lord of the year, and is in Cancer, or in its triplicity, Albumashar said that whatever he signifies, whether it is good or bad, will be in the northern parts. But if he is in Cancer, it signifies the multiplication of waters, rains, fish, locusts, and those things creeping on the earth. And if Mars does not aspect him, the cold will become more severe, and the locusts will be multiplied; and there will be infirmities in the lands which are in the division of the sign in which Saturn is placed, and the signs in his opposition, and square aspect. And if he is retrograde, the death of the king of this region will be feared. If however, Mars aspects him, without the aspect of benefics, it signifies mortality in the aforementioned lands; and the evil and impediment will be multiplied. If however, he does not aspect the Ascendant, the rains, dew, and cold will be multiplied. If indeed, he is direct, the evil will be reduced; and this more greatly so if he is aspected by one of the benefics (unless the Moon were then in the first: since this signifies that impediment will befall the kings and magnates of this region, and death). If however, he is retrograde and Mars aspects him, it signifies ruin and evil (and even locusts) in the lands of the aforementioned sign, and its opposition, and square aspect. And if he is cadent, and not aspecting the Ascendant, and is direct, with Mars cadent from him, it signifies the security of men; and this will be better if he has already transited the 15th degree of the sign: nevertheless, there will be infirmities in the land of this sign. And if he is retrograde, and Mars aspects him, and the benefics are absent from him, the ignoble men of those regions will meet with tribulations, and evil things, and the cold will become more severe; and the water and locusts will multiply.

And Albumashar said, and there will be impediment in the water from shipwrecks, and from the breaking of boats; and those travelling by water will be in danger; aquatic animals will die, and similar things to these. He said that if Saturn is adapted, without impediment, it signifies the good

for those things which I said, and the conversion of bad into good, and fitness in all of their substances, and his signification of them.

And he said to examine the malefic who impedes him, which is Mars; and the Cauda by conjunction (and Mars by conjunction and by aspect).

And he said, Saturn's peculiar significations are over the wealthy, old things, Jews, the religious, farmers, old men, and the decrepit. And if he is impeded in the hour of the revolution judge their destruction and impediment. And if he is fortunate, judge their fortune.

And if his latitude is northern, it signifies the scarcity of waters and the diminution of rivers and rain. If however, his latitude if southern, it signifies the occupation of men in their necessities, and the scarcity of their acquisitions.

And if he is oriental, it signifies the corruption of the air and its darkness, and a multitude of coldness in its own season. And if he is occidental, it signifies a multitude of rains, and their corruption, and the impediment of things from wind.

And if he is retrograde, it signifies the fortitude of those things which were mentioned: and that the king of the region which is in the division of the sign in which Saturn is placed, will fall into opprobrium and very great disgrace, the greatest which could possibly befall him, and which could be likened to death. And Messala said that there will be the greatest battle, and powerful death.

But if he is direct, it signifies the benevolent disposition of the air, and the goodness of its complexion.

## LXXIV

♄ ♏

Indeed if Saturn is in Scorpio, and his latitude is northern, it signifies a multitude of rains, and the overflowing of waters and rivers, and their corruption. And if his latitude is southern, it signifies that famine will come over men, and the oppression of the market price of things for sale,, and especially those things born of the earth.

And if he is oriental, it signifies a multitude of wars, between the wealthy and the magnates. And if he is occidental, it signifies destruction and impediment in the sea, and in marine matters, and the occurrence of evil in these things.

And if he is retrograde, it signifies pestilences in the earth, and battles.

And Albumashar said that if he is direct, it signifies the salvation of the Bablyonian clime.

## LXXV

## ♄ ♓

And if Saturn is in Pisces, and his latitude is northern, it signifies much blowing of northerly winds, and the severity of the cold in winter. And if his latitude is southern, it signifies a storm in the sea, and the breaking of boats for this reason; and that impediments will arrive to those who spend time on the water, and who work in it.

And if he is oriental, it signifies disputes and contrarieties of the wealthy, and that there will be killings between them. And if he is occidental, it signifies that the country folk, the commoners, and the ignoble will be exalted, and lift their heels against the nobles and magnates, and they will cast them down and suppress them.

And if he is retrograde it signifies tribulations of the religious, and battles between men and servants of God, and those cultivating the ways of religion, and their griefs..

And Albumashar said that if he is direct, it signifies the common people of the houses of religion, and divine worship.

## LXXVI

## What Saturn Signifies In Each House In The Revolution Of The Year, As Much Of The World, As Of Nativities, Or Questions, Whether IIe Is The Lord Of Thc Ycar, Or Not.

When Saturn in a revolution, or in a nativity, or question is in:

The first, if it is a revolution of the year of the world, he signifies the grief of many men because of debt, or because of land. If it is a nativity, or its revolution, or a question, it signifies this for the native or querent.

If however, he is in the second, it signifies the disorder of friends in that year, and men will waste, and subtract from their goods.

If indeed, he is in the third, it signifies that disputes and discords will come between brothers more than usual.

And if he is in the fourth, it signifies the destruction of buildings and the pillaging of lands; and the detriment of seed, and of treasures, and danger and death to come because of these things.

And if he is in the fifth it signifies more abortions than usual in that year; and the detriment of children, and griefs because of them, and contentions with messengers and legates, and that they will not exercise well what they have business with in that year.

And if he is in the sixth, it signifies the ill will of slaves and slavegirls towards their masters, and their disobedience; and many infirmities; and the harming of small animals.

If indeed, he is in the seventh, and it is a feminine sign, and its Lord is a feminine planet, it signifies the ill will of wives towards their husbands, and their disobedience. And if it is a masculine sign, or its Lord is a masculine planet, it signifies the ill will of husbands towards their wives; and the fraudulence of associates; and the harming of enemies, more so against absent enemies than public enemies; and tribulations because of land; and in many cases, a detestable end to things. You will say the same if he is found like this in nativities or questions.

And if he is in the eighth, it signifies litigations for the reason of seeking inheritances, or the things left behind after the dead, and for the reason of seeking ancient things; and affliction because of death; and it signifies matters whose pain and anguish or sorrow will last for a long time.

But if he is in the ninth, it signifies the diminution of faith: and the destruction of mercy and piety, and that certain hermits, or religious people will be moved from their religions, and will neglect them, and take on bad advice, and others will likewise do this; and certain men will strive in base and horrible matters of alien things, as are those who dig up the dead from their graves, and plunder them; and it signifies griefs, sorrows, and anxieties to come over travellers in their pilgrimages, and long delays in them.

If indeed, he is in the tenth, it signifies as much in nativities, as in questions, as in other revolutions, grief, sorrow, contractions, and severities on the part of the king, or the authorities, and the perplexity of prisons.

And Albumashar said that if the Sun is the Lord of the tenth house, the king will kill him in his own prison.

And if the Moon is the Lord of the tenth house, it signifies the same as the Sun, unless she is joined to Saturn.

And if the Lord of the tenth house is Jupiter, the king will kill him, and make him injure himself without guilt.

And if the Lord of the tenth house is Mars, he will die by his own fault.

And if the Lord of the 10th house is Venus, it signifies that prosperity, sublimity, joy, and advancement will follow from this tribulation, and the king will regret having done this, and confess he did not act well, and will humble himself before him.

And if the Lord of the 10th house is Mercury, he will kill him because of an injury without a reason, when he bears false testimony against him. And if Mercury aspects Mars, he will be cut by whips. And if Mercury is with the Sun, under his rays, the king will use force on him, and will take his possessions, and cause his goods to be returned to himself.

And he said to know that amongst the rest of the planets, this peculiar signification belongs to Saturn in the 10th.

And if he is in the 11th it signifies grief and sorrow from friends, and because of friends, and little progress in those things which are hoped for, and in those which is had faith for the good; and complication in matters and their harshness; and great hope in false things, which will be of no benefit.

And if he is in the 12th it signifies impediments which happen on the part of the king or another ruler; it even signifies that he will be captured by enemies; and there will be fear in all of his affairs.

And according to what I have touched on for you above, all of these things can be considered in the revolutions of the years of the world, in revolutions of nativities, and in questions and similar things, in all headings, and in anything by itself. And just as for Saturn, so too for any other planet, both for good and for evil.

## LXXVII

### On The Conjunction Of Saturn And Mars In The Revolution: What It Signifies

You will also examine in the revolution when you revolve the year (whether it is of the world, or a nativity) if Saturn and Mars are corporeally conjunct in one of the 12 houses, since this has the signification of burdens and impediments according to the significations of the house in which they are conjunct.

For if their conjunction is in the first it signifies general evil and impediment is going to come over the country folk and the commoners.

If it is in the second from the Ascendant of the revolution it signifies the destruction of their substance and their homes, and the wealthy and magnates will be forgotten by the people, and almost counted as nothing, and their household members will be exalted, and their soldiers and those serving them; and they will be haughty towards them, and they will not want to obey them, nor observe faithfulness with them, unless only slightly, in fact almost not at all.

If indeed, it is in the third, Albumashar said that it signifies the destruction of the houses of religion, and the fall of horrible things upon religious people and those worshiping God.

But if it is in the fourth, it signifies the destruction of buildings and mansions or houses.

If however, it is in the fifth, it signifies that destruction and impediment will fall upon children; and there will be more abortions than usual in that year; and the change of the will of friends towards each other, and also of persons who love each other, and instead of love, aversion and ill will shall fall between them.

If indeed, it is in the sixth, it signifies impediment and detriment is going to befall small and large quadrupeds, and especially those which men use, as are cattle, horses, asses, camels, and similar animal;, and on slaves and slave girls, and servants and maids; and it also signifies infirmities.

If it is in the seventh, it signifies that disputes, contentions, discord, dissension, and many evils will fall among associates and others who participate with each other in things, and also between husbands and wives, and enmities will rise up between men.

If it is in the eighth, it signifies that a huge number of men will leave their homes, and habitations in which they live, and will go off wandering in foreign lands and regions; and ruin will befall them; and there will be worries amongst men because of the things left behind by the dead, and the goods which are inherited from the dead, and the money of wives.

If it is in the ninth it signifies the detriment of the religious people of the plentiful religions, as are bishops, archbishops, cardinals, and similar people. And it signifies highwaymen and travellers, and the detriment of journeys (especially of long journeys, and pilgrimages which men travel far from their homes, seeking great and famous houses of prayer.

If it is in the tenth, it signifies the detriment of kings and magnates, and the destruction of their condition, and the death of a great king.

If indeed, it is in the 11th it signifies that dissension, anger, and disputes or discord will fall between friends. And Albumashar said that everyone who has a friend will be changed regarding their associate; and it also signifies the bad condition of soldiers and the household members of the king.

If indeed, it is in the 12th, it signifies impediments which will fall upon all quadrupeds, and especially over the aforementioned (namely cattle, horses, asses, and the like; and detriment and deterioration will fall upon all sales of beasts, and especially upon those of large ones, as much those that are ridden as those that are not ridden.

And Albumashar said that all of these things will happen in regions which are in the division of the sign in which they are conjoined; and the planet who is the Lord of the terms in which they are conjoined will be a participator; and these things will likewise happen in the cities or regions which are in the division of the sign in which he is placed.

## LXXVIII

### What Jupiter Signifies In A Revolution, In Each Sign, And In Each Triplicity (If He Is The Lord Of The Year); And In Each House, Whether He Is The Lord Of The Year Or Not

### ♃ ♈

When Jupiter is the Lord of the year, and he is in Aries, or in its triplicity, he signifies the appearance of religions in the eastern parts which are ruled by the sign in which he is placed; and especially when he is in Aries, he signifies their appearance, and that of sects; and the observation of divine precepts, and justice, and good works in that revolution; and he signifies a multitude of winds from the parts of Khorasan; and a cold winter, and rains (yet not driven out), and the flooding of rivers, and the fitness of vineyards and trees, and that the granaries will be good.

And if Jupiter is then in good condition, and well disposed, he signifies the multitude of the substance of the citizens of the regions which he rules over, and the goodness of their condition, and their rejoicing, and gladness, and the love of the country folk or the commoners towards the wealthy and the noble, and the magnates.

And Albumashar said that if he is impeded, or in bad condition, it signifies the contrary of those things which were mentioned. And he said to know that the operations in the matter of Jupiter, and the aspects of the planets to him, is equally like the work in the matter of Saturn.

And he said that Jupiter is the significator of the nobility, and judges, bishops, consuls, the religious, and the citizens of sects. And if he is impeded, all who are signified by him will suffer detriment. And he said that if he is in human signs, or fire signs, he signifies the dejection of the wealthy, and the smallness of their gifts, and the preservation of their rank, and their worries for those close to them; and the destruction of the kingdom of Babylonia and of the Arabs; and the scarcity of substances, and curiosity. And this will be over the citizens of the cities which are in the division of the sign in which Jupiter comes down. And it signifies the practicing of lies in large numbers of men, with assent to evil or injury, and infirmities of the body, and the weakness of acquisitions.

## LXXIX

### ♃ ♌

And if he is in Leo it signifies a cold winter, and a multitude of waters, and strong and raging winds eradicating trees; and it signifies the temperateness of the air, and its brightness in the last half of winter, and its coldness in its end, and more intemperate rains than usual in the spring, and the scarcity of water springs, and the scarcity of grass for animals grazing the fields in winter; and many coughs; and it signifies a sterile year.

## LXXX

### ♃ ♐

And if he is in Sagittarius, it signifies the temperateness of the air in the beginning of winter; and coldness in the middle of winter; and severe winds, snow, and frost in its end; and in spring it signifies southerly winds, and the multitude of grass for animals grazing the fields, and the impediment of vineyards from snow

and coldness, and the scarcity of fruits, and the impediment of trees.

If his latitude is northern, it signifies the good complexion of the air, and the scarcity of rain. And if his latitude is southern it signifies the corruption of the winds and their severity.

And if he is oriental it signifies rejoicing and happiness, and the good condition of the wealthy, the magnates, and the noblemen, and their joy and happiness, and that they will be engaged in games and dances. And Albumashar said that if he is occidental, it signifies the exaltation of the wise, the rich, and the nobility.

And if he is retrograde it signifies impediment in the sea, and sailing will not be completely safe. And if he is direct, it signifies the multitude of fish, and animals spending time in water, and their safety.

## LXXXI

### What Jupiter Signifies In Each And Every Revolution Of The Year, As Much Of The World, As Of A Nativity Or Question, Whether He Is The Lord Of The Year Or Not

And if Jupiter is in the first in a revolution, or nativity, or question, if it is a revolution of the year of the world, it signifies that one person will revere another, according to how it is fitting for them to revere each other according to their condition, and they will maintain honour, beauty, cleanliness, faith, and religion, and will spend their time in instruction and reason, and the purpose of their intentions will to be engaged in those things pertaining to the salvation of souls, unless Saturn and Mars operate to the contrary. And these things will happen to men who are fit for leadership. If however, it is a nativity or a question, or their revolution, it signifies something else for the native or querent.

Indeed, if he is in the second he signifies their striving and intention for the gathering of money, and in their obtaining and accumulation, and all of this with the restraint of a good, licit and fitting mind.

And if he is in the third he signifies good fortune from one brother to another, and between them;

and men will rejoice because of their relatives, and especially those younger than them, and their first or older sisters.

But if he is in the fourth, he signifies the increase of the goods of many men, from those things left behind by the dead, and from inheritances, and estates, or from hidden or unexpected treasures, and from ancient things. And griefs will be removed from men, and things from which they will be able to rejoice, and be happy will happen to them often; and evil and sorrowful thoughts will be removed from them; and also disputes and all horrible things will cease.

If indeed, he is in the fifth, it signifies the increase of children and their good condition, and that there will not be abortions in that year, unless perhaps some happen by chance: and it signifies profit because of children, and that honourable things will be done which merit praise. And it signifies the good condition of the wealthy and of magnates and noblemen, and the utility of things in which men have trust in for good.

But if he is in the sixth he signifies good and profit in quadrupeds, and especially in small ones, as are sheep and similar animals; and he signifies the safety of persons, and the scarcity of infirmity, except in regions and places which are naturally infirm - nevertheless, in these places infirmities will be reduced. And it signifies utility from slaves and slave girls, and the obedience of servants and maids.

However, if he is in the seventh he signifies utility, good things, and joy from women, and marriage or nuptials, and good from associates, and their faithfulness; and it also signifies victory over the enemies of that region; and even those of the native or querent,

If indeed, he is in the eighth, and it is a revolution of a year of the world, he signifies the general removal of evil, death, and suspicion in that region, if it is a revolution of the year of the world. However, if it is a revolution of a nativity, or question, it signifies the bad condition of the native or querent, which will befall him because of enemies; and it signifies that he will fall into their hands unless he guards himself well against this; and that burdens and impediment will follow from this: however, ultimately it will end in a manner which will be controlled, and a manner which will

not be evil, in fact, in a certain way it could be praised.

And if he is in the ninth, it signifies profitable journeys in that year, and especially long and useful ones; and that there will be faith, honour, and good amongst men; and there will be dreams, and many of them true; and the explanation of dreams will fall according to the nature of the planet from which Jupiter is separating at that time, or from that planet which separates from him, if he is separating from any planet; and dreams will be explained in that revolution according to the significations of that planet, and this can even have a place in other visions.

If indeed, he is in the 10th, it signifies the accumulation of possessions and their collection, and men will strive to be praised, and whoever is to be praised, will be praised, according to his condition, and honour will thrive amongst them.

However, if he is in the 11th it signifies praise and good reputation from friends; and that men will rejoice and will be in gladness, and that there will be good effecting and profiting in things which men have trust in, and of which they hope for good things.

Indeed, if he is in the twelfth it signifies impediments which will come from servitude; and it signifies poverty and indigence; and it signifies severity which will occur from slaves, and on occasion of them; and also from servitude into which men fall; and they will be saddened from accidents which will come to them on the occasion of quadrupeds, and especially large animals, as are horses, cows, and the like.

## LXXXII

## What Mars Signifies When He Is The Lord Of The Year, In Each And Every Triplicity, And In Each And Every Sign, And In Each And Every House, Whether He Is The Lord Of The Year Or Not

### ♂ ♈

However, if Mars is the Lord of the year, and he is in Aries, or in its triplicity, it signifies strong winds, and many and various mutations of the air in eastern parts. It also signifies eye pains, and the scarcity of rain; and it signifies war in the same parts, and the abundance of the yearly produce; and it signifies evil, anger, injuries, and disputes in the same parts, in the cities which he rules over, and who are in the division of Aries. And he signifies victory in war for the citizens of those cities, and the inhabitants of those regions, over their enemies who come from other parts to these lands for reason of harming them; and the flight of their enemies; and it signifies their own and their kings engagement in martial matters; and that fathers and aged men will teach and instruct their sons, and other young men, in wrestling and exercises of war.

And if Mars is then in good condition, it signifies that the aforementioned citizens or inhabitants, or their kings, will have victory over their enemies; and that they will prevail over them, and all those who contend with them; and he signifies the greatness of the king's heart, and that he is quick in will, and quickly changing, and fast at apprehending things. It also signifies that the country folk and his subjects will love and revere him, and each one will obey him according to his own condition.

And if Mars is the Lord of the year and the Lord of the Ascendant, and is in good condition and not impeded, it signifies that there will be fertility in the same year, and it will be a rainy year; and there will be pestilences and earthquakes: and this will be moderate. And there will be rejoicing and happiness in the same year, and labourers and carriers of arms will fight, and they will find good; and there will be war and contentions close to the king of this region.

However, if he is in bad condition, he signifies that they will rarely prevail over their enemies, and that it will be good enough for them if they are able to defend themselves from them: in fact, it appears more likely that their enemies will prevail over, or overcome, them. And it signifies that the king will not be stable over the matters which he ought to be engaged in; and especially over the noble, useful, and just things; nor will he keep his secrets well, but rather, he will reveal them, and he will exercise his operations in martial matters more than others.

And if his latitude is northern, it signifies the heat of the air and little rain. However, if his latitude is southern, it signifies thunder, flashes, and lightning.

And if he is oriental, it signifies that war is going to fall between the wealthy, the magnates, and the nobility. And if he is occidental, it signifies disturbance and fears are going to come to men.

And if he is retrograde, it signifies infirmities of the eyes, and of the whole human body. And if he is direct he signifies a multitude of hypocrites, who will appear in sheep's clothing, but inwardly will be rapacious wolves.

## LXXXIII

### ♂ ♌

If however, he is in Leo, it signifies wars, contentions, and the scarcity of the yearly produce in the eastern parts; and there will be death in men, and especially in young men from 40 years up to 50 years. However, this will be stronger in boys.

And if his latitude is northern it signifies the scarcity of water. If however, his latitude is southern, it signifies the multitude of waters from springs and rivers

And if he is oriental it signifies the impediment of animals which men use, and the like. And if he is occidental, it signifies the scarcity of fish; and the death of animals spending time in water.

And if he is retrograde, it signifies impediment and trouble which will befall the wealthy and magnates. And if he is direct it signifies the blowing of westerly winds; and that boats will be safe in the sea.

## LXXXIV

### ♂ ♐

And if Mars is in Sagittarius he signifies that there is going to be a war in western parts; and that there will be little power in these parts; and there will be evil impediment and death in the habitations of this region, and in businessmen; and there will be infirmities, coughs, and eye pains: and there will be intestinal worms killing boys: and they will also harm others; and it signifies the scarcity of rain; and that cold will be generated in its own seasons, so that because of this trees, plants, and the annual produce will be devastated; and that bees will suffer detriment in that revolution.

And if Mars is well disposed (namely fortunate and strong), it signifies the good condition of the makers of war, and their advisors, and the bearers of arms, and warriors, for the reason of war; and the good condition of those who seek injustice, and highwaymen, just as those who do such things consider their condition to be good.

And Albumahsar said that if Mars is in human signs, as are Gemini, Virgo, Libra, the last half of Sagittarius, and Aquarius, he signifies a multitude of wars and battles; and that men will rise up against their own king. He also signifies sudden death, and tertian fevers, and other strong and severe fevers, and a multitude of infirmities; and also a multitude of highwaymen; and the spilling of men's blood; and burning fires, and lightning.

If indeed, he is badly disposed, it signifies that the malice of all of the aforementioned things will be more severe, worse, and more harmful, unless Jupiter operates to the contrary.

Indeed, if his latitude is northern it signifies the goodness of the air, and its excellent disposition. And if his latitude is southern it signifies the profit of businessmen, and the excellence of their wealth.

And if he is oriental, it signifies peace, serenity, and security; and there will be little war, or almost none. And if he is occidental it signifies the safety of trees, and the multitude of fruit.

But if he is retrograde it signifies that coughs will come to men, and pains in the posterior parts of the head. However, if he is direct, it signifies that pestilences are going to come to animals which live next to the seashore.

## LXXXV

## On Another Nefarious Signification Of Mars

It should also be considered in the revolution of the year of the world, as to whether Mars is in Gemini or not. For if Mars is in Gemini in the revolution of the year, and Gemini is the ninth house, and the inferior planets are following him, it signifies that the Roman Church will take up the temporal sword in that year; and will strive to shed the blood of Christians, as much of the guilty as of the innocent.

### On Mars In The Houses

If Mars is in the first in a revolution of the year (whether he is the Lord of the year or not). whatever kind of revolution it is, whether of the world, or a nativity (or if it is a nativity or a question), it signifies a horrible thing to come to men, or the native or querent, in that year; along with sorrow and fears, contrarieties and contentions; and men will strive to take each other's substance, and things which do not pertain to them, by ingenuity and slyness, not in a praiseworthy way.

And if he is in the second it likewise signifies the taking of substance by injustice, and without reason; and there will be poverty and indigence, which will be the reason leading men to do this: and household members and ministers will throw things into confusion against their masters ,or those with whom they live or stay. Certain men wish to say that Mars in the second is not to be cursed: for they say that it signifies trade; but I did not find this in experience, from what I remember.

And if he is in the third, it signifies anger, hatred, enmity, contrarieties and contentions, will fall between brothers and younger relatives; and that many of them will murder each other under the most trifling circumstances: and this more strongly so if the third house is Capricorn or Aquarius. And Albumashar said that if the third house is one of the domiciles of Venus, it signifies joy from brothers and sisters. And if it is one of the domiciles of Jupiter, it signifies the multitude of substances, and acquisitions of businessmen. And if it is one of the domiciles of Saturn, it signifies the pillaging of the dead placed in tombs; and the digging under of walls, and the taking away of other things by means of robbery. And it signifies the engagement of men in making money, and extorting money in any way they can, by way of illicit domination, and by false testimony, and by malicious and fraudulent words; and men will suffer dangers and tribulations. And if it is the domicile of the Moon, it signifies robberies and digging under walls, for the purpose of stealing; and snatching things by misdeeds; and thieves will be secure and bold in their stealing. For they will steal in the forum, and in places of business, not only at night, but also during the day. And if it is the domicile of the Sun, it signifies bandits and highwaymen; and plundering in small towns, and sometimes in cities, and in other habitations: and also in those staying at guesthouses, in the marketplace, and foreigners. And Albumashar said to know that this is particular of Mars amongst the rest of the planets.

And if he is in the fourth, it signifies death and ruin from illness; and killing by swords; and the spilling of blood, and its suspicion; and these things will come to an in the south, from whatever part they are examined, and in Khorasan; and from drawn out tribulations; nevertheless their beginning will be more from the north.

And if he is in the fifth it signifies that there will be fornications in that year, and many children will be born from them, of whom many will be counted as legitimate, when they are from adultery, from which their parents will have little or no benefit; however, the sustenance of men that year will be suitable.

And if he is in the sixth, he signifies hot illnesses in that year, as are hot fevers, and ones of dryness which will be set in motion by corrupted blood, and from cholera that is going to come into men in that revolution. It also signifies griefs and sorrows which will occur because of slaves, slave girls, and servants, and from other causes which are signified by the sixth house.

And if he is in the seventh it signifies contentions and contrarieties, and disturbances in all matters, and harm for this reason. And it signifies business dealings with fraud and deception, and also grief and sorrow in this.

And if he is in the eighth, acquisition from the substance of the dead for some men, and this as much for revolutions of nativities or questions, as for questions themselves, as for revolutions of the years of the world; and justice will be done for those acquiring these things for this reason; and they will lose these things after acquiring them; and fall into poverty and indigence. And it signifies killing, and the mutilation or loss of body parts (namely hands and feet); and that men will fall into disgrace and very shameful and reprehensible censure.

And if he is in the ninth, it signifies the diminution of the status of religious people; and it signifies the seeking of horses and arms for reason of war and battle; and men will likewise seek war: and they will strive to make camp, and go into the army. And it signifies drinking and drunkenness, and incontinence with dishonest and illicit things; and men will be very unfaithful, and mendacious, and will strive to explain dreams, and will explain them falsely.

And if he is in the tenth, it signifies that tribulation is going to come to the country folk and the commoners, from kings or wealthy and powerful men; and it signifies injuries and blows of swords and whips, and anguish from these things, and imprisonment; and the scarcity or want of sustenance. And it signifies war and contentions over matters which do not belong to those who seek them, and which do not pertain to them.

And if he is in the eleventh, he signifies the scarcity of profit or benefit in things from which utility is hoped for; and that they will fall into the enmity of their friends; and it signifies the diminution of substance; and men will lose hope of matters in which they had trust, and of which they hoped. And likewise for a native or a querent.

And if he is in the twelfth, he signifies ingenuity in stealing, and in all things similar to this; and laziness and delay in those things which men ought to do, and are capable of doing; and the diminution of the substances of men; and he signifies mourning and sorrow is going to come because of large animals, as much those which are ridden, as those which are not ridden, unless God averts it.

## LXXXVI

### ♂ ♉

And if Mars is in Taurus, or in its triplicity, those things which are signified will appear in the southern parts, and especially if he is in Taurus. For then it signifies that strong winds are going to come; and the destruction of fruits which are in the places from which they ought to be collected; and likewise of trees; and this because of heat exceeding the natural and required limit; it also signifies the multitude of clouds and gloomy weather; rain also, and thunder and lightning.

And Albumashar said that it signifies the death of women and cattle; and it signifies wars are going to come between the citizens of the east, and the citizens of the west; and it also signifies eye pains, and more so of the left than of the right; and they will abound more in women than in men: and the cultivation of the land will not be very useful; and there will be a scarcity of the yearly produce.

And if his latitude is northern it signifies a multitude of rains and the goodness of plants, and utility from them. And if his latitude is southern it signifies a multitude of northerly winds.

And if he is oriental, it signifies that there will be peace in that revolution in the parts of Babylonia, and in western parts; and it signifies the security of their citizens. And if he is occidental it signifies a multitude of infirmities and death.

And if he is retrograde it signifies the infirmities of boys. And Albumashar said that if he is direct he signifies the hatred of women.

## LXXXVII

### ♂ ♍

And if Mars is in Virgo he signifies battles and bloodshed in the northern parts, and he also signifies eye pains, and the abundance of grain, wine, and butter. And Albumashar said that it signifies mortality in women.

And if his latitude is northern, it signifies impediment in the bodies of men; and seeds will suffer detriment, and also the harvest. And if his latitude is southern, then he signifies the safety of seeds.

And if he is oriental, it signifies the death of old men. And if occidental, the blowing of winds in the parts of Spain.

And if he is retrograde, he signifies battles to come between men. And if he is direct, it signifies the honour and good condition of rich men and magnates.

## LXXXVIII

### ♂ ♑

And if Mars is in Capricorn, he signifies war, pillaging, and tribulations; and death in young men. And he signifies that tremors are going to come in eastern parts; and he also signifies rain in these same parts, and the multiplication of grain, butter, and oil. And there will be the aforementioned wars between the citizens of the east and the citizens of the west.

And if his latitude is northern, it signifies a multitude of snow in the required and usual seasons. And if his latitude is southern it signifies the heat of the air, and its darkness, in its own season.

And if he is oriental, he signifies the killing of the Emperor of the Romans. And this more strongly if the Moon is in the eighth (since the Moon is naturally his significatrix), or joined to the Lord of the eighth, or if Mars himself is in an angle, wherever she is joined to him. And this will be stronger again, if she is joined to him in the eighth, or if the Lord of the eighth aspects her from opposition or square aspect. And stronger again, and infallibly, if there is mutual reception between them (or at least if the Moon receives the Lord of the eighth); and Jupiter will not be able to operate to the contrary; for only God will be able to avert it.

And if he is occidental, he signifies blisters, carbuncles, and similar things are going to befall the bodies of men.

And if he is retrograde he signifies the scarcity of the yearly substance. And if he is direct it signifies the abundance of wine and oil.

## LXXXIX

### ♂ ♊

And if Mars is in Gemini or in its triplicity, it signifies that whatever he signifies, the significations will occur in western parts. But if he is in Gemini, it signifies that impediment is going to befall men from thunder and lightning; and a scarcity of rain; and the severity of heat, and its harmfulness. And there will be wars, contentions, and robberies in northern parts; and their king will be exalted in that revolution, and they will have victory over their enemies: and there will be earaches; and blisters, carbuncles, and similar things.

And if his latitude is northern, it signifies a multitude of rain. And if his latitude is southern, it signifies the scarcity of waters, springs, and rivers.

And if he is oriental, it signifies a multitude of blisters and similar things. And if he is occidental, it signifies the impediment of counsellors, scribes, and judges, and cavalry commanders, and their hiding and flight.

And if he is retrograde, it signifies the dissent of the religious, and their diversity and sects. And if he is direct, he signifies that men will reveal secrets, as much their own, as others, nor will they keep them well.

## XC

### ♂ ♎

And if Mars is in Libra, he signifies winds, infirmities and mortality to come in the cities or regions which are in the division of Libra; and this will be stronger in men than in women.

And Albumashar said that if Mars is there, he signifies rain and winds, also clouds and fog. It also signifies that there will be infirmities and mortality in southern parts; and there will be little wine, butter, and oil; and thieves and highwaymen will be multiplied: and there will be disputes and evil things between men; and there will be fears and tremblings or terrors in them.

And if his latitude is northern, it signifies lightning and flashes which will appear in that year, or in that revolution. And if his latitude is southern, it signifies illnesses in men on the left side.

And if he is oriental it signifies that there will be wars and contentions between wealthy men and magnates. And if he is occidental, it signifies the safety of wealthy men and magnates, and writers of letters, and sages.

And if he is retrograde it signifies that illnesses are going to come to the wealthy, magnates, writers, judges, and sages. And if he is direct, it signifies that the wills of the wealthy and magnates or nobles will differ amongst themselves.

## XCI

### ♂ ♒

And if Mars is in Aquarius, he signifies burdens and tribulations which are going to come to men in that revolution; and that snow, rain, and cold will abound in their seasons; and that grain, wine, and butter will be reduced in western parts, and in lands which are said to belong to businessmen. And he signifies the death, or change of the king or ruler of that region in which you revolve the year. And Albumashar said that if Venus then aspects the Ascendant, and she is northern, it signifies a good spring; but there will be little wine.

And if Mars latitude is northern, it signifies a multitude of snow and coldness in their seasons, and in the usual regions; and locusts in their own season. And if his latitude is southern, it signifies the darkness of the air, and its thickness, and the severity of the heat.

And if he is oriental, it signifies the good condition of the wealthy and the magnates, and the nobility, and their joy and happiness; and it signifies a multitude of branches.

And if he is retrograde, he signifies the severity of the heat, and that impediment will befall trees for this reason. And if he is direct it signifies the impediment of the trees, and that vermin will fall in them: and this more strongly if the Caput Draconis is there, or in Gemini.

## XCII

### ♂ ♋

And if Mars in the revolution of the year is in Cancer or its triplicity (and especially in Cancer), the appearance of his significations will be in the northern parts. But in Cancer he signifies shipwrecks happening suddenly, from strong and sudden blowing of wind; and he signifies disputes, contention, and war, in occidental parts: and men will be oppressed because of rendering tributes; and there will be fevers and other illnesses; and there will be pains of the throat and the chest; and the heat will become more severe, and the rain will be reduced. And Albumashar said that it will be a dangerous year, and there will be little oil, butter, or fat: and it also signifies the death of quadrupeds, but more so of horses.

And if his latitude is northern, it signifies the severity of the coldness in its season, and the scarcity of waters of springs. And if his latitude is southern, it signifies that winds will come, and that impediment will befall trees.

And if he is oriental, it signifies that pestilences will befall field animals. And if he is occidental he signifies the worries and solicitude of the mob, or the country folk and the commoners, about their own business.

And if he is retrograde, he signifies lavisciousness; and that men will delight in sex, and strive after it, and they will fornicate, and similar things. But if he is direct, it signifies the good disposition of the air, and its beauty and clarity.

## XCIII

### ♂ ♏

And if Mars is in Scorpio, it signifies a multitude of clouds, and the severity of the cold in winter, and distemperate heat in summer, and the severity of the yearly produce for this reason, and also of trees. And there will be eye pains; and thieves and highwaymen will be multiplied; and there will be wars and pains, and other infirmities in young men; and there will be a scarcity of wine, butter and fat; and these things will happen more so in northern parts.

And if he is in Scorpio, and his latitude is northern, it signifies the scarcity of waters. And if his latitude is southern, it signifies the multitude of waters of springs.

And if he is oriental, it signifies that a multitude of infirmities will befall men, and especially in the interior parts of the belly. And if he is occidental, he signifies the scarcity of men's piety towards one another.

And Albumashar said that if he is retrograde, it signifies good things in that revolution, and a multitude of commerce (however, with fear and trembling). And he said that if he is direct, it signifies the multitude of taking of wealth, and the plundering of the houses of the substances of the wealthy.

## XCIV

### ♂ ♓

And if Mars is in Pisces, it signifies a multitude of snow and rain; and there will be mortality in the southern parts; and more fish will be caught in the revolution than usual; and more kingdoms will be destroyed; and it signifies the killing of kings, magnates, the wealthy, and nobles (namely those who are fit for kingship). And it also signifies the scarcity of the yearly produce, and wine will suffer detriment and diminution. And so, there will be much less than men would have hoped for. And flying animals that impede will suffer detriment, as are flies, gadflies, and the like. And Albumashar said that if Venus aspects the Ascendant of the year, death and eye pains will abound in men; and thunder and lightning will be multiplied; and the evil of the fruits of the earth will be shattered, and they will undergo increase.

And if his latitude is northern, it signifies the goodness of the air and its beauty or purity. And if his latitude is southern, it signifies the abundance of locusts, but they will not impede much.

And if he is oriental, it signifies the killing of the wealthy and the magnates. And if he is occidental, it signifies that infirmities will befall slaves, slavegirls, servants, maids, and low-class persons.

And Albumashar said that if he is retrograde, it signifies the safety and profit of businessmen. And if he is direct, he signifies the guardianship and safety of sheep and small quadrupeds, and slaves, slavegirls, servants, maids, and low-class persons.

The sages of this profession, and especially that most reverend predecessor of ours Albumashar, did not care to record latitudes, except for the three superior planets: since they did not find proven truth in the others, as they did with these. Therefore Albumashar said that he sometimes found errors in the inferiors; but never with the superiors; whence he warned us to pay attention to the latitudes of the superiors, and not the inferiors.

## XCV

### On The Sun, If He Is The Lord Of The Year: What He Signifies

However, if the Sun is the Lord of the year or revolution, and he is well disposed and in good condition (namely fortunate, strong, and free from impediments), he signifies the sublimities and exaltations of the king, and glory and honour, and its seeking; and that the king of this region will be exalted; and he will be painstaking about increasing his kingdom; and not only the king, but also every person according to his own condition, and according to his nature or birth, to increase his status; and it signifies their utility and success; and that they will turn their faces away from matters displeasing to God, and from injuries, and from dishonourable things. And it also signifies the good condition of the wealthy, and magnates and the nobility, and of those who ought to be honoured by men.

And if he is the Lord of the year and the Lord of the Ascendant, and is free from malefics, Albumashar said that kings will rejoice, and they will have joy and security; and the yearly produce, quadrupeds, birds, and all those things over which the Sun has signification will be increased. If however, he is impeded, it signifies the impediment of all the aforementioned things.

And he said that if Mercury is with Saturn, or aspects him, and is a participant with him and receives disposition from him, the harvest and the country folk will suffer detriment in diverse climes; and thieves will be multiplied, and fear will enter over men, and especially in those men who are of the nature of Mercury, or those for whom he is the significator, and animals will be reduced in the

lands of the west, or in Arab lands, if he is in a sign of the figure of a quadruped, according to the substance of that sign.

And he said that in addition to this you should examine the luminary who has authority: since if he is fortunate and is increased in light and number, and is not impeded, it will repel a great impediment, and defend from a malefic. If however, it is impeded by any of the impediments mentioned above in the hour of the revolution, the aforementioned will suffer detriment and great impediment; and there will be infirmities in the country folk or commoners. And these things will happen more strongly and terribly, if it is in human signs (which are Gemini, Virgo, Libra, the first half of Sagittarius, and Aquarius), and if the Moon has the authority; or if she has authority and the Sun is in Libra. And if it is in Taurus or Capricorn, it signifies the oppression of horses, cows, bulls, and oxen. And if it is in Cancer, Scorpio, or Pisces, aquatic things will be oppressed. And these judgements have a place in the revolutions of the years of the world, in proportion to how they pertain to revolutions.

And if one of the malefics impedes him, examine this malefic, and see which sign it is in, and what house it is in: since the impediment will be according to the significations of the house and the sign in which he is.

And if the Sun is made fortunate, and one of the benefics aspect him, it signifies the good condition and the good disposition of all the aforementioned. For where he signified evil when he was impeded, there he will signify good when he is free; and where he signified falsity, there will be truth; where there was injustice, there will be justice; where there was depression, there will be exaltation; where there was lack, there will be abundance. And apply your mind to understand this well, lest you fall into error regarding these things.

And Albumashar said that if the Sun is in Aries or its triplicity, it will be in the eastern part.

And if the Sun is in good condition in his own place, it signifies the rectitude of the wealthy, and their justice and fitness; and victory over their enemies, and over those who contend with them.

And he said that if he is in bad condition in his place, it signifies the appearance of the wealthy and the magnates; and the scarcity of their winning over their enemies, and the fall of their honour in these cities. And he said that if the Sun is in Taurus or its triplicity, the appearance of the occurrence of those things which I said will be from the parts of the south, and from the cities which are ruled over by that sign, and that which belongs to it from the substance of the earth, seeds and trees. And he said that if he is in Gemini or its triplicity, it signifies the appearance of the occurrence of those things which I said, and all the things which belong to it concerning lofty matters will occur in the parts of the west. And he said that if he is in Cancer or its triplicity, the appearance of the occurrence of those things will be in the parts of the north, out of the animals which are signified by the sign.

And he said that the work in the matter of the Sun in the aspects of the planets to him will be like the work in the matter of Saturn in this, equally regarding good and evil.

## XCVI

### What The Sun Signifies In Each And Every House In The Revolution Of The Years Of A Nativity, And In The Years Of The World, And In Nativities, Whether He Is The Lord Of The Year, Or Not

When the Sun is in Aries, or in the first in a revolution of a nativity or a year of the world, he signifies the chief place and sublimity, and greatness of the matters of the native, and the same in a revolution. Likewise in a revolution of the years of the world it signifies the status and increase of the good of the citizens of the revolution in which the year is revolved - unless Saturn and Mars (or either of them) operate to the contrary; and the Sun planet is maliciously placed.

And if he is in the second, it signifies love amongst men, and their decent condition; however, there will be some deformities in the eyes.

And in the third he signifies change from one region to another, and that the king of that region will perfect his own affairs, and those of his subjects for the good and for the majority; and likewise for the native with his own affairs, in part from the king.

However, in the fourth he signifies praise between men, and their sublimity and honour; and things will appear which had remained hidden, and had not appeared, for a long time; and it also signifies the discovery of treasures, or their aggregation or acquisition.

However, in the fifth he signifies a change in the status of many men because of children; and a native will change his status on account of his own children; and that he will be revered by the commoners; and the commoners will revere those greater than themselves, and honour them; and there will even be rejoicing because of gifts.

Indeed, in the sixth it signifies infirmities and detriments because of slaves and of others who are signified by the sixth house; and that the country folk or the ignoble people will envy those greater than themselves; and likewise for the native.

And in the seventh, he signifies contrarieties which will befall the commoners from the nobility or magnates or kings. Likewise, the same will befall the native.

In the eighth he signifies the depression of the wealthy, magnates or nobility, and powerful people, and their diminution, death, and reproach.

In the ninth he signifies the good disposition of men's minds towards one another, and their thoughts will be pleasing to God, and on those things which pertain to faith.

In the tenth, he signifies the honour of kings and their exaltation, and their glory and advancement.

In the eleventh he signifies men's joy and happiness because of friends and mutual love between them, and because of matters in which they have faith for good; similar things will happen to the native from these things; and good things from magnates and those who are below kings.

Indeed, in the twelfth he signifies the diminution and depression of the wealthy and of magnates, and also of nobles; and their death; and the taking away of their dignities; and injuries inflicted on them by ignoble men; and it signifies contrarieties which befall the native from his enemies, and even from others, and more so from low class people than from magnates.

## XCVII

### On Venus, If She Is The Lord Of The Year: What She Signifies

If Venus is the Lord of the year, and she is in good condition and well disposed, she signifies the good disposition and good condition of women, as much of adults as of girls, as much of the corrupted as of virgins, and likewise of eunuchs. And if she is the Lord of the year and the Lord of the Ascendant, and is free from impediments and from malefics, she signifies a year of security and peace, and that matters will be appropriate in that year; and there will be good in honours, justice, abundance, rectitude and peace. If however, she is received, the country folk will find good from kings, the wealthy, and the magnates; and the country folk will love their king, and be obedient to him; and marriages will be multiplied, and there will be joy and gladness in women.

If however, she is impeded she signifies little good in that year, and there will be earthquakes in diverse lands, because of which buildings will fall; and there will be war, even if it is only a small amount; and the king of this region will be dejected. And these things will happen in the assigned region and her clime. If indeed, she is impeded at the hour of the revolution: she signifies the impediment and bad condition of all the aforementioned things.

And Albumashar said that if she is in a human sign, whatever belongs to her in terms of men will be impeded. If she is in an earth sign, whatever belongs to her in terms of the substance of the earth will be destroyed. If she is in an air sign, whatever belongs to her of the substance of the air will be destroyed. If she is in a water sign, whatever is hers in terms of the substance of the water will be destroyed. And he said that if there is a benefic instead of the impeding malefic, change your opinion, and say good instead of bad, and justice instead of injustice. And he said to examine each planet impeding her to see what kind of sign it is in, and mix them: and speak about him according to what was shown to you in the matter of Saturn

## XCVIII

### What Venus Signifies In Each And Every House In The Revolution Of The Year, Whether She Is The Lord Of The Year Or Not

If Venus is in the first in a revolution, and she is in good condition and well disposed, then she signifies that for men, and similarly for the native, there will be love, joy, and delights, and they will delight in eating and drinking: and will be eager for living in a beautiful way, as much in the necessities and clothing, as in the appearance and displaying of clothing or ornaments of the body, and the use of rings, as in necklaces and similar things, as in fragrant things, as in the appearance of honourable things and everything in which men delight.

And if she is in the second, she signifies utility and acquisition because of women, and from the direction of women, and advancement because of these acquisitions.

But if she is in the third, she signifies the forgetting of religion, and that men will care little for it, and likewise the native: and incontinence in sex, and the anger which follows for this reason; and from this many evil deeds will be perpetrated, and friends will help friends in doing these things.

If indeed, she is in the fourth, Albumashar says that she signifies undeserved mourning and sorrow in matters from the direction of mothers, and its end will be laudable.

Indeed, in the fifth she signifies detriment because of children in the beginning of the revolution, but in the end it will be praised and the mourning will change to joy.

However, in the sixth, Albumashar said that she signifies infirmities and tribulations from the direction of slaves and slavegirls, and from the mother, and she signifies widows. Whence if the Lord of the sixth is in good condition, things will be good for them, and vice versa. And he said that the Lord of the question will not attain all that he sought from things. And he said that if it is a question about an ill person, he will be liberated from his illness. And he said that the reason for his liberation will be according to what I set forth to you in the matter of Saturn in the first book. And he said to know that if a benefic is in the house of illness, the illness will be alleviated, but if a malefic is there, it will become more severe.

And he said that if she is in the seventh she signifies marriage, and joy from women, and from all things sought from participation.

And every matter he wishes for will be perfected for him.

In the eighth she signifies the death of older sisters, mothers, and nurses.

In the ninth she signifies change of the religious from one residence to another, and the truth of dreams; and she signifies far-off pilgrimages.

Indeed, in the tenth she signifies joy from kings and from the direction of kings.

Indeed, in the eleventh she signifies joy and happiness from good things which happen to them; and trust and good hope from the direction of friends, and good fortune from them.

But if she is in the twelfth, she signifies tribulations and enmity from women, and much of the time from low class women, and similar things will happen from a nativity.

## XCIX

### What Venus Signifies In Each And Every Sign In A Revolution Of The Year

#### ♀ ♈

If Venus is in Aries in the revolution, and she is the Lord of the year and in good condition (namely fortunate, strong, and free from impediments), she signifies the good condition of the wealthy, magnates, and nobles; and she also signifies the air to be temperate, and its peace in eastern parts: and she signifies soft and temperate rains, not harmful rains; and the good condition of the Arabs, and extinction of war in those parts, and the abundance of their provisions; and peace amongst men, and rest, tranquillity, games and dances in the countries which are in the division of Aries; and the exercise of their citizens in Venusian matters. If however, she is impeded, it signifies impediment, namely that she will not do good, and she will not be able to resist evils.

#### ♀ ♌

If she is in Leo, she signifies the extinction of wars and contentions, or at least their mitigation and weakness; and mortality in the parts of the east; and there will be gladness and delights in Venusian matters, and especially in the wealthy, magnates, and nobles, unless Mars operates to the contrary.

#### ♀ ♐

And if she is in Sagittarius, and she is well disposed, she signifies peace and tranquillity, and the extinction of war in the parts of the west, and in the Arab lands; and the goodness and salvation of the bodies of the citizens of these regions, and the profit of their businessmen, and the health of their children, unless Mars operates to the contrary; and the abundance of rain, somewhat more than there ought to be; and the coldness of their winter will be tempered; and their honey and wine will bring profit; and she signifies little profit for the bearers of arms of these parts, unless Mars oppresses Venus, or she is otherwise greatly impeded, or badly disposed.

#### ♀ ♉

And if Venus is in Taurus in the revolution of the year, and she is in good condition, it signifies that the appearance of those things which she signifies will generally be in southern parts; they will also appear in the parts of Jerusalem, and in the right side of the east, or in the Turkish lands, and in Roman lands. She also signifies winds to come in these parts, but not harmful ones; and the saving of the fruits of the trees; and this will happen in part from her benign nature; and it signifies the goodness of the air, and the safety of women and cattle in these parts; and also the saving of the yearly produce; and likewise the citizens of these lands will be useful, unless Mars operates to the contrary, or if Venus is impeded or badly disposed.

#### ♀ ♍

And if she is in Virgo, and is well disposed, she signifies the tranquillity and good condition of northern parts; and the abundance of wine, grain, butter, and fat; and there will not be mortality there, unless Mars operates to the contrary.

## ♀ ♑

And if Venus is in Capricorn, she signifies the scarcity of war, robbery, pillaging, highway robbery, and tribulations; and the safety of young men; and the scarcity of rain in eastern and southern parts; and the abundance of grain, wine, and butter: and there will be tranquillity between eastern and southern parts. But if she is impeded, or Mars operates to the contrary, her significations will be destroyed, and she will not be able to benefit.

## ♀ ♊

And if Venus is in Gemini in the revolution of the year, and she is in good condition, it signifies that the appearance of her significations will happen in western parts; and likewise in Arab lands, and in northern parts; and she signifies the safety of men in these parts; and the temperateness of the air and rains; and the diminution of war and contrariety; and the increase of gladness in northern parts.

## ♀ ♎

And if Venus is in Libra and she is in good condition, and free from impediments, she signifies the safety of the citizens which are in the division of Libra; and the safety of men more so than women: and she signifies the safety of men in southern parts, unless Saturn operates to the contrary; and there will be wine, butter, and fat in these parts; and robberies, highway robberies, pillaging, and contention will be mitigated, unless Mars operates to the contrary, or Venus is impeded.

## ♀ ♒

And if she is in Aquarius and she is in good condition and well disposed; she signifies the good condition of men, and the removal (or at least the diminution) of the burdens and tribulations which are going to come to men in that revolution; and the diminution of snow, rain, and coldness in winter; and the salvation of wine and butter in western parts, and in Alexandria, and in the whole land which is said to be of businessmen; and the safety of the king of that region in which you revolve the year. If she aspects the Ascendant, and she is northern, she signifies the scarcity of wine; however, it will be a good, useful, and pleasant spring, unless Mars operates to the contrary, or Venus is otherwise badly disposed.

## ♀ ♋

And if Venus is in Cancer in the revolution of the year, it signifies that the appearance of those things which she signifies will be in the northern parts; and she signifies the salvation of those sailing, and peace between men in western parts; and alleviation from renderings and tributes more than usual; and there will be a diminution of fevers and other illnesses; and heat will be diminished; and there will be rains; and the dangers which are going to come in that year or revolution will be alleviated; and likewise the death of quadrupeds will be alleviated, and especially horses: unless Mars operates to the contrary, or Venus is otherwise badly disposed.

## ♀ ♏

And if she is in Scorpio, and free from impediments, she signifies the lessening of the clouds, and the good disposition of the air, and the alleviation of the cold of the winter, and the heat of the summer, and the salvation of the yearly produce and trees; and illnesses, especially eye pains will be reduced, and especially in youths; and robberies, highway robberies, and wars will likewise be reduced; and wine and butter will be saved; and these things will happen more so in northern parts than in others.

## ♀ ♓

And if she is in Pisces, it signifies the diminution of snow, rain, and mortality in southern parts; and the capture of fish, and the safety of the kingdoms of those parts, and of the wealthy, nobility, and magnates; and the yearly produce will be saved, so that it will not suffer severe detriment (and wine likewise). And if she is impeded and badly disposed, and aspects the Ascendant, she signifies thunder and flashes, and death in men, and pains of the eyes; however, those things born of the earth will be increased (unless Saturn operates to the contrary).

## C

## On Mercury, If He Is The Lord Of The Year: What He Signifies

If Mercury is the Lord of the year or revolution, and he is in good condition, well disposed, and free from impediments, he signifies the good condition of businessmen, sages, writers, those doing great works, mathematicians, those using number by way of teaching, and geometers; it also signifies the good condition of children, according to how he is joined with the planets. For if he is joined with a masculine planet, this will happen in males; if with a feminine planet, it will happen in females; and this will be better if the Lord of the domicile he is in receives him.

But if Mercury is the Lord of the year and the Lord of the Ascendant, and is free from impediments, and one of the benefics aspect him, men will find good from the king; and everyone will find good from their masters: and will be heard from them, and will find honour, praise, and a good and praiseworthy status from them; and the year will be of utility to the aforementioned persons. If however, he is impeded, and is not received, it signifies the contrary of those things which were said: since men will find difficulties from kings, and from their masters, and will be oppressed by them: and the year will be contrary to boys, sages, businessmen, and the other people mentioned above.

However, Albumashar said that if in addition to this he is aspected by a malefic, his condition will be destroyed from the place which I said. And he said that if the Moon is free from malefics, the rain and cold will be multiplied, and the legates will rejoice and find good; and this will be better and more deserving, if he is received: since then they will find dignities from the king (or kings), and it will rain in the season when it is necessary. If however, he is in bad condition, and badly disposed, it signifies the impediment and bad condition of the aforementioned, and their evil disposition, each one according to his own subject. If however, he is joined to masculine and feminine planets at the same time, it signifies that this will happen universally to boys and girls.

And Albumashar said that whatever belongs to him will suffer detriment from this. Next will be the narration on those things which pertain to him, and on the human, air, earth, water and bestial figures he is placed in, and the aspect of malefics and benefics to him, and his clothing by them. And he said that all of this will be narrated in the way I demonstrated to you equally so in the chapter of Saturn.

## ☿ ♈

If he is in Aries or its triplicity (and especially in Aries), he signifies the abundance of waters, or much rain; and the scarcity of the yearly produce in western parts, and the detriment of wine; and he signifies that there will be strong winds in that revolution, and dew and soft and thin clouds; and the death of children, as I said. If however, the Moon is joined to him, it signifies the multitude of fish. If however, he is joined to the Sun, it signifies the abundance of wine, and the safety of women; and this more strongly so, if Mars and Venus are then with the Sun, when Mercury is joined to him. If however, Saturn is there instead of Venus, it signifies the multiplication of waters. If Mars alone is with him, it signifies eye pains, and a multitude of battles and wars.

## ☿ ♌

And if he is in Leo, it signifies the severity of the summer in its seasons, and the severity of the summer winds. And if he is past the tenth house, up to the seventh he signifies impediments in those parts, and the scarcity of the yearly produce, but not the extermination of it. And if one of the benefics aspect him, this malice will be destroyed; and it signifies the scarcity of wine and fat (however, dates will abound in the parts in which they grow); and there will be eye pains; and there will be death in wolves and other quadrupeds living by seizing prey.

And Albumashar said that the condition of the nobility will deteriorate in Khorasen. And the aspect of malefics increases the evil, and the aspect of benefics spares and restrains it, by the will of God.

## ☿ ♐

If however, he is in Sagittarius, it signifies that there will be snow in that revolution in its usual season; and the diversity and inconstancy of the air; and the scarcity of grain, and of the fruits of the trees and lands; and the scarcity of waters. However, there will be wine, butter, oil, and fat, and there will be battles and wars in western parts.

## ☿ ♉

Albumashar said that if Mercury is in Taurus, he signifies a multitude of waters; and the destruction of the harvest, and the detriment of wine, and this could happen because of the diversity of the air, and the diversity of its alterations; and he signifies the scarcity of butter, oil, or fat; and he signifies eye pains from the direction of the east; and the death of nobles (namely princes and magnates or wealthy men), unless Jupiter and Venus operate to the contrary: since if they aspect the Ascendant of the revolution, they will destroy all of the malice and impediment which is signified by Mercury. If indeed, Mars aspects the Ascendant of the revolution, it signifies the severity of war, and he also signifies the death of cattle, and this will happen more so in southern parts.

## ☿ ♍

And if he is in Virgo, Albumashar said that rains and harvests will be multiplied; and there will be an abundance of eye pains; and death in the parts of Animarot.

## ☿ ♑

And if he is in Capricorn it signifies that wars and tribulations are going to come in the parts of Khorasen.

However, Albumashar said that if he is conjoined with Venus and Mars, there will be war in Khorasen from the men of Abagir.

## ☿ ♊

And Albumashar said that if Mercury is in Gemini: he signifies battles on the part of the Latins, from the citizens and magnates of Khorasan; and a multitude of snows, and detriment in the harvest, oil, and butter; and there will be a multitude of wine; and it signifies pestilence and death in women; and a multitude of blisters, and inflammations beneath the skin; it also signifies dew and the humidity of the air.

And Albumashar said that if the Sun and Jupiter aspect the Ascendant of the year, pestilence and death will be reduced: and men will be stronger than usual in eastern parts, and wealthier, and they will make more profit, and make more progress.

## ☿ ♎

And if he is in Libra, it signifies the scarcity of wine and the yearly produce; and signifies that there will be powerful and severe winds in that revolution. And if Saturn aspects him or is joined to him, it signifies pains in the head and stomach are going to come to men. But if the Sun then aspects Saturn, it will repel the malice, and destroy it, and it will not impede.

## ☿ ♒

And if Mercury is in Aquarius he signifies a multitude of locusts in the parts where they usually are; and the scarcity of rain; and he signifies itches and blisters happening to men from the corruption of the air and from its diversity. And if he is then corporeally joined with Venus, it signifies that an earthquake is going to come in that revolution; and this more strongly so, if they are joined with the Sun, and stronger again if Mars or Saturn aspects them from opposition or square aspect); and there will be pestilences, and thieves will be multiplied. And from the conjunction of Saturn it signifies an abundance of rain.

## ☿ ♋

If indeed, he is in Cancer, it signifies that there will be killing in the western parts, and also in Animarot; and the scarcity of grain, fat, and butter; and that impediment will befall trees, and also seeds, and in wine; and there will be infirmities, and especially around the part of the neck and throat because of catarrh, such as sore throats, and similar things. And if he is joined to Mars and Venus simultaneously, it signifies the killing of the wealthy, and the magnates or nobles, in the western parts; unless Venus and the Moon operate to the contrary, which, if they aspect, they will destroy the malice and repel it.

## ☿ ♏

And if he is in Scorpio, he signifies a multitude of snow and rain in their seasons in the usual regions; and he signifies battles and war in the western and northern parts (even if there may be some remission); and if Mars aspects him, the northern parts will be stronger than the western ones; and there will be more thieves and highwaymen than usual; and there will be pestilences in the northern parts, and fevers with strong cold; and there will be abscesses and eye pains with lippitude and redness and ophthalmia.

## ☿ ♓

However if he is in Pisces, it signifies wind and rain, and these things will mostly happen in northern parts.

And Albumashar said that there will be death in the parts of Animarot; and the things crawling on the earth will be multiplied, and also fish. All of these things will come to be if Mercury is the sole significator. But if planets aspect him, the significations will be according to the disposition of the planets, and their aspects to him.

And you should not be surprised that I put down Mercury's placements in the signs: since the revolutions are not only made according to the entry of the Sun into Aries alone: but rather they are made according to his entry into every mobile sign, namely when the revolution is according to halves or according to quarters, just as often happens: and then what I said will be possible, even if it won't always be possible.

## CI

## What Mercury Signifies In Each And Every House, Whether A Revolution Of The World, Whether In Nativities, Or Whether In The Revolution Of A Nativity, Whether He Is The Lord Of The Year, Or Not

If Mercury is the Lord of the year, and he is in the first house in a revolution (or a nativity), if it is the revolution of the year of the world, he signifies the practice of men who are interested in wisdom, and likewise in writing and instruction, and that they will be more eloquent in disputations, and in the sciences of the quadrivium than they are usually. If however, it is in a nativity or revolution of a nativity, it signifies that the native will be wise in literature, eloquent in disputations, and learned in number, measures, harmonies, and in the motions of the heavenly bodies, and what happens because of them.

And if he is in the second, it signifies wealth and profit, and the increase of substance, and the increase of honour, and a good reputation with the king and from the king, and good status and good condition amongst men, as much for the native as for others.

And if he is in the third he signifies the good condition of siblings from brothers and sisters, and of friends from friends. For the native it signifies the abundance of brothers and sisters according to the natural possibility, and a multitude of friends of the native, and of household members, and of those who love him.

And if he is in the fourth, it signifies more verbal altercations between men than usual; and also that contentions, sorrows or griefs are going to befall amongst men.

And if he is in the fifth, it signifies good fortune from children; and from the direction of children; and joy and from rumours coming from somewhere; and that men will rejoice from dances or games, and delightful things; and that the sorrow which they had will leave them; and matters of which they will rejoice and be happy from will come over them. The same thing will happen to the native, as much in a nativity as a revolution, if Mercury is found like this.

And if he is in the sixth, he signifies contentions which will arrive to men, and likewise to the native, from the direction of ignoble men, and deceptions from the direction of slaves and slave girls, servants, maids, and small animals; and the deterioration and diminution of matters and honour.

And if he is in the seventh, he signifies friskiness and delight from the direction of women and from women, and contentions for this reason.

And if he is in the eighth, it signifies contentions which fall between men because of matters now past, which will be renewed between them. And if it is a nativity, or the revolution of a nativity, it signifies that enmity will befall the native from his neighbours, and from the direction of neighbours, which he can hardly or never avoid; and they will speak falsehoods against him, and contentions will befall him for this reason, and because of possessions which are left to him by the dead, or on account of a very ancient thing.

And if he is in the ninth, it signifies mutual praise between men, and honour: and for the native he signifies wisdom, learning, and that if he adheres to the quadrivium, he will advance well in it, especially in astronomy, and also in other sciences: and that he will be praised in this by people he knows, and even by others.

And if he is in the tenth, he signifies that the native will acquire a magistracy or dignities, and great honour, because of literature and writing, and the quadrivium of arithmetic, geometry, music, and astronomy. And he signifies the same in the revolution of the world for those who are experienced in these sciences.

If he is in the eleventh he signifies that there will be mutual friendship between men; and in nativities and in a revolution of a nativity, he signifies a multitude of friends, and joy because of nobles and from nobles.

If he is in the twelfth in a revolution of the year of the world he signifies the insipidity of men in that revolution, and their ignorance. If however, he is in the twelfth in a nativity, or the revolution of a nativity, it signifies the stupidity of the native and the diversity of his mind, and his lack of knowledge or sense, and his imbecility, drunkenness, levity, impudence, and ineptitude in coming and going, and asking about unsuitable things, and those

which lack roots. And if it ever happens that he knows, understands, or discerns anything, it will be more so regarding animals than anything else.

## CII

## What The Moon Signifies If She Is Lord Of The Year

If the Moon is the Lord of the year or revolution, and she is in good condition (namely fortunate namely, strong, and free from impediments), she signifies the good condition of the mob generally; and also the good condition of sailors, mothers, idlers, and also buffoons or gluttons, and their rest during the day; and the goodness of their way of life. However, if she is impeded, it signifies the contrary of those things which I said; and the bad condition of the aforementioned people and of all of her significations. And if she is in human signs, the impediment will be in people according to the sex of the sign in which she is placed. And if she is in fire signs, the impediment will fall upon all of those things which she signifies of fiery things. If however, she is in an earth sign, it will fall upon all that she signifies of earthy things. And if she is in an air sign, it will fall upon all things which she signifies of airy things. Likewise, if she is in a water sign, it will fall upon all things which she signifies of watery things. And if she is in a sign formed in the image of any other animals, the impediment will fall upon the animals of a similar form to this sign.

And Albumashar said that to see in what type of sign the planets are aspected: for the narration will be about all of these things in the way which I revealed to you in the chapter on Saturn. And he said to know this, and understand it well: since all of these things belong to the secrets of the science of the stars. And he said that there will be nothing in them which will be hidden from you, God willing.

However, you can pay attention to a certain thing, the root of which I have not found, and which is not mentioned by any sage: this being that whatever kind of revolution of the year it is, or whatever its Lord is like, if it rains noticeably on the 11th day from the beginning of June, bad things, detriment, and impediment will fall upon the fruits and things born of the earth, and one-sixth of them will be destroyed. And if the Lord of the hour of the Ascendant of the revolution is impeded, one-fifth of them will suffer detriment. And if the Moon is impeded at this time it will befall one-fourth of them. If indeed, the Lord of the Ascendant of the revolution is impeded, one-third of the aforementioned things will be destroyed.

You will consider again whether it rains or not on the sixth day into October: since if it rains by way of rain, judge that there are going to be harmful rains; and this will be stronger and more harmful, if the conjunction of the Sun and Moon, or their opposition is on that day; and this will be stronger if the conjunction is in a moist mansion.

## CIII

## What The Moon Signifies In The Revolution Of The Year Of The World, In Each And Every House, Or In A Nativity, Or A Revolution Of A Nativity, Whether She Is The Lord Of The Year Or Not

When the Moon is in the first house in the revolution of the year of the world, whether she is the Lord of the year or not, she signifies rapid changes of men from place to place in that revolution; and their rapid changes from one thing to another; from one proposition to another; and she signifies the effecting of matters which men involve themselves in. And she signifies the chief place and dignities for those who they are suitable for; and also that men will acquire goods from those greater than them; and those who have mothers will acquire good things from them; and men will rejoice from women. And if it is a nativity, good things will happen to the native. And it will be the same in the native's revolution.

If however, she is in the second, it signifies grief and sorrow which will befall the native because of substance, and that they will lose their goods in that revolution; and it will be similarly diminished for a native.

And if she is in the third, she signifies that men will be friendly to one another, and especially in the countries which are in the division of the sign in which the Moon is then placed; and this will likewise happen between brothers, for their love will be increased. And if there is enmity between them, it will be diminished; and men will perfect matters which they begin, and those which they are longing to perfect; and they will also acquire good things from wealthy men and magnates; and dignities from kings and nobles, and wealthy men and magnates who are fit for kingship. And pilgrimages will be suitable and useful, unless Saturn or Mars operate to the contrary. Say the same about the matters of the native, and that he will strive to be with nobles and wealthy people who are not slaves to money.

But if she is in the fourth, and it is a diurnal revolution, it signifies its beginning will be bad and impeded, however, its end will be praiseworthy. If however, it is nocturnal, neither its beginning nor end will be praised: and men's things will be reduced, and their persons will also suffer detriment, unless Jupiter operates to the contrary. And if it is the nativity or revolution of a native, the same will happen to him. And if it is a question, the querent will be sorrowful for this reason, and he will rejoice in the same way that was said for a diurnal or nocturnal revolution. Albumashar said that things will be like this unless it is a question about acquiring a treasure, or about something that is buried, since in this case it is optimal, for the thing will appear, and be uncovered.

And if she is in the fifth she signifies having children in that revolution. And if it is a nativity, it signifies a multitude of children. And if it is a revolution of a nativity, it signifies having children in it, if the natives nature is fit to be able to do this; and this signifies male children in nocturnal cases, and female in diurnal; and say the same as this in nativities and their revolutions, and of questions. And not many horrible things will appear.

And Albumashar said that it signifies the arrival of rumours from far-away regions from which men will rejoice, and especially parents whose children are absent. And he said if you want to know what these rumours are, examine the planet from which the Moon separates: since the rumours will be according to the nature of this planet. And if you wish to know if the rumours are written on paper, or if they come from the mouth of a legate, examine the Moon and Mercury to see if she is joined to him or separating from him. And if she separates from the Lord of the seventh and is joined to Mercury, the rumours will be written on paper. Indeed, if she is separating from Mercury or from his Lord, a legate will relate the rumours.

And if she is in the sixth, Albumashar said that she signifies disputes and contentions from the direction of fathers, and profit from quadrupeds, and the health of the body.

And he said that if she is in the seventh she signifies profit from the direction of women, and marriage, and success because of these things.

And he said that if she is in the eighth she signifies the ruin, finishing up, and deposition of the king, or his death; and disorder in works, and men will falsely testify against one another; and they will quarrel with each other, and one will strive to chase the other away, and throw him out of his own place. And there will be tribulations and anxieties in men, and infirmities of the soul or the mind: as are those which befall raging people who are not right in the head, who are called "*lunatics*" by the mob. For she signifies enchanters and enchantresses making themselves out to know such enchantments, so that they might extort something from some people - because of which enchantments certain men in tunics falsely condemn astrologers. And there will be evil thoughts in the hearts of men. And if it is a nativity, the native will apply himself to these things. And it signifies the same in the revolution of a nativity.

And Albumashar said that if she is in the ninth, it signifies participation in journeys, evil thoughts, and the change of the king from one region to another; and the command of women; and the knowledge of the ordering of the kingdom and of other affairs. And he said that if the 9th domicile is one of the domiciles of Mercury, it signifies the wisdom of astrologers. And if it is one of the domiciles of Venus, it signifies the loftiness of the sciences and of signing. And if it is one of the domiciles of Mars it signifies the mastery of instruments and work of arms. And if it is one of the domiciles of Jupiter, it signifies divine worship, and knowledge in law, and the pre-eminence of judges. And if it is one of the domiciles of Saturn, it signifies knowledge of alchemy and practicing it: for men will be eager for this in that revolution. And likewise for the natives in whose nativity, or revolution, the Moon is placed in the ninth. And if there is an unimpeded benefic in the second or the fourth, profit will follow from it, otherwise it won't. But if there is a malefic there, harm will follow from it. And if this malefic is impeded, destruction of substance will follow from it, and it signifies

many and diverse professions. And if it is the domicile of the Sun, it signifies knowledge and foreknowledge in all of the disciplines of the quadrivium. And if it is her own domicile, she signifies general knowledge of all matters which are taken from the water, or which proceed from them. And he said to know that the Moon has these particular significations among the planets.

And Albumashar said that if she is in the 10th, it signifies the effecting of matters in questions, but this will be done by the mandates of the king if it is during the day. If indeed, it is at night it signifies the effecting of matters from the direction of the king and women, and this will be done quickly. However, he also said that matters in both times, namely in day and at night, will not be durable. Likewise, if a king begins to reign while she is there, he will be quickly deposed: since this place is effective in the significations of the Sun; with the Moon it is not sufficient, except in a slight way in this signification.

And if she is in the eleventh, it signifies that one friend will follow another; it also signifies the obtaining of things which men hope for, and those in which they have faith; and likewise for the native, as much in his nativity as his revolution.

Indeed, in the twelfth she signifies impediment, harshness, and instability of things, and disputes and imprisonment from the direction of enemies.

And Albumashar said that if you are asked about some matter, and when it will be, and the Moon is your significatrix, and she is in the twelfth, it will be at the hour of her exit from the same place: for the matter will be perfected through this, and it will be, and the absent person will arrive, and especially if this is at the end of the lunar month. And if the Moon is impeded by Saturn, then judge a horrible and evil thing, and you should not doubt this, if God wills it.

## CIV

## What The Caput And Cauda, And Comets Signify In The Revolution Of The Year, Both Of The World And Of A Nativity

I spoke above on the significations of the seven planets, and what each one of them signify in every sign, and in every house in the revolutions of the years, both of the world and of nativities, and in nativities themselves. Now it remains to speak about the Caput Draconis (what it signifies in the revolutions), and on its Cauda, and on the comets (what these hairy or tailed stars signify, and how many there are, just as will be said in its own special chapter).

☊ ♈ ☋

Albumashar said that if the Caput Draconis is in Aries, he signifies the exaltation of great men, and of nobles, and the dejection of the low class or ignoble people.

And if the Cauda is there, she signifies the bad disposition and bad condition of kings and the nobility, and their injury from the country folk or the commoners.

And if one of the comets is there, it signifies the evil and detriment of the wealthy, the magnates, and the nobility in the eastern parts, and Babylonia; and a multitude of sorrows with the country folk. And he said that if its appearance is in the eastern parts, its work will be swift. If indeed, it appears from the western parts, it will be slower, etc.

☊ ♉ ☋

And if the Caput is in Taurus, it signifies the killing of the wealthy and the magnates in the northern parts; and it signifies a multitude of differences between the wealthy men and magnates, and the country folk of the western parts.

And if the Cauda is there, it signifies the scarcity of piety and sympathy in the hearts of men; and pilgrimages will be useless in those parts, of little profit and much labour.

And if one of the comets were to appear in its direction, it signifies the bad condition of men, and the scarcity of their good, and injurious rebellion against those who are in these regions, and if the comet appears in the eastern parts, its work will be quick. And if it appears in the west, it will be slower, etc.

☊ ♊ ☋

And if the Caput is in Gemini, it signifies that infirmities are going to come to the wealthy, and magnates, and this will happen because of winds, earthquakes, and wicked fumes of the earth, and war will fall between ordinary men and the wealthy (or the nobles and magnates); and the occurrence of vermin in trees.

If however, the Cauda is there, it signifies that the country folk will be exalted, and they will resist and rise up against the king, and that they will trick him; and they will rise up against his soldiers and wealthy men, or deputies.

But if one of the comets appears in its direction, it signifies the appearance of wantonness and fornications, and impure sex in men, and the dejection of the religious and of the servants of God, and these men will be despised. And if it appears in the eastern parts, its work will be quicker; and if it appears in the western parts, it will be slower

☊ ♋ ☋

And if the Caput is in Cancer, he signifies the goodness of the king's actions towards the country folk and the commoners, and his generosity towards them, and that they will collect the substance of the king, and after it is collected in its own places, they will disperse it

And if the Cauda is there, it signifies a multitude of pestilences and mortality, and sudden death, and fornication and the abuse of sex, and the scarcity of justice; and the breaking and loss of the wealth; and the destruction of houses, substance, and the movement of the wealthy and the magnates from place to place, and their pilgrimage; and the bad condition of the great works of their hands, and also of writers and other significations of Mercury.

And if any of the comets appear there, it signifies a multitude of locusts destroying the harvest; and vermin in grain and trees, and the scarcity of produce and a multitude of vermin in them. And if it appears in the eastern parts, its work will be faster. And if it appears in the western parts its work will be slower, and it signifies the goodness of the king towards the country folk, and his piety with regard to them.

♌ ♌ ☋

And if the Caput is in Leo, he signifies a multitude of rivers, and the appearance of fire in the air; many injuries; and evil and killing.

And if the Cauda is there, she signifies a multitude of obscurity in the air, and earthquakes; and the increase of waters and the detriment of trees; and the destruction of the harvest.

And if one of the comets were to appear there, it signifies an infestation of wolves; and impediment to men from them; and vermin to infest grain; and the destruction of houses and substance. And if its appearance is in eastern parts, its work will be quicker. And if it is in the western parts, its work will be slower.

♌ ♍ ☋

And if the Caput is in Virgo, he signifies the destruction of the harvest and the rest of the produce; and the scarcity of all things which are harvested; and an infestation of vermin in trees; and the detriment of those things which remain from the first destruction, even after they are stored in a place in which they are believed to be safe or guarded.

And if the Cauda is there, she signifies that hatred is going to fall in the wealthy and the magnates, and there will be wars, dissension, and battles between them; and the churches and great houses of religion will suffer detriment; and there will be diversities and controversies between men, and debates and dissensions in faith.

And if one of the comets were to appear there, it signifies the removal of certain of the king's household members, and certain magnates, and their movement from place to place, or from region to region; and they will be led almost like captives, or as those deported or sent over the borders. And their goods will be taken away, without being returned to them, and they will not be recovered by them or for them. And if its appearance is in the eastern parts, its work will be quicker. If however, it is western, its work will be slower

♌ ♎ ☋

And if the Caput is in Libra, it signifies that the kings, the wealthy, the nobles and the magnates, will exercise their powers on the country folk contrary to justice, and especially against those who they rule; and they will strive to extort things from them which they ought not to; and they will accuse them and say that they have offended them concerning things are not their fault; and they will think that they stole things from them which they did not steal: and for this reason the they will inveigh against them. And they will afflict them with such punishment, that for this reason they will come into poverty and need; and they will dupe them.

But if the Cauda is there, she signifies the mortality and detriment of quadrupeds; and there will be dryness and severe cold in their own seasons, destroying the harvest in the fields, and the plants, the trees, and the seeds, in such a way that little produce will be collected from them.

And if one of the comets appear there, it signifies thieves and highwaymen and pillagers who openly extend their strength to men, and pillage all that they can; and men's thoughts will be in fear lest they fall into poverty; and they will expect harm, and they will have fear at one time because of coldness, at another because of heat, and this will endure long in their hearts. And if its appearance is in the eastern parts, its work will be faster. If however, it is in the western parts, it will be slower.

♌ ♏ ☋

And if the Caput is in Scorpio, Albumashar said that it signifies good and joy in ordinary men, and evil and sorrow in magnates; and it signifies war, battles, and injuries; and the multiplication of fornication with deception. And he said that it signifies that they will fall into the hands of the king, in addition to what befalls them in terms of grief and sorrow.

And he said that if the Cauda is there, she signifies the occurrence of fever in men, and infirmities happening in the chest, and a multitude of catarrhs in the throat; with the joy of the wealthy in that time, and their happiness through much peace, and a multitude of wars; and the collection of substance, and the destruction of their homes.

And if one of the comet stars appear there, it signifies the multitude of wars, battles, and rebels against the king; and the change of soldiers between them; and its search by them in addition to those things which are not in their hands, nor their power; for they will seek impossible things. And if its appearance is in the eastern parts, its work will be faster. If indeed, it is in the western parts it will be slower.

♌ ♐ ☋

And if the Caput is in Sagittarius, it signifies the affliction of the country folk of Babylonia by their king; and that he will oppress them with injuries and torments; and that all of their quadrupeds will be impeded, and especially horses and other animals which soldiers and bearers of arms use (and this more strongly so if he is in the last half of Sagittarius); and there will be impediments and diminution in instruments of war. It also signifies the heaviness of the air, and its obscurity, with much corruption, and the heat will be aggravated in its season.

And if the Cauda is there, it signifies the dejection of the nobility and magnates, and their bad condition: and the exaltation of low class and ignoble people (and this more strongly if she is in the first half of Sagittarius); and wise men, scribes, doctors of law, consuls, or advisors will be saddened, or hidden impediments will befall them, because of which they will be saddened.

And if one of the comets were to appear there, it signifies the depression of the aforementioned, and tribulation falling upon them (and especially scribes); and their annihilation with the loss of substance because of concealment. And if it appears in the eastern parts, its work will be quicker. If however, it appears in the western parts, its work will be slower.

♌ ♑ ☋

And if the Caput is in Capricorn, he signifies the gladness, loftiness, and joy of the wealthy, the magnates, and the nobles, and their exaltation, and the fall of the low class and the ignoble, who are called "tails" or "caudae" by certain people.

But if the Cauda is there, she signifies harmful earthquakes in certain parts of the earth, and especially in the southern parts.

And if one of the comets were to appear there, it signifies fornication in men in those times. And if its appearance is in the east, its work will be quicker. If however, it is in the west, it will be slower.

♌ ♒ ☋

And if the Caput is in Aquarius, it signifies the detriment of the religious, and of the faith of the members of sects; and the death of certain people from them, and of judges and doctors of law.

And if the Cauda is there, Albumashar said that she signifies the investigation of the king against Lords of the estates in that which they ought not to; and their misleading in their wealth; and injuries and afflictions which he will inflict against them, with their capture and whipping.

And if one of the comets were to appear there, it signifies a multitude of battles, killings, and tortures, in the same season. And if its appearance is in the eastern parts, its work will be faster. If however, it is in the western parts, it will be slower.

♌ ♓ ☋

And if the Caput is in Pisces, Albumashar said that it signifies the loftiness of the nobles, and each man excelling in his own rank more than he ought to excel according to his nature, and the collection of substance in the houses of substance.

And if the Cauda is there, it signifies the extension of soldiers over the king; and the multitude of the wealthy and the movement of a huge number of the wealthy from their habitations because of sins; with many discussions in the sects, and the apparition of new ones.

And if one of the comet stars were to appear in this sign, there will be the greatest war over allies of the king; and they will kill each other and there will be enmity in the others; and the arrest of their company of soldiers for obedience. If however, its appearance is in the direction of the east, it will be fast in that which it signifies. And if it is in the direction of the west, its work will be slow in that which it signifies.

However, if you wish to see the part in which the significations of the comet will come, it will be in the part which its tail is. Since in that same part will be what was signified regarding tribulation and pestilence. Indeed, in the remaining works (which were said) Albumashar said that the hour will be when the Sun comes to the sign which was of the substance of those things which I told you; or to the planet whose nature is in the work, just as the nature of the occurrence which appears to you like it ought to happen in that year. And he said to know this and consider it, since it is one of the secrets of the science of the stars, and its truth; a precept of which work is that it should be hidden, and it will not be seen except by you, according to what I explained to you.

## CV

### On Comets

Ptolemy said that there are nine types of comets: the first of which the first are called "*veru*"; the second "*coenaculum*"; the third "*partica*"; the fourth "*miles*"; the fifth "*dominus asconae*"; the sixth "*matutina*" or "*aurora*"; the seventh "*silver*"; the eighth "*rosy*"; the ninth "*black*".

And he said that the first four of them are similar to stars, and all of them signify war, terrors, and great events in the world. And he said that the evil which is to come will be known from their colour, and from the nature of the sign in which they first appear; and when the evil will come will also be known: for if it appears in the east, or the north, and goes toward the south, it will be quick; and if in the west, it will be slow.

Those which are called *veru* are a horrible sight, and go close to the Sun, and appear during the day; and when they appear, they signify changes and diminution of produce, trees, and things born of the earth; and the mortality of kings and the wealthy, and those who are fit for kingship.

Those which are called *coenaculum*, are almost of the colour of Mars, and have rays beneath themselves which are like smoke from things prepared under ashes; and when they appear, they signify scarcity, however, not in an excessive way,

nor famine; and they signify battles in which the religious will involve themselves to a degree beyond their level of competence.

Those which are called *partica* have thick rays, and drag a long staff behind them, and are not very bright; and when they appear, they signify dryness and the scarcity of water, and the scarcity of the yearly produce; and if they are joined with one of the planets, they signify different things according to the nature and disposition of the planet whom they are corporeally joined to. So that if one is joined with Saturn, there will be mortality, and much of it will be in old men, Jews, the religious, and those wearing saturnine vestments. If however, it is joined with Jupiter, its significations will appear in kings and magnates according to good and evil: according to how Jupiter is disposed (whether he is fortunate and strong, or unfortunate and weak). If it is joined to Mars, it signifies very many battles, and mortality by the sword, bloodshed, and burning of fire. However, with the Sun it cannot appear. But if it is joined with Venus, it signifies dryness and a great diminution of waters. If indeed, it is joined with Mercury, it signifies the death of youths, sages, and writers. Indeed, if it is with the Moon, it signifies mortality which is going to fall amongst the commoners and other low-class persons.

Those which are called *miles* are of the nature of Venus, and incline greatly towards the manner of the Moon; and they have long rays, and likewise long tails, which extend out after them; and when they appear, they traverse the twelve signs, and have the signification of the harming of kings, nobles, and magnates; and that men will rise up in the world who wish to change laws and ancient things, and lead in new ones; and its worse signification will appear from the part towards which it extends its tail and hair.

The *dominus aconae* are said to be of the nature of Mercury, and their colour is cerulean; and they appear small in respect of other comets; and they have a long tail, and extend their rays to one side or another in the manner of its wings holding heads underneath it, leading it back to one place. If one appears, it signifies the death of the king, or of magnates and nobles who are fit for kingship, and especially towards the part to which it extends its tail or rays; and it signifies battles. And I saw one appear in the 663rd year of the Arab era, in which year Pope Alexander died; and not long after, King Manfred was killed by a certain brother of the king of France, named Charles; and not long after again, Conradin was killed by the same Charles in the kingdom of Apulia, and this was in the 665th year of the Arab era; and many dukes and barons were killed with him. And there were many battles and dissensions from the time of the appearance of this comet, and they lasted a long time.

Those which are called *matutina* or *aurora* are red; and have a long tail (but less than that of the *dominus asconae)*; and they are of the nature of Mars: for they have his significations. If one of them appear from the eastern part, having its head below it, it signifies battles, and burnings of fire, and pestilences, and famine in the Bablyonian lands, and in the Arab and Phormati lands; and dryness and the scarcity of water in Egypt; and this will be extended up to western parts.

Those which are called *silver* have rays similar to the purest silver, whose brightness exceeds that of all the other stars of the night. And if one appears while Jupiter is located in Pisces or Cancer, it signifies the abundance of grain and produce in the parts which it appears. Indeed, if Jupiter is in Scorpio, these things will happen, but they will be something below this.

Indeed, those which are called *rosy*, are great and round, and the face of a man can be seen in them, and their colour is between the colours of gold and silver. When one of them appears, it signifies the death of the kings, magnates, the wealthy, and nobles, and of those who are fit for kingship; and the occurrence and appearance of great matters; and the causes of ancient things: but they will change for the better.

Those which are called *black* are of the nature of Saturn, almost of a similar colour to him; and if one of them appears, it signifies mortality through natural death, and death by the sword and beheadings.

## CVI

### What The Caput And Cauda Draconis Signify In Each And Every House, Both In Revolutions, And In Nativities Or Questions

In the preceding chapter it was stated what the Caput Draconis, and its Cauda, signify in each and every sign; what will be stated in this chapter is what they signify in each and every house. Whence you must consider in which house each of them is found in each and every revolution.

And Albumashar said that if the Caput Draconis is in the first in any revolution, nativity, or question, he signifies increase, strength, and loftiness in that revolution, and this according to his conjunction with the planets. For if the Caput is joined with benefics, he signifies the increase of good. If however, he is joined with malefics, he signifies the increase of evil - since his nature is to increase.

And if he is in the second, he signifies good fortune in substance, and its increase; he signifies the same in a nativity or question if he is in the second.

And if he is in the third, he signifies that the native will be an interpreter of dreams, and will be of good faith. And there will be useful short journeys in that revolution, and acquisitions and profit: and likewise for a native.

And if he is in the fourth, and the fourth house is Aries, Leo, Sagittarius, Gemini, Libra, or Aquarius, he signifies the increase of the good and profit from land and vineyards, and from other immobile things. If however, the fourth house is Taurus, Virgo, Capricorn, Cancer, Scorpio, or Pisces, he signifies loss and the diminution of profit.

If he is in the fifth he signifies the fortune of children, and from children; and their increase, good, and joy, and freedom from contrary matters and displeasing things.

And if he is in the sixth he signifies the increase of small animals which are not ridden, and also of slaves; and there will be strong and harmful infirmities.

And if he is in the seventh, he signifies the increase of associates, and good from women; and the increase of sexual intercourse; and the strength of enemies, both of the native or querent, and in general.

And if he is in the eighth he signifies the good condition of men in their persons; and the strength of the native or querent in a nativity or question: and he signifies the removal of grief, and its scarcity.

And if he is in the ninth, and is joined with benefics, it signifies religion and good pilgrimages, and useful and profitable long journeys. If however, he is joined with malefics he signifies the contrary of what was said.

And if he is in the tenth he signifies that men will apply themselves to the investigation of divine and hidden matters: and the scrutiny of the truth of God in the highest. It also signifies loftiness, reverence, veneration, strength, and fortune in dignities or professions, and honours.

And if he is in the eleventh, Albumashar says that there is no virtue in the Caput of Cauda for good or evil.

And if he is in the twelfth he signifies the increase of evil and the scarcity of good.

## CVII

### What The Cauda Signifies In The Houses

When the Cauda is in the first in a revolution, nativity or question, she signifies the detriment of men and the native, and separation from the good; and eradication, danger, and tribulations; and if a son were to remain rich after his father's death, he will be reduced to poverty. And if he were a pauper and his father died, he will remain a pauper.

And if she is in the second, she signifies the diminution of all substance, and the poverty of the native, and his indigence, and him being occupied in evils, and his fall from his status; and this will befall him from a direction that he does not fear, and it will not be suspected.

And if she is in the third, it signifies the detriment of brothers, and from brothers and sisters, and because of them and their burden.. And if the third house is a masculine sign, this will happen in brothers. And if it is a feminine sign, it will happen in sisters. And it is possible that they will die from

these things, since the Caudas' nature is to diminish; or a dispute will befall the native from his brothers, or with any of his younger relatives, or with friends or neighbours.

If however, she is in the fourth, she signifies poverty, indigence, enmity and labour which they will endure in the seeking of matters without utility.

And if she is in the fifth she signifies the diminution of fortune and its expulsion, and the fall of horrible things upon children; and that those who have children will be saddened because of this, and they will be in need; and men will carry old clothes.

And if she is in the sixth, she signifies the laziness and weakness of slaves, slavegirls, and small animals, and their diminution. And if it is a nativity, the native will not have fortune in them. And she signifies the diminution of illnesses. And if there are illnesses, they will be decreasing and diminishing, and emaciating or exterminating the bodies of the sick.

And if she is in the seventh she signifies that men will not rejoice with their wives like they usually rejoice with them in other revolutions; and there will be quarrels and contentions between them, and this will happen more so in the country folk and the commoners than in others. And if it is a nativity, it signifies that the native will not rejoice with wives, nor from wives, nor even from other women, but he will have disputes and contentions with them (unless perhaps from those related to him), nor will he rejoice from associates; and she signifies the strength of his enemies. And you can say the same in the natives' revolutions; however, he will not have many enemies, even if he will have some.

And if she is in the eighth, she signifies the loss of things because of death: and that those who ought to inherit the goods of the dead will lose much of them; and you can say that the same things will happen to a native.

And if she is in the ninth she signifies change from place to place (but not exile); and the diminution of faith and religion, and long journeys will not be useful, but will be more likely to be harmful than profitable.

And if she is in the tenth she signifies the impediment of kings, nobles, and magnates, and the diminution of their honour or dignity. And Albumashar said that she signifies deposition and dangers, and pilgrimage, or a fall; and she signifies the same for the native.

And if she is in the eleventh, Albumashar said that there is no operation for her in it.

And if she is in the twelfth, she signifies the detriment of large animals, and their diminution, and of enemies; and that few men will be incarcerated in that revolution. And if there are prisoners, the prisons will be emptied of them. And the same will happen in nativities or their revolutions if the Cauda is in the 12th. Albumashar said that when the Cauda is in the 12th, she signifies the scarcity of fortune, and the scarcity of evil.

And he said regarding the significations of the planets, and the Caput and Cauda, in the 12 houses, that if they are in better condition, say they will be better; and if they are in bad condition, change the content, and say the contrary of the good (namely, evil); and speak boldly, and do not fear, nor should you dismiss what I said to you; nor should you say otherwise; and you will discover it, if God does not resist.

## CVIII

### What The Fixed Stars Signify In The Revolutions Of The Years, And Nativities, And What They Do In Them

Having spoken on the revolutions of the years, and on the significations of the planets, and the Caput Draconis, and its Cauda (as to what they signify in each and every house, and each and every sign), it remains now to speak on certain fixed stars which are found in each and every sign; of which certain signify grave evil and impediment, and certain signify good. And this is a matter in which it is necessary to be greatly concerned, since much of the judgement of the revolutions, and of nativities, questions, and elections depends on these stars and from these stars. For revolutions, nativities, and questions, and their judgments are changed by these stars with a powerful change, much more strongly than by the planets. And in this many good astrologers are

often deceived: since they do not consider these stars in their judgements, but only the planets and the Parts. And this is the reason why they are sometimes deceived, and things happen to the contrary of what they judged, both in good things and bad things; and they are rebuked and held in contempt out of ignorance, when they are not to be rebuked. However, I cannot excuse them from laziness or negligence: however, if you consider them well in your judgements, as much for revolutions as for nativities and questions, you will not err, if God does not resist.

When you calculate for each and every revolution or nativity or question, and you erect its figure, you will consider all of the houses from the first up to the twelfth, and you will see whether you find one of the stars written below in the degree of the cusp of any angle; and you will judge good or evil according to the nature of the star you find in it, according to what I will tell you. And I will tell them to you just as I have observed certain ones of them from the sayings of the wise, and certain ones by reason of experience, and being proven true.

Albumashar said to know that in the head of Aries there are two stars: one of which is at 13 degrees 45 minutes; and another at 14 degrees 45 minutes, which are of the nature of Mars and Saturn: and their peculiar nature is to harm, and they are on the northern side.

Another is at 9 degrees 55 minutes of Taurus which is called "*The Pleiades*". And another is at 13 degrees of the same sign. And both are northern. And another is at 14 degrees 55 minutes and is called "*Diabolus*". And another is at 15 degrees of the same sign which is called "*Caput Diaboli*" or "*Gorgonis*". And another is at 19 degrees 15 minutes which is called "*Aldebaran*". And all of these are of the nature of Mars; but Mercury and the Moon participate in the Pleiades.

Another is at 8 degrees of Gemini which is called "*Humerus Canis*" and is of the nature of Mars and Saturn. And another is at 10 degrees 15 minutes of the same, which is called "*Bellatrix*" and is of the nature of Mars. Another is at 17 degrees 55 minutes: and its latitude is in the south. Another is at 18 degrees 52 minutes which is called "*Malefica*", and it is of the nature of the Sun, Mars, and Saturn.

Another is at 2 degrees 3 minutes of Cancer, and is called "*Camelus*", and is the nature of Saturn and the Moon. And another is at 7 degrees 55 minutes. And another is at 13 degrees which is of the nature of the Sun and the Moon, which is called "*Occidens Camelum*". And there is another in the same degree called "*Pes Canis*" which is of the nature of Saturn; and another at 17 degrees 55 minutes; both of which are northern and of the nature of Saturn.

In Leo there is one star at 15 degrees 55 minutes of the nature of Saturn.

In Virgo there are two stars, one of which is at 7 degrees 11 minutes, and is of the nature of Mars. Another is at 15 degrees, and is of the nature of Saturn.

In Libra there is one star at 26 degrees, and it is of the nature of Saturn.

In Scorpio there are three stars, one of which is at 3 minutes of the 1st degree. And another at 8 degrees 7 minutes. And another at 9 degrees. And all of them are of the nature of Mars.

In Sagittarius there are two small stars, one of which is at 19 degrees 2 minutes. Another is at 21 degrees 1 minute, and they are of the nature of Saturn.

In Capricorn there are two stars, one of which is at 27 degrees 2 minutes, which is called "*Mala*"; and the other is at 29 degrees 5 minutes; and both are of the nature of Saturn.

In Aquarius there is one star at 9 degrees 4 minutes, and it is of the nature of Mars and Saturn.

There is one star in Pisces at 4 degrees and 7 minutes, and it is of the nature of Mars and Mercury.

## CIX

## On The Peculiar Nature Of The Aforementioned Stars In Each And Every House

When you see the Lord of the year or revolution, or the Lord of the nativity or question, joined with one of the aforementioned fixed stars in the same degree in the revolution of the year of the world, know that evil and impediment will fall upon kings, the wealthy and the nobles or magnates. Say the same for matters of the native in nativities and questions, and in revolutions of the nativity. And griefs, sorrows, malignant thoughts, and infirmities from headaches, and fevers, and death will fall upon them. And this more strongly so if it is in Aries. And the more their conjunction is less than one degree, the greater its impediment will be, until their conjunction reaches one minute. And if their conjunction is in one and the same minute, not only does it signify their impediment, but it will even signify their destruction and death. The same will happen if one of the aforementioned stars were to fall in the degree of the Ascendant of a revolution, or of a nativity or question, descending up to one minute by the conditions said above.

And if one of the aforementioned stars is in the degree of the Ascendant of some nativity, that native will be unfortunate, bad, afflicted, and laborious, and of many illnesses; and will never rejoice in his life; and most of his infirmities will be from headaches; and this more strongly so, if the Ascendant of his nativity were the Ascendant of the year in which one of these stars are in the Ascendant of the revolution.

## II

But if one of these stars fall in the second from the Ascendant of the revolution; or if the Lord of the second house is with one of them in the same degree, as was said, it signifies that impediment is going to fall in the substance of men, and the diminution of them; and especially that of the wealthy and the magnates or nobles; and dullness of mind will fall upon them; and they will weep from their need and poverty, and they will believe that everything has forsaken them; and for this reason they will fall into sorrow and censure; and the infirmities in this revolution will be from the impediment of the ears, neck and throat (as are inflammation, dry catarrh, and similar things); and this more strongly so if it is in Taurus.

And if one of the aforementioned stars were in the second in some nativity, or if the nativities' Ascendant is second from the Ascendant of the revolution, or if the Lord of the second of the nativity is joined with one of these stars, it signifies that the native will be of bad condition, a pauper, and of little wealth, and will squander that what wealth he does earn; nor will he be able to increase his own substance from his profit. And he will be dull, lazy, of little talent, and will be reputed for little, in fact he will almost be reputed for nothing in respect of his stock. And if he is wealthy, he will be impoverished; and his substance will slip through his fingers, and he will not know how this happens. Even with him willing and striving to keep or guard it, it will fly away. And he will have many illnesses; with much of his illnesses being from his ears, throat, neck, and arms: and this more strongly so if the second house is Taurus.

### III

And if one of these stars fall in the third from the Ascendant of the revolution; or if the Lord of the third is with one of them in the same degree (as was said about the first and the second), it signifies evil and impediment of houses of prayer, and that short journeys will not be useful in that revolution; and that there will be quarrels and contentions between brothers, and one will be saddened because of another, without a reason why this ought to be so; and there will be severe and chronic illnesses in men; and much of them will be from the shoulders blades, shoulders, and arms; and this more strongly so if it is in Gemini.

And if one of the aforementioned stars are in the third of some nativity, or its Ascendant is the third from the Ascendant of the revolution, or if the Lord of the third of a nativity is joined with one of these stars, it signifies that the native will be bad to his brothers: and to those who place him above themselves, and who count him as their friend; and to his younger relatives, and neighbours. And he will long to see the evil of the matters of others, and will rejoice if he sees adversity or impediment befall anyone; and he will be intent on doing evil, and his thoughts will not be on good things; nor will he see good for himself, nor utility from his journeys, and especially short ones. And if he strives to travel abroad on the aforementioned pilgrimages, he will lose his substance; however, it will not be a great matter for him to lose his substance, if he does not lose his person along with it. And the greater part of his illnesses will be from the shoulder blades and arms.

### IV

And if one of the aforementioned stars are in the fourth from the Ascendant of the revolution, or if the Lord of the fourth is with one of them in the same degree (as was said regarding the other houses), it signifies the evil and impediment of farmers, and the harvest, and the things born of the earth; and it also signifies battles between cities and country estates, and among other habitations: and that there will likewise be quarrels between fathers and sons, and altercations and envy, and one will be saddened on account of the other, and vice-versa. And the end of those things which men do, or which will occur in that year, will be bad. And if someone buys land, or another estate or inheritance, he will not see from it what he believed he would see, or what he hoped or intended to see. And there will be many infirmities of men in the chest, or of the lungs, and of the parts adjacent to them; and this more strongly so if this is in Cancer.

And if one of the aforementioned stars is in the fourth in someone's nativity, or if the nativity's Ascendant is the fourth from the revolution, or if the Lord of the fourth of the nativity is joined with one of these stars in the same degree (as was said for the others), it signifies evil for his parents; and that he will hate them; and that the ends of all things which he involves himself in will be bad; nor will the works which he does be praised, even if they are good and praiseworthy; and much of his infirmities will be of the chest and lungs, and of the parts adjacent to these.

## V

But if one of the aforementioned stars were to fall in the fifth from the Ascendant of the revolution, or if the Lord of the fifth is in the same degree as one of them (as was said regarding the other houses), it signifies evil and impediment which will fall upon children, and the hatred which their parents will have for them, and it signifies the detriment and diminution of sexual intercourse in that revolution; and that discord or litigation, and impediment will fall between lovers, and between those who used to love each other, and between those who were on friendly terms because of gifts and other delightful things. And much of the infirmities which will befall men in that year will be in the belly, the stomach, and in parts which prohibit sexual intercourse.

And if one of the aforementioned stars were in the fifth of someone's nativity; or if the Ascendant of the nativity is the fifth of the revolution; or if the Lord of the fifth of the nativity is joined with one of these stars (as was said regarding the others), it signifies that the parents of this native will hate him, and this will be according to the substance of the sign which is the fifth of the nativity, or the sign in which the Lord of the fifth of the nativity is placed: for if it is a masculine sign, his father will hate him more, and his mother less. And if it is a feminine sign, his mother will hate him more, and his father less. And the native will not be obedient to his parents, nor will he persevere in loving anyone who loves him, nor anyone else. And if he begins to be good, he will not persevere in his goodness. And he will not be fortunate in children, if one of the stars are in the fifth; nor in those things which are signified by the fifth house; and he might lack children completely. And most of his infirmities will be of the chest and stomach, and because of them; and this more greatly so if the fifth house is Leo.

## VI

If however, one of the aforementioned stars were to fall in the sixth from the Ascendant of the revolution, or the Lord of the sixth is with one of them in the same degree (as was said regarding the other houses), it signifies that impediment will fall upon quadrupeds, and especially small ones. And Albumashar said that it also signifies impediment in the body of the king, and in his slaves and slavegirls; and likewise in other slaves; and in servants and maids; and in low-class people, paupers, or persons of the substance of the sign: and there will not be profit for those wishing to trade slaves or animals, especially small animals. And Albumashar said that those who flee in that year will meet with impediment; and certain of them will not return; and there will be an abundance of infirmities in men; and the greater part of them will be from an excessive amount of choler abounding in the intestines.

And if one of them fall in the sixth of someone's nativity, or if the Ascendant of someone's nativity is the sixth of the revolution, or if the Lord of the sixth of the nativity is joined with one of these stars in the same degree (as was said regarding the others), it signifies that the native will not rejoice from slaves, slavegirls, servants, or maids; nor will he be fortunate in them; nor will he care to own one of them, even if he has use for them; nor will he be made fortunate in them or from them; nor in those things or from those things which are signified by the sixth house, if one of these stars are in the sixth of his nativity. And Albumashar said that from his childhood, he will love to flee from his parents, and he will not see good from quadrupeds, but rather he will see evil, and this will be worse from small animals than from others: for they will die in his possession, and in his harm. And the greater part of his infirmities will be in the inferior parts of his body; and this more strongly so if the sixth is Virgo.

## VII

And if one of these stars are in the seventh, or if the Lord of the seventh is with one of them in the same degree (as was said regarding the other houses), it signifies a multitude of battles and a multitude of those waging war upon the king of that region, or its greater magnate; and there will likewise be fights, disputes, and contentions between kings; and there will be inactivity and contentions between associates and those participating with each other; and many men will drive out their wives in that revolution, and will quarrel with them; and it also signifies that kings and magnates will become angry with their subjects, and with their household members, and against them; and the hearts of men will harden; and piety or mercy will not thrive in them; nor will men care to celebrate marriage; nor will they be satisfied to contract marriage; and faith and legality will recede from them. And if someone receives something from another, or if someone else's possession reaches him, he will deny the truth, and will not want to return it. And men will not care to exercise their arts or their sciences, or their professions. And Albumashar said that there will be many infirmities of men in the bladder, kidneys, hips, and rear parts.

And if one of the aforementioned stars were to falls in the seventh in someone's nativity, or if the Ascendant of the nativity is the seventh of this revolution, of if the Lord of the seventh of the nativity is joined with one of these stars, the native will not rejoice from wives, nor from other women; nor will he see good from them, nor from associates, nor from those he participates with, nor from the matters which he is in charge of, nor from any matter which is signified by the seventh house. And most of the time he will lose his fights and his battles, and his lawsuits and contentions; and likewise for those of other people which he is put in charge of. And if he learned in law, he will not be fortunate in his advocacies.

And Albumashar said that much of his illnesses will be of the throat, the kidneys, the legs, and the rear parts; and this more strongly so if the seventh is Libra.

## VIII

If however, one of the aforementioned stars were in the eighth, or if the Lord of the eighth of the revolution is with one of them in the same degree (as was said regarding the other houses), it signifies that impediment and evil is going to fall upon those who habitually travel here and there, harming some people by way of robbery; and their return to places in which they usually stay from their robberies, or from their thefts. And it signifies the taking away of some things of the region in which you revolve the year, and some of the things of the authorities of its cities or communities (if another king is not in charge of it), or those belong to him who manages the affairs of communities or cities; nor will the lost thing be recovered. And it signifies that disputes or discord will fall between those who inherit the goods of the dead; and they will not agree with each other; unless perhaps by the interposition of others. And it signifies the death of lower-class persons and of those who are forced to eat the bread of suffering (namely, that of others), and those in need of others, according to the substance of the sign which is the eighth house, or in which the Lord of the eighth is placed: so that if it is a masculine sign, it will be greater in males; however, if it is a feminine sign, it will be greater in females. And if the eighth is a masculine sign, and the Lord of the eighth is in a masculine sign, it will only be in males. And if the eighth is a feminine sign, and the Lord of the eighth is in a feminine sign, it will only be in females. And if one is masculine, and the other is feminine, it will be in both of them, yet more so according to the substance of the eighth, than of the sign in which the Lord of the eighth is placed; and there will be pestilences in them. And Albumashar said that the impediment will be multiplied upon the substance of those contending with the greater king (of the kings of that clime). And he said that they will need the aid of the greater king (namely of the Babylonians, the Romans, or the Indians). And there will be more infirmities in men and women in the genitals, and the privates, and around the parts adjacent to these.

And if one of these stars fall in the eighth in someone's nativity, or if the Ascendant of the nativity is the eighth of the revolution, or if the Lord of the eighth is joined with one of these in the same degree (as was said regarding the others), Albumashar said that the native will be a vagrant, a vagabond, shunning places to stay, and not entering under a roof. And he said that he will be of those men who collect enemies, and seek to be with demons; and will love being alone, and he will not see in himself that he is loved for his labour and pilgrimage; and this will be more so in places of the dead, and in stinking places of corpses. And he will not rejoice in those things which are signified by the eighth house. And most infirmities will be on account of the private parts, and around the private parts, and the parts adjacent to these. And this more strongly so if the eighth house is Scorpio.

## IX

And if one of the aforementioned stars were in the ninth, or the Lord of the ninth of the revolution is with one of them in the same degree (as was said regarding the other houses), it signifies that impediment, destruction, and evil is going to befall bishops and other religious people, and worshippers of God, and especially those who are signified by the worst disposed planet. So that if it is Jupiter it will befall bishops and similar people; if it is Saturn, it will befall those wearing rough clothing. And the more powerful and famous the religion, the greater the impediment that will fall upon its worshippers will be. And the sects or religions approved by the Roman Church will be diminished and depressed, and also the other religions of men; and dullness, ruin, and the forgetting of those serving God, and His praises; and they will recede from Him, and certain of them will deny Him, and desist from His commands; and doubt will fall in them, and they will believe that something else is better than that which they believe or observe. And detriment and sorrow will also fall upon pilgrims on long pilgrimages, and long journeys will go to the contrary of the travellers, nor will good things happen to them from these journeys, but their thoughts will be in vain and of an evil end. And certain people will rise up and reveal their severity, and plot to bring about the ruin of the king of Babylonia, however, they will not be able to perpetrate the crime planned in that year; and battles and conflicts will be diminished. And most of men's infirmities will be because of the thighs and the hips.

And if one of the aforementioned stars were to fall in the ninth of someone's nativity, or if the Ascendant of the nativity is the ninth of that revolution, or if the Lord of the ninth of the nativity is joined with one of those stars in the same degree (as was said regarding the other houses), Albumashar said that the native will be almost stupefied in his affairs, and in his own care; and change from place to place, and pilgrimages, will not agree with him. And most of his infirmities will be of the thighs and hips. And this more strongly so if the ninth is Sagittarius.

## X

But if one of the aforementioned stars were in the tenth, or if the Lord of the tenth of the revolution is joined with one of them (namely, in the same degree, as was said regarding the other houses), it signifies that dejection, evil, and impediment are going to fall upon kings, the wealthy, the nobles, and magnates or powerful men (those who are preferred to other men), and there will be weakness in them, and discord, contention, and mutual envy will fall between them, and impediment will fall upon their substance and affairs; and their procurements will be few; and little money will be tributed to them, except perhaps that which they extort from some men by violence, or in another reprehensible way; and men will not revere them in the usual, or required custom, and they will suppress their dignities, professions, and kingship, and the country folk or commoners will be elevated, and will resist against them, and condemn, deride, and despise them; and they will change their names with derision. And not only will they do these things, but if magnates pass through streets or town squares, there will not be one commoner from the crowd who will not deride them: and these things will happen to them throughout the whole revolution. And most of men's infirmities will be of the knees and the parts adjacent to these.

And if one of the aforementioned stars were to fall in the tenth in someone's nativity, or if the Ascendant of the nativity is the tenth of that revolution; or if the Lord of the tenth of the nativity is joined with one of them in the same degree (as was said regarding the other houses), it signifies the worthlessness of the native and his dejection, and that he will be despised amongst those who ought to exalt him if they can, and especially with his kin; and he will be laborious in his life, and will have little profit (it will be less than his expenses); and he will not profit in those things in which he has faith in the good; and whatever profit he does make, will not be converted to his utility, unless by accident; and this will only be slight. And Albumashar said that what I have said to you will be according to his nature. And most of his infirmities will be of the knees and the parts adjacent to them. And this more strongly so if the tenth is Capricorn.

## XI

If one of the aforementioned stars were in the eleventh, or if the Lord of the eleventh of the revolution is joined to one of them in the same degree (as was said regarding the other houses), it signifies that discord and anxiety is going to fall between friends. And one will strive to overthrow or contemn the other; and he will direct his efforts to his harm and injury. And the trust of men will be annihilated; and things will not go as intended in the matters in which they have hope. And the substance of the king, and of magnates and wealthy men, will be diminished, and suffer detriment; and likewise the soldiers of the king of that region, and his ministers and assistants; and they will not have good faith towards him, nor goodwill, nor will they use arms to his advantage, nor in his aid, if he were to need it, but they will be unfaithful. And most of men's infirmities will be of the legs and around the legs.

And if one of the aforementioned stars were to fall in the eleventh in someone's nativity, or if the Ascendant of the revolution is the eleventh of the nativity, or if the Lord of the eleventh of the nativity is joined with one of them in the same degree (as was said regarding the other houses), it signifies that the native will be of little trust, in such a way that he will believe that nothing can be of benefit to him; and something good will hardly or never happen to him; and if it does, it will only be slight. And it signifies that he will be hateful and despised by the commoners, and his heart will be so worthless that he will not believe himself to be able to avoid any evil or any contrary danger; nor will his thoughts be on anything good. And he will rejoice when he sees the misfortune of another person; and his intention will be to do evil, even if the cannot perfect it; and he will not praise anyone, nor will anyone praise him; nor will he be promoted to any lay or secular dignity, unless perhaps to such a one that will overflow to his harm, or the contrary. And most of his infirmities will be of the legs. And this more strongly so if the eleventh is Aquarius.

## XII

If indeed, one of the aforementioned stars were to fall in the twelfth, or if the Lord of the twelfth is joined with one of them in the same degree (as was said regarding the other houses), it signifies a multitude of thieves and highwaymen. It also signifies the fraud of slaves and slavegirls against their masters; and fall and detriment; and the diminution of dejected and low class persons; for they will be cast down, and things will go badly for them; and likewise for the incarcerated; and prisons will be emptied with the detriment of the prisoners. And large quadrupeds will suffer detriment. And kings, nobles, the wealthy, magnates, the rational, and the wise, will all be exalted, and raised up over the mob, the commoners, the country folk, and the ignoble, and over all who had earlier derided them to their detriment and catching out. And most of men's infirmities will be of the feet.

And if one of these stars were to fall in the twelfth of someone's nativity, or if the Ascendant of the nativity is the twelfth of the revolution, or if the Lord of the twelfth of the nativity is joined with one of them in the same degree (as was said regarding the other houses), it signifies that the native will be evil, crafty, having an evil slyness, laborious, ingenious, a fraudulent nature; of many anxieties and troubles, and many enemies. And many men will hate him, both with a reason and without reason.

And Albumashar said that everyone who sees him will hate him, from his boyhood up to his old age. And most of his infirmities will be of his feet. And this more strongly so if Pisces is the twelfth house.

*Aspects To The Unfortunate Stars*

Anд Albumashar said that if Jupiter aspects it from the place of the image, and projects his rays to that degree, and he is strong in his own place, it signifies the fortitude of those stars.

And if Venus is weak in her place, she will not operate something of her operations that should appear.

And he said the multitude of the fixed stars' evil will be according to the quantity of strength or weakness of the planet aspecting it.

And if the benefic aspects from a place of enmity and contrariety, it will not repel any of the evil, especially if it is weak in its own place; but it will strive to repel the evil, however, it will not repel any of it.

However, he said that if a malefic aspects it from a place of dejection, everything that I said to you about the matters of the planets will be bad, and it will hasten its work, and one evil will follow another.

And he said that if the malefic aspects from a place of enmity and contrariety, everything which I said will be evil; and there will be contrariety from the beginning of the coming of the evil, and preoccupation with it up to its end.

If indeed, the Sun aspects this place, he will uncover the evil, and will act to bring it to notice. And he said that all who strive to hide what will happen, will not be able to hide it. And he said that this will be general for the same generation and the cities.

And he said that if Saturn aspects it, one tribulation after another will descend on it.

And he said that if Mercury aspects it, it will be mixed and coloured.

And he said, if the Moon aspects it, her operation will be what was said above regarding the work of the Sun. And he said that it will be a small bit less, and faster in everything which she does, on account of the speed of her course. And he said to know that everything which I have said to you, will be in the city which is in the division of the same sign. And he said, therefore consider these things, since you will not err, if God wills it.

## CX

## What The Fortunate Fixed Stars Signify In Nativities, And Questions, And Revolutions Of The Years

Having spoken on the misfortunes which are introduced by the unfortunate fixed stars into inferior things, now we shall speak about the fortune which the fixed stars usually introduce in the same. For just as certain unfortunate fixed stars are found in each and every sign, so too certain fortunate fixed stars are found in each and every sign, which are causes of the contrary, namely of fortune.

Therefore, know that at 15 degrees 6 minutes of Aries, there is a certain star of the nature of Jupiter and Venus, and its latitude is southern, and its peculiar nature is to benefit and aid. Indeed, another is at 26 degrees 1 minute, and is of the nature of Jupiter.

In Taurus there is one star in the first degree and third minute. Another at 8 degrees 7 minutes. The third is at 9 degrees 1 minute. All of which are of the nature of Venus.

In Gemini there is one star at 19 degrees 2 minutes. And another at 21 degrees 3 minutes. Both of which are of the nature of Jupiter, and are of the second magnitude.

In Cancer there is one star which is called "*Bona*", at 27 degrees 2 minutes. And another at 21 degrees 3 minutes. Both of which are of the nature of Jupiter and do good.

In Leo there is one star of the nature of Jupiter and Venus at 9 degrees 4 minutes, and it is called "*Benevola*".

In Virgo there is a certain star at 4 degrees 7 minutes of the nature of Venus and the Moon.

In Libra there is a certain star of the nature of Jupiter and Venus at 13 degrees 40 minutes. And another at 14 degrees 40 minutes of the same nature. And both are southern, and helpful.

And in Scorpio there is one star at 9 degrees 55 minutes. And another at 13 degrees 1 minute. And another at 14 degrees 45 minutes. And another at

19 degrees 15 minutes. All of which are southern, and of the nature of Jupiter.

In Sagittarius there is one star at 10 degrees and 15 minutes which is called "*Pacifica*" and is of the nature of Venus. Indeed, there is another at 17 degrees 55 minutes, and it is northern, and of the nature of Jupiter.

In Capricorn there is one star at 2 degrees 3 minutes which is called "*Bos*", and is of the nature of Jupiter. And another at 7 degree 55 minutes. And another at 17 degrees 55 minutes. Both of which are southern, and are of the nature of Jupiter.

In Aquarius there is one star at 15 degrees 55 minutes, and it is of the nature of Jupiter.

In Pisces there is one star at 7 degrees 11 minutes, and it is of the nature of Jupiter.

## CXI

## On The Peculiar Nature Of The Fortunate Stars In The Twelve Houses

### I

If you see the Lord of the year or revolution, or of a nativity or question, joined with one of the aforementioned stars in the same degree in the revolution of the year of the world, you will know that good things and fortune will befall the kings, the wealthy, the nobles, and the magnates. You will say the same in nativities about the affairs of the native; and in revolutions of questions and nativities. And happiness, gladness, health, and safety of their bodies will be allotted to them. And the more their conjunction is less than one degree, and closer to one minute, the better and more well adapted their status will be.

And if one of the aforementioned stars were to fall on the degree of the Ascendant of someone's nativity, or if the Lord of the nativity is joined with them in the same degree, the native will be fortunate and good: and will lead his life in peace, joy, and tranquillity and every good condition; and this more strongly so if the Ascendant is Aries.

### II

And if one of these stars were to fall in the second from the Ascendant of the revolution, or if the Lord of the second of the revolution is with one of them in the same degree (as was said), it signifies the increase of the things and substance of men, and especially of the wealthy, the magnates, and the nobles; and this more strongly if Taurus is the second house.

And if one of the aforementioned stars were to fall in the second in someone's nativity, or if his Ascendant is the second of the revolution; or if the Lord of the second of the nativity is joined with one of them in the same degree (as was said in the first house), it signifies that the native will be of good condition, of a good status, wealthy, having much property and profit. And he will retain his acquisitions, and his substance: and he will be of good intelligence and painstaking in his business, and will be reputed amongst other men: and they will listen to his words and they will be pondered; and this more greatly so if Taurus is the second house.

### III

But if one of these stars were to fall in the third from the Ascendant of the revolution, or if the Lord of the third is with one of them in the same degree (as was said regarding the others), it signifies the good condition of houses of prayer, and that short journeys will be agreeable and useful to those making them, and that brothers will be good to one another; and one brother will rejoice because of the other: and they will be healthy in their bodies, and they will be of sound mind; and this more greatly so if Gemini is the third house.

And if one of the aforementioned stars were to fall in the third house in someone's nativity, or if the Ascendant of the nativity is the third of the revolution, or if the Lord of the third of the nativity is joined with one of the aforementioned stars, it signifies that the native will be useful and benevolent to his brothers, and his younger relatives, and neighbours, and to those who place him above themselves, or who count him as their friend. And he will not long to see the evil of another, and he will be compassionate to those to whom evil things happen; and his intention will be mostly benign, and not to the contrary; and his journeys will be useful to him, and especially his short ones; and they will be safe and advantageous, both in his affairs and his person; and he will be sound of body, and especially around the shoulder blades and arms; and this more greatly so if Gemini is the third house.

## IV

But if one of the aforementioned stars were to fall in the fourth from the Ascendant of the revolution, or if the Lord of the fourth is with them in the same degree, (as was said regarding the other houses), it signifies the good condition of farmers, the harvest, and the things born of the earth. It also signifies peace and tranquillity in cities and between cities and other habitations; and that fathers will be good with their sons, and towards their sons, and they will rejoice and be happy with one another, and on account of one another. And the ends of things began in that year (which were to happen in that year, or in that revolution) will be for the good. And if someone buys land, or another estate, or some inheritance, what was intended will follow from it; and more men will be healthy, especially around the chest and lungs; and this more greatly so if Cancer is the fourth house.

And if one of the aforementioned stars are in the fourth in someone's nativity, or if the fourth of the revolution is the Ascendant of the nativity, or if the Lord of the fourth of the nativity is joined with one of these stars in the same degree, it signifies that the native will be good to his parents (namely, his father, grandfather, and father in law, and other older people); and that he will love them, and that he will be obedient and favourable to them: and the end of those things of which he involves himself will be praiseworthy; and his works will be praised, even if sometimes he does less well, nevertheless he will be praised by men; and he will be of a sound body, and his health will thrive, especially around the chest and lungs, and the inferior parts of the chest.

## V

But if one of the aforementioned stars were to fall in the fifth from the Ascendant of the revolution, or if the Lord of the fifth is with one of them (as was said regarding the other houses), it signifies that good things and fortune will happen to children, and the love which their parents will have for them; and it signifies the increase of licit sexual intercourse, and delight in it in that revolution; indeed, love and good will shall be increased between those loving each other; and there will be more friendship, and gifts between them than usual; and there will be health in their bellies; and this more greatly so if Leo is the fifth house.

And if one of the aforementioned stars are in the fifth of a nativity, or the Ascendant of the nativity is the fifth of this revolution, or if the Lord of the fifth of the nativity is joined with one of these stars, it signifies that the parents of this native will love him, but the parent who is of the nature of the sign of fifth house will love him more; and he will be obedient to his parents, and he will not ignore their orders; and he will love this parent, and persevere in the good; and he will be fortunate in children, and in those things which are signified by the fifth house, and he will be sound of body, and especially around the chest, belly, and back, and around the genital parts; and this more greatly so if the fifth house is Leo.

## VI

If however, one of the aforementioned stars were to fall in the sixth from the Ascendant of the revolution, or if the Lord of the sixth is with one of them in the same degree, (as was said regarding the other houses) it signifies that increase and good things are going to come to quadrupeds, and especially small ones. And Albumashar said that this is also signified in the king and in his slaves and slavegirls; and likewise in other slaves, and in servants and maids. And the status of low class persons will be good, according to the substance of the sign (whether it is masculine or feminine). And there will be profit for those wanting to trade slaves or small animals; and it will be good for those wanting to flee; and infirmities will be decreased, and especially those which usually occur from choler abounding in the intestines.

But if one of these stars fall in the sixth house of someone's nativity, or if the Ascendant of the nativity is the sixth of this revolution, or if the Lord of the sixth of the nativity is joined with one of them in the same degree (as was said regarding the others), it signifies that things will be good for the native from slaves, slave girls, servants, and maids; and he will be fortunate in them, and in those things which are signified by the sixth house. And he will willingly stay with his parents; and he will be healthy, mostly in the inferior parts of his body: and this more strongly so if the sixth house is Virgo.

## VII

And if one of these stars are in the seventh, or if the Lord of the seventh is with one of them in the same degree (as was said regarding the other houses), it signifies tranquillity and good, and the diminution of conflicts and battles; and that there will be tranquillity and peace between associates and those participating together, and between other men; and that there will be good will between husbands and wives, and fewer disputes than usual; and kings and magnates will be reconciled to their subjects, and they will be humbled by their subjects, and they will obey them more freely than usual; and piety will thrive in men, and they will be intent on celebrating nuptials, and contracting marriage; and faith and legality will thrive in them; and they will use truth somewhat more than usual; and they will be content to exercise their arts and their professions; and health will thrive in men, and especially around the bladder, kidneys, hips, and rear parts.

And if one of the aforementioned stars were to fall in the seventh in someone's nativity, or if the Ascendant of the nativity is the seventh of the revolution, or if the Lord of the seventh of the nativity is with one of them, the native will rejoice from wives and other women, and he will see good from them, and from associates and participants, and from all those who are signified by the seventh house, and he will win in his legal cases. And if he is an advocate or learned in law, things will go well for him in his advocacies. And he will be healthy in his throat, kidneys, legs, and rear parts; and this more strongly so if the seventh house is Libra.

## VIII

If however, one of the aforementioned stars are in the eighth, or if the Lord of the eighth of the revolution is with one of them in the same degree (as was said regarding the other houses), it signifies the good condition of vagrants, namely of those who usually travel here and there, and harm others by means of robbery; and something of their malice will be mitigated. It also signifies them staying in the places where they usually live, more than they usually do; and they will not exercise whatever evil they can from their robberies. It also signifies the safety of the king of this region in which you revolve the year, or the ruler or authorities of that place, or who is managing the republic. And if he loses any of his things, they will be recovered. It also signifies concord between those who inherit the goods of the dead. It also signifies the guarding of the lives of low class persons according to the substance of the sign; and there will not be people who strive to defraud the substance of the greater kings (namely the king of the Romans, the king of the Babylonians, and the king of the Indians); and there will be health in men and women, and especially around the genital parts, and around the privates, and the parts adjacent to these.

And if one of these stars were to fall in the eighth in someone's nativity, or if the Ascendant of the nativity is the eighth of this revolution, or if the Lord of the eighth of the nativity is joined with one of them in the same degree (as was said regarding the others), it signifies that the native will be one of those men who eagerly associates with others, and who flee from solitude, and who gladly stay with good men. And he will see what he wants in his own person; and he will rejoice from those things, and in those things which are signified by the eighth house: and he will be of sound of body, and especially around the private parts, and the parts adjacent to these; and this more greatly so if Scorpio is the eighth house.

## IX

And if one of the aforementioned stars are in the ninth, or if the Lord of the ninth of the revolution is with one of them in the same degree (as was said regarding the other houses), it signifies the rejoicing, happiness, and good status of bishops and other religious people, and those serving God, according to how the planet signifying them is well disposed: so that if it is Jupiter, it will be greater in bishops and other clerics who are called secular. If it is Saturn, it will be more in the religious wearing rough vestments, and more strongly in those wearing blacker vestments, and in more famous men. And the sects approved by the Roman Church will be increased; and they will serve God and praise Him. And pilgrimages or long journeys will be useful and profitable, and the citizens of Babylonia will be obedient to their king; and men will be healthy, especially around the thighs and hips; and this more greatly so if the ninth house is Sagittarius.

And if one of the aforementioned stars were to fall in the ninth in anyone's nativity, or if the Ascendant of the nativity is the ninth of the revolution: or if the Lord of the ninth of the nativity is joined with one of them in the same degree (as was said regarding the other houses), it signifies that the native will attentively regard his own affairs, and choose the better part regarding them, and he will also do this for the affairs of others; and pilgrimages and long journeys will be useful to him. And his health will thrive around the thighs and hips; and this more greatly if the ninth house is Sagittarius.

## X

And if one of the aforementioned stars were to fall in the tenth, or if the Lord of the tenth is joined with one of them in the same degree (as was said regarding the other houses), it signifies that good and the increase of good is going to come to kings and magnates who are fit for kingship; and there will be strength in them for the good. And there will be peace and security between them, and it will be good for them; and tax will be returned to them without contention and without impediment; and men will revere them, and their dignities and professions, or their kingdoms will be exalted; and health will thrive in men, and especially around the knees and the parts adjacent to them.

And if one of the aforementioned stars were to fall in the tenth in someone's nativity, or if the Ascendant of the nativity is the tenth of the revolution, or if the Lord of the tenth of the nativity is joined with one of them in the same degree (as was said regarding the others), it signifies the goodness of the native and the greatness of his mind, and the increase of his honour; and he will be honoured by his own, and even by strangers; and he will lead his life without great labour, and will live as though at rest; and he will be a man of profit or acquisition, and what he earns will be converted into his utility; and he will even be of a sound body, and especially around the knees and the parts adjacent to them; and this more greatly so if the tenth house is Capricorn.

## XI

If indeed, one of the aforementioned stars were in the eleventh, or if the Lord of the eleventh of the revolution is joined to one of them in the same degree, (as was said regarding the other houses), it signifies that good things and fortune is going to come amongst friends, and one will try to support the other and exalt him; and one will strive to assist and help the other; and the substance of the king, and the wealthy or magnates, will likewise be increased. And the soldiers of the king of this region, and his ministers, and his assistants, will have good faith and good will towards the king; and they will eagerly exercise arms in his utility; and they will be faithful to him. And men will be healthy in the legs and around the legs; and this more greatly so if the eleventh house is Aquarius.

And if one of the aforementioned stars were to fall in the eleventh in someone's nativity, or if the Ascendant of the nativity is the eleventh of this revolution, or if the Lord of the eleventh of the nativity is joined with one of them in the same degree (as was said regarding the others), it signifies that the native will have great confidence, so that in all the things which he involves himself in, he will hope to be able to get good things and utility from them; and it will hardly ever happen to the contrary for him in those things which he has hope for, and with those things which he involves himself in; and he will be loved by the mob, and he will have such trust, and such boldness, that he will not believe that anything evil or anything contrary could possibly happen to him. And his thoughts will be on good things, and he will have pity for those for whom things go adversely; and his intention will be in doing good; and he will be praised by others, and he will praise them. And if he strives to have an office or honours, he will be promoted to them. And his health will thrive in his legs, and around his legs; and more greatly so if the 11th house is Aquarius.

## XII

Indeed if one of the aforementioned stars are in the twelfth, or if the Lord of the twelfth is joined with one of them in the same degree (as was said of all the others), it signifies the diminution of thieves and highwaymen, and their detriment; it also signifies the obedience of slaves and slavegirls towards their masters. And it signifies the good condition of low-class persons, and the alleviation of the conditions of prisoners, and large quadrupeds will be saved. And it also signifies that kings, or magnates and nobles, will be good to the country folk or commoners. And there will be health in men, and especially in the feet and around the feet; and this more greatly so if the twelfth house is Pisces.

And if one of them falls in the twelfth in someone's nativity, or the Ascendant of someone's nativity is the twelfth of the revolution, or if the Lord of the twelfth of a nativity is joined with one of them in the same degree (as was said regarding the others), it signifies that the native will be good, ingenious, having good, lawful, and laudable talents; of little labour, few difficulties, and few worries; he will lacking little; having few enemies, (especially hidden ones); but rather, he will be loved by men, both as a young boy, and an old man; and health will thrive in him, especially in his feet and around his feet; and this more strongly so if the twelfth house is Pisces.

### Aspects To The Fortunate Stars

And if Jupiter is in good condition, and aspects the degree in which the star is in at that time, or if the Caput Draconis is there, their fortune will be increased.

If indeed, Saturn aspects it, or if the Cauda is there, the fortune will be decreased.

If Venus aspects it, it will increase it a little, almost insensibly.

The rest do nothing which can be sensed. However, if the Sun aspects this place, he will make what is signified by the fixed star come into act more quickly. And if the Moon aspects it, the significations will be quickened even more.

## CXII

### On The Varieties Of Customs

Albumashar placed this chapter in his book of revolutions, and it does not seem that we should omit it; since I am following in his footsteps, even if I am employing a longer discussion than he did. And he said that in the circle there are customs which are not similar to other customs. For he said that in a king there is a custom which is not likened to the custom of household members; and in household members there is a custom which is not likened to that of a king. And in a kingdom there is a custom which is not likened to the custom of nativities. And in nativities there is a custom which is not similar to the custom of questions.

## CXIII

### On The Impediments Which The Lord Of The Ascending Sign Of The Revolution Introduces When He Is Impeded (Whether He Is The Lord Of The Year Or Not)

If the Lord of the Ascendant of the revolution of the year of the world is impeded at the hour of the revolution (whether he is the Lord of the year or not: since if another planet is the Lord of the year, the Ascendant Lord is a participator in these matters; and the significations are more naturally taken from them, even if they are taken from the Lord of the year), and if he is impeded in one of the angles, he will introduce tribulation upon men. For if he is combust in the tenth, the impediment will be because of kingship, or something equal to kingship. And if the Sun is in the Midheaven, or if the Sun is otherwise the Lord of the tenth, it signifies that men will meet with sorrow or difficulties from the king, or because of the king.

If however, it is combust in the fourth (this being closer to the cusp than to the end of the fourth), mortality will be feared in that same revolution, and this will be according to the substance of the sign of the Ascendant, and the planet who is its Lord: so that if it is a feminine planet, it will be more so in females, and if in addition to this its Lord is a feminine planet, it will be entirely in females. If however, it is a masculine sign, and in addition to this its Lord is a masculine planet, it will be entirely in males.

And if the Lord of the Ascendant is Mercury, it will be more in boys up to the beginning of adolescence. And if the Lord of the Ascendant is Saturn, it will be more in the elderly and the decrepit, and in those who are signified by Saturn. And if the Lord of the Ascendant is Jupiter, it will be more in wise men, those learned in law, and men of completed youth. And if the Lord of the Ascendant is Mars, it will be more in youths from the twenty-first year up to the forty-fifth. And if the Lord of the Ascendant is Venus or the Moon, it will be more in women. Indeed, if Venus has the signification, and she has escaped from combustion, and is outside of the rays of the Sun, and she is oriental, it signifies that this will happen in young women. And if she is occidental it will happen in aged women.

But if the significator is the Moon, and she is from the new moon up to the first dichotomy, it signifies young women up to 30. And if she is from the first dichotomy up to the fullness of her light, it will be in those women who are from the thirtieth year up to the forty-fifth. And if she is from the fullness of her light up to the third dichotomy, it will be those from thence until they have begun to grow old. And if she is in her fourth dichotomy, it will be in elderly or old women. And if this happens in men, she signifies their ages by the same method.

### On The Significations Of The Lord Of The Ascendant If It Is Combust In The Seventh Or The Ascendant

And if the Lord of the Ascendant is combust in the seventh, it signifies that battles, pillagings and contentions are going to fall between men. If however, he is combust in the first, his impediment will be less harmful. You will also see what the nature of the sign of the Ascendant is: since impediment will fall in the substance which is signified by this sign: so that if it is Aries or Capricorn, it will be in small animals. If however, it is Taurus or the last half of Sagittarius, it will be in large animals, and especially in cows and the like.

And if it is Gemini, Libra, or Aquarius, or the first half of Sagittarius, it will be in men. And if it is Cancer or Pisces, it will be in aquatic animals which men use in their utility. If however, it is Scorpio, it will be in venomous animals, both terrestrial and aquatic. And if it is Leo, it will be in wild animals preying on living things, such as lions, wolves, and similar beasts. And if it is Virgo, it will be in seeds and things born of the earth, and in uncorrupted girls.

And know that if the impeded planet is received by a strong unimpeded planet, that reception will remove the malice, and destroy it. If however, a malefic aspects it without perfect reception, it will increase the malice, and this more strongly so if the aspect is a square or opposition.

## CXIV

### On The Impediments Which The Lord Of The Midheaven Will Introduce, If It Is Impeded In The Revolution

After you have examined the Lord of the Ascendant of the revolution, and you have seen his significations, it remains for you to examine the significations of the Lord of the Midheaven. For if he is combust in one of the angles, he signifies that the king will meet with destruction in that revolution: so that if he is combust in the first, and the Sun is the Lord of the first, it signifies that the country folk, commoners, or subjects, are going to kill the king in that revolution, and at least plot to ruin and betray him. Whence, for your judgement to be of benefit to him, and for discretion to triumph, and for free will to be believed (that you can avert evil which is set to happen according to the stars), advise him not to believe the commoners nor trust of them.

And Albumashar said that if you want to know what exactly should be feared over him, see which of the planets aspects the Sun at the hour of the revolution. And if Mars aspects him, or is corporeally joined to him, it signifies that the murder of the king will be because of the mob, or commoners, persuading daytime robbers, murderers, and highwaymen (who kill men for a price), to kill the king. If however, Saturn aspects him, or is corporeally joined with him, a fearful infirmity will be feared regarding the king, or possibly that he will be poisoned. And he said that if the Sun burns up the Lord of the Ascendant of the year, what I said will also be feared for him, in the same way that I described it. However, he said that what there would be of this will be in the region in which he is, someone will not come from another land to him.

But if the Lord of the tenth is combust in the fourth, or in the seventh, these things will occur because of those arriving from another land to the one in which he is in; and it signifies that the aforementioned will come according to what was said above. And again he said to speak of the evil things according to what I said in the chapter of the Sun on the king and his country folk; except that in the chapter on the malefics you will look to the revolution of the year. And he said that if the Lord of the Midheaven is joined to a malefic in an angle in the way mentioned in the first chapter, and the aspect is from opposition or square, the aspect of malefics is more severe than the conjunction in this place. And he said that if the Sun is the significator of the king, and Jupiter aspects him from opposition in the revolution, the king will be inimical to the substance of the same planet, and he will destroy it like the Sun destroys Jupiter.

### On The Significations Of Mars In The Revolution

Albumashar said to know that if Mars is in Gemini at the hour of the revolution, and is in the Midheaven, he signifies that many men will be tortured in that year. And if he is in the first or the seventh, the hands of many men will be cut off, and many will be mutilated. And if he is in the fourth (namely in the angle of the earth), he signifies the severing of the hands and feet of many men. And he said to say likewise in the entrance of two magnates or kings in their rule. Say the same in the entrance to any position of power, or rulership. It can be said that many malefactors will arrive with whom it will be necessary to deal with in the manner mentioned. Know these things and do not forget them.

## CXV

### How The Evil Or Horrible Accidents Which Are Going To Come In That Year Can Be Known From The Hour Of The Revolution

If you wish to know the severe and horrible accidents which are going to come in the year which you are revolving, know that the accidents will be according to the disposition of the two malefics (namely, Saturn and Mars). Which if they are found in the superior circle (that is, in the northern half), and with them being placed above the earth (and this more strongly so if they are northern), it signifies that harshness and horrible things are going to come in that year. And the more they are elevated above the earth (and especially Saturn), the more their significations will be extended to far away and diverse regions.

And Albumashar said to know that the condition of the year will be oppressed if the two malefics are in the high circle (where the pole is), in the images themselves, which, if they go out to the end of the circle, will return; and signify destruction.

Therefore, when you see the two malefics in the superior part of the circle at the hour of the revolution, you will then know that the condition of the year or revolution will be oppressed, and there will be severe and horrible accidents. And if one of them is in square aspect to the other, their condition will be worse, for then it will signify the lack of activity of all living things, and tribulations will appear in all subjects which are on the earth, and this will be prolonged and slowed down; and this more strongly so if Saturn is in Virgo and Mars is in Gemini, and the revolution is nocturnal, and Mars commits his disposition to Saturn, and he receives him, and both of them are retrograde (or at least one of them, but Saturn is more harmful): since then it signifies matters exceeding the limit in evil, both in burnings and in killings; nor will Jupiter be able to shatter their malice by his aspect, unless perhaps one of them are in Cancer, in the trine or sextile aspect of Jupiter, and Jupiter is in good condition and well disposed: for then he will be able to shatter the malice of that planet which he aspects, or at least diminish it by a noticeable diminution.

And the weakening of the condition of the king of that region in which you revolve the year will be signified, and that of other magnates and wealthy men or nobles. And kings and magnates will seek assistance from the commoners; and religion will be reduced; and piety will be taken away from men; and mercy will not be found in them; and this will be prolonged until one of them (namely Saturn or Mars) arrives at the degree which was the cusp of the tenth house at the hour of the revolution; or it will begin then, and last long after: at least for one transit of Mars through the zodiac.

If however, Saturn is then in Virgo, and Mars commits disposition to him from Gemini (as was said), and the Moon commits disposition to Saturn, while she is in Sagittarius, then it will signify the most horrible of horrible things, and the most pestilent of pestilences; and it signifies the destruction of kingdoms and kings, and the transmutation of certain kingdoms from certain kings to certain other kings.

Moreover, if the Moon commits her disposition to Saturn, and if she is joined to him, or in his square aspect or opposition, and the Lord of the sign in which she is placed is impeded at the time when she perfects her conjunction with Saturn degree for degree and minute for minute, it signifies that many diverse impediments are going to come in that revolution.

And if the Moon suffered an eclipse in the most recent prevention, or if she is going to suffer one in the next prevention, the significations of the malefic will be prolonged for as many months as the eclipse of the Moon lasted in hours.

But if the Part of Fortune is impeded, and the Lord of the sign that it is placed in is impeded, when the conjunction of the Moon with Saturn is perfected (whether it is perfected by conjunction or aspect), then the conjunction signifies the increase of impediment and destruction.

And Albumashar said to examine the Sun and his condition, and his aspect to the impeding malefic, and the Lord of the malefic in the way I told you regarding the Moon, and the perfection and the Lord of the perfection.

And make the Part of Fortune and its Lord participants with them, and let them assist by the dignities of the seven planets who are assisted. and who signify the time.

And he said that if the significator is in an angle, the evil will be prolonged, and in the rest of the houses it will be shortened.

Likewise, examine the Sun to see if he suffered an eclipse in the preceding conjunction, or if he will suffer one in the next: since the significations of the malefic will be prolonged for as many years as his eclipse lasts in hours.

And he said that the Lord of the course and perfection signify according to what the significator signifies in terms of good or evil.

Likewise the Lord of the Ascendant and the Lord of the domicile of the division if he receives the Moon from Saturn in an optimal place of the circle, in a strong place, signifies the repulsion of evil by the will of God, and the prohibition of the destruction of the malefic by their fortune.

And he said that likewise in nativities if the Moon is like this, in a place of the testifying of the Ascendant, and is assisting, and she is made fortunate by the Lord of the Ascendant, and it is a good complexion, it signifies the long length of life and the kingdom. And he said that the native will be wise, and he will be fortunate. And he said that benefics dissolve the evil of the planet which is pushed, if it is strong and in an opportune place, and if it's testimony is direct. Indeed, if it is to the contrary, they will be weakened and will not be perfect.

### On The Cazimi Of The Sun, According to Albumashar

Albumashar said that when a star is united under the rays of the Sun, and especially Mercury, it will be strength and kingship for him, unless the Sun is with Saturn (whose nature is contrary to the nature of the Sun). And if there are 15 degrees between Mercury and the Sun, he will be in a praiseworthy place, if he is received.

### When A Planet Goes Out From Under The Rays Of The Sun, According To Albumashar

Albumashar said to ensure that the significator (or any planet) is gone out from combustion, and that he is not aspected by a malefic; since then it will be like a delicate boy. If however, any malefics aspect him, he will lose him and it will end. And likewise if he enters into combustion or is joined to him, he will be like a decrepit old man who is suffering with a disease.

### On The Condition Of The Higher Planets In The Revolution Of The Year Of The World, And Particularly Of Saturn

You will examine the condition of the higher planets in the revolution of the year of the world, when you revolve it, and see where they fall in the circle, beginning from Saturn: who, if he falls in the degree of his exaltation, and receives the disposition of Venus, will be the dispositor and significator of a great matter. For he will signify great things to come in that revolution: chiefly in the Roman Empire, secondarily in the Bablyonian kingdom

It will be in the detriment of men, and a detriment to their utility. And if it is like this (even if is very rare) it will be the greatest signification, almost exceeding measure in the exaltation and increase of the kingdom or empire, and it will be a matter of long duration. And this will be possible to perceive from the substance of the sign in which Venus is placed; and from the terms of her place: since if she

is occidental from the Sun, direct, fortunate and strong, in the terms of a benefic, free from impediments, recently having gone out from under the rays of the Sun, then she signifies that such things ought to occur; or if some planet aspects her who receives her from two dignities, and commits its own strength to her, and this planet is free, fortunate, and strong, and well disposed, so that nothing bad can be said about it, he will be the participator; if indeed, it is otherwise, the signification will be otherwise, namely being such that you would pray for God to avert it.

### On Jupiter

You will also see if Jupiter falls in the degree of his exaltation, and is fortunate, strong, and free from impediments: since if so, it signifies that the greatest of changes are going to come in that revolution, in that kingdom and empire, and for good. And this more strongly and more fully so if the Moon aspects him, and she is free, fortunate, and strong; and another planet who receives him, and who commits its strength to him (and this planet is free from impediments), and this planet will be a participator. If indeed, things are otherwise, Jupiter will not keep his promise, except according to how he is disposed.

### On Mars.

Then examine Mars; who, if he falls in the degree of his exaltation, signifies great changes, but they will be less than the aforementioned; and they will be of his nature, as are battles, burnings, fire, highway robberies, bloodshed, and similar things - unless Saturn aspects him from a trine or sextile aspect, and Saturn is fortunate, strong, and free from impediments, so that nothing bad can be said of him; or if Mars is aspected by another planet who receives him, and commits its disposition to him, and this planet is free from impediments, fortunate, and strong. If it is otherwise, the malice of Mars will be increased, and worse things will happen.

## On The Other Planets

There is nothing to be said regarding the Sun: since it is impossible for him to be in the degree of his exaltation in any revolution.

Regarding the inferiors I found nothing said by the ancient sages, only what Albumashar said about Mercury: that you will examine Mercury in the revolution, to see if there is some planet in his exaltation who receives him, and receives his disposition: for this planet will be the master of the condition of his significations (which I told you), God willing; since he comes together with his exaltation in the revolution of the years, and of the quarters. If there is a planet who receives him is in its own exaltation, it will be similar for him.

And he said this regarding the condition of the malefics in the conjunction of the planet who is in his own exaltation in the conjunction of malefics, and their aspects, the which planet is in the degree of its exaltation, according to what has been shown.

And he said that if the Moon is pacified, and the Sun is strong in his own place in a nocturnal revolution, the Sun will commit his rulership and regency to the Moon.

## CXVI

### What The Planets Signify In A Revolution Of The Year In Which A Solar Or Lunar Eclipse Is Supposed To Take Place

When you revolve a year of the world, see whether there is going to be an eclipse of the Sun or the Moon in that year. Since if an eclipse is not going to come, the judgement of the revolution will not be changed, but it will remain in its own condition; however, if one is going to happen, see in what sign it is going to happen in. Then you will calculate the planets and houses for the hour of the middle of the eclipse; and then examine the sign and its Lord, and see how it interacts with the Lord of the Ascendant of the eclipse; and how it interacts with the Lord of the year (or with its significator), and how it interacts with the significator of the king; and how it aspects with them, and with other planets.

Albumashar said that if some planet who is impeded aspects the hidden luminary at the time of the eclipse, and afterwards a malefic aspects it,

what it signifies will be made worse, and the impediment will be multiplied; and this will be more severe if the significator of the king is the Lord of the sign in which the eclipse is made: since if this is so, and one of the malefics aspect him, and this malefic is Mars, the death of the king will be feared in that revolution. And if it is Saturn, severe infirmity will be feared for him, or another very serious accident: and this will be when the Sun reaches the degree which was the cusp of the Medium Coeli at the hour of the middle of the eclipse. And if the Lord of the year is the Lord of the sign in which the eclipse is going to occur, the ruin of the commoners and their great impediment (besides death) will be feared, and this will be when the Sun arrives at the degree of the Ascendant of the middle of the eclipse. And if this Ascendant of the eclipse is Gemini, Virgo, Libra, or the first half of Sagittarius, or Aquarius, this will happen according to the kind of persons who are signified by the sign of the Ascendant; and according to other significations of the signs, as I explained to you above in the chapter on impediments which the Lord of the sign of the Ascendant of the revolution introduces when he is impeded. And these significations will last according to the number which we said above, namely if it is a lunar eclipse for each and every hour, it signifies a month; if it is a Solar eclipse, for each and every hour it signifies a year.

And Albumashar said that after this you will examine the part of the ecliptic over which you measured from the place of the eclipse and the place of its Lord, according to the substance of both signs. And he said to examine the flying stars which are the stars of Jupiter and always appear in the place of Mercury. And if Mercury is in the east, they will be seen in the east; and if he is in the west, they will be seen in the west; and the combustion of Mercury will be their receding..

## On The Portions Of The Planets In An Eclipse

Regarding the portions of the planets in an eclipse, if they are in the inferior journey, it will be bad for the function of Mars and Venus, which are southern and northern; and if they are on the upper journey, it will be bad for the function of Saturn, the Moon, and the Sun. And he said that after this you will see what kind of sign they appear in, and what is the condition of the Lord of the same sign in its place like, and what kind of aspects the malefics and the benefics have to the Lord of the sign and place where it is staying. If it is a sign of kings, and the Lord of the sign aspects it from a strong place, it signifies that he will leave from the side which contends in the kingdom, and will be one of the household members of the king, and he will be famous. And he said that if it is in the sign of a kingdom, in the way that I said, and the Lord of the sign did not aspect, he will be of the sons of nobles, and he will be fit for kingship. And he said, and judge likewise with all of the signs. And he said to know that the signs of the Sun, Jupiter, and Mars signify the sons of kings; and the signs of Saturn signify those famous in bygone days; and the domicile of the Moon is beneath [worse than] the domicile of the Sun, and the domicile of Mercury is beneath the domicile of Jupiter, and the domicile of Jupiter is beneath the domicile of Saturn. And their circles are below the circles which I stated. And he said that Saturn in Aquarius is notable, and is assigned to sages; in Capricorn he is evil. And he said, and the places of staying in their rising only signify the condition of the mob, and the general condition kings and magnates. Whence you ought to consider the ascending sign, or the place of staying, and judge about the people mentioned above according to its planet.

## How To Discern The Hour

Again, Albumashar said that the investigation of the hour in which it will appear, is to count from the Ascendant of the eclipse, or from the place of the eclipse, to the Ascendant of the middle of the eclipse to each and every sign and month. And he said that when you get to the sign itself in which it is (or to the Ascendant of the middle of the eclipse) without a doubt this will be it, whether it is good or bad: or perhaps this thing will appear if it when it is faster; toward the entrance of the Moon to the Ascendant, (especially in an eclipse which is in day): there will be battles, corruption or mutation in weather, and adversity.

## CXVII

### How One Should Proceed Regarding The Significators Of The King And The Country Folk, According To Albumashar

Albumashar said that if the Sun has signification over the country folk, and you understand it, the significator of the king will be clear to you, and it will reveal to you what will happen in his kingdom in the same year. And he said to know from the reception of the planets towards each other through their light, and the falling of their rays in the twelve houses of the circle, and what there is in the signs regarding climes and cities, so that their destruction can be shown to you; and adaptation by the rays of the malefics being inimical, and by the rays of contrary ones, and likewise by the rays of the malefics being friendly, and likewise by the rays of the benefics being friendly and inimical, and speak according to their friendship or enmity towards the domiciles. For if the benefics are pacified toward the domiciles (that is, if they aspect the places by a trine or sextile aspect), they signify a multitude of good; and if they are inimical (that is, if they aspect from square or opposition). And likewise, if the malefics are inimical to the houses (that is, if they aspect from square or opposition), they signify a multitude of evil. If however, they are pacified towards the houses (that is, if they aspect them from a trine or sextile aspect), they signify a scarcity of evil.

And he said to then examine what is in each sign in terms of lands, in the east and west. And if a sign is impeded in the west, it signifies impediment from the lands which are in the direction of the east and the west. And if the impediment is in the Medium Coeli, it signifies impediment in lands which are in the east and west, and especially towards the north and south (namely in the regions of Mars and Venus, and in the Aethiopian lands).

And he said that this is an admirable example through which you can contemplate a revolution of the year, namely with twelve days remaining of the month of Ramadam (which is the ninth lunar month) in the 35th year of the Arabs. And the year arrived to Scorpio, and the Ascendant was 15 degrees Libra, in the terms of Jupiter, and the planets and the their rays were according to what they are in this figure

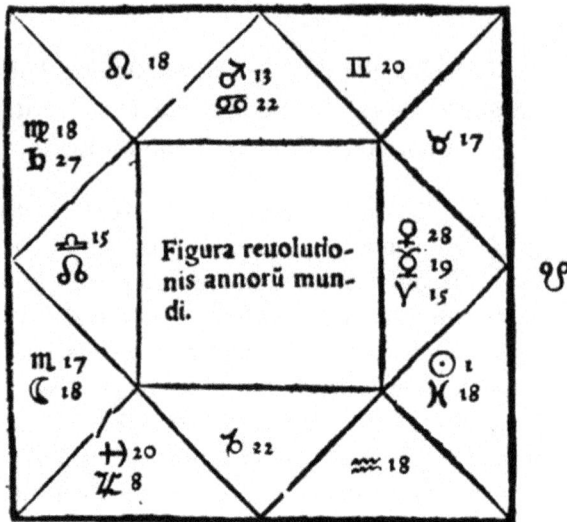

And he said, that the revolution was following Benesaphar, according to one equal hour and 12 minutes from the beginning of the night of the Sabbath, which dawns on the 18th of the aforementioned month.

And the Ascendant (by the ascensions of Toledo) was 15 Libra, the planets were according to what I will tell to you. For Saturn was in 27 degrees 29 minutes of Virgo. Jupiter in 8 degrees 16 minutes of Capricorn. Mars in 13 degrees Leo. The Sun in the first degree of Aries. Venus in approximately 28 degrees of Aries. Mercury in 19 degrees 35 minutes of Aries. The Moon in 18 degrees 7 minutes of Scorpio. The Caput in 15 degrees 33 minutes of Libra. And the Cauda in Aries at 15 degrees 33 minutes.

The year arrived at Scorpio. And the erected angles, that is, the same signs, were by division and by number in the revolution of the year of the 35th year of the Arabs, which 12 days remained of the month of Ramadam. And the Sun was in opposition to the Ascendant receding. And the revolution was at night, and the Moon was in her descension in the second sign; and the benefics were absent from her, and she was joined to malefics; and she was the Lord of the Medium Coeli. And Venus and Mercury were in opposition to the Ascendant. And Mars in the 11th (namely in Leo) received, And Jupiter was in the fourth, in his own descension, cutting off the light of the Sun from Mars. And Saturn was cadent in Virgo, not received, in the twelfth house. And Mars was the Lord of the domicile of the Lord of the Ascendant (namely Aries, which contained Venus, who was the Lord

of the Ascendant), and the Lord of the domicile of the Sun and Moon.

And the Lord of the year, the significatrix of the commoners, was Venus, who had more in terms of testimony; and she was in an angle, in opposition to her own domicile, going from the east to the occidental angle, not received.

And the significator of the king was the Moon, since the revolution was at night, and she had the authority; and she was the Lord of the Medium Coeli, and was joined to Saturn, who was cadent in the twelfth house; then she was joined to Mars, and he was retrograde in the eleventh. Therefore this signified that the king of the same clime would be killed by his own country folk: because Mars being retrograde signified his killing (Mars was the Lord of the domicile of the luminaries, and the Lord of the domicile of the Lord of the Ascendant). And on account of the falling of the Moon from the angle, it signified that he would be killed without contention, and would not subdue the aforementioned citizens.

And he said that on account of the place of Venus, and her deposition from her rank, and the opposition, and her being the Lord of the year, and the significatrix of the country folk, it signified that after this the country folk would be given to battles, and the complication of war and contention in the kingdom.

And he said that on account of the placement of the Moon from Saturn, and the rays of his sextile aspect, it signified that these things would happen in the first quarter of the year.

And from the place of the Sun (who is the Lord of the eleventh), in the square aspect of Jupiter, committing disposition to him, it signifies that he who will succeed the king will be just, and the country folk will be improved in his time.

And he said that on account of the light of retrograde Mars in the eleventh from the Ascendant, it signifies that he will scatter the house of the king's treasures after killing him by a powerful killing and shedding of blood. And he said that on account of the presence of Mars in the house of the Sun, it signifies the contention of the nobles with their king.

And he said that the light of the opposition of the Sun, Mercury, and Venus in the Ascendant, and the rays of the second square aspect of Jupiter, and the rays of the first sextile aspect of Mars, signified that there was going to be a contention in the climes of their signs, and bloodshed. And that there would be a battle in the regions of Marmon, Sagesten, and Aafon, and their cattle would be benefitted, and the land would be fertile; and there would be infirmities in boys, and an improvement in the condition of their businessmen.

The second from the Ascendant was Scorpio, and the Moon was there, impeded, and also the rays of the second trine aspect of the Sun, and the rays of the second sextile aspect of Jupiter, and the rays of the first square aspect of Mars, and the first sextile aspect of Saturn. And this signified bloodshed and battles. And the beginning of these things will be in the clime of the Arab climes. After that it will change, since the Moon is impeded outside of the sign in which she is placed; it will be magnified, and there will be much bloodshed, and the condition of the clime of the Arabs will be made worse, and there will be death of their cattle, and the coldness of their winter will be more severe, and this will be because of the place of Venus from the Ascendant. And on account of her presence in an angle, it signified that a foreign enemy would not enter upon them, and he would be in the east, and death would be from his role, and the greater part of it would be in women.

The third was Sagittarius, and in it were the rays of the second trine aspect of Mercury, the rays of the first trine aspect of Mars, and the first square aspect of Saturn; and its Lord Jupiter was in his descension. This signified infirmities and severities which the citizens of the first clime, and the citizens of Spain, would meet with; and a multitude of thieves and the death of beasts; and this would be multiplied in the land, such as in Upper Armenia; and more boys would die in this year.

The fourth was Capricorn, and Jupiter was in it, and the rays of the second square aspect of the Sun, and the rays of the second square aspect of Venus, and the light of the first trine aspect of Saturn, and the light of the first sextile aspect of the Moon. These signified the safety of the clime in the day, and the goodness or fineness of their condition; and the fitness of the condition of their king; and the felicity of their lands, and that they will conquer those who contend with them; and it signified the multitude of their profit, and the fertility of the lands of the citizens of Asamilier and Almedehai, and the security of their citizens together with their high spirits, and the abundance of necessities; and the fitness of their king.

The fifth was Aquarius, and no planets were in it, but the light of the second sextile aspect of the Sun was there, and the light of the second sextile aspect of Mercury, and the light of the first square aspect of the Moon, and the light of the opposition of Mars, and the light of the second sextile aspect of Venus. Which signified contention and war in the region of Alcuphus, and in its country folk; and war, rebellions, and feasting. And he said that perhaps this will be in Egypt, and Gurgan, and on account of this occasion there will be much bloodshed. And he said that many pilgrims will gather to those regions.

The sixth was Pisces, and there were no planets in it, but there was the light of the opposition of Saturn, and the light of the first sextile aspect of Jupiter, and the light of the first trine aspect of the Moon. And he said that the place of the opposition of Saturn signified the severity of the cold in Tabaristan, and in its direction, and the severity which its king will meet with in this land, and this on account of the place of Jupiter and the weakness he is in. And it signifies the bad condition of its citizens, and they will have power over their king, and will resolve things amongst themselves; and there will be dissensions, and their rains and profits will be multiplied; and their cattle will be fit; and likewise things will occur in the regions of India, and the lands of Armenia (those which approach toward Romania).

The seventh was Aries, and the Sun was in it remote from the angle; Mercury and Venus were also in it; and the light of the first square aspect of Jupiter, and the light of the second trine aspect of Mars (who is the Lord of the second). And on account of the placement of Venus, who is in an angle, and the trine aspect of Mars, who is the Lord of the second domicile (who is retrograde in Leo), the Sun signified the ruin of the king of Babylonia, and that there would be contention, war, and much bloodshed in the clime of Babylonia, and the destruction of their kingdom. And the beginning of these things would be in another clime, and this on account of the placement of Mars, and on account of the placement of Mercury (who is the Lord of the ninth). And the light of Jupiter (who is the Lord of the third domicile), signifies that there will also be a loss of many men on occasion of these wars. And he said that there will be religion, and boys and camels, and all hairy things, will be benefitted; and they will be oppressed by heat. And what I said will also be in the mountains and in Azerbaijan.

And the eighth was Taurus, and none of the planets were in it, and its Lord Venus was cadent from it. However, the light of the first sextile aspect of the Sun was there, and the light of the first trine aspect of Jupiter was there, and the light of the second square aspect of Mars (who is the enemy of this domicile), and the light of the opposition of the Moon (who is the exaltation Lord of this domicile), signifying that the king of Antiha and the city of Ortona (which are said to be next to Nueria and Segesten, and particularly Cabrus (since it is in the western regions), will go out upon all enemies who are close to them, and they will find severity from them; and thieves, the arrogant, and contradictions will be multiplied in that place; and their harvest will be destroyed; and the country folk will put down their king, and their cattle will perish; and they will be safe from the king; and they will find good from pilgrimages.

And the ninth was Gemini, and none of the planets were in it, but the first sextile of Mercury was there, and the light of the second square of Saturn, and the light of the second sextile of Mars. The mixture of the light of Mercury (who is the Lord of the ninth) signified that those from Adaliam and Exanos, and their regions, and Thebut, would be strengthened over those who are inimical to them, and who are of their opposition and are enemies, and this will be on account of the strength of the place of Mercury and his reception. And on account of the mixture of Mars with Saturn, it signifies many infirmities and pains in these regions, and that many men will die; and this will particularly be in youths. And since the second square aspect of Saturn has more degrees, it signifies that they will acquiesce to their king and be obedient to him. And he said and those things which I said will be in Gurgen and Lower Acebirutaba, Upper Alem, and Amacil.

And the tenth was Cancer, and no planets were in it, but the light of the trine aspect of the Moon (who is the Lord of the tenth, and impeded in her descension) was in it, and the light of the second sextile aspect of Saturn, and the light of the first square aspect of the Sun, and the light of the first square aspect of Mercury, and the light of the first square aspect of Venus. And he said that it signifies what I said by the malignity of the Lord of the domicile, and the Lord of the exaltation, in addition to what the square of the Sun signifies; that the king of the clime of Iraq will perish, and their kingdom will be destroyed and mixed together, and there will be contention between them in their princes, and there will be infirmity in men generally from cold and moisture; and their produce will be destroyed, and the condition of men will be oppressed, and acquisition will be decreased, and likewise for the lands of Balab and Allaharara (that is, of the two seas), and Egypt, Emarius, and Addul.

And the eleventh was Leo, and Mars was in it, retrograde; and the light of the first trine aspect of the Sun, and the light of the first trine aspect of Mercury, and the light of the second square aspect of the Moon, and the light of the first square aspect of Venus. And he said that it is signified by the placement of Mars, and the light of the second square aspect of the Moon (who is the nocturnal luminary, and the significatrix of the king), that in the clime of Altoio and in Aeratus, there will be war, bloodshed, and detriment from thieves; and these things will be in Albafrah; and many men will perish in the same year, and there will be contention in the kingdom. And this will be on account of the light of the second square aspect of the Moon - understand this.

And the twelfth was Virgo, and Saturn was here, retrograde; and the light of the first trine aspect of Venus, and the light of the second trine aspect of Jupiter, and the second sextile aspect of the Moon: which signifies infirmities from coldness and dryness according to the nature of this sign, And he said that on account of the placement of Mercury they will be freed, God willing, and will not be destroyed: and they will not be strong in the heat of the summer- understand this.

## How The Condition Of The King Can Be Examined In That Year

The tenth of this figure was Cancer, and the Moon (who is its Lord) was the significatrix of the king, and was cadent in the second place. And he said that therefore we should examine whether her light is in the Medium Coeli (which is her place) or in the Ascendant. And the light of her trine aspect was in the eighteenth degree and seventh minute of Cancer. Therefore we examined to see who she committed her disposition to in this place, and the light of the first square aspect of Mercury was closer to her than the light of the others, and it was in the 19th degree and a fraction. We subtracted the light of the Moon from this, and one degree and a fraction remained. We divided this by 59 minutes and 18 seconds: and one day and a fraction remained. Therefore the Moon disposed one day and a fraction through her own light out of the Midheaven. And because the disposition was committed to Mercury (who was the Lord of the house of enemies, and the Lord of the house of pilgrimage and faith), this signified the sorrow of the king in this disposition from the accusations of the religious and people of faith, and from their sayings, and from enemies. After this, Mercury will receive disposition from the Moon by its first square aspect. And he is the Lord of the ninth and the twelfth; and his rays are in the ninth domicile from her, and this signifies that every work which is hoped for will have a good measure of accusations from penance, prayers, and fasting, and they will find marriage celebrations in this disposition.

Then Saturn will receive disposition by the light of his second sextile aspect, from the light of Mercury's first square aspect, and he will dispose the remainder sign in which his light is, in the following sign from the same place. And he is the Lord of the fourth and fifth (which is the eighth from the place of disposition). Therefore, in the disposition it signified in this place, since he received the light of Mercury's square aspect, that little notes and rumours will come on these days from the direction of the west which will make him sorrowful; and he will be disturbed about them, and he will be of a bad mind over it, and he will hinder the citizens in their work, and his own children, which will make him sorrowful.

After this, the Sun will receive disposition from Saturn by the light of his first trine aspect, and he is the Lord of the second house from the Midheaven; and is also the second from the house of the king, which has the signification of expenses because of women, and this is on account of the place of the Sun, and since he commits disposition to Venus, and Venus receives the light of (her/his?) first square aspect, and the light of the first trine aspect of the Sun, and Venus is the Lord of the Ascendant, and is in its opposition.

Therefore she receives disposition from the Sun, and renders it to the Moon, and this signifies the entrance or involvement in this disposition, and contention with the country folk because of the kingdom, and the marriage of his son from the direction of women, and their consolation by the light of the second square aspect of the square aspect of Venus; and the Moon is the Lord of the Midheaven, and she is in the second from the Ascendant, which signifies of the entry of the king into these matters in the same year, and in the same disposition, and generally into the disposition of the planets from the Midheaven up to the place of the cutting of the light by her[his] rays up to 73 days, and a half day, and one-sixth of a day.

Therefore consider it by this, and what is necessary for you to use in it, in a revolutions of the years of the world, if you work it out in the disposition of the days by the projection of the rays according to what I said to you regarding the domiciles and their Lords, and the reception of light and its sending to reception from trine or square aspect, or from opposition. After this, know the light of reception and its impulse and work in the lights of the contrary and inimical malefics, and in the lights of the harmonious and pacifying malefics And he said to say likewise regarding the inimical benefics: that if they are inimical to the houses, there will be little good; and in the lights of the malefics if they are inimical to the houses, there will be a multitude of evil, and if they are pacified, a small amount of good.

## The Same On The Two Parts In A Revolution Of The Years Of The World

Albumashar said that if you find two Parts in one place or in one sign, those whose significator is better disposed will prevail. And he said the better disposed (as far as it pertains to this) is the one who better aspects its Part, or who is corporeally joined to it. And Albumashar said that this is like if a Part is joined with its Lord in the water triplicity, and their presence or conjunction coincides in one of the signs of the triplicity from which the conjunction was changed: so that if it is Gemini, the conjunction is changed from it, and it will summon its presence or conjunction in the circle of the conjunction, or in two others outside of this triplicity in Aquarius. Therefore in addition the citizens of this triplicity will be strengthened. And he said that if it is Saturn, and the conjunction is in Scorpio, they will be strengthened. If however, he receives the disposition of Mars in Scorpio, and is in the Medium Coeli and rules over the year; and Mars is in the Ascendant and rules, with the commission of his disposition to Saturn in the Medium Coeli in Scorpio, it signifies that the king will perish in the direction of the east, and leave his kingdom. And if it happens that in addition to this Venus is strong in her exaltation, and the conjunction is in Scorpio, it signifies the strength of the Arabs and their seeking in the kingdom.

## Another Chapter On The Revolution Of The Years Of The World According To Albumashar

If you erect the figure of the revolution of one of the years of the world, examine the significator or Lord of the year, which is called the significator of the country folk; and examine the Sun and the significator of the king. Also see if one of them falls in opposition to Mars, unless perhaps Mars is truly fortunate, so that nothing bad can be said about him (which only occurs very rarely): since this signifies wars, terrors, and bloodshed. And if two of the aforementioned significators fall in the opposition of Mars, it will signify greater evil.

And Albumashar said that the removal of the malefics from the angles into the third or the ninth, signifies war and little religion, as much for the king as for the country folk. You ought to consider the Sun and his condition, who, if he is well disposed (namely fortunate and strong), signifies the good disposition and fitness of the lands of Babylonia and of its citizens. If however, he is impeded, it signifies their bad condition and their detriment, and the same for their king. If the Sun is alone, and impeded, in the second, the sixth, or the twelfth, or is impeded somewhere from the conjunction, square aspect, or opposition of one of the malefics, he signifies the bad condition of the aforementioned king, namely the king of Babylonia.

You will also examine the disposition of the Moon: for if she is free (namely fortunate and strong), she signifies the strength of the Romans and their king, and the weakness of their enemies. If however, she is alone, and impeded in whatever place she is in (but more so in the aforementioned houses), she signifies their impediment and evil, and the same for their king, and the strength of their enemies.

But someone might say "Why does the Sun signify the king of Babylonia, and the Moon the king of the Romans, since the kingdom of the Romans is a bigger kingdom than any other, and the Sun is the bigger luminary" The response to which is that the Sun is the higher luminary, but is not the universal participant in things like the Moon is; and the kingdom of Babylonia existed before the kingdom of the Romans, and it not a universal kingdom: and so the Sun was attributed to it as its significator. Indeed, the Moon, since she is the universal luminary participating in all things, was attributed to king and kingdom of the Romans: since this kingdom is universal beyond all other kingdoms, to which all other kings and all other kingdoms were then subjected to and placed under.

You will also see the disposition of Saturn, who, if he is well disposed and in conjunction with benefics, and especially from the Ascendant, and is the Lord of the year free from impediments, will not impede, nor will he then be an evildoer, and the impediments which he introduces in the in inferior subjects by nature will be removed if he is not impeded; and this more strongly so if he is in Scorpio, and Scorpio is the Medium Coeli: since then the Ascendant will be Aquarius, and he will be the Lord of the year. For it signifies that bloodshed and other pestilences are going to come in that revolution; and it seems that this evil ought to begin when Saturn reaches his own terms. However, if Mars aspects him from opposition or square aspect, it will increase the evil: but if the aspect is a trine or sextile with reception, it will not introduce as much, and the evil will be reduced.

You will also examine Mars, and you will see if he falls in Cancer (which is his detriment and descension): since if this is so, Albumashar said that it signifies that the citizens of the clime of Iraq will fall into oppression due to a leader, and likewise Sagittarius. And he said that since these signs belong to their clime, and Mars is the significator from the leader; and he said that Mars in the Ascendant signifies the diminution of the eastern direction in the same year. And he said that the fitness of Venus in Pisces, or in one of her own domiciles, signifies the fertility of the Arab regions, and their security. And he said that if she commits disposition from a place similar to a planet who receives her in the Medium Coeli, and she is in an angle, receiving, and not remote, and the luminaries in the signs of the profection from Scorpio, the Arabs will contend in the kingdom, and seek it from their own citizens, since she is joined to the planet in the Medium Coeli, and falls in a good place; and this will be better if the sign of the Medium Coeli agrees with her nature.

And he said that the fitness of Venus signifies the fitness of the Arabs in their bodies, and the fitness of their sustenance. However, he said that if she falls in enmity to the Ascendant, she signifies war and changes in the middle of the year, and in the ignoble men and thieves. And he said that the impediment of the Lord of the Ascendant in a malignant place in the Medium Coeli signifies the oppression which the country folk will meet with from their masters. And he said a planet were to fall in the seventh from the Ascendant (which is the place of its enmity), it signifies that the king will contend - if the signification of the planet in its place concerns the kingdom or the year. And he said that if the first side is in the Medium Coeli in its own dignity, and the second side is in the fourth, it signifies that war will generally abound on earth.

Similarly, you will see if one of the malefic planets fall in the second from the Ascendant of the revolution: since if this is so, and it impedes the Lord of the second from opposition or square aspect, it signifies the diminution of substance, and its dispersion or expense, and mostly on useless things.

You will also consider the malefic planets, and you will see if one of them is in opposition to the other: since if this is so, it signifies the occurrence of a great thing in the world, in a time that is not far off. Likewise you will see whether Mars is found to be combust (unless perhaps he is in the cazimi of the Sun), and he is the Lord of the sign of the tenth house and remote from the angle: since if this is so, it signifies that someone will go out from the kingdom who will punish it, and the end of this affair will be by the sword. And if the Sun then commits disposition to Saturn, and Saturn is the significator of the country folk, and the Ascendant is Capricorn or Aquarius, and he aspects the Ascendant from a friendly aspect, and is in a good place from it, and the Moon has authority, and she commits disposition to him from the Ascendant, it signifies that the country folk will plot together to kill their king, death by them will be feared for him in that revolution.

And if Saturn is the Lord of the year, and the Almutem of the Midheaven is impeded by him, and does not receive him, but there is no testimony on the condition of the country folk from Venus and the Moon to the Lord of the tenth, and Saturn is in the eleventh, and the Moon (who has authority) is in the Ascendant, Saturn will be given more testimony in the condition of the country folk.

And Albumashar said that if Mars does not aspect his own place, and is not received, and the Moon is also like this, Saturn will signify from the place of the Moon (who is the luminary of the night) what the matter of the Sun signified. And by the committing of disposition and strength to Saturn, the king will perish in that year, and the country folk will kill him. And he said that there will be poverty and tribulations in men, and likewise oppression and battle; and there will be oppression of the yearly produce, and it will be in the sixth month, on account of there being six degrees between them. And he said that cattle will be profitable in the same year; and the coldness of the winter will only be slight.

You will also see in the hour of the revolution if Saturn is the significator of the mob, or the Lord of the year, or the Almutem over the Ascendant of the year, and is not impeded by Mars, and there are benefics in the Ascendant, and Mars is cadent from them, and from the Ascendant: since this signifies the fitness of the affairs of the mob; and this more strongly so if he is in an angle or in another good place from the Ascendant, and Saturn receives these benefics.

And Albumashar said that the moist and watery planets in the Ascendant signify a cold year in the same city or region, and locusts and the fitness of cattle: and likewise if the benefics descend in the Ascendant with the Sun. And he said the presence of the Lord of the Medium Coeli falling into the third with Jupiter signifies the levity of the king and his despatching in ruling.

## SECOND PART OF THIS TRACTATE

### On The Projection Of The Parts And Their Significations

### I

### What We Should Consider First In Particular Revolutions, And It Is A Chapter Related To The Entire Work

Since by the grace of God we have sufficiently dealt with these things which precede from the universal revolution (even if was by way of a long, but not tedious, discussion) it is fitting (lest something might be seen to be missing from the treatment of revolutions) that we expand more on the particulars. And the works of our ancients must be examined by way of particular revolutions, just as they were considered in general ones for they considered it a very useful, fitting, and opportune matter: and this was the extraction of Parts regarding things which we use in the revolutions of the years, and which fall to us (and they occur frequently in the work of astronomy), and from which those wishing to, will be able to attain very great utility in revolutions.

And Albumashar said that this is done in two ways. One way being when one planet is joined to another, or when it is separated from the other by a perceptible quantity: since then it acquires some signification of good or bad, since a planet signifies one thing when it advances toward another planet, another when it is with it, and another when it recedes and is separated from it. For the planets signify certain things by nature, certain things by accident, certain things according to more, certain things according to less, certain things according to equality. Because if two planets have equal signification over one and the same thing, the stronger (namely, the one who is stronger by nature, power, or dignity) is let loose to act. Or if one is diurnal and the other is nocturnal, or if one is the Almutem over that Part, or if one signifies the beginning, and the other the end. or if it is stronger or more deserving in some other way, it will be preferred: just as you will see in the extraction of the Part of the Father, which the Sun and Saturn signify equally (since each of them signify fathers). However, it begins from the Sun in the day, since he is stronger than Saturn in the day, for the Sun

signifies clarity and splendour, and rejoices in these things; Saturn signifies obscurity and darkness, and rejoices in these things which are the contraries of the aforementioned. And you should understand similarly about the others, as will be discussed in its own time and place.

The other way which the extraction of Parts comes to be is that if there are two or three significators, who signify one matter, and the virtue of one is equal to the virtue of the other; or if one is more deserving or stronger than the other - Albumashar said there will be similitude in signification, and for these reasons the extraction of the Parts is necessary.

For the extraction of the Parts is the knowledge of the longitude which is between two significators who naturally signify one matter; and the effect of a Part would not be known well enough through two significators, unless a third is added on, namely, one who naturally signifies the matter on account of which the Part is extracted.

For from two significators naturally signifying a matter, derives a space of longitude between them: and the significator from whom the measurement is begun is called the first significator of this matter; the second is called the other. And these two are called "immobiles". The one from which begins the projection of degrees of distance which are between the first natural significators, is called the third significator. And the third is the Lord of the Ascendant or the Lord of another house from which the projection of degrees of distance begins - which is "mobile", just as will be handled below in a suitable place. And therefore it was said to take what is between this planet and that planet, and add on the degree of the Ascendant, and project from the Ascendant (or from such a place to such a place; or from such a planet to such a planet), giving each sign 30 degrees by equal degrees. And where the number finishes, there will be the Part.

And this was done in three ways, and for two reasons: one of which was to know what must be judged regarding the good or evil that is signified by the Lord of the sign from the Ascendant in which this part falls, or from the other place from which the part is projected. Indeed, the second reason was since the Ascendant signifies bodies and the beginning of all things; however, sometimes the projection was from planets or other places, since that same house or that same planet could be of the same kind or complexion with the place of the Part.

And Albumashar said that since the Ascendant and the house of the circle from which the longitude between the two natural significators is projected changes every hour, the third significator is named "mobile" from its signification. They also used equal degrees in the Parts for the reason that the planets are moved about the axis of the circle of signs, and the Ascendant is considered according to the degrees of the circle of signs, and the degrees of the circle of signs are equal.

And therefore Albumashar said that one planet is in this sign and this degree; and the Ascendant is this or that degree of some sign. And he said that the whole of the circle of signs is spoken of by equal degrees. However, he also said that the degrees of ascensions are from the degrees of the circle surrounding the circle of signs, and this moves the circle of signs and the other circles. And Albumashar said that the ancients of Babylonia, Egypt, and all the rest, used 97 parts, according to what is found in their books.

And there are three ways of projecting the Parts: the first of which is the projection of the seven Parts of the seven planets; indeed, the second is comprised of the Parts of the twelve houses; the third is comprised of the parts of the rest of the matters, which there is no mention or reminder of in the twelve houses (which are Parts necessary in certain places, both in revolutions and in nativities). There are seven parts of the first way; twelve of the second; and ten of the third. And the parts of the seven planets are first to be discussed.

## II

## On The Parts Of The Seven Planets And On Their Particular Significations, And First On The Part Of The Moon, Which Is Called The Part Of Fortune

Albumashar said to know that one part is not extracted except from two significators naturally signifying the matter on account of which the part is extracted. For if two planets naturally signify one thing, and they concord in diurnality or in other qualities, the extraction of the part ought to begin from the stronger one of them, following what was said elsewhere about the Sun and Saturn, who are equal in signification of the father, and diurnality: however, the extraction of the part of the father is begun from the Sun, since he is stronger on account of the reason assigned above. And if they are equal in signification just as was said, and one is diurnal and the other is nocturnal, the extraction of the part in the day is begun from the diurnal one, on account of the day prevailing over the night, and since it must be preferred to it. Indeed, in the night it is begun from the nocturnal one, on account of its equality in signification with the diurnal one, just as in the extraction of the Part of Fortune, which is extracted from the luminaries: and the luminaries, according to what the ancients said, are of equal strength in fortune.

But since the Sun is the diurnal fortune, it begins from the Sun in the day; and since the Moon is nocturnal, it begins from her at night. And this part is set out in advance, and preferred to all other parts, just as the luminaries are preferred to all other stars: and so, this part overshadows all other parts, just as the luminaries could be said to overshadow all other stars by virtue of their brightness. And likewise the Sun is more splendid than all the rest of the stars, and it is called the luminary of the day, since by his rising it becomes day; and by his setting the day is taken away, and it becomes light; and he signifies natural life, and the rest of the things which are said in the chapter on his significations. And the Moon is the luminary and fortune of the night, and the significatrix of bodies, and of all things which are said elsewhere in her chapter.

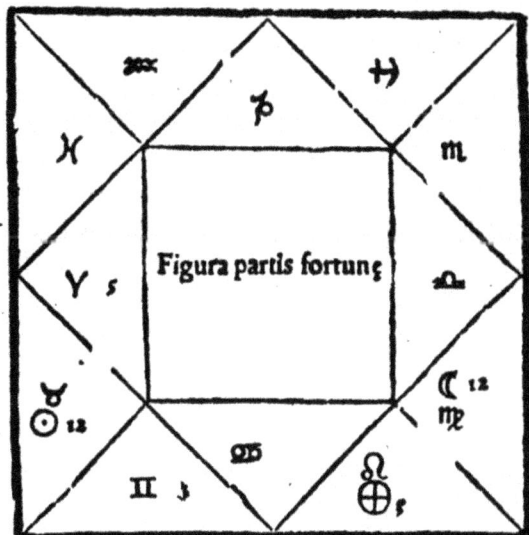

Figura partis fortunç

And I will give you an example of the extraction of the Part of Fortune: posit that the Sun is at 12 degrees 5 minutes of Taurus; and the Moon is at 12 degrees 5 minutes of Virgo; and have the matter on account of which you wish to extract the Part of Fortune be in the day. And so you ought to subtract the place of the Sun from the place of the Moon, and 4 signs will remain; and 5 degrees 5 minutes from the ascending sign. And begin to project from the beginning of the same sign by equal degrees, giving each sign 30 degrees, and where the number finishes, there will be the Part. And it is to the contrary at night: namely, subtract the place of the Moon from the place of the Sun, and add on the degrees of the ascending sign, and project from the Ascendant, and where the number finishes, there will be the Part of Fortune. However, if both luminaries are in one degree, the Part of Fortune will be in the degree of the Ascendant, and in a like minute.

And this part signifies life, body, and soul; strength, fortune, substance, and success; Also riches and poverty; gold and silver, and the severity or ease of things for sale in the marketplace; also praise, good reputation, honours, and loftiness; good and bad, present and future, hidden or manifest. And it has signification over every matter; however, it does more for the wealthy and magnates than it does for others. Nevertheless. It works for each and every man according to the condition of each and every one of them.

And if this part and the luminaries are well disposed in nativities or revolutions, there will be good in a notable way. And it is called the Part of the Moon, and it is the Ascendant of the Moon; and signifies good fortune.

And Albumashar said that if what is absent from the hours of the day in its parts of the hours (that is, of the day) is multiplied, and the result is projected from the place of the Moon by equal degrees, it will fall in the place of the Part of Fortune, or close to its place.

And if one significator is stronger than the other in the place of the part, the part will begin from the stronger one, both in the day and at night. However, if the signification is from the sign and its Lord, this will begin more so from the Lord of the sign up until the degrees of the sign: since the signification of the sign is strengthened by the signification of the planet. And if it happens that the sign is stronger in signification, it will begin from the sign, and the Ascendant will be a participant with it (or another place of the circle to which it is extended). And this will be discussed more widely, clearly, and openly below in the Tractate on Revolutions on the Parts of the twelve houses, and of the things born of the earth, according to what occurs to each of these parts when they are dealt with, if God permits.

### On The Part Of Future Things, Which Is Called The Part Of The Sun

After the Part of Fortune (which surpasses all other parts in strength and fortune), next to be discussed is the Part of Future Things, which is called the Part of the Sun. And this Part, immediately after the Part of Fortune, surpasses all the other parts, and prevails over them: even if certain astrologers seem to care little for it, which does not seem fitting to me, since it is reputed as a very useful thing by the wise. And this Part is extracted to the contrary of how the Part of Fortune is extracted: for just as the Part of Fortune is extracted in the day from the Sun to the Moon, and at night from the Moon to the Sun, so the Part of Future Things is extracted from the Moon to the Sun in the day, and from the Sun to the Moon at night, and what has ascended from the sign of the Ascendant is added on to this, and the result is projected from the beginning of the ascending sign, namely by giving each sign 30 degrees by equal degrees; and where the number finishes, there will be this Part.

The parts of the luminaries are set out in advance of the parts of the other planets since even though things to be generated are generated through corruption, and corruption comes to be through the motion of the planets; and the operations which come to be through the other planets do not appear as manifestly; likewise, they are not similar to those things which come to be through the luminaries.

And you should know that the peculiar nature of the Part of Future Things is to signify the soul and the body (after the Part of Fortune), and their condition; and faith, prophecy, religion, worship of God, and secrets, thoughts, intentions, hidden matters, and everything that is absent, and courtliness, liberality, praise, good reputation, heat, and cold.

And Albumashar said that the significations of the Part of Fortune and the Part of Future Things are more apparent regarding all matters absent and future, than they are over what is present. They also reveal more over the beginnings of work, and over revolutions of the year, both of the world as of nativities. And he said that the significations of the Part of Fortune appear more in the day than the Part of Future Things; and the significations of the Part of Future Things appear more in the night than the significations of the Part of Fortune. And whatever mutations and alterations happen by seasons, by the changes of the planets from sign to sign, generations and corruptions come to be, and life comes to be for animal and the rest of the vegetative things (and for this same reason generated things fail and are corrupted): nevertheless the luminaries operate more manifestly and perceptibly in them than the rest of the planets. And these two parts, as much for good as for evil operate beyond the rest of the parts: and their significations are similar to those of the luminaries.

## On The Heavy Part, Which Is Called The Part Of Saturn

The Part of Saturn, which the sages named the Heavy Part (on account of the heavy and ponderous things which are signified by this part) is taken in the day from Saturn to the Part of Fortune; and vice versa at night, and projected from the Ascendant, giving each and every sign 30 degrees according to equal degrees. And where its number

and minute fall, there will be this Part. The significations of which are: memory, profundity of intellect and counsel; faith, religion, and continence in them, and constancy and durability. And it signifies matters which have perished, or which have gone astray, or which have been stolen, or which have fled, or have been submerged in the sea or in a river, or which have fallen into a pit or a similar place; or have died. And it signifies the condition of the dead, namely what death the native should die of, or is going to die of. And it signifies the condition of lands and the harvests of others, and things born of the earth. And it has the signification of inheritances, especially those which are purchased; and it signifies heavy buildings, and especially those which are not elevated much above the earth; and ditches and accumulations of earth, and carrying these things up high; and productions of waters and the like. It also signifies avarice and difficulties of wretched men living miserably. And it signifies praise and slander; and it signifies old age and the age making to grow old, and all bound and imprisoned matters, or things placed in prison, and liberation from prison or binding.

## On The Part Of Jupiter Which Is Called The Part Of Blessedness

The Part of Jupiter, which the philosophers called the Part of Blessedness and Assistance, is taken in the day from the Part of Future Things (which signifies fortune) to Jupiter (who signifies blessedness and assistance), and vice versa at night; and projected from the Ascendant. And its signification is over honour, attainment of matters, victory, assistance, blessedness, and benignity; and the praiseworthy end of matters; and the seeking of faith and its fitness, and whatever there is concerning its nature; and belief in God; eagerness for all good works, and love of it and of justice and of just judgement between men; and houses of prayer. And it signifies wisdom, the wise, and the loftiness of the wise; also trust and hope in all good things which men enjoy, and participate in the good with each other.

## On The Part Of Mars, Which Is Called The Part Of Boldness

The Part of Mars, which is called the Part Boldness by the ancients, is taken in the day from Mars to the Part of Fortune, and vice versa at night, and projected from the Ascendant. The significations of which are: the disposition of armies, battles, and conflicts; and the uprightness and acuity of the mind; and boldness, strength, anticipation, greatness of heart, with rapid motion and haste; it also signifies lascivious lewdness from slyness and seductions.

## On The Part Of Venus Which Is Called The Part Of Love And Of Concord.

The Part of Venus, which is called the Part of Love and Concord, is taken in the day from the Part of Fortune and the Part of Future Things: and vice versa at night, and projected from the Ascendant. The significations of this Part are as follows: delights, desires, and longing in matters of sex, and the practice of such things, as much licit as illicit; and in those things which Venusians love, and in which they delight, and which the mind desires; and marriages; and general things which pertain to the sex drive; and rejoicing from games, lively things, and delights.

## On The Part Of Mercury Which Is Called The Part Of Poverty And Middling Intellect

The Part of Mercury, which is called the Part of Poverty and Middling Intellect, is taken in the day from the Part of Future Things, to the Part Of Fortune, and vice versa at night; and projected from the Ascendant. And it has these significations: poverty and smallness of talent and intellect; and it also signifies war, fear, hatred, contentions, injuries, and anger in the hour of injuries, and enemies. And it also signifies business, buying and selling; also thoughts, whether intelligent or crafty; and writings and calculation, and the pursuit of astronomy and of diverse sciences.

This is the way of extracting the parts of the seven planets, and these things which were said in them are their significations. Whence if you ever extract the Part regarding one of aforementioned significations, and you project it in some figure, judge on it according to how you see its conjunctions, or its Lords conjunctions, with the planets or their aspects for good or bad. Nor do I want to bring forth the diverse opinions of the ancients to you: since this is the more correct way which was maintained by our most reverend predecessors Hermes, Valens, Albumashar (who is the flower of the Latins, even though he studied at Athens, where study then flourished), and likewise their followers. Indeed, other significations of the parts will be discussed below after this, in their proper places and in their proper chapters, if God permits it.

## III

## On The Significations Of The Parts Of The Twelve Houses

Having spoken of the significations of the Parts of the seven planets, and of their extraction; the next to be discussed are the significations of the parts of the twelve houses, and their extraction. And above the parts which are more useful and more necessary were extracted. And while it was noted that the place of every Partis taken from such a planet in such a place, or from such a place to such a place, and projected from the Ascendant, now I say to always add on what was left over between each place, to that which is from the beginning of the sign from which you project, as was said in the work of extracting the Part of Fortune, according to how they extracted the others.

Nor does it appear to me that the diversity of opinions are to be recited here, but only to apply the mind to the ones of greater utility. For the ends of all individual things are not those things which are signified by every house, but different ones. Even if some might have a beginning or origin from the same house, and certain others from others, just as on the significations of death, the ends of which will not be the same, but they all signify death. For certain people die from infirmities, in their beds or elsewhere; others from brief infirmities, others from long infirmities; others die from sudden events; others die by iron; others by fire; others are suffocated; others drowned; others are hanged; and men die in almost innumerable ways. And even if they are not the same ways, nevertheless every one of them is death. And so too of the offices which are signified by the tenth house: since a magistracy is one thing, a kingdom is another, a rulership is another, a generalship is another, a position in the imperial retinue is another, one of the crafts is another, and so on. And even if all of the ways are not the same, nevertheless they all have their origin from a matter signifying honour and dignity. And so too for any of the significations of any house, each one according to its own nature, and according to the nature of the house whose significations it was necessary to know.

And many other parts will be found, which would take a long to list; however, you will consider them just as they will come into your hands through your own industry; and do not let what I have said to you be a burden to you. And if everything that is signified by the houses cannot be revealed to you at one and the same time; so many will be explained to you that they will suffice for you to extract the parts of all the houses. Since from this, any able man will see the Part of the significators of some matter signified by one of the houses of the circle, and from his own industry he will be able to openly comprehend that which has not yet been expounded to him

## IV

### On The Parts Of The First House, That Is The Ascendant, And On Their Extraction And On Their Significations

Now on the extraction of the parts of the twelve houses, and first on the first house, namely on the Ascendant and on the significations of its parts, and on their extraction.

The first house, just as was said above in the chapter on the twelve houses, signifies natural life. And I say "natural" on account of the fact that a chance occurrence or some accident often (in fact, mostly) is the power of nature, just as was said above in another chapter. And therefore from this the Part of Life will be considered, and its extraction. For through it the quality of the life of the native is discerned, and what his condition is going to be like. And it is extracted from Jupiter and Saturn on account of their height and far remoteness from the earth; and on account of their motion being slower than that of the rest of the planets. And therefore virtue is given to them over matters whose long duration and durability we seek. And because of the reason above, the Ascendant participates with them. And this Part is

taken in the day from Jupiter to Saturn, and vice versa at night; and projected from the Ascendant. And this Part is a significatrix of natural life, and it signifies the condition of the body and its sustenance. Which, if it is well disposed, signifies the long length of life and its continuation, and the soundness of the body, and the liveliness of the soul. However, if it is impeded, it signifies the scarcity of life, and its brevity, and it's bad condition with a multitude of diverse infirmities, and with the grief of the soul, and its sorrow. It signifies the same about the condition of men in revolutions of the years, both the years of the native and the years of the world.

Having spoken on the first Part of the Ascendant, which is the Part of Life, the next thing to be discussed is its second part, which is called the Part of Durability and Stability. And it is the Part of Trust of the Ascendant. For since it is the most noble and worthy accident that can happen in this world, it is necessary that it is perfected in a more noble manner, by durability, and stability. And it is necessary that this is from the joining together and complexion of the body and the soul; and this is not possible to come to be, except by the stronger of the supercelestial bodies: and these are the luminaries, whose parts are found to be stronger and fortunate than the rest. And like the luminaries are stronger benefics than the rest of the benefics, in accordance with their effects being sensed more strongly and manifestly than the rest of the effects. And their parts signify the body and soul, just as the luminaries themselves signify these things. Nor can durability come to be, or last, without the joining together of the body and soul in living things, and so, they come to be and endure through their complexion or joining, just as they are corrupted by their dissolution or separation. And this was the reason which moved the ancient sages to the extraction of this part. And they counted it from the Part of Fortune (from the more deserving, as it were) in this way: the Part of Durability (which is the Part of the Trust of the Ascendant) is taken in the day from the Part of Fortune to the Part of Future Things, and vice versa at night, and projected from the Ascendant.

And Albumashar said that this Part coincides with the Part of Venus. And certain other things are taken up with this Part which are not taken up with others. And this Part signifies the beauty of the native and his deformity; and his resemblance to his parents. And if this Part or its Lord are well disposed in someone's nativity, the native will have a beautiful body, a beautiful face, and will be surrounded everywhere by beauty and health in every Part of his body, and this will be extended up to his descendants: and this will endure up until some malefic resists them and impedes them. And he will abound in good things, and this more strongly so if the Part of Fortune and the Part of Future Things are well disposed; and greater again if their Lords are fortunate: for then he will have all that he wishes for from everything: however, there will be much and the greatest profits, as much on journeys and pilgrimages as in other places. If however, this Part is impeded, it signifies the deformity and ugliness of the form of the native: his body will be badly joined together, and surrounded by infirmities; and he will be unfortunate, and everything will go to the contrary for him according to the position and disposition of the aforementioned Part and the aforementioned significators. And these things might be extended to his descendants up until some benefic encounters their significators in one of their nativities.

And Albumashar said that if it declines to the significator of the mother, he will be similar to his mother, and more friendly with her.

And he said that if you wish to know the durability of any matter, whether it is the life of the native, or a querent, or a revolution; or whatever other way you wish to know something's durability or defect, whether the matter is known or unknown, whether it is manifest or hidden - examine this part, and see if the Lord of its domicile, exaltation, or two other dignities of the sign it is in aspects it; or if it is with the Lord of the Ascendant of the year or with one of the Lords of the angles. And if it is in an angle, it signifies the stability and durability of the matter; and this more greatly and firmly if it is in the first or the tenth. If however, it is cadent, it signifies its removal and destruction. If however, it is in a succeedent; and this more strongly so if it is in the second or eighth, it signifies that the durability of the thing will always be doubtful and fearful. If however, it is impeded in an angle, it signifies durability with sorrow and horribleness. But if a benefic is with it, or aspects it from a trine or sextile aspect, or even from a square with reception, and this benefic is not impeded, there will be durability in the house, even if it is with fear or suspicion. And Albumashar said that if it is

made fortunate in its receding, it will find enjoyment by means of the benefic according to its receding. If however, it is impeded, it will be evil and horrible according to the quantity of its approach. And if it is in some revolution, as was said regarding the Part, this will be in men beyond what their condition is usually, and they will be more stable, more constant, and more firm than usual.

Having spoken about the first and the second Part of the Ascendant, the third Part will be discussed now, which is called the Part of Reason and Sense. And since a man cannot truly be human without reason and sense, the wise men considered from where they could extract the Part of Reason and Sense. And since they saw that Mercury was naturally the significator of both (and also of thoughts, speech, and thinking), and Mars was the significator of heat and motion, they extracted the Part which they called "The Part of Reason and Sense" from these two planets (this Part can also be called the Part of Cognition and Speech) - which is taken in the day from Mercury to Mars, and vice versa at night; and projected from the Ascendant. And they said that this Part signifies sense and reason; and it also signifies knowledge, thought, cognition, and speech. If this Part is well disposed in someone's nativity, and it is with the Lord of the Ascendant, or the Lord of the house in which it is placed, or the Lord of the Ascendant aspects the Lord of the Part in its own dignity, and Mercury then aspects the Part and the Lord of the Ascendant, or the Lord of the part, from a trine or sextile aspect, or at least a square with reception; and Mercury is fortunate, strong, and not impeded, the native will be rational, knowledgeable, talkative, thoughtful, and knowing. And if Mars then aspects the Ascendant or its Lord, or the Lord of the part, the native will be wise, as said, and he will be of acute intellect, easily learning; and those things which he learns he will retain well, and he will not be forgetful.

And if it is in some revolution, as was said in nativities, men in that revolution will be of better ability, and better intellect, and of better memory, than they usually are.

Having spoken about the first, the second, and the third Part of the first house, it remains to discuss the fourth part, which is called the Part of the Hylech: regarding which not many of the ancients cared to make mention of, since it is so joined with others, that none of them can exist without her. Indeed, without the others it can exist well, for she is to them as matter is to form. And the wise men would have been able to set the Part out if they wished, but they set it aside on account of the aforementioned reason. For it is the root of the others, and is taken in the day and night from the degree of the conjunction or prevention which is before the nativity, question, or revolution, to the degree of the Moon, and projected from the Ascendant. And this Part is called the "root of life", since it generally comprehends the whole condition of the life of the native or querent; and even the revolution. Which, if it is well disposed, signifies the general good condition of the life of the native, and of the other things subject to it. If however, it is badly disposed, it signifies the contrary of the aforementioned.

## V

## On The Parts Of The Second House And On Their Extraction And On Their Significations

After having spoken above on the parts of the first house, next to be discussed are the parts of the second house, which is called the house of substance, since the first thing man needs after his birth is substance (life is the first thing) and therefore the signification of substance was given to the second house.

Its first Part is called the Part of Substance, and it is taken in the day and the night from the Lord of the house of substance up to the degree of the house of substance; and projected from the Ascendant. And this Part signifies the sustaining of the life of men, and their profit, and the rest of the things which men use for their sustenance. Which, if it is well disposed and well placed, it signifies the good condition of the native and querent, both in sustenance and in profit and the like. If however, it is impeded, it signifies the contrary of what was said. And Albumashar said that the other significators of substance and fortune signify the rest of the types of fortune appearing from substance (namely what is hoarded up and saved). The same happens in revolutions. And the Part of Poverty is one of the parts of Mercury.

The Part of Moneylenders is taken in day and night from Saturn to Mercury, and projected from the Ascendant: which, if it is fortunate and well disposed, signifies profit and the increase of substance because of usury and moneylenders. If however, it is impeded, and the Lord of the house of substance is impeded, it signifies that the native will lose the greater Part of his substance because of usury and moneylenders, and the like; and likewise for the querent. The same thing will happen in revolutions, for the substance of men will be disposed according to the disposition of the aforementioned part.

The Part of Blessedness, which elsewhere is called the Part of Jupiter, and is also called the Part of Triumph and Victory, is taken from Saturn to Jupiter during the day, and vice versa at night; and projected from the Ascendant.

The fourth Part of the second house, which is called the Part of Collection, is taken in the day from Mercury to Venus, and vice versa at night; and projected from the Ascendant. And this Part signifies lost things or semi-dispersed things which people sometimes find on journeys on roads, fields, the seashore, or river banks, in mountains, or by digging, or another unplanned way; or a thing which had fallen or fled from someone, or is forgotten by them, or has gone away from its master in a similar manner, or gone out of his hands. Which part, if it is in an angle, and one of the Lords of some dignity of the sign in which it is placed (or one of the luminaries) are joined to it (unless it is combust), and it is aspected by them from a trine or sextile aspect, the aforementioned things will arrive into the hands of the native or querent, and he will be made fortunate in them; and will find his own things, it they fall from him or are forgotten by him, or flee from him (as was said regarding other people above). And if the significators of the parts are in good condition in the places in which they are, and in the root nativity, the discoverer or the rediscoverer will have good, profit, utility, and fortune from the things which he finds in this way. If however, the aforementioned significators are badly disposed, it will not be agreeable to him to find them, nor will he profit from it, but rather the contrary and harm will befall him. The same will happen to men in revolutions, if the aforementioned Part or significators are so disposed.

## VI

### On The Parts Of The Third House, And On Their Extraction And On Their Significations

The third house has three parts. The first is the Part of Brothers, and it is taken in day and night from Saturn to Jupiter; and projected from the Ascendant. And the Lord of the domicile of this Part signifies the matter of brothers and their concord. And if this Part falls in a sign of many children, there will be many brothers; and the number of brothers is known by the number of signs which are between this Part and the Lord of the sign in which it is in, giving one brother for each sign between them.

The second part, the Part of the Number of Siblings, is taken from Mercury to Saturn, and it is joined etc., and projected from the Ascendant. And if it falls in a sign of many children, there will be more brothers and sisters according to the number of signs and planets; and perhaps the number will reach the quantity of the lesser years of the planets, or the middle or greater years. And the aspecting planets increase their years. And if this Part falls in a sign of few children, there will be few siblings.

The third Part is the Part of the Death of Brothers and Sisters: which is taken in the day from the Sun to the degree of the Medium Coeli, and vice versa at night; and increased and projected from the Ascendant. And it signifies the cause of the death of brothers and sisters: and when this Part reaches the significators of the brothers and sisters, or vice versa, according to profection by sign, and according to direction by degree, brothers and sisters will have evil.

## VII

### On The Parts Of The Fourth House, And On Their Extraction And On Their Significations

Now the parts of the fourth house are to be discussed, and first regarding the Part of the Father, which is taken in the day from the Sun to Saturn, and vice versa at night; and projected from the Ascendant. And this Part is taken from these two planets for the following reason: since Saturn signifies agedness and males, and the Sun signifies natural heat, which is the cause of the life of animals; and fathers are more aged than children, and are the cause of children. If however, it happens that Saturn is under the rays of the Sun, then the Part of the Father is taken in the day from the Sun to Jupiter, and vice versa at night; and projected from the Ascendant. And Albumashar said that the Lord of the house of the Part of the Father signifies the fortune of the father, and his substance and labours. If the Part is in good condition, the father will be noble. And if its Lord is in good condition, he will be fortunate and long lived. If however, it is impeded or badly placed, he will be laborious, unfortunate, and short lived. And he said that its Lord signifies the kingship of the native and his honours and strengths.

The second Part of the fourth house, which is called the Part of the Death of the Father, is taken in the day from Saturn to Jupiter, and vice versa at night; and projected from the Ascendant. And this Part signifies the cause of the death of the father. And whenever the profection of the year arrives at this part, or to its Lord, it signifies danger and something horrible for the father: and likewise if one of them comes to the significators of the father.

The third Part of the fourth house, which is called the Part of Grandfathers is taken in the day from the Sun to Saturn, and vice versa at night; and projected from the Ascendant. If the Sun is in Leo, in the day it is taken from the first degree of Leo to Saturn, and vice versa at night; and projected from the Ascendant. And if the Sun is in Capricorn or Aquarius, in the day it is taken from the Sun to Saturn, and vice versa at night; and projected from the Ascendant. And you will not care whether Saturn is under the rays of the Sun, or not. This Part signifies matters of grandfathers. Whence, whenever this Part is joined to benefics, they will find the good of the grandfather. And whenever it is joined to malefics, they will find dangers of the grandfather.

The fourth Part of the fourth house, which is called the Part of Parents, or Kindred, or Stock, is taken from Saturn to Mars in the day, and vice versa at night; and projected from the Ascendant; and added on to this are the degrees which Saturn has travelled through in the sign which he is placed, and it is projected from the beginning of the same sign; and where it falls, there will be the Part.

And Albumashar said that after this you will examine to see if the Part is in an angle, and if it is aspected by one of the Lords of the dignities of the sign in which it is in: either the Sun or the Lord of the tenth, or one of the Lords of the angles, by a friendly aspect: for if it is, the native will be of noble progeny or of honest lineage. If however, the Part is cadent from an angle and joined to malefics, or if none of the Lords of the dignities of the sign in which it is in, or none of the Lords of the angles aspect it, the native will be scorned in his parentage, kindred, or stock.

The fifth Part of the fourth house, which is called the Part of Inheritances or Possessions, is taken in day and night from Saturn to the Moon, and projected from the Ascendant.

And Albumashar said that this Part coincides with the Part of the King or Kingdom, or what kind of work the native will do. If it is in good condition and well disposed, and likewise its Lord, the native will be made fortunate because of inheritances and because of the cultivation of the land, and seeds, and he will acquire substance. However, if the Part is in bad condition and badly placed, it signifies griefs, sorrows, and dejections or evil and horrible things because of the aforementioned things.

Moreover, there is another Part of Inheritance according to the Persian sages, and this is the sixth Part of the fourth house. And this Part is taken in the day from Mercury to Jupiter, and vice versa at night; and projected from the Ascendant. This Part is not considered in kingship, nor in professions, nor in cultivation of the land, nor in seeds, but only in matters which are called hereditary.

The seventh Part of the fourth house, which is called The Part of the Cultivation of the Earth, is taken in day and night from Venus to Saturn; and projected from the Ascendant. If it is fortunate, and its Lord is fortunate, the native or querent will have good things and utility from the cultivation of the earth, seeds and planting, and he will be fortunate in these things. Similar things will happen to men generally from the aforementioned things in the revolutions of the years of the world, and to the native in revolutions of nativities, if it is disposed as said above. If however, it is impeded, good things will not befall the from the aforementioned things, but the contrary will follow from them.

The eighth Part of the fourth house, according to Alchabitius, which is called the Part of the Nobility of the Native (and of him of whom it is doubted whether he is the child of the father to whom he is attributed, or of another) is taken in the day from the degree of the Sun in the degree of his exaltation, and projected from the Ascendant. [and at night from the degree of the Moon to the degree of her exaltation; and projected from the Ascendant. If the Sun is in the degree of his exaltation in the day, or if the Moon is in hers at night, the signification goes to the degree of either of them, and the degree of the Ascendant.]

The ninth Part of the fourth house, which is called the Part of the End of Matters, is taken in the day and night from Saturn to the Lord of the house of the conjunction (if it is conjunctional), or to the Lord of the house of the prevention (if it is preventional); and projected from the Ascendant.

And Albumashar said that if this Part and its Lord are in signs of direct ascension, or are otherwise fortunate, the end of the matters of the native or querent will be of a good and praiseworthy nature. If however, they are in crooked signs, or if they are impeded, their ends will be bad. And if one of them is in a direct sign, and the other is in a crooked sign, their ends will be intertwined, neither wholly good nor wholly bad. And Albumashar said that after this the matter will revert to what is signified by the sign in which the Lord of this Part is placed.

## VIII

## On The Parts Of The Fifth House, And On Their Extraction And On Their Significations

The parts of the fifth house will be discussed here, and first the Part of Children, which is taken in the day from Jupiter to Saturn, and vice versa at night; and projected from the Ascendant. For through this Part it is signified whether the native or querent will have children or not.

And Albumashar said that if this Part or its Lord is in a sign of many children, he will have many children, and if it is in a sign of few children, he will have few children. And if it is in a sterile sign, he will not have children. If however, this Part signifies children, and it is fortunate and in good condition, the children will live. If however, it is impeded, it signifies that they will not live. And he said that it also signifies the general condition of children, and how they will behave towards their parents, and how one will love or hate the other. And he said that what there is in terms of signs between this Part and its Lord is taken, and a child is given for each sign. And he said that if there is a common sign between them, the number of that sign is multiplied - since two children will be given to him, where one was posited before. And he said that if there is a planet between them, count it as one child, as was said above regarding brothers.

The second Part of the fifth house, which signifies the hour in which their ought to be a child, and the number of children, and whether they are males or females, is taken in the day and the night from Mars to Jupiter, and projected from the Ascendant. And this is because the effecting of children is signified by Jupiter on account of the temperate heat and moisture of his nature, and this is the cause of growth; and Mars on account of his signification over heat, and on account of his motion, delight, and desire for sexual intercourse (or which comes to be more in men). And since a child cannot be made except through the sexual intercourse of men and women, and through the natural heat and moisture connected to it, these things came to be the reason for the extraction of this Part from these planets.

And Hermes said that if the first Part and the rest of the significators of children signify children for the native or querent, that this Part signifies the number of them; and additionally, when Jupiter arrives to this Part or its place by body, or by trine or sextile aspect (and this more strongly so if it is with reception); it signifies that if the native has sexual intercourse, he will generate a child in the same hour (if age permits).

And Albumashar said that if it is in a masculine sign, more of his children will be males; and if it is in a feminine sign, more of his children will be females. And he said that if the significators signify a multitude of children for the native or querent, examine what sign this Part and its Lord are placed in: since this signifies when he will have the children according to the number of the lesser years of the Lord the part, or the number of the medium or greater years. And he said that perhaps the ones aspecting will increase for him, according to their number of years.

The third Part of the fifth house, which signifies male children, is taken in the day and the night from the Moon to Jupiter, and projected from the Ascendant. Alchabitius said that it is taken in the day from the Lord of the house of the Moon to the Moon, and vice versa at night; and projected from the Ascendant. And this Part is extracted in this way, since the Moon signifies youth and the lesser age; which, because it generates, is stronger in generating than old age, or even the mature age. And the operations of nature ought to be more noble or more powerful in this age than in others, on account of its proximity to the nativity. Moreover, generating males is more noble than generating females: since males are agents, and females are patients - and action is more noble and more deserving than passion. And Jupiter is the significator of the effecting of children, and of creation, and their increase (and especially of males). Therefore the sages counted this Part from them.

Indeed, Theophilus and certain other Persian sages seemed to want to say otherwise. But Albumashar held the sayings of the Hermes as being more authoritative. Likewise, they said that this Part assisted the fortune of the native in the manner of the Part of Fortune; and this is not impugned by the sages of that time.

The fourth Part of the fifth house, which (according to Alchabitius) signifies the condition of daughters, is taken in day and night from the Moon to Venus; and projected from the Ascendant.

The fifth Part of the fifth house, by which it is known whether a conceived child is male or female, is taken in the day from the Lord of the house of the Moon, to the Moon, and vice versa at night; and projected from the Ascendant. And if it falls in a masculine sign, then the person born, or the quesited person, will be a male. If it is in a feminine sign, it will be a female.

## IX

### On The Parts Of The Sixth House And On Their Extraction And Their Significations

I will narrate the parts of the sixth house, and first on the Part of Infirmity and Accidents and Inseparable Defects, which is taken in the day from Saturn to Mars, and vice versa at night; and projected from the Ascendant.

The second Part of the sixth house, which is called The Part of Infirmities both Separable and Inseparable, is taken in day and at night from Mercury to Mars; and projected from the Ascendant.

The third Part of the sixth house, which is called the Part of Slaves (according to Alchabitius and Theophilus), is taken in the day from Mercury to the Moon, and vice versa at night; and projected from the Ascendant. Indeed, according to Hermes (whose opinion was held as being more authoritative by the sages), it is taken in the day and the night from Mercury to the Moon; and projected from the Ascendant. And this for the reason that himself and other sages of the time considered slaves and slavegirls, and most assistants, footmen, and legates not to be very faithful, and to be quickly changing, and this to the contrary of their masters more so than to their utility. And they attributed all of these things, and other swift, and swiftly changing things to the lighter planets. And therefore they extracted the Part from these planets. Which part, if it is fortunate and in good condition, and its Lord is in similar condition, signifies that the native or querent will have good things from the aforementioned significations of the part. If however, they are impeded, it signifies the contrary. And if the Part is in good condition, and its Lord is impeded, or vice versa, it signifies that he will have good things from them, and then the contrary will befall him. And if this Part is in a sign of many children, he will have many slaves and slavegirls, or other servants. And if it is in a sign of few children, he will have few servants. However, if it is in a sterile sign, he will lack them altogether. And the same will happen in revolutions regarding the aforementioned parts to those who have slaves.

Theophilus and certain others said that this Part is taken from Mercury to the Part of Fortune. Albumashar praised the sayings of Hermes more.

The fourth Part of the sixth house, which is called the Part of Captives and The Bound, is taken in the day from the Lord of the domicile of the Sun to the Sun, and at night from the Lord of the domicile of the Moon to the Moon; and projected from the Ascendant. Which Part, if it falls in a good place from the Ascendant, and is with one of the benefics, the querent or captive will be freed from captivity. But if it falls in a malignant place, and with malefics, it signifies evil and something horrible for the captive or bound person; and it might signify the death of the prisoner (especially if the Lord of the tenth aspects it).

However, Albumashar said that if the Sun is in its own domicile in the day, or the Moon at night, one of them will be the significator. And he said that after this you will examine the one of them who is the significator, to see in what kind of place of the circle it is in, and from whom it is separating, or to whom it is joining, and operate according to that. Understand the same in revolutions.

## X

## On The Parts Of The Seventh House, And On Their Extraction, And On Their Significations

I will discuss the parts of the seventh house, and first on the Part of Marriage of Men, which is taken in the day and the night from Saturn to Venus, and projected from the Ascendant: and Hermes and other sages extracted it from these two planets: since Saturn signifies antiquity and durable things, and marriage ought to be a durable thing; and Saturn also has signification over masculinity, and Venus has signification over femininity, and masculinity ought to precede femininity by the nature of masculinity and action. Which part, if it is in good condition and well disposed, signifies the marriage to be suitable and fortunate; and that it will benefit the native or querent; and that good will follow from the marriage. And it also signifies that he will contract marriage with a beautiful and decent woman. However, if it is impeded, it signifies that the marriage will be bad and harmful; and that harm, danger, and disturbance with adversities will follow from it. You will also see if Jupiter arrives at this part, or aspects it by a praiseworthy aspect: since the marriage will be praiseworthy, if it is consummated at that hour. And Albumashar said that if this Part is with the Lord of the sign in which it is placed, or the Sun, the Moon, and its Lord aspect it by a strong and praiseworthy aspect, it signifies that the native or querent will join with one of his relatives. Understand the same regarding marriages which are made in revolutions when the aforementioned Part or its Lord are disposed as was said.

Albumashar said that the second Part of Marriage of Men, which Valens described, is taken in the day and the night from the Sun to Venus; and projected from the Ascendant.

The third Part of the seventh house is the Part of Cleverness and Trickery of Men towards Women, and is similar to the Part of Marriage of Men according to Valens.

The fourth Part of the seventh house is the Part of Men's Sexual Intercourse with Women, and is similar to Valens' Part of Marriage of Men.

The fifth Part of the seventh house, which is called the Part of Luxury and Fornication of Men, is taken in day and night from Venus to Saturn; and projected from the Ascendant. If it is in a good place, the marriage will be praiseworthy, and the man will get the woman he wants. If however, it is badly placed, it will be a blameworthy marriage, and he will not be able to get the woman he wants. However, Albumashar said if it is in a sign signifying impeded sexual intercourse, he will be a man of much sex, lascivious, and a fornicator. However, if it is fortunate, he will be a man of much sex; and his sexual intercourse will be of the praiseworthy kind. And he said in regards to the significations of the Part of Lasciviousness and Fornication of Men, that if the Lord of the Part of Marriage of Men (which Hermes described) were to fall with the Part of Valens, or if the Lord of this Part aspects the Part of Marriage of Men, he will fornicate with a woman before she is joined with him by way of marriage, and after the matter it will be made public that he is a fornicator.

The sixth Part of the seventh house, which is called the Part of Marriage of Women, Hermes said that it has a similar reason to that of the Part of Marriage of Men, and is taken in the day and the night from Venus to Saturn; and projected from the Ascendant.

And Albumashar said that this Part is congruent with the Part of Cultivation of the earth. Valens took it in the day and the night from the Sun to Mars, and projected it from the Ascendant. Nevertheless, Hermes was more authoritative than him. If this Part and its Lord are well disposed and in good condition, it signifies a fortunate woman by marriage. Indeed, if it is impeded, it will signify griefs, sorrows, afflictions and tribulations which he will meet with because of the marriage, and she will be a lascivious woman.

Moreover, Valens took the same in another way, and a better way: for he took it in day and at night from the Moon to Mars; and projected it from the Ascendant. Ad this way was more pleasing to Albumashar; and this is the seventh part.

The eighth Part of the seventh house is called the Part of Trickery and Slyness of Women towards Men. Hermes said that it is similar to the Part of Marriage of Women.

The ninth Part of the seventh house, which is called the Part of Pleasure and Delight, is taken in the day and the night from Venus to the degree and the minute of the seventh house; and projected from the Ascendant.

The tenth Part of the seventh house, which is called the Part of Lasciviousness of Women and their Shamefulness, Valens said it is similar to the Part of Marriage of Women, which is taken in the day from Venus to Saturn, and projected from the Ascendant. If it is in good condition and well disposed, the woman will be pleased with her marriage and she will praise it. Indeed, if it is in bad condition, and badly disposed, she will be displeased with her marriage and will revile it, and will be saddened and afflicted because of it, and will strive with slyness and trickery in the deception of men. And if this Part is well placed, or is in signs of slyness and trickery, which are Leo, Sagittarius, Capricorn, and Pisces, the woman will seduce whatever man she wants. Indeed, if it is outside of the signs of slyness and trickery, or is otherwise badly placed, she will not be able to seduce any of them.

And regarding the signification of the Part of Conjoining and their Sexual Intercourse, if it is in a sign signifying impeded sexual intercourse, she will be a shameful fornicatrix, by means of evil lasciviousness. Indeed, if it is fortunate in a sign signifying sexual intercourse, she will have much pleasure in sexual intercourse, nevertheless, it will be of a suitable sort.

And in the signification of the Part of Lasciviousness of Women and their Baseness, Albumashar said, that if the Part of Marriage of Women (which Hermes described), is with the Part which Valens narrated, and if the Lord of this Part is with the Part of Marriage of Women, she will fornicate with a man, then she will be conjoined with him in marriage.

The eleventh Part of the seventh house which is called the Part of Women's Religion and Honour, is taken in day and night from the Moon to Venus; and projected from the Ascendant. And he said that this Part is the Part is of Daughters, which, if it falls in a fixed sign, or in the aspect of one of the Lords of the dignities of the sign in which it is, or the aspect of any benefic, the woman will be honourable and religious, even if she is desirous of sexual intercourse. If indeed, malefics aspect it without reception, and it is in a mobile sign, she will be a woman desiring sexual intercourse too much, giving herself to men and inviting them for sexual intercourse, and for a cheap price; and she will be in every way a fornicatrix.

The twelfth Part of the seventh house, which is called the Part of Marriage of Men and Women (according to Hermes), is taken from Venus to the degree and minute of the angle of marriage (that is, the seventh); and projected from the Ascendant. If it is joined to benefics, the woman will marry, and good things will be said regarding her marriage. However, if it is in bad condition and badly placed, and joined to malefics, or if they aspect it without perfect reception, her marriage will be made common knowledge and meet with reproach among the peoples. Indeed, if the Lord of the sign in which the Part is placed is in a malignant place, and Venus is under the rays of the Sun, or impeded by Saturn, the woman will never marry, but will lead her life in a shameful manner.

The thirteenth Part of the seventh house, which is called the Part of the Hour of Marriage, is taken in the day and at night from the Sun to the Moon, and projected from the Ascendant. Which, if it aspects Jupiter by a praiseworthy aspect, or is corporeally joined to him, and he is in good condition, and it is for a man, he will marry a beautiful, honourable, pleasing, and desirable woman.

However, Albumashar said that this Part is used in this manner: since if a nativity of a man signifies that he will marry, this will be the reason for it. Since one luminary is hot and masculine; the other is moist and feminine. However, he said that through the conjunction of heat and masculinity with moistness and femininity, generation universally happens in this world; and therefore this Part is named thus.

The fourteenth Part of the seventh house, which is called the Part of Ability and Ease of Marriage is taken in both day and night from the Sun to the Moon; and projected from the degree and minute of Venus. Which Part, if it falls in a sign of cleverness, and is in good condition and well disposed, it signifies that it will be perfected for him who was inclined to marriage with ease, according to how it was planned. If however, it is impeded and in bad condition, his marriage will be with duress and affliction; and he will hardly or never be able to arrive at that which he intended.

The fifteenth Part of the seventh house, which is called the Part of the Father in Law, is taken in both day and night from Saturn to Venus; and projected from the Ascendant.

And Albumashar said that this Part coincides with the Part of Marriage of Men, which is dealt with by Hermes. And if it is fortunate, strong, and well disposed, and concordant with the Lord of the domicile in which it is placed, he will be more concordant and benign to the parents and relatives of his wife than he is to his own. Indeed, if it is impeded, he will be an enemy to them.

The sixteenth Part of the seventh house, which is called the Part of Contenders and Contention, is taken in the day from Mars to Jupiter, and vice versa at night; and projected from the Ascendant.

And Albumashar said that if this Part is in the Ascendant, or with the Lord of the Ascendant in one of the angles, the native will be given to much contention. Which, if it is unfortunate, evil and horrible things will follow from the contentions. But if this Part falls with the Lord of the seventh in the Ascendant, he will be one of those people who openly contend in person before kings and judges.

## XI

### On The Parts Of The Eighth House, And On Their Extraction And On Their Significations

The parts of the eighth house are to be discussed in this chapter, and there are five parts. And the first is the Part of Death, which is extracted from three significators. For it is taken in both day and night from the Moon to the degree of the eighth house; and the number of degrees Saturn has travelled through in the sign in which he is placed is added on to this; and it is projected from the beginning of the same sign. And it is extracted in this manner, since the Moon is the significatrix of the body, and the eighth house is the significator of death, which has destroys the body; and Saturn has signification over the end of matters, and over grief, sorrow, bewailing, lamentation, anguish, dissolution, and destruction - all of which follow from death. For this reason

these three significators were given signification over the matter of death. If this Part and its Lord are free, in good condition, well disposed or placed, the native will die a natural death in his own bed. If however, they are impeded and the benefics (or at least one of them) do not aspect them, the native will die an ugly death. If the mentioned significators are badly disposed (as was said) in some revolution, many men will die such a death in that revolution.

The second Part of the eighth house, which is called the Part of the Killing Planet, is taken in the day from the Lord of the Ascendant to the Moon, and vice versa at night; and projected from the Ascendant. This Part is extracted in this way since the Lord of the Ascendant signifies the soul, and the Moon the body (even though sometimes one is put as the other). While the soul embraces the body it signifies the temperament; and they will remain during the time in which they are united; however, when they are divided, the body will perish, even though the soul will remain. And for this reason this Part was extracted in this manner by the sages.

And Albumashar said that if the Moon alone aspects this Part, and she (or the Lord of the sign in which the Part is placed) is impeded in a sign of severed limbs, or if the Lords of the signs they are in were to impede each other, he will die by suffering. However, if they are not impeded, nor impede each other, he will be mutilated according to the body Part assigned to the sign which the Moon is then placed in, but he will not die from this.

The third Part of the eighth house, which is called the Part of The Year in which Death (or affliction, impediment, or heavy oppression) is Feared for The Native, is taken in the day from Saturn to the Lord of the domicile of the conjunction or prevention which was before the nativity or question or revolution; and projected from the Ascendant. And the reason why this Part is extracted in this way is that Saturn (and likewise the degree of the conjunction or prevention) is the significator of cold and death, and the end and affliction (which makes for destruction): therefore they calculated this Part from these two places.

And Albumashar said that this Part agrees with the Part of the End of Things. And he said that if this Part and its Lord are with the Lord of the

Ascendant, and impeded, the native will have many infirmities and afflictions in his body and in his substance, and he will often come close to the destruction of his body and the loss of his substance. And whenever the year arrives at this part, or the Part arrives to the Ascendant or its Lord by profections (through which one sign is given to every year), or by direction (which is made by degrees of ascensions), the native will meet with danger in his body and his limbs from infirmities; and he will find difficulties and horrible things in his substance; he will also fear death from diverse directions.

The fourth Part of the eighth house, which is called the Part of the Heavy Place, is taken in the day from Saturn to Mars, and vice versa at night, adding on the degrees which Mercury has travelled through in the sign in which he is placed; and projected from the beginning of the same sign.

And Albumashar said that this Part is similar to the Part of Relatives. And he said that if this Part and the Lord of the Ascendant are impeded in someone's nativity, he will have an inseparable infirmity which is called "*azemena*" in the body Part assigned to that sign in which the Part is placed; and he will be unfortunate in all of his business dealings; and he will be occupied and worried in them; and he will not be able to lead them to a good end. And whatever he does lead to an end, whether it is good or bad, will be delayed, and he will hardly be able to do it.

And Albumashar said that when the year from the Ascendant reaches this part, or if the Part reaches the Ascendant or its Lord by profections in which each sign is given one year, or by the direction of significators, the natives will be occupied by his affairs in that year; and whatever he hoped for from his works will be delayed; and griefs, sorrows, and afflictions will find him for this reason; and nothing that he begins in the same year will be perfect prosperously for him, but rather they will be perfected harmfully. And he will meet with infirmities in the body Part assigned to the sign in which the year of the revolution arrives to that part. And if malefics aspect it, distress and loss will find him.

The fifth Part of the eighth house, which is called the Part of Trouble, Oppression, and Destruction, in the day is taken from Saturn to Mercury, and vice versa at night; and projected from the Ascendant. And if the Lord of the Ascendant happens to be with this part, and impeded, in the root nativity, it signifies that the native will be in evil and oppression for the entire time of his life. And if he is working at something of which he has the hope for good things, he will find oppression and evil from it, and what he intended will not follow from it. And if the year of the profection (namely a year which is had according to the succession of the signs, by giving a year to every sign) ever arrives to them, or to one of them; or by degrees of direction (as will be discussed in the tractate of nativities when the degrees are directed through the terms to some places), and the direction arrives at this part, the native will find evil from which he will not be liberated from in that revolution. And if he is liberated from it, he will fall into another, perhaps being no less severe than the last. And if benefics aspect this place from strong places, they will alleviate the evil, but will not destroy it completely.

## XII

### On The Parts Of The Ninth House, And On Their Significations, And On Their Extraction

The parts of the ninth house, of which there are seven, are to be discussed in this chapter. And the first to be discussed is the Part of Pilgrimage, which in the day and the night is taken from the Lord of the ninth sign to the degree of the ninth house, and projected from the Ascendant. And this Part and its Lord signify the pilgrimages of the native and querent; which, if they are in good condition and well disposed, signify his pilgrimages to be useful and successful. Understand the same in revolutions of the years. If they are badly disposed, say the contrary.

The second Part of the ninth house, which is called the Part of Journey and Pilgrimage by Water, in the day is taken from Saturn to the fifteenth degree of Cancer, and vice versa at night, and projected from the Ascendant. If this Part falls in a water sign with benefics, the native will see good, utility, and success from sea journeys and employing them; and also wealth and safety. And a certain one of the ancients said that if Saturn is in the fifteenth degree of Cancer, that the degree of the Ascendant itself and the degree of Saturn will be the significators:

therefore examine them and their condition, and the aspects of the planets to them, and operate according to them.

The third Part of the ninth house, which is called the Part of Religion, in the day is taken from the Moon to Mercury, and vice versa at night; and projected from the Ascendant. And if this Part and its Lord fall in the Ascendant, or with its Lord, or with the Almutem over it, the native will be religious. And if the significators of the Part aspect the Part and the Lord of the Ascendant, he will likewise be religious. However, if the Part is impeded, nothing will come of the aforementioned, but it will be to the contrary.

The fourth Part of the ninth house, which is called the Part of Prayer and Profound Counsel, in the day is taken from Saturn to the Moon, and vice versa at night; and projected from the Ascendant. This Part in particular signifies reason, consideration, examination of profound matters; and the profundity of praiseworthy counsel; and even the discovery of wisdom. And this more strongly so if Saturn is above the earth in the day, and even more again if he is oriental, aspecting the part, and receiving it; or if the Moon aspected the Part from an optimal place from the Ascendant.

The fifth Part of the ninth house, which is called the Part of Wisdom and Patience, in the day is taken from Saturn to Jupiter, and vice versa at night; and projected from Mercury. And this Part is taken in this way, for this reason: Saturn signifies stability, philosophy, and profundity in matters: and scrutiny in speech, and prolixity of thought; and Jupiter has wisdom, patience, and reason; and Mercury signifies writings, wisdoms, and experience in things - and so it ought to be extracted from them. Which if Saturn and Jupiter aspect it, or are joined to it, and they both receive it, or one of them, the native will be wise, patient, and rational. And if Mercury aspects it, or is joined to it, he will be wise, of sharp and profound intelligence, the greatest expert or investigator of profound matters; and he will be quick in discovering all things which can be discovered.

The sixth Part of the ninth house, which is called the Part of Histories, and Knowledge of Rumours and Stories, in the day is taken from the Sun to Jupiter, and at night vice versa; and projected from the Ascendant. And Albumashar said that this Part

agrees with the Part of the Father, if Saturn is under the rays. If this Part falls in an angle in the aspect of Mercury and Venus, and the Lord of the Ascendant aspects it, the native will be a keeper of ancient history, and men's rumours; and will be an inventor of stories and beautiful narrations, which listeners will love, and they will laugh and rejoice from them. However, Albumashar said that if it is otherwise, it will be to the contrary.

The seventh Part of the ninth house, which is called the Part of Rumours (whether they are true or false), is taken in both day and night from Mercury to the Moon; and projected from the Ascendant. And Albumashar said that this Part is similar to the Part of Slaves. Which, if it is in an angle or in a fixed sign, or a sign of direct ascension, the rumours will be true; and this more greatly so if the Moon is joined to a truth speaking planet; and they will be even more true again, if in addition to this there is a truth speaking planet in the first, second, fifth, or ninth. If things are otherwise, it will be to the contrary.

## XIII

## On The Parts Of The Tenth House, And On Their Significations, And Their Extraction

A discussion will be had in this chapter about the parts of the tenth house, and first on the Part of Nobility, which in the day is taken from the Sun to the nineteenth degree of Aries (which is the degree of his exaltation), and at night from the Moon to the third degree of Taurus (which is the degree of her exaltation); and projected from the Ascendant. And this Part is extracted in this way for this reason: because the Sun (who is the diurnal luminary) in the day is the significator of the life of the native and his durability, and it signifies the soul, honour, loftiness, kingship, and victory; and the Moon (who is the nocturnal luminary) signifies at night what the Sun signifies in the day. And therefore this is called the Part of Nobility: since it is extracted from the luminaries (which are more noble bodies), and from the degrees of their exaltation. For through this Part the nobility and stock of the native is known, and whether he is the son of who he is said to be, or not. And his honour, his exaltation, his kingship, his loftiness, and victory are known through this Part. Which Part, if it falls in a good place (such as the tenth house), or is with a benefic in good condition and well placed, signifies that the native will attain honour, nobility, exaltation, riches, and that his good reputation will become widely known - each native to his own degree. So that if he is one of those men who is fit for kingship, he will attain this. And if he is one of the other people, he will arrive at honours and dignities fitting for him, and he will even transcend them. The same will happen if this Part is so disposed in someone's revolution. If this Part falls in the aforementioned degrees, and it is a diurnal nativity, Albumashar said that the signification of those degrees will be like the signification of the degree of the Ascendant. Which if the significators of this Part aspect it, and they are in good combinations with it, the native will be born of the father to whom he is attributed; however, if it is to the contrary, he will not be his.

The second Part of the tenth house, which is called the Part of Kingship, in the day is taken from Mars to the Moon, and vice versa at night; and projected from the Ascendant.

And Albumashar said, this Part and its Lord, if they are in good condition, and they are mixed with the Lord of the tenth and the Ascendant, the native will be a king or a duke, and he will be with wealthy men who will receive his words, and listen to him.

The third Part of the tenth house, which is called the Part of Kingship, and Kings and Dispositors, is taken in the day from Mercury to Mars, and vice versa at night; and projected from the Ascendant. And this Part is extracted from these planets, since the signification of giving, receiving, writing, prohibiting matters, pursuing consulships, reading letters, sending and receiving orders, and counting monies, and shrewdness of intellect, is given to Mercury. And the signification of fear and terror is given to Mars. Therefore this Part is counted from these planets. When this Part and its Lord are well disposed, and in good condition, and well placed with the Lord of the Ascendant, the native will be of good intellect, teachable, and rational, and he will be made a consul, if he is fit for this; and he will be a scribe of kings, or a tax collector, or guardian of their wealth, or of the substance of greater kings. And if he is fit for a kingdom or empire, he will obtain this, and his fame will traverse on high, and will be extended up to the ends of the earth, and he will raise up certain men,

and will exalt them beyond measure; and he will depose certain powerful men and press them down; and soldiers and men's affairs will pass through his hands.

The fourth Part of the tenth house, which is called the Part of Kingship, Victory, and Assistance, in the day is taken from the Sun to Saturn, and vice versa at night; and projected from the Ascendant.

And Albumashar said, this Part agrees with the Part of the Father, if Saturn is not under the rays of the Sun. Which Part, if it is well disposed and in good condition, and especially with the Lord of the tenth house, and with the Lord of the Ascendant, signifies kingship for the native (if he is one of those who are fit for kingship); it also signifies honour and exaltation for each person according to his own condition; and that he will be extended beyond, and preferred to, and prevail over those of his own kind. Albumashar said that if it is in a sign in which the Lord of the Ascendant, or the Lord of the tenth house have dignity, it will signify victory for the native over those who will contend with him; the same will happen in revolutions, if this Part is so disposed.

The fifth Part of the tenth house, which is called the Part of Those Who Are Suddenly Exalted, is taken in the day from Saturn to the Part of Fortune, and vice versa at night; and projected from the Ascendant. And Albumashar said that this Part is similar to the Part of Saturn. Which, if it is in an optimal place from the Ascendant, and from benefics, in someone's nativity or question, he will be suddenly exalted. And if the Lord of the Ascendant is with it, or aspecting it from a friendly aspect and from a praiseworthy place, and the Lord of the Ascendant is well disposed, his loftiness will be increased from an unknown place: and he will attain power very quickly, and in the shortest space of time, in such a way that men will be amazed from it.

However, Albumashar said that you will examine this Part when you know that someone will be exalted, and that he will acquire kingship and honour.

And he said that if this Part is impeded, the native or querent will suddenly meet with evil, and impediment, and horrible things, and depression. You will understand the same in revolutions: since if this Part is in good condition and well disposed, the native and others will suddenly acquire good in that revolution; and if it is impeded, they will likewise be impeded.

The sixth Part of the tenth house, which is called the Part of Nobles (or of those who are noted amongst men or of honoured men) is taken in the day and the night from Mercury to the Sun; and projected from the Ascendant. If it and its Lord are in good condition and well disposed, the native will be noble, and honoured amongst kings, nobles, and wealthy men. And Albumashar said that if this Part is with a planet who has great dignity in the Midheaven, he will he will get a chief position through which he will be celebrated in the manner which a division of the people of a city is celebrated amongst its own citizens. However, if it is to the contrary, the contrary will happen. You can understand the same in revolutions.

The seventh Part of the tenth house, which is called the Part of Soldiers and Agents, (according to Albumashar) is taken in the day from Mars to Saturn, and vice versa at night; and projected from the Ascendant. And he said that if this Part and its Lord are mixed with the Lord of the Ascendant, the native will be a follower of the king, or will be one of his soldiers or agents.

The eighth Part of the tenth house, which is called the Part of Kings (and what works the native might do), is taken in day and night from Saturn to the Moon; and projected from the Ascendant. And this because Saturn signifies labour, adversity, necessity, poverty, and generally laborious works, such as the directing of houses, digging, operations of iron and its extraction from minerals, and other hateful and tedious works, since he is the significator of labour and affliction. And he is the significator of the wealthy whose riches are heavy and ponderous. And the Moon signifies labours, and quickness in matters on account of the speed of her motion; and she is the significatrix of the mob - and for this reason the sages counted this Part from these planets.

And Albumashar said that this Part signifies kingship, honour, and magnificence; and what kind of work the native will do for the reason of these things; and what profession he will exercise: and whether he will acquire wealth from his profession or kingship or not. And he said that if this Part is in

Gemini or Virgo, or in signs of arts or professions, the native will be exalted by works of his hands which are necessary for the wealthy (by which they are adorned); and he will be with wealthy men and magnates because of his expertise and his ability. And if the Part is mixed with the significators of substance, he will acquire a great quantity of wealth from his profession. And he said that if it is to the contrary, he will be poor and unfortunate in his profession, hardly acquiring his sustenance for the day; yet he will not be able to tire: and if he were to be fatigued, he will die of starvation. For there will not be anyone who will offer food to him. You will understand the same in revolutions, for there are sometimes years in which fortunate men do not earn money: and this is when this Part is badly disposed in the revolution. And there are sometimes years in which unfortunate men earn something: and this is when this Part is well disposed.

The ninth Part of the tenth house, which is called the Part of Businessmen and Those Working With Their Hands, in the day is taken from Mercury to Venus, and vice versa at night; and projected from the Ascendant. And Albumashar said that this Part is similar to the Part of Collection. This Part signifies men who are talented, and artisans in their professions, namely Venusian and Mercurial ones, such as are working gold, silver, precious stones, and similar things; and those who know how to do business, namely buying and selling precious and selected merchandise of this kind, as are pearls, rings, and similar things; and those who know how to make beautiful garments, and how to adorn them (especially those which pertain to women); and how to paint, and write, and make coins, and sculpt statues, and similar things which pertain to the nature of Mercury and Venus. If this Part and its Lord are in good condition and well disposed, and are mixed with the Lord of the Ascendant by conjunction, or a trine or sextile aspect, the native or querent will be exalted from works and businesses of his own hands. For he will make beautiful instruments and beautiful works through them, which will be fitting for nobles, magnates, and the wealthy. However, if it is to the contrary, he should not involve himself with these things, since they will turn out to the contrary for him. If this Part and its Lord are well disposed in any revolution, both of nativities and the world, the aforementioned creators will profit from the aforementioned businesses, however, if it is to the contrary, the contrary will happen.

The tenth Part of the tenth house, which is called the Part of Business, and Buying and Selling, in the day is taken from the Part of Future Things to the Part of Fortune, and vice versa at night; and projected from the Ascendant.

And Albumashar said that this Part is similar to the Part Of Mercury. And he said that these parts (which belong to business), if they are in the aspects of Mercury with reception, signify that the native will be skilled in business matters; and he will have knowledge of buying and selling. If they are fortunate and well disposed, these things will be beneficial to the native, and he will profit from them, and because of them. However, if they are in bad condition, and badly disposed, even if he will know these things, he should not involve himself with them, since it will be to the contrary for him. The same is to be understood in revolutions, both of the world, and of a nativity.

The eleventh Part of the tenth house, which is called the Part of Work (and of matters which are necessary to come to be completely), is taken from the Sun to Jupiter in the day, and vice versa at night; and projected from the Ascendant.

And Albumashar said that if Saturn is under the rays, this Part is similar to the Part of the Father. And he said that if this Part is with the Lord of the Ascendant, the native will be remarkable in his works, since he will know them better than others, and will pant and be troubled in every matter which he wants to do, and he will intend to complete it quickly, and will always fear that it won't be perfected until he sees it completed. Whence, if someone wants to do something, and they want to know what will come of it in the future, examine this Part: which, if it is in good condition, and especially if it is with benefics, it will benefit him if he does it, and especially if he hurries up doing it. However, if the Part is with malefics, or otherwise impeded, he will meet with evil, detriment, and horrible things if he does it (because of hurrying), and the more he hurries doing it, the worse and more horrible things will happen to him from it. And this is not only effective in nativities, it is even effective in questions and revolutions, both of the world and of nativities.

The twelfth Part of the tenth house, which is called the Part of the Mother, is taken in the day from Venus to the Moon, and vice versa at night; and projected from the Ascendant. And this Part signifies the condition of the mother. Which, if it is in good condition and well disposed, signifies the good condition of the mother. And if in a nativity it is in the trine or sextile aspect of the Lord of the Ascendant, it signifies that the mother will love the child. And if the Lord of the tenth receives the Lord of the Ascendant (namely that neither the Lord of the first nor the Moon receives the Lord of the tenth), it signifies that the mother will love the child; however, he will not love the mother. And if the Lord of the Ascendant (or the Moon) receives the Lord of the tenth, and the Lord of the tenth does not receive him, it signifies that the son will love the mother more than she loves him. If both of them receive each other, they will both love each other. If neither of them receives the other, neither of them will love the other. The same is to be said in questions and revolutions as in nativities. And the sages put the Part of the Mother in the tenth, since it is opposite to the 4th, which signifies the father.

The thirteenth Part of the tenth house, which is called the Part Signifying Whether There is a Reason of Kingship or Not, is taken in the day and the night from the Sun to the degree of the Midheaven; and projected from the degree of Jupiter.

The fourteenth Part of the tenth house, which is called the Part of the Mothers Death, is taken in the day from Venus to Saturn, and vice versa at night; and projected from the Ascendant.

## XIV

## On The Parts Of The Eleventh House, And On Their Extraction And On Their Significations

In this chapter we will discuss the parts of the eleventh house, and first on the Part of Excellence and Nobility.

Albumashar said that it is taken in the day from the Part of Fortune to the Part of Future Things, and vice versa at night; and projected from the Ascendant. And he said that this Part is similar to the Part of Stability and Duration, and the Part of Venus. And this Part is extracted like this, since if it is noble, stable, and very useful, it is necessary that it is extracted from the two Parts more noble and more excellent than the other parts - which are the Part of Fortune, and the Part of Future Things. And if this Part is in good condition and well disposed, and is well placed with the benefics; and this will be better if it is in the 10th, or the 11th, without any malefics impeding it, the native will surpass other men, and will be noble and fortunate, and his fortune will endure, and he will be praiseworthy and of good condition.

And Albumashar said that he will be one of those men who others need on account of his good fortune, and who men revere, and he will practically be a prince amongst the mob. And he said that his name will remain through the ages for many years, and he will see good things and joy from all works which he does, and that it will please him. However, if it is to the contrary, the contrary will befall him. You will understand the same in general questions, and it can also play a role in other things; and likewise in revolutions. And depending on how this Part is disposed, good things or the contrary will happen to each person according to his own condition.

The second Part of the 11th house, which is called the Part Signifying How The Native Or Querent Will Be Loved By Men (or how they will hate him), is taken in the day (according to Albumashar) from the Part of Fortune to the Part of Future Things, and vice versa at night; and projected from the Ascendant. And he said that this Part is similar to the Part of Venus. If this Part falls in the domicile, exaltation, or triplicity of some benefic,

and this benefic aspects the Part; and is not impeded by any of the malefics; he will be loved by men and will be lovable to them, and sweet and pleasing in their eyes. Indeed, if it falls with malefics, or in their evil aspects, he will be hateful and burdensome amongst men; they will almost not want to see him, and much of whatever he does or says, will displease men, even when he says or does good things.

The third Part of the eleventh house, which is called the Part of the One Known Amongst Men, and his Honour Among Them (and through whom their matters and business matters are completed), is taken in the day

from the Part of Fortune, to the Sun, and vice versa at night, and projected from the Ascendant. Which, if it is well placed, namely received by the Sun, Jupiter, Venus, Mercury or the Moon, with them being benefic, or if they aspect it and the Lord of the Ascendant from a trine or sextile aspect, the native or querent will be honoured, both by magnates and commoners, and they will love him, and run to him for their affairs, and place many things in his hands, and much business matters to perfect or determine, and will trust greatly in him.

The fourth Part of the eleventh house, which is called the Part of Luckiness and Profit, is taken in the day from the Part of Fortune to Jupiter, and vice versa at night; and projected from the Ascendant. Which, if it is with the Lord of the Ascendant, or if the Lord of the Ascendant aspects the Part from a trine or sextile aspect (or at least a square with reception), and is not otherwise impeded, it signifies that the native will be lucky in all matters, and will profit in them, and will obtain the generality of what is necessary for him from temporal things, and not only will his own affairs be perfected through his hands, but also those of others, according to his wishes. If in addition to this the Part is aspected by benefics, he will obtain whatever he wants with ease, so that practically nothing will seem to be lacking from what he desires. And Albumashar said that perhaps he will easily acquire something more than what he desires. Indeed, if it is not with the Lord of the Ascendant, nor in its aspect, he will not obtain these things; if malefics aspect it, it will be to the contrary. The same will happen in questions and revolutions.

The fifth Part of the 11th house, which is called the Part of Concupiscence (and inclination or appetite in the love of the world and temporal matters), in the day is taken from the Part of Fortune to the Part of Future Things, and vice versa at night; and projected from the Ascendant.

And Albumashar said that this Part is similar to the Part of Venus. Which, if it is in an optimal place in a nativity, question, or revolution, he will conquer his desires and lusts. And he said, indeed, if it is in a bad place, he will be conquered by his desires, and will be inclined towards the world and its delights, and will have an appetite for them, and he will lose whatever he has in this

The sixth Part of the eleventh house, which is called the Part of Trust and Hope, in the day is taken from Saturn to Venus, and vice versa at night; and projected from the Ascendant. Which, if in anyone's nativity or question, if this Part and its Lord are in an optimal place, fortunate, and strong, the native or querent will attain everything which he hopes for, and in which he has trust. If they are in bad condition and badly placed, he will not attain what he hoped from these things (what would benefit him in a perceptible way). And the same will happen in revolutions. For if they are well placed and in good condition, men will obtain enough of the things they want in that revolution; however, if they are impeded it will be to the contrary.

The seventh Part of the 11th house, which is called the Part of Friends, is taken in both day and night from the Moon to Mercury, and projected from the Ascendant. And this Part is taken in this manner because Mercury is a shapeshifter of many diverse things, namely, significations. For at certain times he signifies masculinity, at certain times femininity; and at certain times he signifies swiftness, at certain times slowness; at certain times heat, at certain times cold; at certain times fortune, at certain times misfortune; and he always inclines to the nature of the planet to which he is joined. Likewise, the Moon does the same on account of her swift motion, and on account of her being quickly changeable. Whence, since the wills of men with their friends change quickly, and they do not remain long in the same condition, the sages extracted the Part of Friends from these two planets, since they are swifter and more changeable than the rest. Which part, if it is in good condition and well disposed, and its Lord is well disposed, and they are in mobile signs, the native or querent will have many friends. If they are fortunate, his friends will benefit him, and he will benefit them, and they will enjoy good things with each other. And if they are received, he will be praiseworthy amongst them and be loved by them. Indeed, if it is to the contrary, you will judge to the contrary.

The eighth Part of the eleventh house, which is called the Part of Concord of Friends (and also of the husband and wife) And Their Discord, is taken in both day and night from the Part of Future Things to Mercury, and projected from the Ascendant. This Part is one of the more difficult ones to comprehend, since it is necessary to know the nativity of the native, and of those who are posited as his friends (or of the husband and wife), and to see if this Part falls in the Ascendant of nativity of the native, or with its Lord, without the impediments of malefics; or is in the sign which is the Ascendant of their nativity; or is in the 11th or joined with its Lord; or is joined with the Lord of the Ascendant, with the Lord of the Ascendant in good condition and well disposed, and placed in the aspect of benefics, and in a good place from the Ascendant, and not impeded by any of the malefics; or if the Part is in the sign of the exaltation of one of the planets; or, as Albumashar said, if it is in signs that agree with each other. Since if this is so, he will have mutual love with his friends and with his wife. But if it is in a sign of the descension of one of them, or in the sign of its fall, or in opposition to the Ascendant, or in signs that are contrary, they will be inimical to one another.

The ninth Part of the 11th house, which is called the Part of Bounty and Abundance of Good in the Home, is taken in both the day and the night from the Moon to Mercury, and projected from the Ascendant.

And Albumashar said that this Part is similar to the Part of Friends. And he said that if this Part and its Lord are in a good combination with the Part of Fortune and the Lord of the Ascendant, the native will have abundance in the home, with all bounty; and if it is otherwise, things will be to the contrary. If this Part is so disposed in a revolution, the same will happen.

The tenth Part of the 11th house, which is called the Part of the Honesty of the Mind, in the day is taken from Mercury to the Sun, and vice versa at night; and projected from the Ascendant. Which part, if it falls in a good place with one of the benefics, and especially with Jupiter, or if Jupiter or the Sun aspect it from a trine or sextile aspect, the native will have a pleasant, sweet, and patient mind.

And Albumashar said that if this Part and its Lord fall in a sign of honesty, he will have an upright mind; and if it falls with malefics or in signs contrary to honesty, it will be to the contrary. Understand the same in revolutions.

The eleventh Part of the 11th house, which is called the Part of Praise and Gratitude, in the day is taken from Jupiter to Venus, and vice versa at night; and projected from the Ascendant. Whence, if this Part and its Lord are in good condition, and well disposed; and the benefics (especially Jupiter) aspect them or are joined with them, the native or querent will be praiseworthy, and thanked for everything which is put to him; and will be praised for his works, and will be benefited from this. If however, they are badly disposed, or malefics aspect them, he will not be praised for his works or for this services, and not only will he not be praised or benefitted from his services which he does, but he will not even be thanked from them; and it will be possible that from services which he does provide, instead of being rewarded, contempt will be brought to him, and he will acquire hatred from it. The same will happen to men in revolutions if this Part and its Lord are so disposed, as was said.

The twelfth Part of the eleventh house, which is called the Part of Necessity and Love of Matters, according to the Persians, is taken in the day and the night from Venus to the house of brothers; and projected from the Ascendant. According to the Egyptians it is taken in the day from Mars to the house of brothers, and projected from the Ascendant.

## XV

## On The Parts Of The Twelfth House, And On Their Extraction, And On Their Significations

Mention shall be made in this chapter of the Parts of the 12th house, and first on the Part of Hidden Enemies, which is taken in the day and the night from Saturn to Mars; and projected from the Ascendant.

The second Part of the 12th house (according to Hermes) is taken in the day and the night from the Lord of the house of enemies to the degree of the house of enemies; and projected from the Ascendant.

And Albumashar said that both of these Parts ought to be used; and that if they are in opposition or square aspect to their Lords, or to the Lord of the Ascendant, the native or querent will have many enemies; if however, both of them are free from their Lords, and with the Lord of the Ascendant, he will not have enemies easily. The same will happen in revolutions, since if they are badly disposed, as was said, men will be inimical to each other in that revolution.

The third Part of the 12th house, which is called the Part of Labour and Affliction, is taken in both day and night from the Part of Future Things to the Part of Fortune, and vice versa at night; and projected from the Ascendant.

And Albumashar said that this Part is similar to the Part of Mercury. Which if this Part and its Lord are well disposed, it signifies that the native or querent will be fortunate in his labours, and will profit from them, and they will be beneficial to him. However, if it is corporeally joined with the Lord of the Ascendant without reception, or is in its opposition or square aspect, he will be laborious for the entire time of his life; and his labours will not be beneficial to him; nor will he rejoice from his goods or profit from them; nor will his fortune be beneficial to him.

## XVI

## On The Recounting Of Certain Parts According To Albumashar, Of Which Mention Was Not Made Above, Which Are Called "The Fifth Category"

In this chapter mention is to be made of certain other Parts which are not distinctly listed above, which are the ten Parts according to Albumashar, which often fall into the work of the masters of this science when they want to judge on some nativity or general question, or any revolution.

Of which parts, the first is called the Part of the Ylem, and this is a matter which was strongly observed by the ancient sages of this science, and they found it to be truthful. Which is taken, if it is a conjunctional nativity, question, or revolution, from the degree of the conjunction to the Moon; if it is preventional, from the degree of the prevention, to the Moon; and projected from the Ascendant (in both the day and the night).

And Albumashar said that this Part is directed in the way that the Ylem is directed. And when its direction (or its profection) arrives at benefics, it signifies good; when it arrives at malefics, it signifies evil, impediment, and danger for the native or querent, or for the person for whom the year is revolved (or even if it is a general revolution). And this is the reason why many capable men are sometimes deceived: since sometimes they see many contrary things happen, which ought not to happen according to the Ylem. For they only considered the Ylem; they do not care for the Part of the Ylem. However, you will not neglect this, but always direct the Part of the Ylem, as much in nativities, as in questions and revolutions; and you will not err. For it has its own peculiar significations apart from the others, which are of great efficacy.

The second Part of the fifth category, which is called the Part of Lean Bodies, in the day is taken from the Part of Fortune to Mars, and vice versa at night; and projected from the Ascendant.

And Albumashar said when this Part is with the Lord of the Ascendant, or with a planet who has some dignity in the Ascendant, or in the alcocoden, and the planet is in its own dignity, or in a moist sign, the native will have large limbs. And he said that if it is otherwise, or it is with Mercury or Mars, or if these planets rule it, he will be lean in body.

The third Part of the fifth category, which is called the Part of Warfare and Boldness, in the day is taken from Saturn to the Moon, and vice versa at night; and projected from the Ascendant.

And Albumashar said that this Part is similar to the Part of Reason and Profound Counsel, and the Part of the King, and what Work the Native Will Do. Which, if it is the sextile of Mars or Jupiter in animal signs, it signifies that the native will be brave, and a soldier, and a keeper of animals, and will be a gladiator, practicing with spears, arms, and swords.

The fourth Part of the fifth category, which is called the Part of Boldness and Strength and Rulership, in the day is taken from the Lord of the Ascendant to the Moon, and vice versa at night; and projected from the Ascendant. Which Part, if it is in the sextile aspect of Mars or Jupiter, or received in the houses of malefics in strong signs, signifies that its master will be spirited and strong in his body.

The fifth Part of the fifth category, which is called the Part of Cleverness, Talent, Acuity, and Learning (of all arts and memory, and the like), in the day is taken from Mercury to the Part of Future Things, and vice versa at night; and projected from the Ascendant. And the sages took this Part in this way, because all of these things are signified by Mercury, and are attributed to him, and are rendered to the soul: and the Part of Future Things signifies the condition of the soul; and all of these things proceed with the authority of the soul. Which, if it is in good condition and well disposed, and is with Mercury in a nativity or question, and Mercury is in good condition, it signifies that the native will be clever, with a good cleverness, of sharp intelligence, teachable, acting in many arts, of less labour than others in learning anything that he wants, and in which he applies himself to; and he will retain that what he learns well, and all of these things will be of benefit to him. But if it is unfortunate and badly disposed, he will be fit to learn, but they will not be useful to him; in fact, he will come upon evil and horrible things because of the aforementioned things. If Mercury is joined to Mars by conjunction or aspect, and if Mars has some testimony in the place where the Part falls, it signifies that the native or querent is going to be a thief, and will be a very keen thief, and will know how to open gates and bars on doors by craftiness and precise skill without a key. However, if the aspect is a trine or sextile aspect with reception, he will know how to do all of these things, but will not use his knowledge in an evil way. The same will happen in revolutions: for if this Part is so disposed, as was said, the aforementioned things will happen more in that revolution than they usually do in other times.

The sixth Part of the fifth category, which is called the Part of Investigation of a Matter (and whether a matter will generally be perfected, or destroyed, or deferred, or led to effect), in the day and the night is taken from Saturn to Mars; and projected from Mercury. This Part is extracted from these three planets because the malefics have signification over destruction. Which planets, even if they sometimes impede by square aspect or opposition, nevertheless sometimes perfect a matter (even if it might be with slowness and harshness); but if the malefics do impede, they destroy a matter; and if they do not destroy it, they will delay it until all hope is lost. And since Mercury participates in matters, the Part is projected from him. Which Part, if it is in good condition and well disposed, free from malefics (namely Mars in the day, and Saturn at night), signifies the effecting of the matter. And if it is impeded by one of them, as was said, it signifies its destruction, and that it will not be perfected. And if it is perfected, it will not last.

And Albumashar said this Part is used in unknown matters, and matters whose kind is unknown. However, if it is a known matter, consider whether it is substance, or marriage, or any other matter: for the matter will be examined from its own place, and this Part will assist the significator signifying it.

The seventh Part of the fifth category, which according to the Egyptians is taken in the day and the night from Mars to the degree of the house of brothers; and projected from the Ascendant; has the signification of the laziness and inertia of the native. If this Part is so disposed in a revolution, it signifies that men will be so disposed in that revolution.

The eighth Part of the fifth category, which (like the aforementioned Part) is called the Part of Necessity, and of the Delay of Matters, (according to the Persians) is taken in both day and night from the Part of Delay to Mercury; and projected from the Ascendant.

And Albumashar said that each of these Parts are employed. Which, if they are in good condition and well disposed, signify that the native will be semi-painstaking in carrying out his business. However, if they are badly disposed, joined with malefics, or with one of them; or if its Lord is with one of the malefics (particularly Saturn); or if the Part and its Lord are with the Lord of the Ascendant, this signifies that the native will be lazy and inert, and will hardly be moved to do anything, and especially to those things which are necessary for him to do, unless perhaps he is forced by necessity. Nor will he freely do any of those things which men do with the hope of utility; nor will his heart suffer to get involved with any mercantile matters, or other lucrative things, because of the fear that he might lose money for this reason; nor will he believe that he can profit from anywhere; and will hardly or never believe himself to be able, or to know how, to make a living.

And Albumashar said that if the Lord of this malefic impedes the Lord of the house of substance, the native will destroy his own substance, and will not know how he did so; or will lose a great deal according to his condition. The same will happen in questions and in revolutions. For if this Part is as was said, men in that year or revolution will be lazier and more fearful than usual.

The ninth Part of the fifth category, which is called the Part of Retribution, in the day is taken from Mars to the Sun, and vice versa at night; and projected from the Ascendant. Which, if it is in good condition and well disposed in an angle (especially in the first or the tenth), or in the succedents of the angles (especially in the 11th or the 5th), with the Lord of the Ascendant in one of its own dignities, signifies that the native will gladly repay those who did good for him, or who have rendered a good service to him. However, if it is in bad condition in the cadents from the angles (especially in the sixth or the twelfth), and is not with the Lord of the Ascendant or in one of its dignities, it signifies that if he receives any favour from someone, he will not repay the good deed done to him. Say the same in revolutions, that if this Part is so placed, that men will observe this manner in that revolution. Understand the same in questions.

The tenth Part of the fifth category, which is called the Part of Truth and of Good Works, is taken from Mercury to Mars in the day, and vice versa at night, and projected from the Ascendant.

And Albumashar said this Part is similar to the Part of Reason and Sense. Which Part, if it is in good condition and well disposed, and strong in an angle, signifies that the native or querent will be observant of truth, and will direct his efforts to honest works, and will recoil from the contrary of these things, and utility and profit will happen to him for this reason. However, if this Part is in an angle, and is impeded, he will exercise and observe the truth and good works, and harm and evil will follow from this. And if it is outside of the dignities of the Lord of the Ascendant, he will know good things, but will not exercise them. If this Part is so disposed in revolutions, men in those revolutions will be so disposed and will act accordingly.

And Albumashar said that these are the divulged Parts which were described by the ancients; and these are employed in nativities and in many places in revolutions of the years and questions, namely each one of them in the places where they are necessary. And he said to know that in many things from the significations of the twelve houses, and of questions, beginnings, and revolutions of the years, there are Parts which we have not mentioned here. Since it is necessary for us to describe these Parts in other books. And he said that what we have spoken of regarding the significations of the Parts in this book are summaries of investigations: since the places of these Parts in the signs which they are in, and the conjunctions of the planets with them, or their aspects to them, change much of their significations for good or for evil. And he said that we will describe the investigations of their significations in their own places from the signs in every books according to what is necessary.

## XVII

## On The Knowledge Of Certain Extraordinary Parts, Of Which Mention Was Not Made Above

What will be examined in this chapter are certain extraordinary Parts of which mention was not made in the Parts of the seven planets, nor in the Parts of the twelve houses, nor in the recollection of the ten Parts of the fifth category. And they are very useful parts, and ones with which someone wishing to profit from a revolution can greatly profit from. For through these Parts you will be able to judge the cheapness or dearness or mediocrity of the price of certain things born of the earth, and of certain other things for which it is often necessary for men to have recourse to for their sustenance and necessities, such as grain, wine, oil, and the like. You will even be able to see whether there is going to be an abundance or scarcity of them. Likewise you will be able to know why it sometimes happens that a thing is in abundance, and is dear, and sometimes it is in abundance and cheap. And sometimes it is not in abundance, in fact there is a small quantity of it, and it is cheap; and sometimes there is a small quantity of it, and it is dear.

The abundance of something is signified by the aspect of benefics (or the Moon) to its Part or to the Lord of its Part, or their corporeal conjunction, and this more greatly so if the benefic (or the Moon) which aspects the Part or its Lord, is the Lord of the domicile in which the Part falls. The scarcity or lack of it is signified by the aspect of malefics to the Part, and their corporeal conjunction.

You will be able to judge the dearness or cheapness of a thing by the place of the Lord of the domicile or exaltation in which the Part falls (or the significator). Which, if it is in its own domicile or exaltation, or is otherwise fortunate and strong, or is in an angle (and this more seriously if it is in the 10th), signifies the dearness of the price of this thing. If however, one is fortunate and the other unfortunate, the condition of this thing will be changed little. But the Lord of the exaltation is below the Lord of the domicile: however, the term Lord and triplicity Lord add or subtract something. However, if it is in the 12th, or in its fall or descension, or in a cadent from an angle (and this more strongly so if it is in the 12th, or combust), it signifies the cheapness and smallness of the price of this thing. And by however, much the significators are weaker, by that much more will it signify the greater cheapness of the thing and the smallness of its price. If however, it is in a succedent of an angle, unless it is otherwise impeded, it will neither be made more dear, nor greatly cheapened. But if all the significators are fortunate and strong, the thing will be made dear, and will exceed measure in price: and this more strongly so if they are in the 10th, as I said. Indeed, if they are unfortunate, weak, and badly disposed, they signify the ultimate cheapness of the thing and the smallness of its price.

And always make it your concern to consider the matter of each and every one of the significators, since every one of them gives and takes according to its condition. The significators are: the Lord of the domicile, the Lord of the exaltation, the Lord of the terms, and the triplicity Lord - of the planets from which the Part is extracted; and the planet who is the Lord of the domicile from which you begin to project the Part. However, there is little force in the Lord of the face, so one needn't have much concern for that, however, the Lord of the domicile in which the Part falls, is to be preferred to the rest, and it should be judged more according to him, even though the others add and subtract something, as was said. and this more strongly so, if he is one of those planets from which the Part is extracted, since it will be greatly strengthened in significance from this.

## XVIII

### In Which There Is An Example Of The Method Of Extracting Some Of The Parts

Now I will give you an example of one of the Parts for all of the other extraordinary parts, and I will begin from the Part of Grain. Whence, if you wish to know the status of grain in some revolution, namely whether it will become cheaper or more dearer, or have a mediocre price, subtract the place of the Sun from the place of Mars; and add on the degree and minute of the ascending sign, and project the sum from the beginning of the ascending sign, giving each sign 30 degrees by equal degrees, and where the number finishes, there will be the Part of Grain. Therefore,

you will consider how the Lord of this sign is disposed: since the better it is disposed, the more expensive grain will be, and the more badly it is disposed, the cheaper it will be, and the less it will be worth. You will also examine how the other significators (which I named to you) are disposed: since those who are well disposed, will make for an increase in the of the thing, and will make it more scarce; and those which are badly disposed will make the price cheaper, and will make the thing more abundant. And you will judge the rest according to this (or any other thing whose Part you seek), namely on each one in its own place and in its own condition, with the aforementioned aspects, and the Moon being saved. If the significator of the Part of Grain (or any other matter), namely the Lord of the domicile in which it falls, is impeded, and in bad condition and badly disposed; and a fortunate and strong benefic, and the Moon aspect the Part, it signifies that there will be an abundance of grain (or any other thing whose Part you seek), and it will be cheap. However, if a malefic aspects it, there will not be an abundance, but there will be little of it; however, it will be cheap. And if its significator is fortunate, strong, and well disposed, and a malefic aspects it, it signifies that grain (or whatever other thing whose Part you seek) will be scarce and dear. But if a benefic aspects it, it signifies that it will be in abundance; however, it will be dear. Understand the same for each and every individual Part.

### On The Part Of Barley

If you wish to know whether barley will be cheap or dear in the revolution which you seek, or what its status will be like, subtract the place of the Moon from the place of Jupiter; and add the degrees and minutes of the ascending sign to the remainder; and project from the Ascendant. And where the number finishes, there will be the Part of Barley. Which you will judge according to the condition of the Lord of its sign by the aforementioned conditions.

### On The Part Of Beans

If you wish to know whether beans will be cheap or dear in the revolution wish you seek, subtract the place of Saturn from the place of Mars, and add the degrees of the Ascendant to the remainder; and project from the Ascendant, giving 30 degrees to every sign according to equal degrees, and where the number finishes, there will be the Part of Beans. Then you will judge as was said with the others.

## On The Part Of Onions

You will find the Part of Onions and the Part of Peas in the same way as the Part of Beans - therefore it is not necessary for you to make another rule for them.

## On The Part Of Lentils

If you wish to know what the status of lentils will be like, subtract the place of Mars from the place of Saturn, and add the degrees of the sign of the Ascendant to the remainder; and project it from the Ascendant, and where the number will finish, there will be the Part. You will judge according to it as was said with the others.

## On The Part Of Rice

You will take the Part of Rice from Jupiter to Saturn; and project from the Ascendant. And where the number falls, there will be the Part of Rice. You will judge according to it as was said with the others.

## On The Part Of Sesame Seeds

The Part of Sesame Seeds is taken from Saturn to Jupiter; and projected from the Ascendant; and it is a seed along the lines of flaxseed, but is white, and is used by doctors in certain antidotes.

## On The Part Of Sugar

The Part of Sugar is taken by subtracting the place of Mercury from the place of Venus, and adding the degrees according to the ascending sign to the remainder; and projecting from the Ascendant. And where the number finishes, there will be the Part of Sugar, which you will consider as was said of the others.

## On The Part Of Dates

If you wish to know the condition of Dates, subtract the place of the Sun from the place of Venus, and add the degrees of the ascending sign to the remainder, and project from the Ascendant, and where the number ends, there will be the Part.

## On The Part Of Honey

However if you wish to know the condition of honey, subtract the place of the Moon from the place of the Sun, and add the degrees of the ascending sign to the remainder, and project from the Ascendant, and where the number finishes, there will be the Part.

## On The Part Of Wine

Indeed if you wish to know the condition of wine (which is had from the condition of grapes), subtract the place of Saturn from the place of Venus, and add the degree of the ascending sign to the remainder, and project from the Ascendant; and where the number arrives at, there will be the Part which you seek. Judge on it as was said of the others.

## On The Part Of Olives

If it is your heart's desire to know whether there will be an abundance of olives or not; and you want to know whether oil is going to be cheap or dear, subtract the place of Mercury from the place of the Moon, and add the degrees and minutes of the ascending sign to the remainder, and project from the Ascendant, giving each sign 30 degrees by equal degrees, and where the number ends, there will be the Part.

## On The Part of Nuts

If you wish to know whether or not there will be an abundance of nuts in that year or revolution, subtract the place of Mercury from the place of Mars, and add the degrees of the ascending sign to the remainder, and project from the Ascendant, and where the number ends, there will be the Part - which you will judge as was said of the others.

## On The Part Of Silk And Woven Things

And if you wish to know the disposition of silk and its condition, and the rest of the small, lifeless, overly dry things, and those things loving temperate humidity, as are millet, Italian panic grass, melic, beans, and the like (even though silk does not like excessive humidity, however, it is counted among these things): it is taken in this way

- namely, subtracting the place of Mercury from the place of Venus, and adding the degrees of the ascending sign to the remainder, and projecting from the Ascendant, and where the number finishes, there will be the Part.

### On The Part Of Melons, Watermelons, Cucumbers, And Gourds

To know whether there will be an abundance of melons, watermelons, cucumbers, and gourds, or not, subtract the place of Mercury from the place of Saturn, and add the degrees of the ascending sign to the remainder, and where the number ends, there will be the Part: which you will judge just like the others

### On The Part Of Poisoned Things

If you wish to know whether there will be a poisoning in that revolution or not, subtract the place of the Caput Draconis from the place of Saturn, and add the degree of the ascending sign to the remainder, and begin to project from the Ascendant; and where the number ends, there will be the Part. You will judge regarding it as with the others.

### On The Part Of Wetness And Dryness

To have knowledge of the wetness and dryness of the revolution, in the day subtract the place of the Moon from the place of Venus, and vice versa at night; and add the degrees of the ascending sign to the remainder, and project from the Ascendant; and where the number ends, there will be the Part which you seek. Judge regarding it as you do of the others.

### On The Part Of Salted Things

To know the market of salted things, through which you will be able to perceive the status of them and of salt (even though it might not be to a point, nevertheless it will be to a useful degree), subtract the place of Mars from the place of the Moon, and add the degrees of the ascending sign to the remainder; and project from the Ascendant. And where the number ends, there will be the Part.

### On The Part Of Sweet Foods

To know the condition of sweet foods, subtract the place of the Sun from the place of Venus, and add the degrees of the ascending sign to the remainder, and where the number ends, there will be the Part.

### On The Part Of Bitter Foods

To know the condition of bitter foods, subtract the place of Mercury from the place of Saturn, and add the degrees of the ascending sign to the remainder, and where the number ends, there will be the Part.

### On The Part Of Sour Foods

To know the condition of sour foods, subtract the place of Saturn from the place of Mars, and add the degrees of the ascending sign to the remainder, and project from the Ascendant, and where the number ends, there will be the Part.

### On The Part Of Pungent Foods

To know the condition of pungent foods, and herbs having a pungent taste, subtract the place of Mars from the place of Saturn, and add the degrees of the ascending sign to the remainder, and project this from the Ascendant.

### On The Part Of Sweet Medicines

To know the condition of sweet purgative medicines, subtract the place of the Sun from the place of the Moon, and add the degrees of the ascending sign to the remainder, and where the number ends, there will be the Part.

### On The Part Of Sour Medicines

To know the condition of sour medicine, subtract the place of Saturn from the place of Jupiter, and add the degrees of the ascending sign to the remainder, and project from the Ascendant, and where the number ends, there will be the Part.

### On The Part Of Salty Medicines

To know the condition of salty medicine, subtract the place of Mars from the place of the Moon, and add the degrees of the ascending sign to the remainder, and project this from the Ascendant, and where this number ends, there will be the Part.

## On The Part Of The Disposition Of The Year

And there is another Part which seems to comprehend all of the aforementioned ones; and seems that it is so correlated with them, and them with it, that this Part is generated from them, and that they are generated from it. And this is called the Part of Good Disposition, or Productiveness of the Year, which is taken from the Moon to Mercury and projected from the Ascendant; and where the number ends, there will be the Part. Whose judgement will be like the others.

## On The Extraction Of Parts

If it ever happens that the planet (whose place you wish to extract from the place of another's), is in more in signs and degrees and minutes, than the other planet from whom you have to extract him, add twelve signs to the lesser planet which you extract from. Afterwards you will be able to extract what you wish, and add the degrees and minutes of the ascending sign to the remainder, and project from the Ascendant, giving each sign 30 degrees by equal degrees; and where this number ends, there will be the place. You will judge this as was said with the others.

## On The Regions Where These Will Be

To know in which regions the aforementioned accidents will happen, you will consider from what direction the Lord of the Ascendant, or of the tenth, the seventh, or the fourth is. Whether in the eastern direction, or the southern, or the western, or the northern; or in eastern signs - which are Aries and its triplicity; or southern signs - which are Taurus and its triplicity; or western signs - which are Gemini and its triplicity; or northern signs - which are Cancer and its triplicity.

## On The Time When They Will Be

To know the time in which the significations of the aforementioned Parts ought to happen, and in which quarter this signification will arrive, examine the Part which you want: which, if it falls between the Ascendant and the fourth, its signification will occur in the first quarter of the revolution of the year, or that time in which the signification ought to occur. If however, it is in the fourth, or between the first and the seventh, it will happen in the second quarter. Indeed, if it is in the seventh, or between the seventh and the tenth, it will happen in the third quarter. But if it is in the tenth, or between the tenth and the Ascendant, it will happen in the last quarter of that time. And the closer to an angle, the faster it will happen; and the more remote it is from them, the slower it will happen.

## On The Number Of Significators Of Any Part

Every Part will naturally have at least two significators, even if there are some of them which are sometimes content with only one significator, like the Part of Substance, if it falls in the second; and like the Part of Journeys if it falls in the ninth.

And there are certain Parts which have three significators: the two from which the Part is extracted; and one from the domicile in which the Part will fall (if the domicile does not belong to either of the other two). And there are some Parts which have four significators: two from which the Part is extracted; and a third ruling the place to which it arrives; and a fourth from which it begins to project.

And a Part which is content with one significator is strengthened when it is aspected by its significator. Indeed, a Part which has two significators, is strengthened when it is aspected by both of its significators, and they give more hope of perfecting what the Part intended: however, the Lord of the domicile in which the Part falls will be more deserving. If the Part has three significators, and two aspect it, but the third does not, there will not be such strength in the Part in perfecting what the Part intended. But if only one aspects it, and two do not aspect it, its strength will be less again for it. Indeed, if none of them aspect it, there will be even less, and what is done of the matter in the revolution will come to be with burdens and harshness. You will say the same if the significators are saved according to their safety. But if they are impeded, you will speak according to their impediment. For if they are all impeded, the signification of this Part will hardly or never appear. And if the significators aspect the Part from a praiseworthy aspect, he who has hope, will see what he intended from it. However, if they aspect it with enmity, evil and contrarieties will befall him because of it.

It could be that none of the planets having a role in the Part aspect it; and another planet who naturally signifies that which the Part signifies aspects it - then something of it will happen, even if it is not in whole. So if Jupiter (who naturally signifies substance) aspects the Part of Substance, and no other significators aspect it; or if Venus aspects the Part of Marriage, and none of the other significators aspect it, it will signify some kind of effecting of the matter. Or if it were knowledge of the Part of Slaves or Servants, and none of the significators of the Part aspect it, but Mercury (who naturally signifies slaves and servants) aspects it. But this will be below the signification of the significator of the Part; and it will be on the occasion of someone who involves himself in the matter, perhaps unrequested. And if the planet aspecting the Part has any dignity in the domicile in which he is, this will happen from the direction by which the person intended was hoping for. If however, the aspecting planet is peregrine, it will happen from a direction unknown to him. And if the planet aspecting the Part is unfortunate, not receiving the Part, or IF it is impeded, there will be movements and rumours in it, and nothing which is signified by the Part will be perfected.

And Albumashar said that after this you will examine if the unfortunate planet is in an angle, or a succedent of an angle, and it is direct: for if it is, there will be destruction, or impediment after it is thought to be perfected. If this unfortunate planet is Saturn, the impediment will be because of someone of greater age. However, if it is Jupiter, it will be because of a religious person or a judge, or others coming between them. Indeed, if it is Mars, it will be because of some contention of his. Indeed, if it is the Sun, it will be because of the king, or the wealthy. But if it is Venus, it will be because of women. But if it is Mercury, and he is impeded, it will be because of some business matter. And if it is the Moon, and she is increased in light and number, she will be the cause of the matter being increased. And if she is decreasing in light, she will be the cause of the matter being deteriorated and diminished.

## Parts Of Kingdom And Empire

Alchabitius said that the Part which is called the Part of Kingdom and Empire, which is used in the revolution of the years of the world, is taken from Mars to the Moon, and projected from the Ascendant of the conjunction, which signifies the change of the kingdom. Understand the same in sects, since in a certain way they are similar to rulership and dominion. According to others, it is taken from the degree of the Ascendant of the conjunction, and projected from the degree of the Ascendant of the revolution. However, according to certain others it is taken from the degree of the Sun to the degree of the Midheaven of the revolution; and projected from the degree of Jupiter - and this opinion appears more fitting to me.

The Part of the Time of the Elevation of The King, which signifies his durability, in the day is taken from the hour of his elevation or entry from the Sun to the fifteenth degree of Leo; and projected from the degree of the Moon; indeed, at night it is taken from the degree of the Moon to the fifteenth degree of Cancer; and projected from the degree of the Sun.

And there is another Part of the Kingdom or Empire, which in the day is taken at the hour of his elevation, from Jupiter to Saturn, and vice versa at night; and projected from the Ascendant of the revolution of the year in which the king or emperor is elevated (and for any other person promoted to a lay dignity).

And Alchabitius said that if Jupiter is in a common sign, and it is a diurnal revolution, and Jupiter is cadent from an angle, it is taken from Saturn to Jupiter, and 30 degrees are added on; and it is projected from the Ascendant of the revolution of the year in which the king rose up. Indeed, if Jupiter and Saturn are opposed to each other, and both are cadent from the Ascendant, then half of the degrees between them are taken, and projected from the Ascendant. If Jupiter is in Cancer, and it is a nocturnal revolution, this Part is taken from Jupiter to Saturn, and projected from the Ascendant.

Alchabitius said that the first of the Parts by which the durability of the king is examined from his elevation, is to examine the hour of the elevation of the kingship, by which the profection of the year has arrived from the conjunction of the triplicity which signifies the kingdom or sect, in terms of a count by which a year is given to every 30 degrees, and one month is given to every two degrees and 30 minutes. And when you know in which sign or degree this is, save this; since this will be the place from which you calculate the first Part. And when you wish to apply it, determine the Ascendant of the revolution of the year in which the king rose up or was elected. After this, take the distance from the planet (either Saturn or Jupiter) which is more oriental from the Sun in the figure of the year, up to the degree of the calculation of the first Part which you saved; and project from the Ascendant of the revolution. And where it arrives, this will be the place of the first Part.

Indeed, the second Part is, to examine in the month or day in which the king arose, from the conjunction of Saturn and Jupiter in which the kingdom or empire arose, to see to what sign or what degree the profection of the year arrives from the count by which every 30 degrees is given a year: and this is the place of the calculation of the second part - save this also. After this take the distance from the planet more occidental from the Sun (from Saturn and Jupiter), up to the place of the calculation of the second part (which you saved), and project it from the Ascendant of the revolution. And where this arrives at, is the place of the second Part. These are the Parts which signify the strength of the king, and his durability.

# GUIDO BONATTI'S

## BOOK OF ASTRONOMY

## PART FIVE

*On Nativities And Their Accidents, And Other Things Which Seem To Pertain To Nativities, In General And Particular*

### Preface

ince almost the entire purpose of astrology appears to revolve around two things, namely nativities and revolutions (but principally with nativities, and secondarily with the others), to me it seems fitting and very appropriate to explain faithfully, with an honest intention and the entire effect of my mind, which was given to me by divine goodness (according to what my little bit of knowledge can demonstrate), for the utility of those who are eager; and to follow in the footsteps of our predecessors, namely according to Ptolemy, Albumashar, Hermes, Aomar, Alboali, Alchindi, Yergis, Dorotheus, and others who dedicated themselves both generally and particularly for our benefit in this work.

### I

### Excusing Why This Tractate Has Been Delayed Up Until Now

None of those wishing to study should wonder, nor should any hostile person, nor any slanderer or detractor, rise up asking, why the tractate of nativities is placed after the other tractates mentioned above: even though nativities precede all of the accidents named in the other tractates: Because even though the nativity and all the accidents of the native come first, nevertheless of the knowable things taken together it is found to be more weighty and powerful. And therefore this tractate merited being placed after all the previously stated knowable things. For it cannot be known by the unskilled, nor by those who need to be introduced, or those without some kind of introduction or fruitfulness, nor by any others, except for the wise and the advanced. And therefore it is placed after the other tractates: since they can be known by those of less knowledge - this tractate cannot. Indeed, no matter contained in the luminous circle is found to be more powerful than a treatment of nativities. For through nativities it is necessary that all of the native's accidents, which ought to happen to him naturally from the hour of his nativity up to the hour of his death are known; and likewise what is said about him after his death.

### II

### That Two Things Are Principally Required For The Being Of Every Man

Since for the being of each and every man two things are principally required (namely the first beginning, and the second beginning), I believe that it is fitting in this chapter to make mention of each one (namely, first to make mention of the first, and the second of the second), and in which things it might be effective (even if I touched somewhat on these things elsewhere), and how they differ, so that from these things which will be said, the order will be more rightly understood - since it is from God, and since whatever is from God, is ordered.

## FIRST PART

### *On The First Beginning*

Therefore, the start of the first beginning is the fall of the seed in the womb, after which the foetus is generated (not immediately, but in time). Whence, if you have the hour of this, which seldom happen, it will be known through this beginning what is going to be regarding the conceived child up until the hour of its exit from the womb of the mother. And the accidents of this conceived child will be according to the disposition, and according to the condition of the surrounding stars, which will signify the accidents of the body up until it is ensouled, and those of the body and soul immediately after the soul is infused, and from this point onwards, for as long as it remains in the womb.

Since after the seed falls in the womb, arrangement, variation, enlargement, growth, and the composition of the members and their natural division take place in it (and the adaption of nutrition of like to like), regarding which certainty cannot be had, as it can with the nativity. For indeed, the nativity is entirely an internal end, but its cause is an external end; its operation is both an internal and an external end. For the beginning of the nativity is certain, the other is untrustworthy; wherefore, if the fall of the seed in the womb is a complete beginning, then it would seem that the beginning of the nativity superfluous. However, the fall of the seed can be said to be an incomplete beginning, and likewise the other beginnings which are prior to the nativity. Nevertheless, it is possible to have knowledge of them through a question, just as a business matter is renewed, or as a case is renewed after the sentence by an appeal.

And even if certain pretenders and detractors might say that the fall of the seed in the womb is the beginning for all of the accidents of the native up to the end of his life (which is manifestly contrary to all truth, and it is consonant with falsity that the seed of man could make a legal appeal), it is not as they say: for no whole (or whole-like) part can advance something without the assistance of the other; for incompleteness does not make for nobility. For one form cannot be in diverse materials; and regarding those things of theirs which they have as a mutual connection, one can be destroyed without the other, before they are connected. For indeed, the fall of the seed is like a journey to the accidents of the person being born; the infusion is like a door; the nativity is like the entrance through this door. However, it is superfluous, that something which can be had by one thing, or comes to be by one thing, comes to be by many; for it is not the intention of nature, which is always intent on better, to impede or complicate herself.

### *On The Second Beginning*

The other beginning, namely the second, is in respect of the accidents of the native from the hour of his nativity up to the end of his life. Whence, the two beginnings differ in this: since the first is in respect of the accidents of the conceived child from the hour of the fall of the seed, up until the hour of the nativity - and at that hour its disposition expires. Indeed, the second one, which is more effective, more true, and more noble than the first in the whole being of the native (even if it is caused in the sense of form being "caused" by matter); and therefore it is considered more noble from the hour of his birth up to the end of his life.

Whence it is necessary at the hour of the nativity that each and every one of the accidents which are going to happen to the native can be had in it. Wherefore, this beginning is said to be the most certain; and the nativity is said to be such a beginning that it comprehends all of the natives future accidents, which does not happen in any of the other beginnings.

And it is a complete beginning for which nothing is lacking as regards the composition of the number of members: wherefore, in a nativity is found: sameness of quality, certainty, and one and the same cause (therefore, not diversity); whereas in the other beginnings a diversity of causes are found. And therefore the diversity of causes diversifies the effect, and they are multiplied according to how the causes are diversified and multiplied. For the purpose of completion of the conceived child in the womb, many and diverse things are aggregated into one before the birth. But the aggregation is preserved by the nativity alone, which is the peculiar property of nature's intention - who, insofar as she is in herself and from her own intention, always intends to prefer the more deserving and the better things. And perfection makes for nobility: wherefore, as long as the conceived child remains in the womb, it is in motion, and what is in motion, is not in a limit, or in an end, but is on a path - namely in the operation of something which is incomplete which is conjoined to motion. However, if it is in a limit, it is in perfection: for a limit or perfection, and a path and motion, are contraries of each other. Whence perfection cancels motion. For the conceived child in the womb, is on a path until the cotyledon is severed by the natural order - and then it is in a limit: since then it is perfected or completed, and the conceived child has ceased being on the path.

Then another beginning begins, namely the second one, which is the life of a man, in which it grows, is increased, is diminished, and withdraws, nor can the child be said to be "perfected" before it is ensouled by a rational soul, since this is the first perfection. And knowledge and virtue are the second. Indeed, in a nativity both can be found, even if it may not be found everywhere or blessed in every way. However, in the fall of the seed no perfection can be found; indeed, the fall of the seed is an imperfect thing, from which much is lacking. And on account of its imperfection, it cannot truly be called perfect: since it lacks something.

And this beginning is called the being of man, since at this time the native begins to use the five natural senses of the body, which he could not use freely while he was in the womb (and the delay of this is clearly sensed), and increase, and also certain other accidents, which he could not use, as are speaking, laughing, crying, and similar things.

The being of the native is also assisted by the virtue of the stars having power at the hour of the nativity in his qualities, even it may seem to certain idle men that the stars do not help anything in the making of the native (which is far removed from the truth). For the stars assist the conceived child in perfecting himself; and after the perfection they assist in safely leading him out of his mother's womb. And just as they help him by forming him after the fall of the seed in the womb before his rise from it; so too do they help him in nourishment after the nativity. And since the truth of the matter is had in this manner, it is necessary for you to observe the condition of the stars at the hour of the exit of the infant from the womb, in order to perceive the quality of the body and soul of the native; the nourishment through the triplicity Lords

of the Ascendant, and direction through the term Lords. And through this you can prognosticate the status of his life for him, and everything of his being as long as he lives, according to the truth of the course of nature; and to arrive at those things which will be mentioned regarding the diversities of the nativity: and I will do this below in its own time and place, by means of dissimilar natural accidents and by the natural path of truth.

Whatever the condition and disposition of the stars is like at the hour of the nativity, such will be the all the things of the natives being up until the end of his life. Since the condition of the stars and their disposition is like a container with respect to the condition of the native and his condition; and the condition of the native and his disposition is like the things contained in this container - and the things contained are changed by the container. Whence the disposition of the stars changes the disposition of the native, and they sway his own being, unless perhaps free will operates to the contrary.

For there are many diversities and dissimilitudes, so that all things which come forth from the many stars by an intimately connected reason, seem almost infinite - the investigation of which seems to pertain more to the natural philosopher than to the astrologer - therefore it shall be left to natural philosophers: even if the astrologer cannot pass over this without getting his feet wet and without making some mention of these things, wherefore it cannot easily be fully expressed by his intention.

## III

## How The Condition Of The Native Should Be Examined

Now you must see by which method (according to each kind of prognostication and according to the figure of its extent) the condition of the native can be examined and clearly observed, and the powers of the stars over these can be narrated, and by a natural path, as it pertains to the astrologer, the accidents of the native can be truly comprehended, in order to reach an understanding of the truth which we intend, both in generally and in particular.

And since particulars are in universals particularly, according to the nature of each of them, it will be examined concerning both of them below in its own time and place. Nor does it seem opportune here to have a distinct discussion of each and every one of the places of the figure: but concerning the Lords of the dignities and which of them would prevail in this matter, and what is their peculiar nature - it shall be stated in the required order which pertains to them, and they shall be distinguished according to the revolving of the alachir (which belongs to the acting of the stars of heaven) rather than those signifying the virtues of nativities, in the natural order together, and step by step, according to the successive significations of the houses. And by a precise investigation it can be known more certainly, together with everything which is going to happen to the native in the entire time of his life, from the hour of his nativity up to his last day.

But what is to be investigated first in the aforementioned accidents? It seems more fitting to me in the investigation of these accidents, to make the first instruction of the investigation of the degree of the Ascendant of the nativity; then to instruct on the rest in a suitable order.

## IV

## On The Investigation Of An Unknown Ascending Degree

So that your mind may be at ease in the alleviation of a certain doubt (which seems to happen very often) regarding the finding of an uncertain degree of someone's nativity (as exact as we can be with it), it is fitting, as I remember having said to you above (following the rules of the ancient sages, and also how it seemed to me), that a special chapter should be added so that you can be made truly certain as to the degree of the sign of the Ascendant of any nativity.

And since the nativity is the first accident which happens to the conceived child after its completion and the rupture of the cotyledon, it is necessary for you to be rendered certain on the degree of his Ascendant, so that you can avoid all error, and also to make the native certain about all the accidents for the whole time of his life. And I want you to know the discovery of this matter is going to be of a most precise investigation, even more so than is found written in the books of the ancient sages - not that they were ignorant, but they left it to the industry of the wise.

## What Is The Degree Of The Ascendant Of A Nativity

The degree of the Ascendant of the nativity is the degree of the sign which is on the eastern line, when the cotyledon is ruptured by the birth of the child. Nor is he said to be born immediately when he begins to appear from the womb of the mother, nor when he is completely out of it; but he is said to be born when two-thirds of him have appeared out of it, and the remaining third remains hidden, naturally, without prolonging the time of his exit.. And if you place the Ascendant immediately when his final one-third exits, not much noticeable error will fall in your work, nor will it be noticeably impeded. If however, some impediment supervenes which impedes the natural way of birth being carried out by two complete thirds, and the last third remains to come out, from your great judgement, you shall be able to find out what you seek: for the degree which is then on the eastern line is said to be the Ascendant of the nativity (however, with the aforementioned method about the appearance of the infant being observed).

## The Method Of Finding The Aforementioned Degree

The method of finding this degree, according to the authority of our predecessors, is as follows. For you will take the hour of the exit of the infant from the womb of the mother, just as best and as certain as you can, with the astrolabe or any other instrument is suitable for this, such as the quadrant or water-clock, or any other instrument by which hours are discerned (but with the astrolabe you can be made more certain than with any of the others); however, with this you will not be able to be made completely certain to a point without hesitation: whence to remove every hesitation of doubt, and to have a certain and constructive reckoning, and so you can be ensured to a point on the aforementioned (from which you would have the hour of the nativity as close as you can), by your investigation or by that of another (such as by midwives or similar people), and so a certain and examined calculation could be exhibited to you - you will calculate the planets to the not very certain hour, and you will verify their places, and the twelve cusps, and you will erect the figure according to the ascensions of the region in which you are, and you will then take the degree of the nearest conjunction to that nativity - if the nativity is conjunctional; or if the nativity is preventional the degree of the prevention (namely the degree of the luminary which was above the earth at the hour of the prevention). Next you will examine the Almutem in that degree by domicile, or exaltation, or term, or triplicity, or relationship to the Sun in the figure which you erected for this. If the aforementioned significators are impotent, impeded, and unfortunate, then you will use the Lord of the face.

## Instruction On Finding The Aforementioned Degree

The instruction on this matter is as follows: you will see if the Lord of the domicile aspects the sought degree (namely of the conjunction or the prevention), or if he is presently in that degree: since the Lord of the domicile is to be preferred over all other significators. If this is not so, and the Lord of the exaltation aspects the degree, the Lord of the exaltation is to be preferred over the Lord of the domicile and all of the other significators. But if neither of them aspect it, and are not in it, and the triplicity Lord aspects it, or is in it, you will consider him. Indeed, if he does not aspect it, you will observe the term Lord by the aforementioned conditions.

However, you will not judge according to this, unless you first see the fortitudes of all of these: since you ought to observe the one who has more fortitudes in the aforementioned degree, unless the aspect of another operates to the contrary, However, if all of the aforementioned planets (or many of them) equally aspect the aforementioned degree, he who has more dignities or fortitudes in that degree, will be said to be the significator; and if they are in diverse degrees or minutes and are different in number, you will take him whose number of degrees in the sign in which he is placed is closer to the degree of an angle (if he is in an angle), or closer to the Sun (if he is oriental). If this is not so, see which of them is closer to the degree of the terms in which they are in, you will place the last or first degree first. But if they are all equal in fortitude and dignity, you will place him first who is closer by aspect or presence.

Then you will examine the Almutem itself over the degree of the conjunction or prevention, and see to which of the degrees of the cusps of the angles he is closer to - namely, the Ascendant, or the 10th, or the 7th, or the 4th. If the degree of the planetary Almutem is closer to the degree of the cusp of the Ascendant than to the degree of one of the other angles, and the number of degrees which he had travelled through in the sign you find him in, are equal to number of degrees of the sign of the Ascendant you found for the uncertain nativity (which you had previously discovered by your consideration or by the instruction of another), this will be the Ascendant sought. However, if they are different, abandon the uncertain degree of the Ascendant, and place the Ascendant like the number of degrees of Almutem planet over the degree of the conjunction or prevention; and establish the rest of the houses according to this.

However, if it is closer to the cusp of the tenth house, place it as the degree of the 10th house: and establish the angles and the rest of the houses according to this. You will give judgement likewise with the 7th and the 4th.

Then, by your most precise investigation you will discover what hour and what minute of the hour the degree which you examined was ascending; or when the degree which was the cusp of one of the angles (namely the 10th or its nadir, or the nadir of the Ascendant) was ascending - since that will be the hour of the examined nativity. And you ought to calculate the planets for this, and establish the houses according to the ascensions of the region in which this nativity is in: and this will be its natural Ascendant - I say this, if you begin from the Ascendant. If you begin from the degree of the 10th house, you will start from the beginning of Capricorn, and you will operate according to the direct circle, always leading back in degrees of equal ascension; or you will find it according to the circle of the region, starting from the beginning of Aries up to the degree sought.

However, you will get the degree of the conjunction from the degree in which the conjunction of the luminaries was. Indeed, you will not be able to find the degree of the prevention as easily. For as Ptolemy attests, it will be necessary for you to know the degree of the luminary which was above the earth at the hour of the prevention: since this will be the degree sought. However, if one of the luminaries was in the eastern degree, and the other was in the western degree, the eastern degree will be preferred, and it will be the degree of the prevention.

Indeed, Papiensis said that the degree in which the Moon was at the hour of the fall of the seed in the womb, will be the degree of the Ascendant of the nativity, and vice versa.

## V

### On The Narration Of The Divisions Of Nativities And Certain Accidents Of Theirs

Our most reverend predecessor Ptolemy, wishing for the accidents of nativities to be divided up according to a natural approach, took up the following method of division. For he said that whoever wants them to be divided naturally, will find what pertains to the practice of this work. For he said that there are certain accidents which happen before the birth, and also after the birth.

Before birth, such as speaking about brothers - since it is possible that certain of them are born before the native from the same parents, and certain ones will be born after him.

And there are certain accidents which happen to him at the hour of his birth hour (and these are not one and the same, but diverse). And he said that the accidents which happen to the native in the hour of his birth (which the astrologer intends to know) are many and diverse, such as speaking of males and females; and whether the woman giving birth will give birth to twins (or more children), or not; and on monstrous forms, and those which are not separated.

And he spoke on the accidents which occur after the birth: which are to declare regarding the life, concerning which a rule is given in two ways: one according to quantity: another according to quality.

Indeed, quantity is not varied, only according to what it is given from the ylem and the alcocoden: for either it is long, brief, or mediocre in length. Quality is varied in many ways, according to dispositions and directions of the Lords of the terms of the figure of the nativity in many ways, for one is good, another is bad; one easy, another laborious; one large, another small; one miserable, another covetous; one for the good, another for the bad; one chaste or religious, another unchaste or self-indulgent; another thieving and pillaging; one profiting and saving; another in dissipation and devastation; one in ruling, another in serving; one

in praise, another in slander, and in many other ways which are almost innumerable. The qualities of the life of the native are varied according to the diverse human accidents, just as they descend from the diversity of the diverse motions of the supercelestial bodies, and by the actions of men and their free will, as will be sufficiently discussed below in its own time and place.

Then he spoke about the form and figure of the native, then about the infirmities and impediments happening to the body, then about the qualities of the soul and on its accidents, then about the fortune and misfortune of the native, and likewise about his kingship, exaltation, and loftiness, then about his works, then about his marriage, and his manner of acting with his spouse, then what will happen to him from children and from his familiarity with men, and about friends, and about his pilgrimages; and lastly judging the manner of his death.

And some of the sages followed in his footsteps. I however, not by a contrary approach, even if it is a different one, but tending towards the same end, will make mention to you of all the things (or at least most of them) which pertain to the accidents of the nativity, following the succession of the houses and their significations, beginning from the first up to the twelfth, so that the work of nativities may be rendered easier, and that you may more easily succeed in pursuing what you intend

## VI

### On The Causation Of Natives' Stay In The Womb Of The Mother

The stays of conceived children in the womb of the mother are caused by the dispositions of the supercelestial bodies, according to their three principal differences: which are the greater, the middle, and the lesser; to which certain other middle ones between these are subordinated

For if you see the Moon in the upper part of her epicycle, moving from the east to the west at the hour of the fall of the seed in the womb, or at the hour of a question made after conception, it signifies that the stay of the infant in the mother's womb was the greater one, which consists of 288 days from the hour (of the fall of the seed) up to the hour of birth. However, if you find her in the lower part of the epicycle, moving from west to east, it signifies that the stay was the medium one, which consists of 273 days - and this if the Moon differs in the question from the degree in which she was at the hour of the fall of the seed, or from the degree which was ascending at that time by exactly 90 degrees. However, if she is distant by more or less than this, it signifies that the circular motions will not be completed, and then it was a certain other stay in the middle between these (namely between the greater and the medium). And if the Moon is in the degree of the Ascendant at the fall of the seed, then it signifies that it was the lesser stay, which consists of 258 days. If she is above the earth, more than 5 degrees away from the east or the west, it will be a certain other stay in the womb, in the middle between these (namely the medium and the lesser). But if the Moon is right in opposition to the degree of the Ascendant at the hour of the fall of the seed, you could then be off by one month.

Whence Haly said that to avoid this error you ought to take the degrees which are between the degree of the occidental line and the degree of the Moon, and double them; and divide the result by 24, and what you come out with will be the days, and how many remain below 24 will be the hours - since the Moon passes through one degree in two hours, calculated according to her medium course. Therefore add these days and these hours to the hour of the lesser stay, and the sum will be the stay sought. Then subtract this stay from the days of the nativity, and you will have what you intend. Indeed, if it is an intercalary day, then add 5 hours and 59 minutes, and that which you arrived at within the tables, and calculate the Moon: for the degree in which you find her then, will be the degree she was in at the hour of the fall of the seed. Therefore see which degree is ascending then, since this was the Ascendant at the hour of the fall of the seed.

If the Moon is under the earth tending from east to west, then you will take what was between the degree of the Ascendant and the Moon (in terms of degrees and minutes) and divide by 24 as was said, and add on the medium stay, and subtract the sum from the days and hours of the nativity: and enter what remains into the tables, and calculate the Moon to this hour; and according to the place in which you then find her, you will find the Ascendant for the fall of the seed, as was said above.

## On The Narration Of The Four Species Or Varieties Of Nativities

It is said above that there are four species or varieties of nativities. Now mention is to be made of them individually.

For as the ancient sages testify, the first of them will be abortions, who are born practically dead, or half-dead, or those of which their lives do not last long enough for them to take in any nourishment.

The second is that of those who take nourishment, but do not last long enough in life for any perceptible benefit to follow from it.

The third of them is that of those who take nourishment and live for a few months or years, but do not go beyond the years of childhood; and if they do go beyond them, they still do not reach long life.

The fourth of them is that of certain ones who take nourishment, and life lasts in them until they reach youth (and sometimes they reach old age. And another group is subordinated to this, namely, those who reach the decrepit years, and die from old age: even though this only happens to a few, of which my grandfather was one, who I saw die without any clear occasion, only that his vital breath went away, leaving his corpse behind, for he had 120 years. Concerning all of whom, I believe will be looked at in a suitable order.

And even though I said above that I will spread my wings in this tractate, and show my powers, nevertheless I wish for you to understand my words well. For the business of nativities is a very lofty and precise one, in need of investigation: whence I do not take up the highest manner of expression, lest it impedes; nor an altogether humble one, lest you disparage it; but a middle way, so that you might better succeed in pursuing what you intend, and you will not judge that I have not kept my promise to you.

## SECOND PART

### I

### How To Examine Regarding The Four Species Of Nativities, In Order

With mention having being made above that there are four distinctions of nativities, according to the four determinations made in the first part of this tractate which preceded this one (to which this is subordinated). In this second part it remains to speak about all of these things in order; and first about those whose life does not last long enough in them so that they can take any nourishment.

The knowledge of which matter is to examine the degree of the Ascendant of any nativity and its Lord; and the triplicity Lords of the degree of the Ascendant, and the other angles and their Lords; and also the degree of each of the luminaries and their Lords.

And Aboali said that you are to examine the triplicity Lords of the Sun, and likewise Jupiter and Venus, and the diurnal and nocturnal planets (according to whether the nativity is diurnal or nocturnal). You will also examine the Part of Fortune and its Lord; and likewise the Lord of the conjunction or prevention which was before the nativity.

Then you will examine the planet who is stronger than the rest in the aforementioned places, or in any of them: and you will see whether it is only one, or if there are two or three. Which, if there is only one, and it is cadent from the Ascendant, or only from the angles, and one of the malefics are with him in the same degree impeding him; or if the degree of the Ascendant is impeded - namely so that one of the malefics is in it who does not have any dignity there, or such a malefic is aspecting it from square aspect, or from opposition, it signifies that the native will die before he takes any nourishment. You can say the same if the degrees in which the luminaries are placed are impeded.

Indeed, Ptolemy seemed to think something different from that which the other sages thought, even if it was not something contrary. For it appeared to him that if the luminary who has authority, and the degree of the Ascendant, were impeded; and the Lords of the degrees in which the luminaries were, were receding from angles, that the native would not taste anything until he died. And he said that the hour of this matter would be when the luminaries reach a malefic.

However, other ancients said that if all three triplicity Lords were receding from angles, and the luminaries and their Lords were receding, and the conjunction or prevention and its Lord were receding, then the native would not taste anything until he died; or the native would not be a human, or he would be of those people who are born with some unnatural signs, as are those who have more limbs than they ought to, or lack them, or have them transferred, just as I have seen many times, certain ones of which lacked arms, others even lacked hands, certain others lacked feet, others lacked legs, others lacked knees, others had backwards knees, others were missing eyes; and I saw a certain one who had three arms, and another who had a hip-bone and a leg in place of an arm, and another who did not have an anus: and there was a certain foolish lay surgeon who wished to make one for him, and he was so foolish that he perforated him below with an iron instrument, and killed him in this way. And likewise in my time there was a certain monster which from above the navel was two men, and only one person below it; and a certain creature that had one head, and from the head below there were two bodies. Or the native will be one of those who are born with some brute animal, as sometimes happens: as with a monkey or a cat or similar things; or if a woman births a monstrous thing; or if the native himself is a brute animal.

If this is so, and the aforementioned significators are all cadent as was said, and one of the malefics impedes the Lord of the Ascendant, or the Moon, or the Almutem over the aforementioned places; or if the Almutem itself is a malefic, he will be a wild and rough animal, not wishing to associate with others, and especially with men, as are wolves and similar beasts. Indeed, if benefics and malefics rule (and especially if Mercury has some dignity in these places), he will be one of those who associate with men (as Aomar says) as are dogs and the like. And my mother (who seemed to be a truthful enough woman) told me that in her time a certain woman gave birth to a cat!

## On The Second Species Or Distinction

The second species or distinction is to examine the ascending degree and the rest of the angles, and their Lords; also the degree of the luminaries and their Lords, and their triplicity Lords (in accordance with the nativity being diurnal or nocturnal), also the triplicity Lords of the ascending degree, and the Part of Fortune, and the conjunction or prevention which was before the nativity; and the triplicity Lords of the place in which they fall; Jupiter also, and Venus; and you will examine the planet who is stronger in these places by multitude of dignities (which is called the "*almudebit*"), and see if it is cadent from an angle, and one of the malefics rule over them, and there were some distance between the Almutem and the malefic, this signifies that the native will take some nourishment for himself, and will live until this Almutem reaches the malefic (or until the malefic reaches him) by body, or by aspect, whichever happens to him first degree for degree; for then it signifies that the native will perish after that many days, or that many months, or that many years.

If this malefic is impeded in an angle and in a fixed sign, they will be years according to the quantity of degrees which are between the Almutem and the malefic.

However, if it is in a succedent and in a common sign, they will be months.

Indeed, if it is in a cadent and in a mobile sign, they will be days.

But if it is in an angle and in a common sign, it will subtract one-sixth of these years.

Indeed, if it is in a succeedent and a mobile sign, it will subtract one-quarter of these months.

And if it is in a cadent in a mobile sign, it will subtract one-third of these days.

If it is a benefic instead of a malefic, and it is in a cadent in a common sign, it will prolong the days by one-sixth. However, if it is in a cadent in a fixed sign, it will prolong them by one-fourth. But if it is cadent in a mobile sign, it will prolong them by one-third.

You will say the same regarding the degree of the Ascendant, and likewise regarding the degree in which the Moon is in at that time, if it is joined with a malefic.

And if all of these (or most of them) are cadent from angles, he will taste food, but he will not be nourished. However, if any of the triplicity Lords of the Ascendant are on the cusp of the angle of the Ascendant, or of the tenth, or the eleventh, or the fifth; or if Jupiter or Venus is there, and is free from impediments, and from malefics, it signifies nourishment, but not determinately (namely, whether it is going to be long or short), unless according to other testimonies which signify nourishment.

And if the aforementioned significators are impeded, examine the triplicity Lords of the Part of Fortune, and judge according to their condition, and according to how the Sun aspects the Part. You will say the same with regards to the triplicity Lords of the conjunction or prevention. You can say likewise if the Moon is besieged by two malefics (one of which is in the first, and the other in the seventh), since his life will be short.

## When These Things Will Be Done

To know the time and hour when these things ought to be done, the degree of the Ascendant should be directed to the body of the impeding malefic, or to its square aspect, or to its opposition, namely, by giving a day, a month, or a year, to one degree, according to whether days, months, or years are signified. And if the native has passed one year, you will consider afterwards according to profections - namely giving one year to every 30 degrees according to equal degrees, a month to every 2 degrees and 30 minutes, and a day to every 5 minutes, and an hour to every 12 seconds or thereabouts, and where the number ends, then the native will perish.

And Aomar said to also examine certain benefics in that hour, to see if they are in angles or in the best places from their own dignities, or examine the planet who is more deserving in the degree of the Ascendant and the Part of Fortune, since this signifies according to the quantity of its strength and weakness, that the life of the native will reach to years, or months, or days, according to the quantity of the gift of this planet from its lesser years.

And he said that perhaps they will be days, according to what Dorotheus though: if the triplicity Lords of the Ascendant (namely the first, second, and third) are cadent, it signifies that the native will not be nourished (and especially if Saturn is in an angle in a nocturnal nativity, or Mars in a diurnal ones). And the hour of his death will be when the profection of some other year arrives at the angles, since when the malefics are in an angle, and when the year comes to one of the angles, and there is a luminary there in the square aspect of the malefic, if the native did not die in the first year, then he will die in this year.

And he said, and it is thought in the *Book of Likenesses*, that if there are two Almutems, and one of them is impeded, the native will die, and the other one would not suffice. Likewise if there are three, and one of them is impeded, even if the other two are strong, the native will last, but his life will not be prolonged. Also if there are four, and one or two of them are impeded, and the others are useful, the child will remain longer, but his life will not be prolonged. However, if three are impeded, even if the other is strong, the native will not live (unless a strong benefic aspects the significator of this nativity); and this more strongly so if the Moon is impeded and not received (however, if she is free and received, it signifies the prolongation of life with respect of its brevity).

## On The Third Species Or Distinction

Indeed the third species or distinction is that the native does not have a Ylem, nor an Alcocoden from his own nativity, but the Lord of the Ascendant, the luminaries, and the Lords of the houses which they are in, are free from the aforementioned impediments (namely retrogradation, combustion, the corporeal conjunction of malefics, and their square aspect and opposition), and free from the Lords of the houses in which the malefics are in, even if they are cadent from the angles, or from the Ascendant, or if they are impeded in the angles, it signifies the stay of the native in the world, and his nourishment, but his life will not be prolonged; and it will hardly or never happen that his life is prolonged beyond twelve years, but he will die beforehand according to the quantity of degrees which are between the Lord of the Ascendant and the angle from which it is cadent.

And Tiberiadis said that if the nativity were according to what we have said, we will defer speaking about such a nativity until the Ascendant reaches one orb (namely twelve years), namely giving one year for each sign - and this on account of the significators being cadent. And he said that for as often as the orb of the Ascendant reaches the bodies of malefics, or their square aspect, or opposition, it will be feared for the native until the Ascendant passes through one orb. And he said that whenever it were to transit one orb, we will direct for him from the Ascendant, giving one year to each and every degree by the ascensions of the region in which the nativity was, until it arrives to malefics, as was said in the other species.

## The Fourth Species Or Distinction

Indeed the fourth species or distinction is when the native has a Ylem and Alcocoden, and the aforementioned significators are free: namely, the degree of the Ascendant and its Lord, the triplicity Lord of the degree of the Ascendant, and of the rest of the angles, and their Lords, and the degrees of the luminaries and their Lords, and Jupiter and Venus and the Lords of the domiciles in which they are placed; and the diurnal and nocturnal planets (according to whether the nativity is diurnal or nocturnal), and the Part of Fortune and its Lord; and likewise the Lord of the conjunction or prevention which was before the nativity, and the planet who is the Almutem in these places.

## On Finding The Ylem

The discovery of the Ylem is to seek it in diurnal nativities from the Sun: which if you find in the 1st, 11th, or 10th, will be fit to take the Ylem from (whether he is in a masculine or feminine sign). Indeed, if he is outside of these places in the 7th, 8th, or 9th, and in a masculine sign, he is not to be placed as Ylem.

And Aomar said to know that the Sun and the rest of the places which are used for the Ylem, cannot be the Ylem unless they are aspected by the Lords of their domiciles, or exaltations, or triplicities, or terms, or faces (according to how things seemed to Aboali regarding the Lords of the face). However, if the Lord of one of these dignities does not aspect him, the Sun will not be fit to be the Ylem, nor will the Lord of that dignity. You will pronounce likewise regarding the Moon in the day and night;

and regarding the Part of Fortune; and regarding the degree of the Ascendant; and even the degree of the conjunction or prevention.

Again, if the Sun is not fit to be the Ylem, you will take the Ylem from the Moon; which if you find in an angle or a succedent, and in a feminine sign, and one of the Lords of the four aforementioned dignities aspect her, she is fit to be the Ylem.

And if the nativity is preventional, then the Ylem is to be sought from the Part of Fortune. However, if it is conjunctional, seek it from the degree of the Ascendant, which will signify the Ylem if the Moon or one of the aforementioned significators aspects it, and if this is so, it should be preferred to the Part of Fortune. If however, none of them aspect it, it will not signify the Ylem.

If the degree of the Ascendant is not with the Ylem then, you will consider the Part of Fortune: which, if it is with the Ylem, or with the degree of the Ascendant of the nativity, will be the Ylem, if not, then it won't.

If neither of these can be the Ylem, then seek it from the degree of the conjunction (if the nativity is conjunctional), or from the degree of the prevention (if it is preventional). However, it appeared that Aomar wished for it to be sought from the degree in which the Moon was at the hour of the prevention in this case.

If again one of the aforementioned significators do not aspect the aforementioned degrees, then the Ylem will be useless and the native will have a short life.

And if one of them aspect the degree of the ylem, he himself will be called the alcocoden and the giver of years. But if all of the aforementioned significators (namely the domicile Lord, the exaltation Lord, the term Lord, and the triplicity Lord) aspect the degree, he who is closer in degrees by aspect or by conjunction will be the alcocoden or giver of years, whether the aspect is in front or behind. However, if all of them aspect equally, and if they have equal dignity (namely, one exactly) the alcocoden will be the one who is stronger in his own place. However, if one of them has more dignities than the others, it will be said to be stronger than the rest, and ought to be preferred to the rest, provided that he aspects the aforementioned degree, even if the distance between the degree of the ylem and the other of the aforementioned significators (who only has one dignity in the degree of the ylem) is lesser.

## On The Certification Of The Years Of The Native And His Life

Indeed after you have done this, and you are certain of the ylem and the alcocoden, you will be able to be made certain of the years of the native and his life; and concerning his life, namely, whether it will be long or short, safe or dangerous; and of his good or bad accidents; and you will even be able to be made certain of his prosperities and adversities. For the Ylem signifies the root of life, the Alcocoden the number of years: wherefore the status of life is taken from the Ylem, and the giving of years is taken from the Alcocoden: but still, neither of them are sufficient to give life to the native without the other. For just as a man alone is not sufficient for generation, neither is a woman alone sufficient for conception or begetting - for one cannot beget without the other. For the Ylem gives life formally, the Alcocoden gives it effectively.

## Again On The Certification Of The Years Of The Native

When you perceive the years of the native and their number, you will consider the disposition of the Ylem and the Alcocoden, and you will see how many years are attributed to the native. You will also see if he is given years by the Alcocoden or by another, as sometimes happens. Since if he is given them by the Alcocoden, it will be clear what you ought to do. Indeed, if he is given them by the another, you will see whether the years of the alcocoden are equal to the lesser, middle, or greater years of this planet (which happens most rarely), or if they are a little less.

And you will see in which of those years the Ylem arrives to the bodies of malefics or to the places in which they were in the nativity, or to their square aspect, or opposition; or to the Cauda Draconis, or to the degree in which she was in the nativity; or to the square aspect of the place in which the Moon was in the nativity, or to her opposition, namely by giving one year to every degree according to the degree of this region - and if none of the benefics project their rays to the terms in which the Ylem reaches the impeding malefic, it signifies that the native will die in that year, month, or day, namely at the hour in which the arrival of the Ylem to aforementioned places (or to one of them) is perfected.

But if the aforementioned years are not equal to the years of the Alcocoden, nor similar to them, and the Ylem arrive at the impeding malefic as was said, or arrives to the aforementioned places, without the aspect of one of the benefics, the native will be oppressed by the strongest impediment, so that it will almost all hope will be lost of him not being endangered; and he himself will fear the same - that he would die. However, ultimately he will escape, unless perhaps he is endangered by error. But if a benefic projects its rays to the Ylem the native will be oppressed at that time, but there will not be as much fear about him.

## II

## On The Diversity Of Opinions Regarding The Ylem

However there were differences among the sages regarding the Ylem, even if there is no contrariety. Since it seemed to Ptolemy that the Ylem was not to be sought in the eighth, since the Ascendant does not have any assistance there, and it is a dark place, and it does not aspect the Ascendant. However, in the ninth it is different, since it is of the same triplicity as the Ascendant, and of its kind; and since the Sun rejoices in it, and it is his foundation. Which if the Sun is in the ninth in someone's nativity, and he is otherwise well disposed, the native will have a good and honourable life, and one of good durability.

Indeed, it seemed to Dorotheus that the Ylem was not to be sought from the eighth, nor from the seventh, unless it is in masculine signs. And he said, that if the Sun is in these two houses, in feminine signs, he is not fit to be the Ylem: since his strength is weakened in feminine signs, and he is made effeminate. And it seemed to him that the Sun would be Ylem in nocturnal nativities in places opposite to these, in masculine signs.

But Ptolemy did not make mention of the sex of the signs, wherefore it seems fitting to me that you observe the opinion of Dorotheus, if you can, for it is more secure; however, the opinion of Ptolemy is not to be abandoned.

However, in diurnal nativities, if the Sun is not in masculine signs in the aforementioned places, he is not fit to be the Ylem. Then it will be necessary for you to seek the Ylem from the Moon. Who, if you find her in one of the angles or succedents, will be fit to be the Ylem; and you will not care about the sex of the signs (namely, whether they are masculine or feminine), however, in a woman's nativity she will be more useful in a feminine sign, and in a man's nativity she will be more useful in a masculine sign.

And in this everyone agrees - that the Moon is fit to be the Ylem in the third, as she rejoices here, and it is her foundation. However, regarding the ninth, there were diverse opinions among them. For to Dorotheus is seemed uncertain as to whether the Moon could be the Ylem in this place, since she is then impeded; indeed, it appeared to Ptolemy that she could be the Ylem in the ninth, but it is necessary for her to be in a feminine sign.

And Aomar said that if the Moon is not in these places, and it is a nativity is conjunctional, the Ylem should be sought from the degree of the Ascendant of the nativity. Indeed, if it is preventional, it should be sought from the Part of Fortune (which is called the "Ascendant of the Moon"); and you will put the degree of the Ascendant last. And the sages put the Part of Fortune first in preventions, since the Moon is then in the full amount of the whole of her light from the side which we see of her, and is in charge of the whole night. However, in conjunctional nativities, it should begin from the Ascendant: since then the Moon is deprived of all of her light.

But if the Ylem is sought from the Part of Fortune, and it signifies the Ylem, and it is in the angles or the succeedents of the angles, you will not care whether it is in a masculine or feminine sign. If you seek the Ylem from the Ascendant of the nativity, and the Ascendant is not impeded, even if the Part of Fortune is not there, it will still be the Ylem. And Aomar said that you will not care whether it is cadent from an angle or not, since the Ascendant itself will be an angle. And he said that there is nothing which must be sought in the Ascendant which is feared concerning the condition places of the Ylem - namely from what is profitable or unprofitable. For it is possible that the aforementioned places are in profitable or unprofitable places; indeed, the Ascendant does not cease being a place of profitability.

And he said that if the Sun, or the Moon, or the Part of Fortune, or the Ascendant, are not suitable for the Ylem, examine the conjunction or prevention which is before the nativity, and see which of them are aspected by the Sun, or the Moon, or the Lord of Ascendant (or another one of the benefics), and is in an angle or a succedent of an angle: for this will be the Ylem (and you will not care whether it is a masculine or feminine sign).

## On The Knowledge Of The Alcocoden

And when you know the Ylem, and you wish to know the Alcocoden (which is called "the divisor"), you will consider the said four significators (namely the Lord of the domicile in which the Ylem is placed, the Lord of the exaltation, the term Lord, and the triplicity Lord), and whichever one of them you find more fit, place it as the Alcocoden, beginning from the Lord of the terms: who, if you find him projecting his rays to the terms, put him as the Alcocoden. If you do not find him as such, then examine the Lord of the domicile, and operate through him as you did with the term Lord; then through the Lord of the exaltation; and then by the triplicity Lord. If you find none of them fit for this, you will lastly use the Lord of the face (even if his signification is weak). And understand this if their dignities are the same and equal (namely each and every one of them).

However, if all of them aspect equally, and one of them has more than one dignity, he who has two, will be preferred to the he who only has one dignity; and he who has three, will be preferred to him who has two, and will be said to be stronger. However, if they are all equally strong in terms of dignities or testimonies, he who is in an angle or a succeedent will be preferred. Indeed, if all of them are in angles or succedents, he who is closer to the cusp of an angle or succeedent will be said to be stronger. Indeed, if they are equal in strength and dignity in the place of the Ylem, and they are equally in an angle or a succeedent, he who is in his own dignity will be preferred to another who is peregrine, or in less of his own dignities than the other.

But if all of them are equally equal in all the above mentioned fortitudes, he who is oriental will be preferred. And if all of them are oriental, he who is closer to the Sun will be preferred, whether rising cosmically or helically. And if the Sun is on the eastern line, he will be preferred to the rest of the significators. And if one of the planets is in the Ascendant, or the tenth, not distant from the line of the cusp by more than 3 degrees before, or by more than 5 after, make him a participator with the Ylem, whether he has dignity there or not; but if he has dignity there, he will be stronger than one outside of the aforementioned places, even if their dignities are equal; and not only if they are equal, but even if the planet not present in the places has one, or even two more dignities than him, the present planet will still be stronger in the aforementioned place, as was said. However, if he does not have dignity there, his participation will be weak, and will be of little benefit.

And if one of the three superior planets are oriental, and are in the cazimi of the Sun, or before their second station, or after it by a space which he can travel in seven days, and has some dignity in the place of the Ylem, and is otherwise well disposed, the Ylem and Alcocoden can be found from him, unless the term Lord of the degree of the Ylem operates to the contrary.

And it seemed to Ptolemy that an aspect is one fortitude of a planet in the matter of the Ylem and Alcocoden; and that a planet who has three dignities, even if he does not aspect it, is stronger than a planet who only has one and does aspect it; however, this does not contradict the other philosophers who said that a planet who has one will be stronger if he is in the aforementioned places; since Ptolemy understood this with regards to the planets aspecting, and not the planets present in these places. And he said that the planet is more deserving (so that he would rule), who has more dignities in the Ascendant, and in the places of the luminaries, and in the Part of Fortune, and in the degree of the conjunction or prevention which was before the nativity. And he said, that if there is some planet who has dignity in three or four of the places, or at least in two, we will establish him as the Almutem over the nativity.

# Tractate IX

## On The Knowledge Of The Years Of The Native

After this we will examine the place of the Almutem in order to know the years of the native: which, if it is oriental and in an angle, and in addition is in its own aym (as is a masculine planet in a masculine sign, and above the earth; and a feminine planet in a feminine sign and below the earth), and it is in one of its own dignities (which were mentioned above, and which are domicile, exaltation, triplicity and face - as it seemed to certain men seen regarding the face), and is in the Ascendant, or in the tenth, and in its own aym, then it will give its greater years.

And Aboali said that if the Sun is the Ylem, and is in Aries or Leo, and none of the Lords of his five dignities aspect him, then he will be the Ylem and the Alcocoden. And it will be likewise with the Moon if she is in Taurus or Cancer with the aforementioned conditions.

And Ptolemy said that if it is oriental and in a succedent of an angle (and especially in the 11th), and in one of its own aforementioned dignities, and is free from impediments, then it will give its medium years.

If it is in the cadents, even if it is otherwise free, then it will give its minor years. If it is cadent, and is otherwise impeded (namely retrograde, or in opposition to one of its own domiciles, or to its exaltation, or is peregrine, or besieged by two malefics), then it will give months instead of years, or perhaps it will give weeks instead of months. But if in addition to one of the aforementioned impediments it is combust, it will signify and give hours instead of those years; or at most it signifies days.

Aboali considered all the angles as equal in giving greater years; and all succeedents in giving medium years; and indeed, the cadents in giving lesser years.

## When The Planets Increase The Years

After you have recognized the alcocoden (who is called the giver of years), see whether he is aspected by any of the planets, or if he is corporeally joined to any of them. You will also see whether it is a benefic that he is joined to, or who aspects him; and by what aspect it aspects him: since if the planet aspects him by a trine or sextile aspect, and the planet is a benefic, and this benefic is fortunate and strong, it will add its lesser years to him, and as many months as are its medium years. However, if it does not receive him, but it was still with the aforementioned conditions, it will add its own lesser years to him, and on top of this, as many days as are its greater years. You will say the same if it receives him from a square aspect or from opposition. However, if that benefic is impeded, it will add months to him, according to its own lesser years,

## When The Planets Decrease Years

Indeed if the planet who aspects him is a malefic, and it aspects him from a square aspect or from opposition, or is corporeally joined to him, it will decrease his years according to the number of its own lesser years. However, if the malefic is fortunate and strong, he will only reduce them according to one-third of his own lesser years. And Mars is of greater harm than the other malefics. Indeed, Mercury is convertible, since if he is with increasing planets, he will increase the years of the native according to the number of his lesser years. Indeed, if he is with decreasing planets, he will decrease the same.

## On The Caput Draconis And Its Cauda

Alchindi said the Caput Draconis, if it is with the Alcocoden by 12 degrees before or after, will subtract one fourth of the years of the alcocoden - which, did not prove true for me, as far as I remember; but regarding the Cauda this is true. And it harms more if it is with the Moon than if it is with any of the other significators.

The years of the native are also altered in other ways, and are given on account of the virtue of someone's nativity by his own children coming after him (of those who are living), just as the years are altered by revolutions after nativities: and on this you will find discussed below in the chapter on the father.

## On The Direction Of The Degrees To Planets, For Knowing The Accidents Of The Native

After you have discovered the number of the years of the native's life which are signified by the Alcocoden, and if you wish to know about the accidents of the native, and about his condition, direct his Ylem to the rays of the malefics from square aspect, and opposition, and from their corporeal conjunction in one sign, and even from their trine or sextile aspect. And you will give one year to each degree of distance between them, up to the completion of their conjunction minute for minute, by the degrees of that region; and a month for every five minutes; and six days for every minute; and one day for every ten seconds; and one hour for every 25 thirds.

And see when the Ylem arrives to the rays of malefics, or to the degrees in which the malefics or their rays were at the hour of the nativity, since if the Ylem or the Alcocoden is then badly disposed, the accidents of the nativity will be oppressed,, and horrible things will happen. If the Ylem arrives to one of the malefics, or to one of the aforementioned places to be feared, and none of the benefics project their rays to this place, and that year is the last of the years of the native which are given to him by the Alcocoden, the native will die in that year, and in that month, and in that day, and in that hour, by such a death as the giver of years signified for him in his nativity. This being if he lives up until the time when he ought to, that is, that he is not overcome by an accidental death (as often happens), and this more strongly, and certainly, and infallibly, if that malefic impedes the Lord of the Ascendant of the nativity, and the Lord of the Ascendant of the revolution of that year, and the Lord of the profection of the same; or if himself and another malefic impede all of the aforementioned significators, there will only be one cure for him - that is, if the malefic is in a greater or lesser latitude than the Ylem is, so that they do not block other by a straight diameter, so that the deviation of one from the other is more than one degree (unless perhaps it is by a divine miracle); but if their deviation is as said, he will not die unless perhaps by the fault of those erring, or if it is done by a force of nature; nevertheless, he will be endangered by a danger similar to death.

You will even employ the fixed stars which are of the nature of the impeding malefic, in their own latitudes, just as you employ the impeding malefic. And do not make your direction, unless you first examine the latitudes of the planets and of the fixed stars, as I said.

However, in other years, if the Ylem arrives to the aforementioned places without the projection of the rays of any benefic, the natives' condition will be oppressed, and horrible contrary things will befall him (not dangerous things however). But if a benefic projects its rays to this place, the native will not be impeded by a severe impediment. And however, often the Ylem arrives to benefics, or to the places in which they were (or to the places in which their rays were) at the hour of someone's nativity, without the projection of the rays of a malefic, so often will prosperous and pleasing things happen to him. However, if a malefic projects its rays to it, it will reduce something of that goodness, yet it will not greatly reduce it (nevertheless, it will reduce it by more or less according to how it is disposed). Likewise, whenever the Ylem arrives to malefics, or to the places in which the malefics were (or where there rays were) at the hour of the nativity, without the projection of the rays of some benefic, so often will contrary and horrible things happen to him, and his condition will be made worse.

If a benefic projects its rays to the aforementioned places, it will reduce the malice of this malefic, according to how it is disposed. If the Ylem arrives to a malefic who was impeding at the hour of the nativity, or to any one of his aspects, and the malefic does not receive it by perfect reception, and the malefic itself is impeded, it signifies the death of the native in that year, as is said elsewhere.

### III

### That All Planets Are Givers Of Years, But Not All Of Them Are Preservers Of Them Simply; But Rather Sometimes They Are Killers, Some Naturally, Some Accidentally, And Likewise The Caput And Cauda

All of the planets are givers of years (and even the Caput and the Cauda) but according to a diverse order; but not all of them are guardians or preservers of them simply; in fact certain of them are naturally killers (namely Saturn, Mars, and the Caput and Cauda Draconis). And there are even certain other killers besides the aforementioned, even if not naturally so, but rather by accident, and there are thirteen of them - so that altogether there are seventeen killers, namely the aforementioned four naturally, and the other thirteen by accident: certain by time, certain by position of places.

For the Sun kills by corporeal conjunction, and by square aspect, and by opposition.

The Moon likewise kills by corporeal conjunction with the Sun, whether she is the Ylem or not (unless she is in the cazimi of the Sun), and when she is in his square aspect, or opposition.

The Moon also kills if she arrives to the degree of the Ascendant without the aspect of a benefic, if she is the Ylem in the nativity, and if it is the degree of the Ascendant of some revolution: then the native will perish, since she is inimical to the Ascendant, on account of the difference of each of their natures. For the Ascendant is friendly to the Sun, and is of the nature of heat and of the day. And the Moon is inimical to the Ascendant, and is friendly to its nadir (namely the seventh), and is of the nature of cold and night. And one of them is inimical to the other, and they are contrary to each other.

Indeed, the Caput Draconis and its Cauda kill on account of their stricture in the section of the circles, when the Ylem is joined to one of them in the nativity or revolution, unless benefics were then to aspect the degree of the Ylem.

And you may understand the same about the degree which was the 12th house (namely at the hour of the nativity), or of the sixth or the eighth.

Cor Tauri and Cor Scorpionis do the same on account of the excessive abundance of heat prevailing in them.

Indeed, Mercury kills, if he is corporeally joined to one of the malefics, or in its square aspect, or opposition without perfect reception, or without the aspect of some benefic, and is in the degree which was the Ascendant at the hour of the nativity, or is joined to the Ylem, or is in its square aspect or opposition. If he is with benefics he will not kill.

Even the Ylem kills if it is joined with the degree of the nadir of the Ascendant of the nativity.

You can say the same of the Moon if she is joined with this degree, and this will be more so if the planet whose degree you were directing to the Ylem is badly disposed at the hour of the nativity.

Certain other degrees which you would direct to the Ylem will also kill if they are badly disposed. Whence Aomar said that if the direction is completed at the end of a sign with half of the lesser, medium, or greater years of the Alcocoden, it kills.

And he said that if the disposition is changed from the Ylem from the terms of a malefic to the terms of a malefic, it kills in the entrance of that malefic.

And he said to know that it seemed to Ptolemy that the Moon is always to be directed to the rays of malefics and benefics in order to know the condition of the body in health or infirmity, and the condition of the mother. And the Part of Fortune to know the acquisitions of the native (namely of his wealth or poverty). And the Sun to know the condition of the father or kingdom. The Midheaven to know the condition of his kingship and his profession. And he said that it seemed to him that the direction of the degree of the Midheaven should be by ascensions of the right circle.

Again it seemed to him and others generally that to know his condition one should direct from the degree of the Ascendant according to the divisions of the terms, to the rays of benefics and malefics. So that if the divisor and the dispositor are benefics, it would signify the health and safety of the body in the division or disposition, and his good condition (whatever circumstances it is in), and that time will be of a greater and better condition, and a better complexion, than the preceding ones. And this will happen more so in kings, the wealthy, and magnates, than in small men and paupers, or low class or mediocre men. And this will be better and stronger if the rays of some benefic are there, and the better condition this benefic is in, the better the natives' condition will be. However, if the divisor or dispositor is a malefic, and the division is found in the rays of some malefic, it signifies the bad condition of the native in that division or disposition; it also signifies infirmities and the bad temperament of the complexion of his body, according to the nature of this malefic, and according to its disposition; and the worse its condition is, the more oppressed his disposition will be in that time; and this will be worse if the rays of another malefic are present.

If the divisor or dispositor is a malefic, and the rays are of a benefic; or if the divisor is a benefic, and the rays are of a malefic, the condition of the native will be mediocre, that is, the native will sometimes be healthy, sometimes infirm, sometimes wealthy, sometimes poor, sometimes abounding, sometimes in need, sometimes losing, sometimes acquiring, sometimes putting his affairs in order, sometimes devastating or ruining them, sometimes miserly in things he should not keep, sometimes generous with things he should not spend.

However, if the benefic is impeded, his condition will incline more to the side of adversity, than to the side of prosperity. Indeed, if the malefic is well disposed, his condition will incline more to the side of prosperity than adversity.

## IV

### On The Knowledge Of The Directions Of The Rays Of The Planets To The Ylem

If you wish to direct the degree of some planet to the Ylem, in order to know the life of the native and his condition for the whole time of his life, and his disposition with his accidents, see whether the Sun or the Moon is the Ylem (or whichever other one of the planets or degrees). Since it is necessary for you to consider the disposition of the rays of the planets, and of their projection to the Ylem, and to examine for the place of the planet or the degree which is the Ylem, and see in what place or in what degree he is by equal degrees and their minutes. And when you have done this, see which planet projects its own

rays to it by whatever aspect it is (even opposition), by equal degrees and their minutes, and reduce them to equal degrees by the ascensions of the region: and those will be called the rays of that planet. Then we ought to examine in what degree of that sign the planet is in, and reduce them into degrees of ascension, and this will be called the degrees of the body of that planet. You will even find the Ascendant and the rest of the houses by degrees of ascensions of that region.

And many of the ancients operated according to this method, and especially those who were following in the footsteps of Dorotheus, who was one of the few more noble men who applied themselves to this work. Nor was this contrary to the opinion of Ptolemy, even if it might seem somewhat different from it; but it is an easier method, and therefore many of the ancients followed in his footsteps.

An example of such a matter is this: posit that the Ylem is in the seventeenth degree of Leo, and the planet whose direction you intend to make is in the twenty-eighth degree of Pisces. The seventeenth degree of Leo (in which the Ylem) is placed, is to be directed to the twenty-eighth degree of Virgo, to the rays of the aforementioned planet (whether it is a benefic or a malefic, provided that benefic is then a killer, which sometimes happens). Then subtract the ascensions which are in the straight line of the degree of the Ylem from the ascensions which are in the straight line of the twenty-eighth degree of Virgo, where the opposition of the killing planet is; and the natives years (absolutely) will be as many as the degrees which remain, of which there are forty one. Likewise you will see if one of the increasers of years add any years, or if one of the decreasers of years diminishes something of these years, and you will judge the number of years of the native's life according to this - regarding which I will tell you below when the directions of the planets according to the terms is dealt with.

Aomar said that Ptolemy used another method, however, it was contrary to this, even if it seemed different from it (it might have seemed more difficult to some). For I say that the intention of Ptolemy was according to the disposition of the Lords of the terms, and according to the division of their disposition in them. For he said, that all rays are congregated in the centre point of the earth, and become one thing; and that it is necessary for us to know the diversity of rays according to the position of the place, beginning to operate on the rays by the longitudes of the planets from the angles by the ascensions of the city in which we are, and by the ascensions of the right circle. And when you do so, and you arrange the places of the planets, you will direct the Ylem and the degree of the Ascendant according to these longitudes, as was said. And if you see it arrive at benefics, judge good. And if you see it arrive at malefics, judge the contrary, according to what you see of their condition, and of their strengths or weaknesses, and of their fortune or misfortune - and this, if the Ylem is from the 10th to the 7th, according to the succession of signs. Indeed, if it is between the 7th and the 10th, these things are done backwards, namely against the succession of signs, namely subtracting the ascensions of the degree of the Ylem from the ascensions of the degree of the malefic, if it is in the aforementioned places to which you were directing, even though certain men appear to want something else.

And understand the same as this for the Caput Draconis, that is, if you direct the Ylem to the Caput, whatever kind of Ylem it is, whether it is the degree of the Ascendant, or the degree of the Moon, or another, you will direct backwards (namely, against the succession of the signs), subtracting the ascensions of the degree of the Caput from the ascensions of the degree of the Ylem. Indeed, for the Cauda you will direct according to the succession of the signs, just as I told you above; and you will give years according to the number of degrees of distance.

And if the Ylem arrives to the western degree, or to the degree of the malefic who was between the tenth and the seventh (to which you directed the degree of the Ylem), then the native will die, unless a strong benefic then aspects that degree from a trine or sextile aspect, and with reception: since then it will not kill, but the native will be endangered by a danger similar to death; and if he does not watch himself, then he will die by the required rule, even if the error is slight.

## V

## On The Number Of Malefics And Benefics

The ancient sages said that there were four malefics, however, it seems to me that there can be said to be seven of them. Since even though they said that there were four, nevertheless they did not seem to exclude others. Whence I say that there can be seven: namely two naturally, which are Saturn and Mars; two accidentally, which are the Sun and Mercury; one by misfortune, which is the Moon; and two again by placement, which are the Caput Draconis and its Cauda.

The Sun specifically if he is corporeally joined with Mars, or in his opposition, or in his square aspect without perfect reception. And Mercury if he is combust, or in those aforementioned aspects with or without reception.

And the Moon if she is made unfortunate, as was said in the chapter on the impediments of the Moon. And Tiberiadis said that if these are congregated above Venus without the aspect of benefics, then the native will be a eunuch. If the primary triplicity Lord of Venus is strong, this will be of benefit to him: without this however, in addition to suffering this, he will be laborious, and in need of food for his belly for all the days of his life.

Indeed, the Caput Draconis is malefic if it is with malefics, and likewise the Cauda if it is with benefics.

Indeed, there are eighth benefics:

Four naturally, as are Jupiter, the Sun, Venus, and the Moon.

Two accidentally, as is Mercury when he is with the first four, or corporeally joined to one of them, or in their trine or sextile aspect with reception, or without reception; or in their square aspect or opposition with perfect reception; and if one of the malefics did not impede him without reception. And as are Mars and Saturn when they are both effectively united by body, which is if both of them are in the same minute, in the domicile or the exaltation of either of them, or in two of their lesser dignities, or even if there are five minutes or less between them (but with Mars moving towards Saturn), but in other places they are not made benefic, unless they are received by a benefic, but their malice will be withdrawn. And from this it is said that two malefics joined together make one benefic.

And two are malefic by place, as the Caput is, by increasing with benefics, and the Cauda is, by decreasing with malefics.

And they are called benefics because they help the works of the virtues and even the operations of nature. And therefore Jupiter and Venus are called benefics: since they always do this, each one of them according to its own power. And Saturn and Mars are called natural malefics: since each one of them by its own nature always strives to harm and impede the works of the virtues and operations of nature. The others can conduct themselves as either.

And you should know that it is said by the jealous and the ignorant, that all external goods are goods of a benefic; but they are prejudiced, since they are ignorant of what others know, loving neither those who know, nor knowledge, or in knowledge: since nothing is loved except what is known.

## VI

## On The Knowledge Of The Life Of The Native, And His Condition According To The Lords Of The Terms

To know the condition of the life of the native and his disposition according to the division of the terms of the planets, it is necessary that you first consider the projections of the rays of the planets; then that you direct the Ylem and its degree, as was said above, which I will repeat for you.

For if you wish to direct the Ylem to one of the planets, or to its rays, you will consider how many degrees of distance are between them according to the ascensions of the region of the nativity by the oblique circle, and you will give one degree to each year, and one month to every five minutes, and six days to every minute, according to this method.

For you will begin from the first minute of Aries for both the Ylem and the degree of the planet or its rays to which you are directing, and you will subtract the lesser from the greater; and that which

remains will be the distance or longitude which is between them; then you will give a year to each degree; and so on with the others, just as I have said to you now.

And Aomar said that you should always direct the degree of the Ascendant in nativities so that you can know the condition of the life of the native, since the degree of the Ascendant is the divisor, which is called algebutar. Of which work, even if I took it briefly from the ancients, I handed down such a teaching to you: namely, for you to examine whose terms the degree of the Ascendant and its minute are in, and how many degrees of those terms are left to be ascended in it by the oblique circle, to be ascended. Since that planet who is the Lord of these terms, will dispose the life of the native from the day and hour of his birth up until as many years and as many days and as many hours, as are those degrees, minutes, and seconds. Then you will subtract the ascensions of the last degree of those terms from the ascensions of the last degree of the following terms and their minute, and you will give one year to each degree of it which is left over, and one month to every five minutes, and six days to every minute, and the Lord of these terms will dispose the life of the native according to what his condition is, and his disposition for as many years, as many months, and as many days. Then you will subtract the ascensions of the last degree of the second terms from the ascensions of the last degree of the third terms, and you will give one year to each degree remaining which is left over, and the rest as was said above. For the Lord of these terms will dispose the life of the native for as many years, as many months, and as many days; and you will operate like this from terms to terms up until the end of the signs, for as long as the natives' life lasted. And you will always consider the condition of this planet who rules the terms, since according to whether he is good, bad, or mediocre, so will the life of the native be disposed, unless impeded by another. If this work exceeds the end of Pisces, you will start again from the beginning of Aries, and do as I said.

## If The Division Is With A Benefic

However, if you find the division to which you directed to be with one of the benefics, or in one of their rays, without the aspect or presence of one of the malefics, and the algebutar or divisor is a benefic, in those years the native will be in a good and praiseworthy condition in those years, and in tranquillity and the goodness of his life, and likewise in the increase of his affairs; and this will endure until the degree of the direction reaches a malefic or its degree. However, if a malefic aspects, it will subtract something of the goodness according to what its malice is, unless those degrees are his dignity. Indeed, if it has dignity there it will impede less.

## If The Division Is With A Malefic

And if this is with one of the malefics without the aspect of a benefic, and the divisor of those years is a malefic, the native will be in bad and detestable condition in those years; and he will be in difficulties, griefs, tribulations, and sorrows, and he will meet with evil, and diminution of his affairs, and want. However, if a benefic aspects it, it will reduce this malice according to what its goodness is. And if these degrees are its dignity it will be of more benefit.

## If It Is The Dignity Of Many Planets

However if many planets have dignity there, and they aspect this place, the planet who has more dignities or fortitudes there will be more deserving in the disposition of that time. Indeed, if one planet has one dignity, and aspects it, and another has more than one, and does not aspect it, each will be a participator, and deserving in disposition, and each one of them will dispose the life of the native according to its own condition, namely, according to its good or bad condition, just as said above.

## THIRD PART

### On The Form And Figure Of The Natives Body: And Likewise On Its Accidents, Generally And Particularly, And On The Qualities Of The Soul And On The Things Adjacent To These

It was discussed above (in the parts which preceded this part) about the determinations or species of nativities, and the things adjacent to them; and how many years and how much a space of life is attributed to each native. In this part it is fitting to make mention of the accidents, and the form and figure of the native's body, both in particular and in general, and on the qualities or accidents of the soul.

### I

### On The Form And Figure Of The Native

Therefore, if you wish to know this, you will consider the Ascendant in someone's nativity and its Lord, and you will see which planets are the Almutem in it, and according to the form and figure which it attributes, and according to the figure which the sign of the Ascendant attributes.

You will attend to the future form of the native generally, since natural action is according to the necessity of the form; but also by conjecturing from the signification of the planet to the sign, and the sign to the planet, and also from the added essence of the natives ancestors - since from similar causes are produced similar effects. And this can last until the seventh generation of their descendants; and each descendant can give something of his own essence to his descendants up to his own seventh generation; however, according to more or less, both in one and in another of its individuals: since a person proceeds from another person; for a person is an individual substance of rational nature. The same nature can be in the species of the man; nor does it seem discordant that individuals of a species draw likeness or appearance or complexion from the mothers more so than from their other ancestors, since they are nourished from the humours of the mothers in their wombs, even if the members are arranged from the seed of the father: for it is necessary that it follows from the necessity of matter. And since the truth of all the forms of figures of the world, and of the two kinds of humans, cannot be straightforwardly said or described (unless perhaps by an extremely long discussion generating boredom in the reader), it is necessary that you consider the mixture of significators from your industry and likewise your own discretion, both of planets and of signs, and of the places of the circle, coming together to attribute a form and figure to the native.

For everything which is established for this, is established so that it might do what is given to it by the Establisher. For you will not find anyone who is simply Saturnine, or Jupiterian, or Mercurial, or Solar, or Venusian, or Martial, or Lunar, and who is free of the significations of all the other planets, so that they have no part in him. And the sign also interposes some of its influence, and also the place of its position in the circle of the signs, and what I have just touched on above - the essences of the relatives. Whence Ovid

*"The son often tends to be like the father"*

Therefore consider the planetary Almutem in the hour of the nativity of him whose accidents you wish to know, and the ascending degree of this nativity; and you will take the signification of the form and figure of the native's body from the planet who is the ruler at that time. And it seems fitting to me that the form of the body of the native, on account of its density, is mentioned before the qualities of the soul, for the reason of certain accidents which will appear in its combination, which naturally precede the qualities of the soul. However, the qualities of the soul do not appear as manifestly, as the qualities of the body, but those things which the native acquired from the stars after his creation and nativity are perceived bit by bit, and step by step (which combined his body together, and which we see appearing).

## II

### On Those Things Which Are Outside Of The Body Which Are Not Of Its Substance Nor Of The Substance Of The Soul

Indeed other things existing outside of the body, such as gaining wealth, marriage, generating, and the like, usually happen a long time after the aforementioned things, all of which can naturally be known, and ought to be known, from the hour of the nativity and its Ascendant; but by accident or by habit sometimes nature tends to be taken away. Whence for this, so that we might know them, that we consider the stars which are in it, and those which are aspecting it, and likewise to rightly consider the condition of the Moon, just as each one will be discussed in its own place below. For the operations of nature are diversified in many ways: for they are diversified by the planets and the fixed stars, by customs, by nourishment, by the position of the regions, by preservation, and similar things; all of which would be useful to know, if possible.

We can even know each one of the knowable things better when we know its cause: for the act of cognition is the cognition of what is cognized or cognizable; for a place is owed to every mixed body according to the person and disposition of what is operating - since the perfection of a matter is taken up from its totality, since operating is more noble than the action which follows an agent. Whence by the actions of the supercelestial bodies their more noble effects or operations are made. For indeed, the stars regulate the inferior corruptible things collectively, namely every individual nature: wherefore the operations of stars in this respect are the same; according to the operations they are diverse. Wherefore, the form and figure of the bodies of natives are comprehended from the nature of the figures of the Ascendant, and from the planets and their conjunction with others, and from the signs, and from the fixed stars appearing in these places.

## III

### On The Form And Figure Of The Body Of The Native; And First On Those Which Saturn Bestows

If Saturn is the sole significator of a nativity, without the support or mixture of another, and he is oriental in the world, and from the Sun, Ptolemy said that the native will be of a temperate size, middling thickness, and a honey colour; his hair will be black, but it will be thick on his chest; curly hair on his head; coldness and dryness will prevail in his complexion.

However, if he is occidental in the world, and from the Sun, he will be lean, somewhat black, having a small body; having thin and straight hair on his head; his limbs suitably joined together; his eyes will be black, and dryness will prevail in his complexion.

And Dorotheus said he signifies a man with a very hairy body, with a unibrow. And Adila said that Saturn gives men a swarthy nature, making the hair thin on the beard; having a grey colour, sometimes a thin chest; rough and unkempt hair on his head; having sores or fissures in his heels.

### On The Participation Of Jupiter With Saturn

And if Jupiter is participating with Saturn, it signifies a man having a face which is not truly white, whose colour will be chestnut or olive, yet with a praiseworthy comeliness; his eyes will be blackish, of medium size, yet comely; his stature will be more than average, he will also be half-bald, some of his teeth not truly white, semi-curled, chestnut coloured hair on his head; his body hair not totally black, and it will be between thin and thick - and this, if both of the planets are oriental. If one of them is oriental and the other is occidental, it will be something below this. Indeed, if both of them are occidental, it will be much below this.

### On The Participation Of Mars With Saturn

Indeed if Mars is participating with Saturn, it signifies a man not very upright, semi-thick, whose colour will be blackish, with a certain unsightly redness participating. He will sometimes have some unsightly palestras on his face; his body hair semi-thin; the hair on his head will not be very black, but rather they will participate with a certain dark redness.

## On The Participation Of The Sun With Saturn

If the Sun is participating with Saturn, it signifies a man having an average stature, inclining more to the side of largeness than the side of smallness; whose colour will be almost imitative, so that it will seem to be able to participate with every other colour, but more so with blackish. And he will be of a more comely stature than with any of the other planets; and he will be semi-fleshy; having semi-thick eyes, a semi-full beard; chestnut or honey coloured hair on his head, between semi-curly and long. And the Sun adds something in the way of fatness to the body and form of the native, and beauty - more so than the rest of the planets.

## General Remarks

Moreover, if the Sun is oriental in the world, and even if the other planets are oriental in the world, or from the Sun, and are participating with Saturn, they add something to the size of the natives body. And if they are in their first station, they assist the bodies of the natives in making them stronger and more vigorous than at other times. Indeed, if they have passed their first station, the aforementioned things will be moderated, and made lesser according to how much more remote they are from it. And if they approach the second station, they will make the natives' bodies weaker according to how close they are to their second station. But if they fall into combustion, they will detract from the beauty and the form of the natives' bodies, and make them oppressed, impeded, and likewise wretched.

And even the places and the degrees in which the significators or dispositors of the natives (and the Moon) are, make for the disposition of the form and the figure of the body of any native, and his complexion, according to the nature and complexion of the signs in which these places or degrees are.

Indeed, if the significator had no latitude at the hour of the nativity, so that it is in the degree of its zenzahar or in its opposition, it signifies that the native will be lean. However, if its latitude is in greater latitude, he will be fat. Indeed, if it is between a great and a small latitude, he will be fleshy, and light on his feet, and easily bearing the burden of this fleshiness. And if it is between a greater and middle latitude, it will add on fleshiness up to fatness, according to its closeness to the greater latitude, and remoteness from the middle. And if it is between the middle and lesser latitude, he will diminish in fleshiness according to its remoteness from it, and its closeness to the zenzahar, until he reaches leanness.

And these things will occur more strongly if the Ascendant is at the end of a sign, or around it, and the Lord of the tenth house is occidental. And if the Lord of the Ascendant and the other significators are in a closer longitude, they will make for fatness. And if they are in a further longitude, they will make for leanness. However, it the latitude is southern, that is, so that the significator is from the point of its zenzahar up to its opposition, from the southern half (which is 179 degrees or less), the native will be light on his feet, as Haly attests, and this lightness will be according to more or less, just as his latitude is greater or lesser or in the middle: since the southern half is hot and dry, for which reason it lightens those things collectively which are perfected in it. However, if it is northern, namely from its own "cauda" up to the zenzahar, so that its distance is 179 degrees or less, he will be heavier and burdened on his feet, and slow in motion: since this half is most cold and moist, from which those things (collectively) which are perfected in it are made worse: and this according to more or less according to if its latitude is greater or lesser.

And you should know that the first station, and retrogradation, make for fattening; while the second station and being direct, make for thinning out. Nor should it be hidden from you that the relationship to his predecessors sometimes, in fact often, does much for the fattening and thinning out of the native, insofar as it precedes (and likewise for fleshiness).

## On The Participation Of Venus With Saturn

However if Venus is participating with Saturn, it signifies that the native will have such a bodily form that his colour will be almost blackish, or honey or olive, yet comely; and his hair on his head will not be truly greyish, nor truly chestnut; his face almost round, a middling jaw; his eyes praised for beauty by the majority of those seeing them; their blacks greater than if Saturn alone is the significator; having a becoming head of hair; and he will more often be semi-fleshy.

## On The Participation Of Mercury With Saturn

And if Mercury is participating it signifies that the native will be of a blackish colour, having a semi-raised forehead, a semi-long face, and his nose likewise semi-long; and semi-becoming eyes, inclining more so to black than to another colour, a black and thin beard, semi-long fingers, and of a suitable stature.

## On The Participation Of The Moon With Saturn

Indeed if the Moon is participating with Saturn, is signifies that the native will be said to have a white colour: yet his whiteness will not be bright and true, it will be in a certain sense tinged with cloudiness, with some mixture of redness; and he will have beautiful eyebrows, black eyes, a round face, a fine stature, comely enough; and he will have limbs suitably put together.

You should always understand this in any of the aforementioned planets, if any of them are well disposed. However, if they are badly disposed, all of these things will be much below what was said, according to the quantity of the impediment of any of them. And this will signify that the native will be deformed, inept, unsightly, horrible, and of a vile appearance, and disordered in the composition and unison of his members. And however, much it is Saturn or the planet who participates with him. in the aforementioned places or the ones to be stated below, by that much will it increase the deformity and ineptitude of the form, and likewise of the figure of the native's body.

Moreover, the sages said that the Moon assists the form of the native and his figure in the mixture of the combination, and makes him leaner than Saturn does when he is the sole significator: and this more greatly if she is separating by conjunction from any planet, or by aspect (but by conjunction more so), and is joined to Saturn, and this according to more or less, according to whether her body is illuminated, or her elongation is greater from him; up until she transits the projection of his rays upon her own rays.

## IV

## On What The Quarters Of The Circle Of The Signs Operate In The Disposition Of The Form And Figure Of The Natives Body, And First On The First Quarter

And even the quarters of the circle of the signs operate and make for the disposition of the form and the figure of the body of any native. For the first quarter (which is from the beginning of Aries up to the end of Gemini), which is called the vernal quarter, makes for the goodness and betterment of the form of the body of any native. Whence, if the Moon and all the other significators are in this quarter at the hour of the nativity, they will assist the form and figure of this native by increasing the beauty of his body, and the fitness of his stature, and his goodness, and the comeliness of his eyes; and they will give him a suitable fleshiness; in whose complexion, as Ptolemy attests, heat and moisture will prevail. However, if only certain ones of them are in it, they will perform the aforementioned things according to how they are found. The ones who are in the other quarters will operate according to the nature of those quarters in which they remain.

### On The Second Quarter, Namely The Summer Quarter

Indeed the second quarter, namely that which is from the beginning of Cancer up to the end of Virgo, makes for the goodness and betterment of the form and figure of any native's body. Whence, if the Moon and all the other significators are in this quarter at the hour of the nativity, they assist the form and figure of the body of the native, giving a temperate quality of the body, and a medium size of stature, and a suitable fleshiness, and a largeness of the eyes (yet not an unsightly largeness); and a thick and curly head of hair; in whose complexion, as Ptolemy attests, heat and dryness will prevail. However, if only certain ones of them are in this quarter, they will perform the aforementioned things according to what their nature is. Those who are in the other quarters will perform the aforementioned according to the nature of the quarters in which they are found.

### On The Third Quarter, Namely The Autumnal Quarter

Indeed the third quarter, namely that which is from the beginning of Libra up to the end of Sagittarius, which is called autumnal, makes for the goodness and improvement of the form and figure of the body of any native. Whence, if the Moon and all the other significators are in this quarter at the hour of the nativity, they will assist the form and figure of the body of the native, giving him a honey colour, a stature somewhere between average and thin, large shoulders, somewhat more than is fitting (yet not exceeding measure), his eyes suitable for his form; and an average head of hair; in whose complexion coldness and dryness will prevail. If however, only certain of them are found in this quarter, they will perform the aforementioned things in accordance with how it proceeds from their nature. Those who are placed in other quarters will operate according to the quarter in which you find them.

### The Final Quarter, Namely The Wintry Quarter

Indeed the final quarter, namely that which is from the beginning of Capricorn up to the end of Pisces, which is called the wintry quarter, makes for the goodness and betterment of the form, and also of the figure, of any the natives body. Whence, if the Moon and all the other significators are in this quarter at the hour of someone's nativity, they will assist the form and figure of the body of this native, giving him a colour inclining to black; and a becoming and temperate quality and size of his body, straight and thin hair on his head; a fit unison of his limbs; in whose complexion coldness and moistness will prevail. However, if only certain of them are in this quarter, they will perform the aforementioned in accordance with how it proceeds from their nature. Those who are found in other quarters will operate according to the nature of the quarter in which they are found.

## V

### On The Other Aids To The Forms And Figures Of Natives' Bodies, Besides The Aids Of The Quarters

Again, Ptolemy said that there are certain other supports which assist the aforementioned according to the places and positions in which they are found: and these are the signs which are likened to human figures, as are Gemini, Virgo, Libra, the first half of Sagittarius, and Aquarius. For they make for the symmetrical fashioning of the natives body, and also for the fitting unison of the members. Whence, if the Moon and the other significators are in these signs at the hour of someone's nativity, they will assist all of these things, and make the bodies of the natives more suitable for exercising them, and more apt.

Indeed, those signs which are not likened to the human form, as are Aries, Taurus, Leo, Scorpio, the final half of Sagittarius, Capricorn, and Pisces, make for the goodness of the natives body: for they render the body parts (which are assigned to these signs in which the Moon and the significators are placed), stronger and more temperate, and more ready and fitting for the actions assigned to them.

### Those Things Which Assist Particularly According To Largeness

Again, there are signs which help particularly in the form and figure of the body of the native, and its members in making them big, as do Taurus, Leo, and Virgo: since their forms are big in the heavens, but Taurus and Leo likewise assist them in making them strong.

### Those Which Assist According To Smallness

Indeed certain signs make for the smallness of bodies and limbs, as do Cancer, Capricorn, and Pisces: since their forms are found to be small in the heavens, yet they are smaller from the rear part than from the foremost part. Moreover, the first part of Aries, the first part of Taurus, and the first of Leo, assist the members of the native by making them more inclined to, and more apt in, taking up fat. Yet the final half of each of them inclines the body of the native towards leanness.

Indeed, the first half of Gemini, the first half of Scorpio, and the first half of Sagittarius enable the natives' body to support leanness. Indeed, their latter halves adapt the native's body to take on fat. Again, Virgo, Libra, and Sagittarius prepare the natives body for a temperate complexion of the body, and a good and fitting unison of the members. Indeed, Taurus, Scorpio, and Pisces impede them, and slacken them from temperateness, even if the slackening does not exterminate the temperateness. For it will seem fitting that you, from your own industry, together with the aforementioned, might skilfully perceive the aforementioned taken together in your mind, rightly and deliberately, according to more or less, according to the closeness of the significators to the aforementioned places, or their remoteness from them, according to how they are strong or weak, fortunate or unfortunate, so that you could judge more truly, more certainly, and more securely about the accidents of the native according to the condition of his nativity.

## VI

### On The Form And Figure Of The Native Which Jupiter Bestows

However, if Jupiter is the sole significator of a nativity, and he is oriental in the world and from the Sun (or either of them), it signifies that the native will be of a white colour, fitting, of a moderate stature and average height, having a white (and becoming and comely) head of hair; his eyes will be average, neither very big nor very small; in whose complexion heat and moisture will prevail. Indeed, if he is occidental, his whiteness will not be as fitting, as when he is oriental; the hair on his head will be straight; and he will be bald; having average eyes, average stature, in whose complexion moisture will prevail.

### On The Participation Of Mars With Jupiter

If Mars is participating, there will be some mixture of redness in his colour, and he will have eyes somewhat wider than when Jupiter is the sole significator. If Mars is oriental, he will have a mark on his right foot. If he is occidental, he will have it on his left (this rarely fails).

## On The Participation Of The Sun With Jupiter

But if the Sun is participating with Jupiter, it signifies that something will be taken away from his whiteness; however, he will be more comely than when Jupiter is the sole significator; and his stature will be somewhat less than average, yet it will be becoming, and comely. Having a somewhat curly head of hair, and his eyes will have some orangeness.

## On The Participation Of Venus With Jupiter

However if Venus is participating with Jupiter, it signifies that the native will have a colour inclining more to blackness; indeed, more comely than if it was inclining to another colour; a beautiful head of hair, almost honey coloured; yet it will not be of a determinate colour, for tis colour will be imitative. He will have a handsome stature, a semi-round face, not a big jaw, but a becoming one; beautiful eyes, apart from their blacks being somewhat bigger than they ought to be (yet they will not be unbecoming); a comely and handsome face; and he will be semi-bald.

## On The Participation Of Mercury With Jupiter

Indeed if Mercury is participating with Jupiter, it signifies that the native will have a colour slightly differing from the first; a semi-raised forehead, a semi-long face, a semi-long nose; comely eyes, not wholly black; a black and thin beard; semi-long fingers, a semi-slim body, an average stature, and thin lips.

## On The Participation Of The Moon With Jupiter

Indeed if the Moon is participating with Jupiter, it signifies a man not truly white, with a certain not true redness; becoming eyebrows; eyes not truly black, sometimes one bigger than the other, or flawed; with a round face and an average stature.

## On The Participation Of Saturn With Jupiter

And if Saturn is found to be participating with Jupiter, it signifies that the native will have a colour somewhat more beautiful than honey; sinking his eyes to the earth while walking along the road; having crooked feet, and joining them when he goes:;eyes which are not big; a unibrow; skin which is not decent, almost dry; thick lips; visible veins; a beard which is not thick; a rough and unkempt head of hair.

## What Form Jupiter Bestows Upon The Native If He Is Impeded

And if Jupiter is impeded in a nativity, and is unfortunate, in bad condition, and badly disposed, it signifies the contrary of those things which were said. If the planet who participates with him is likewise impeded, there will be even greater defect again in the form and figure of the native's body, and greater deformity. And the greater the impediment is, the more the natives deformity will be increased; and many contrarieties will befall him, just as is said above in the chapter on Saturn.

# VII

## The Form And Figure Of The Natives Body Which Mars Bestows

Indeed if Mars is the sole significator of the nativity, and he is oriental in the world (namely that he is above the earth), and from the Sun (that is, that he rises in the morning before the Sun), or either of them, it signifies that the native will not be of a healthy colour; and it will participate with a certain whiteness which is not very bright, and a certain redness which is not true.

And Ptolemy said that his body will be of a good size, and fitting fleshiness; his eyes will be varied, he will have a thick and average head of hair; in whose complexion heat and dryness will prevail.

## If Mars Is Occidental

And if he is placed occidentally, it signifies that the native will be of red colour; moderate stature; having small eyes; straight and thin head of hair; yet with a certain golden yellow; in whose complexion dryness will rule.

And Messala said that of the forms and figures of man it signifies a man who has a red colour, a red head of hair, a round face, wide eyes, a horrible glare [or countenance], a mark or blemish on his foot. Indeed, Dorotheus said the same about his glare [countenance].

However, Sacerdos said that Mars gives men having a crooked and semi-brown body, so that it is neither truly red, nor truly black, like those who stay too long in the Sun, or travel in the heat for a long time, and sometimes the Martial man has red grains on his face, and often wearing a thin beard, like a eunuch.

### On The Participation Of The Sun With Mars

If the Sun is participating with Mars, it signifies a man having a colour not truly white, nor truly red, nor truly brown, covered by a not truly red colour; semi-bald and semi-thick; a stature inclining to beauty and comeliness; a head of hair inclining to greyness more than another colour; eyes not truly black.

### On The Participation Of Venus With Mars

Indeed if Venus is participating with Mars, it signifies a man having a semi-red colour, with a certain becoming whiteness; an average and handsome stature; much, and becoming hair on the head; a semi-round face, an average jaw; decent eyes, and their blacks will be bigger than they ought to be, yet not unsightly; well fleshed, so that he could be said to be semi-thick; his face will be cheerful.

### On The Participation Of Mercury With Mars

Indeed if Mercury is participating with Mars, it signifies a man having a semi-slim body, an average stature; a colour inclining more so to that of Mars than to another, unless the conjunction of other planets operate to the contrary; a beautiful beard, even if it is thin and small; thin slips, and likewise a thin nose.

### On The Participation Of The Moon With Mars

Indeed when the Moon is participating with Mars it signifies a man having a beautiful and white colour, with a certain mixture of semi-redness; semi-wide eyes; beautiful eyebrows; a face that is almost round; and a decent stature.

### On The Participation Of Saturn With Mars

If Saturn is participating with Mars, it signifies a semi-thick man, not very upright, having an unsightly colour, sharing in a certain redness with a mixture of blackness; sometimes having unsightly marks on his face; semi-sparse body hair; a head of hair tinged between black and a certain dark red.

### On The Participation Of Jupiter With Mars

However if Jupiter is participating, it signifies a man having a colour with a certain amount of redness; semi-wide eyes; having a mark on one of his feet. I say all of these things if Mars and his participator are well disposed and in good condition; however, if they are in bad condition and badly disposed, say the contrary, as was said above in the chapters of the others.

## VIII

## The Form And Figure Of The Natives Body Which The Sun Bestows

However, if the Sun is the sole significator of the nativity, and he is oriental in the world, he signifies a man having a colour between saffron and almost black, covered with a certain redness or imitative colour (and according to certain men it signifies a white colour); an average stature, and sometimes inclining to the side of largeness rather than smallness; a beautiful and comely stature, and also bald.

And Dorotheus said that if you wish to know the figure of the Sun and the Moon, know that it will be just like the figure of the planets who are with them. And he said that if the Sun is in the Ascendant of someone's nativity, there will be a mark on the natives face; he will have a head of hair between saffron and the participation of a certain redness; eyes somewhat saffron.

Indeed, if he is occidental in the world, he signifies a man having a stature greater than average, an imitative colour, a blonde and long head of hair, sometimes a bit curly.

### On The Participation Of Venus With The Sun

If Venus is participating with the Sun, and she is well disposed, it signifies a man having an average and beautiful stature; a mixed colour of whiteness and redness, semi-bright, and becoming; with much and fitting hair on his head: appearing to participate with a certain baldness in the front, yet he will not be truly bald; his face almost round, and happy; not a big jaw; beautiful eyes; fleshy in such a way that he could nearly be called fat.

## On The Participation Of Mercury With The Sun

Indeed if Mercury is participating with the Sun, and he is well disposed, it signifies a man having a honey colour; and his colour will participate with the colour which is signified by the planet aspecting Mercury, or who is corporeally joined with him; he will have a beautiful beard, yet not big, nor overly thick; semi-wide and becoming eyes.

## On The Participation Of The Moon With The Sun

And if the Moon is participating with the Sun, and she is in good condition, it signifies a man having a beautiful and fitting colour, with a certain semi-clear whiteness, and with some admixture of redness; beautiful eyes; beautiful eyebrows; and a round face.

## On The Participation Of Saturn With The Sun

If Saturn is participating with the Sun by a good condition, it signifies a man having an average stature, and suitably comely; a honey colour; semi-wide eyes; semi-fleshy; a chestnut or honey coloured head of hair, and curly in a certain way.

## On The Participation Of Jupiter With The Sun

Indeed if Jupiter is participating with the Sun, it signifies a man having a honey, olive or chestnut, colour, which is almost the same, with some kind of whiteness mixed in, and decent enough; and a becoming enough stature; eyes somewhat saffron; a head of hair inclining to curliness in a certain way.

## On The Participation Of Mars With The Sun

However, if Mars is participating with the Sun, it signifies a man having blackness, but inclining to redness, not far from an imitative colour; stature following an average one, and comely; a semi-thick head of hair, almost grey; semi-wide eyes.

## IX

## On The Form And Figure Of The Natives Body Which Venus Bestows

And if Venus is the sole significator of a nativity, and she is oriental in the world, and from the Sun, it signifies a man having a colour (as Ptolemy says) which is beautiful and becoming, more so than the colour which Jupiter bestows; and his face will be soft, and formed more like the face of a woman than that of a man; and he will have a beautiful and becoming stature; blackish eyes, likewise becoming.

And Messala said, that of the figures of man, it signifies a white man, tending towards a shade of blackness; and from this he will appear more decent; having a beautiful stature; beautiful eyes, the blacks of which are found to be bigger than in others, yet fitting; a beautiful head of hair; a round face, yet not big, nor will his jaw be big.

And Dorotehus said that it signifies a man having a beautiful face; beautiful eyes, whose blacks will be greater than they ought to be; and a beautiful head of hair, dense, white, complete with a redness; in whose complexion moisture prevails. But if she is placed occidentally, her significations will be below the aforementioned; in this case coldness will prevail in his complexion.

## On The Participation Of Mercury With Venus

If Mercury is participating with Venus, and he is will disposed, it signifies a beautiful and decent man; having a beautiful colour; having a somewhat raised forehead; a long face, and likewise a long nose (and sometimes a thin one); beautiful eyes, not totally black; and long fingers.

And Sacerdos said it signifies a man having a slim body; average stature; a beautiful, yet thin beard (but not small); sometimes having thin lips.

## On The Participation Of The Moon With Venus

Indeed if the Moon participates with Venus, and she is in good condition, it signifies a man having a beautiful colour of whiteness and redness mixed together; semi-black eyes; beautiful and pleasing eyebrows; and a beautiful and average stature; but a round face; sometimes having one eye somewhat bigger than the other, or even defective.

## On The Participation Of Saturn With Venus

If Saturn is participating with Venus, it signifies a man having a honey or blackish colour, yet this colour will be fitting and becoming; a head of hair between greyish and honey; having a beautiful and decent quality from them; a semi-round face; average jaw; beautiful eyes, the blacks of which will be of a fitting size; and he will be semi-fleshy.

## On The Participation Of Jupiter With Venus

And if Jupiter is participating with Venus, it signifies a man having a blackish and decent colour; a beautiful head of hair, indeed, its colour will be imitative; a beautiful stature and blessed with beauty - for beauty is a harmony of parts, with a certain pleasantness of colour; a semi-round face; an ordinary and decent jaw; beautiful eyes, however, their blacks will appear somewhat bigger than they ought to, yet this will not detract from their beauty; a very beautiful face; and he will be semi-fleshy.

## On The Participation Of Mars With Venus

However Mars is participating with Venus, it signifies a man having a fitting colour, mixed of a whiteness and redness; a beautiful and average stature; much, and decent hair on his head; an average jaw; a semi-round face; beautiful eyes, their blacks somewhat overabounding, though not in an unsightly, way; semi thick; having a cheerful face.

## On The Participation Of The Sun With Venus

Indeed if the Sun is participating with Venus, it signifies a man having a beautiful colour, mixed with redness and whiteness, not very clear; an average and beautiful stature; a beautiful and decent head of hair; a happy face, which will be almost semi-round, semi-fat; with beautiful eyes.

# X

## On The Form And Figure Of The Body Of The Native Which Mercury Bestows

However, if Mercury is the sole significator of the nativity, and he is oriental in the world or from the Sun, and otherwise well disposed, it signifies a man having a honey, chestnut, or olive colour; his limbs united together fittingly enough; small eyes; an average head of hair, as much in quantity as in colour; with heat prevailing in his complexion. If he is occidental in the world, or from the Sun, it signifies a man having a saffron colour with a certain mixture of blackishness; lean; having a feeble voice; hollow eyes, the pupils of which will be goat like; inclining to the side of a certain redness; in whose complexion dryness will dominate.

## On The Participation Of The Moon With Mercury

But if the Moon is participating with Mercury, and she is oriental in the world, and from the Sun, and otherwise well disposed, it signifies a man having a beautiful colour, in which whiteness will prevail with a mixture of redness; with beautiful and benevolent eyebrows; eyes not totally black; a round and decent face; a fitting and beautiful stature. Indeed, if she is occidental, the significations will be below this; and this more so, if the Moon is impeded.

## On The Participation Of Saturn With Mercury

Indeed if Saturn is participating with Mercury, and oriental, it signifies a man having an almost blackish colour; his forehead somewhat elevated; an average face and nose; semi-decent eyes, inclining to blackness; a thin and black beard, average fingers; a fitting stature. Indeed, if he is occidental, the significations will be below the aforementioned.

## On The Participation Of Jupiter With Mercury

If Jupiter is participating with Mercury, and he is oriental, it signifies a man having a colour inclining to a certain decent blackness; imitative hair; a semi-round face; an average and fitting jaw; beautiful eyes, in which blackness will prevail; a fitting and beautiful face; a decent stature; and he will be semi-fleshy. If he is occidental, his significations will be something below the aforementioned.

## On The Participation Of Mars With Mercury

And if Mars is participating, and he is oriental, it signifies a man having a colour determined more to a certain untrue redness, with an admixture of a certain not true white, rather than to any other colour; a thin and small beard, yet not unsightly; thin lips and nose; an ordinary stature; often a slim body.

## On The Participation Of The Sun With Mercury

Indeed if the Sun is participating with Mercury, and he is oriental in the world, it signifies a man having a colour like honey; an average and beautiful beard, even if it is thin; decent and semi-wide eyes. However, if he is occidental in the world, all of his significations will be below the aforementioned.

## On The Participation Of Venus With Mercury

If Venus is participating with Mercury, and she is oriental in the world, or from the Sun, it signifies a man having a beautiful and decent colour; a long face, and likewise a long (and thin) nose; a raised forehead; beautiful eyes, not totally black; long fingers; a beautiful and decent stature.

And Sacerdos said, it signifies a man with a slim body; average stature; a beautiful but thin beard (yet not short); sometimes having thin lips.

And if Venus is occidental, all of the significations will be below the aforementioned.

## XI

## On The Form And Figure Which The Moon Bestows Upon The Native

Indeed if the Moon is the sole significatrix of a nativity, and she is oriental in the world, or from the Sun, and otherwise well disposed, it signifies a man having a white colour, mixed with a rosy red; inclining to leanness; benevolent eyebrows; eyes not totally big; a round face; and a wholly beautiful stature.

## On The Participation Of Saturn With The Moon

If Saturn is participating with the Moon, and they are well disposed, it signifies a man having a colour inclining to whiteness, yet not true whiteness, it will have a mixture of a certain redness; beautiful eyebrows; black eyes; a round face approaching leanness; a fitting stature; an apt unison of his limbs. However, if they are badly disposed, it signifies the contrary of those things which were said, for the native will be of vile appearance, nor will his members be fittingly united; and the more they both (or either of them) are unfortunate, all the more will be native be inept, deformed, vile, and horrible.

## On The Participation Of Jupiter With The Moon

However if Jupiter is participating with the Moon, it signifies a man having a colour which is not truly white, with some bright redness mixed in; beautiful eyebrows; semi-black eyes; a round face; a fitting stature; sometimes with one of his eyes defective.

## On The Participation Of Mars With The Moon

Indeed if Mars is participating with the Moon, it signifies a man having a beautiful colour; beautiful eyebrows; semi-wide eyes, in a certain way inclined to blackness; a fitting stature; a semi-round face.

## On The Participation Of The Sun With The Moon

But if the Sun is participating with the Moon it signifies a man having a decent colour with a certain agreeable whiteness and redness; beautiful eyebrows; beautiful eyes; and a round face.

## On The Participation Of Venus With The Moon

Moreover, if Venus is participating with the Moon, it signifies a man having a colour coming from a mixture of whiteness and redness, and very beautiful; decent eyebrows; eyes which are not truly black; an average and beautiful stature; a round face; suitable eyes, even if they are not completely equal.

*On The Participation Of Mercury With The
Moon*

Lastly, if Mercury is participating with the Moon, and he is well disposed, it signifies a man having a colour mixed of an agreeable whiteness and redness; beautiful eyebrows; semi-black eyes; a round face with decently symmetry; a decent stature, surrounded with beauty.

Understand all of these things which were said about the form and figure which the planets bestow upon the native as being common to both sexes. For you should know that such things ought to happen in a way otherwise than was said, if the planets are fortunate and well disposed; if it is to the contrary, you will judge to the contrary according to the quantity of the contrariety.

Having considered each and every one of the things which were said about the planets, and the rest (as I have touched on for you above), with the others having being introduced by conjecturing, by your discretion, and with the help of our Redeemer, Jesus Christ, you will even know a certain other thing, which sometimes impedes the natural course of the nativities - of which it is necessary for you to beware, this being, that the years of the nativities are changed in the nativities of children, practically according to how they are changed in the revolutions of the years (just as will be touched on below when the matters of the father are dealt with).

## ON THE FIRST HOUSE

### I

### On The Qualities Or Accidents Of The Natives' Soul

Having made mention in the preceding chapters about the form and figure of the body of the native and of its accidents, I think what we should discuss next are the qualities or accidents of the natives' soul, and to write about these to the best of my ability. On the rational soul first (as the more deserving and noble), subsequently about the sensible and vegetable soul.

Therefore it should be said that those things which particularly pertain to reason and intellect are perceived through Mercury.

However, that which is sensible and vegetable is perceived through the luminary who has authority. And if it is a diurnal nativity, it is perceived through the Sun only; indeed, if it is nocturnal, through the Moon and through the planet to whom she is joined, and who is alithirat with her, or even contrariety, or alitisal (whether conjunction or application).

However, we cannot arrive at cognition of it by one path alone, but by many. For there are six ways:

The first of which is to consider the condition of the Moon and Mercury.

The second is to consider the signs in which they are (namely one of them, or more).

The third is the consideration of the Lords of these signs.

The fourth is the conjunction of the planets in the figure of the hour of the nativity.

The fifth is what is the peculiar signification of each of the planet which is a participant in the figure of the nativity which the astrologer intends to consider.

The sixth is the consideration of the angles and their Lords, since the aforementioned significators, and likewise the signs, in which the qualities of the soul and the accidents are greatly assisted and helped.

Whence the significators are to be considered, and the signs in which they are placed are to be considered, and likewise the angles.

### On The Three Superior Planets

If the three superior planets are oriental from the Sun, or from the Lord of the Ascendant, or are in the Ascendant or in its angles, or in the almuguea of the Sun. the Moon, or the Lord of the Ascendant, they make the soul liberal, fit for freedom, fierce, and confident of his own counsel; generous and frank, bringing forth his thoughts into the open, but not very discreetly

### On The Signifying Stars

And if the signifying stars are in their first station, and they are fortunate and strongly placed (and this more so if they are found around the cusp of the tenth house), they will announce the natives' soul to be a thinking one, and a steward of goods, and of good memory, and good capacity; and of good intellect; stable, calm, and immovable; magnanimous, unconvertible, not deceptive, lawful, understanding, a lover of works, a truthful dream interpreter, and very experienced in such and similar things.

### On The Three Inferior Planets

Indeed when the three inferiors remain in the aforementioned places, and they are direct, occidental, and strong, and particularly in nocturnal nativities (even though in diurnal nativities they will do something less than this), they will make the native's soul weak, easily changing itself from one proposition to another, cowardly and unfortunate, false; slow and sluggish at things to be understood, or known; timid and scared; a lover of great tempests of falsity; gladly remaining alone.

Indeed, Ptolemy appeared to say that when the three superiors are in opposition to the Sun (namely in the middle of retrogradation), then they are hidden in the beginning of the day. However, when they are united with the Sun, then they are hidden in the beginning of the night (this is true), and then they become as weak as they can be, and make the soul useless and of little goodness. And when they are oriental, or in their first station, they are strong, and make the soul strong. And when they are retrograde, they are weak, and make it inert. And when they are in their second station they make it average. However, when they are direct and oriental, then they are stronger, and make the soul strong and skilful at exercising its strengths.

## On Venus And Mercury

With regards to Venus and Mercury, Ptolemy said that if they are in their first station and the nativity is diurnal (or if they are in their second station and the nativity is nocturnal), then they are mediocre, and make the soul mediocre, neither good nor bad, but fit to be inclined to both the good and the bad.

Abohali seemed to say that if they are in their first station, and the nativity is nocturnal (or if they are in their second station and the nativity is diurnal) they are very strong, and make the soul strong. And if they are in the middle of their direct motion, they are weak, and make the soul weak, agile, and easily changing itself from one proposition to another, faint-hearted and unfortunate, and loving faint-heartedness, gladly remaining alone.

## On The Three Superiors

However if the aforementioned three superior stars are in their second station, and they are in the tenth around its cusp; or Venus and Mercury when they are retrograde and entering under the Sun's rays, or are under them, and the nativity is diurnal, or if they are direct and entering under the aforementioned rays, or are placed under them, and the nativity is diurnal - make the natives' soul pure, sensible, and gentle; but it will not have a perfect memory; avoiding and fleeing labour; and it will be an investigator of secret matters, and the most precise investigator of occult things, and especially of the sciences: as are necromancy, magic, and other profound and hidden sciences; it will even be effective in certain wondrous and precise things, as are the judgements of the stars, interpretation of dreams, and similar things.

## On Fixed Signs

For if the significators and the angles they are in fixed signs, they make these accidents, or these qualities come into the soul: wherefore they make it benevolent, upright, legal, not deceiving, not easily changing itself, stable, enduring many difficulties and labours, and much efforts; easily understanding and talented, true and rigid, and achieving its goals; often free of malices, optimally defending itself from pleasures. A collector of things which it sees or hears, and of words, as much the worthless as the precious, leaving behind little or none of them, and committing them to memory; jealous in useful matters, and especially in the sciences, for it does not want to be outdone by others; a lover of honour and matters from which praise is acquired; and in a good part contentious in lawful matters; passing beyond the abilities of other souls; only changing itself with difficulty from one proposal to another.

## On Common Signs

However, if the Ascendant and the aforementioned significators are in common signs, on account of their multiformity and mutation they will make the soul multiform, slow and burdensome to act, difficult to be understood appropriately, easily loving, and easily leaving love behind; unstable, cunning, wanting this one minute, that the next; persevering well in few things; and it will be suited to gaining knowledge of music; easily regretting of things, both good and bad; however, it will be of perspicuous intellect.

## On Mobile Signs

Indeed if they are in mobile signs, they will make a man eagerly staying in cities, and associating with others on account of the mobility of these signs; they make the soul loving matters of communities and societies; likewise desirous of praise, and they make it a ponderor of the divine, and it will be of praiseworthy intellect, and fit to move itself towards those things which it ought to; an investigator of matters; and liberal, and of a good opinion towards almost everyone indifferently; and sharp sighted and prophetic in the judgements of the stars.

## On The Stars Disposing The Soul Of The Native

Again, the Moon and Mercury are to be considered, as to whether they (or the planets in whose domiciles, exaltations, terms, or triplicities they are placed) are in the aforementioned places, or their own peculiar dignities, or if they are in their aym: since then they will make the natives' soul generous and frank; the peculiar characteristics of which will be: free, prosperous, and effective; nor could this be frustrated, unless something contrary to its nature checks this. And this more greatly so, if one and the same significator were the Lord of the places in which the Moon and Mercury are, or is associated to them, or at least if one of them has alitisal with the Moon. However, if it were otherwise than what was said: that is, that the aforementioned stars (namely, one of the five other planets) are not the rulers of the places of both of them (namely the Moon and Mercury), or one of them; and are not associated to them, nor to either of them: you will examine which one of those two planets one of the others is closer to, since the natives' soul will be disposed according to how Mercury or the Moon, or the planet associating with them is disposed.

However, if the aforementioned five planets are outside of their dignities, or otherwise badly disposed, they will signify and make the natives' soul contrary to what was said: since his qualities will be harsh, hidden, and imperfect, without prosperity.

Indeed, Baruch said that the star ruling the places in which the Moon and Mercury are, or who were elevated over them, will make the natives' soul do rigid and harmful works (I say this if they are malefics or made unfortunate), and they will make the native do unjust things, and the soul of this native will easily move itself to impede others, and willing to harm them, nor will it be reformable from through its own discernment, nor will it seem troublesome to hurt others, but it will delight in these things.

But if those impeding them in the places of stars are malefics which are in the aym contrary to them, they will make the natives' soul weak and detestable, and easily changing from one proposition to another (and this will more likely be to a bad one than a good one); and from these occasions unfortunate things will befall the native, with torments harming him. The way by which the natives' soul becomes inclined to the aforementioned things, will be the way by which it will become joyous in the good deeds of others, and inclining towards the good when benefics are the significators, and he himself free from impediments, and nothing impeding were elevated above them. Then it will please the natives' soul to do good for others, and it will delight in this; nor will disagreeable things will not follow from these good deeds, in fact utility and good praise will.

But if the significators are benefics, and malefics are elevated above them, it will not be the same condition for the natives' soul with the aforementioned, for it will be altered, and the qualities of the natives' soul will be soft and benevolent, not rigid, not harsh, in fact it will be quiet; but something of those things which I said to you will befall the native, since on account of his humility, level headedness, softness, peacefulness, benevolence, abstinence from evil-doing, piety and love which he has for men, he will be reviled, spurned, and blamed by them, and accused when he is innocent, and people will rashly believe the evil things which are falsely said of him, and discernment will be found in almost none, or very few, in excusing him; nor will his words be listened to, and he will almost be reputed for nothing in everything (even when he should be praised and reputed as genuine, and his counsel will be found to be sound); and many false pretexts will be imposed on him. And his friends will easily leave him, practically without cause, and the more he is of service, the less he will be thanked, and his service reputed as nothing; and men will often strive to harm him, not only others, but also those who he served well; and most of what he involves himself in will turn out badly for him.

This is the way through which the general qualities of the minds of the natives are known and forecasted. However, with regards to the particular qualities which are to come about according to the nature of the stars or planets, we must examine them one by one below.

## II

## On The Qualities Of The Natives' Soul Occurring Particularly, According To The Natures And Significations Of The Stars

Having already spoken about the qualities generally happening to the natives' soul, now mention is to be made of the particular qualities happening peculiarly to it, which tend to happen to the natives' soul according to the natures and qualities of the stars.

### On The Signification Of Saturn If He Is The Sole Dispositor Of The Qualities Of The Native's Soul

Therefore, you can say, that if Saturn alone is the dominator or dispositor of the qualities of the natives' soul, and is the Almutem of the places in which the Moon and Mercury are placed, and is oriental in the world and from the Sun, and in an angle, and is otherwise well disposed, and not impeded, according to Ptolemy it will make the natives' soul a lover of just and good men; of solid and profound counsel; confident its own counsel; a debater; sustaining labour; not always using truth, for it will not be but that it will keep something of its own malice to itself; loving enrichment; desirous of having dignities; not keeping its promises well, nor remaining firm in them; eagerly treasuring things; jealous; hiding its secrets from others.

### If Saturn Is In Bad Condition

And if Saturn in those things mentioned above is found to the contrary, and he is detestable in his condition, or in the place in which he is placed, he will make the natives' soul base, impure, faint-hearted in knowledge, only trusting in its own counsel; yet not knowing what kind of counsel this is; and always believing itself to be deceived in the counsel of others; jealous, timid, not brave; recoiling from association with men; a lover of secrecy and mourning; unfortunate; cunning, shameless, laborious, a deceiver; loving nobody, malevolent; never knowing for the entire time of its life how to use its goods so that it might rejoice in them or from them.

### If Saturn Is Neither Good Nor Bad

Indeed if Saturn is found to be neither totally well disposed, nor totally badly disposed, you will announce what the qualities of the soul will be according to his condition. But if he inclines more towards freedom than towards impediment, you will judge the good to be less removed; however, if he inclines more towards impediment than towards liberation, you will judge the evil to be less removed.

### On The Signification Of Saturn If He Is Joined To Jupiter

If Jupiter is joined to Saturn, and he is in good condition and well disposed (namely oriental in the world, and from the Sun), and is in an angle, he will make the natives' soul just, eagerly honouring elderly and decrepit men; and it will be of sound counsel, eagerly coming to the assistance of others and helping them; having good renown; a giver of gifts; magnanimous, patient, tranquil, a lover of friends, and desirous of philosophy.

### If Jupiter Is Badly Disposed

However, if his disposition is contrary to what is said above, it makes the natives' soul unacquainted with doing good, irrational in matters, and eagerly applying itself to, and conversant with, and delighting in diabolical words; loving hypocrisy, pretending to gladly spend time in houses of prayer, when internally it is found to the contrary; even predicting the future without having knowledge of letters; not inclined to delights; recoiling from having children; in no way wishing to have friends; desiring to live in places remote from habitations; not wishing to associate with men. And although he is stupid, sometimes he will have words similar to those of the wise; not seeking honour; not caring for praise; choosing evil things rather than good things, and eagerly adhering to them; weak and malicious; and if he ever exercises any good things, he will quickly regret of them; laborious, and not loving peace.

## If Jupiter Is Neither Well Disposed Nor Badly Disposed

Indeed if Jupiter is found in a disposition which is neither totally good, nor totally bad, he makes the quality of the natives' soul the quality of his own condition. If his condition inclines more to good than to bad, then the qualities of the soul will incline more to good than bad. But if his condition inclines more to bad than to good, it makes the qualities of the soul incline more to bad than to good. And you will always be able to prognosticate according to his condition.

## On The Significations Of Saturn If Mars Is Joined To Him

However if Mars is joined to Saturn, and he is in good and praiseworthy condition, namely in an angle, and oriental in the world and from the Sun, and not impeded, as Ptolemy says, on account of the malice of both of them, it makes the natives' soul not understand that which it ought to understand; miserable, ineffective, harmful, laborious, faint-hearted, hardly ever attempting anything (and if he does, it will be with the greatest fear); impious, grave, an imposter, and if it contains magnanimity in himself, it will be criticizing almost everything, having no organised method in itself, and with a certain hypocrisy against its own nature, making itself out to be bellicose, while it is timid in all things; but still pretending to be the contrary, and therefore it will be said to be bellicose (when it is a frightened little girl); loving disturbances; jealous with the worst jealousy; a traitor; persevering in its malice, nor easily moving itself away from it; a laborious native, and gladly making others to be laborious; loving hypocrisy; having hatred for kings, princes, rulers, magnates and all of his superiors; bragging about himself from others victories, or ascribing them to himself; having nothing in goodness or depth; full of rusticity, grave in things to be tolerated; unfair; gladly harming men, and hating them, scorning them and despising them; nor will it be altered or changed from the above said things, but will always persevere in them; involving itself in trades and many and diverse other things, and he will not persevere well in any of them.

## If Mars Is In A Condition Contrary To What Is Said Above

Indeed if Mars is in a condition contrary to what was said, he will make the natives' soul a pillager, and make the native a highwayman; and Mars will make him of awful qualities, not knowing God, nor revering Him, nor fearing Him, nor loving Him; eagerly profiting by unlawful means; a blasphemer; disturbing; not truly loving anyone; given to stealing; a traitor, a deceiver, a killer, immodest, impure, evil, sacrilegious, a necromancer; the native himself murdering his own; a fornicator, a violator of tombs, and generally wretched in all matters.

## On The Signification Of Saturn If Venus Is Joined to Him

If Venus is joined to Saturn, and she is well disposed, and is oriental in the world and from the Sun, and likewise in an angle, it will make the natives' soul peaceful, benevolent, faithful, modest, abstinent, considerate, a lover of knowledge, abstaining from impurities, loving God, and fearing Him, and having reverence for Him.

## If Venus Is In The Contrary Condition

However if Venus is in a condition contrary to what is mentioned above, it will make the natives' soul of evil undertaking, and of evil opinion, and of evil law; shameless, impure, irksome, loving itself, recoiling from women, desirous of disgraceful and unclean sexual intercourse, as is that horrible and blameworthy sodomitical kind, and similar things (and this will be with old and filthy men): with regards to women, choosing an unsightly and deformed one, not caring for the beautiful ones; and sometimes allowing himself to be deceived by women; separating himself from everyone; only confident in his own counsel; a fornicator of every shameful and perverse fornication; ignorant, adulterous; shameless, and delighting in shameless things; lewd, and carrying out his lewdness with his own relatives rather than with others; attracted to disgraceful sex acts, and those against nature, not only with rational beings but also with brutes; and proud, worthless, insulting, sinful, hiding his thoughts from others, not having reverence for God, despising dreams and other secret things, involving himself in necromancy and of many other different things.

## *On The Significations Of Saturn If Mercury Is Joined To Him*

And if Mercury is joined to Saturn, and he is in good condition and well disposed, and is oriental in the world and from the Sun, and likewise in an angle, and not otherwise impeded, he makes the natives' soul an inquirer into the law and legal matters, and investigating of necromancy; a lover of medical science; a deliberator of hidden matters; and hiding itself from others; a sophist; a necromancer; demonstrating itself to do wondrous things both in the presence of men, and without their presence; of good intelligence; easily explaining things to be explained; a good investigator of things to be investigated, but having an acute bitterness in himself, a lover of understanding almost all works; and things turning out well for him from this.

## *When Mercury Is Badly Disposed*

If however, Mercury is disposed to the contrary of what was said above, it will make the natives' soul turbulent, jealous, laborious, hateful of men (and especially his own relatives); nor will he desire to see them; and he will be pained by their good things, and will rejoice from their bad things; a lover of sorrows; seeing fantasies in the night which will disturb him; a deceiver, a traitor, a concealer of his own business matters; eagerly adhering to necromancy, and utility will not follow from it, but the contrary.

## III

## On The Significations Of Jupiter If He Is The Sole Significator Or Dispositor Of The Qualities Of The Soul

If Jupiter is the sole dispositor of the qualities of the natives' soul, so that he is the Almutem over the places in which the Moon and Mercury are, and he is oriental in the world and from the Sun, and likewise he is in an angle, and otherwise well disposed, and not impeded, it will make the natives' soul just, generous, magnanimous, even, modest, and it will make the native famous; benevolent, liberal, fair, gentle, distinguished, pious, having great thoughts of his own works; lovable to men, gladly doing good, knowing how to establish rule, and a conductor of matters, and the like.

If Jupiter is in contrary condition to what was said above, it will make the natives' soul weak and hidden, without good intellect; wasteful, demonical, and exercising his services in demonic matters; of evil opinion, deceitful and something to watch out for; loving delights and desires; obstinate; disdaining and ignorant of knowledge; he will be wishing to be similar to the other things mentioned above, but it will be much below this.

## *On The Significations Of Jupiter When Mars Is Joined To Him*

And if Mars is joined to Jupiter, and he is in good condition and well disposed (namely oriental in the world and from the Sun), and he is in an angle, in no way impeded, it will make the natives' soul cunning, an appeaser; eagerly litigating; and delighting in controversies; bellicose and of an arranger of wars; and a leader of armies (and especially of those who are on the side of justice); very strong, humbling himself to no one; loving revenge and overcoming others; not wanting to be placed under others, or subject himself to others; wishing to promote himself to dignities and rulerships; not ignorant of the truth of matters; seeking honour and influence, with prosperity following from this; prudent, irritable and deceitful; commanding many men to do many things.

## *When Mars In The Aforementioned Is Placed In Contrary Condition*

Indeed if Mars is placed in contrary condition to what was said above, he will make the natives' soul blasphemous, shameless, a malicious divulger of his own words, and his own secrets and those of strangers; comprehending things which are to be comprehended; explaining things which are to be explained; despising others; hypocritical, proud, a deceiver, disobedient, a highwayman, a plunderer, losing his own things, a confuser of men (using evil words); low-class, unfaithful, unstable, of ill-repute, and bad counsel; irrational, easily changing from one proposition to another, having an existence of diverse qualities, and a certain way of life will not be found in him.

## On The Significations Of Jupiter If Venus Is Joined To Him

However if Venus is joined with Jupiter, and she is in good condition and well disposed (namely oriental in the world and from the Sun), likewise in an angle, and free from impediments, it will make the natives' soul polished, simple, without malice, loving professions and the investigation of things; desirous of games, songs, feasts, foods, and drinks; and it will be of good capacity and good opinion, and good counsel; pious; a lover of God, and serving Him, and labouring in His love; humble, rational, obliging, eagerly reading books and thinking about matters while at leisure; temperate with regards to sexual matters, and acting according to His law; and a lover of his relatives; desirous of honour and a good reputation; just and upright.

### If Venus Is Impeded

If Venus is contrary to the condition above, it will make the natives' soul irritable, and his anger will be similar to the anger of women; irrational; and wasteful (especially in matters of women); libidinous, shameless or ill-mannered; ;easily making jokes in stupid matters; a gift giver; offending; ornamenting his body; ignorant of friends; extolling himself; not very free of trouble amongst men (for he will blush in their presence); allowing himself to be impeded for a trivial reason; having a feminine sense; competent in matters pertaining to the oversight of the Church - if he adheres to them, he will prevail; and loving of these things; faithful, ignorant of evil things; submissive in all of his acts, both in serving others and in his own affairs; dignified; yet in all of his own works he could be said to be something other than commendable.

### On The Significations Of Jupiter If Mercury Is Joined To Him

Indeed if Mercury is joined to Jupiter, and he is in good condition and well disposed, namely fortunate and strong, oriental in the world and from the Sun, and is in an angle, not otherwise impeded, it will make the natives' soul apt for syllogisms, geometry, eagerly reading books at leisure, and studious of them, expert in all areas of mathematics, a sermoniser, a versifier; good-natured; an arranger; a lover of associations; providing sound counsel; good quality, and of good opinion, and good belief; having a bountiful and good nature; and gladly and quickly finishing all things which he begins; and if he adheres to medicine he will make progress greatly in it, and honour and utility will follow from it; and the native will be called by kings, magnates, nobles, and the wealthy for this reason, and they will gladly submit themselves to his care; loving God, and holding Him in reverence and fear; and he will love his relatives and neighbours; having riches, and be a rational lover of the sciences.

### If Mercury Is In Contrary Condition To What Is Said Above

Indeed if Mercury is in a condition contrary to what was said above, and he is impeded, it will make the natives' soul stupid, ignorant, irrational, and speaking a lot in his discussions; often and more often deceived; and he will easily lose that small bit of sense which he has; impetuous; wishing to adhere to divine things, yet not knowing how to do so; morose; proud in persevering in his stupidity; reputing himself as wise; placing himself in the service of another; disorganised in his own actions and movements; verbose, feigning to the public; for he will not know how to hide what he is feigning; yet he will have some bit of memory, and even some bit of erudition.

## IV

### The Qualities Of The Soul If Mars Is The Sole Significator

If Mars is the sole significator or dispositor of the qualities of the natives' soul, and he is in good condition and well disposed, namely oriental in the world and from the Sun, and in an angle, and not otherwise impeded, it will make the natives' soul very strong, very powerful, hot-tempered, courageous, one that seeks arms, indeed, appropriating all arms to himself; humbling himself before nobody; putting himself in danger of death for the sake of any matter; caring little or nothing for financial profit; destroying almost everything; wanting to be first in war; despising everything; wanting to bring violence into everything, trusting more of his own powers than of the entire rest of the world.

## If Mars is Badly Disposed

Indeed if Mars is in contrary condition to what is said above, it will make the natives' soul proud, stupid, irrational, a whisperer, irritating, a blasphemer, garrulous, impious, a pillager, a deceiver, a waster and destroyer of things, delighting in bloodshed, rejoicing in the harm and detriment of others, recoiling from his relatives, ignorant of his Creator, and not holding Him in reverence.

## On The Significations Of Mars If Venus Is Joined To Him

Indeed if Venus is joined to Mars, and she is in good condition and well disposed, namely oriental in the world and from the Sun, and in an angle, and not otherwise impeded, it will make the soul cheerful and pleasant, good-natured, making the native good, lovable; even rejoicing, and of a happy or peaceful life, with games; loving his associates; well disposed according to the complexion of the natives body; and a fit form of the body; desiring dancing and feasting, and loving them and eagerly engaging them; eagerly adhering to beautiful women, and gladly spending time with them and reasoning with them; pursuing delights, and knowing how to lead a good and praiseworthy life; easy in sexual intercourse, with benefit following from this; wise, modest, understanding what ought to be understood, knowing how to guard himself against useless, illicit, and dangerous or unnecessary things; but easily angered, meanwhile a selfish destroyer of his own matters, abusing men by means of sodomy, sometimes destroying their goods.

## If Venus Is Badly Disposed

And if Venus is in a contrary condition to what was said above, it will make the natives' soul offending, and remaining in the contraries of what was said above: for it will make it excessive in sexual intercourse, bending itself now to this kind, then to another; a blasphemer, a deceiver, betraying and deceiving both his own and others; scornful; desirous of illicit things; easily desiring things; and easily and quickly retreating from what was sought; a doer of illicit and prohibited sexual intercourse, or a corruptor of women (such as of nuns, virgins, and brides); disordered, sly; sharp, even in malices; and always striving in the qualities of its own vices;

and falling into shame many times on this occasion; making the native of worthless intellect, almost irrational, impetuous, eagerly committing disgraceful things, and eager to ornament his body.

## On The Significations Of Mars If Mercury Is Joined To Him

If Mercury is joined to Mars and he is well disposed and in good condition, and is oriental in the world and from the Sun, and likewise free in an angle, and not otherwise impeded, it will make the natives' soul of mixed and diverse qualities: for it will make it wise and able, a lover of things to be loved, an understander of things to be understood; knowing how to govern; easily changing from one proposition to another, desiring to arrive quickly at what was proposed, sometimes, in fact often, gladly engaging in evil; cunning, a traitor, sharp, unstable, frenzied, having a shallow intellect, a deceiver, loving hypocrisy, obstinate, astute, a shapeshifter delighting in disputes and discord, a great investigator of any matter; nevertheless things will turn out unfortunately for him from all of these reprehensible things; loving those like himself, and eagerly benefiting them and assisting them; hating those inimical to him, and intending to harm them in all ways, and knowing well how to do this.

## If Mercury Is In Contrary Condition To What Is Said Above

And if Mercury is in a contrary disposition to what was mentioned above, it will make the natives' soul appear to know something, when it knows almost nothing; for it will be irrational, almost foolish; making itself out to be obedient when its obedience does not come from obedience, but rather from a certain foolishness; quickly regretting everything that he does or begins; not knowing how to choose the good part of them; wishing to be called wise, when he knows almost nothing; a deceiver, disordered, a destroyer, maintaining no right order in his movements, thieving, deceptive, sly, wretched, falsely speaking, a perjurer, loving discord and controversies; base; yet wishing to be called virtuous; a blasphemer, a pillager: eager to misuse roads and dig under walls; performing incantations; a traitor, a killer or murderer; a necromancer; not having reverence for God.

## V

### If Venus Is The Sole Significatrix Of The Qualities Of The Native's Soul

Indeed if Venus is the sole significatrix of the qualities of the natives' soul, and she is in good condition and well disposed, namely oriental in the world and from the Sun, and is in an angle, and not otherwise impeded, she makes the natives' soul just, humble, and likewise peaceful, rational, having riches, and using them in a good way; suffering injuries; deliberating wisely in matters; a lover of games, dances, and feasts; recoiling from impieties; having reverence for God; pursuing knowledge of professions; bestowing a beautiful form and good quality to the native; dreaming good dreams; lovable, pious, doing good, prospering; nevertheless, lazy with all of these things; impudent; making the native effeminate, and his qualities similar to those of a woman's, not courageous, and not well acquainted with this; and not making the native magnanimous, in fact his name will almost be nothing amongst other names; and making him easily rushing into the majority of his professions.

### On The Significations Of Venus, If Mercury Is Joined To Her

And if Mercury is joined to Venus, and he is in good condition and well disposed, oriental in the world and from the Sun, and is in an angle, and not otherwise impeded, it will make the natives' soul a lover of professions and sciences, and especially the quadrivium; and of good intellect, a versifier, desiring music; loving all commendable things; and in the same way it will be desirous of delights, and it will be well suited for them, commendably using them; and likewise it will make him a lover of peace, and delighting in these things; cheerful; loving his friends; likewise intelligent, and having a good law and good worth; a lover of horses, entering on the correct path and deviating in nothing; eagerly learning as much from himself as from others, and eagerly applying himself to learning; imitating the ways of good and virtuous men, likening itself to just souls; eager to make public speeches and fit in speaking; loveable, temperate in the quality of the soul, fair, magnanimous, a helper of the needy, nevertheless corrupted in desiring to abuse boys, and committing disgraceful acts with them, desiring them over women; and he will be selfish.

### If Mercury Is Badly Disposited

However if Mercury is in bad condition and badly disposed, namely in contrary to what was said, he makes the natives' soul two tongued, slanderous, sly, duplicitous, crafty, mendacious, a deceiver, deceptive, a traitor, a perjurer, a disturber, considering all evil things profoundly and to the root, evil in all things, loving nobody and loved by nobody, a deceiver of women; and if the native is a woman, she will be a suffocator and destroyer of her own children; blaming and condemning others, doing all evils that it can, wishing to do and to try everything - yet sometimes (albeit rarely) for the good, but mostly (in fact, almost always) for bad; eagerly committing disgraceful acts, and will be blamed for many things, yet he will be sometimes blamed when he did not commit the thing he is blamed for; but this will happen on account of his evil habit of committing guilty things.

## VI

### The Qualities Of The Natives' Soul If Mercury Is The Sole Significator

However if Mercury is the sole significator of the qualities of the natives soul, and he is in good condition and well disposed, namely oriental in the world and from the Sun, and is in an angle, and is not otherwise impeded, it will make the natives' soul of much uprightness and knowledge; having a sharp intellect; a good memory for ancient matters, and a recorder of experiences; one elucidating natural things, an understander, explainer or interpreter of them, beneficent; a deliberator and investigator of the sciences; able to learn the quadrivium; a evaluator of goods; and a good, true, and secret concealer of things which ought to be concealed.

### If Mercury Is In Contrary Condition To The Aforementioned

If Mercury is in contrary condition to what was mentioned above, namely that he is in bad condition and badly disposed, it will make the natives' soul worthless, a deceiver, eagerly making others err, confident in its own counsel; having shallow and hasty motives; easily changing himself from one proposition to another; ignorant, deceptive, mendacious, unstable, disorganised in his qualities, unfaithful, not having reverence for God; disobedient, unjust, using falsity with all things and through all things.

### When Mercury Is Joined With Any Of The Aforementioned

If Mercury is joined with any of the aforementioned, whatever condition it is found in, Mercury will be converted to the nature of the planet with whom he joins, and you will judge the qualities of the soul according to the other planets disposition and condition, whether it is good or bad.

### What Each Of The Planets Do In The Qualities Of The Soul If They Are Contrary

Indeed, if any one of the other planets are joined with any other planet, and one is well disposed and in good condition, and the other is badly disposed and in bad condition, it will not signify such qualities of the soul as are said above, but they will be between both of the participants (or wise in the nature of each), it will be a certain medium between those extremes, neither truly good nor totally bad.

## VII

## On The Significations Of The Luminaries Concerning The Qualities Of The Soul Of The Native, And First On The Sun

With regards to the significations of the luminaries concerning the qualities of the natives' soul, a rule is given to each of them, which is different from the rule of the other. For with the Sun naturally having the signification of religion, and since the qualities of the soul seem to pertain to religion, he has participation in the qualities of the natives' soul with the dispositor of these qualities. Whence, if he is in good condition at the hour of the nativity, and well disposed, namely in the world and in the angles, and is joined with the dispositor of the qualities of the natives' soul, he will assist the soul in making it more discerning, more mindful; and separating itself from unjust and illicit things; likewise more liberal and more powerful, having a better and more faithful law.

### If The Sun Is In Bad Condition And Badly Disposited

If the Sun is in a condition contrary to what was said, he will help the dispositor of the qualities of the natives soul (if he is joined to him) in making the soul miserable, and having evil qualities; base in its harm, laborious, trusting in its own counsel, doubting others, stupid, grave, having a wicked will against others, and not desisting from its vices easily.

## VIII

## On The Significations Of The Moon Concerning The Qualities Of The Natives' Soul

Indeed the Moon is given signification over the qualities of the body and the soul, yet not individually over the qualities of the natives' soul as are the others; but she has other significations, of her own supports, assisting according to what her disposition is like: namely, if it is a good disposition to the good, and if it is a bad disposition, to the bad. Whence Ptolemy said in Tetrabiblos, if the Moon is in the bending places (that is, the beginning of her return to the circle of the signs when she is in her greater elongation from it, namely to the north or to the south), she will assist the qualities of the soul, and make them change suddenly. However, if the Moon is in one of the two Nodes, or the places of the transiting of the circle of the Moon through the path of the Sun, she will help the qualities of the natives soul, so that it might operate the things which it ought to operate more quickly. Moreover, if the Moon is above the earth, increased in light, or is in her fullness, or in the opposition of the Sun, she will help the qualities of the soul in making them more truthful and frank, and suitable for those things which are necessary. And if she is below the earth, or decreased in light, under the rays of the Sun, she will assist the qualities of the soul in making them more hidden, or coming into act less, and so that they will be less quick.

## On The Significations Of The Moon If She Is
## Joined To Planets From Their Dignities

*On The Significations Of The Moon If She Is*
*Joined To Planets From Their Dignities*

Indeed, to know the significations of the Moon (what she bestows upon the native) with the planets when she is in their dignities, examine her place in the circle in nativities, and see in whose domicile, or exaltation, or in two of the other dignities she is placed.

For if she is in any of the aforementioned dignities of Saturn, joined to him by aspect or conjunction, it will make the natives' soul sorrowful, laborious, stupid in inquiring into living, anxious, cold, and it will make the native cold unless Saturn is oriental at the time - for then the condition of the native will be improved.

But if she is in the dignities of Jupiter, joined to him or applying to him, it will make the native magnanimous, mixing with kings and magnates; religious and fortunate, praised by everyone in his actions.

However, if she is in the dignities of Mars joined or applying to him, it will make the natives' soul bold, a lover of disputes, loving labour and pilgrimages, gladly mixing with bellicose men, and acquiring good things from this.

Indeed, if she is in the dignities of the Sun, and is joined to him or applying to him by a good aspect, she will make the natives' soul make him mix with kings, magnates, and lofty men; or he himself will be the same as these men. However, if she is applying by a bad aspect, it will make the soul make the native be of a bad condition, of a short life and many infirmities.

Indeed, if she is in the dignities of Mercury joined to him or applying to him, it will make the natives' soul clever, ingenious, wise in contentions, with fortune and good things resulting from them.

## ON THE SECOND HOUSE

## I

## On The Signification Of The Prosperity and Substance Of The Native, And On Its Acquisition

I spoke in the preceding chapters on the form and figure of the native's body, and of the qualities of his soul. It remains to make mention of the substance of the native, and his prosperity; and likewise from where the native would acquire it, and how, and in what part of his life, since this happens after the nativity, amongst the rest of the principle things; and is more necessary for the native.

For indeed, Ptolemy says that we ought to apprehend what kind of substance, and how and whence substance will come to the native from the Part of Fortune; nor is his saying is not contrary to what Aomar or Aboaly said, since Ptolemy was speaking in a general sense. Indeed, the others followed in his footsteps, but added on certain things (which were proven in their time) affirming what he said, not contradicting it.

The investigation of the arrival of his substance is to examine the Part of Fortune and the Almutem planet over the degree in which it is in, and its strength and weakness, and the planets which are conjoined with the Almutem at the hour of the nativity, or those which are elevated over it according to the aforementioned method, and to see whether they are of its aym or not. Since if the Almutem over this place is in good condition and well disposed, namely fortunate, strong, and free from impediments, you can judge that the native will be abounding in many riches - and this more greatly so, if the aspect of some benefic intervenes: and especially Jupiter, both in the day and the night; or the Sun in the day, or the Moon at night.

And if the significator of substance is Saturn, or the Almutem over it is Saturn, and he is in good condition as we said, it signifies that the native is going to acquire riches from oppressive labours or from great buildings.

However, if it is Jupiter, it will demonstrate that the native is going to attain riches from offices, and the bearing of burden, both extraordinary (as are deputyships of castles, the office of a judge), and from other honest ordinary means.

But if Mars is placed as the significator of the natives' riches, you will have no doubt that they will increase from leading armies and from rulership, both cities as of others.

Indeed, if the Sun is the significator of the natives' substance, it will bring riches to him from the discovery of raw gold, either unexpected, or bought at a cheap price. And if the Sun is in the fourth he will find it underground.

Likewise if Venus is the significatrix of the native's wealth, it will make him gather substance from women or from gifts.

Yet, if the native were to acquire money, and Mercury is his significator, it will announce that riches will come to the native from merchants and mercantile dealings, and from scientific industry.

However, if the Moon is the significator of the wealth of the native, it will bring it to him from unexpected silver, or from journeys, sailing, or managing merchandise.

Again, if Saturn is the Almutem over the Part of Substance, and Jupiter is joined to him, and this more strongly so if it is in the angle of the Ascendant, or in the tenth, or in another good place in a common sign, it will signify inheritances which are inherited from strangers, and especially through women; and this more so if Jupiter has Ytisal with the Moon; and even more so if the planets who are from the aym of the significators of substance are in conjunction with her: and this even signifies that the inheritances will remain in the natives possession. Indeed, if another one of the planets, who is not of their aym, but of the contrary one, are elevated above the Almutem, or following him from the neighbouring sign, it signifies that the native will lose what he acquired in the aforementioned way, nor will they remain in his possession for very long.

As to when this ought to happen (what was said about substance, or its loss), you will be able to perceive through the aforementioned significators: for these things will happen when they arrive to the angles of the figure of the nativity. For example, by their distance from the angles - having considered this, years or months are signified.

Tyberiadis said that if you wish to examine the matter of the natives substance, examine the second from the Ascendant of the nativity, and the Part of Substance, and its Lord; also Jupiter and the Part of Fortune, and likewise its Lord. Then examine the Almutem over these places, whether it is one or more, and after this examine to see what the condition of the Almutem is like: whether it is free from impediments (namely fortunate and strong), and see how he interacts with the Lord of the Ascendant, whether they aspect each other, or are corporeally joined together, and whether this is with reception or not (since reception signifies the effecting of the matter); or if they are joined from opposition or square aspect (since these signify the detriment of the matter); and you will judge according to what you see concerning their substance.

However, Aboaly seemed to wish for you to examine in the matter of the prosperity and substance of the native, to see from where it would come to him, and its multitude or scarcity, from the triplicity Lords of the sign in which the luminary who has authority is placed, as will be said below. And in order to explain this more easily: which planets, if you find them in angles, namely fortunate and strong, signify the prosperity and riches of the native for the whole time of his life, and especially if they are in the first 15 degrees in front of the cusp, (namely those degrees which move towards the angle, not those which have already passed the angle) - yet more in the seventh than the fourth, more in the tenth than in the seventh. And even more in the first than in the tenth: since then his accidents will be made more prosperous. Also, the closer they are to the cusp, all the greater and more praiseworthy will be his status, prosperity, and fortune. And if they are after the aforementioned 15 degrees up to the end of the angle, the more they are remote from the angle, the more his prosperity and fortune will be below this.

Therefore you will consider all the aforementioned things which I have already told you to consider, namely all the aforementioned methods and all the aforementioned significators: which, if you find them all fortunate, strong, and free from impediments (which hardly or never tends to happen), you will be able to judge that immense and immeasurable wealth is going to come to the native; and that his prosperity and his status will be most excellent and sublime to such an extent that nothing will be able to resist him from promoted to rulership over the whole world, of whatever family or condition he is, even if he is found to be from the lowest stock; and he will remain in this state for the whole time of his life; unless perhaps one of the fixed stars which I listed for you above diminish this somewhat (or even Cor Leonis), namely in the Ascendant, or in the tenth one degree before the line or three degrees after it, for this will increase his sublimity to be practically immense; yet ultimately it will end in evil (unless perhaps a strong benefic aspects it by a trine or sextile aspect): since this signifies that the native will die an evil death, or at least that he will fall from all his dignities, powers, and sublimities. However, if it is aspected by a benefic it will reduce the malice of the Cor Leonis by one-fourth. But if malefics aspect it, it will increase its misfortune.

And if all the aforementioned significators are not placed safe and free, but a portion of them are, you will be able to judge the strong prosperity and status of the native, and the abundance of his riches, according to the quantity of them which are safe.

Therefore, I will render the individual factors individually, so that you can rightly discern the prosperity of the native and his riches and status.

## If You Wish To Consider The Prosperity And Substance Of The Native

Whence if you erect the figure of someone's nativity, and you wish to consider his prosperity and substance, first examine the Part of Fortune: for it is to be preferred to the Part of Substance, since the Part of Fortune signifies the natives substance, prosperity, and status, and his whole condition; the Part of Substance is attributed to his riches alone.

And see in whose domicile, exaltation, terms, or triplicity you find it to have fallen in, and consider which of the aforementioned significators is stronger in that place by multitude of dignities, or fortitudes: since he will be called the Almutem, and he will be the significator of the prosperity and substance of the native, and his condition. Wherefore, if it is in the Ascendant, or in one of the other angles, or in one of its own domiciles (and especially in the one where the Part of Fortune is), free from impediments, fortunate, and strong, it signifies the prosperity of the native, and his profit, and likewise a great quantity of riches to come. And if the Lord of the Ascendant or one of the benefics aspect him, and this aspecting planet is free from impediments, fortunate, and strong (and this more greatly if the aspect is a trine or sextile, and greater again if it is with reception), it will increase his substance by a half of its total. Indeed, if it is the exaltation Lord, it will be increased by one-third, but it will be with greater fame. However, if it is the term Lord, it will be increased by one-fifth. And if it is the triplicity Lord, it will be increased by one-seventh. Indeed, if it is the face Lord, it will be increased by one-twelfth. However, if this aspect is a square, or from opposition, it will be much below this, and even more so, and worse, if the aspect is without reception.

### If The Lord Of The Domicile Does Not Aspect, Or Is Impeded

However, if the Lord of the domicile does not aspect it, or is impeded, then examine the Lord of the exaltation; and if he is impeded, examine the term Lord; indeed, if the term Lord is impeded, examine the triplicity Lord; and if you find him impeded, lastly examine the Lord of the face. And speak about whichever one of them, and their significations, just as I have told you now. Indeed, if the Part of Fortune and all the aforementioned significators are impeded (and especially the Almutem over the place of the aforementioned Part), you will firmly announce that it is going to be the contrary of what was said of them above (which you found); and according to the same method in a bad way, you will predict according to what was judged above in the good one.

### If The Part Of Fortune Cannot Be The Significator Of The Substance Of The Native

Indeed if the Part Of Fortune cannot be the significator of the substance or riches of the native, and of his condition; nor the planet which is the Lord of the domicile in which the Part is placed, nor the Lord of the exaltation, term, triplicity, or face, nor the Almutem over this place, then examine the Part of Substance, and you will examine in whose domicile (or one of the aforementioned dignities) it falls in; and you will consider the Almutem over this place according to the method which I told you for the Lord of the domicile: since such a planet will be the significator over the prosperity and substance of the native.

### If The Part Of Substance Cannot Be The Significator Of The Substance Of The Native

If the Part of Substance, or the planet in whose dignity it is placed, cannot be the significator of the prosperity and substance of the native: examine the second and its Lord, or a planet who is in it. If one of the benefics are in the second, or joined with the Lord of the second by a trine or sextile aspect, it signifies that the native is going to acquire much substance, and this more greatly so if that benefic is Jupiter. However, if it is the Sun in the day, his signification will be below that of Jupiter. Indeed, if it is the Moon at night, her signification will be below that of the Sun. Indeed, if it is Venus, it will be below that of the Moon.

### If The Second, Or Is Lord, Or The Planet Who Is Placed In It, Cannot Be The Significator Of The Substance Of The Native

And if the second, or its Lord, or the planet who is placed in it, cannot signify the substance of the native, then examine Jupiter, who naturally signifies substance: who, if you find in the second, judge confidently that the native will have a copious abundance of wealth: however, this will be according to Jupiter's disposition - nor will he ever fall into poverty at any time; and this more strongly so if Jupiter is the Lord of the Ascendant. In agreement with this, Almansoris said:

*"He will never be a pauper or needy, the Lord of whose nativity is Jupiter"*

And even more greatly and sublimely if the Ascendant is Sagittarius and Pisces is the fourth house: for this does not receive the contrary. If Jupiter is impeded, so that he cannot be the significator of the aforementioned things, and the nativity is diurnal, then examine the Sun; who, if he is in any good place from the Ascendant, free from impediments, fortunate and strong, signifies that the native is going to obtain money or substance; but this will be below what is naturally signified by Jupiter. Indeed, if the nativity is nocturnal, then examine the Moon; who, if she is in the second, fortunate, strong, and free, or in another good place from the Ascendant, signifies that great riches are going to come to the native; however, what is signified by her will be below what is signified by the Sun.

## If Neither The Sun Nor The Moon Can Signify The Substance Of The Native

If neither the Sun nor the Moon can signify the substance of the native, then examine the planet which is the Almutem over the place in which the Almutem over one of the aforementioned Parts is placed (the Part of Substance, or Fortune), and this will establish the significator of substance. Which if he is fit for this, will signify that the native is going to acquire much substance; but what he signifies will be below what the Moon signifies.

## If This Planet Cannot Be The Significator Of The Substance Of The Native

Indeed, if such a planet is not fit to signify the substance of the native, examine the planet in whose domicile the Moon is placed: who, if he is in the Ascendant, or in the second, or in an angle, or in another good place from the Ascendant, and is free from impediments, fortunate, and strong, will bring much money to the native; however, what he signifies will be below what the aforementioned Almutem signifies.

## If The Planet In Whose Domicile The Moon Is Placed Cannot Be The Significator Of The Substance Of The Native

Indeed if this planet cannot be the significator of the natives substance, examine the planet who is in the second: which, if it is free from impediments, fortunate and strong (and this more so if it has some dignity in the second, or if it is a benefic), will signify that the native is going to attain a good quantity of money, however, what it signifies will be below what the planet in whose domicile the Moon is placed signifies.

## If The Planet Who Is In The Second Cannot Be The Significator Of The Natives' Substance

However if the planet who is in the second cannot be the significator of substance, then see if the Lord of the Ascendant, and the Lord of the fourth house are the same planet: since he will deserve to be called the significator of the prosperity and substance of the native; which, if

you find this planet free, namely fortunate, and strong, you will have it as a sure thing that the native will gather much money, equally as well as when there is a benefic in the second.

## If The Lord Of The Ascendant And The Lord Of The Fourth Are Not The Same Planet

However, if you do not find this, then examine the triplicity Lords of the house of substance: which, if you find them all free (namely, fortunate, and strong), will signify that riches will come to the native in abundance, in accordance with what his condition is, or beyond it. However, if only two of them are safe, riches will come to him in two parts of his life, but not in the third. But if only one of them is safe, riches will only come to him in a single one-third of his life, but not in the others. If none of them are safe, riches will never come to him (as much as it is from this); however, riches could come to him from other causes besides the aforementioned, namely, from the ones said below.

## If The Triplicity Lords Of The House Of Substance Cannot Be The Significators Of The Substance Of The Native

And if the aforementioned triplicity Lords of the house of substance cannot be the significators of the substance of the native, then examine the triplicity Lords of the sign in which the Sun is (if it is a diurnal nativity); or the triplicity Lords of the sign in which the Moon is (if it is a nocturnal nativity); and judge according to what I said to you about the triplicity Lords of the house of substance.

## If The Triplicity Lords Of The Sign In Which The Sun Or Moon Is, Cannot Signify The Native's Substance

Indeed, if the aforementioned planets cannot be the significators of the native's substance, and are not fit for this, then examine the triplicity Lords of the sign of the Ascendant, and judge those according to how you judged the aforementioned triplicity Lords of the Sun and the Moon; but what is signified by them will be below what is signified by the triplicity Lords of the Sun in the day, and the Moon at night.

### If The Triplicity Lords Of The Sign Of The Ascendant Cannot Signify The Native's Substance

However if the triplicity Lords of the sign of the Ascendant are not fit to signify the substance of the native, then examine the sign in which the Part of Fortune is placed, and its Lord: which if it is in the second or in another good place from the Ascendant, and free from impediments (namely fortunate and strong), will be the significator of the natives' substance and prosperity, and bring an suitable quantity of substance to him. However, what was signified will be below what the triplicity Lords of the Ascendant signified.

### If The Lord Of The Sign In Which The Part Of Fortune Is Cannot Signify The Native's Substance

Indeed if the Lord of the sign in which the Part of Fortune is cannot be the significator of the natives substance, then examine the sign in which the Part Of Substance is placed, and its Lord: who, if you find in the second, or in another good place from the Ascendant, free (namely, fortunate and strong), put him as the significator of the natives substance and the giver of it. For his signification will be comparable to the signification of the Lord of the sign in which the Part of Fortune is: indeed, he will vary little from it.

### If The Lord Of The Sign In Which The Part Of Substance Is Cannot Signify The Native's Substance

And if the Lord of the sign in which the Part of Substance is placed cannot be the significator of the substance of the native, then examine to see if the Sun is on the line of the tenth house, two degrees before, or five or less after, and that the Moon is moving towards him from the left, from a trine or sextile aspect; and that the Lord of the house of substance is in its own domicile or exaltation, moving to a conjunction with the Lord of the Ascendant, or to his trine or sextile aspect; and this more greatly and strongly if Jupiter is the Lord of the house of substance. Since this will signify that the native will have a great name, great fame, and be very powerful. However, if in addition to this the significator of substance is other than Jupiter, immense substance will arrive to the native, but there will not be the exceeding fame in addition to this. If the nineteenth degree of Aries is the 10th house, and the Ascendant is the twenty-fifth degree of Cancer (or at least the Sun and Jupiter), and they (and their Lords), are free from malefics, the name of this native will be exalted, and greatly expanded, and his fame will spread throughout the world.

And Ptolemy said certain words which seem to differ from the consideration of this house, but they do not seem to differ from the opinion. For he said that if the planetary rulers of the houses or signs which give children (which will be described below in a chapter on the topic of children) are in their own places (which are tenth, the eleventh, the first, and the fifth), and they are oriental, the native will be powerful and have a great name.

However, if they are occidental, in a place of the aym contrary to them, the native will be miserable and unknown.

However, if the aforementioned planetary rulers of the places taught, and the Part of Fortune, are in the Ascendant, or with the Lord of the Ascendant, the native will live until he takes a wife; and will be loved by his parents and will be made their heir.

However, if it is not so, or if they are contrary to each other, or they aspect each other from square or opposition, the native will be a litigator, and accumulate the height of hatred with regard to his parents, and will treat them badly; nor will he obtain their inheritance.

### If The Aforementioned Planets Cannot Be The Significators Of The Native's Substance And The Sun Is Not In The Tenth

If neither the Lord of the sign in which the Part of Substance is placed, nor any of the other aforementioned planets, are able to be the significators of the natives' substance, and the Sun is not in the tenth by the method which I told you, then examine the planets with whom the aforementioned significators are joined, or who are elevated above them - that is, who precede the others in conjunction with the Almutem which I told you; or who are northern from him: since they will be the significators of the native's substance, and especially the one who is stronger among them in dignity or fortune: but what he signifies will be very much below what the planet in whose domicile the Part of Substance is signifies.

### If The Aforementioned Planets With Whom The Significators Are Joined Cannot Signify The Native's Substance

Indeed if the aforementioned planets cannot be the significators of the substance of the native, then examine the Almutem over the aforementioned places, or over one of them: which, if it is free from impediments, fortunate and strong, will signify the natives substance; but what it signifies will be below all of the aforementioned.

### Which Of The Mentioned Significators Should Be Preferred To The Others

Indeed, from the mentioned significators the principal and stronger ones are the Part of Fortune, the Part of Substance, the second and its Lord generally (and more in matters of substance); and likewise Jupiter, who, even if he might not always be stronger than the others, nevertheless, in the signification of substance he is always more general than the others.

### If All Of The Aforementioned Significators Are Impeded

If all of the Lords of the aforementioned domiciles, and all the aforementioned significators are so impeded, that none of them can signify matters of the native's substance, then examine the exaltation Lords (nor is this going to be repeated). However, if the exaltation Lords are impeded, examine the term Lords; indeed, if the term Lords are impeded, examine the triplicity Lords; but if the triplicity Lords are impeded (which would be astounding and unheard of), lastly examine the face Lords, and judge by them, just as you judge by the others, as I touched on above.

### If Malefics Are The Significators Of The Native's Substance

And you should know that if malefics are the significators of the natives substance, even if they are found well disposed, they will still not convey as much good as benefics. Indeed, if they are unfortunate and badly disposed, they will bring in the contrary - intolerable conditions and poverty. Indeed, if you find a malefic, or the rays of

malefics are found in the second (or even in one of the aforementioned places signifying substance) which do not have dignity there, without the presence or aspect of a benefic, or if the significators themselves are impeded: you will expect, and ought to judge, the contrary of those things which were said.

### If Benefics Are The Significators Of The Native's Substance

Indeed, if the benefics are strong, they will present much good to the native; however, if they are impeded, they will present little good to the native.

## II

### From Where The Native Will Acquire Substance, Or Money, And By What Means, And In What Part Of His Life

The last things to be examined are the planet and the place signifying from where the native will acquire substance, and by what means, and in which part of his life, and in what part of time. Therefore, after you have found the significator of the natives substance, consider in what house you found him to have fallen: for according to the significations of this house, and even according to the significations of the Almutem planet over this house; and likewise according to the significations of the planet found in that house, you ought to announce from where, and by what means the natives substance ought to come.

## III

### In Which Time Of His Life, And In What Part, The Native Will Acquire Substance

Indeed, you can assess in which time and in what part of his life the native will acquire substance, by the triplicity Lords. For the first will bring substance in the first part of the native's life, the second in the second, and the third in the third; and so for each one of them, according to how you find them, you will be able to judge how fit they are to provide the native with wealth in that third part of his life. If you find all of them well disposed, the native will delight in the advantage of substance for the whole time of his life. Indeed, if you only find two of them fortunate, you will predict that he is going to attain substance in two parts of his life. But if you only find one of them fortunate, you could affirm that substance is going to arrive in the single third part assigned to that significator.

## IV

## Why The Ancients Avoided Certain Of The Mentioned Significators

The ancient sages, not because they were ignorant, but because they avoided labour (in the matter of the signification of the native's substance) only used the Lord of the Ascendant, the Lord of the second, the Part of Fortune, the Part of Substance, and their Lords, and likewise Jupiter, leaving almost everything else touching on this to the industry of the wise. And because of this it often happens that things are not judged rightly and to a point by astrologers, regarding the matter of substance. Since they do not care to consider the other significators, except those which I just told you now. However, you will be able to see, if you wish to rightly consider, that the riches or substance of the native do not always come down exactly according to the significators above.

For we will see certain extremely wealthy men, certain rather wealthy men, certain wealthy men, certain who are moderately wealth, certain who are neither wealthy nor poor, certain who are moderately poor, certain who are poor, certain rather poor, and certain very poor, certain who are in need, certain who are even more in need, certain who are the neediest, certain men always abounding, certain always wanting, certain men sometimes abounding (and these same men sometimes in need), certain who escape from need by great labour, certain who escape it with ease, and similar things: which does not happen, except from the significators named above, and from their dispositions and what falls with them (even if those which the ancients use are more principal).

Whence, you could judge regarding the natives prosperity and substance according to which of them you find fortunate. And according to which of them you find unfortunate, you can announce on his adversity, according to their succession and order which I demonstrated to you: since just as the above mentioned significators of substance, if they are fortunate and strong will bring substance; so too if they are unfortunate and weak, and badly disposed, they will take it away; and will convey want, misery, labour, sorrow and poverty. Therefore, be industrious and wise, so that you know how to consider these things.

You will even consider if the Part of Fortune is with the Moon in nativities, and if Jupiter aspects it, and the nativity is diurnal; or if Venus aspects it and the nativity is nocturnal: since this will signify the good nourishment of the native (and this more strongly so if the Part of Fortune is in a good place from the Ascendant).

Likewise you will examine the disposition of each and every one of the aforementioned significators (namely the triplicity Lords, and the others): for if one of the triplicity Lords are well disposed, and the Lord of substance, or the Part Of Fortune, or its Lord are badly disposed, it will take from the Lord of the terms, and vice versa according to his own condition.

And if the significator of a nativity in a diurnal nativity is in a masculine sign, and in a feminine sign in nocturnal nativities, and is not otherwise impeded, its strength will be greater, and its testimony more affirming of the truth of the goodness of nourishment, whether the natives' life is long of short.

## V

## Whence And Because Of What The Native Will Acquire Substance

Having examined the acquisition of the native's wealth, and its accumulation of quantity in the preceding chapters, what is to be examined from this point onwards is to see whence the native will acquire it, and by what means, and for what reason.

Therefore you will consider the Lord of the house of substance, or whichever other significator of it you find, and you will see in what house you find him to fall; and likewise with which of the planets you find him joined: since this will signify how, and whence the native is going to acquire money.

## If The Significator Of The Natives' Substance Is In The First

For if it is in the first, as I remember having touched on for you above in the Tractate on the significations of the twelve houses (summarising the same), it signifies that the native is going to acquire substance from his own person, namely by his own industry, with little solicitude, and little labour, or by one of the things which are signified by the first house.

## If The Significator Of The Natives' Wealth Is In The Second

However, if it is in the second, he will find it because of his own substance, and his own goods, and trade, and other arts with which are exercised with money, and the like; or one of the things which are signified by the second house.

## If The Significator Of Substance Is In The Third

And if it is in the third, he will find it because of brothers or sisters, or neighbours not related to him, or from short journeys (which are of two days or less), or because of his own relatives or those related to him through marriage, who are lesser than him in riches and power, and likewise in age, or those who consider him as their elder; or one of the things signified by the third house.

## If The Significator Of Substance Is In The Fourth

Indeed if it is in the fourth, he will find it because of fathers, or grandfathers, or fathers-in-law, or other ancestral relations older and of greater age than him, or from use of merchant activities of lands, or of houses or things which are dug up from the ground: or perhaps he will find a treasure underground (even though this happens most rarely); or from the use of furnaces and similar things; or from one of the things which are signified by the fourth house.

## If The Significator Of Substance Is In The Fifth

And if it is in the fifth, he will acquire substance because of children, and carrying out the affairs of kings and magnates, or because of moderate journeys (which I consider as being between two and four days), or because of foodstuffs or drinks which are sold in taverns and similar places; or because of games and the like; or because of one of those things which are signified by the fifth house.

## If The Significator Of Substance Is In The Sixth

If it is in the sixth, he will acquire it because of slaves, slavegirls, or servants, or small animals which are not ridden, as are sheep, goats, pigs dogs, birds, and the like; or because of one of those things which are signified by the sixth house.

## If The Significator Of Substance Is In The Seventh

But if it is in the seventh, he will acquire it because of women, or associates, or enemies, or because of one of those things which are signified by the seventh house.

## If The Significator Of Substance Is In The Eighth

Indeed, if it is in the eighth, he will find it because of dowries of women, or because of their goods, or the goods of associates or enemies; or because of someone's death; or because of goods which are inherited from the estate of the dead; or because of one of those things which are signified by the eighth house.

## If The Significator Of Substance Is In The Ninth

But if it is in the ninth, he will acquire it because of religion, or religious people, or because of long journeys, as sometimes merchants and others travelling far tend to make; or because of one of those things which are signified by the ninth house.

## If The Significator Of Substance Is In The Tenth

However, if you find it in the tenth, say that he will acquire it because of a king, or a profession, or a magistracy, or an office, or another lay dignity (as are generalships, or positions of authority, and the like); or because of one of those things which are signified by the tenth house.

### If The Significator Of Substance Is In The Eleventh

Furthermore, if it is in the eleventh, he will find it because of friends, or the soldiers or household members of the ruler; or by means of business or lending, and harvests; or he will acquire it from unexpected fortune coming to him; or even because of matters in which he has hope of profiting; or because of one of those things which are signified by the eleventh house.

### If The Significator Of Substance Is In The Twelfth

Lastly, if it is in the twelfth, he will acquire it because of prisons, or prisoners, as sometimes guards of prisoners tend to do, or those who release prisoners from their prisons for profit; or because of hidden enemies, or large animals, or some low-class or shameful duty; and from stealing; or because of one of those things which are signified by the twelfth house.

What the significations of all of the twelve houses are, you have above in the tractate on the twelve houses, it is not necessary to repeat them all here for you.

## VI

## By What Means Will The Native Acquire Substance

The next thing to be examined is the means by which the native will acquire substance. For you will consider the significator of substance, whether it is the Lord of the Part of Fortune, or the Lord of the Part of Substance, or the Sun or Moon, or one of the triplicity Lords, or any other one of the aforementioned significators.

### If Saturn Is The Significator Of Substance

Since if Saturn is the significator of the natives substance, and is in good condition, and well disposed, free from impediments, fortunate and strong, and joined with benefics, and is in an angle or a succedent of an angle, the native will acquire substance and riches from the aforementioned labours (or the like), by justice and by licit and suitable means. However, if he is impeded, unfortunate and weak, retrograde or combust, or joined with malefics, cadent from the angles, and in

bad condition and badly disposed, the native will gather substance by wickedness rather than by anything else; even by means of deception and lies, and thievery.

### If Jupiter Is The Significator Of Substance

Indeed if Jupiter is the significator of the natives' substance, and he is in good condition and well disposed, namely fortune, strong, and free from impediments, the native will gather riches by justice and by licit and praiseworthy means. Indeed, if he is impeded and in bad condition and badly disposed: namely, unfortunate and weak, retrograde or combust, or joined with malefics, and cadent from the angles, the native will sometimes acquire substance by justice, sometimes by wickedness; sometimes by licit means, sometimes by illicit means.

### If Mars Is The Significator Of Substance

If Mars is placed as the significator of the natives wealth, and he is in good condition and well disposed, namely fortunate, strong, and free from impediments, the native will apply himself to the acquisition of substance by licit and illicit means, nor will he care much about where he gets it, as long as he gets it. For he will say that it is good to extort money everywhere:

"*A denarius in the purse and a peasant in the ditch*"

However, if he is found in bad condition and badly disposed, namely unfortunate and weak, impeded by the mentioned impediments, he will investigate the ways of acquiring money by justice and wickedness, by stealing, by highway robbery, by fire, by illicit bloodshed, and by every way he can, and from whoever he can, irrespective of sex, rank, or dignity.

### If The Sun Is The Significator Of Substance

If indeed, the Sun signifies the natives' substance, and is in good condition and well disposed, free from impediments, fortunate and strong, the native will acquire wealth by licit, required, and reputable means. Indeed, if he is impeded, in bad condition, and badly disposed, he will acquire it by any means he can, practically not caring whether by justice or wickedness: yet he will know how to disguise his wickedness, so that it will not appear as manifestly as maliciousness would.

### If Venus Is The Significatrix Of The Natives' Substance

If Venus is the significatrix of the natives wealth, and she is in good condition and well disposed, namely fortunate and strong, the native will gather substance (namely riches) in a praiseworthy way, and by licit means. Indeed, if she is found in the contrary condition, he will seize it in a reprehensible way, and in which falsehoods are committed, nor will he be ashamed of such profiting.

### On Mercury And The Moon

However, with Mercury and the Moon it is not like the others. For whichever of them is the significator of the native's substance, it signifies that the native is going to acquire substance according to the condition and significations of that planet with whom the Mercury/the Moon is joined. Indeed, if Mercury/the Moon is joined to nobody, and Mercury/the Moon is the significator, it will show that the native is going to acquire wealth by carrying the smallest of wares, and by short journeys.

And always make it your concern to see if the planetary significator of substance is joined with one of the planets: since the planet with whom he is joined, will throw in its lot. For if the significator of substance is good, and is joined with a good planet, its goodness will be increased. However, if it is bad, and is joined with a bad planet, its malice will be increased. Indeed, if it is a benefic and is joined to a malefic, its goodness will be reduced. Indeed, if it is a malefic and is joined to a benefic, its malice will be reduced.

## VII

## At What Age Or In Which Part Of His Life The Native Is Going To Acquire Substance

The last thing to be examined is at what age or in which part of life the native is to acquire wealth. To certain ancient sages it seemed that you should consider the triplicity Lords of the Sun in the day, and indeed, the triplicity Lords of the Moon at night; to certain others it appeared differently, according to how

their opinions pleased them. However, I do not contradict their statements, nor do I wholly agree with them, nor wholly disagree with them. However, it seems to me that the one who is more powerful in any matter, is by nature more powerful in the judgement of his effect. For the triplicity Lords of the house of substance seem to signify it more effectively and more naturally than the others do. And so it seems more fitting that the triplicity Lords of the house of substance should be preferred to the other significators in signification of the time (or in what part of life) in which the native or querent is going to have or acquire substance.

For if the first one of them is in good condition and well disposed, he will acquire it in the first one-third of his life, in the others he will be in need of it. If the second, he will acquire it in the second third of his life, in the other two he will be in need. Indeed, if the third is in good condition, he will acquire it in the final third of his life, in the other two he will be in need.

However, if only two of them are fortunate, and the third isn't, he will acquire it in the thirds assigned to the fortunate ones, in the other he will be in need. For if the first and the second are fortunate, he will acquire it in the first and second one-thirds of his life, and be in need of it in the last third. If it is the first and the third, he will acquire it in the first and last third of his life, in the middle he will be in need. If it is the second and the third, he will acquire it in the second and third one-thirds of his life, and indeed, he will be in need of it in the first.

However, if all of them are fortunate, he will acquire it and abound in it for the whole time of his life. Indeed, if all of them are unfortunate, he will be in need of it for all of his life, and always live in misery.

And if the Almutem over the place of substance is a planet other than the triplicity Lords of the house of substance see whether he is oriental or not, since if he is oriental, it signifies wealth in youth (that is, the first half of the natives life). However, if he is occidental, it signifies it in the latter half of the natives life. Whence you will make him a participator in the signification of the time of acquisition of substance, with the triplicity Lord of the house of substance. Indeed, if both concord in the good, substance will be increased in that time, and will be made more than could be signified by one of them alone. However, if they are discordant, the better signification will be reduced, and there will not be as much substance for the native as there ought to be at that age.

## VIII

### When Other Significators Will Increase Or Diminish The Substance Of The Native, With The Triplicity Lords Of The House Of Substance

Likewise, you will consider the significator of the natives' substance, whatever way he is, and you will mix his virtue with the virtue of the triplicity Lord of the house of substance who is the significator of the time in which the native is going to acquire substance. Which if they both agree, and are in good condition, the substance will be increased then, and in that part of the native's life, and it will become more abundant. However, if they are both in bad condition, the substance will be diminished more in that time than it seems it ought to be diminished, and the native will become more needy. Indeed, if one is fortunate and the other is weak, the goodness of the fortunate one will be reduced. Indeed, if the more deserving significator of substance is fortunate, and the other is unfortunate, the goodness of the good one will be reduced, and the quantity of substance signified will be less. But if one is unfortunate and the other is fortunate, the malice of the bad one will be reduced, and the scarcity of substance will be signified as less.

And Aboali said (with regard to the signification of the time of the natives' substance) that if the triplicity Lords of the luminary who has authority are all safe, free from impediments, and are in angles, it signifies the prosperity of the native for all the days of his life. And this more so, and more strongly, if the significator of the substance of this time is in the degree of the cusp of an angle; and the more it is elongated from the angle up to the end of the house, the more his prosperity and fortune will be something less, according to his elongation from the angle, diminishing it degree by degree.

However, if the first Lord of this triplicity is free, and the second and third are impeded, it signifies the fortune and prosperity of the native in the first one-third of his life, in the second and the last one-third of his life, he will be in need (just as was said). If the second is free, and the first and third are impeded, the native will prosper in the second one-third of his life, and will be in need in the first and last one-third. However, if the third is fortunate, he will prosper in the last one-third of his life, and in the first and second he will be in need.

If the first Lord of the aforementioned triplicity is impeded, and the other two are safe, it signifies the impediment and bad condition of the native, and his detriment, in the first one-third of his life, but not in the others. Indeed, if the second Lord of the same triplicity is impeded, and the others are safe, the native will be impeded in the second one-third of his life, indeed, not in the others. Indeed, if only the third is impeded, it signifies his impediment in the final one-third of his life, however, in the other parts of his life he will prosper. And if all of the mentioned significators are impeded, it signifies the evil and detriment of the native, and his indigence for the whole time of his life, and the diminution of his life, as was said above regarding the triplicity Lords of the house of substance.

If in addition to these misfortunes there are benefics in the angles, and the malefics are cadent, and the luminaries are well disposed, the malice of the malefics will be decreased, and the native will almost always prosper, nor will his life be diminished because of it. You can say the same if the Lord of the Ascendant and the Moon are in angles, free from the impediments of malefics, or if they apply to planets in angles (and this will be better and stronger if reception intervenes).

### If The Lord Of The Ascendant Applies To The Luminaries, Or They Apply To Him

However, if the Lord of the Ascendant applies to the luminaries, or they apply to him, and the Sun is in Aries or in Leo, and the Moon is in Taurus or Cancer, when the luminary applies to the Lord of the Ascendant; or if the Lord of the Ascendant is in its own domicile or exaltation when it applies to the luminaries; or one of them is in two of its own minor dignities, when one is applying to the other (as was said), it signifies the fortune and prosperity of the native for all the times of his life, unless the triplicity Lords of the house of substance operate to the contrary: for if its triplicity Lords are impeded, it will detract somewhat from this disposition, and his prosperity and fortune will be somewhat below this.

## If The Part Of Fortune And Its Lord Are Oriental

If the Part of Fortune and its Lord are oriental, and free from the impediments of malefics, and are in angels, and aspect the Ascendant, and benefics are aspecting them, it signifies the prosperity of the native, and the durability of his fortune; and the increase of the goodness of his life; and his firmity, constancy, and vigour. And if the Moon is in her own domicile or exaltation, safe from malefics, and unimpeded, it signifies the exaltation of the native and the greatness of his name. However, if the mentioned significators are cadent and impeded, it signifies that the native's life will be laborious and of little utility, and this more so if they do not aspect the Ascendant.

If benefics and malefics together aspect the Part of Fortune and its Lord, and they are in angels, judge the native's fortune and prosperity to be mediocre. Indeed, if the triplicity Lords of the Ascendant are joined to planets in angels, and they are cadent from them, they will signify the fortune and prosperity of the native, but after labour and fatigue. You will say the same about the Lord of the Ascendant, if he is joined to a planet in an angle, in its own domicile or exaltation, while he himself is cadent and in his own descension. Indeed, these things are true, unless the aforementioned significators of substance operate to the contrary (or if one of them does), since each one throws in its own lot according to how it is disposed. Indeed, if it is well disposed, it will increase the significations of the benefics for the good, and reduce the significations of malefics. However, if it is badly disposed, it will increase the significations of malefics in their evil, and reduce the significations of benefics.

Nor should you forget to consider how all of the aforementioned significators are disposed. Since if they are all well disposed, the native's prosperity will be increased, and his fortune will be augmented. Indeed, if they are all badly disposed, the prosperity of the native and his fortune will be diminished. But if the more principal significators are well disposed, and the less principal ones are badly disposed, his prosperity and fortune will be diminished, and he will profit less. Indeed, if the more principal ones are badly disposed, and the less principal ones are well disposed, their misfortune will be diminished, and they will harm less.

## If The Nativity Is Diurnal Or Nocturnal

You will also see if the nativity is diurnal or nocturnal, for if it is diurnal, you will examine the triplicity Lords of the sign in which the Sun is placed, as said above. However, if it is nocturnal, then you will examine the triplicity Lords of the sign in which the Moon is placed. Which planets, if they are in angles, fortunate, and strong, and aspected by benefics (and this will be better and stronger if the benefics receive them), signify the fortune prosperity and blessedness of this native, If they are in succedents of the angles, they will judge moderate fortune. However, if malefics are in the angles, and benefics in the succedents, it signifies the indigence of the native, and his labour, in the first half of his life; and fortune and good condition in the latter half. However, if benefics are in the angles, and malefics are in the succedents, they will judge the contrary. Indeed, if they are in the natives' cadents, they will signify his misfortune and his bad condition, and a laborious life, unless the mentioned significators operate to the contrary.

## When To Examine The House Of Substance

Likewise, examine the domicile of substance, which is the second sign from the Ascendant, and the second sign from the domicile in which the Part of Fortune is placed, and likewise the second sign from the domicile in which the Sun is placed (in diurnal nativities), or from the domicile in which the Moon is placed (in nocturnal nativities). And see if any of the malefics are in any of the aforementioned places: since if the native has other good significations, this has the signification of their diminution, and of the diminution of his good condition. Indeed, if he does not have other good significations, it signifies the fall of his prosperity, and also his detriment and bad condition, unless this malefic has domicile, exaltation, or two other lesser dignities there

And Alboali said that if the Sun does not aspect the Part of Fortune or its Lord, or its Lord the Sun in diurnal nativities (or the Moon in nocturnal nativities), it signifies detriment, and the diminution of the natives fortune and prosperity. You will be able to say the same of the Moon if she is besieged by malefics, both in diurnal and nocturnal nativities. Likewise, the Alcocoden signifies the same, if it is cadent from the angles, or from the Ascendant, and in a bad place from it, and in the aspect of some malefic. Indeed, if you find the malefics in angles, and benefics in the succeedents of the angles, it signifies the native's labour and his impediment in the beginning of his life; but prosperity and good things in the end. You will be able to judge the same if the Sun in diurnal nativities, or the Moon in nocturnal nativities, is separating from malefics and joining to benefics. You can speak likewise about the triplicity Lords of the luminary who has authority, if they are cadent from the angles, or from the Ascendant, and they are joining themselves to planets placed in their own domiciles or exaltations, or in two of their other dignities.

### If The Planet Who Is The Significator Of Substance Is Oriental

You will also consider if the planet who is the significator of substance is oriental and above the earth, since then it will signify the fortune and good of the native, and his prosperity in the beginning of his life. Indeed, if it is occidental and under the earth, then it will signify it at the end of his life. If it is oriental under the earth, or occidental above the earth, then it will signify it in the middle of his life.

## IX

## On What Is Signified By The Places Of The Circle

Indeed the places of the circle signifying the times are as follows:

For the Ascendant and the second signify the beginning of the native's life up to the end of his adolescence.

The tenth and the eleventh signify youth up to the end of the mature age.

The seventh and the eighth signify from the end of youth up to the middle of old age.

The fourth and the fifth signify from the middle of old age up to the end of the native's life.

And Alboali said that the Part of Fortune signifies the beginning of life, its Lord the end.

And each one of the aforementioned significators signify the condition of the native in their own time according to how they are disposed at the hour of someone's nativity. And if you knew the accidents through those things which you have perceived regarding the dispositions of his significators of the hour of his nativity, when and in what time they ought to be prosperous and useful, or fortunate; or the contrary, or laborious or unfortunate, or unlucky; and you saw the direction of the rays of the planets to the places signifying his fortune or misfortune; and you saw the distance which is between them in terms of signs, degrees, and minutes; and you saw in which times of his life good or bad accidents ought to happen to him through these significators - then examine the Part of Fortune, which you will direct to the bodies of benefics and malefics, or their rays. And if you see the Part of Fortune joined to a benefic (and especially Jupiter or Venus), then judge the good condition of the native. If you see it joined to malefics (and especially Saturn or Mars), you can judge the contrary, unless the aforementioned significators operate to the contrary; for when benefics or their rays come to it, and the significators are joined to benefics, or their rays, his prosperity, his fortune, and his good will be increased twofold. When malefics or their rays come to it, and the significators are joined to malefics or their rays, his misfortune, his evils, and his labour will be increased twofold, and his goods will be diminished. However, if the Part of Fortune is joined with benefics, and the significators with malefics, or the Part with malefics, and the significators with benefics, the significations of each will be reduced, you will not doubt.

### For What Reason The Native Is Going To Acquire Money

Having seen in these preceding chapters from where the native will acquire substance, and by which method, the last thing to be seen is for what reason he will acquire it. And even if this might seem to wish to be likened to those preceding things, nevertheless it is not the same as them, but something else.

## If The Part Of Fortune Is In The Dignities Of Saturn

Therefore you will consider the Part of Fortune at the hour of someone's nativity, which if you find in the house or exaltation of Saturn, or in two of his other lesser dignities, and Saturn is joined to it, or aspects it, it signifies that the native will acquire substance because of slaves, slavegirls, or middle aged men (namely from 50 years and older up to the middle of old age), and from low-class persons, and his fortune will be in them, and mixed with them; and his signification will be stronger if the Part of Fortune is in his exaltation than if it is in his domicile or other dignities. If the Part of Fortune is in an angle, the fortune of this native will be elevated, and greatly exalted.

## If The Part Of Fortune Is In The Dignities Of Jupiter

And if it is in the dignities of Jupiter according to the aforementioned method, he will acquire it because of mixing with, and working with great men and nobles, and even bishops and the like, and other wise men, and his fortune will be in them and with them.

## If The Part Of Fortune Is In The Dignities Of Mars

And if it is in the dignities of Mars according to the same method, he will acquire it because of generals of armies, and bellicose men, and warriors, and those who delight in wars; and exercises of wars, and his fortune will be mixed with them.

## If The Part Of Fortune Is In The Dignities Of The Sun

If it is in the dignities of the Sun according to the aforementioned method, he will acquire it because of mixing with and working with kings, and other princes similar to kings; and his fortune will be in them and with them, and the like.

## If The Part Of Fortune Is In The Dignities Of Venus

However if it is in the dignities of Venus according to the same method, he will acquire it because of women, eunuchs, and likewise effeminate men; and his fortune will be in them and with them, and the like.

## If The Part Of Fortune Is In The Dignities Of Mercury

However if it is in the dignities of Mercury according to the aforementioned method, he will acquire substance because of mixing with sages and writers, and also businessmen; and his fortune will be in them, and with them, and the like.

## If The Part Of Fortune Is In The Dignities Of The Moon

Indeed if it is in the dignities of the Moon according to the aforementioned method, he will acquire it because of mixing with men learned in the law, and legal men; and his fortune will be in them and with them, and the like.

## That The Aforementioned Will Be Signified By The Aforementioned Significators, However, They Are Disposited

And know that whatever the condition of the aforementioned significators is like, and wherever the Part of Fortune is in their dignities, those things which were said will be signified naturally, and according to their disposition, and according to their places in the circle. For if they are in angles, and in good condition, and otherwise well disposed, and likewise the Part of Fortune, they will signify the increase of the native's fortune, and his prosperity. However, if they are in succeedents, they will signify the moderate fortune of the native. Indeed, if they are in cadents or otherwise badly disposed, it will signify the laboriousness, burden, impediment, and diminution of this native's fortune.

## X

### On The Same Topic, According To Aboali

Moreover, another thing, almost the same as the last (even if it is not simply for knowing the status of the native's life at the signified times), by the triplicity Lords of the Ascendant. For its first triplicity Lord signifies the beginning of the natives' life, namely the first third of it. The second signifies the middle, namely the second third of it. The third signifies the end, namely the last third of it.

If one of them is in its own domicile or exaltation, or in two of its other dignities, in the angles, joined to benefics, free from impediments, it signifies the good and prosperous condition of the native in the times it signifies. However, if it is in succeedents, his condition will be something below this. If it is in cadents, it signifies that his condition will be much below this. But if one of them is in a cadent from angles, or in its fall, or in its descension, or in a bad place from the Ascendant, or is retrograde, or peregrine, or combust, or joined to malefics, it signifies the natives' bad condition, and his impediment in the times it signifies, but in cadents it will be increased more.

His impediment will be increased more greatly again, and more strongly, if the Lord of the Ascendant is impeded, along with the first Lord of the mentioned triplicity, or the Lord of the tenth with the second Lord of the triplicity, or the Lord of the seventh Lord with the third Lord of the triplicity.

However, if the first Lord of the mentioned triplicity is impeded, and the Lord of the Ascendant is safe, or vice versa, the misfortune of the impeded planet, and the good fortune of the safe planet, will both be reduced.

Indeed, if the second Lord is impeded, and the Lord of the tenth is safe, or vice versa, the misfortune of the impeded planet, and the good fortune of the safe planet, will both be reduced.

But if the third Lord is impeded and the seventh Lord is safe, or vice versa, it will reduce the misfortune of the impeded planet, and the good fortune of the safe one. But if all of them are safe, it will increase their fortune, and the fortune of the native will be prosperous. Indeed, if they are impeded, his misfortune and bad condition will be increased.

You will also examine the Moon, since she has great signification over the condition of the fortune of any native. For if she is in good condition and well disposed, joined to benefics, she signifies generally over the prosperity and fortune of any native, adding to the goodness of the benefics, and detracting from the malice of the malefics. Indeed, if she is joined to malefics, it signifies the native's adversity, and his bad condition, adding to the malice of the malefics, and detracting from the goodness of the benefics. If she is void-of-course, and in malignant places in the circle, she signifies the impediment of the native, and the adversity and detriment of his fortune.

You will also examine the Lord of the sign in which the Moon is placed: who, if you find well disposed and in a good place from the Sun (namely in his trine or sextile aspect), and otherwise fortunate, strong, and well disposed, joined with the benefics (or the benefics joined to him), signifies the good of the native and his prosperity. But if you see the contrary you can judge to the contrary.

## XI

### On Another, Almost Extraordinary Thing Regarding The Condition Of The Nativity

Indeed you will perceive the condition of the natives' nativity by the Lord of his nativity, and through its place in the houses according to which one of them you find it in.

For if it is in the first, it signifies that the native will be powerful amongst his kin, household members, and those known to him, and those of the same age as himself.

Indeed, if it is in the second, and is in good condition and well disposed, joined to benefics, and is received, it signifies that he will be fortunate in the acquisition of substance. If it is in the contrary condition, you will judge the contrary, and that he will be a destroyer of substance.

However, if it is in the third, it signifies that he will be fortunate among his brothers, and what's more, he will be fortunate when he will go away, and that he will gladly travel on short journeys, and sometimes moderate length ones.

But if it is in the fourth, it signifies that he will not be malicious, and that he will be loved by his father (and good will follow from his father) and by his older ancestors.

If it is in the fifth, it signifies that he will rejoice in children, and because of them, and that he will be loved by men (in a good way).

Likewise, if it is in the sixth, it signifies that he will be a laborious man, wrapping himself in thoughts, and he will have many infirmities.

In the seventh it signifies that he will be an argumentative, contentious man, irritable, a debater, permitting himself to be with women here and there, drawn to obey their will.

But if it is in the eighth, it signifies that he will be fainthearted, a deceiver, crafty, sorrowful, not caring about others, rejoicing in the troubles of others, pained by their prosperities.

Indeed, if it is in the ninth, it signifies that he will be a man of the sciences, and a lover of them; he will also make many pilgrimages, and especially long journeys, loving to go on pilgrimages.

However, if it is in the tenth, he will be a man eagerly having dealings with kings and magnates, and with those who are fit for kingship, and he will wish to lead his life with them.

Indeed, if it is in the eleventh, it signifies that he will be a good natured man, of good dealings, loved by men, amongst whom he will count many as friends, and he will have few children.

Finally, if it is in the twelfth, it signifies that his life will be severe, laborious, impeded; he will be able to count many as enemies, but none as friends, and if he has any friends, they will be very few in number.

## XII

## On The Acquisition Of Substance, Again According To Aboali

Another method on the natives acquisition of substance, according to the opinion of Aboali, almost tending towards a like end. For he said, that the second domicile from the Ascendant should be examined, and it should be seen which planets are in it.

For if benefics are in it, and if malefics (and likewise their aspects) are absent, and its Lord is free, and in a good place from the Ascendant, and likewise from the Sun, it signifies the fortune of this native with substance and in substance. However, if it is to the contrary, it signifies the misfortune of the native with substance and in substance. After this you will see whether the Lord of the Ascendant is joined with the Lord of the second from the Ascendant, since this signifies that the native will easily acquire a multitude of substance, almost without fatigue. You will also examine the lighter planet out of them, namely he who is in an angle, since he will signify the quantity of money, or wealth, that is going to come from the matters already known (as Alboali testifies), not things happening fortuitously. If this lighter planet is in a succeedent, his acquisitions will be below the aforementioned, nevertheless it will be from good, fair, and licit things. However, if it is in a cadent, or in another bad or wicked place from the Ascendant, his acquisition of substance will be from wherever he can acquire it, acquiring it by justice and by wickedness, and he will be stingy and avaricious with it.

If there is not a conjunction or application between them, then examine the Lord of the house of substance: who, if he is in an angle, free from impediments, and the Moon is in similar condition, signifies that the native is going to acquire a moderate amount of substance. Indeed, if it is in a succeedent, it signifies that he will acquire a small amount of money. But if it is in a cadent, it signifies his labour, distress, and oppression in acquiring substance from which he can live, and he will hardly be able to obtain it, and this will be worse and more severe, if the Lord of the house of substance is impeded by malefics, or joined to them by aspect or rays.

Again you will examine the Lord of the Ascendant, and likewise Jupiter: which, if one is joined to the other by body, or by aspect, and they are fortunate, strong, and in good condition and well disposed, it signifies the prosperity of the natives' life, and much acquisition of substance (and this stronger, and more greatly, if the one applying to the other is received). However, if they are not in such a condition, as I said, their signification will be below that which was said, according to the quantity of the diminution of their strength and goodness.

You will be able to say the same about the Part of Fortune and its Lord, if they are in good places from the Ascendant, free from malefics, and from their rays.

And likewise for the Moon, if she is in a good place from the Ascendant, aspecting it; and especially if she is received; and this will be stronger and better if she is received by a benefic. For the Moon has this prerogative, since if she is in an angle, or their succedents, increased in light and number, and committing her disposition or virtue to a planet receiving her, she signifies the goodness of the native's fortune, and the multitude of his goods, and the abundance of things flowing to him.

Also examine the eleventh sign from the sign in which the Part of Fortune is placed: since if there is some benefic in this sign, it signifies the honesty of the acquisition of the natives' substance, and his good way of acquiring it. If one of the malefics are there, it signifies the contrary, namely a dishonourable way of acquiring it (nor will the native be ashamed of acquiring it whatever way he can, as long as he can seize it), and often by injustice, and from illicit things; and this more strongly so, if this sign in which this malefic is placed, is its domicile or exaltation, or has two of its other dignities there.

You will also see whether the mentioned Lord of substance, or the Lord of the sign in which the Part of Fortune is placed, or the Lord of the 11th sign from the domicile of the Part of Fortune, enters into combustion: since this has the signification of the destruction of the fortune and prosperity of the native, and likewise of his substance, and his good condition.

Likewise, you will examine whether the Part of Fortune is joined with any of the benefics, or is in

their opposition or square aspect; and the malefics are cadent from it. Since this signifies the good fortune and prosperity of the native, and the increase of his substance. If it is to the contrary, you could rightly judge to the contrary.

You will also consider whether the Lord of the Ascendant and the Lord of the house of substance are joined, or apply to each other at the same time, since this signifies the good condition of the native. However, if they are not joined together by body or by aspect, and the benefics are cadent from the Ascendant and from the house of substance, and from their Lords, it signifies the detriment of the native and his bad condition, and his laborious and painful life, and his indigence for the whole time of his life: since the Lord of the Ascendant and the Lord of the second house (which naturally signifies the natives profit, and his wealth) are not joined nor applying together.

These things which were said will happen as was said, unless the aforementioned significators of the native's substance operate to the contrary (these significators being the triplicity Lords of the luminary who has authority, the Part of Fortune and its Lord, and likewise Jupiter and his Part). If you find these significators, or the majority of them in good places from the Ascendant (and especially the more authoritative of them, and who has more dignities in the places in which they are), they will operate against the malice of the aforementioned planets - namely the planets who are in the 11th sign from the Part of Fortune, the Lord of the Part of Fortune, and the planets to which they are joined, or to which they are conjunct, or in whose opposition or square aspect they are in. However, if you find them impeded in the places in which they are, they will operate against their goodness, detracting from it.

## XIII

### On The Same

**M**oreover, you will examine the Lord of the house of substance, or the planet who is the Almutem over the substance of the native, and you will consider where it is.

For if it is in the first, it has the signification that the native will acquire wealth without labour, fatigue, or solicitude, and this more strongly and fruitfully, if it is received by a benefic placed in an angle or a succedent.

And Aboaly said that if it is in the second, it will be from the things of the native.

And if it is in the third, it signifies the badness of the brother.

And if it is in the fourth, it signifies the good condition of the father, and that he will remain living in the house he is in.

And if it is in the fifth, he said the native will have children who are known in the palaces of kings.

And if it is in the sixth, it signifies the flight of slaves, and the loss of docile small animals.

And if it is in the seventh, it signifies the turning around of matters because of injustice, and their dispersion, because of women and contentions.

And if it is in the eighth, it signifies the acquisition of things from the things left behind by the dead, nor will he care how he profits or how he spends his wealth.

And if it is in the ninth, it signifies acquisition because of pilgrimages and religions (from sects). And he said that he will only care for hidden things, and his business will be from pilgrimages.

And if it is in the tenth, he will pursue substance from kings, and because of them.

And if it is in the eleventh, he will find substance from friends, and business matters, and leasings, and from merchandise.

And if it is in the twelfth, it signifies that he will earn money from prisons, and humble hidden enemies, and from all low-class and disgraceful works. And he said that he will be a thief and a pillager.

## ON THE THIRD HOUSE

### I

### On The Matter Of Siblings Of Either Sex And Of Their Multitude And Scarcity

Having spoken in the preceding chapter about the natives' substance and his prosperity, and by what means and from where he would acquire it. What will be examined in this chapter is the matters of his siblings' condition, and their multitude or scarcity, according to what we can know about them, and even what we should acquire their affairs from.

Therefore, you should examine the third sign from the Ascendant of the nativity of the native whose nativity you intend to investigate, and the Part of Siblings and its Lord; you will also examine Mars, since he has participation in the signification of the matter of siblings. And likewise the triplicity Lords of the sign, and the planetary Almutem of the aforementioned places (whether there are one or many of them); even the planets who are in them, or who aspect them from opposition or from square aspect, or even from other aspects.

Since if there are benefics in these places, or aspecting them from a praiseworthy aspect, namely a trine or sextile (whether they have dignity there or not), or from a square (if they have domicile, exaltation, term, or triplicity there, but term and triplicity are below domicile, and below exaltation), it signifies the good condition of the natives siblings, and their prosperity. However, if they aspect from trine or sextile aspect, and they have dignity in these places, it signifies an even better condition of the siblings and the increase of their prosperity. However, if there are malefics in these places, or if they aspect them from a square aspect, or from opposition, they will judge the contrary of the aforementioned; and this more greatly, and strongly so, if they do not have dignity in them.

You will also consider the third sign from the Ascendant of the nativity, to see if it is one of the signs signifying many children, and its Lord is in any of those signs (those signs being Cancer, Scorpio, and Pisces). And consider if between the Lord of the Ascendant and the aforementioned Almutem, one of the 14 ways signifying the effect and detriment of matters (which I narrated to you above in the Tractate on The Considerations Which Fall over Judgements etc.; of which there are 16): if there is, it signifies that the native will have many brothers and sisters. You will be able to say the same if Mars is in a sign of many children, and you the planet in whose domicile you find him is oriental, and the Moon is not in a sign of few children (since then she will diminish the number of siblings).

### II

### On The Masculinity And Femininity Of Siblings

Moreover, you will examine if the aforementioned places are masculine signs, and if the significators are in masculine signs, since these will signify that the majority of the siblings are going to be of the masculine sex. However, if the aforementioned places and the aforementioned significators (or the majority of them are in feminine signs), they will signify that the majority of the natives siblings will be of the feminine sex. But if the significators are in signs of few children (which are Gemini, Leo, Virgo, Capricorn, and Aquarius), they will signify a scarcity of siblings for this native, indeed, the rest of the signs show a middling amount.

If the house of brothers is a common sign, and its Lord is in a common and masculine sign, it signifies that the native will only have siblings from the same father. However, if they are both masculine signs, it signifies the siblings to be males; if both of them are feminine signs, it signifies them to be females. Indeed, if one is masculine and the other is feminine, it signifies they will be male and female. However, if the house of brothers is a feminine sign, it signifies that the native will only have siblings from the same mother. If in addition to this, Venus and the Moon are in feminine signs, it signifies only female siblings. Indeed, if the Moon is in a masculine sign and Venus is in a feminine sign, or vice versa, it will judge the native to have male and female siblings. And this more greatly so if the Ascendant is one of the signs signifying many children, and the Moon is in one of these signs.

Again I say that if the Ascendant and the house of brothers are masculine signs (or either of them), and their Lords (or either of their Lords), and the Lord of the fourth is in them, and Venus and the Moon are in feminine signs, or vice versa, it signifies that these siblings will be from the same father, and from the same mother.

You will also examine the Lord of the Ascendant, and the Lord of the house of brothers, to see if they concord with one another, or are of the planets loving each other, for if this is so, or if they aspect each other from a trine or sextile aspect, it signifies that there will be concordance, love, and good will between the native and his siblings. However, if you find to the contrary, you can judge to the contrary, and judge that they will be deceivers and grave enemies in the future. Indeed, if they aspect each other from square, it signifies that there will be some kind of friendship between them, yet not perfect, even if reception intervenes. Likewise examine the Lord of the house of brothers, to see if it is combust, or entering into combustion in nocturnal nativities: since it will signify the scarcity of his siblings, and their detriment and destruction, and this more strongly so if the Moon is separating from Saturn, with him placed in an angle, in nocturnal nativities (or from Mars in a diurnal nativity, with him likewise placed in an angle).

And Alboali said that when Mars enters combustion, it signifies the scarcity of brothers. And he said that if a malefic, peregrine planet is placed in the third sign from the Ascendant, it will signify the scarcity of brothers, and the death of the older brothers.

And Aomar said to examine whether the native or his brother is of greater dignity from the strength of the Almutem over the Ascendant, or the Almutem over the house of brothers, since the stronger of them will be in charge.

And Aboali said that if Mars and his triplicity Lords are in a good place in the circle, and from the Sun, it signifies the good condition of brothers, and their fitness and prosperity, and a multitude of them. And if he is in his descension, or entering into combustion, and his triplicity Lords are in bad places, it signifies the scarcity of brothers and their weakness and bad condition. Say the same if the triplicity Lords of the Ascendant are cadent; and if they are in signs of few children, they will signify a scarcity of siblings (and in those signifying it moderately, judge their moderate quantity).

Then examine the Part of Siblings and its Lord, and see if they concord will the Lord of the house of the natives substance, since this will increase his virtue. Indeed, if it is to the contrary, it will reduce the virtue of the Lord of the house of brothers, but it will prevail over the Lord of the Part of Siblings, even if their virtue appears to be of one quality, according to what the triplicity Lords do.

And Aomar said to examine the triplicity Lords of Mars (namely the first, second, and third) and see which of them is stronger and in better condition, since he signifies the matter of brothers: for the first signifies older brothers, the second middle brothers, the third younger brothers.

You will even examine the Lord of the Part of Fortune: for if he is with the Part of Fortune it signifies that the older brothers will hate each other.

## III

### Who Will Die First Amongst The Siblings, Or Who Will Have A Longer Life

And he said to know which of them will last and which of them will be consumed by death (and the rest of the things which happen to them), examine if there is a planet between the Midheaven and the Ascendant, since if a benefic planet is there, it signifies that children were born to the natives father before him, and are still alive. And if a malefic is there, it signifies that they have already died. Indeed, if the benefics or malefics are in common signs, there are two siblings who remain or who have died.

Aomar also said to examine those who are born afterwards by what is between the Ascendant and the angle of the earth. If there are planets there, brothers and sisters will be born after him according to the quantity of stars which you find there. If you find some of the planets in common signs, double their number. However, if there are malefics there, it signifies their death. And if there are benefics, it signifies their durability.

And he said that the Sun and Saturn signify the father; and Venus and the Moon signify the mother. He also said that the Moon separating from planets (especially from the Sun or Saturn), signifies those who are born before him. Indeed, the conjunction of the Moon with other planets, signifies those who are born after him, and those who are younger than him.

And he said that you will also examine the triplicity Lords of Mars (namely the first, second, and third) and you will take the stronger of them. And the one who has more testimony, will be the one in the first, fourth, or seventh or tenth, and understand this about the rest. And he said that if it is in an angle, he will be the first child (or according to the number of angles, just as was said). And he said that if it is in the Ascendant, he will be the first or the fourth. He also said that if it is in the Midheaven, it signifies that he will be the first, or fourth, or more. Again he said, and if it is in the seventh, it signifies that he will be the seventh, or fourth, or first. Indeed, if it is in the fourth, it signifies that he will be the first or the fourth. Moreover, he said that all of these places signify according to the quality of the place, but to me this appears to be a mistake or the scribe.

Indeed, Aboali said to examine the triplicity Lord of the Ascendant, for it is in the Ascendant, he will be the first born of his mother; and if it is in the Midheaven or in the angle of the earth, he will be the first or the fourth; and if it is in the seventh, he will be the first, or the seventh. And he said that if it is in an angle, examine the planets who are between the degree of the Ascendant and the degree of the Midheaven, which, if they are benefics, signify that he will have living brothers; and if they are malefics, it signifies he will have them, but that they will die; and if there are neither benefics nor malefics there, say that he is his mother's first-born.

## IV

### On The Matter Of Siblings

Indeed Ptolemy was of the opinion that the matter of siblings is found from the matter of the mother, making mention of siblings from the same mother; and he did not care to make mention of the same father, since we are more certain that brothers are from the same mother than from the same father (it sometimes happens not to be true, as is commonly thought).

Ptolemy seemed to want it to be so that the eleventh house signified the mother, just as the tenth does: and since the third from the Ascendant is the fifth from the eleventh (which signifies the mother, just as the tenth does), therefore the third is the house given to the natives siblings, and the children of the same mother, since it is the fifth from the eleventh.

Whence the tenth and the eleventh are to be considered, which, if benefics are found to be in either of them, will judge a multitude of siblings, and their prosperity (if malefics are there, you will undoubtedly announce the contrary of what was said). If Jupiter is in these places, you will say this without a doubt or a scruple - or if Venus is there in the day, or the Moon in the night, both of which signify the purpose of the mother. Indeed, if they aspect Saturn from a trine or sextile aspect, and they are fortunate and strong, they will signify the goodness of the good number of siblings (however, it will be below the aforementioned, nor will their condition be as prosperous). Indeed, if they are badly disposed, and remain in the aforementioned places, or if the malefics look forward from square aspect, or opposition, they will show the scarcity of the siblings and their weakness (and this more strongly so if they are placed under the rays of the Sun). Indeed, if these, or one of the malefics (Saturn for the first born, Mars for the latter born) are found in one of the angles (but more strongly in the Ascendant), they will judge their scarcity and bad condition. And Mars for the most part reduces their number through death.

And even though I touched on the same thing for you above, again I say this: that if the planets who are the significators of the siblings are well disposed, and aspect the place of the brothers from a trine or sextile aspect, this signifies that the native's brothers will be virtuous and powerful and exalted amongst other men. However, if the significators of the brothers are in contrary condition, the natives brothers will be found to be imbeciles and powerless. If many malefics impede the significators of the brothers, they signify the shortness of their lives.

## V

### On The Masculinity Of Natives And Siblings, According To Ptolemy

And Ptolemy said the givers of males are the masculine planets, clean in their qualities (that is in their condition), free from impediments; however, the bestower of females are the feminine planets.

And he made a certain statement which almost appears uncertain, when it is not: that if the planetary significators of siblings are conjoined in the figure and joined with Saturn (namely from a trine or sextile aspect), the siblings will love and honour each other. However, if they are not conjoined with each other, or if they aspect each other from a square or opposition, the native will be a bringer of adversity.

Nor did he express the reason why the significators of children have to act in the matter of brothers.

And he said that eastern planets impart older siblings, western planets younger ones.

And Aboali said to examine the planets who are between the Ascendant and the angle of the earth: who, if they are benefics, signify that his mother will give birth to children after him, and they will live. Indeed, if they are malefics, it signifies that she will give birth again: but those who are born after the native will not live; or if the mother conceives, she will abort the child, and if there are neither benefics nor malefics, it signifies that the mother will not conceive after having the native.

And Aboali said to examine the Lord of the house of brothers, which if it is in the Ascendant or in the seventh, say that the native does not have siblings; and if it is in the Midheaven he has siblings older than him; and if it is in the fourth he has siblings who are born after him.

Again I tell you, that if the Moon is in someone's Ascendant, separated from benefics, it signifies the good condition of the natives' siblings (and especially the older ones) and the good disposition of their lives. And if she is separating from malefics, it signifies their detriment and the closeness of their death.

## VI

### On The Prosperity Of Siblings

You will examine the prosperity and goodness of the siblings according to the triplicity Lords of their domicile (namely the first, second, and third), since the first signifies siblings older than the native, the second middle siblings, and the third younger siblings. For the condition of the natives brothers will match the condition of the triplicity Lords of their domicile at the hour of the nativity of the native whose nativity you are investigating, and such things ought to be discovered. For if the first one of them is in good condition and well disposed, it signifies the good condition of the natives' older siblings; if the second, the middle siblings; if the third, the younger siblings. For if the first triplicity Lord of the house of brothers is in its own domicile or exaltation, or in two of its other dignities, or in an angle, or a succedent, and in good place from the Sun and from the Ascendant, and free from impediments, it signifies the good condition of the older siblings and their good disposition, and likewise their exaltation and fame.

If it is joined with one of the planets which are in good condition, and well disposed in its own domicile or exaltation, or placed in two of its other dignities, it signifies the increase of their prosperity and their exaltation, and their association with princes, magnates, noblemen, kings, and wealthy men fit for kingship, and being recalled to memory by these men. Indeed, if it is joined with a malefic planet not receiving him, or made unfortunate, or cadent, or placed in its own descension, or placed in one of its detriments, it will judge their worthlessness, weakness, and contact with the most worthless of persons, and stay with them.

Indeed, if the second Lord of this triplicity is so impeded, it shows the detriment of the middle sibling; if the third, of the younger - according to what was said of the older siblings. But if the Moon is then void-of-course it signifies the bad condition of the siblings, and their impediment.

And Aboali said that if the Caput Draconis is in the house of brothers, it signifies that the condition of the native is going to be below that of all of his siblings, and weaker than it. And if the Cauda is there, it signifies that the condition of the native will prevail over the condition of all of his siblings. And if the Lord of the house of brothers is a benefic, and is free from malefics and from impediments, or if there is a free benefic in the house of brothers, and it is applying to an unimpeded benefic, it signifies the fitness of the siblings' condition, and of the native. Indeed, if it is a malefic, and another malefic (or both malefics) aspects it, and it is impeded, it signifies the bad condition of his siblings, and their detriment and destruction, and the bad condition and impediment of the native.

In order to know whether the native or his siblings are of greater value, examine the triplicity Lords of the house of brothers and the triplicity Lords of the Ascendant: for whichever one them is in better condition and better disposed, he will be preferred, and will be of better health and more exalted.

## ON THE FOURTH HOUSE

### I

## On The Condition Of Fathers And Their Accidents, And From Which Place Of The Circle It Is Taken

With a narration on the matter of siblings having been set out in the preceding chapters, it seems fitting to me to subsequently make mention of the matter of the father, and from which place in the circle the matter of the father ought to be taken.

Indeed, Aomar said that you ought to examine it from the fourth sign from the Ascendant of the natives' nativity, and its Lord, and from the Part of the Father, and from the Sun and Saturn (from the Sun in the day, and Saturn at night), and we ought to examine the Part of the Father, and the sign of the fourth house in both the day and the night.

For you will examine the place of each one of these in the figure of the aforementioned nativity, and you will consider the Almutem over the place of each one of them, and whichever one of them you find stronger, operate by him - namely, beginning from the Lord of the fourth house, then from the Part of the Father and its Lord, and so from the Sun, and afterwards from Saturn, and lastly from the planet who is in the fourth. For by the planet through which you operated, you will be able to know the span of the natives' fathers life (and especially of the first born), and whether it will be long or short; and this more freely if the nativity of the father is unknown: since the life of the father will vary in the aforementioned nativity, just as the years of the world and of the nativity vary by their revolutions (just as was dealt with above in the chapter on the form and figure of the body of the native). For the stronger of them will be the one who is in an angle, not remote from the cusp of the angle by more than three degrees before, or five degrees after; or who is in the succedents (likewise not remote), or one of the Lords of the other four dignities of the degree in which he is in.

Indeed, after you have seen the quantity of the fathers life, and you wish to know what the condition of his life is going to be like, you will examine the degree of the Part of the Father, and the degree of the fourth house, and the degree of the Sun (or Saturn), and you will examine him who is more fit to be the Ylem; and direct him to the places of the benefics and malefics. And according to what you see of the quantity of his years (which are signified by the aforementioned Almutem), you will speak about the end of the life of this natives' father (which is hardly or never in disagreement to that which is found in his own nativity). And to know the true condition of the father for every year, you will likewise direct the degree of the profection of the father to the degrees of benefics and malefics: and according to what you see of the condition of the mentioned year of the profection (or even of a revolution), so you will be able to judge of the condition of his father, and the soundness of his body.

In the cognition of his dignity and sublimity or honour, you will consider the Sun's dustoria of by the diurnal planets (if the nativity is diurnal), which is signified by planets which are oriental from the Sun. And if it is nocturnal, you will consider it from Saturn's dustoria from the Sun in particular. If there is dustoria, it signifies that great dignities and great honours are going to come to the father. But if you find the contrary, you can judge the contrary.

### II

## On The Time Of The Things Mentioned Above

Indeed to know at which time these things ought to occur, you will consider the triplicity Lords of the Sun, if it is a diurnal nativity; however, if it is a nocturnal nativity, you will consider the triplicity Lords of Saturn, and according to what you see of their condition (namely of the first, second, and third) so you will announce.

### III

## On The Kind Of Death Of The Father

If you wish to examine the matter of the fathers' death, as regards it severity or agreeableness, you will consider the Almutem over the matter of the father; namely, whether it is free from impediments or not: since if it is free, this signifies that the father will pass away in his bed from a decent death, and this more greatly so, and more certainly so, if Jupiter or Venus are found in the eighth from the house of the father. But if it is impeded, the contrary of what was said will be suspected, and this more so if Saturn or Mars are placed in the fathers eighth house. For if it is impeded by Mars in the day, or by Saturn at night, from opposition or square aspect without the presence or aspect of one of the benefics, and if this malefic doesn't receive him, it signifies evil of the father's death, and its severity. However, if this malefic who impedes the mentioned Almutem is the Lord of the Ascendant, or the Almutem over the Ascendant, it signifies that this native will kill his father, or will be the reason for his death.

Indeed, for their harmony, you will examine the Almutem over the Ascendant, and over the house of the father: which if they agree with each other, and are concordant, it signifies that there will be concord between them, and likewise benevolence (and this more strongly so if they receive each other). If this is not so, and they are discordant, it signifies that there will be discord, lawsuits, and hatred between them. And Aomar said that then you will be able to say that he is not a legitimate son. And if the Sun is impeded by Mars in the day, or by Saturn at night, the father will suspect that this will befall him from native. Likewise if the Moon is impeded by Mars in the day, or by Saturn at night, he will not believe him, and will always suspect evil of him.

And Aomar also relates that certain of the sages said that if the Lord of the Part of the Father does not aspect the house of children, and the Sun does not aspect the Lord of the domicile in which he is placed, and if the Lord of the Part of the Father does not aspect the Part, the native will not be the son of this father; but if either of them aspect, the native will be legitimate.

## IV

### On The Condition Of The Father And Mother

Aboali truly said, that you ought to examine matters of the father from the Sun if it is a diurnal nativity, however, if it is a nocturnal nativity, you ought to examine it from Saturn, and as much in the day as at night you ought to examine the father from the fourth and the Part of the Father, and their Lords.

And again, Aboali said that you ought to examine the matter of the mother from the fourth, just as in the matter of the father; and in day and night from the Part of the Mother and its Lord - which Part is taken in the day from Venus to the Moon, and vice versa at night, and projected from the Ascendant.

Indeed, if you find the significators of the father and mother, or the Lords of the signs in which they are placed, or most of them, in angles, or in their succedents, and one of the benefics is in the house signifying the father, and the triplicity Lords of the domicile where the luminary who has authority is placed are safe and well disposed, and in a good place in the figure of the nativity - it signifies the prosperity and good condition of the father, and his gladness, and a multitude of joy. Indeed, if you see to the contrary, you can judge the contrary of the father's condition, and the durability of his misfortune and infirmity.

But if the Sun is in a good place of the figure of the nativity (and I say that he is in good condition and well disposed), and the triplicity Lords of the domicile in which he is placed are badly disposed and impeded, it signifies the good condition of the father, namely at the time of the nativity; but you will undoubtedly judge the contrary for the future. However, if the Sun is impeded, and his triplicity Lords are found to be safe, it signifies the bad condition of the father, and his impediment at the time of the nativity, but his good condition, fortune, and good disposition in the future.

## V

### On The Condition Of The Father By Direction

However, if you intend to know what the condition of the father will be like in the future, and what his disposition will be like, according to direction, if it is a diurnal nativity you will direct from the place of the Sun, and from the place of the Part of the Father. However, if it is a nocturnal nativity, direct from the place of Saturn, and from the place of the Part of the Father (as you do when you direct from the place of the Sun) to the bodies of benefics and malefics, and to their rays: since from these will be adopted the significations of benefics or malefics which are going to befall the father after the child's nativity; which, when they arrive to the body of any of some benefic, or to its rays, without the presence of a malefic or its rays, then it will signify good accidents, prosperity, and benefit, and the safety of his body, and pleasing things which ought to happen to the father (and this more strongly so if the Part of the Father and the Lord of the domicile in which it is placed is found in an angle or their succedents).

Indeed, when it arrives to the body of some malefic, then it will signify the contrary of all of those things which were said, and that infirmities, impediments, and vile things will befall the father; and this more greatly and strongly so if the Part of the Father and its Lord are in places which are cadent from the Ascendant.

And Aboali said that the same is to be examined in the matter of the mother, namely in the day from Venus and the Part of the Mother; and at night from the Moon and the Part of the Mother. And he said that we ought to examine the degree of the conjunction and or prevention; which, if the benefics aspect it, and the malefics are cadent from it, signifies the good condition of the father and his exaltation. However, if malefics aspect it, and the benefics are cadent from it, it signifies his worthlessness. However, if benefics and malefics aspect it at the same time, it signifies the mediocre condition of the father. And he said that the sign of the conjunction and its Lord signify the affairs of the father, the sign of the prevention and its Lord signify the affairs of the mother.

And he said to examine the fourth sign, since if Jupiter, the Sun, or Venus are placed there, or if one of them aspect it by a praiseworthy aspect, it signifies the exaltation of the father and his loftiness and fortune. But if one of the malefics are there, or they aspect it by an evil aspect without the presence or aspect of any benefic, or if the fourth sign is the domicile or the exaltation of the planet in whose domicile the Lord of the fourth is placed, it signifies the weakness and fall of the father and his servitude. However, if the fourth sign is Taurus or Cancer, it signifies the bad condition of the mother, and her weakness and fall, and likewise her servitude.

And if the Sun and the Moon are in mobile signs, it signifies that the father will not be of the same stock as the mother, but one will be of lower parentage than the other; and according to how they are in a more worthless or weaker place, it will signify lower stock. For it is the Sun, it will signify the father, and if it is the Moon, it will signify the mother.

And Alboali said that the Sun in the day, and the Moon at night, signify the affairs of the father at the time of the birth of the child; and the Lords of the houses in which they are in, signify that which will be with regards to the father in the future. And when the significators of the father, which in diurnal nativities are the Lord of the domicile in which the Sun is placed, and its triplicity Lords, and the Lord of its exaltation; and in nocturnal nativities the Lord of the domicile in which Saturn is placed, and its triplicity Lords and exaltation Lord; and the Part of the Father, and the Lord of the domicile in which it is placed both in day and at night - are in their own domiciles or exaltations, free from malefics, and benefics aspect them, signify the exaltation and sublime dignity of the father, and the acquisition of substance. And this more greatly and strongly if the Part of Fortune and the Lord of the domicile in which it is placed are fortunate and strong. And greater again, if in addition to this, the Part of the Father and its Lord are fortunate: for it will be signified by this that the fortune, dignity, and honour of the father will be of great durability and constancy after the birth of this child.

You will also examine for the strength of the father, and likewise his value, in diurnal nativities, by seeing if some diurnal planet is in the dustoria of the Sun, since this signifies the greatness and exaltation of the fathers' strength - unless the fathers' nativity operates very much against it; which if this is so, then the aforementioned will be diminished. However, if the figures agree, they will be increased. But if the aforementioned significators (especially the luminaries) are impeded, and in bad places void-of-course, and in their falls, and their descensions and detriments, it will signify the fall, impediment, or detriment of the father, and his worthlessness, and his life will miserable, and the diminution and loss of his goods; and this more strongly so if Venus and Saturn are in bad condition, and badly disposed. And greater again if Mars ascends after the Sun, or Saturn after the Moon, and if benefics do not aspect the Sun or the Moon.

And always examine the condition of the father from the Sun in the day, and the Lord of the domicile in which he is placed, and its triplicity Lords. Indeed, at night, from Saturn and the Lord of the domicile in which he is placed, and its triplicity Lords.

And Aboali said to know that the Sun and the Moon and the Lords of their domiciles, and the triplicity Lords of the same, if they are in angles, free from malefics and impediments, signify the fortune of the native' father and mother. And when they are impeded and joined to malefics, and are cadent and void-of-course, signify the bad condition of the native and his parents, and the destruction of their matters.

## VI

## On The Death Of The Father

And Ptolemy said to examine in whose nativity the Sun in the day aspects the Ascendant, and direct him to the bodies of malefics, and to their rays by degrees of ascension, giving one year to each degree. And if the Sun does not aspect the Ascendant, and Saturn does aspect it, direct him as you directed the Sun. If Saturn does not aspect the Ascendant, then direct the degree of the angle of the earth. Then examine to see how much comes to him in terms of years. If that which comes forth is exactly as much as that which is signified by the planet who has more dignity in the day from the Sun and from the Lord of the house in which he is placed; indeed, at night from Saturn, and from the Lord of the domicile in which he is found; however, in day and night from the fourth and its Lord, and from the Part of the Father and its Lord, or close to it, it signifies that his father will die in the same year.

## VII

## On The Death Of The Mother

And Ptolemy said that if it is a diurnal nativity, to examine the life of the mother from Venus, who, if she aspects the Ascendant, direct her to the bodies of malefics, and to their rays by degrees of ascension, giving each degree one year. However, if Venus does not aspect the Ascendant, and the Moon does aspect it, direct her as was said of Venus. However, if the Moon does not aspect the Ascendant, then direct the degree of the tenth house. And in nocturnal nativities begin from the Moon, and then from Venus, and then from the degree of the tenth house. After this you will examine what is brought forth for her in terms of years; which if it is equal to the years which the planet who has more dignity in the day from Venus and the Lord of the domicile in which she is placed, and at night from the Moon and the Lord of the domicile in which she then falls; and in the day, and the night from the degree of the tenth house and its Lord, and from the Part of the Mother and the Lord of the same domicile in which it is placed, or close to them, signifies the death of the mother in the same year.

## VIII

## On The Knowledge Of The Years Of The Fathers Life

In order to know the years of the fathers life, if it is a diurnal nativity, you will examine if the Sun is in an angle or a succeedent, and the Lord of the domicile, exaltation, terms, or triplicity aspects him: since then you will be able to take the Ylem from him, whatever kind of aspect it is. Indeed, if none of these planets are aspecting the Sun then, and the Lord of the face aspects him from a trine or sextile aspect, and he is otherwise in good condition and well disposed, you will also be able to take the Ylem from the Sun and direct him for the life of the father, and the planet who is the Almutem over the degree of the Sun will be called the Alcocoden, and the significator of the years of the life of this natives' father.

But if what was said about the Sun is not so, then you will examine Saturn, who if you find in one of the angles or the succedents, and one of the Lords of the aforementioned dignities are aspecting him, you will be able to take the Ylem from Saturn; and the planet who is the Lord of this dignities of this degree will be the significator of the years of the fathers' life.

However, if Saturn is not so disposed (as was said), then you will examine the Part of the Father, which, if you find in one of the angles or their succeedents, and aspected by one of the Lords of the aforementioned dignities, it will be the Ylem. And the planet who is the Lord of this dignity, and aspects it, will be the significator of the years of this natives' fathers life.

And Aboali said that if what was said of the Part of the Father is not so, then examine the degree of the house of the father; and if one of the Lords of is dignities aspect it, this degree will be the Ylem, and the planet aspecting the Lord of the dignity will be the Alcocoden.

Indeed, if it is a nocturnal nativity, you will begin to examine from Saturn first, then from the Sun, after that from the Part of the Father, and indeed, lastly from the degree of the house of the father.

And Ptolemy said that if the benefics aspecting the Sun or the Moon, aspects the Part of Fortune in nativities, it signifies that the substance of the parents will last, and that it will be saved usefully. If you find things to be to the contrary of the aforementioned, namely that benefics, or the luminaries do not aspect the Part of Fortune, and this more strongly so if malefics aspect it, the native will not enjoy the goods of his parents, nor will they benefit him.

## IX

### On The Length Or Brevity Of The Fathers Life

For the length or brevity of the fathers life you will examine if Jupiter and Venus are joined to the Sun or Saturn, or if Jupiter is joined with Venus, or if the Sun and Saturn are joined together by such a conjunction (namely an aspectual or corporeal one) that they receive each other by mutual reception, and both of them are fortunate and strong, they will signify a long life for the natives father. However, if you observe the contrary, you will be able to judge to the contrary, except that you will not be able to be certain to a point on the length or brevity of the fathers life: however, one should fear for its brevity, rather than hope for its length.

You will be able to say the same if Mars is northern from the Sun or from Saturn, or if he is oriental from Saturn, and occidental from the Sun, or is following them in the figure (that is, if one of them is in one domicile of someone's figure, and Mars is in the domicile which immediately succeeds it), and likewise if Saturn is joined with the Sun by a square aspect, or from opposition. However, if the conjunction is from a trine or sextile aspect, it will reduce the malice, and this more strongly so if reception intervenes. And if the Sun and Saturn are cadent from the angles, they signify the bad condition of the father and his weakness.

And Ptolemy said that if the Sun and Saturn are in angles, or in places ascending to angles [i.e. succeedents], they will signify the short life of the father (yet this is not contrary to what Ptolemy said above, that when the Sun and Saturn are in angles, they signify the life of the father, since there he spoke about the Ylem, here he spoke about the life after the Ylem). Or they signify some detriment of his, or harm similar or equal to it, and this more greatly so if they are in the first, the tenth, the second, or the eleventh (since these two angles are faster than the others). However, if they are in the 7th, or the 4th, the 8th, or the 5th, they judge the fathers life to be less short.

But if Mars aspects the Sun from square or opposition, it will signify either of two things for the father - that a quick and unexpected death will befall the father, or the impending detriment of his eyes. Indeed, if the aspect is from the eighth it will signify death (and this more strongly so if the eighth is Scorpio). However, if it is from the sixth, it signifies the aforementioned impediments (and this more strongly so if the sixth is Virgo). Indeed, if Mars aspects Saturn from the aforementioned aspects, it will judge death for this natives father, or at least a fever, with very cold recurrences, or mutilation, or being burned, or damage from robbery. If the conjunction is from the eighth, death; if from the sixth, fever; if from any other places besides the 12th, mutilation; if from the 12th, by robbery, or by hidden enemies. But if Saturn and the Sun are joined by the aforementioned aspects without perfect reception, from whatever houses the conjunction is, they will announce that the father's death will be because of illnesses (and especially cold ones).

## ON THE FIFTH HOUSE

### I

### On The Matter Of Children And Their Condition

**E**ven if it seemed to some of the ancient sages to defer the chapter of children, since children follow marriage, it still seems fitting to me that after a narration on the father, to make mention of the children; nor it is in vain, since children are loved by parents more tenderly and deeply than spouses; and the house signifying children precedes the house signifying marriage.

Annuz and Baruth said in the chapter on children (and they did not appear to dissent from Ptolemy's' opinion) that in the matter of children you ought to examine the tenth in the nativity of any native, and likewise the 11th, the 1st also, and the 7th; and see if one of the planets or one of the significators signifying children are found in any of the aforementioned places (which are Jupiter, Venus, the Moon, Mercury, the Lord of the fifth, and the Part of Fortune and the Part of Children, and the Lords of these Parts) or if there is one of the child-denying planets in them (which are the Sun, Mars, and Saturn). For if the aforementioned significators of children (or one of them) are in the aforementioned places, or in one of them, or even in the fifth, and they are fortunate and strong, and one of the benefics aspects them from a trine or sextile aspect with or without reception, or even from a square with reception, it will signify that the native will undoubtedly have children, unless the significator is with one of the fixed stars of the nature of Mars or Saturn in the same minute. However, if they are weak, they will judge that he will have little children.

But if one of the aforementioned significators are not there, and the Part of Fortune or the Part of Children is there, and one of the malefics are aspecting it, it will totally deny children, whether it is weak or strong; unless perhaps one of the benefics aspect the malefic from a trine or sextile aspect, with reception, or if it is with one of the fixed stars of the nature of Jupiter, Venus, or the Moon, in the same minute; and it should not be in Leo, Virgo, Libra, Capricorn, Aquarius or Taurus. Yet this varies in the signification of Mercury,

since if he is in one of the aforementioned places he will incline to the nature of that planet with whom he is joined.

And if one of the aforementioned significators signifying children is in one of the aforementioned places, and he is void-of-course, it signifies that the native will only have one child.

### II

### At What Age The Native Is Going To Have Children

**I**f Mercury signifies the native to have children, you will consider whether he is joined to an oriental planet, since this signifies children in youth. However, if this planet is occidental, it signifies them after youth. You will be able to say the same as this regarding the triplicity Lords of Jupiter, since if the first is oriental, it will signify them in youth, if the second, in middle age, if the third, in old age. However, if all of them are oriental, they will be signified at any age, but more so in the first 25 years; indeed, if they are all occidental, they will signify children for him after youth is completed.

Likewise if the Almutem over the house of children, or Jupiter, or the Planet in whose domicile the Almutem is placed, are oriental, or if the Part of Children is in the Ascendant, it will signify that the native is going to have children in his youth.

If that planet appears in the morning before the Sun, distant from him by three signs or more, or if the Part of Children is in the 10th, it will signify children for him in his middle age. Indeed, if it is occidental, or if the Part of Children is in the 7th or the 4th, it will signify him to have children in his old age; and you will conjecture according to the rest of these houses.

Indeed, Aboaly said that if the Part of Children is in the Ascendant, it will signify children in youth; if it is in the Midheaven, it will signify them in middle age; and if it is in the fourth, or the seventh, it will signify them in old age. However, you will be able to connect all of their sayings together, and so by conjecture you will be able to judge more rightly and securely.

## III

## On The Multitude Or Scarcity Of Children

However, for the multitude of children you will examine Jupiter and Venus, and you will judge according to their condition. Indeed, for their scarcity you will examine Saturn and Mars, and speak according to what you see with regards to their disposition. Indeed, for a moderate amount of them, you will seek the Moon. However, you will speak regarding Mercury just as you see him, as was said above.

However, if the aforementioned places are common signs (provided that they are not sterile signs), and the significator of children is likewise in a common sign, it will signify that he will have twins; and their sex will be signified by the aforementioned places, or the aforementioned significators.

And if these places are in signs which signify children (which are the water signs, namely Cancer, Scorpio and Pisces, which signify a greater quantity of children than the rest), it will signify that the native is going to have many children.

If the planet signifying children is feminine, and the place signifying children is a masculine sign, or vice versa, you will announce that he will have children of both sexes. And if the planet and the place are of the same sex, they will judge the children to be of this sex.

And if the givers of children are in the above mentioned sterile signs, or if malefics are elevated over them, or if they are the Almutems over the places signifying children, they will try to not to forsake the native having children. If they cannot prevent him from having children, they will hardly or never permit him to have more than one child, and the father will see the death of this child, and he will not live long; and if he does live, he will be unfortunate and troubled, and evils will befall him. However, if Mars and Saturn or the Sun are in the Ascendant, or in the tenth, or the seventh, or even in the 11th or the 5th, or if they aspect these places without the conjunction or aspect of some benefic to the places, or to the aforementioned planets, or if the Ascendant is a sterile sign, and the places signifying children are sterile signs, this signifies that the native will not have children.

And Ptolemy said that if the mentioned malefics are placed in masculine or sterile signs, even if benefics aspect them, they signify that he is not going to have any children, since masculine signs, almost like sterile signs, speak against children. But if they are in feminine signs (for feminine signs, like water signs, bestow children), or signs of many children, and benefics aspect them, they will signify that the native will have a child with some defect in his person which he will suffer; or this child will not be long lived, but short lived.

But indeed, if there is a masculine or sterile sign in one of the aforementioned places signifying children, and a feminine sign or a sign of many children in another, it signifies that the native will have some children, whose friendship no men will desire, in fact they will completely recoil from them; or his children will be aborted. And this will happen according to whether the greater part of them are in signs of the aforementioned natures (such as if the greater part are in masculine and sterile signs), or according to one of the planets being stronger than the other, or being elevated over him, or being greater in number, or being stronger in these places, or according to the majority of them being oriental, or closer to the aforementioned angles, or moving towards them by the aforementioned conditions, so will the quantity of their significations be greater.

And Aomar said that after this you should examine the sign of children and the sign of the Almutem over the matters of the condition of the native, and the Ascendant: which if they are signs of many children, the native will abound in children. If there is no concord between the Almutem of the Ascendant, and the Almutem over the house of children, and Jupiter is combust and Venus is impeded, it signifies that the native will be sterile and without children; and you will observe this for both sexes.

However, Ptolemy said that particular matters of children can be understood by an appraisal, if we place the planet who is the giver of children as an Ascendant. For then all of the particulars of the children taken together will be discerned, just as they are generally known from a nativity.

Indeed, Aomar said to examine the planets who are the Almutem over the house of children, whether there are one or many. If one or more of them agree with the Lord of the Ascendant, the children will be good and just, and loving of their father; if it is to the contrary, they will impede him. And he said that if the significator of children is a malefic impeding the Ascendant and its Lord, the children will introduce diverse impediments to their father. And if it impedes the Moon, they will introduce diverse impediments to their mother. And he said that if the significators of children are safe, the children will be safe, and they will not perish. And if the significators of the children are impeded, the children will rarely be agreeable.

You will be able to say the same about the Part of Children: which, if it is in the angles or the succeedents of the 10th or the 4th, signifies the multitude and goodness of children, and rejoicing with them. However, if it is in the other six places, it signifies the scarcity of children, and their quick death. If it is void-of-course, it signifies the death of the natives' first born, or perhaps his mother will abort him, and she will be sorrowed over children, or because of children.

And Aboali said that if the Lord of the Ascendant is applying with the Lord of the seventh, it signifies a multitude of children from concubines. However, if it is applying with the Lord of the sixth, it signifies them from his own handmaids or slavegirls. You will also examine the triplicity Lords of Jupiter, who, if they are in angles, or in succeedents of angles, signify a multitude of children. However, if they are in other places, besides the 6th and 12th, in their own dignities, and not impeded by malefics, signify a suitable quantity of children. But if they are cadent from angles, or otherwise impeded by malefics, or if they are combust, it signifies the scarcity of children, and their unfitness.

Moreover, Aboali said that if Jupiter and Mercury are in their own domiciles or exaltations, in angles or their succedents, and their triplicity Lords are in good places from the Ascendant, not impeded, namely fortunate and strong, it signifies a multitude of children, and good things and rejoicing with them.

You will be able to say the same about the Part of Children if it is well disposed in good places (namely that it is in angles, or their succeedents), since then it will signify a multitude of children, and their aptitude and their good behaviour. And if it is cadent from the Ascendant, and especially in the sixth, or in the twelfth, it signifies the scarcity of children, and the brevity of their lives. But if one of the benefics, which is free, fortunate, and strong, aspect the Part of Children by a trine or sextile aspect, and especially with reception, it will signify a great multitude of children. However, if this benefic aspects the part from the mentioned aspects without reception, or from a square with reception, the significations will be well below the aforementioned, however, it will be a suitable quantity. However, if it aspects from a square aspect without reception, it signifies children, but its signification will be much below this. However, if this benefic is impeded, or if a malefic is aspecting the Part of Children (and this more strongly so if this aspect is from opposition), it significations will be weaker again, and it will signify fewer children. If Jupiter does not aspect the Part of Children, and Venus is impeded by Saturn, you can announce the sterility of the native or the smallest quantity of children; and even more so if the Moon is impeded in addition to this.

And Aboali said that if Jupiter, Venus, and Mercury are free from malefics, retrogradation, and combustion, the native will have many children. However, if they are impeded by malefics or in their own detriment, or in their own descension, or under the rays of the Sun he will not have children; or if he has them, they will die before their father.

You will also examine the fifth: if there is a benefic placed there, and its Lord is free from the aforementioned impediments, and it aspects the tenth house, it signifies the native will have many, and benevolent children. However, if there is a malefic in the fifth, and its Lord is impeded, it signifies the scarcity of children, and their hastened death (and especially if the impediment is in the third or the sixth). Likewise if the Sun or the Moon are impeded by malefics without the aspect of some benefic, it signifies the scarcity of children, and the diminution of the natives' substance.

**IV**

## On The Time Of Children According To Aboali

Moreover, Aboali said, summarising the aforementioned, to examine the planet who is more deserving in the significations of children: who, if he is oriental, signifies children in youth; and if he is occidental, signifies children in old age. And if he is in the tenth or eleventh, he signifies children in youth, and if he is in the fifth, the eighth, or the ninth, he signifies children in middle age. And if he is in the fourth, or the seventh, he signifies children at the end of life.

And he said that if the Part of Children is in the Ascendant, it signifies children in youth; and if it is in the Midheaven, it signifies children in the middle age of life; and if it is in the fourth or the seventh, it signifies children at the end of life. And he said that in the revolutions of the year, if Jupiter or Venus arrives to the place of the Part of Children, or aspects it from a square aspect or opposition, it signifies that he will have children at that time (but Jupiter has greater signification in children). And likewise if the year arrives to the sign in which Jupiter or Venus is placed in his nativity, it signifies children in the same year.

And he said in the agreement of children with their father, examine the planet who is more deserving in the significations of children, and the Lord of the Ascendant; and if either of them make the other fortunate, it signifies their concord; and if one impedes the other, it signifies their discord and enmity. However, you will turn your intention to this, by conjecturing from house to house, from signification to signification with industry and discretion - for it not possible for all of the things which happen in these works to be written down individually; for the effort would be led back to nothing.

## ON THE SIXTH HOUSE

### I

## On The Natives' Slaves And Slavegirls, And Servants Or Assistants; And On Small Animals Which Are Neither Ridden Nor Yoked; And On His Infirmities, And Likewise Illnesses

Having discussed the matter of children in the chapter which preceded this one, it seems fitting to me in this chapter to subsequently deal with and make mention of the matter of slaves, slavegirls, servants, assistants, small animals which are not ridden or yoked, and of the infirmities of the native and his illnesses.

For Aboali said, with regard to the matters of slaves and slavegirls, or servants and assistants, that you ought to examine the sixth and its Lord, and likewise Mercury and the Moon, and see if Mercury is oriental and in the Ascendant or in the tenth, joined to Jupiter by corporeal conjunction or by aspect, in a mobile or common sign; or if one of the luminaries, or one of the other benefics are in the sixth or the twelfth; or if the Lord of the house of slaves is fortunate, and is free from impediments, joined to Mercury in one of the angles; or if Mercury is free, joined with one of the benefics or seeking their conjunction; or if the Lord of the house of slaves is in a good place from the Ascendant, or if he is in the Ascendant, or is in the sixth free from impediments (namely fortunate and strong), joined to one of the benefics - since his signifies that the native will abound in slaves, slavegirls, servants, household servants, and assistants, and that he will have good, profit, rejoicing, and utility because of them, for them, and from them.

But if Mercury is retrograde, combust, or joined with malefics in a fixed sign, or seeking their conjunction, or if one of the malefics are in the house of slaves, or in the 12th, or if the Lord of the house of slaves is a malefic, or if he is retrograde, or otherwise impeded by malefics, or is cadent from the angles or the Ascendant, without the aspect of some benefic; or what was said about the Lord of the house of slaves is true of Mercury, or if the Cauda is in the house of slaves - this signifies a want of slaves, and their scarcity, and that anger, sorrow, and troubles to befall the native because of them, and from them.

And Aboali said to examine the natives inconveniences, impediments, and profit with slaves, from the planet who is more deserving in the sixth house, and from the Lord of the sixth, the Part of Slaves and its Lord, the planet who is in the sixth, Mercury, and the Lord of the Ascendant; and you will see if they make each other fortunate - since if this is so, it signifies the profit, goodness, and concord of the native with slaves. However, if they impede each other, you will be able to judge to the contrary. And according to what you see regarding the goodness or malice of each (namely the Lord of the Ascendant and the other significators which were mentioned) in terms of the multitude of testimonies (namely good or bad), you will judge according to this. For if the Lord of the Ascendant behaves well towards the significator of slaves, and the significator of slaves towards the Lord of the Ascendant, it will signify the goodness of both of them towards each other. However, if they behave badly towards each other, they will judge evil for both parties. If one behaves well towards the other, and the other behaves badly towards him, good will follow for one, and evil will follow for the other from his contrary And so it will judge that one will be benevolent to the other, and the other will be malevolent towards him.

### II

## On Domestic Animals And Other Animals Which Are Signified By The Sixth

Having examined in the preceding concerning the slaves and slavegirls and the others in what has preceded, what is to be examined next are domestic animals and other beasts which are signified by the sixth house, before arriving at the infirmities of the native. For it seemed to the ancient sages (with whom I agree in a friendly enough manner), that the matter of domestic animals, goats, pigs, and other animals, both bipeds and quadrupeds, which are not ridden or yoked, and domestic and tamed birds, are taken from the sixth house.

Whence the sixth house is to be examined, and its Lord is to be examined, and likewise Mars, and how they are disposed, and in which places from the Ascendant they (or one of them) are found, and whether Mars is direct or retrograde, since he naturally has signification over the animals mentioned above.

Whence, if he is in Aries or Capricorn, in the Ascendant, or in the 10th, or even in the sixth, and Jupiter or the Sun aspect him from a trine or sextile aspect, and he is otherwise fortunate and strong, free from impediments, it signifies that the native will be fortunate in having a multitude of the aforementioned animals, and that goodness, utility and joy will follow from them, and because of them. And this more greatly so if Mars is in one of his own dignities (it is even praised if he is in Leo). And likewise if the sixth house is one of the aforementioned signs, and its Lord is in one of them, joined with one of the benefics or in its trine or sextile aspect: and this signifies that he will have profit and benefits from them, and they will be multiplied for him and for his utility.

But if the sixth house is Taurus, or Leo, or Scorpio, or Aquarius, and Saturn is there, or aspects it from opposition or square aspect, it signifies that the native will be saddened and impeded because of the aforementioned animals, and will suffer loss from them, and this will be stronger in Leo than in the others; and less so in Aquarius.

And if Mars and Jupiter then have dignity in the sixth, the impediment of Saturn will be greater, unless one of them aspect him from a trine or sextile aspect, and with reception, and with them being fortunate and strong.

And Aboali said, that if one of the bestial signs are there, and the Ascendant is suitable, and the Lord of the Ascendant is with Mars or in his aspect from praiseworthy places, the native will love beasts and rejoice with them. Likewise if the Moon is in the aforementioned places, it signifies this just as much as the Lord of the Ascendant.

## III

## On The Infirmity Of The Native And On His Illnesses

Having spoken on those things which preceded in that chapter about the slaves and slavegirls of the native, and his small animals, and those which are not ridden, now it remains to speak about his infirmities and illnesses.

And infirmity and illness differ.

For an infirmity is an accident or weakness of the body which comes and goes.

An illness is an infirmity or accident of the body coming and not going away,

Whence it is necessary for you to consider that you ought to examine the Ascendant and its Lord in someone's nativity; the sixth also and its Lord, the Moon and the Lord of the domicile she is placed in, and the planet who is in the sixth (if one is found there), even Mercury and the Part of Infirmities, and the planet in whose domicile it is placed (both for the natives infirmities as for his illnesses), and likewise the places in which the aforementioned significators are.

Examine the Almutem over these places, and especially over the sixth house, which signifies the infirmities of the native and his illnesses. Which, if it is a benefic, and there is a conjunction between him and the Lord of the Ascendant (and this more strongly so if reception intervenes), signifies the health of the native and his prosperity (at any rate, his salvation from infirmities and illnesses) and that his infirmity and illness will be few and light.

And Aomar said that he will be fortunate in animals, slaves, and servants, if the Almutem over the aforementioned places is a benefic, or agrees with the Lord of the Ascendant. However, if the aforementioned Almutem is a malefic, whichever kind of the aforementioned significators he is, and is joined with the Lord of the Ascendant, or is in one of the angles or succeddents impeding the Lord of the Ascendant (or the Ascendant itself), it signifies that the native will be surrounded and impeded by many infirmities.

If Saturn is the Almutem, most of them will be caused by coldness and dryness; likewise they will be extended, as are cancer, gibbosity, gout, epilepsy, hiposacra, anasacra, oprphea, elephantiasis, paralysis, and similar incurable illnesses (or almost incurable, or very difficult to cure).

But if Mars is the Almutem, and is in one of the angles, joined with the Lord of the Ascendant and impeding him, it signifies that the natives' infirmities and illnesses will arise from heat and dryness, as are those which come to be from red cholera, or even from blood; as are sharp fevers, frenzy, and abscesses which do not easily mature.

And Aomar said that if the Part of Azemena (which is an inseparable accident), with the Moon in the ninth and Mars in the eighth, were in signs of severed limbs in the nativity, it signifies that the native will have one of his limbs cut off by an iron blade. Likewise if Mars is with the Moon in another quarter, and the Ascendant is impeded by some malefic, the native will meet with accidents in the body part of the sign in which the Moon is placed, or in the left eye in diurnal nativities, and in the right eye in nocturnal nativities. And he said that if the luminaries are in conjunction or prevention, and malefics are in square aspect to the conjunction or prevention, and the malefic ascends, the native will later lose his right eye from the Sun, and his left eye from the Moon.

Moreover if either of the luminaries are impeded from the square aspect of malefics, or by their opposition, or by corporeal conjunction, he will lose the eye signified by that luminary. However, if both luminaries are impeded, he will lose both eyes.

And Aomar said that if the Moon is impeded in a nativity (understand this is as her being impeded in any sign by the malefics, without the projection of the rays of a benefic to the terms she is in), the body part which pertains to the sign which the Moon is placed in will be destroyed. And he said that if the Moon is in signs signifying impediment in the eyes (as are Cancer, Leo, Scorpio, Sagittarius, Capricorn, and Aquarius), it signifies impediment to the eyes; and likewise for the Ascendant.

And he said that if the Moon is in Sagittarius, whether she is impeded by malefics or not, impediment will befall him in the eyes; and understand that blindness will be feared for him unless she is aspected by benefics. If the Moon is in Gemini, Libra, or Aquarius, impeded by Mars, it signifies the putrefaction of the eyes and their inflammation. And Aomar said that it signifies leprosy unless she is aspected by one of the benefics. But if she is impeded by Saturn while she is in Cancer, Scorpio, or Pisces, without the aspect of a benefic, it signifies cancers, gout, swelling, leprosy, albaras, and the quinsy.

And Tiberiadis said that if the Moon is in the square aspect of the Sun, or with him in the same sign (understand combust) or in the square aspect of Mars, or his opposition, the native will be burned by fire.

And if Venus is impeded by Mars, Saturn, the Sun, and Mercury at the same time in someone's nativity, without the aspect of a benefic, the natives' genitals will be cut off. If the Lord of the 8th aspects this, or if one of the aforementioned planets are the Lord of the 8th, the native will die from this severing. Indeed, if the triplicity Lords of the sign in which Venus is then placed are fortunate, strong, and well disposed, dignity and honour will result for the native from this severing. And if they are impeded, evil upon evil will follow from it, since he will fall into sorrow and distress because of it, and labours, afflictions, depressions, and detriments which he will not be able to avoid. If it is a woman, she will not provide milk for her child, nor will she care for men nor will she want to *make use* of them, nor will she care for any sexual matters.

And Aomar said that if the Moon is in the first degree of the signs, or in their end, and malefics cast their rays to these terms (and especially Saturn) she will love with the greatest love and will be made known for this.

But if Saturn is in the house of infirmities, or in the sixth from the sign in which the Moon is then placed, or is in opposition or square aspect to these places, it signifies a multitude of illnesses to befall the native because of coldness, and more so if he is in moist signs.

If Mars is in the sixth from the Ascendant, or in the sixth from the sign in which the Moon is placed, or in square aspect or opposition to the aforementioned places, it signifies a multitude of illnesses to befall the native because of heat, and quickly to end for good or bad. For if the Lord of the Ascendant or the Moon aspect Mars by a trine or sextile aspect, and they do not receive him, it signifies their end being for good. However, if he aspects them from a square aspect, or opposition, or any other aspect, and he is received, it signifies their end being for the bad, and that they will more likely die from these illnesses than not.

And if the Moon and the Lord of the domicile in which she is placed, and likewise the sixth sign, are free from malefics, it signifies the liberation of the native from his illnesses. Indeed, if the Moon and the Lord of the domicile in which she is placed, and the Lord of the house of infirmities, are impeded by malefics, it signifies a diverse multitude of illnesses for the native.

And Aboali said that if a malefic is in the Ascendant (and especially if it is Mars in diurnal nativities, or Saturn in nocturnal nativities), joined to the Sun or the Moon, it signifies the weakness of vision or the destruction of the eye. However, if the luminaries are impeded by malefics, or if the Cauda is joined to them, it signifies the weakness of the vision or the destruction of the eyes.

However, he said that if the Moon is joined to malefics, or in their square aspect or opposition, and in a moist sign, it signifies that most of the natives' infirmities will be from coldness and moisture. And if she is in a dry sign, it signifies illnesses from heat and dryness.

## IV

### At What Age These Things Will Happen

And if the planet who signifies infirmities is oriental, the infirmities will be in the first half of the natives life. However, if it is occidental, they will be in the last half of his life. And if it is in the Ascendant, they will be in the beginning of life. Indeed, if it is in the 10th, they will be in the mature age of his life. If it is in the seventh, they will be in the decline of his life. Indeed, if it is in the fourth, they will be around the end of his life.

You will also examine his significator, since according to its strength and weakness, the illnesses will be weak or strong.

You will also see if the Part of Infirmity and the Lord of the domicile in which it is placed, are free from impediments, since this signifies the salvation and health of the native, and his salvation from infirmities. However, if they are impeded, it signifies that severe infirmities and pains are going to come, and this more strongly so, if none of the benefics aspect them (or at least one of them).

And Aboali said, and it is true, that the Ascendant and the Moon are the significators of the body, and the Lord of the Ascendant and the Lord of the domicile the Moon is in are the significators of the soul. And if the Ascendant and the Moon are free from malefics, and their Lords are impeded, it signifies the health of the body, and the fear and sorrow of the mind. And if the Ascendant and the Moon are impeded by malefics, and their Lords are safe, it signifies the infirmity of the native's body, and the health of his soul.

Indeed, Ptolemy said that we ought to consider the Ascendant, the seventh (and even the sixth, which naturally signifies infirmity, since it has no friendship with the Ascendant). Likewise you ought to consider Saturn and Mars, and see how they are disposed: for if one or both of them are in one of the aforementioned places, or aspecting one of them from a square aspect, or from opposition (wherever this aspect comes from), it signifies that the native will be infested with many infirmities and impediments, and this will be more certain, if in addition to this you find the Sun and the Moon impeded. And more strongly again, if this impediment is the angles or their succeedents. And greater again if one of the aforementioned malefics aspect them (or one of them). And even more if these malefics are in angles or their succeedents, and aspect them from square aspect or opposition, and even from a trine or sextile aspect without reception. And those illnesses will be weak which are signified by the Ascendant, or by the seventh, or by the sixth, or by the malefics themselves, according to which of the aforementioned places the Almutem over infirmities is found, as said above.

## V

### In Which Body Part The Above Mentioned Things Will Occur

And the illnesses will occur in that part of the body which is signified by the sign in which the Almutem is made unfortunate or impeded.

If the Almutem signifies one part of the body, and the sign in which he is placed signifies another, the aforementioned will occur in both of the body parts signified by them: like Aries, which signifies the head, Taurus the neck, Gemini the arms, etc.; and Saturn the right eye, the spleen, the bladder, etc.,; and Jupiter the right hand, the lungs, the ribs, etc.; and Mars the left eye, the left ear, the male genitals, etc.; and the Sun both eyes (but more so the right), the face, and almost the entire right part of the body (and this on account of his diurnality),etc.; Venus the buttocks, liver etc.; Mercury the tongue, the interior of the nose, etc.; the Moon the interior of the throat, the epiglottis, and in women the belly, the private parts; and the entire left part of the body on account of her nocturnality.

And Ptolemy said that the impediments will happen for the most part if the unfortunate stars which are the occasion for them are oriental in the figure, or from the Sun. However, infirmities, for the most part (if not always), will occur when the same stars (namely the unfortunate ones), are occidental, whether in the world or from the Sun, since there is a separation or distinction between the both of them. For the impediments only happen once, nor do their pains last long; infirmities either last forever, or come and go, namely in intervals. And he said that in matters by which particular accidents are perceived, when the peculiar figures are experienced and observed, and the qualities are discovered, there are infirmities and impediments signifying what was understood in terms of the accidents which follow, and they will happen for the most part according to the similar positions of the stars in their qualities.

For there will be a loss of vision in one eye, if the Moon alone is impeded in the aforementioned angles (namely the oriental or occidental ones), and she is in the hour of a conjunction or prevention; or if she in another figure with the Sun, and she has Alitisal (or is in trine or sextile aspect, or square) with one of the stars which are similar to clouds: like the cloudy star which is in Cancer, and the Pleiades which are in Taurus, and the point of the arrow of Sagittarius, also the tail of Scorpio, and that which is around *Aldhasera* (and almost the cord or tresses from the parts of Leo), the Calbem, and the Jug of Aquarius. And if the Moon is impeded in one of the angles (namely the fourth), occidental from the Sun, and Mars and Saturn are oriental, and the Moon is also moving to Mars and Saturn (or either of them); or if the Sun is in the fourth angle, and the two mentioned malefics ascend before the Sun, or are joined to him, and the luminaries are conjoined in one and the same sign, or are opposite to each other, and the two mentioned malefics are occidental from the Moon, impediments will befall the native in both of his eyes; and this will happen with some strike or blade. And if it is in Aries, Leo, or Sagittarius, this will happen because of fire. And if the mentioned malefics (or at least Mars) are joined with Mercury, this will happen because of a battle, or a game which could be likened in some way to a battle; or it will happen from something which will be moved unfairly against the native. However, if Mercury is joined with Saturn, this will happen from a flow of water into the eye, or from the torture of the eyes themselves, and the like. And if the Moon is in the oriental half joined to Mars, and Venus is joined to Saturn and joined to Mercury in the aforementioned manner; and Mars is northern from her, or if they aspect each other by opposition, the native will not have his sex organs, or will have the function of both sexes, or will be born without an anus, or it will be overly constricted. And if it is a woman, she will not have her privates as she ought to. And if Venus were to have herself like this with Mercury, Mars and Saturn, as was said, and Venus is seeking the conjunction of the Sun, and the luminaries are in masculine quarters and signs, and Venus and the Moon are occidental (from the Sun I say), and the malefics were in following degrees, and Venus and the Moon are impeded, and Ptolemy said, if the native is a male, he will be mutilated, or suffer impediments in his testicles (especially if this is in Leo, Aries, Scorpio, Capricorn, or Aquarius). But if it is a woman, she will be sterile, and perhaps she won't escape impediment in one of her eyes.

You will also consider whether Mercury and Saturn are in the aforementioned angles with the diurnal luminary, and Mercury is retrograde, occidental, moving to a conjunction with the Sun, and the Moon is in their conjunction (namely of Mercury and Saturn): since if this is so, it signifies that the native will be a stutterer, and a holder of his tongue, but he will not be completely deprived of speech. However, if Mars is joined to them, it signifies that he will hold his tongue less, even if it will not be completely resolved. However, if Jupiter aspects, his tongue will only be slightly impeded.

And Ptolemy said that this is known by the degrees of direction which are between him and the luminary who has authority. Again, if the aforementioned malefics are in the beginnings of signs, or close to them, it signifies that the natives' impediments will be from the navel upwards. However, if they are in the end of the signs, or close to it, it signifies that they will be from the navel downwards. However, if the Moon is impeded in these places, you will be able to judge the same.

## VI

### Again On The Above Mentioned Impediments - Where Will Be, And For What Reason Will They Will Occur, According To Ptolemy

You will also consider whether the luminaries are moving towards the conjunction of the mentioned malefics (Mars and Saturn), with them being placed in angles, or if they are in their opposition; and with the Moon in the zenzahar of any of them, or placed in its cauda, or in the Caput or Cauda Draconis, or in signs of infirmities (which are, as Ptolemy says, Aries, Taurus, Cancer, Scorpio, and Capricorn): since this signifies that the native will be a hunchback, or have one of his limbs destroyed, or an Azemena will invade him, as is lameness, dislocation, or the diminution of the function of some official limb. But if the malefics are joined with the luminaries, corporeally, or from opposition or square aspect, in the hour of the nativity, you will be able to announce the same. If the mentioned malefics are in the tenth, and they are northern from the luminaries, or the luminaries are in the fourth, it signifies that these impediments and these infirmities, will often come from accidents, often great ones from which follow from the greatest and ultimate terrors, as are drowning, falling into the

hands of deadly enemies or desperate thieves, or highwaymen with no mercy; or falling from, or being trampled by a horse, or being gored by a bull, and similar things. If Mars is northern from these luminaries, and is the Almutem over one of the aforementioned places, the aforementioned impediments will happen on the occasion of fire or some burning or great injuries being delivered. However, if Saturn is northern, and is the Almutem, impediments will happen which could befall the native on the aforementioned occasions, of submersion, or falling, and paralysis.

The impediments which happen more frequently if the Moon is placed in the two equinoctial points and the two solstial points (if only the Moon and these signs are impeded), are these: since if she is in the vernal equinoctial point, then the impediments which will befall the native will be a peculiar morphew, and peculiar white spots, and leprosy, and they are curable. And if she is in the summer solstitial point, it will be impetigo or erysipelas and the like. And if she is in the autumnal equinoctial point, it will be albaras and the like. And if she is in the winter solstitial point, the more frequently occurring will be lentigo.

You will also consider if the mentioned malefics (Saturn and Mars), are in angles joined with the luminaries (or with either of them), if they are oriental from them, since if it is Saturn, it will signify illnesses emaciating the native on account of the coldness of the humours, and drying out his limbs and wounds, and that the natives body will be full of infirmities, jaundice, coughs, intestinal injuries, and other hidden injuries, and certain other illnesses exterminating the natives body, and drying it out, and sometimes making him a leper. If the native is a woman she will fall ill in her privates. If the planet is Mars, it will signify most of the illnesses to be from a hot and dry cause, bloody and indeed, foul spit, ulceration of the lungs and the arteries of the windpipe, the loss of sense, itches, blisters of the lungs and cavities, things coming from inflamed and choleric blood; and impediments will even befall this native from injuries, cuts, and burns inflicted on him or done to him on account of his illnesses (and especially hidden ones, as are kidney stones, haemorrhoids, and the like, which are born in the body and grow), and hot fiery ulcers will be present, also ulcers which grow by corroding; and in women, illnesses which befall them on account of abortion and other incomplete births.

You will also consider Mercury: who, if he is with one of the aforementioned malefics in one of the aforementioned places, and none of the benefics aspect them, it will support this malefic in increasing its malice in exercising the illness and impediments, by increasing its malice in every kind of illness.

Even the signs will assist the mentioned malefics in increasing their malice in illnesses. For if the Ascendant, or the seventh, or the sixth, or the conjunction of the aforementioned planets, are in Cancer, Capricorn, Pisces, Leo, or Scorpio (which are the signs of illness, yet not the only ones), the aforementioned malefics will be supported in the illnesses which are increased by corrosion, as are cancer, kidney stones, impetigo, and similar things corroding the natives flesh, and leprosy. Indeed, Gemini and Sagittarius will assist them in making epilepsy, or falling illnesses, and the like. And if the aforementioned stars are in the final parts of the signs, they will signify that the natives infirmities will be in his extremities, and this will happen on account of impediments touching upon them, and on account of the disorder of the humours - of the occasion of which there will be leprosy, gout, and arthritis, unless one of the benefics then aspects the malefics, or is corporeally joined to them. And the infirmities and impediments which appear because of this will be severe and incurable.

And Ptolemy said that the same will happen if benefics are joined with them, and malefics are elevated above them, or are stronger than them. However, if the benefics are in their own dignities and are stronger than the malefics (which are the occasions for the operations), then the impediments will not be disgraceful, or shameful, but will be light infirmities: however, this will happen if the benefics are oriental. For he said that Jupiter hides impediments, and makes infirmities quiet down, namely with external aids (such as physicians, and even with expenses), and this more greatly so if Mercury is with him. However, he said that Venus beautifies impediments, namely, since on that occasion the native will consecrate himself to God, and thus he will be freed from impediments and infirmities (or at least they will be alleviated); and sometimes she even makes them conceal themselves by means of incantations of the just, or exorcisms, and divine pronouncements and experiences, and medicines, just as sometimes in dreams and apparitions, such as if something says to him while he is sleeping to "Go to such a cross, to such a Saint, or to such a place, and you will be freed", and sometimes it happens in this way. However, even if these things depend on faith, they are not to be cast aside for this reason: for faith does much and is powerful in every matter. And he said that if Saturn is joined with Venus, this will be known and manifest, or their equivalent. But if Mercury is with her, this will be with benefit and profit to the patient, which will come to him from because of this illness.

## VII

## On The Impediments Of The Soul, And Of Its Infirmities And Ways

Mention having been made above on the infirmities of the body, and of its impediments, now it remains to examine something subjoined to the above, concerning the infirmities and impediments of the soul. And infirmities and impediments differ, for infirmities of the soul, as the astrologer takes them, are principally two, magnanimity and pusillanimity; and these two can hardly or never possible be cured, even if perhaps someone may sometimes be cured of them. For the magnanimous man despises great things, the pusillanimous man esteems small things (as is said elsewhere). Certain others are secondary, such as ardour, sorrow, irascibility, and similar things, which are easily cured and removed from the soul, and go away. Indeed, impediments of the soul in most cases do not go away, but they remain in it almost inseparably, such as if the soul ought to be wise, following fairness and goodness, but is exceedingly wise, so that from this excess it is deceived; or is less wise than it ought to be, so that it does not beware of doing evil; or is more impulsive than it ought to be, or less fearful than it ought to be. All of these, and similar impediments, belong to the soul, and are such that they hardly or never go away from it.

Whence you ought to examine in the nativity of any native to see what the condition of Mercury and the Moon is like (since this signification concerns them) and see how they interact with each other, and whether they are in angles or in their succedents; and whether they are corporeally joined with malefics, or joined with them by aspect. Since if they are both joined together, or are joined with malefics in the Ascendant, and these malefics are northern from them, or besiege them, or are opposite to them, it will signify that this native's soul will have many impediments. You will be able to say the same if the Almutem over the Ascendant is impeded by the mentioned malefics by one of the aforementioned means.

However, the other qualities of the soul, the limit of which neither exceed measure, nor subsist exceedingly low, are said to be commendable or worthy of approval. However, if the other qualities (which are not made by the aforementioned means, but on account of the excessive nature of the temperament), were to supervene, they could be stated as infirmities of the soul. However, these things befall the irrational soul and not the rational soul.

And certain illnesses sometimes happen, which do not belong to the rational mind, even if they might seem to be able to receive impressions in the suitable parts of the native, as we see in certain epileptics, in whose nativities the Moon and Mercury are not joined together, nor with the Lord of the Ascendant, nor with its Almutem, (and the Almutem is Saturn in diurnal nativities, and Mars in nocturnal ones). However, Ptolemy said, that he (namely Saturn in diurnal nativities, Mars in nocturnal ones) will rule this quality.

And those illnesses which then come over the soul are called insanity, and similar things, if the nativity is nocturnal and Saturn rules the quality (or if the nativity is diurnal, and Mars rules it), and this more so if the Moon and Mercury are not joined together, nor with the Lord of the Ascendant, and one of the aforementioned malefics is in an angle, and this is in Cancer, Sagittarius, or Pisces. However, Saturn will cause possession by evil spirits more, Mars will cause fury more. And in the case of Saturn, these things will happen from the overabundance of moisture in their brains. And their occasion will be the placement of a malefic in the angles with the aforementioned quality; and this more so if Saturn is in his own condition (or Mars is in his), elevated above the Moon; with her just after exiting from under the rays of the Sun; and the Lord of the domicile in which she is placed is joined to Saturn if the nativity is conjunctional, or

Mars if the nativity is preventional, with Saturn or Mars being placed in Sagittarius or Pisces. Indeed, if Saturn and Mars predominate in nativities, and both are the Almutem over it, there will be the aforementioned infirmities (namely, epilepsy, insanity, mania, and the like) will be incurable, yet not very intense, nor will they be calmed very much.

If it were Jupiter and Venus instead of the aforementioned malefics, and they were in the Ascendant, and the malefics were in the seventh, the aforementioned illnesses will be curable, even if they often seem to be intensified. If only Jupiter is joined with the Moon, it signifies that these illnesses will be cured, both by diet and by medicine, but they will be less. But if Venus alone is joined with the Moon, it signifies that it seems he can only be cured by Psalms, exorcisms, or incantations, or the prayers of some saint, or intercessions, or divine prayers and similar things. Indeed, if the aforementioned malefics are in the Ascendant, and Jupiter and Venus are in the seventh, with the aforementioned quality existing, it signifies that the aforementioned illnesses are going to be incurable and intense, and very strong and manifest, and loud and fearful in the future, and that such infirm people will be unstable, nor will they be restrained, unless they are chained up or imprisoned; and that they will say disgraceful and shameful things, both to their own, and others, and will perform disgraceful acts also. Indeed, in the case of demonic infirmities, it will be said that its cause is a certain moistness which takes away sense, and after the removal of the sense, makes him raging (nor does it dismiss him from the sense of the body): and so sometimes while spirits are tormented, and even sometimes when they are not vexed, they predict the future; and sometimes they make attacks on men, and strike them, and do other things similar to these.

And there are other qualities of other stars assisting the aforementioned qualities. For if the Sun is with Mars in the aforementioned places, or in angles (and especially in the Ascendant or the seventh), they will increase insanity. Indeed, if Jupiter has association with Mercury, it will increase epilepsy. Venus increases those things which were said above about the aforementioned infirm people. Indeed, if Saturn is placed with the Moon in the aforementioned places, they will increase demonic passions and the abundance of harmful moisture;

and likewise they will increase the harmful impediments to the rational soul, and its infirmities. And these aforementioned infirmities are those which are usually cured by the care of the aforementioned qualities. Those which differ from the aforementioned (namely, those which receive disposition in the non-rational soul. with increase or decrease), are considered in things happening naturally, and they will appear in both sexes, for the examination and knowing of which, it is necessary for us to assume such a method by which we can arrive at cognition of them: namely, we should examine if the Sun is not joined with the Moon, nor with the Lord of the Ascendant, and is not in the Ascendant; and Saturn is in an angle in diurnal nativities, and Mars in nocturnal ones; and either of them is the Almutem over the Ascendant, or over the domicile in which the Lord of the Ascendant is placed; and Mars or Venus aspect the Sun or the Moon; and the Lord of the domicile in which the Moon is placed is joined to Saturn (if the nativity is conjunctional), or Mars (if it is preventional) and principally in one of the domiciles of Jupiter; and the aforementioned malefics are conquering in the figure of this nativity, and the Moon and the Sun are in masculine signs, it signifies that the illnesses of the non-rational soul will be exceeding the natural limit in sexual acts, and using them beyond what it is permitted by nature. Indeed, with a female native, that which is naturally permitted to them (the womanly nature having been transformed into that of a man), will become accustomed to the way of men; however, she will unduly involve herself with those things which nature prohibited for her.

Moreover if in anyone's nativity Mars or Venus are in masculine signs, and in masculine quarters, and none of the luminaries, nor the Lord of the Ascendant, nor the Lord of the sign in which he is, are joined with them, it signifies that the native will be overly excited with regards to sex acts, and place his intention in them, and spend his time in them, and will commit these disgraceful things against the permission of the law, and will commit them gladly and indecently - if he is a man that is. Indeed, if it is a woman, she will desire unnatural sex acts, and will engage in them more that she ought to, and she will mix freely and disgracefully with women. And Ptolemy said that if Venus alone is masculine, what is perpetrated from it will be hidden and ignored. But if Mars is masculine, it will be so that it is clear that sometimes women will consort with them as if they are demonstrating them to be their wives. But however, if both are masculine, things will be between the two, namely not totally manifest nor totally hidden.

Moreover, Ptolemy said that if the same stars are in the contrary of the aforementioned (namely that only the luminaries with the aforementioned qualities are placed in feminine signs), women will do that which is natural to them, however, men will commit what is contrary to their nature, and with softness and femininity of the soul hey will transgress nature. However, if only Venus is feminine, women will perform too many illegitimate sex acts, and with anyone, so that she will deny no sexual intercourse, regardless of whether it is deformed, or against the law. However, men will be effeminate and weak, and very prone to sex acts, nor will they prohibit themselves from any illicit sexual intercourse nor from its disgracefulness, excepting for this - that they will perpetrate it secretly. Moreover, if Mars is femininely placed, and Venus isn't (namely of these two) they will engage in fornication, disgraceful things, and illicit, uncovered acts, and without blushing, so that they will be reproached for excessive exposure.

Oriental in the figure (namely from the Sun), the qualities of Venus and Mars in masculinity help with detection; and their evening and occidental quality (from the Sun) in the figure, helps hiding (by femininity). Likewise, even if Saturn is with them, he will assist them (namely the male and female native) to incur horrid, rotten, and very shameful things, since his nature assists each one of these with their bad ways. But if Jupiter is with them, it will increase the beauty and decency of matters, and give suitable modesty. And if Mercury is with them, he will assist in the detection of matters, and the hastening of what is going to be, and the multitude and increase of their kinds.

## ON THE SEVENTH HOUSE

## I

## On The Native's Marriages, And His Associates, And His Enemies Openly Opposing Him

**M**ention having been made in the preceding chapter on the slaves, small animals, and the infirmities of the native, to be examined immediately is the natives' marriage, his associates, and likewise his enemies openly opposing him.

Therefore, in these things you will consider the seventh and its Lord, and which of the planets are found in it (namely one or more), the Moon also, and Venus, and also the Part of Marriage, and also the Lord of the domicile in which you find it. And you will examine the planet who is the Almutem over these places, or over the angles of the figure of the nativity which you seek (and of their suceedents), and you will see if they are free from the impediments which have been stated many times, and also if they are fortunate and strong.

Which if all of them, or some of them (and especially the Lord of the seventh or the Almutem over it) are joined with the Lord of the Ascendant of the nativity, or with its Almutem, by a trine or sextile aspect, and this more greatly so if reception intervenes, and this planet is lighter than the Lord of the Ascendant, it signifies that the native will marry a good and suitable woman, and one with whom he will rejoice to his wishes. However, if the aforementioned aspect is without reception, or if it is a square aspect with reception, it signifies that the native will marry, but his marriage will be much below the aforementioned. However, if it is a square aspect without reception, it will be even more greatly below the aforementioned. But if the Lord of the Ascendant is joined with the Lord of the seventh, so that it is lighter than the Lord of the seventh, it signifies that the native will desire to couple with women.

Indeed, if the seventh sign is Cancer, Scorpio, or Pisces: or there is a conjunction of the Lord of the seventh, or its Almutem, with the Lord of the first, it signifies that the native will have many wives, or a great abundance of other women. Indeed, if you find the contrary of what was said, you will be able to judge to the contrary.

If Venus is then in an angle or in its succedent, namely, fortunate and strong, and the triplicity Lords of the sign she then possesses, and she and they are oriental, then it signifies that the native will contract marriage in his youth, and he will be fortunate with women, and will be loved by them. You will say the same, if you find the Moon in the first quarter of her month, or in the third (namely in her separation from the Sun up to the half of her light, or from the prevention up to the middle of her decrease), which two quarters (just as is testified elsewhere by Ptolemy) are said to be oriental: nevertheless his marriage will be delayed somewhat more, and he will contract it with a young girl, and his fortune will be with women, however, it will be less than the aforementioned.

However, if Venus is impeded (namely cadent or combust, or retrograde, or joined to malefics), and the triplicity Lords of the sign in which she is placed are impeded, or if she is occidental, and the others are occidental, or if they are between the Ascendant and the fourth, or between the seventh and the tenth, or in the second quarter of the lunar month, or in the last quarter (which two quarters Ptolemy called occidental), it signifies that his marriage will be postponed, and he will marry after his youth at a great age, and to an old woman; and he will be unfortunate because of women.

But if Venus is free (namely, fortunate and strong), and is in an angle or its succedent, and the triplicity Lords of the sign which she then occupies are impeded, it signifies that the native will marry with a good, suitable, and beautiful woman, however, evil and detriment will follow because of this marriage. If Venus alone is impeded, and the triplicity Lords of the sign she is placed in are free from impediments, it signifies that the native will marry with an unsuitable and disagreeable woman, but he will be fortunate because of this union; and utility and suitable good will follow from it.

And Aboali said that if Venus is free from malefics and from impediments in the nativities of men and women, and in fit places, it signifies a good and fitting marriage. However, if she is impeded and in a bad place, it signifies the destruction and malignity of marriage.

Indeed, if Aomar said that if Venus is exalted above Saturn from the tenth, marriage will be in middle age, in a suitable time for it, and it will be a medium marriage (and likewise the children). However, if Venus is in a mobile sign in someone's nativity, and especially in Cancer or Capricorn, it signifies the firm stability of the native over one wife. Indeed, if the Moon and Venus are mutually opposed, or in square aspect, it signifies evil and impediment in marriage. And if they are in Gemini, Virgo, Sagittarius, or Pisces, it signifies that the native will contract marriage with more than one woman.

## II

## On The Manner Of The Natives Sexual Intercourse

You will also examine whether Venus is in Aries or Scorpio, and Mars is in Taurus or Libra, since this will signify the excessive abundance of sex in the native, and impediment in his person and the destruction of his things for this reason. If Venus is in Capricorn or Aquarius, and Saturn is in Taurus or Libra; or if she is in Gemini or Virgo, and Mercury is in Taurus or Libra; or if Venus and Mercury are in Capricorn or Aquarius, and they are joined together, and one is seeking the conjunction of another, it signifies the filthiness of the native's sexual intercourse, and his engagement in the sin of sodomy, and he will delight more in the filthy sexual intercourse of men than in that of women.

Indeed, if Venus is in her own house or exaltation, the wife will be elevated over this native, and will predominate over him. And this more so, if the Lord of the seventh is northern from the Lord of the Ascendant. However, if she is in her terms or triplicity, the wife will predominate over him, but much less so. But if she is in her own face, the wife will predominate even less.

And Aomar said that if Venus, and the Sun, and the Part of Marriage (or many of the significators of the native) and the Lord of the house of marriage are in Aries, Leo, Libra, or Capricorn (which are the signs signifying disgusting sexual intercourse), it signifies that the native will be overflowing in sexual intercourse, with a shameful and filthy overflowing.

If Venus is corporeally joined to Mars, or in his opposition or square aspect, and Mars is in Aries, Scorpio, or Capricorn, it signifies that the native will be disgraceful, and abusing shameful sexual intercourse, and this more greatly so if Venus is in a masculine sign, since then this disgrace will be made more disgraceful by the sin of sodomy. However, if she is in a feminine sign, he will be deceived by women. Indeed, if the native is a woman, and Venus is in a feminine sign, she will be insatiable in sexual intercourse, and she will become a prostitute. However, if she is in a masculine sign, she will misuse women, and desire to rub against them, and will also delight in being bent down over men.

And Aomar said that if Mercury is the Almutem over Venus and the Moon, and the house of wives, of the Part of the same (or over most of them), the native will delight in boys, and will delight in deceiving them.

## III

## What The Native's Wife Will Be Like

However if the Moon is combust, and Saturn aspects her from opposition or square aspect, and Jupiter is not aspecting her, and Saturn does not receive her, it signifies that the native will not take a wife.

However, if the Moon is joined with benefics from a trine or sextile aspect, and she is in good condition and well disposed, and with reception, it signifies that the native will take a good, useful, agreeable, and fit wife. However, if she is joined with malefics, you will prognosticate the contrary.

For if she is joined to Saturn from a trine or sextile aspect, it signifies that the native will have a laborious, feral, and rigid wife. However, if it is from square or opposition, it signifies that she is low-class, foul, and dull.

Indeed, if she is joined to Mars, it signifies that she will be unlearned, unruly, badly understanding, unstable, and a devastator. If Mars is in good condition, it will reduce this malice; and if he is in bad condition, it will add to the malice, and make her a fornicatrix.

Indeed, if she is joined with Jupiter, and he is not impeded, it signifies that the wife will be good, suitable, and proper, and shrewd and wise with regards to running the affairs of the household.

If she is joined with Venus, it signifies the wife to be humorous, happy, and very beautiful. However, if Venus (or Mercury) is impeded, the signification will be below what I said.

But if she is joined with Mercury it signifies her to be studious, well attentive, and intelligent.

And Ptolemy said that if Venus is placed with Jupiter, Saturn, or Mercury, in those things which pertain to life, she will well benefit him (namely the wife to the husband), and she will love him and the children greatly.

And Aomar said that if Venus is in the houses of Saturn, and Saturn aspects her, the native will be frigid in sexual intercourse. Likewise if Saturn conquers, and he is the Almutem over the house of marriage.

While if the Lord of the seventh does not aspect the seventh, and the Lord of the Moon the Moon, and also the Lord of the Part of Marriage, the Part of Marriage, and Venus the Lord of Venus, then the native will not taste the taste of women, and will not marry. And he said that if the Almutem which is the victor over the Ascendant, the Moon, the Sun, the Part of Fortune, and also the conjunction or prevention which was before the nativity, according to the condition which I said, and most of the planets are unfortunate, the native will be effeminate and soft. And if masculine planets conquer in the above mentioned places in feminine nativities, the girl that is born at that time, will be masculine, almost like a male.

## On The Aforementioned Through The Part Of Marriage

You will also examine the Part of Betrothal, and the Lord of the domicile in which it is placed, or its Almutem: which, if you find in angles or in their succedents, namely fortunate, strong, and joined to benefics, it signifies that the native will be married with good, beautiful, and agreeable women. However, if the Part is cadent, and the aforementioned planet is safe, or if the planet is impeded and the Part is safe, it signifies the mediocrity of the aforementioned. If the Part and the planet is cadent and impeded, and benefics don't aspect them, it signifies that the native will

consummate marriage with low-class and defiled women. However, if the planet who aspects the Part of Betrothal, or the Lord of the sign in which it is placed, is benefic, and is direct and in an angle, it signifies that the native will contract marriage with many women, and with good women who are free of vices. Indeed, if it is malefic, and is impeded (namely cadent, retrograde, or combust), it signifies that the native will contract marriage with women of no utility, no goodness, no profit, and full of vices.

If Venus then aspects Saturn (and this more greatly so if this aspect is from square or opposition), and either of them are cadent from the Ascendant, and Jupiter does not aspect one of them, it signifies that the native will have little delight in women, and if he marries, he will delight very little in sexual intercourse or pleasure, almost not at all.

You will also consider if Venus is in Taurus, Cancer, Libra, or Pisces: since this will signify that the native will contract marriage with a women related [or neighbouring] to him.

However, if Venus is in Sagittarius or Pisces, or Jupiter is in Taurus or Libra it signifies that the native will marry a woman more verging on the side of being older than him than younger, and on the side of goodness rather than malice; and he will be praised by men with a fitting praise.

But if she is in Capricorn or Aquarius, it signifies that the native will couple with an aged woman.

If she is in Gemini or Virgo, it signifies that he will contract marriage with an ignoble and low-class woman, or a handmaid or perhaps a slavegirl.

However, if the planetary significator of women is free, in its own domicile or exaltation, it signifies that he will contract marriage with a noble woman. However, if it is in one of its other dignities, it signifies that he will contract marriage with other women corresponding with the dignity. However, if it is received, it signifies that he will couple with a low-class (albeit not very low-class) woman. Indeed, if it is peregrine, without reception, it signifies that he will contract marriage with a slavegirl.

However, if it is in Cancer, it signifies that the native will contract marriage with an unsuitable and malignant woman, nor will she permit him to rejoice or have any peace.

And moreover, if Venus is in Taurus, Libra, or Pisces, and is in an angle or its succedent, free from impediments (namely combustion, retrogradation, and the conjunction and aspects of malefics), say that the native will contract a good and fitting marriage, and this more greatly so if Jupiter aspects her then, and he is not impeded in any bad way; and even greater again if reception intervenes.

But if Venus is oriental, it signifies some kind of rulership of the wife over the husband, yet by means of gladness, games, and feasts. Indeed, if she is occidental, or if she is in Virgo, it signifies the scarcity of the native's delight with his wives, and even with other women, unless perhaps Jupiter then aspects Venus.

If you observe her to be impeded (namely retrograde, combust, or cadent) say that the native's marriage will be delayed, and it will be with burdens and something contrary for him.

However, if the Ascendant is Aries or Scorpio, and Venus is combust, whether from in front or behind, but rather from behind, it signifies that the native will contract marriage with an ill woman (but it will be a hidden illness).

## IV

### On The Time When The Wife Will Be Taken, And On The Number Of Wives, And On Their Durability In General

And the contracting of the marriage will be when the year of this nativity arrive to his seventh, or if its seventh is the Ascendant of the revolution of the nativity, it signifies marriage in this year; or it will be when it is signified by the direction of the Moon to the planetary significator of marriage.

And Aboali said that if the seventh sign is mobile, it signifies marriage with many women. You will say the same if the Moon is joined to many planets in the same sign, or has alitisal with them from trine or sextile aspect. However, if it is a common sign, he will only marry two women. Indeed, if it is a fixed sign, or the Moon is void-of-course, or is only joined with one planet, or has alitisal with one planet, it will judge that the native is going to contract marriage with only one woman.

You will also examine the seventh and the fourth (if it is a man's' nativity), and see if one of the malefics is placed there: since this signifies the death of the natives' wives. However, if it is a woman's nativity, it signifies the death of her husband. If Venus is occidental, and is peregrine, joined to malefics or in their square aspect or opposition, it will signify their hastened death.

You will also see in nativities of males, if all of the significators, or the greater part of them, are feminine: since this will signify that the native will be worthless, effeminate, soft, stupid, lazy, and watery and weak, in such a way that he will not seem to have any bones and as if he is totally flesh. And Aomar said that the lives of such men tend to be cut short, on account of the multitude of moisture prevailing in his complexion. However, in women's nativities, if the greater part of their significators are masculine, the native will be a virago, almost like a man: indeed, apart from her sex, she could be said to be a man rather than a woman, and the lives of such people are usually cut short, on account of the multitude of dryness predominating in them.

### On The Marriage Of Women

Ptolemy said that in marriages of women we ought to consider the solar qualities in their nativities, saying that it is necessary for us to see whether the Sun is found in either of the two oriental quarters (which are, as said above, from the 10th up to the Ascendant, and from the 4th up to the 7th): since this will signify that this native will marry a man in her youth, or that she will marry a young man in her old age; and will not take an old man as a husband. But if the Sun is between the Ascendant and the fourth, or between the seventh and the tenth, her marriage will be delayed, or she will be married to an old man while she is a young girl. If the Sun is from the beginning of Aries up to the middle of Taurus; or from the middle of Leo up to the end of Virgo; or from the middle of Scorpio up to the middle of Aquarius; and the significator of the native is oriental, the aforementioned will be done in her youth, or with a young man. However, if the Sun is from the middle of Taurus up to the middle of Leo; or from the beginning of Libra up to the middle of Scorpio; or from the middle of

Aquarius up to the end of Pisces; and her significator is occidental, this will happen in her old age, or with an old man.

And Haly said that if the significator is under the rays, it signifies that she will have none. But if the Sun is in a fixed sign, she will be signified to only couple with one man. If there is an oriental planet in that sign, you will announce that he will be a youth, and it will be possible that she will acquire another after him. However, if an occidental planet there, he will be past youth. Indeed, if the Sun is in a common sign, you will announce that she is going to have two husbands. If an oriental planet is found in such a sign, for each one of them you will adjoin another husband. But if they are not in good condition, they will signify fewer husbands. Indeed, if the Sun is in a mobile sign, you will judge that the native will have many husbands.

## *What Will Her Husband Be Like*

You will also see if Saturn then has an association with the Sun from a trine or sextile aspect, since this will signify that the natives' husband will be wise, upright, just in his deeds, and concerned about others, and laborious.

However, if the Sun is joined with Jupiter, this will signify that this natives husband will be humble, gentle, magnanimous, and of good judgement.

But if the Sun is joined with Mars, it signifies this girls' husband will be unruly, cruel, someone who can't be pleased, disobedient, and of bad judgement.

Indeed, if the Sun is joined with Venus, it signifies that her husband will be upright, decent, handsome, and beautiful.

But if the Sun is joined with Mercury, it will demonstrate that he will be laborious and profitable in the things which pertain to human life.

If Venus is joined to Saturn, it signifies that the natives husband will be tired, and will refrain himself from sexual matters.

Indeed, if she is joined to Jupiter, it signifies that her husband will be good, chaste, honourable, and modest.

If she is joined to Mars, it signifies that her husband will be of a hot complexion, a fornicator, freely engaged in, and soliciting sexual intercourse.

However, if Venus is joined to Mercury, it signifies that he will be inclined to love his wife, but will not be a stable lover, nor will he continue well in his loving; however, he will love his children, and he will have affection for them.

However, if the Sun and Moon aspect each other from trine or sextile aspect in both nativities (namely those of men and women), it signifies that that the marriage which either native contracts will not dissolve unless this happens for some great reason.

Indeed, if the Sun and Moon do not aspect each other, or aspect each other from square aspect or opposition aspect, or malefics aspect any of them, it signifies that there will be a separation or litigation in their marriage.

For if malefics aspect the Moon in a man's' nativity, there will be dissension on the side of the man. However, if they aspect the Sun in a woman's' nativity, the dissension will be on the side of the woman. And if the marriage remains, it will remain with litigation, harshness, contention, and hatred.

But if benefics aspect the Sun or the Moon, it signifies that the marriage of the man (if it is the Moon), or of the woman (if it is the Sun) will remain in jocularity, happiness, love, and health.

However, if malefics and benefics simultaneously testify to the Sun or the Moon, it signifies that the marriage will dissolve, even if not simply; and after this dissolution it will be restarted, and it will endure in peace and love.

If malefics aspect the Sun from a square aspect, or from opposition (unless there is reception, which diminishes their malice), it will signify that the divorce will be with a lawsuit and harshness, and likewise with great ferocity and complaint.

Whence if Mercury then aspects these malefics, this divorce will become public knowledge and will fall into the rumours of the people. Indeed, if Venus testifies to these malefics, it signifies that the divorce will occur from the suspicion of adultery or similar things.

## V

## How The Marriage May Be Perceived By The Significations Of Venus, Mars, And Saturn

In this matter, examine if Venus, Mars, or Saturn are conjoined corporeally, or from good aspects, by agreeable mixture, since this will signify that the native will be joined in a good, useful, and legitimate marriage.

If Venus and Mars are joined by a good aspect, and the Moon aspects Mars or Venus from the mentioned aspects, it signifies that he will contract marriage with a young girl.

If Venus is joined to Saturn, he will marry an old woman.

And if the Sun is joined with them, or with any of them, it signifies the female native will do the same with a young man.

If Mercury is joined with them, the aforementioned things will happen openly and will be made public.

And Ptolemy said that if these are both in signs common to them, as are Capricorn and Libra, it will signify that he is going to marry with his own sister, or his own relatives, or he may commit incest with them.

If the Moon is joined with Venus, Mars, and Saturn, in masculine nativities, it will signify that the native will commit something impure with two sisters, or with two of his relatives or those related to him by marriage.

However, if in the nativity of some woman the Moon is found in a sign common to Venus and Mars, it signifies that the native will commit something impure with two brothers or with two men closely related to each other.

And if Venus joins Saturn in the aforementioned signs it signifies a suitable marriage, and one lasting for a long time. And if in addition to this, Mercury applies to Venus and Saturn, this marriage will be with profit, and good and proper utility. If in addition to this Mars is also joined with the same, it signifies that the natives' marriage will not be a useful union, nor a durable one, but rather one which quickly comes to an end, and a harmful one.

However, if the disposition of Venus is like the disposition of Mars and Saturn, and she is in the domicile, exaltation, terms, or triplicity of one of them, or in a sign common to him and her, it signifies that the woman will marry a man of the same age as her. If all of them are placed oriental, and Venus is more oriental from the Sun, it signifies that the woman will adhere to a man younger than her. However, if it is a man's nativity, it signifies that he will take a wife younger than him. But if they are occidental, and she is more occidental than the others, it signifies that the woman will contract marriage with a man older than her, and the man will marry a wife more aged than himself.

And Ptolemy said that if Venus and Saturn are placed in signs common to them, as are Capricorn and Libra, the marriage will be between relatives. If however, the Moon belonged to the aforementioned qualities, and this quality remains in the Ascendant or the Midheaven, the native will transgress sexually with his mother, stepmother, or aunt, or a woman with her own offspring, or father, or her sister's son, or her own descendant, or uncle, or mother's husband. And he said that if the Sun is placed with this aforementioned quality, and the planets are occidental, the native will defile the bed of his daughter, or the daughter of his brother or sister, or his own child's wife.

But if the aforementioned quality is in masculine signs (which are Aries, Gemini, Leo, Libra, Sagittarius, and Aquarius), or in naturally feminine signs (which are Taurus, Cancer, Virgo, Scorpio, Capricorn, and Pisces), or in places which are accidentally masculine (which are the eastern quarters), or places which are accidentally feminine (which are the western quarters), or in the accidentally masculine houses (which are the 1st, 3rd, 5th, 9th, and 11th), or the accidentally feminine houses (which are the 2nd, 4th, 6th, 8th, 10th, and 12th), or if they are in their own dignities, so that Venus is in masculine signs, and Mars and Saturn are in feminine signs, or vice versa, it signifies that the native will be subjected to more sexual activity than is proper, nor will the man in being active, nor the woman in being passive, show themselves to be burdened in all of the ways they indulge.

But if the aforementioned quality is placed near the fixed star Aldebaran, or placed close to the end of the sign of Leo, or close to the beginning of Capricorn, it signifies that the native will engage in sexual activity in a disgraceful, shameful, and reprehensible manner. However, if it is in the Ascendant or the tenth, his shameless sexual activity will be made known amongst the people. And if it is in the 7th or the 4th, he will engage in the aforesaid acts as secretly as he can, or the native may be found without strength, or sterile. Indeed, if Mars is found with them in the aforementioned places, it signifies that the male natives penis will be cut off, with the testicles; in the case of a woman, her female parts will be unsuitable, or she may be castrated.

Again, if you find Venus separating from Mars, or Mars separating from Saturn, in a man's nativity, and Jupiter testifies to them, it will signify that the native will be moderate in sexual intercourse, and will only engage in sexual activity, in the natural and proper way, and will only desire it in the proper way. But if Mars is joined to Saturn alone, it will judge that the native will not be eager, nor willing, nor passionate, in sexual activity, and he will be lazy in it.

However, if Mars is joined with Venus and Jupiter, it will show that the native will be easy for sexual activity, and willing to do it, even if he will refute these words; and will strive as much as he can to restrain his own desire and malice, but will not be able to do it well, and will pretend to abstain from impure and disgraceful acts.

And if Mars is joined with Venus and Jupiter at the same time, or with only one of them, provided that Saturn does not aspect them, it will seem that the native will be eager for, and delight in, adultery or debauchery; and that he will eagerly use delightful foods and drinks.

But if Venus, Mars, or Jupiter are occidental, and the other is oriental, it signifies that the native is going to have a disgraceful manner of sexual intercourse, both with men and with women.

However, if only Mars and Venus are occidental, and Jupiter is oriental, he will abhor from disgraceful sexual intercourse with men, and will engage in sexual activity with women.

Indeed, if aforementioned significators (namely Mars and Venus), are joined together in signs which are called feminine (or even in feminine quarters), it signifies that he will submit himself to disgraceful and wicked sexual intercourse.

If both Mars and Venus are oriental, the native will desire to perpetrate these things more so with men than with women.

Moreover, if the aforementioned planets are oriental and placed in masculine signs, and Mars is stronger than Venus, and she is more remote from the Sun, the native will place women after men in every way, and he will concern himself with engaging in disgraceful sodomitical sexual activity with men.

But if they are occidental, and Venus is more remote from the Sun, the native will desire women instead, however, he will gladly subject himself to low-class and ugly ones, even maids and slavegirls, rather than noble or beautiful ones.

However, if Mars is more occidental than Venus, it signifies that the naive will carnally adhere to noble women, or married ones, or his own mistress who is in charge of him.

Indeed, if the nativity is of a woman, examine if Venus is joined with Jupiter and Mercury at the same time: since this signifies this native will be humble and modest in her manner of sexual intercourse, and all of her sexual activity will be performed with purity.

If Venus is joined with Mercury, or Saturn is participating, it signifies that the native will eagerly adhere to sexual activity, but it will be with remorse of conscience, and the restraint of her will, and the omission of all indecent foulness of sexual intercourse.

But if Venus is joined to Mars only, or in any way associated with him, then she will eagerly exercise sex activity, and will delight in them indecently.

However, if Jupiter aspects them, and if Mars is covered by the rays of the Sun, this girl will be greatly excited around sexual activity, and will freely and more eagerly engage in it, nor will she avoid low-class men, or other servants or slaves, nor even strangers.

Indeed, if Venus is found under the rays with Mars, she will lie with her own Lord, or with other noblemen.

But if the aforementioned Venus and Mars are placed in feminine signs or quarters, and they are occidental she will delight in sexual intercourse with men.

Indeed, if Saturn is joined with Venus and Mars simultaneously, it signifies that this girl will be horrid and wild. If Saturn is oriental, it signifies that she will desire adultery, and will love men that she finds in solitude.

However, Ptolemy said that Jupiter always mitigates these impediments; however, Mercury assists their delights, and likewise their baseness.

## VI

## What Will Happen To The Native Because Of His Associates, And From His Associates, And Those Participating With Him

Indeed, to know the condition of the native with associates and his participators, and what happens to him because of them, examine the Ascendant and its Lord, and also the Moon, for the native; and the seventh and its Lord for his associates and his participators. You will know what their condition will be like in partnerships and participations from the tenth and its Lord; however, you will perceive the end of these things from the fourth and its Lord.

For if the Lord of the Ascendant (who is the significator of the native) and the Moon are in fixed signs, and the Lord of the Ascendant is a benefic, and the Moon is free, and unimpeded, it signifies that the native will have associates with whom he participates with by a good and durable participation, but he will not profit much with them, nor will they profit much with him: however, they will have some kind of profit, namely below a moderate amount. However, if the Lord of the Ascendant is a malefic, and the Moon is impeded, it will judge the contrary.

Indeed, if they are in common signs, it will signify that the native will have good and faithful associates, and he will profit with them, and they will profit with him, unless something else impedes; and things will work out well for them in every respect, and their trades will be turned over often and more often, and mostly with utility and profit.

But if they are in mobile signs, it signifies that this participation will not be uniform, but sometimes there will be litigation between him and his associates, and likewise there will be suspicion and confusion; and after this there will be reconciliation and durability between them.

If there is a malefic impeding them in the Ascendant, it signifies that treachery and fraud, and cause for separation and regret is going to come from the side of the native. Indeed, if it is in the seventh, you will be able to judge the same to come from the side of the associates and participants.

Indeed, if you see that there ought to be separation between them, and you wish to know what it will be like, and what will be the means of it - examine the Moon; who, if she is joined with the Lord of the domicile she is placed in, or the planetary Almutem in this sign, and this planet is in good condition and well disposed, it signifies that his separation from his associates or participants will be with delight, a full spirit, and with utility and profit. If the Lord of her domicile (or its Almutem) do not aspect her, or if this planet aspects, and it is unfortunate and badly disposed, it signifies that the native will separate from his associates or participants by means of their ill will, and by the suspicion which one has for the other that their associate might deceive them, and defraud them of their goods - and this more strongly, if these impeding malefics are below the earth: for then the bad estimation one has of the other will be the cause of their separation, nor will they remain good friends, but they will turn their backs on each other.

And Zael said that if there are benefics in the Midheaven, their profit will be multiplied; and indeed, if malefics are there, it will be reduced. And he said that if the Moon is joined to the Lord of her domicile, and a malefic is joined to them in one sign or aspects them, they will not be separated, except by death.

## VII

## What Will Happen To The Native From Enemies Openly Opposing Him, Or Because Of Them, And Whether He Will Have Them Or Not

However in the qualities which must be perceived regarding whether the native will have enemies openly opposing him or not, and what will happen to him because of them or from them, it is necessary for us to consider the indications which lead us to know this, namely the Ascendant and its Lord, and also the seventh and its Lord; also the places of the luminaries; the place of the Part of Fortune, and its Lord; the Part of Enemies and its Lord; and Saturn and his Lord.

For if the mentioned places and the aforementioned significators (or the majority of them) are badly disposed, that is, that there are malefics in them, or with them, or aspectsing them from opposition or square aspect (but the square aspect is less malicious than the opposition); or if the Lord of the Ascendant and the Lord of the seventh aspect each other from the aforementioned aspects; or if the Lord of the Ascendant is in the seventh, and the Lord of the seventh is in the first; and this more strongly so if the Lord of the seventh is malefic, or if there is a malefic in the seventh, or in the place of the Part of Enemies; or if one of the aforementioned significators is a malefic, or impeded by malefics, and aspects the Lord of the Ascendant - it signifies that the native will have many enemies openly opposing him, and he will suffer contrarieties, loss, and detriment from them and because of them.

But if there is a benefic, or a well disposed planet (namely a fortunate and strong) in the aforementioned places, or in any one of them, and it aspects the Lord of the Ascendant, and this planet is not the Lord of the seventh, and the Lord of the seventh does not aspect the Lord of the Ascendant, it signifies that the native will have few enemies openly opposing him.

If the Lord of the seventh or the Almutem over the seventh aspects the Lord of the first, or the Almutem over the first, impeding him, it signifies that harm, impediment, and destruction will befall the native from enemies, and it seems that on this occasion he might be ruined; and this more greatly so if the Lord of the eighth house aspects it then; and even more so if the Lord of the first has any dignity in the eighth besides face (which will not impede much), and the Lord of the eighth impedes him, since then it will signify the natives' death by the hands of enemies. And this will be even more certain if Mars is the Lord of the eighth house: since then the native will hardly or never be able to evade it, so that it doesn't befall him, and this will happen more so in war than any other situation.

Indeed, if the significator of the native and the significator of his enemies, or the Lord of the Part of Enemies, are more than 17 degrees distant from each other, and are not in places aspecting each other from noted aspects, or are opposite to each other, it will signify that the native will have public enemies, between whom there will be enmity lasting a long time, and it will be possible that the enmity will not end at that time. But if it is from a square aspect, it will judge a lesser enmity between them, and one of lesser duration; and the root and beginning of this enmity will be jealousy, and this will be because one of them is making more money than the other.

You will also examine if there is any noted aspect of any of the luminaries with the aforementioned significators: since if there is not any noted aspect between them (namely a trine or sextile), or some harmony or association, it signifies that inextinguishable enmity will fall between them, which will never be ended.

Likewise, you will examine if the Ylem of the native is separating from the Ylem of the enemies, since this signifies that the enmities of the native will be temporary, and not of long duration. If Saturn is the Ylem of the native, and Mars is the Ylem of the enemies, or vice versa, the enmity between them will occur for almost no reason, on account of the contrariety of their natures. But if Mars is the Ylem of one, and Mercury is the Ylem of the other, it signifies that enmity will fall between them because of knowledge and similar things.

You will consider the same in nativities of a native with regards to enmity, Wherefore, if the significator of the native is a malefic, and impedes the significator of enemies, it signifies that the native will have many enemies, but he will overcome and conquer them all, and evil and detriment will follow from this; and by his hands his enemies will be endangered, killed, and they will perish.

Moreover, you ought to examine where the Part of Enemies falls: since the native will hate this sign, and what it signified by it, and its image.

And if Saturn or Mars are in the house of enemies, he will destroy them; or if this planet impedes the house of enemies, the native will never cease to rejoice from his enemies, and he will send them to their deaths before him, and he will see their ruin. Indeed, if the significator of enemies is in an angle or a succeedent of an angle, and has any dignity there, it signifies the nobility and strength of the natives enemies opposed to him. If it is peregrine or cadent from an angle, and it is combust, or is in its own descension or fall, it will signify their durability and bad condition, and that they will fall into poverty and indigence; and it signifies the prosperity of the native and his power against them; and this more greatly so if one of the malefics are in the house of enemies, or if the enemies significator is impeded by malefics: since then the native will prosper against them, to their detriment and adversity.

Indeed, if a benefic is found in the house of enemies, and their significator is joined with it, it will signify the prosperity and strength of the enemies and their overcoming of the native. But if their significator is in the Ascendant, or in the opposition of one of the luminaries, it will signify that the native will have many enemies, and also those who despise him. If there is a malefic there, it signifies that they will be inimical for great and famous matters. However, if it is not a malefic, they will be as much from great matters, as from small and middling matters, and sometimes their enmity will come from almost nothing.

## ON THE EIGHTH HOUSE

### I

### On The Native's Death, And On The Accidents By Which Death Usually Occurs

**M**ention having been made in the preceding chapters about the life of the native, and his substance, and about brothers, fathers, children, slaves, and about his marriage, it seems fitting to me, to deal with his death and on its occasions and means. And even though death is the final accident which can befall the native, it is fitting that it is placed in the eighth, which is called "the house of death" by the sages.

Therefore you will consider those things which occur to you to be considered, and these are: the Ascendant at the hour of the nativity of any native, and its Lord, and likewise its Ylem and the projection of the rays of the planets to it, and its arrival to the seventh of his nativity: since if it is signified that death ought to arrive on account of the projection of the rays of the planets to the Ylem, or by its conjunction with one of the killing planets, then it is necessary for us to consider the places in which the Ylem conjoins with the killing planet: for the signification of the house in which the killer falls, will be the cause of death; and this more greatly so if such a conjunction or aspect happens when the Ylem reaches the seventh of the nativity.

You will also examine the Part of Death, and the planet in whose domicile you find it, and the eighth sign from the Ascendant of the nativity and its Lord, and the planets which you find in the eighth, or the planets which aspect it (whether they are benefics or malefics). Likewise you will examine the triplicity Lords of the fourth house from the Ascendant of the nativity, and the eighth sign from the Sun (if it is a diurnal nativity), or from the Moon (if it is a nocturnal nativity), and the planets in whose domiciles you find these planets. For if all of the aforementioned significators, or the majority of them, are in good condition, well disposed, and free from impediments (namely retrogradation, combustion, and the conjunction or aspects of malefics), or if there are benefics in the eighth, the native will finish his life and pass on to the next in his own bed. But if the aforementioned places and the aforementioned significators (or the majority of them) are impeded, or if one of the malefics is in the eighth, he will die an evil, horrible, and strange death [or a death outside of his home].

If Saturn alone is stronger in the aforementioned places, and is the Almutem over the place signifying the natives' death, it will come from cold and dry humours. However, if he is impeded, it signifies that the native will die from active or unnatural coldness or moisture (as is snow, ice, or drowning), or from a chronic infirmity, or catarrh, or excessive decay of the body, or on account of a long quartan fever (not a true one), or a spleen pain or dropsy, or something similar. And if it is a woman, from an illness of the womb or its orifice, and this type of illness which usually comes on the occasion of great coldness. Nevertheless, Saturn (or any one of the other planets), could not be the sole significator of death, without the Lord of the terms in which he falls participating with him.

But if Jupiter is the Almutem over the domicile signifying the native's death, and he is in good condition and well disposed, it signifies death will befall the native on the occasion of the liver, pneumonia, or *stomatica*. However, if he is in bad condition and badly disposed, a famous death will befall him from the orders of a king, or another man of great power, or even the judgement of the people, or perhaps a tertian fever (especially the recognised one) or angina, or another suffering of the throat, or heart disease, or colic, or iliac passion, or even from some other illness which can come on the occasion of much obstructed wind; or from continuous fever, or any of the infirmities which tend to occur on the occasion of an overabundance of blood.

But if Mars is the sole significator of the native's death, and is in good condition and well disposed, it signifies that the occasion of his death will be a tertian fever, or even a quotidian fever, or delirium, or suffering from spitting blood, or some death arriving suddenly or unexpectedly. However, if he is in bad condition, and badly disposed, it signifies that the natives death will be by the sword or some instrument of war.

Indeed, if the Sun alone is the Almutem over this domicile, and he is in good condition and well disposed, it will signify that the natives' death will be on the occasion of a fever, or an overabundance of heat, or from some infirmity from the overabundance of blood coming over him. However, if he is in bad condition and badly disposed, it signifies that his death will be because of his own parents, or a king, or powerful person, or some leader, or a heart attack, or that the end of his life will be imposed by heat of the stomach. Or Aboali said that he will die in horrible places.

Indeed, if Venus is the sole Almutem over the domicile signifying the death of the native, and she is in good condition and well disposed, it will signify that the death of the native will be from stomach pain, or from intoxication or drunkenness. But if she is impeded it signifies that the death of the native will approach from a poison given to him by women; or from an overabundance of sexual activity consuming him; or a stomach, liver, or heart illness, or because of too much bloodshed from the above things; or perhaps kidney stones, or some blister, especially one which is born from the material of blood; or from the consumption of a poisonous draught; nor from these illnesses alone, but it will even come from any other ones, arriving from the malice and overabundance of the humours.

But if Mercury is placed as the sole significator of the natives' death, and he is in good condition and well disposed, then you will be able to judge that the native's life will end by means of a true frenzy, or by diverse pains from being an overabundance of diverse humours mixed together coming over him. If Mercury is impeded, then you can announce that the native will die from indeterminate pains, and almost imperceptible ones. However, if he is joined with another planet, he will commit what is his to the partner, and the natives' life will end according to the partner planets nature, or perhaps by a manic passion, or the loss of sense, or swooning, or consumption, or (as Ptolemy says) an overabundance of phlegm, or tuberculosis, or even from any other illness which comes over him from an excess of dryness.

Indeed, if the Moon is the sole significatrix of the native's death, and she is in good condition and well disposed, the native will be led to death by an overabundance of sexual activity, or excessive consumption of food, or an inordinate manner of taking food. But if she is impeded by one of the malefics, it will judge that the native's death will be according to the significations of the impeding

planet. However, if the Moon is not impeded by planets, but is impeded in another way, death will be judged to come over the native from sailing, hunting, fatigue, or from repeated changes from place to place.

And Aboali said if the authors of death mentioned above are in their own domiciles or exaltations, free from malefics, his death will be amongst his parents and close ones. Indeed, if they are peregrine, and impeded by malefics, his death will be on a pilgrimage. If they are cadent, it signifies that the death of the native will be due to a fall from a high place. However, if they are in their own descension, it signifies that his death will be in a well, or a pit, or a cavern, or deep water. Indeed, if the aforementioned planets are the significators of the nativity, death will befall him from the occasion of killing, since he will be murdered, or perhaps stoned.

However, other significators of death, whose significations do not arrive into act by the aforementioned means, but who signify death in a natural way, are those over whom planets signifying an evil death are not elevated, since this death which is to supervene contrary to nature, and happen otherwise than from the aforementioned means, is when Mars and Saturn are both in the place signifying death, or are ruling this place, or aspecting it from opposition, or from square aspect, or rule over the place of the Sun or the Moon, or aspect them from the mentioned aspects. However, if any of the other planets aspect the aforementioned malefics, they will assist the natives death according to their nature, and according to the signs from which they aspect them. Moreover, if Saturn is placed in a fixed sign, and the sign is not in his Aym (nor in the Aym of the Sun), and is in square or opposition aspect, the native will be undone by a rumour of the mob, or he will be strangled, or he might even be killed by the hands of some commoner. The same will happen if he is placed setting, and the Moon approaches him, and if he is also the Lord of the place signifying death.

Indeed, if he is placed in Leo or Scorpio, it signifies that the native will die from the bite of a wild animal. However, if he is in Aries, Taurus, the last half of Sagittarius, or Capricorn, it will signify that the native will die because of domestic animals. Indeed, if you find him in Cancer, or Pisces, you will be able to announce that he will die because of fish or animals spending time in water. But if he is in Scorpio, he will be signified to die from venomous animals, either terrestrial or aquatic ones. If Jupiter is then joined to Saturn, and he is impeded, he will strengthen Saturn's malice, and it will even signify that the native will likewise be killed by the aforementioned beasts, but on a festival or holy day.

Indeed, if the Sun or the Moon are placed in the Ascendant, and Saturn in its opposition, it signifies that the native will die because of imprisonment.

Indeed, if Mercury is joined to Saturn in the figure of a nativity (and this more strongly so if their conjunction is in Leo or Scorpio, or with the Cauda Draconis), it will signify that the natives life will be ended on the occasion of a venomous or rapacious animal. However, if Venus adds on her powers, it will signify that the native will be subjugated to death from a poisonous draught given to him by women.

If Saturn is in Gemini, Virgo, Libra, the first half of Sagittarius, or Aquarius, or even in Pisces (as Ptolemy says) and the Moon is joined to him in the natives figure, the native will end his life by drowning.

If the Moon is in Leo with the Cauda, it will signify that the native will die from poison given to him with purgative medicines.

And Aboali said that if the triplicity Lords of the angle of the earth, or the degree of the Ascendant and its Lord, or the Sun in diurnal nativities, or the Moon in nocturnal nativities, are impeded, the native will complete his life with a strange [or foreign] death. But if the significators of the natives death are above the earth, or if they are in air signs, or if Mars is in the fourth or the tenth, and is the Lord of the aforementioned quality, this signifies that the natives death will occur openly and publicly, or will happen in a torture device similar to a yoke, or in some wooden thing similar to this, or in a place elevated from the earth. And if Mars is below the earth and in an earth sign, it will signify that his death ought to be hidden, or perhaps that it will be under some collapsed building. Indeed, if he is in a fire sign, this signifies that he will be burnt, or die because of fire in some other way.

But if one of the benefics are in the eighth, or with its Lord; or in the fourth, or with its Lord, it will signify death to come pleasingly to the native. But if one of the malefics are in the aforementioned places, or with their Lords, they will indicate an evil death for the native. If this malefic is Mars, his death will happen by fire or iron. However, if it is Saturn, it will be from poison or a collapse of a building, or a fall, or a stormy inundation of the sea, or some other submersion.

But if Saturn is from the fourth degree of Sagittarius up to the fifteenth degree of Capricorn, or from the twentieth degree of Cancer up to the fifteenth degree of Leo, or in Aries or Taurus, corporeally joined to the Sun, or if Mars is in opposition to him, or if the same Saturn is in opposition to the Sun, it signifies that the native will die by the fall of some ruin. But if Saturn is in the tenth, and Mars is in the 4th, or corporeally joined to him, and Mars himself is the Lord of the aforementioned quality (namely that he is the Lord of the domicile or terms of the degree signifying death), it signifies that the natives will end his life with a fall.

If Mars is in the fourth from the Ascendant of the nativity, and is the Lord of the quality of the natives death, or if one of the luminaries are opposite to him, and he is outside of his Aym, and is in Gemini, Virgo, Libra, the first half of Sagittarius, or Aquarius, it signifies that the native will enter the gibbet on the occasion of a dispute or altercation, or contingent death, that will be born amongst his relatives, or on the occasion of some war, and he will not avoid his head being cut off.

And Ptolemy said that either he would kill himself by his own hand because of a woman, or he will be killed by the hands of a woman. And he said that this will occur if Venus will again testify to Mars. If Mercury is joined with Mars in the figure, he will be torn to shreds by thieves, pirates, or those lying in ambush.

But he said that it will be by the severing of limbs if Mars was in Caput Algol, or the signs of imperfect forms, or if Mars is with the Caput Draconis; and he is placed as the Lord of the aforementioned quality, the natives head will be cut off, or he will die on the occasion of the maiming of another limb. However, if the signification of death is placed in Taurus or Scorpio, and Mars is in the same place by the aforementioned conditions, it signifies that the native will be deprived of his life from burning, or from cauterisation or other severings or puncturings, or doctor's cuts rendered to him by way of remedy applied to him, or perhaps by convulsion.

But if Mars is in the Ascendant, or the seventh, and the Almutem over one of these, and Saturn is testifying to him from a fire sign, it signifies that the native will be sent alive into fire, so that he might be burned.

Moreover, Ptolemy said that if Mars is in quadrupedal signs, the natives will be crushed by a fall. And if Jupiter testifies to Mars, and he is placed unfortunately, the judgement of death will be entered because of kings or powerful person, and this will be public, and not hidden.

And if Mars and Saturn are joined in the place signifying the natives' death at the hour of the nativity, or they are opposite to each other (just as is said above), or if either of them have dignity in the place signifying death, or if either of them are the Almutem over it, it will make the manner or quality of the natives death severe, and this severity will be double what it would have been if the aforementioned malefics were not so disposed, nor will his body be buried; and this more truly so if a benefic does not aspect the aforementioned malefics, or if one does not have dignity in the place signifying death; and his body will be made bait or food for rapacious quadrupeds, and birds living by seizing prey (and this more so if the aforementioned malefics are in Leo or Scorpio, or in other places in which the forms of the aforementioned birds are depicted). However, if benefics aspect the mentioned places, or the mentioned malefics, and the benefics are below the earth, it will not go as was said, but rather, the native will die in any way, and it will signify him to die in an agreeable and proper way.

Indeed, if the mentioned killing planets are in the third, or the ninth (and this more greatly if the Moon is in the aforementioned places of journeys, or if she aspects them from square or opposition), this will signify that the native will not die amongst his own relatives, but amongst foreign people.

And Ptolemy said to examine the Almutem over the place signifying the natives' death, since if it is impeded in a place which is called "Audax" (which

is close to the head of Scorpio), or if the Moon herself is placed there, it signifies that the native will lose his life from a snakebite, or the blow of a poisoned dagger, or poison presented to him in some clever way. And if it is impeded close to the place which is called the "Vultur Cades", which is in Capricorn, or the "Vultur Volans", which is at the end of Capricorn, his body will not be buried, but will be made into the food of crows and other birds living by seizing prey, as are vultures, kites, and the like. And if it is impeded, joined to Caput Algol (which is in Taurus), the natives' head will be cut off. If it is joined to the Sun in the aforementioned places, or the Moon, or Jupiter, and they are impeded, it signifies that the native's death will be truly awful. And if they are in opposition to him, it signifies that the native will die by the hands of a king or another powerful person.

## ON THE NINTH HOUSE

### I

### On The Religion And Faith Of The Native, And His Knowledge, And Likewise On His Pilgrimages Or Long Journeys

Since the natives death and its occasions have been discussed sufficiently in the preceding chapter, in this chapter I think it is fitting to deal with the subject of his religion and faith, and likewise his pilgrimages or long journeys.

It is necessary for you to examine the Ascendant in the aforementioned nativity which you wish to investigate, and see whether the Lord of the Ascendant and the Moon (or the stronger one of them), is in the ninth, or joined with its Lord (which signifies the faith of the native and his knowledge and religion). For if both of them are as said, and are in a good place in the circle, and especially in the aforementioned good condition, and well disposed, and the planet is a benefic, it signifies that the native will adhere to a fitting, proper, or lawful religion.

For if Saturn is the significator of religion, it will signify that he will adhere to a severe and laborious religion, especially the religion whose followers think that they are better and more worthy of God than all other religious peoples, and especially those clad in black vestments.

However, if Jupiter is the significator of religion, it signifies that he will adhere to the religion whose followers are called secular clerics (as are bishops, archbishops, and others who preside over churches), on account of its liberality.

Indeed, if the Sun is the significator of religion, it signifies that he will adhere to a liberal and noble religion, namely one of the religious people spending time between spiritual and temporal things, and the like.

If Venus is the significatrix, it signifies that he will adhere to religions in which he will be able to preside over women spending time in it, and the like.

Indeed, if Mercury is the sole significator of religion, and is in good condition, it signifies that the native will adhere to a religion of youths, or learned men and the wise, and the like.

But if the Moon is the significator of religion, it signifies that he will adhere to a religion of unstable men, and those easily and quickly changing themselves from one proposition to another, nor observing their own religion well.

However, if the significator of knowledge or religion (namely the Almutem over the ninth house), is joined to Jupiter or the Sun by a trine or sextile aspect, and with reception, and is in the first, whichever one of the planets it is (apart from Mars Mars), it will judge that religion will come to the native casually, and without him knowing, and unexpectedly, and this will occur almost inevitably.

### II

### On The Natives' Faith And The Depth Of His Knowledge

In the investigation of the faith of the native and depth of his knowledge, you ought to examine Mercury, and see how he is disposed: since he, before all other planets, it the Almutem over the signification of the natives' faith and the depth of his knowledge: who, if he is oriental, free from impediments, fortunate, and strong, will signify that the native will be of good faith, and eagerly adhering to the sciences, and that he will be profound in them, and eagerly associating with religious men, and that he will love them.

You will likewise examine the Part of Faith, and the place in which you find it, and its Lord, and see how he is disposed, since if he is safe, removed from impediments, and the third and the ninth houses and their Lords are free from impediments, and if they (and the Lords of the houses which you find them in) are fortunate and strong (namely free from combustion, retrogradation, and likewise fall, and the aspects of malefics), this will signify that the native will be (as I said) religious and very profound in the sciences, and distinguished, and there will be few like him found. But if you find the contrary, you will be able to judge the contrary.

If Mercury, as was said, is free, fortunate, and strong, and you find the significator of the native's religion, faith and knowledge free, see in which of the signs, or in the aspect of which planet Mercury falls.

For if he is in Capricorn or Aquarius, and Saturn aspects him from a trine or sextile aspect, and Saturn is in good condition and well disposed, it signifies that the native will be religious, of good faith, and very profound and distinguished in the sciences; and he will commit these sciences to memory very well; and will eagerly read and study while at leisure; nor will he desire the monetary advantage from these sciences, and if he does desire it, he will not attain it; and he will be a solitary man, fleeing from temporal delights (as are laughter, games, and worldly joys), nor will he desire them in any way, and he will withdraw from them in every way; and he will also be humble, and will sustain well almost everything which befalls him, however, adverse as these things may be, nor will he easily be saddened on such an occasion, and he will bear difficulties, tribulations, labours that are introduced easily and in peace; and will not care to avoid them.

Indeed, if he is in Sagittarius or Pisces, and Jupiter aspects him from trine or sextile aspect, and Jupiter is in good condition and well disposed (namely fortunate and strong), it signifies that the native will adhere to civil and canonical laws, from which he will obtain praise, honours, good fame, and likewise lofty and famous clerical dignities, and in addition to this he will be generous, good minded, of good faith, and rejoicing in these things which he will have - unless Mars operates to the contrary. Since if Mars aspects him, it signifies that he will despise his own law, and he will be a transgressor of it.

However, if Mercury is in Leo, and the Sun is well disposed (namely fortunate and strong), and aspects him from a trine or sextile aspect, it signifies that the native will be wise, humble, discerning, and of good faith, a lover of religion, and profound in matters of faith, and he will understand them well, and will eagerly associate with religious men.

But if he is in Taurus or Libra, and Venus aspects him from a trine or sextile aspect, with Venus being well disposed (namely fortunate and strong), it signifies that the native will adhere to a religion in which he will not persevere well in, and it will hardly happen that he doesn't leave it; nor will he eagerly study while at leisure, nor will he become profound in sciences, even if he will be found to be of good beliefs. he will delight much in lively things.

If Mercury is in Gemini or in Virgo, and Mercury himself is in good condition and well disposed (namely fortunate and strong),and he is the sole significator, it will signify that the native will be of good faith and religious, blessed in every respect with the gift of knowledge, and he will understand books of the sciences well, and will wondrously expound both the divine ones and others, and praise and a good reputation will follow from this. And these things will occur more strongly, if Jupiter regards him from a trine or sextile aspect: but with Jupiter in good condition, fortunate and placed free

Indeed, if he is in Cancer, and the Moon is in good condition and well disposed (namely fortunate and strong), it signifies that the native will be in good condition and of good faith, and of good belief, and desirous of a good reputation.

And Aboali said that if the ninth domicile is a common sign, signifies that the native will be unstable in faith, or to the religion to which he adheres, and this more so if Mars aspects it from a trine or sextile aspect: since then he will deride and despise the law or religion which he takes up, nor will he observe it well, but rather he will deride and despise it. And even more so, if Mars is unfortunate and weak, aspecting it from a trine or sextile aspect, or from opposition, since he will then remove all goodness from the native, and will make it so that he sheds the blood of strangers, and eagerly inflicts injuries on others; and this after he has gnawed off the collar of the religion which he took up. However, if Mars (when he aspects this house) is free from impediments, the native will fashion many lies (even when he is placed in the religion), which will never seem credible, nor they be known to be invented by anyone else.

But if it is in a mobile sign, and its Lord is in a mobile sign, it will signify that the native will not follow any faith will, and that he will easily and quickly be changed from one opinion to another; nor will he persevere well in any of them; nor will he know how to select the better of them.

Indeed, if it is in a fixed sign, it will signify his constancy or firmity in the faith and religion to which he adheres, and he will do good in it, and he will be firm in his counsel and propositions, and also in those of others, since he will perceive its truth, unless Mars operates to the contrary.

And Aboali said that if the Lord of the ninth or the third is in the Ascendant, or in the Midheaven, free from malefics, it signifies the rulership of the native over his associates, and that he will be of good sense, and the best morals, and perfect in faith, especially if Jupiter is the Lord of the ninth, or if the Lord of the ninth is in the Ascendant in the aspect of Jupiter.

And know that if it is as was said, and Mercury is oriental, the native will manifestly and visibly do well and observe his faith and law, and likewise the religion in which he spends time, and those things which are of that law and faith. And if he is occidental, he will hide and conceal his law and faith.

You will also examine whether Mercury is in Gemini, Cancer, or in Virgo, with the Moon, and the Part of Faith or the Part of Knowledge is with them in one of the aforementioned places, since this will signify that the native will be profound in knowledge and wisdom, and likewise almost prophetic. If Jupiter aspects them from noted aspects, or if he is corporeally joined with them, it will signify that the native will appear truthful and lawful, and experienced in profound, exalted, lofty, and even great matters; and witness, and a trusted counsellor; and even if he isn't, nevertheless he will be believed and his counsel will stand, nor will it be believed that anyone else knows better than him.

Likewise, you will examine in diurnal nativities if the Caput Draconis is in the ninth, or if it is in the third in nocturnal nativities: since this will signify that the native will be of good memory, and will be firm in his proposals, and will observe his faith and law well; and this more strongly and more reverently, if Jupiter, the Sun, and Mercury aspect this place from noted aspects: since then his goodness and reputation will be exalted on high, and will fly across many regions or provinces.

And Aboali said that if the ninth house is a domicile of Jupiter, and the Moon is there (in nocturnal nativities), it signifies that the native will be a wise astronomer, and announcer of divinations and future things. Likewise if Mercury is the Lord of the 9th and is placed in the ninth.

And if you find the Moon in the Ascendant, and the Ascendant is a sign having a human form, it signifies that the native will be horrible and of an evil mind. Likewise if Saturn is in the Ascendant in nativities, or in the angle of the earth.

You will also see if the Part of Faith is with Saturn, since this will signify that the native will be an investigator of profound and precise matters, and he will be a precise investigator of them, and he will be grave in his discussions, and bringing forth ponderous words, and full of thoughts.

But if the Part is with Jupiter, it signifies that the native will be an observer of good law, of good faith, bringing forth beautiful and honourable words.

Indeed, if it is with Mars, the native will be of bad faith, bad opinions, and a wicked character.

However, if it is with the Sun, and the Sun is then fortunate and in good condition, it signifies that the native will be of great appearance, even more so than is the truth of the matter; however, he will be of good faith, good law, and extolling good religion.

If it is with Venus, it will signify that the native will be benevolent, and a lover of games and joys.

However, if it is with Mercury it will signify that he will be excellent in the science of measurement, in number, and in trade.

But if the Moon is with the mentioned part, it will indicate the liberality of the mind, and the purity of the native.

Indeed, if the ninth house is Aries, Cancer, or Pisces, and the Sun, or Jupiter, or Venus (namely whichever one of them is the triplicity Lord of the sign in which the luminary who has authority is placed) is in a good place in the figure of the nativity - it signifies that the native, on account of his way of life, and on occasion of his faith or law, will be good and honourable, and he will get and acquire the notice and praise, and likewise the love of men; and this more greatly, and more strongly so, if one of the benefics are then found in the third or in the ninth, and even more strongly if the Lords of the ninth and third houses are safe and free from impediments.

And Aomar said that if Mercury is the Lord of the ninth house, and agrees with the Lord of the Ascendant, the native will be one contending in faith and will be a debater having discipline in words. However, if Mercury is then fortunate and oriental , he will be prudent in this, and will acquire wealth from it, and even his condition will be good and praiseworthy. Indeed, if he is impeded, and occidental, he will meet with evil from this.

And Aboali said that if Saturn is the Lord of the ninth, it signifies that the native will be wise, and especially if he is in the aspect of benefics, and not retrograde, nor under the rays of the Sun.

And Bernardus said that a planet placed in combustion in anyone's nativity signifies the laziness, and even the idleness of the native, and his illegality; indeed, if it is retrograde, it signifies that he will be deceitful.

And Remigius said to examine the third and ninth sign, and also their Lords, and the Part of Faith and the Lord of the sign containing it. However, if these three planets are in good condition and well disposed (namely fortunate and strong), free from malefics and from other impediments, it signifies that the native will be of good faith and good law, and likewise of good religion. However, if they are impeded by the conjunction of malefics, or from their square aspect or opposition (and especially in the ninth or the third) it signifies that the native will be of bad faith, of bad law, and of much corrupt hypocrisy, wavering in a mixed condition in faith.

And Valens said that if Cancer is the third or ninth house in anyone's nativity, and the Moon or Mercury are in one of them, and Jupiter or Venus is in the Ascendant or the tenth, and is free from impediments, namely fortunate and strong, this will signify that because of this natives faith, law, and religion, he will ascend to a great dignity or prelature.

And Bernardus said that if you correctly consider the condition of the triplicity Lords of the Part of Faith, you will be able to see in what third of the native's life he will be of better faith, of better law, and of better religion.

And Aomar said to examine from the ninth and the third, and the planets which are in them, and from the Part of Faith and its Lord. You will also examine the Almutem over these places: who, if it

is Saturn, and he is safe, namely from malefics, combustion, and retrogradation; or if it is Jupiter, Mars, or the Sun are free from malefics, the native will be a worshipper of one God, without a division of intention, and the native will be saved because of this faith, and he will observe it, nor will he be changed to another.

## III

### On The Pilgrimages Of The Native, And On His Long Journeys

Having looked in what preceded regarding the faith of the native, and his religion, I believe it is fitting to subsequently elucidate something regarding his pilgrimages and long journeys.

Indeed, in the pilgrimages of the native and his long journeys, examine the ninth house from the Ascendant of his nativity, and its Lord, and if any planet is placed in this house, you will consider it likewise; and likewise Mars and the Part of Pilgrimages, and the Lord of the domicile in which you find it, and see which of the planets is the Almutem over these places, or over one of them (whether the Almutem is one or many). And you will also see how they interact with the Ascendant, or with its Almutem, and what is their simultaneous aspect, conjunction, or application like: since if they are in good condition and well disposed (namely fortunate and strong), and applying well together, or corporeally joined, or aspect each other from noted aspects (and this more greatly so if it is with reception), it will signify that the native will eagerly engage in pilgrimages and long journeys, and especially in regions distant and remote from his own land, and even more greatly so if the Moon is placed setting in the figure of the nativity, or remote from the angle of the 10th house, and especially if she is in the ninth from the Ascendant of the nativity. You will be able to give a similar judgement if you find Mars in the 9th, the 8th, or the 7th, and if he is in opposition or square aspect to the Sun or the Moon, yet he will not desire journeys or pilgrimages as fervently.

If a benefic is in the ninth, or joined with the Lord of the ninth, or if the Lord of the ninth is a benefic, or if one of the benefics aspect the aforementioned places, or if it aspects Mars, the Sun, or the Moon, this will signify that his journeys will be safe, useful, and salubrious, and that the native will return from his pilgrimages safely and in a short space of time, and with profit, no matter how little journeys or pilgrimages he carries out. But if you find the contrary, you will be able to judge to the contrary. For his journeys will be believed to be burdensome and useless, and likewise laborious, and also fearful, and with a delayed return. If you find none of these things, say that the native will avoid the mentioned pilgrimages and journeys, and that he will search for his profit in his own place of habitation.

Likewise you will examine the triplicity Lords of the domicile in which Mars is placed; and according to the place, disposition, and condition of the one of them which is stronger, more fortunate, and better disposed, you will announce that in the period of his life attributed to that planet, his pilgrimages will be better, more useful, and more profitable; and likewise you will announce the contrary if it is to the contrary. Still, if one of the benefics are joined with the aforementioned significators outside of any of the aforementioned places, they will increase the good and diminish the bad. However, if they are malefics, it signifies that they will perform the contrary, and that evil, harm, and the diminution of substance will befall the native because of his journeys; and it signifies that he will be of little faith.

You will even examine to see if the Sun and the Moon are from the angle of the tenth house facing towards the Ascendant, or in the Ascendant up to the fourth house, since they will signify that most of his pilgrimages and his long journeys will be towards the east and the south. Indeed, if they are from the aforementioned angle of the tenth house towards the west, up to the angle of the fourth house, or in the seventh itself, you will not doubt that his journeys will be toward the west and the north.

If the aforementioned third and ninth houses are fixed signs, and their Lords are benefics, and likewise in the aforementioned domiciles, or in any others in fixed signs, and in good places from the Ascendant, this will signify that the native will not make frequent journeys or pilgrimages, and if he does go on a pilgrimage, he will go on pilgrimage intermittently. But if the aforementioned places and the aforementioned significators are in common signs, it signifies that he will make frequent journeys or pilgrimages. And if the aforementioned places, or the places of the Sun and the Moon, are Taurus, or Cancer, or Libra, or Sagittarius, or Pisces, this signifies that his journeys and his pilgrimages will be according to what the native wished for, prosperous and secure.

And Aboali said to examine the Moon on the third day of the nativity: who, if she is applying to Mars, or is in his house or terms, and he is aspecting her, signifies many pilgrimages and journeys. And he said that if the Lord of the Ascendant is contrary to the Ascendant, and the Lord of the domicile of the Moon is contrary to the Moon, or if the Lord of the Ascendant is in its own descension, it signifies that that the native's livelihood will come from foreign regions. And he said that if the Lord of the domicile of the Sun is contrary to the Sun, it signifies that the native will travel on many journeys. And if the aforementioned Lord of the domicile of the Sun is fortunate, the native will attain good and profit from his journeys. Indeed, if it is a malefic, you will judge badly. And he said that if the Moon is applying to Mercury on the third day after the nativity, and she is impeded by Mars, it signifies that horrible things will befall the native on his journeys. However, if the Moon, or the Lord of her domicile, is in the angle of the seventh house, it signifies that the native will love journeys. Likewise the Lord of the Ascendant, if it is in the ninth, or the Lord of the ninth, if it is in the Ascendant, signifies that the native will desire to travel and to move from region to region.

## IV

## Which Of The Planets Assist Journeys And Which Don't

And know that the planets assist journeys, and sometimes they impede them.

For Saturn and the Sun, if they are in good condition and well disposed (namely fortunate and strong), will assist journeys made towards the east; however, if they are impeded, they will work to their contrary.

Jupiter provides his assistance to journeys made towards the north.

Likewise Venus assists journeys which are made towards the south.

However, Mars and the Moon strive to strengthen those which are made towards the west.

Mercury provides assistance to journeys according to the nature of the planet who he is joined to.

You will even consider the aforementioned planetary significators supporting of journeys or pilgrimages: since if it is Saturn, and he is in good condition and well disposed, it will signify that the native will perform his journeys and his pilgrimages in the service of great prelates, and especially those clad in black vestments, or old men, or Jews.

However, if it is Jupiter, he will perform them in the service of magnates, wealthy men, and nobles, or great and famous jurists, or their friends.

Indeed, if it is Mars he will labour in the services of bellicose soldiers, and leaders of armies.

If it is the Sun, he will tire in the service of great kings and wealthy men who are fit for kingship.

But if it is Venus, he will render his services to great ladies and even their friends.

Indeed, if it is the Moon he will perform his service for the commoners or those of low birth.

However, if it is Mercury, he will serve those who he is attached to, and also learned men and youths.

In the same way, you will see if Jupiter or Venus assist the aforementioned significators of pilgrimages or journeys, and whether Mercury is applied to them, and he is placed in good condition and well disposed: since this signifies that the native will obtain great good and utility from the aforementioned journeys or pilgrimages; and he will perfect them well and in accordance with his wishes, and he will acquire honour and contributions from them.

But if the Sun and Moon assist the aforementioned significators, and they are in Aries, Scorpio, Capricorn, or Aquarius, and Mars or Saturn are in their opposition, it signifies that great inconveniences and also impediments will befall the native because of his journeys or pilgrimages.

If Mars stays in Cancer or its triplicity, the aforementioned things will happen to the native from inundations of the sea, or even other waters, or on account of unsuitable or intolerable journeys, or on account of thieves or highwaymen, or submersions.

But if Mars and Saturn are in Gemini or its triplicity, the aforementioned things will occur from strong gusts of wind.

However, if they are placed in Taurus or its triplicity, they will portend those things to occur from the collapse of buildings.

Indeed, if you find them in Aries or its triplicity, say that impediments will befall the native, which will surround him because of a fall from a high place, or from an unexpected or accidental fall.

And Ptolemy said that if Saturn and Mars are in solstial or equinoctial signs, we will not doubt that this will happen because of their things for which they will be in want of (namely, men's want and privation); and on account of the corrupt qualities of the air bringing in illness. However, if they are in signs of a human form, we will say that they will occur because of highwaymen, or from men's insults or aggressions, or betrayals or pillagings. And he said that if they are in signs whose forms are similar to the forms of wild animals, it will happen from rapacious wolves or from earthquakes, or any matter which will fall down on him.

And Aboali said that if the Moon is applying to benefics on the third day of the nativity, and she is in a good place, namely fortunate and strong, it signifies the success of the native on his journeys. Indeed, if it is to the contrary, it will indicate to the contrary. And he said to examine the ninth domicile, which, if there is a benefic there, or in its square aspect or opposition, it signifies the profit of the native because of journeys, especially if the Lord of the Ascendant is a benefic, or if he is aspected by benefics. However, if you observe the contrary, you will be able to judge to the contrary, especially if the Lord of the ninth is a malefic, or if malefics aspect him. And if the Lord of the ninth is in the Ascendant, or in its tenth, it signifies the love of the native in journeys.

Indeed, if Venus is the Lord of the ninth, and she is in the Ascendant, it signifies the rejoicing of the native, and his marriage on his journeys, and marriage.

Indeed, if Jupiter is the Lord of the ninth, and is in the Ascendant or in the tenth, it signifies that the native will acquire praise and a good reputation on his journeys.

But if the Sun is the Lord of the ninth, and is in the Ascendant or the tenth, it will signify that the native will acquire knowledge and things of nobility, and things from the nobility, on his journeys.

If Saturn is the Lord of the ninth, and is in the Ascendant or the tenth, in the aspect of Jupiter, it signifies that the native will acquire substance on his journeys from watery and earthy things, and beasts.

Indeed, if Mars is the Lord of the ninth, and is in the Ascendant or in the tenth, it signifies that he will acquire substance on his journeys because of bellicose soldiers, and those by whom wars are engaged in, and armies.

And Aboali said that if the Lord of the domicile of the Sun does not aspect him, and the Lord of the domicile of the Moon does not aspect the Moon, and the Lord of the Ascendant does not aspect the Ascendant, or if Mars is in the third or the ninth, and the Lord of the Part of Journeys is contrary to its own domicile, it signifies a multitude of journeys with labour, fear, and the loss of substance.

And if the Part of Journeys is in one of the angles joined to the Lord of the Ascendant and the Moon, it signifies that the native will love journeys and travelling.

## ON THE TENTH HOUSE

### I

### On The Profession Of The Native, And On His Work, And His Duties, And On His Strength, Likewise On His Prosperity And Kingship And On The Condition Of The Mother

If you wish to be made certain on what the matter of the profession of the native and his work, will be like; and on his strength, prosperity, and kingship, and likewise on his duties and on maternal matters, examine the Ascendant of his nativity, and see if one of the planets are found in it. Since the planet who you find in the Ascendant will be the one that ought to be considered, and you will take the signification of the aforementioned things from him. If there is not a planet in the Ascendant, then examine the tenth: if one of the planets are placed in it, the signification of the aforementioned is to be taken from this planet, however, the tenth signifies the laziness of the native in his work, and likewise the fourth. And the aforementioned significators should be oriental from the Sun and occidental from the Moon.

If none of the planets are in the Ascendant or in the tenth, then examine the fourth or the seventh, for if you find one of the planets in either of them, you will be able to take the signification of the natives' work from it; however, their significations will be weaker than the aforementioned. If there are no planets in any of the aforementioned places, examine the Almutem over each of them, whether it is the Lord or the Almutem over the Ascendant, or over the tenth, or the fourth, or the seventh.

Then, even examine the planet to whom the Moon is first joined after her corporeal separation from the Sun (if the nativity is diurnal), or the planet who is first joined with the Part of Fortune (if the nativity is nocturnal). You will also examine whether any planet is recently appearing from under the rays of the Sun, not more than 20 degrees remote from him - and if it is one of the superiors, it should be oriental from him; however, if it is one of the inferiors, it should be occidental. And see if this planet (which I just mentioned), or the planet who is in the first, the tenth, the fourth, or the seventh, has alitisal with the Moon.

However, if you find one of the planets (whether it is one of the aforementioned, or if it is one of the others), to whom two of the aforementioned accidents pertain to, you will consider him alone, and you will omit the others, since these should not be cared about much.

If you only find one of them so disposed, namely that this planet alone is in one of the aforementioned places, or with one of the aforementioned conjunctions, or if he is the Almutem over one of them, you will consider him, and you will take the natives profession and each one of the aforementioned things from him, and especially if you find Mars, Venus, or Mercury in the Ascendant or in the tenth; and even more so if they have domicile, exaltation, term, or triplicity there (yet face, even though it does something in this, its signification will be much below the aforementioned).

And if one of the three aforementioned planets are in one of the noted aspects with the Sun, or with the Moon (and this more strongly so if reception intervenes), it will signify that the native will adhere to whatever profession, work, or office that he wants, and he will be able to attain it well and easily; and he will be able to accept utility and profit which is pleasing to him from whatever one he wants, according to how one of the planets signify it.

If there are more than one of the planets in the aforementioned places, you will prefer the one who has greater authority or more dignity there.

If you find none of the aforementioned, and the nativity is diurnal, you will take the signification from the planet which is joined with the Sun. But if it is nocturnal, then you will take it from the planet with which the Moon is joined. Indeed, if the Moon is not joined with anyone, the signification will be taken from the planet which she has most recently separated from, or from the Lord of the domicile in which the Part of Fortune is placed, or namely from the planet who is better disposed.

If this planet is fortunate, in good condition, and strong (and this more greatly so if Mercury is fortunate and strong, and if he is aspecting the planet by a friendly aspect), it signifies that the native will have a good profession, good work, and good mechanical works, and that in this profession, and from this profession, he will succeed, and likewise he will obtain wealth, utility, and great benefit from it. And he will be learned in the science of numbers, and a precise operator in writing, and fortunate in all of the aforementioned things, and he will be of good talent and good intellect.

And if Saturn aspects the aforementioned significator of the native by a praiseworthy aspect, and Saturn is in good condition and well disposed (namely, fortunate and strong), it will signify that the natives' fortune will prevail in the cultivation of the land and trees, and planting. And if Saturn aspects the 10th, or is in the 10th, it will signify that the native will reach great rulership and great duties and great burdens.

Indeed, if Jupiter regards from the mentioned aspects, it signifies that the native will be honourable and wise, and will be a writer who will prevail over others, and he will be in the households of princes (namely, kings, and magnates).

If Mars aspects the planet from the aspects and places mentioned above, or if he himself is the significator of the natives work, it will signify that the native will be excellent in medicine (and especially in surgery), and likewise in theology; and of a common enough nature, and one applying itself to those things he wants (and not with difficulty); and he will be crafty and ingenious.

And Aboali said that if the Sun aspects the planet, or is with him in one sign, so that he does not burn him up, it signifies him to have a great and lofty profession, and a scribe for kings, and highly valued among them.

And if Venus aspects the planet, or is the significatrix of the work of the native, it signifies the condition of the native will be mixed with the women of kings and nobles, and he will be strengthened to the greatest extent with them, and will attain profit from them.

However, if Mercury testifies to this planet, the native will be excellent in knowledge of writings, and in number, and bartering, and similar things.

But if the Moon aspects the planet, it signifies the native's knowledge and complete fortune in those things which end quickly.

But if any of the malefics aspect the planet from an evil aspect. It signifies labour and striving in the profession. For if Mars aspects it, and he is in bad condition and badly disposed, or Mars himself is in the Ascendant or in the tenth, and the nativity is diurnal, it will signify that the native will incur harm and danger because of his profession: for he will be whipped from it, and chained, or clubbed to death or condemned.

However, if it is Saturn, and he is in bad condition and badly disposed, and is in the first or the tenth, and it is a nocturnal nativity, it signifies that the native will be bound for the aforementioned reason, he will be fettered by strong fetters, and imprisoned or hanged, or tortured like a hanged martyr.

And Aboali said that the year in which the root Ascendant arrives to the sign of the Midheaven, and if there are any of the planets signifying the profession in it, the native will renew his profession according to the substance of the planet who is there.

And Ptolemy said that when we take the signification of the profession and work of the native from the tenth alone, the native will be idle in his profession and work, and that we ought to take what kind the natives profession and work will be, principally through Mars, Venus, and Mercury, and by the sign in which they are - I say secondarily through the other planets and places.

For if Mars is placed as the sole significator of the natives work and profession, and is in his dignities, it will signify that his profession and work to be perfected by fire or iron, and it will indicate that he will know how to cut stones and sculpt statuettes.

But if Mars is in the dignities of Saturn, and Saturn is testifying to him, and is in good condition and well disposed, it will signify that the natives profession will be in the building of ships (and especially the ships of pirates and pillagers), and by way of robbery on the seas. And Ptolemy said that the native will be a navigator, a swimmer, or a painter [or a fisherman - pictor vs piscator] and that he will eagerly stay in great waters and in the baths.

However, if Mars is in the dignities of Jupiter, and Jupiter is testifying to him, and one of them is well disposed, and the other is badly disposed, it signifies that his work will be in the military, and in inflicting punishments, both on the innocent and the guilty; and will pretend to be a host to travellers, and will eagerly pilfer what he can from them. And likewise he will be a toll operator, so that he will acquire something for himself.

If he is in the dignities of the Sun, and the Sun is testifying to him, and in addition to this the Sun is weak, this will signify that the work of the native and his profession will be in the kindling of flames, and in those things which are made by the kindling of fire, and especially the fire in which the metal and minerals are smelted.

Indeed, if he is in the dignities of Venus, and Venus is testifying to him, this will signify that the work of this native and his profession will be in women's jewellery and precious metals (namely gold and silver), and in games and inventing songs, and making musical instruments and compositions.

And if he is in the dignities of Mercury or the Moon, and one of them is testifying to him, it signifies that the work and profession of the native will be in engraving coinage, and making rings and necklaces, and likewise in sculpting precious stones.

And Ptolemy said that if two planets come together in the profession of the native, and they are Venus and Mercury, he will engage in music or games: he said this for the reason that Venus signifies delights, and Mercury signifies number; or his exertion will be in songs or investing songs, or in any manner of finding songs - however, especially when they will be interchanged in their lyrics: for then the native will be a joker, especially if Venus is in the dignities of Mercury, and Mercury is in the dignities of Venus; or an actor (as are those who use the *barbastellis)*, and he will be a composer or maker of citharas, viols, drums, organs, levitarum, other musical instruments. And he will be excited for defiling, deceiving, and deluding women, but (as Ptolemy says) not for marrying them. He will also be a painter, and a good operator or maker of the aforementioned stringed instruments, he will even be a preacher [or a proclaimer/crier] and he will mix in flattery and lies in his preachings.

And Ptolemy said that if Saturn testifies to them, so that he is a participator in the natives' profession with the aforementioned significators, his work and profession will be in the aforementioned things, in trade, and he will sell those things with which women are adorned.

And he said that if Jupiter is testifying to them, and he is in the dignities of Mercury, he will be a pleader, and always eagerly remaining in places where men congregate. However, if he is in his own dignities he will stay around the gates of the royal palace, and will teach boys. However, if Jupiter is weak, he will be concerned with matters of the mob.

But he said that if Mars and Mercury have rulership over the work of the profession, he will be learned in the making of statuettes and arms, and he will be a sculptor of things which are used in the house of the divine, and will make statuettes of animals; and he will be a wrestler, a doctor, a surgeon, an evil doer, a fornicator, and a forger of documents.

And he said if Saturn testifies to them, the native will be a murderer, and will tear off the clothes of others, and he will be a highwayman.

And he said that if Jupiter testifies to them, that he will esteem arms and duels, on account of Jupiter, he will also be a leader, an administrator, and cunning: and this since one is a malefic and the other is a benefic; he will love works, and will be concerned with others affairs, and will profit in this way.

However, Ptolemy said that if Venus is the significator of the natives work and profession, and Saturn and Mars (or at least Saturn) are testifying to her, and Venus is in one of the dignities of the Sun, or the Moon, or Saturn, and this planet is in good condition and well disposed, it signifies that the native will be a buyer and seller of gold and silver goods, and even if the luminaries do not specifically signify these things, they do signify them generally, and especially in a case like this. However, if Saturn is not in good condition, provided that he is not otherwise made unfortunate, it signifies that he will be a dyer, and a trader of lead, iron, and similar things, and other works in which dark things are handled. And he will be a sacrificer for divine will, and a lamenter for the dead, and will be concerned in the dressing of the dead for funerals, and preparing for the burial; and performing funeral songs in a lay manner, and he will eagerly spend time in hidden places, and likewise he will divine there by means of *tyrisia* (*tyrisia* is a certain assembly of diviners).

However, if Venus is in the dignities of Jupiter, and he is testifying to her, it signifies that the native will frequent houses of religion, and will eagerly stay in them, and contract a stay with religious people, and from this he will pursue his living, and those things which are appropriately necessary for him. He will also know how to contract marriage, and sagaciously lead it to effect, and from thence utility will follow for him; and he will also be an augur.

However, if Venus is in the dignities of Mars, and Mars is testifying to her, it will signify that the native will have power in medical science in a suitable way, and that he will delight in the bearing of arms; however, more so in bearing them rather than using them - he will delight in bearing them on account of Mars, and will not care much to use them on account of Venus.

And it is not only the planets that signify the work or profession of the native, indeed, even the signs assist them (as Ptolemy attests).

For if the significator of the work of the native or his profession is running through any of the signs which are likened to the figure of man, all the professions which pertain to the native will be assisted by this.

Indeed, if it is in a quadrupedal sign, and the native adheres to a profession of minerals or the trade of metals (namely gold, silver, copper ore, lead, and iron), constructions, and the use of pickaxes and similar things, he will know them perfectly, since quadrupedal signs, especially those of domestic animals, assist the aforementioned things.

And Ptolemy said, the equinoctial and solstial signs assist the professions of translations and variation of interpretation, geometry, and likewise matters of houses of prayers.

And he said that the signs which are likened to the figures of wild beasts and aquatic animals, assist the professions which are for moist things (as are fishing and sailing); and those in which moistening agents are put, and oil and water presses, and the like; and the expertise in plants, (as is the guarding of gardens and crops), and also shipbuilding; and salting, such as salting fish, and salting things in any way, and things that salt, and making salt.

And he said that if the Moon is close to the place ruling the profession (I say that she has dignity in the Ascendant or the tenth), and is exiting from under the rays of the Sun, and after separating from him joins with Mercury first, and you find her in Capricorn, Taurus, or Cancer, this signifies that the native will be wise in the subordinate sciences, such as augury, and will become a haruspex, or a geomancer, or a hydromancer, a chiromancer, an agurgusticus, a spatulamancer, an enchanter, conjurer, or a sacrificer, and this in the following way: for if there is a conjunction of the aforementioned significators of the natives work and profession, and the Sun and the Moon in Taurus (since it is the domicile of Venus, and the exaltation of the Moon), it will signify that the native will be a soothsayer or an augur. But if it is in Capricorn (since it is the house of Saturn, and the exaltation of Mars, and the triplicity of the Moon), it signifies that the native will be a sacrificer. Indeed, if it is in Cancer (since it is the house of the Moon) it signifies that the native will be a hydromancer. And Ptolemy said that if it is in Sagittarius or Pisces, he will divine by the dead, and he will act to move malignant spirits from place to place by his incantations. But if it is in Virgo or Scorpio, it will make him an astrologer and a necromancer, and he will judge hidden things and predict the future (even if he has little or no knowledge of letters). If it is in Aries, Leo, or Libra, he will be a prophet or sage, and a dream interpreter.

And this is the way (according to Ptolemy) which we ought to observe in rationally recognising the quality of the natives' professions and their kinds are.

However, if you consider it well you will assess the qualities of the natives' work or profession by the planets of their significators and by their disposition. For if you see them well disposed, namely fortunate and strong, oriental, direct, in angles (and especially in the tenth, or even in the first), or in one of their own dignities (namely domicile, exaltation, term, or triplicity), it will signify that the works or professions of the native will be from dignities, strengths, and rulerships. However, if you find them cadent or occidental, outside of the aforementioned dignities, you will announce that his works or professions, and he himself in them, will be subordinated to others, and this more greatly and strongly so, if one of the malefics aspect the mentioned significators, or if the malefic are elevated above them: since the native's works or professions will be signified to be low-class, contemptible, and despicable, and that he will not be able to be secure in them, and he will be despised in them and from them, and because of them. If this malefic is Saturn, and he is of the same triplicity as the significator of the natives' profession, it will signify that this will occur from his laziness, his apathy, and his cold disposition and evil complexion. But if it is Mars, and he is in a suitable sign of his nature, this will occur because of the timidity of the native, and his uselessness and faint-heartedness, and he will suffer evil and destruction from this. Indeed, if both of the aforementioned malefics are impeding the significators of the natives' work and profession, his works and professions will be despicable to almost everyone indifferently and always.

You will perceive whether the native is going to have a multitude or scarcity of works or professions, and whether or not he will be called to establish or exercise a profession or work, from the condition or disposition of the significators of works. For if they are well disposed, they will indicate good things, however, if they are badly disposed, they will promise the contrary. Indeed, if benefics aspect them, or are elevated above them, the natives' works will be signified to be suitable and likewise favourable, and that the native will be commended from them, and he will be secure in them and because of them, nor will he suffer any shame or scandal from them, but will gain honour and utility in proportion to the profession or work is in his nature, and this more greatly so if Jupiter and Venus aspect them: and on this occasion he will be raised up, and he will be called "master" on account of it.

## II

## On The Natives' Strength And Prosperity, And On His Duties And His Kingship

If you wish to investigate the natives' strength and the prosperity, and his duties and kingship, examine the Sun in diurnal nativities (the Moon and Saturn in nocturnal nativities), and the tenth and its Lord and the Part of the Kingdom, and the planet in whose domicile you find this Part. And if you see the mentioned significators (namely the Sun and the Moon, or either of them) in angles, namely fortunate and strong, joined to benefics (or even to well disposed planets), and with reception, and the oriental ones are aspecting the Sun, and the occidental ones are aspecting the Moon and Saturn, this will signify that this native is undoubtedly going to be a king.

If it is not as I said with regards to the luminaries, then examine the Lord of the tenth, and the planet in whose domicile the Part of the Kingdom is placed, and examine the tenth and the Ascendant, and the planetary Almutem (whether there are one or more) over the mentioned places, and its mixture over the Ascendant or the tenth, or with their Lords. Since if they are as I said to you (or if a portion of them are), it will signify that the native will be a king, or a prince similar to a king, and that his dignity will be found to be long lasting. And if benefics aspect the luminaries (as was said), and they are in angles, or aspect one of the aforementioned significators placed in the tenth, and this significator is well disposed (namely fortunate and strong); and this more strongly so if the benefic aspecting him is placed above the earth, and even more so again, if it is corporeally joined with the significator in the tenth, and this more strongly if reception intervenes, and the luminaries are in masculine signs, and the mentioned significators (or the majority of them) are well disposed, this will signify that the native will have a great name, great strength, and great power, and likewise that he will be a king, or at least similar to a king. However, if the Lord of the Ascendant does not aspect the aforementioned Almutem, it will signify that the native will have little power and little strength, and he will have little fellowship with kings and magnates.

However, if other planets besides the luminaries are placed in angles, or having commixture with planets placed in angles, and the Sun is in a masculine sign and the Moon is in a feminine sign, and only one of them is in an angle, it will signify that the native will not be a king, but rather he will have governance in which he will be permitted to spill the blood of the wicked and guilty, and to hang and decapitate them, and he will be able to kill by other methods by means of his governance. And such men are those to whom kings commit their own position in affairs of the kingdom, and make them their deputies, and they give them authority of governance, and ratify what they do.

If the aforementioned stars are not in angles, nor the planets who testify to the luminaries, and the angles are not of their aym, this will signify that the native is going to be renowned, indeed, his ability or his power, will not be possible to be surpassed by those who have no governance, for his rulership will be like that of those who rule in the manner of a great and powerful Lord.

Indeed, if the luminaries are not in angles, but planets are in them who testify to them, or who have mixture with them it will signify that the native will not be of such great strength in the aforementioned matters, but he will be strong in the governances of cities and the like, and will even have moderate knowledge of how to set his own house in order, and likewise his own life.

Indeed, Haly said that if the luminaries are not in angles, but very many of the stars are in them, surrounding or joined with them, then the native will be of moderate strength; but if the luminaries were there, and the surrounding stars are in their own dignities, he will be middling in the management of affairs which pertain to cities.

For example, if Mars is the giver of substance, he will be of middling acquisitions, and middling in the rectifying of the weights and measures of the city. However, if it is Jupiter, he will be middling in practicing justice. If it is Saturn, he will be middling in the activity of building. Indeed, if it is Venus, he will be middling in religion. If it is Mercury, he will be middling in writing. And he said that if the luminaries and the surrounding stars are not in their own dignities, the native will be middling in his condition, such as in trade, and so too in the rest of his duties.

And Ptolemy said that if all the stars which surround the luminaries have no similitude with the

angles, the native will be miserable and unlucky in all of his works. If the luminaries are not placed in either angles or masculine signs, and benefics do not surround them, he will be in an extreme of misery and lack of prosperity.

And he said that therefore the path which is to be taken in the investigation of these matters, is what we have shown in the increase and decrease of the native's strength. However, we ought to observe the very many qualities which are between increase and decrease, by those things which are found in that kind of particular alteration which the luminaries have (and the stars which surround them, and which are disposed in the surrounding planets). For if the dispositers are the Lord of the aym of the place of the Sun, and the Moon, or of another benefics, the natives' force will be of greater duration. Indeed, if the stars which are contrary to the aym of the luminaries are the dispositers, or if they are malefics, the natives' strength will be weak, and will quickly end, and easily pass away.

And Ptolemy said that the matters of future force are to be observed from the peculiar qualities of the stars which surround the luminaries.

For if Saturn is the dispositor of the natives' prosperity (which is going to come to him) and he is in good condition and well disposed, (namely fortunate and strong), he will signify that the fortune of the native, and his strength, and prosperity will be because of inheritances which will come to him, and even from the gathering up or accumulation of other substance. However, if he is weakly disposed, what he signifies will be much below the aforementioned.

Indeed, if Jupiter or Venus disposes the natives' strength and prosperity, he will approach it in pleasant things, lively things, and gifts given to him, and honours conferred upon him, and his magnanimity.

If Mars is placed as his significator, it will signify that his force and prosperity will come because of victory over his enemies, or those contrary to him, and from those subject to him who fear and revere him.

But if Mercury is the ruler of force, it signifies that he will be raised up from his own intellect and instruction, and managing matters, and he will be made prosperous, and will be held as strong.

You will even examine whether the Lord of the first is joined with the Lord of the tenth or vice versa. For if the Lord of the first is joined with the Lord of the tenth (namely so that he is lighter than it), from a trine or sextile aspect, with or without reception, or from a square aspect with reception, it signifies that the native will attain good things, utility, and profit because of kings, and from kings, but not without his own seeking or petition. However, if the Lord of the seventh is lighter and is joined to the Lord of the first by the mentioned aspects, it signifies that he will obtain the aforementioned without seeking or petition, and this more strongly so if reception intervenes, unless they are cadent or otherwise unfortunate.

And Aboali said that if this application is from angles (and especially if it is from the Ascendant or the Midheaven) the dignity which he acquires will be great and furnished with a surname And he said that if the Lord of the Ascendant is in an angle, and the Lord of the Midheaven is cadent, it signifies that the natives name will be great and his work will be worthless. And if the Lord of the Midheaven is in an angle, and the Lord of the Ascendant is cadent, it signifies that his work will be great and his condition will be worthless. However, if both are cadent it signifies that both the native and his work will be worthless.

And he said that if the Lord of the Ascendant is in the Midheaven, it signifies that the native is born of a royal family (or mixes with royalty). And if the aspect which is between them is good, it signifies the friendship between the native and the king; if it is bad, it signifies enmity and severity.

And he said that if there is no application between the Lord of the Ascendant and the Lord of the Midheaven, examine the application which is between the Lord of the Ascendant and the Sun, and judge over that, just as you judged over the application of the Lord of the Ascendant and the Midheaven above.

And he said that if the Lord of the Ascendant is conjunct with the Sun, it signifies that the native will be a household member of the king, and faithful and knowledgeable to his secrets, and the king will be receptive to his words.

And he said, if the Lord of the Ascendant is one of the superior planets, and it is in the Midheaven, applying to the Lord of its domicile, it signifies that he will be mingled with both noblemen and kings, and that he will have a dignity around them seizing things for the public treasury, occupying a position in this area, or collecting things. Indeed, if one of the inferior planets is the Lord of the Ascendant, and is placed in the Midheaven, and applying to its Lord, it signifies that the native will hold some office of the king below that which was mentioned above.

And if there is an application between the Lord of the Ascendant and one of the luminaries, it signifies mingling with kings; and if it is with reception, he will attain the greatest good from it, otherwise he will not.

And for the strength of the native, examine the planet who has application with the Lord of the Ascendant, or who is the Lord of the domicile in which the natives Part of Work and Kingship is placed: who, if you find in his own exaltation, will signify that the native will have strength, greatness, and a title of his strength, and mingling with kings and magnates. But if he is in his own domicile, it signifies something below this, and the mingling of the native with those who are below the aforementioned. And if he is in his own terms it signifies something further below this. However, if he is in his own triplicity, it signifies something again below this. But if he is in his own face, it will signify something very much less than and below the aforementioned. However, if the Lord of the Part is void-of-course, it signifies much ferality of the native, and his solitude, and that he will love solitary places according to the nature of the sign in which he then occupies.

Then examine the Part of the Natives Work and Kingship, and its Lord: which if you find in a good place from the Ascendant, and free from malefics and from other impediments, or if he and the Lord of the Ascendant are in angles free from the aforementioned impediments, it will signify that the native will be of much work and little rest.

And Aomar said to also examine the Sun: if he is in eastern quarters, the native will find honour, sublimity, and kingship in his youth. And if he is in western quarters, this will be in his old age, and at the end of his life. However, you will examine his condition in his work, and in what time he will be of greater dignity and honour, from the triplicity Lords of the Sun. Which if all three are strong, his kingship and honour will endure for the whole time of his life. However, if you find them all weak, say that he will suffer detriment, weakness, and misfortune for the entire time of his life. However, if the first is weak, he will be surrounded by misfortune, and of fragile memory, in the first third of his life. Indeed, if there is a fortunate planet ruling that one-third, announce that prosperity will befall him; the same for the second and the third.

And Aomar said that if Saturn is in an angle at night, or if Mars is in an angle during the day, and especially if this is in the Ascendant or the Midheaven, he will not gather either work or kingship up until the completion of the lesser years of the planet. If it passes this period of time, it will be according to the ascension of the sign in which the planet is placed. And he said that if Mars is in an angle (and especially in the Ascendant or in the Midheaven) in the day, the native will be endangered on account of his work, and his body will be whipped and he will die. And he said that if the Sun is in opposition to the Moon, the native will not be directed to a kingship, nor a profession, nor a chief place; and if is directed to it, the wealthy men and magnates of that region will act contrary to him.

And he said that if you see that a profession or kingship is signified for the native, examine the planetary Almutem over the Midheaven and the Sun, and the Part of Work or Kingship. And see what substance the Almutem over these places is of: since the natives' work or kingship or duties, will be according to the signification of the aforementioned Almutem. For if it is the Sun, the native will be a prince or king, and he will be a wise manager of matters, and of good discretion.

And Aomar said that you will speak likewise of the nature of this Almutem, and of those aspecting it, whether there is one, or more (namely two or three). And he said to likewise examine the Almutem, and see which of the planets aspect him, and mix their work with the work of the Almutem, and speak according to this.

And Ptolemy said that the native will even have a profession if an oriental planet in the morning is placed in the Midheaven with the Moon, or if the Almutem over the Midheaven is oriental; and if this Almutem does aspect like so, generally there will not be a profession for those natives.

However, Aomar said that if the Almutem over the Midheaven is mingled with the Almutem over the Ascendant, or agrees with him, then he will not lack a profession, and this will be better if the Almutem is oriental from the Sun, and from the Ascendant, or from either of them. For the substance of the profession was generally examined from the quality of Mars, Venus, and Mercury to each other, and in their mixture and aspect. And he said the qualities are like when one planet is in square or sextile aspect with another, or in the same sign.

Indeed, certain sages wished for the angle of the Midheaven to fall in the eleventh, and were in dread of it falling in the ninth: for its fall into the ninth reduced the quality of the dignity of the divisor, and its fall in the eleventh increased his honour and his condition. Likewise all places, when they are removed towards the receding places, and the malignant ones (as are the sixth, the second, the eighth, and the twelfth), will be bad - for the 11th in the twelfth is bad, and the 11th in the Midheaven is good.

### III

### How You Should Examine In The Matter Of The Mother

Since matters of the father are examined from the fourth of the natives nativity, and we wish to examine the matter of the mother; and the wife is examined from the 7th from the house of the man; it is necessary that in the matter of the mother we examine from the tenth - since the tenth is the seventh from the 4th.

Whence if it happens that you have to examine the matter of the mother, examine the Ylem from the tenth and its Lord, and likewise from the Moon and Venus, and likewise from the Part of the Mother, and the planet in whose domicile it falls, and from the planet who is the Almutem over some one of the aforementioned places, since it will be regarded as the significator of the mother.

Then examine to see which of the planets is the significator of the years of the mother, and if any of the others adds on any years, or months to it, or reduces them from its own years or months. For if one of the benefics aspect it from a trine or sextile aspect, and it is in good condition and well disposed (namely fortunate and strong), and is in an angle, it will add on its lesser years to him, and add on as many months, as are its medium years; and this more strongly so if he received it. However, if it is in a succeedent, instead of years it will add on months. Indeed, if it is not received from the mentioned aspects, it will add on to him by his lesser years, but it will not add on any months on top of this. But if it is impeded, it will not add on years, but instead of years it will add on months.

Indeed, if the planet who aspects the significator of years is a malefic, and he aspects it from square or opposition, he will reduce from its years according to the number of his own minor years. If this malefic is in good condition and well disposed (namely fortunate and strong), he will only reduce them according to one-third of his lesser years.

After this you will examine in the status and strength of his mother, and her condition or work or profession and dignity, and her fortune, from the dustoria of the planets from the Moon. For if you see Mars or Venus in the dustoria of the Moon (or Mercury if he is joined with one of them), and they are in good condition and well disposed, this will signify the increase of the mothers dignity, and her exaltation and the greatness of her value and honour. Then examine the Ylem of the mother, and the planet from whom you took the Ylem, and you will direct it to the places of benefics and malefics; and in which place you see it reach benefics, judge good in all the aforementioned things, from the significations of this house. However, if you see it reach malefics, it will judge the contrary in all the aforementioned things to come to the mother, from the significations of the house.

And Aomar said that if the Moon and the Part of the Mother are not in the place of the Ylem, and you wish to know the place to which you will direct for the mother, you will direct from the degree of the Moon: whenever it arrives to malefics it will signify the danger and death of the mother.

After this examine the concord and love of the mother towards the child, and her hatred against him, from the Almutem over the Ascendant and the Almutem over the place of the mother. If there is harmony between them, and they love each other in turn, judge that there will be love between them. However, if they hate each other, you will judge the contrary. You will also examine with regards to the harmony between the natives father and his mother, and you will announce on what will be between them according to what you see of the harmony of their significators.

However, regarding the death of the mother, whether it is in the near future or remote, Dorotehus said that it is signified by the entry of the Almutem below the earth.

And Aboali said that you will examine the life of the mother from Venus (in diurnal nativities): which if she is aspecting the Ascendant, direct her to the bodies of malefics and their rays by degrees of ascension, giving one year to each degree. However, if Venus does not aspect the Ascendant, but the Moon aspects it, direct her just as you would have directed Venus if she were fit to direct. Indeed, if the Moon does not aspect the Ascendant, then direct the degree of the Midheaven. And in diurnal nativities you will begin first from Venus, then from the Moon, and lastly from the degree of the Midheaven. Indeed, in nocturnal nativities you will begin first from the Moon, then from Venus, and lastly from the degree of the Midheaven. Then you will examine if the years signified by the Ylem are equal to the years signified by the Almutem over the degree in which Venus is placed; or, in diurnal nativities, over the degree in which the Lord of the domicile in which Venus is in is placed; in nocturnal nativities, from the degree in which the Moon is placed, or the degree the Lord of the domicile (in which the Moon is placed) is in; and both in the day and the night, from the degree of the Midheaven, or the degree its Lord is in: for by this, the death of the natives' mother will be signified to be before the completion of one year from the day of the nativity.

However, you will examine the condition of the mother from the triplicity Lords of the sign occupied by the Moon. For according to how you see them disposed, according to that you will judge (namely regarding the good, or the contrary to good): since if they are all in good condition and well disposed, fortunate and strong, you will announce that things will always be good for the entire time of her life. However, if they are in bad condition, they will judge evil. Indeed, the first triplicity Lord will show its signification in the beginning of life from the nativity of this native. The second in the middle of his life. Indeed, the third in the final part of the mother's life, you will predict what it signifies in the last part of the mothers' life.

You will perceive what kind of death the mother will die (namely whether it will be easy or severe or ugly), from the condition of the Moon, and from the Lord of the domicile she occupies, and also from the Part of the Mother and its Lord, and from the Part of the Death Of The Mother and its Lord. Since if they are in good condition and well disposed, they will judge a common and praiseworthy death. Indeed, if they are impeded and badly disposed, they will signify that the mother will die an evil and ugly death, nevertheless the significator of death in her nativity will throw in its lot.

You will perceive who is to die first out of the father and the mother from their significators. For whichever one first feels the misfortune of combustion, or who first arrives at the angle of the fourth house of the natives' nativity, will signify that the parent it signifies will die first.

## ON THE ELEVENTH HOUSE

## I

## On The Natives Friends And Likewise On His Good Fortune And His Hope

Having looked in the preceding chapter at the profession of the native, and his duties and his strength, and even the matter of the mother, and the rest. In this present chapter it seems suitable and fitting to me to deal with the matter of friends, and the natives' good fortune and his hope, and to make mention of all of these things.

Whence if you wish to busy yourself over any of the aforementioned things in anyone's nativity, you will examine in this way. Indeed, you will consider the eleventh from the Ascendant of the nativity of any native, and its Lord; and the Part of Friends and its Lord; and likewise Venus, who naturally signifies friends, since we delight in them. Likewise, you will examine the planets who are in the 11th, and in the house in which the Lord of the 11th is placed; and the Lord of this domicile, and the Lord of the domicile in which the Part of Friends is placed, and the Lord of the domicile in which the planet (in whose domicile this Part is) is placed. Likewise you will examine the planet in whose domicile Venus herself is placed. You will even examine the luminaries and their Lords (namely the Sun in the day, and the Moon at night).

Having inspected these, you will see which planet is the Almutem over all of the aforementioned places, and which of them is in better condition and better disposed, since from him you will be able to take up the significator of the matters of the natives friends and his good fortune, and also of his hope; beginning first from the 11th and its Lord, then from the planet who is in the 11th, then from Venus, then from the Part of Friends and its Lord, then from the Lord of the domicile in which Venus is placed, then from the luminary who has authority, and indeed, lastly from the Lord of the domicile in which this luminary is placed.

For if benefics are in the 11th, and there is a friendly mixture between the Lord of the Ascendant and the Lord of the eleventh (or an application from conjunction, or from any friendly aspect) especially with reception which is made from domicile or exaltation, or from two of the other lesser dignities - it will signify that the native will have a multitude of friends loving him; and this more greatly so if the 11th house is Cancer, Scorpio, or Pisces; however, if the 11th house is Aries, Taurus, Libra, Sagittarius, Capricorn, or Aquarius, it will reduce the number of the natives friends by a one-fourth. Indeed, if the 11th house is Gemini, Leo, or Virgo, it will reduce the number of his friends by one-third. And if there are no benefics in the 11th, but they aspect it by a noted or praiseworthy aspect, and these benefics are in good condition and well disposed (namely fortunate and strong), they will signify almost the same that was said about the number or multitude of the natives' friends. However, if what was said above regarding the 11th house is not so, you will consider its Lord: for you will announce on the matter of the natives friends towards him according to how you see the Lord of the eleventh and the planet in whose domicile you find him disposed.

You will even examine the Part of Friends and its Lord, which if you find one or both of them well disposed, you will be able to judge regarding the matters or friends - for they will indicate good things to come for the native from his friends.

Then examine Venus: who, if she is in good condition and well disposed, and is aspecting the Ascendant or its Lord, or the 11th or its Lord by a friendly aspect, signifies that the native will have many friends, and the majority of them will of the feminine sex, from whom utility and good things will follow, and his friends will be fortunate themselves.

Likewise examine the Lord of the domicile in which Venus is placed: since he will assist in the signification of the good of the friends.

But if the luminaries and their Lords are well disposed, they will do the same without a doubt. For if the Sun is in good condition and well disposed, it signifies that the greater part of his friends will be wealthy and noble, namely those who are fit for kingship.

However, if the 11th house is the house of one of the seven planets, it signifies that the natives' friends will be according to the substance and signification of the planet whose house the 11th is.

For if it is the domicile of Saturn, the natives' friends will be according to the image, condition, and disposition of Saturn: for they will be old men, slaves, Jews, and other low-class people.

Indeed, if it is the domicile of Jupiter, they will be according to the condition, disposition or image of Jupiter, and they will be nobles, or bishops, and people similar to Jupiter.

Indeed, if it is the domicile of Mars, they will be according to the nature and disposition of Mars, and according to his image and condition: namely princes and bellicose men.

But if it is the domicile of the Sun, they will be according to the nature, disposition, and condition of the Sun, and his image, and they will be nobles, kings, and wealthy men, as was said.

And if it is the domicile of Venus, they will be according to nature, disposition, and condition of Venus, and her image, as are women and effeminate men.

But if it is the domicile of Mercury, they will be according to the condition, nature, and disposition of Mercury, and his image, and they will be sages, merchants, and scribes.

However, if it is the domicile of the Moon, then the natives' friends will be signified according to the nature and disposition of the Moon, and likewise her condition and her image.

And if all of the aforementioned significators, or the majority of them are in fixed signs, it signifies that the natives' friends will love him, and their friendship and love will be firm, constant, and durable. However, if they are in bicorporeal signs, it will signify the mediocrity of the aforementioned things and their durability. But if they are in mobile signs, it signifies that his friends will quickly depart from his friendship, and that they will be made contrary to him, and will be inimical to him.

And Aomar said that if the Almutem over the Ascendant is a malefic, and harms the Almutem over the house of friends, evil will come to the friends from the native. And if it is to the contrary, speak to the contrary. And he said that if these significators are made fortunate by one another, they will get good things, advancement, and reverence from each other. However, then he said

that if the Lord of the 11th does not aspect the 11th, and Venus does not aspect her own domicile, and the Lord of the Part of Friends does not aspect the Part of Friends, the native will be one of those men who has no mingling with friends, nor will he be sociable with men, but will mostly remain solitary, and will do so gladly. And if benefics are then in the 11th, then you will be able to judge, that his friends will be good, and of good suitability, and of good character, and that they will abound in wealth; and this more strongly so if a benefic is in the 12th. However, if a malefic is there, this will signify that the natives' friends will be evil, of much discord and want.

## II

## On The Kinds Of Friends

And Ptolemy said that there are three kinds of friendship and enmity: namely, on account of the harmony of spirits, by which it is necessary that a man loves his friend; or on account of advancement; or since joy or sorrow compels them together.

And he said that those who love each other on account of harmony of spirit, are those in whose nativities it happens that the Sun and Moon transfer from their places - that is, so that the Sun is in the sign or place in which the Moon was in one of their nativities, and the Moon is in the sign or place in which the Sun was in the other; or that their significators or luminaries are in trine or sextile aspect; and this will be made stronger if reception intervenes. Then their friendship will be constant and naturally durable, and even more so if one of the benefics aspect the mentioned significators or the luminaries in the aforementioned nativities, without the aspect of one of the malefics.

Then he said that those whose love is on account of joy or sorrow, are those which it happens that their Ascendants are one and the same sign, or if the sign of the Ascendant of one nativity aspects the sign of Ascendant of the other from a trine or sextile aspect, and benefics aspect the sign of both the nativities from a trine or sextile aspect, with the aspects of malefics being completely removed.

However, those whose friendship was harmonised on account of advancement are those in which the sign where the Part of Fortune is placed in one nativity, is the same as that of the other (or in its triplicity, or in its trine or sextile aspect), and there will be harmony between them, and they will profit from one and the same thing, or the same merchant activity; and both will strive to profit and benefit from it, and for this reason their friendship will occur, and love will fall between them. Or something unfortunate will happen to them (or to one of them), from one and the same cause, because of which both of them will suffer, and one will have compassion for the other, and for that reason they will be made friends - which will happen if the benefics aspect the Ascendants of their nativities, or their significators, without the aspect of any of the malefics.

Moreover, if the Almutem of each nativity aspect each other from noted aspects, they will be friends and love each other, and this more strongly so if both of them receive each other. If their aspect is from square or from opposition (and especially if they do not receive each other), ill will shall fall between them for one and the same reason; and this more strongly so if one of the malefics aspects their significators, and even more so if this aspect is without the intervention of reception, and greater again if this is from square or opposition, or if it is a corporeal conjunction.

Indeed, if Saturn is the malefic which aspects, and he is in some sign in both nativities which is the domicile, exaltation, terms, or triplicity, of the significator of the nativity of one of them, and it is some dignity (namely one of the aforementioned) of the other one, and the aspect is a trine or sextile (and this more strongly if reception intervenes) - there will be friendship between these natives because of waters, or land, or other estates, or on account of old men, or old age, or on account of fathers who will be the occasion of their friendship, or on account of other suitable things or familiarities occurring between them. But if this aspect is from opposition or square aspect, or if it is a corporeal conjunction (and this more strongly so if the conjunction or aspect is without reception), enmities will fall between them, and likewise discords and contentions, because of the aforementioned reasons.

However, if it is Mars, the aforementioned will occur because of one those things which are signified by Mars.

If one of the benefics aspect him, and it is Jupiter, the friendship and concord between them will occur for the reason of wealth, or acquisitions and profit, or one of the other significations of Jupiter.

Indeed, if it is the Sun, they will occur because of some lay dignity, profession, or office, or raw gold, or one of the other things which are signified by the Sun.

Indeed, if it is Venus, they will occur on the occasion of weddings, or some delightful matter which is signified by Venus.

But if it is Mercury they will occur because of writings, or sculptures, or exchange of a moneychanger, or one of the other sciences which are signified by Mercury.

But if it is the Moon, the above-mentioned things will happen because of legates, or orders imposed on them, or some other distinguished ministry, or because of one of those things which are signified by the Moon. And you will examine her significations according to her disposition in the quarters and the dichotomies of every lunation.

You will also consider the condition and disposition of the aforementioned benefics, since the aforementioned ought to occur according to how they are disposed.

But Ptolemy said that in matters of the natives' friends and his friendship, there are four places in the figure of his nativity which are said to be greater, or greater matters, namely those which have greater rulership and greater power over the native and his friends. These are: the place of the Sun, the place of the Moon, the place of the Lord of the Ascendant, and the place of the Part of Fortune. For if all of these places, or the majority of them are in one sign, or places exchange with each other, namely so that the Sun in one nativity is in the place in which the Moon is in the other nativity, or vice versa, or if the Lord of the Ascendant of one nativity is in the place of the Part of Fortune of the other nativity, or vice versa, and there are 7 degrees or less between them and the places, this will signify that the love between the natives will be fixed, unfailing, and inseparable. However, if the mentioned significators aspect from a trine or sextile, or the Lords of the aforementioned places aspect each other, there will be friendship between them, yet not as true as the aforementioned will be.

But if the Almutem of the Ascendant and the Almutem of the 11th, or even the Almutem of the 7th, regard each other by a trine or sextile aspect, and especially if they receive each other, and are not otherwise unfortunate or impeded, you will undoubtedly announce a friendship of joy and gladness between them in the future.

If you see one of the planets transferring light or virtue between the significators of the two significators of the nativities, and this planet is in good condition and well disposed (namely fortunate and strong), friendship will fall between them, even if it will not last forever, but only for a time (but it won't be very short).

However, if you find Jupiter or Saturn to be the significator of the friends, or the natives' friendship, and one transfers from his own domicile to the domicile of the other, or from the place in which he was, to the place in which the other was, there will be friendship between them because of estates, or some other durable matter, or if the significators are suitable for it, because of agriculture.

But if Saturn is the Ylem, and Venus, and you find them so disposed that one occupies the place of the other, friendship will happen between the natives because of blood-relation, but since one is a benefic and the other is a malefic, it will end in a brief space of time.

Indeed, if Saturn is placed as the significator of the native, and Mercury is the significator of friends, and he is joined to Saturn, you will announce friendship between them because of mercantile dealings, because of giving and receiving, and similar things: and this because their domiciles aspect each other from a trine aspect.

And Ptolemy said that if Jupiter and Mars, are the Ylems, this will happen because of riches or a rulership - since their domiciles likewise aspect each other by trine.

However, if Jupiter is placed as the significator of the nativity with Venus, and has mixture with the Almutem of the 7th or 11th, friendship will occur between them because of women, or another delightful matter, or because of divine obedience, or religion, or the construction of houses of the religious, or similar things.

But if Jupiter is the Ylem with Mercury, with an application of the Almutem of the 7th or 11th, they will love each other of their own free will because of the sciences of the trivium or the quadrivium, and philosophy.

And he said that if Mars and Venus are the Ylems, and they are with the aforementioned Almutem, as was said, there will be esteem between them because of sexual activity, namely fornication or adultery, or perhaps the disgraceful crime of sodomy, nor will their friendship be of long duration - which will happen to them since Mars is a malefic, and Venus is a benefic.

If Venus and Mercury are the significators of the nativity, or the Almutem over the Ascendant, and are with the aforementioned significators, as was said, they will have a mingling because of women, or perhaps because of music or the study of books, or the friendship between them will be confirmed because of the necessities which men use for nourishment.

You will consider all of the aforementioned things according to how you see the mentioned significators in good condition and well disposed (namely fortunate and strong), and in good aspects with the Sun and the Moon, or in the Ascendant, or with its Almutem, or with the Part of Fortune, since according to the condition of the aforementioned four, or according to how they aspect the aforementioned four places, their significations will appear according to that. And if they do not aspect them, their significations will disappear completely.

## ON THE TWELFTH HOUSE

### I

### On Matters Of Hidden And Jealous Enemies, And On The Considerations Which You Ought To Have In The Significations Of The Twelve Houses, And Likewise In The Judgements Which Result From The Aforementioned Significations

In the matter of enemies and jealous people, and likewise the judgements which result from the significations of the houses and their Lords, you will examine the 12th house from the Ascendant and see what the condition of the Almutem of the 12th is like with the Almutem of the Ascendant. You will also examine how Saturn, and the Part of Enemies and its Lord are disposed.

For if the Almutem over the 12th, or over the house in which the Part of Enemies (or Saturn) is placed, is in bad condition and badly disposed, or if some malefic impedes one of them, and this more strongly so if it impedes the Lord of the Ascendant or its Almutem, or the Moon, and even stronger if the impediment is from opposition or square aspect; or if the Almutem of the 12th is in the Ascendant, or in opposition to one of the luminaries, this will signify that the native will have many hidden enemies, and many jealous ones, and that many will be able to secretly harm him, and will strive to harm him, and they will harm him, and this more so if that malefic has any dignity in the 12th, and even more so again if the planet impeding the Almutem over the Ascendant is the Lord of the 12th. However, if the Almutem over the 12th does not aspect the Almutem over the Ascendant, nor the Moon, or if one of the benefics aspects them, or if one of them is the Almutem over the 12th (and is unimpeded), it signifies that the native will have few hidden enemies and few jealous ones.

If Saturn is the Almutem over the 12th, it signifies that the natives' hidden enemies and jealous enemies will be old men, Jews, low-class men from the mob, religious men clad in black vestments, and uncultured and wild men, and the like.

If it is Jupiter, they will be men who appear to be wise, and jurists, secular clerics, and even mediocre and lesser nobles, and similar people.

However, if it is Mars, they will be bellicose men, evil doers, whisperers, and those speaking evil, and the like.

But if it is the Sun, they will be nobles and magnates and the like, and this more so if the Almutem of the 12th is in an angle, or the succeedent of an angle, in which it has some dignity.

But if it is Venus, they will mostly be women, and effeminate men, and drunkards and gluttons and the like.

However, if it is Mercury, they will be learned men, youths, writers, and the like.

Indeed, if it is the Moon, they will be unstable men, and common and low-class persons, and the like.

However, if the Almutem of the twelfth is retrograde, combust, or besieged by malefics, or peregrine, or in a cadent from an angle, or in its fall, or in its descension, or it is in a cadent from the Ascendant, or in the 2nd or the 6th, or in the 8th, or if the Almutem of the Ascendant impedes him, or if one of the malefics is in the 12th (who is impeded by malefics), it signifies that the native will prevail over all of his hidden enemies and jealous enemies, and will crush them, and that they will be able to do little or no damage to him, but he will impede them. And if the Lord of the Ascendant is a benefic, and impedes the Lord of the 12th or its Almutem, they will suffer harm and detriment from him. Indeed, if Saturn and Mars (or either of them) are in the 12th, and they are in bad condition and badly disposed; or impeding the Lord of the 12th or its Almutem, it signifies that the native will see from his hidden enemies and his jealous enemies, what they wish to see from him.

## II

### On The Judgements Which Result From The Significations Of The Twelve Houses And Their Lords

Having examined in the preceding chapters regarding the matter of the natives hidden enemies and those jealous of him, now it remains to examine the judgements which result from the significations of the twelve houses, and the placements of the planets in them (which are comprehended under this chapter), and the method which is necessary for you to observe in this matter, according to what our ancient and wise predecessors, seem to have advised. For it seemed to them that we ought to examine the aforementioned houses and their Lords, and to judge regarding them according to their disposition.

Whence you ought to examine all of the houses in the nativity of every native, when you have erected the figure of the nativity, and seen in which houses the planets are received, and how they are disposed, and what is their condition like (both the benefics and the malefics). For in whatever house you find a benefic, or whatever house a benefic aspects from a friendly aspect (namely a trine or sextile), and this planet is free, fortunate, and strong, and not beset by any impediments, and there are no malefics in place where the benefics aspect, and this place is not aspected by a malefic, and the superior benefics are oriental (and the inferiors occidental), and not otherwise impeded, and the Part of Fortune is in good condition and well disposed, free (namely from the conjunction of malefics and their aspects) - this will signify that good things, utility and prosperity will befall the native from the significations of those houses in which the aforementioned benefics are found.

However, if the mentioned significators are not fortunate (provided that they are not unfortunate), they will still signify good things and utility for the native, but much below what was said. And if they are impeded, they will signify some benefit, but a small amount, and with the mixture of many contrary things.

However, if they are malefics, and they are aspected by benefics, and are not otherwise impeded, and are in their own dignities, fortunate and strong, again they will signify some that some good is going to come from the significations of the houses in which they are in, or which they aspect from a good aspect; but with great fatigue, and likewise complications and burdens, so that it will hardly seem to the native that he is benefitted. But if they are impeded they will signify that from the significations of these houses of the nativity, all evils, all contrary things, unlucky things, harms, and likewise misfortunes, will befall the native.

# ♄

# SATVRNVS

## ♑    ♒

If it is a diurnal nativity, and Saturn is the significator of this nativity, and he is in good condition and well disposed (namely fortunate and strong), and he is in Capricorn, Aquarius, or Libra, and in the Ascendant, this will signify that nobles, magnates, and the wealthy will eagerly make friends with this native; and that he will remain healthy and sound in body and mind; and it will also signify that he will come to be a great accumulator of substance, and this more strongly so if he has mixture with the Part of Fortune or with the Part of Substance in the Ascendant, or the second, or in another praiseworthy place in the figure. Indeed, if his disposition is contrary to the aforementioned, it will indicate a multitude of illnesses of the body and mind, and also the contrary of all the aforementioned things.

## ♐    ♓

And if he is in Sagittarius or Pisces, and the nativity is diurnal, it signifies that the native will have a beautiful body and a beautiful stature, and a son of truth, and an accumulator of substance from something just, suitable, and licit. Indeed, in nocturnal nativities it signifies that the native will freely stay with nobles or magnates and the wealthy, and that he will send his own father to death before him.

## ♈    ♏

Indeed if he is in Aries or Scorpio, it will signify that that native will have strong propositions, and will be hard hearted, with little or no mercy, no compassion, and very irascible. And if the nativity is nocturnal, he will be found to be twice as worse and cruel.

## ♌

Indeed if he is placed in Leo in a diurnal nativity, it will indicate that the native and his father will be fortunate, unless the nativity of the father in his own peculiar matters operates to the contrary. However, if it is a nocturnal nativity it will portend the contrary of the aforementioned, and it will indicate their depression.

## ♉    ♎

Indeed if you find Saturn in Taurus or Libra, both in diurnal nativities and nocturnal nativities, it will show that the native will spend time in sexual activity, especially with low-class women, and will suffer harm because of them, and the native himself will be badly complexioned, and will often be semi-sick, and he will be of bad faith.

## ♊    ♍

If you find him in Gemini or Virgo, whatever kind of nativity it is, it will signify that he will be gifted in the investigation of sciences, and in the investigation of books, and will reveal their secrets. And you will be able to say that from much sturdy and much fatigue over these things, his tongue will be impeded; and this labour and this study will often overflow to his own harm, and his reproach. Ad he will made unfortunate by men, and especially from those who he serves, who, not wanting to respond to his services, will find pretexts for speaking ill of him, and criticising him, thinking that he has perpetrated evils which he has never devised; on which occasion he will be made to have a bad conscience, bad thoughts, and a bad soul.

## ♋

And if you find him in Cancer (since Cancer is the sixth sign from his own domicile), it will signify that the native will often be burdened by infirmities, and his mother will incur a wicked illness on the occasion of his birth; or perhaps that the native will destroy her goods while she is alive, and will disperse her wealth in a bad way, or possibly kill her.

# ♃

# IVPITER

## ♑  ♒

If Jupiter is in Capricorn or Aquarius, and he is placed as the significator of the nativity, free from impediments, it will signify that the native will be anxious, gasping for breath, distressed about making money, and always showing himself to be indigent and poor to men, and living a low-class and miserable life, and always thinking bad thoughts, and he will be worthless and feeble in all things by which men have power, and for this reason many inconveniences will come to him.

## ♐  ♓

And if he is in Sagittarius or Pisces, and it is a diurnal nativity, it signifies that the native will be wealthy and fortunate in substance, and will accumulate it in great quantities, and he will also be a discerning man, knowing how to fare well amongst nobles, magnates, and the wealthy. However, if it is a nocturnal nativity, it signifies that he will be fortunate in the aforementioned things, but it will be much below what was said above; nevertheless, he will be familiar with the religious and those worshipping God, and will gladly stay with them.

## ♈  ♏

Indeed if he is placed in Aries or Scorpio, whatever kind of nativity it is, it signifies that the native will be fortunate amongst kings, nobles, magnates, and bearers of arms; and he will be a man of great stability and much constancy, and this all the more so, if Jupiter is then placed in the angles or their succedents, and in a masculine sign, and he will be a good warrior, and likewise a good combatant, and a good leader of armies (and especially great and famous armies).

## ♌

Indeed if you find him placed in Leo, in a diurnal nativity, it will signify the native to be renowned, famous, wise, and of profound intellect; and that he will freely stay with kings, and that he will be loved by them, even without serving them much - and not only by great men, but even by commoners. And

Aboali said that if in addition to this he is in the angles or their succedents, free from malefics and impediments, he will be more fortunate, namely being a king namely or similar to a king: yet his lineage should be considered, since he will surpass it much more than men had expected. But if the nativity is nocturnal, the aforementioned things will happen, but will be much below what was said, nevertheless he will be fortunate and well disposed.

## ♉  ♎

Indeed if the nativity is diurnal, and Jupiter is in Taurus, or in Libra, say that he will eagerly adhere to noble and wealthy women, and those with dowries, and will consummate marriage with them, and will be made rich from this. Indeed, if it is a nocturnal nativity, he will gladly stay with religious people, and he will be a possessor of good faith, and for this reason he will profit and become rich.

## ♊  ♍

However if he is found free from impediments in Gemini or Virgo, both in diurnal nativities and nocturnal ones, it signifies that the native will be a great accumulator of substance, and for this reason he will be preferred before many other men, and will almost seem to be a king.

## ♋

If you find him in Cancer, namely fortunate and strong, and well disposed, in a diurnal nativity, it will signify that the native will be a fortunate man, fortunate almost beyond measure, and this more greatly so if he is in the angles or the succeedents of the angles. But if it is a nocturnal nativity, the aforementioned things will happen, but they will be much below that which was said above; nevertheless, he will be a man having a great name and great reputation, however, the utility which follows from this will not be of much benefit to him.

# ♂
# MARS

## ♑ ♒

And if Mars is found in Capricorn or Aquarius, and he is the significator of the nativity, and he is in good condition and well disposed (namely placed fortunate and strong), it will signify that the native will be magnanimous and bold, arrogant with all arms; and will wish to bring about whatever he plans in his heart, and he will perfect and complete many of those things which he wishes to begin; and his fame will be exalted, and he will bear a royal manner. And if he is of the stock fitted for it, he will be made a king, and his fame will fly to far off places, and he will be a great disperser and dissipater of both his own substance and that of others. And if he has older brothers, he will send them to their death before himself, or perhaps he himself may be the cause of their death, and especially if the Lord of the eighth aspects their significators, or is corporeally joined with them.

## ♐ ♓

If Mars is in Sagittarius or Pisces, and he is the significator of the nativity, and he is fortunate and strong, whatever kind of nativity it is, he will signify that the native will mingle with kings, magnates, and wealthy men, and that he will be greatly loved by them: for they will prefer him to their own tradesmen and the leaders of their armies; and this more greatly and strongly so if Jupiter is then placed in Aries or Scorpio, fortunate and free.

## ♈ ♏

And if Mars is placed in Aries or in his other domicile, and this more greatly so if the nativity is nocturnal, he will signify that the native will be a master of instruments of war, as are trebuchets, war-machines, and similar things, and will be very clever, and likewise perspicacious in geometrical science. However, if the nativity is diurnal, and he is oriental in the world or from the Sun, and he is not aspected by one of the benefics, it will signify that the native will be evil, diabolical, a whisperer, and an injurer of men, and that he will appear to be gladly applying himself in their evil; and will be sick with hidden illnesses (such as hidden cancers, and the like). And if he is in Aries, the native will fall from a high place, and because of this fall he will injure his body according to the body part attributed to the sign of the Ascendant. If he is in Scorpio, it will reduce his malice.

## ♌

Indeed if Mars is in Leo, and is placed as the significator of the nativity, whether this nativity is diurnal or nocturnal, it will signify that disagreeable things will befall the native, and the destruction of his person and his things, and that eye illnesses will beset him (and especially of the right eye); and his illnesses will also thrive in the stomach; and his professions will be more in those things which operate by fire and iron; and likewise it will signify that he will die an unexpected or sudden death, or perhaps he will be decapitated or hanged (and this more strongly so if Mars is then in the tenth), or he may be killed at the hands of men in another way. And Aboali said that either him or his father will die on a pilgrimage.

## ♉ ♎

If Mars is in Taurus or Libra, and he is the significator of the nativity, it signifies that the native will be self-indulgent, fornicating, a sodomite, and wicked in all abusive sexual activities. And a betrayer and deceiver of women (and he will be deceived and betrayed by them), and will marry someone so that he can commit adultery on them; and he will commit adultery on them, and afterwards he will marry his mistress; and in all these things and things like them, he will observe an evil method; and from this he will suffer harm and detriment. And Aboali said that if he is in Taurus, it signifies that the native will be a traitor, false, malignant, a threathener, and a fornicator. Indeed, if you find him in Libra, it signifies that he will suffer injuries to his body in the hidden and private areas; or perhaps he will be burned in some part of his body.

## ♊ ♍

And if you find him in Gemini or Virgo, whatever kind of nativity it is, it signifies that the native will be negligent, yet he will be carnal, and one who is occupied in temporal matters; and he will be sly, not very legal, and will strive to profit whatever way he can, both by way of thieving and from other illicit means. If he adheres to writing he will make a good writer; he will learn foreign languages easily, and he will even understand books of diverse discourses well, and will make their meanings clear; and he will be of a very good intellect, and perspicacious in science beyond the others who study with him.

## ♋

Indeed if you find him in Cancer, it signifies that the native will be fickle, easily changing himself from proposition to proposition; he will have profound ingenuity in all sciences, and will advance in them, and will eagerly direct his efforts to evil acts. And Aboali said that he will suffer evil or impediment in hidden parts of his body; and he will die a sudden death; and he will dissipate his mother's goods, and his mother will suffer a long infirmity because of the birth of this native.

# ⊙

# S O L

♑    ♒

If the Sun is the significator of someone's nativity, and you see him placed in Capricorn or Aquarius, I say with the nativity being diurnal, it signifies that the native will be a man of good quality, and benevolent, cheerful, good commerce, and of good mingling; even he delights with a certain seriousness; making others delighted, and perfect in administration or mechanical arts if he wishes to admit himself to them. However, if the nativity is nocturnal, it will signify that the native will be unstable regarding whatever matter which he wants to do or begins, and quick to change himself to something else.

♐    ♓

However if you find the Sun placed in Sagittarius or Pisces, and the nativity is diurnal, it will signify that the native will be the most excellent of all of his relatives, and will be very famous among men; and will freely mingle with nobles and magnates; however, he will assent to sexual activity more than is fitting, and to such an extent that for this reason he will be called a fornicator, and will commit something impure, nor will he avoid fornication with the wives of those close to him, nor even with his own stepmother.

♈    ♏

Indeed if you find the Sun in Aries, and it is a diurnal nativity, and he is placed as the significator of this nativity, and is placed in good condition and well disposed (namely fortunate and strong), it will signify that the native will be fortunate, exalted, and have a great name, and especially among kings, nobles, and magnates eagerly wishing to wage war; and he will remain like this as long as he lives, unless a triplicity Lord of the Ascendant operates to the contrary: who, even if it cannot destroy the aforementioned things, can still diminish them. However, if the nativity is nocturnal, it will signify the aforementioned will be one-third below what was said above.

Indeed, if you find him placed in Scorpio in a nativity (I say a diurnal one) it will signify that he will not have good fortune, unless the aforementioned triplicity Lords offer their support. But whatever kind of fortune it is, it will signify that he will have illnesses of the joints, and likewise that he will have liver disease. And Aboali said that his father will be weighed down by the worst of deaths. If the nativity is nocturnal, it signifies the aforementioned will be suppressed or increased according to the disposition of the triplicity Lords.

♌

And if the Sun is in Leo in someone's nativity, and is the significator of the nativity, and he is in good condition and well disposed in an angle (and chiefly in the tenth), or in a succedent of angle (and especially the succedent of the tenth), it signifies that the native will be a great, strong, and exalted king (if he is of such a stock that great offices or lofty dignities are suitable for him). However, if the native is of ordinary stock, even if he will not reach the ultimate kingship, he will still reach the greatest honours, the greatest dignities and riches, and unexpected revenues. If he is of worthless stock, he will reach great offices, and great dignities, regarding which men will be truly amazed: however, it will be feared that inconveniences will befall him from this great occasion. And Aboali said that in nocturnal nativities it signifies the stupidity of the father, and that he will be quickly seized by death, and will obtain good on pilgrimages.

♉    ♎

Indeed if you find him placed in Libra or Taurus, and he is placed as the significator of this nativity, whether the nativity is diurnal or nocturnal it signifies that the native will be good and truthful, an interpreter of dreams and secret things, and also a discoverer of hidden things; however, he will sin in disgraceful sexual intercourse.

♊    ♍

And if you find the Sun placed in Gemini or Virgo in someone's nativity, and it is diurnal, and he is the significator of this native, it will signify that the native will be very skilful in the sciences, and a perfect teacher of them beyond all other teachers of his time, and also of good morals and good works. And Aboali said that perhaps he will be a well-known and loved astronomer among kings and nobles. Indeed, if the nativity is nocturnal, it will signify him to be indigent and unfortunate, gladly doing evil things. And Aboali said that in his youth he will be a pauper: however, when he arrives to middle age, he will abound in riches; and pains will befall him in the aforementioned and the hidden parts of his body; and he will be an exorcist, loosening men who have slipped into the work of demons.

# ♀
# VENVS

### ♑ ♒

Indeed if Venus is placed in Capricorn or Aquarius in someone's nativity, and she is placed as this natives significator, whatever her condition or disposition is like, and whatever kind of nativity it is, it signifies that the native will desire low-class women, nor even will he recoil from ugly ones, and will easily acquire them for himself, and marry them; and will send his first wife to the grave before him.

### ♐ ♓

However if you find Venus is in Sagittarius or Pisces in anyone's nativity, and she is placed as the significatrix of the nativity, in a nocturnal nativity it signifies that this natives parents will hate him, and without a just cause; nevertheless, it will signify that he will obtain riches by means of noble women, or belonging to nobles, or even by wives or marriage, or by his mother in law or grandmother. However, if it is a diurnal nativity, the aforementioned things will occur, but they will be weaker and below this.

### ♈ ♏

If you find Venus in Aries or Scorpio, whether the nativity is diurnal or nocturnal, and whatever her condition is like, and if she is placed as the significatrix of this nativity, it signifies that the native will be ill-behaved towards women, not associating well with them; and will make much use of low-class, ugly, and unsuitable women, and much harm and inconvenience will follow from this, and he will hardly or never marry; and if he does marry, he will pursue it with difficulty and complications, and because of this he will meet with many contentions and disputes; and on the occasions of these contentions, many unfortunate things will happen to him; and he will fall into suspicion of his wife, and it will be possible that because of this suspicion he will kill her.

### ♌

And if Venus is placed in Leo, and she is the significatrix of the nativity, whatever her condition is like, and likewise whatever kind of nativity it is, it signifies that the native will burn with the love of women, and that he will abound in sexual activity, and that he will be unsuitable wanton, and will desire to abuse boys.

### ♉ ♎

And indeed, if you find Venus placed in Taurus or Libra, and she is placed as the significatrix, whatever kind of nativity it is, and whatever her condition is like, it will signify that the native will desire wicked women, and prostitutes [or witches - *affaturatrices*], and whores, fornicators, and other harlots;, and from this he will be defamed, and his infamy will be made common knowledge. And Aboali said that he will be fortunate and acquire good things in all the times of his life.

### ♊ ♍

Indeed if she is found in Gemini or Virgo in someone's nativity, and it is a diurnal nativity, and she is in good condition and well disposed, and she is the significatrix of this nativity, it signifies that the native will be a painter of diverse pictures, and likewise a writer, and will know how to do the work of women and effeminate men, and how to make women's jewellery. And he will stay with the religious under a certain kind of hypocrisy, however, he will be oppressed by the vice of luxury. Indeed, if it is a nocturnal nativity, and she is in bad condition and badly disposed, the native will know how to do none of the good aforementioned things, but he will more eagerly act on the bad ones.

### ♋

Again, if Venus if found in Cancer, and is the significatrix of the nativity, whatever kind of nativity it is, and whatever her condition is like, it will signify that the native will be unstable and quickly changing from one matter to another, and from place to place; he will also be depraved, profiting shamefully, and disgracefully wanton.

# ☿

# MERCVRIVS

## ♑ ♒

And if you find Mercury placed in Capricorn or Aquarius in anyone's nativity, both in diurnal and nocturnal nativities, and he is placed as the sole significator of the nativity, whatever his condition is like, it will signify that the native will be of an evil suspicion, and a grave tongue; nevertheless, he will eagerly have mingling with religious men and the wise.

## ♐ ♓

However if you find Mercury in Sagittarius or Pisces in anyone's nativity, and he is the significator of the nativity, and this nativity is diurnal, and he is placed in good condition and of good qualities, it signifies that the native will have mingling with kings, and the management of their affairs, and of men's legal cases, and he will be wise in judgements and in judging. Indeed, if the nativity is nocturnal, whatever his condition is like, it will signify this, but it will be very much below the aforementioned.

## ♈ ♏

If you find Mercury in Aries or Scorpio, whether the nativity is diurnal or nocturnal, whatever the condition is like of the nativity that he is the significator of, it will signify that the native will be a thief, a wooer, false, deceitful, sly, and surrounded by malice everywhere, and many evil things will follow from this.

## ♌

Indeed if you find Mercury placed in Leo, and he is placed in good condition and well disposed, and he is the significator of the nativity, whatever kind of nativity it is, it signifies that the native will acquire the friendship of magnates and nobles, and will freely stay with them. If you find him badly disposed, whatever kind of nativity it is, it will signify that he will turn out to be a wooer and foolish.

## ♉ ♎

And if you find Mercury in Taurus or in Libra in anyone's nativity, whatever kind of nativity it is, and if he is placed as its significator, it will signify that the native will be lively and humorous, and knowledgeable in all the sciences and all the things because of which and in which men delight.

## ♊ ♍

Indeed if you find Mercury placed in Gemini or Virgo, and he is placed as the significator of the nativity, and is in good condition and well disposed, it will signify that the native will be excellent and perfect in all the sciences, both the doctrinal and theoretical ones, and the mechanical ones.

## ♋

However if you find Mercury in Cancer, and he is the significator of the nativity, and in good condition and well disposed, it will signify that the native will know well how to prepare banquets, and daily nourishment, and will be of good will, not delighting in sexual activity, and he will be faithful and benevolent.

☽

# L V N A

♑  ♒

If you learn that the Moon is placed in Capricorn or Aquarius, and she is well disposed, and the nativity is nocturnal, and she is the significatrix of the nativity, and in the decrease of her light, it signifies that the native will suffer illnesses of the eyes, and kidney pains, and will suffer greatly because of these things. However, if the nativity is diurnal, he will be less impaired by these illnesses. In both nativities, whatever her condition is like, she signifies that the native will not be commended by men, but they will strive to reproach him, and will slander him, even if he is doing good and speaking good.

♐  ♓

However if you see the Moon placed in Sagittarius or Pisces as the significatrix of the nativity, in both diurnal and nocturnal nativities it signifies that the native will prevail amongst all of his relatives, and that he will almost be seen as a king amongst them (in respect of them), and his fame will be exalted. However, he will be tainted with the vice of wantonness, and will revel with prohibited women.

♈  ♏

Indeed if you find the Moon in Aries or Scorpio, and she is placed as the significatrix of the nativity (whatever kind it it), and whatever her condition is like, it will signify that the native will be a wooer, a thief, avoiding good works, applying himself to evil, freely staying with bandits and other wicked men, and desiring to associate with them.

♌

Indeed if you learn that the Moon is placed in Leo, in both kinds of nativities, and she is placed as the significatrix of the nativity, it signifies that the native will have mingling with kings, the wealthy, and magnates, and this more greatly so if the Moon dwells in the first or last terms of Leo.

♉  ♎

If you see the Moon in Taurus or Libra, whatever kind of nativity it is, and if she is the significatrix of the nativity (but not placed impeded) it signifies that the native will be ablaze with the love of women, and will delight in rejoicing with them, and good and utility will follow from them.

♊  ♍

And if the Moon is placed in Gemini or Virgo, and she is likewise the significatrix of the nativity (but not impeded) it signifies that the native will be benevolent, observing a good life, striving to harm nobody, of good intelligence, and good ability, eagerly revelling with girls and young women.

♋

Indeed, if you see the Moon in Cancer, and she is in good condition, and placed as the significatrix of the nativity, it signifies that the native is going to have mingling with kings and magnates, and will obtain good things, utility, and profit from them.

And Aboali said that if she is conjoined or applying to malefics, it will signify diverse illnesses for the native. Indeed, if she is conjoined or applying to benefics, it signifies the health and equilibrium of the body.

## III

## On The Years Of Fidaria And Their Dispositors

The ancient sages considered certain years in nativities, which were not called greater years, nor medium years, nor even lesser years, but they called them years of fidaria, that is dispositors years. For every planet disposes its own portion of the natives life, according to its portion of the years of fidaria in this manner: since whatever kind of nativity it is, the disposition of the years of fidaria will begin from the luminary who has authority; and this planet will dispose the life of the native according to the years of its fidaria, but not without the participation of other planets.

For if the nativity is diurnal, it will begin from the Sun (who is the diurnal luminary), who will dispose the years of the natives' life according to the quantity of the years of his Fidaria (which are 10), with the participation of all the other planets; but he will obtain the chief place, and especially in the first one-seventh of those years.

In the second one-seventh, Venus (who succeeds him in the order of the circles) will participate with him in the disposition of the natives' life.

In the third one-seventh, Mercury (who succeeds Venus in the order of the circles) will participate with him.

In the fourth one-seventh, the Moon (who succeeds Mercury in the order of circles) will participate with him.

In the fifth one-seventh, Saturn (who succeeds the Moon circularly in the order of the circles) will participate with him.

In the sixth one-seventh, Jupiter (who succeeds Saturn in the order of circles) will participate with him.

And indeed, in the seventh and final one-seventh, Mars (who succeeds Jupiter in the order of the circles) and is the seventh planet from the Sun, will participate with him.

After this, Venus (who succeeds the Sun in the order of the circles) will disposit the life of the native, according to the years of her fidaria (which are 8), and all the other planets will participate with her in the disposition of these years, each one of them according to their own one-seventh, just as was said regarding their participation with the Sun.

Then Mercury will disposit the natives' life according to the quantity of the years of his fidaria (which are 13); and the others will participate with him, namely each one of them according to their own one-seventh of these years.

Then the Moon will disposit according to the quantity of the years of her fidaria (which are 9); and each one of the others will participate according to their own one-seventh of these years.

Then Saturn will disposit according to the quantity of the years of his fidaria (which are 11), with the participation of the others, just as was said regarding the Sun.

Then Jupiter will disposit according to the quantity of the years of his fidaria (which are 12), with the participation of the other planets, as was said regarding the others.

Then Mars will disposit according to the quantity of the years of his fidaria, which are seven, with the participation of the other planets, as was said above.

Then the Caput Draconis will disposit according to the quantity of the years of his fidaria (which are three).

Then its Cauda will disposit according to the years of her fidaria (which are two).

After this, the disposition will revert to the Sun, and so it will be done (as was said) successively up until the end of the native's life.

### On Nocturnal Nativities

If the nativity is nocturnal, the disposition will begin from the Moon (who is the nocturnal luminary), and it will be done in everything, and by everything, as was said when the disposition begins from the Sun: both regarding the participation of the planets with her, and their succession in the order of the circles. And all of the aforementioned significators or dispositors, will dispose according to the condition and disposition of each one of them, so that if they are well disposed they will increase good fortune and diminish misfortune; and if they are badly disposed they will increase misfortune and decrease good fortune.

And this is a laborious matter, but it is still something to be well observed: since certain astrologers, avoiding labour, sometimes do not consider this in their judgements, whence they slide into deception.

And the years of fidaria all added together are 75, which sometimes (although it rarely happens) are all given to certain natives; and then years are not given to the native by the Alcocoden: for it could be of such great weakness, that it is not sufficient to give the years which are given by the fidaria - whence it is possible for the astrologer to sometimes be deceived in perceiving the number of the natives' years, if he does not take precautions (and it is not surprising).

## IV

### On The Eminence Of The Planets, Or The Transit Of One Over Another

In the eminence of the planets, or the transit of one over another, Alchabitius said that you ought to examine the average course of any superior planet, and likewise the place of its equation. For if its equated place is less than the medium course of the planet, and this planet will be ascending from the middle of its epicycle to its summit, approaching to a further longitude. If its equated place is more than its average course, the planet will be descending from the middle of its epicycle to its lower part, approaching a closer longitude. But if both of them are equal, the planet will be in the middle of its epicycle, namely between a further and closer longitude: which, having been found most truly and certainly, subtract the lesser of them from the greater, and multiply the difference by 7, and divide the result by 12, and what you get from this division will be the quantity of the ascending or descending of the planet in its circle.

### On Venus And Mercury

Alchabicius said that you ought to take what is between the place of the Sun and the place of Venus, and likewise what is between the Sun and the place of Mercury, and subtract the lesser from the greater, and multiply and divide just as was said above: since by this we will know which of them is stronger in the circle. And he said that if Venus and Mercury are oriental, and the equated place of one of them is less than the place of the Sun, we ought to take the remainder which is between the place of the Sun and the place of this planet, and do with it (in terms of multiplication and division) just as was said above for the superior planets.

And he said that the signification of the planets will be stronger and closer while they go away above each other (namely one over another) in conjunction; however, in prevention, and in square aspect, their significations will be weaker and less apparent. And when one of them is ascending and the other is descending, then the ascending one goes over the descending one; and when both are descending, he who is of less descension, goes over him who is of greater descension. However, when both are ascending, he who is of greater ascension goes over him who is of lesser ascension.

### On Another Manner Of Elevation Of One Planet Over Another

A planet is said to be elevated over another planet in another way (even if I have touched on this for you elsewhere) and it is stronger than the other one. For if one planet is northern, and the other is southern, the northern one travels over the southern one. And if both are northern, he who is more northern will go above him who is less northern. However, if both are southern, he who is less southern will go above him who is more southern. And for this reason it is said that the Moon goes above all the planets, and each one of them goes above all the others in these two ways.

Likewise if one of the planets is in the middle of its epicycle (that is, in the extreme of the further or closer longitude), or is in its zenzahar, then the one ascending in his epicycle will go above him who is in the further or closer longitude, and the northern one will go above the southern one, and even above the descending one, and above him who is in his zenzahar, and he who is in his own zenzahar will go above the southern planet, and even above the descending planet, and above him who is in a closer longitude.

## V

### On The "Opening Of The Gates" According to Alchabitius

The "opening of the gates" follows the aforementioned, and this is when two planets whose domiciles are opposed to each other are joined together: as are Saturn and the luminaries, Jupiter and Mercury, and Mars and Venus - when a lighter one of them is joined with one of the aforementioned heavier ones, and he finds him in his own domicile or exaltation, or two of the other lesser dignities, he receives him, and is said to open the gates to him; just as someone would do if he found his enemy in his own house - he would honour him, lest he does something uncivil; provided that he is not a mortal enemy (unless he is an insolent or wild or feral man, who does not have domesticity with men, as was that Ezzelino da Romano, who did not spare sex, age, rank, or dignity). And all of what is said above is called "*the opening the gates*".

## VI

### On The Twelve Hours Of The Sun And The Moon Which Are Applied To The Sun

Then follows on the 12 hours of the Sun and the Moon, which Alchabitus called *Albuim*, which follow immediately after the separation of the Moon from her corporeal conjunction with the Sun. And Alchabitius said that the ancient sages divided these 12 hours in threes, that is, into three equal parts, each one of which consists of 4 unequal hours; which 12 hours they applied to the Sun. And they judged these hours according to the Lords of the triplicity in which the Sun was placed at the hour of his conjunction with the Moon; beginning from the Sun, giving him the first four hours, giving the second four to the second Lord of the same triplicity, and indeed, the last four hours to the third Lord of his triplicity.

Then the aforementioned sages gave Venus another 12 hours after the 12 hours of the Sun; and divided them into three divisions (as was said of the Sun), and they judged regarding each one of these divisions, giving the first 4 hours to Venus, the second four hours to the second triplicity Lord of Venus, and the final four hours to her third triplicity Lord, and they judged according to how

the aforementioned triplicity Lords, and the others, were disposed.

They did the same with Mercury and with his triplicity Lords. And likewise with the Moon and her triplicity Lords. Then with Saturn and his triplicity Lords, and likewise with Jupiter and Mars, and with their triplicity Lords. Then the circle reverts to the Sun,, and so on up until another conjunction.

### On The Twelve Combust Hours After The Conjunction

And Alchabitius said that certain men said that the albuim is this: namely that after the conjunction of the Sun and Moon there were 12 unequal hours which are called "combust", and it is not fitting to begin any work in these hours.

### On The 72 Incombust Hours

And after these 12 combust hours there are 72 incombust ones, and after the 72 incombust hours are likewise another 12 combust ones, and so on, repeated until the succeeding conjunction. After this they divided the above mentioned 12 combust hours into 3 equal divisions, and they said that whoever begins to battle in the first four hours, will fear for the loss of his soul. And whoever begins in the second four hours will fear for the detriment of his body without the loss of his soul. And whoever begins to plough in them, will fear great detriment in everything he possesses, and his body, without the loss of his soul, and the ruin of those who belong to him will be feared. And who begins in the last four hours is to fear the detriment of his substance, just as touched on elsewhere.

## VII

### On The Profections Of The Years, Both Of The World, And Of Nativities

Having made mention above of the number of years which are attributed to every native, it appears fitting and right to me, to subsequently speak about the profection of their years. However, a profection is the signification which results from those things which happen from the sign which immediately succeeds the sign which was the Ascendant of the nativity, and its Lord - whether good, bad, or mediocre, just as said in the chapters above. It is called a "profection" since it advances (Latin - *proficit*) by moving itself by one sign every year, following the succession of signs; whose Lord offers support to the significator of the revolution of the year, both for good and bad, sometimes increasing one, sometimes decreasing. Whose interpretation is the alcocoden, which is a participator of the accidents which will come to the native in every year of any one of his revolutions. The knowledge of whose discovery, is as follows:

You will consider the year, the day, the month, and the hour, of whatever nativity you wish, and you will observe how many solar years the native has now completed; and you will take one sign from the Ascendant of the nativity for every solar year. And you will begin from the hour of the nativity of this native according to the succession of signs, giving one sign to each year, and where this number ends, the sign which immediately succeeds this one is the sign of the profection from the Ascendant of this nativity, and will be the Ascendant of the profection of the year which then follows (which you will not have yet sent forward in your count); and the profection of this year will be in such a degree of this sign, as was the degree of the Ascendant at the hour of the nativity. And understand this for every profection, since every year will always be in such a degree of the sign in which it falls, as it was in the sign which preceded it in the year which has just passed immediately before this one which you seek; and the planet who is the Lord of this sign will be called the alcocoden, which is the assistant of the planet who is the Lord of this sign which is the Ascendant of the revolution of the year which you revolve. And by such a planet the disposition of the status of this native in that year will be shown to you, even if it happens that you have to make more revolutions in that year.

Indeed, for the annual honours and dignities of the native, you will examine the sign of the profection from the Sun (namely one full sign for each solar year) in order to perceive his profection.

Indeed, for the condition of the body and soul of the native, you will examine the sign of the profection from the Moon.

Indeed, for his professions and offices, you could examine the sign of the Midheaven.

However, to know his wealth and prosperity, you will examine the sign of the profection from the Part of Fortune, and from the sign of the house of substance.

For the profection of brothers, you will examine from the sign of the profection from the house of brothers.

For the profection of the father, you will examine from the sign of the profection from the house of the father.

For the profection of children you will examine from the sign of the profection of the house of children.

For the profection of slaves and slavegirls, you will examine from the sign of the profection from the house of slaves.

For the profection of wives, associates, and enemies, you will examine the sign of the profection of the house of wives.

For the profection of their substance, you will examine from the sign of the profection from the house of the substance of wives.

For the profection of the religious, you will examine from the sign of the profection from the house of religion.

For the profection of kings, you will examine from the sign of the profection of the house of kings.

For the profection of friends, you will examine from the sign of the profection of the house of friends.

However, for the profection of hidden enemies, you will examine from the sign of the profection of the house of hidden enemies.

And know that a profection is a certain way of altering the revolution, which is done individually according to the succession of signs. For whatever kind of Ascendant it is, the profection will only be made from one sign to the sign which follows it immediately, which does not happen so in revolutions.

And a profection alters a revolution according to this method: that if good is signified by the revolution in that year, and good is signified by the profection, it will increase the good which is signified by the revolution. Indeed, if the profection signifies the contrary, it will diminish the good which is signified by the revolution. Indeed, if evil is signified by both the revolution and the profection, it will increase the evil signified by the revolution. But if the revolution signifies evil, and the profection signifies good, it will reduce the evil signified by the revolution; and so, according to this, the profection is a different revolution.

## VIII

### On The Order Of The Profection

The order of the profection is like this: let us posit that someone is born with the Ascendant at 10 degrees of Aries, in the following year Taurus, at 10 degrees, will be the sign of the profection. But it will not be the Ascendant of the revolution, yet it will be in a certain way managing the year in turn with it. In the third year Gemini (at 10 degrees) will be the sign of the profection, but it will not be the Ascendant of the following revolution. And so on by this order up to the end of the signs. After completing the twelve signs, the profection will return to the first sign, and in this way you will order it up to the end of the native's life. And therefore I will give you a certain true example.

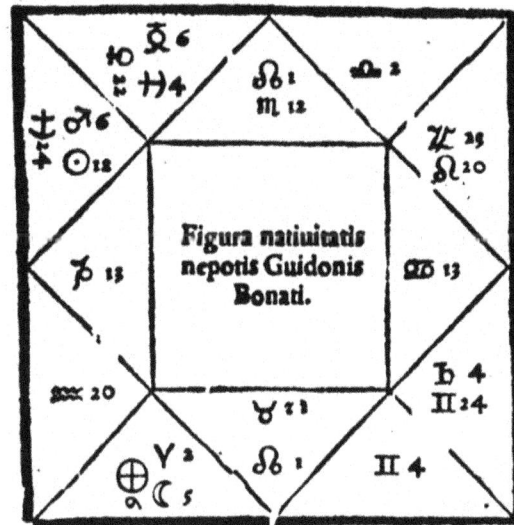

Figura natiuitatis nepotis Guidonis Bonati.

A certain nephew of mine was born in the era of the Arabs, in the 665th year, in the 9th day of the third month; and the era of Christ 1267, the 6th day of the entrance of January. Whose nativity had 13 degrees Capricorn as the Ascendant; and Mars there at 6 degrees and 5 minutes; the Sun there at 12 degrees 10 minutes. The second house was 20 degrees Aquarius. The third house was 2 degrees Aries. The fourth house was 12 degrees Taurus, with the Moon there at 5 degrees 5 minutes, and the Part of Fortune at 6 degrees 5 minutes. The 5th house was 4 degrees Gemini, with the Cauda there at 1 degree 31 minutes. The sixth house was 24 degrees 15 minutes Gemini. The seventh house was 13 degrees Cancer, with Saturn there at 4 degrees 15 minutes. The eighth house was 20 degrees Leo, with Jupiter there at 23 degrees 20 minutes. The ninth house was 2 degrees Libra. The tenth house was 12 degrees Scorpio. The eleventh house was 4 degrees Sagittarius, with the Caput there at 1 degrees 31 minutes, and Mercury there at 6 degrees 55 minutes, and Venus at 22 degrees 16 minutes. The same Sagittarius was the twelfth house, at 23 degrees.

Whence, when he had already passed five solar years, I examined a certain revolution of his. And the fifth year from his Ascendant arrived to Gemini (which is the sixth sign from Capricorn), to its thirteenth degree; and the profection of the Sun likewise arrived at 13 degrees of Gemini. And Mercury was the Alcocoden, or the Lord of this year or revolution. And the profection of Mars arrived to Gemini at its seventh degree. And the profection of the Moon arrived to the sixth degree of Libra, (which is the sixth sign from Taurus).

And the profection of the Part of Fortune arrived at the seventh degree of Libra. And the profection of Saturn arrived to the fifth degree of Sagittarius (which is the sixth sign from Cancer). And the profection of Jupiter arrived to the twenty-fourth degree of Capricorn (which is the sixth sign from Leo). The sign of Virgo was enclosed. And the profection of Mercury arrived to the sixth degree of Taurus (which is the sixth sign from Sagittarius). And the profection of Venus arrived to the thirteenth degree of the same Taurus. And the profection of the tenth house arrived to the twelfth degree of Aries (which is the sixth sign from the Midheaven of the nativity). To say everything that happened to him in that year would take a long time to narrate, wherefore I will not persevere in it, but will proceed to more useful things.

Therefore you will consider every profection of whatever kind you wish, since it always will be in such a degree, in the sign in which you find it, as it was in the sign in which it was at the hour of the nativity, changing itself from one sign to the next one which immediately and successively follows it, in each year (namely solar ones), by one complete sign. And the planet who is the Almutem over this place, or who is in it, or who projects his rays to it, will be said to be the co-assistant of the significator of this revolution with the Alcocoden. But the other planets will not be called the Alcocoden, except the one which is the Lord of this sign. And if one of the planets is in this sign, or its rays, and you wish to know when the profection will arrive to him or to his rays, Alchabitius said that you will examine how many degrees and minutes are between the degree to which the profection of the year has reached, and the planet in question: and you will multiply this by twelve and one sixth of one day, and what results will be the days of this year in which you are in.

## IX

## On The Profection Of The Years Of The World

However the profection of the years of the world differ somewhat from the profection of the years of the nativity: for the profection of the years of the nativities is taken from the Ascendant of someone's' nativity, then moved by one whole sign for every solar year, just as was said. However, the profection of the years of the world is taken from the first minute of Aries, or even from any inception of another great matter, such as some kingdom or empire, or some sect, or some religion - such as when the reign of Nebuchadnezzar began, or the reign of Ptolemy, and the reign of Philip, and the reign of Alexander, and the reign of King Yazdigrid, and the kingdom of the Romans; and like when the sect or religion of Augustine began, or the sect of Benedict, or the sect of the Minor Brothers, which began in 609th year of the era of the Arabs, in the month of the latter Rabbae, the era of Christ 1211 years: whose beginning was such an Ascendant, that it will uproot all other sects, and all other Orders existing under the Roman Church; but I do not dare to speak of its end, fearing lest I fall into the rumours of the mob. Nevertheless, it will be very public when it comes, and the rumour about it will be immense.

And for similar things, whose beginnings are had, their general accidents will be known forever; and their annual accidents will be known by their annual revolutions, having considered its beginning. And the profection will throw in its lot according to its condition: sometimes increasing, sometimes decreasing or detracting from the revolution. By considering it from sign to sign successively (as I said), the accidents of that matter whose revolution you desired, could be known in that revolution. However, this profection is not simply of such beginnings as is the profection of the years of the world, but is likened to it in a certain way, on account of its long duration.

However, on the profections proceeding from the Ascendant, and regarding the significator which is in one of the angles, or in one of the other places besides the angles, and concerning the significator of the right circle, and the significator of the oblique circle, and on certain other things which are in the fourth chapter of the *Introduction* of Alchabitius for the judgement of this art, I will say nothing for the minute, since it is determined enough with regards to them in that Tractate, by a long discussion, so that it is not necessary that I should sweat about them now, and also since this work, even though it would be useful and profound in knowledge, nevertheless it would return more work than manifest benefit; but I will resolve the things which are more manifestly useful which.

It was discussed above concerning the direction according to the Lords of the terms in the Second Part, in the chapter on the knowledge of the life of the native and his condition. Therefore it will be discussed below regarding the significators to be directed, and how, and in what way we ought to direct them.

## X

## On The Direction Of The Significators To Be Directed In The Circle, And How Many Are The Significators Which We Must Direct, Which Were Directed By The Sages

There are seven significators which are to be directed: namely the degree of the Ascendant, the degree of the Sun, the degree of the Moon, the degree of the Part of Fortune, the degree of the Midheaven, the degree of the conjunction, and likewise the degree of the prevention.

And the degree of the Ascendant is directed to know the accidents which are going to happen to the native in his own person (namely good, bad, or middling ones). For if you see the direction come to good planets, say that the accidents of his body will be good. However, if it comes to malefics, you will judge the contrary. Indeed, if it arrives to bicorporeal or convertible ones, or mediocrely disposed ones, you will announce middling accidents: that is, neither truly good, nor truly evil.

Indeed, the Sun is directed to know to what dignities, or exaltations, which seem to pertain to lay honour and fame, the native ought to arrive at. Whence if the Sun is in good condition and well disposed, and the direction arrives at well disposed benefics, it will signify that the native will arrive to great and famous honours. And if you find the contrary, you will be able to judge the contrary.

However, if the Sun is mediocrely disposed, or the benefics to which he arrives, it signifies that the native will arrive at some kind of dignities, yet they will not be very famous.

Indeed, the Moon is directed to know the disposition of the body of the native, and the quality of his soul, and likewise his marriage. If the Moon is in good condition and well disposed, and the direction is to well disposed benefics, it will signify that the disposition of the natives body will be good and praiseworthy, and so too will the qualities of his soul, and that he will be well married - if the Lord of the seventh is in good condition and well disposed, and in a good aspect with the Lord of the Ascendant, or with the Moon herself, or with the Lord of the Part of Marriage. Of the contrary however, you should understand the contrary; of what is mediocre, say what is mediocre.

Indeed, the Part of Fortune is directed to know the wealth of the native and his pecuniary profit, and also his acquisition. Whence if the Part of Fortune is well disposed, and the direction arrives to well disposed benefics, it signifies that the native will acquire and accumulate much money by just means. However, if the benefic is impeded, it signifies that he will acquire it, but after the acquisition he will dissipate it. But if you observe the contrary, you will be able to judge the contrary; however, if you find mediocrity, you will announce mediocrity.

However, the Midheaven (as Alchabitius says) is directed to know the works of the native, and his arts or professions, and for all particular dispositions and their condition. Whence, if the Lord of the Midheaven is well disposed, or the Midheaven itself, and the direction arrives to well disposed benefics, the native will conduct himself well with regards to professions, and with regards to offices, and to all matters related to the mechanical arts, and lay matters, and those things which pertain to them.

However, the degree of the conjunction is directed to know general matters, and to consider all the aforementioned things up to the middle of the natives' life - if the nativity is conjunctional. Whence if it is well disposed, it will increase the signification of those things signifying good, and decrease the signification of those things signifying evil.

You will be able to say the same about the degree of the prevention after the middle of life (if the nativity is preventional), and you will add the aspect of benefics or malefics with the Almutem over the aforementioned degrees and their significators, since they will add or subtract according to their natures, and according to their dispositions.

Therefore these aforementioned things are to be considered in nativities generally, and in the beginnings of other things of which an end is expected.

Indeed, if you wish to consider the aforementioned things in revolutions of the years, both those of the world and those of nativities, examine the Ascendant of whichever one of these years. For you wish to direct a year of the world, Alchabitius said that for knowing the condition of the country folk ahead of time, we ought to direct the degree of the Ascendant of the revolution, and give one day to every 59 minutes and 8 seconds. And according to the direction arriving to benefics or to malefics, you will be able to judge regarding their condition and status in those days, up until the end of that revolution - and this according to the oblique circle.

However, if you want to examine the direction of kings, you will examine them from the degree of the Midheaven, according to the direct circle, giving one day to every 59 minutes and 8 seconds, and thus you will know the accidents which ought to happen to kings in that revolution, with regards to them as kings. But for their own personal matters, and in their persons, you ought to examine them, just as for other individual persons, and according to how you see the direction arrive to benefics or malefics, so you will judge regarding their condition (whether good, bad, or mediocre), both for kings and the country folk.

You will be able to say the same for the condition of the revolutions of nativities: however, it is necessary that you consider the revolutions of the nativities from the Ascendant of the nativity, and the Ascendant of the revolution. But the revolutions of the world from the Ascendant of the revolution of the years of the world to know the condition of the mob according to the oblique circle; but the revolutions of kings according to the right circle for

knowing their condition, according to what was said.

## XI

## On The Nature Of The Degrees Of The Signs, In Any Sign

And there is something else to be known, which the ancient sages (and especially the Indians), considered in nativities, and questions, and beginnings of matters, and called them the twelfth-parts of the planets and domiciles, or the twelve signs. For every sign is divided into twelve divisions, each one of which consists of two and a half degrees. And these divisions are given to the twelve signs, so that each one of the signs has its own twelfth-part in every sign, and in this twelfth-part it signifies that sign to which is attributed that which pertains to the peculiar quality of its own nature, according to how Albumashar appeared to want it.

Whence, if you wish to know in the nature of what sign is any degree or any sign, according to what he said, you should take the degrees which are from the beginning of the sign up to the degree whose twelfth-part you seek, and multiply them by 12, and divide the result in this manner: namely giving 2 degrees 30 minutes to each sign. And see where your number leads you, since there will be the nature of the same degree of the sign in whose twelfth-part it falls.

Which matter seems to certain of the modern sages to be understood in this manner: namely that the degree of the Ascendant (or any other house, according to what this house signifies), of whatever sign is to be taken, and it is to be multiplied by 12; and that what resulted was to be added to the degree of the sign of the Ascendant (or the degree of the house it began from), and projected by 30, namely giving each sign or house 30 degrees. And this number is projected from the Ascendant or from the domicile in which you wished to begin, and where the number ends, there will be the signification of the twelfth-part of the signs and planets. Then see in the twelfth-part of which sign the number falls, since this sign and its Lord will provide support to the Ascendant or the other house from which you began, and its Lord. Whence if this sign and its Lord are well disposed, they will add something in the good, and reduce something of the bad. However, if the sign and its Lord are badly disposed, they will add something in the bad, and reduce something of the good: by one-twelfth. If the sign is well disposed, and its Lord is badly disposed, or vice versa, they will add or diminish in the good or in the bad by one twenty-fourth. But if one is well or badly disposed, and the other is neither good nor bad, but mediocre, it will neither add nor diminish.

And all this will be according to what is the nature of this sign or this planet.

And the sages understood this to be the twelfth-part of the planets and the houses. And even if this chapter does not seem to be of great utility, and is difficult, it is still fitting for you to know this: for in a certain way, it will render you more eloquent.

## XII

### On The Ninth-Parts Of The Signs And What They Will Signify

Mention having been made above in the preceding chapter of the twelfth-parts of the signs (or of the nature of the twelve signs in each sign), their ninth-parts should not be overlooked.

Indeed, the ancient sages said that we ought to know how much a planet had ambulated in the sign in which you found him, from degrees and minutes, or how many degrees have ascended, from the house whose ninth-part you wish to know.

Then divide the sign into nine divisions, each one of which consists of 3 degrees and 20 minutes; and you will begin to project from the beginning of the sign in which the planet or degree of the house in which you began from is placed; and see in which ninth-part this degree falls, and give this ninth-part to the Lord of the mobile sign of the triplicity of the Ascendant, or the of the aforementioned domicile; and you will give the second ninth-part you to the Lord of the sign which immediately succeeds the Ascendant or the aforementioned domicile. And the third ninth-part to the Lord of the third sign which succeeds the second; and the fourth to the fourth sign which succeeds that; and the fifth to the fifth sign which succeeds that; and the sixth to the sixth sign which succeeds that; and the seventh to the seventh sign which succeeds the first sign; and the eighth to the eighth sign which succeeds the first;

and the ninth Lord to the ninth sign which succeeds the first - and you will always do this until you find the planetary ruler of the ninth-part which you seek. Below is such an example.

The Ascendant or the domicile from which you begin was Aries, Leo, or Sagittarius: Mars is now the Lord of the first ninth-part, since he is the Lord of the mobile sign of this triplicity (namely Aries). Venus is the Lord of the second ninth-part, since she is the Lord of Taurus, which is the second sign from the first (namely from the Ascendant), and succeeds it immediately. The third ninth-part belongs to Mercury, who is the Lord of Gemini (which is the third sign from the first). The fourth ninth-part belongs to the Moon, who is the Lord of Cancer (which is the fourth sign from the first). The fifth ninth-part belongs to the Sun, the Lord of Leo (which is the fifth sign from the first). The sixth ninth-part belongs to Mercury, the Lord of Virgo (which is the sixth sign from the first). The seventh ninth-part belongs to Venus, the Lord of Libra (which is the seventh sign from the first). The eighth ninth-part belongs to Mars, the Lord of Scorpio (which is the eighth sign from the first). The ninth ninth-part belongs to Jupiter, the Lord of Sagittarius (which is the ninth sign from the first).

### On The Second Triplicity

However if the Ascendant or the aforementioned domicile is Taurus, Virgo, or Capricorn, the first ninth-part will be Saturn, the Lord of Capricorn. Indeed, the second ninth-part will belong to the same Saturn, the Lord of Aquarius. The third ninth-part will belong to Jupiter, the Lord of Pisces. The fourth will belong to Mars, the Lord of Aries. The fifth will belong to Venus, the Lord of Taurus. The sixth will belong to Mercury, the Lord of Gemini. The seventh will belong to the Moon, the Lord of Cancer. The eighth will belong to the Sun, the Lord of Leo, and the ninth will belong to Mercury, the Lord of Virgo.

And so understand for the third and fourth triplicity, if the Ascendant or the house were some sign of the mentioned triplicity. always starting from the mobile sign of the triplicity of the Ascendant or the house, and proceeding in order, as was said.

Therefore you should see an example of the aforementioned: therefore posit that some planet or the beginning of some house from which you wish to begin, is in the twenty-first degree of Taurus. You will divide the whole of Taurus into nine divisions. Therefore the first division, namely the first ninth-part, will belong to Saturn, the Lord of Capricorn, and you will have 3 degrees 20 minutes of Taurus. The second ninth-part will belong to the same Saturn, the Lord of Aquarius, and now you will have 6 degrees and 40 minutes. The third ninth-part will belong to Jupiter, the Lord of Pisces, and behold, you will have 10 whole degrees. The fourth ninth-part belongs to Mars, the Lord of Aries, and you will have 13 degrees and 20 minutes. The fifth belongs to Venus, the Lord of Taurus, and you will have 16 degrees and 40 minutes. The sixth belongs to Mercury, the Lord of Gemini, and you will have 20 full degrees. The seventh belongs to the Moon, the Lord of Cancer: and look, you will have 23 degrees and 20 minutes.

Thus the planet or degree of the aforementioned house will necessarily fall in the ninth-part of the Moon, whence it is necessary that the Moon is the Lord of this ninth-part: and according to how the Moon is then disposed, she will either provide support to the Ascendant and its Lord; or the house from which you began

the matter, or the Almutem of the nativity or question, or of any other inception - or she will detract from its signification. For if she is well disposed, and the Ascendant is well disposed, she will support it for approximately one-seventh in the good. However, if both are badly disposed, she will detract from it according to a similar portion. However, if one is well disposed, and the other is badly disposed, they will neither add nor diminish.

However, you will always consider the triplicity Lords and the term Lords, since they will always remain in their own condition, and in their own significations, just as was said above.

I will not say anything here on the "*dorungez*", since it seems to pertain to the consideration of the faces - which was widely and sufficiently discussed above in the First Tractate, in the chapter on the faces.

## XIII

## On The Lord Of The Circle Or Of The Orb Of Signs

You will consider in nativities the Lord of the orb or circle of signs, in this manner. You will examine the Lord of the Ascendant of the nativity of whatever native, and its first hour; and you will give the Ascendant and its Lord, and the Lord of this hour, to the first year of that native, since these two signify the condition of the native, and what it will be like in the first year of his life. Whence if both are well disposed, his condition will be good in that year; however, if they are to the contrary, you will judge to the contrary. But if one is well disposed, and the other is badly disposed, then you will be able to judge that the natives condition will be mediocre, unless the Moon or the triplicity Lords or term Lords operate to the contrary. You will be able to say the same about the good or bad health of his body. Then you will examine the Lord of the second house, and the Lord of the second hour, to see how they are disposed: for if their disposition is good, the native's substance will be well disposed in the second year; if they are to the contrary, you will judge the contrary. If one is well disposed, and the other is badly disposed, then the native's substance will be deposited in a mediocre way. After this examine how the Lord of the third house, and the Lord of the third hour are disposed: for the condition of the brothers will be disposed in the third year according to their condition. And so on in order, proceeding according to the dispositions and the condition of the Lords of the houses and the hours, up to the twelfth. You will judge on the significations of all the houses in their years, according to the aforementioned method, which was just stated for the first, second, and third house.

## XIV

## On The Lord Of The Twelve Remaining Hours

However, regarding the twelve hours remaining after the aforementioned ones, you will consider them in this way, successively, just as you considered the aforementioned hours and their Lords.

For you will give the 13th hour and its Lord to the first house, and the Lord of the first hour: for it will provide support to the Ascendant and its Lord, in the increase of the good for by one twenty-fourth, if they both (namely the hour and the Lord the hour) are well disposed, and even the Ascendant also and its Lord. However, if the Ascendant and its Lord are badly disposed, it will subtract one-fourth from their malice. But if the Lord of the thirteenth hour is badly disposed, it will subtract one twenty-fourth of the good, and increase the evil by the same amount, in the first year: and understand this with regards to the rest of the hours successively proceeding in order. For according to how themselves and their Lords are disposed, so will they assist or impede the disposition of the other significators, according to the significations of the twelve houses in their years, just as even according to natural things it can happen in those years - just as was said concerning the thirteenth and its Lord, which were given to the Ascendant and its Lord, and so the 14th and its Lord are given to the second house, and so on in order.

And according to this method you will look ahead to all of the houses and their Lords, and all of the hours and their Lords. For every Lord of these houses, and these hours (just as Alchabitius testifies), is a Lord of the orb, and will have a signification for every year over everything signified in the year to which it is assigned, according to what the Alcocoden has, and he will disposit the significations of the native, according to how he is well or badly disposed, adding or subtracting in good or bad, by the portions named above.

And Alchabitius said that certain astrologers make the Lord of the Ascendant of the root nativity the Lord of the orb in the first year; and in the second year the planet who succeeds the first (just as was said for the Lord of the hour), and it seems to me

that this could be suitably upheld; not that they are the Lords of the orb absolutely, but are co-assistants of the aforementioned ones.

I would even say certain things according to what has been handed down, which seem fitting for you to know; and even though it will bring more work than utility to you, nevertheless it will make you more profound in the science of profection. And he spoke about the profection of certain ones of them, and even about certain other things, as I will recite to you in what follows.

For indeed, the mentioned philosopher said, that Alchindi said, that between the year of the conjunction which signified the sect of the Saracens, and the year of Hijra (which was the first year of the years of the Arabs), there were 51 complete solar years. And the Ascendant of the year of the conjunction of the aforementioned sects in that region, was Gemini. And the profection of the same year arrived to Virgo. And between this first year of the years of the Arabs, and the first year of Yazdigird, the king of the Persians, were 3264 days. Therefore if you wish to have knowledge of this matter, take the years of Yazdigird, and turn them into days (as was explained in the book the courses of the planets), and add on the days which were between the first year of the years of the Arabs, and Yazdigird, and divide this by 365 days and one-fourth of a day, and however, many divisions result, that is how many solar years there are; and how many remain in term of months and days, will be of an imperfect year. And what is conjoined or collected in terms of years, they are the solar years from the beginning of the years of the Arabs. Therefore project one sign for every year, and begin from Virgo, and to whatever sign your count leads you, that will be the sign to which the year or the world arrives from the ascension of the conjunction of the aforementioned sect.

However, to others, as were Albumashar and his followers, it seemed that we should add on top of the years of Yazdigird, 51 perfect years and two months, and 12 days, and 18 hours from the years of the Persians (which are without fractions and without a quarter of a day), and they extended these years into days, and they will turned those days into solar years (as was said), and they began to project from the beginning of Libra.

If you wish to know the profection from the sign of the conjunction of such a sect, make the profection from Scorpio, since the conjunction of the planets which signify the sect began from Scorpio. Indeed, if you want the profection from the ascension of the kingdom, subtract 118 complete years from the years of Yazdigird, and turn them into solar years, just as was said before, and begin to project from Virgo.

However, it should be known that Muhammed was not the aforementioned king, but a prophet, and so the kingdom did not begin from his own time, but began long after, perhaps by 117 Persian years, and the Arabs began to reign; and the Ascendant returned to Virgo. And it seemed that there was an error in this literature: for this is not so, but then the reign of the Arabs changed to the blackness of that day; and this is had in the second figure of the three figures of the last section of the book of Alalraren.

### The Profection From The Ascendant Of The Change

Again if you want the profection from the Ascendant of the change of the conjunction from the water triplicity to the fire triplicity, subtract 176 perfect years from the complete years of Yazdigird, and change those which remain into solar years, and begin to project from Leo; and where the number arrives in that same sign will be the profection of each beginning, of those which were mentioned.

## XV

## On The Direction Of A Significator

And after this, we will move on to the direction of a significator. That is, that you direct the significator which you want, to some place of the signs. And you should know what there is between them in terms of degrees of the direction, and you will take one year for each and every degree.

Therefore if you wish to know this, and the significator which you want to direct to some part of the circle is in the Ascendant, subtract the ascensions of the degree (in which the significator is placed) by ascensions of the region, from the ascensions of the degree to which you want to direct him. And what remains will be the degrees of the direction.

If the significator is in the opposition of the degree of the Ascendant, subtract the ascensions of the opposite degree (in which the significator is placed), from the ascensions of the opposite degree to which you want to direct him, in that region (since the setting of any sign concords with the rising of its opposite one).

And it should be known that the degrees of the direction (for which one year is taken for each), are the degrees of the equatorial day. And the degrees which are directed, and the degrees which are directed to, are degrees of the oblique circle.

Indeed, if the significator is in the tenth or the fourth, you will subtract the ascensions of the degree of the significator from the ascensions of the degree to which you want to direct him, by ascensions of the right circle; and what will remain will be the degrees of the direction.

But if the significator which you want to direct is not in one of the angles, you will examine his longitude from the angle he is least far away from (namely from the angle of the tenth house, or from the angle of the fourth house). Which, if he is between the Ascendant and the tenth, subtract the ascensions of the degree of the significator by the right circle; and if he is between the seventh and the tenth, you will subtract the ascensions of the degree of the significator by the right circle, from the degrees of the tenth house (likewise by the right circle). And what remains from whichever of these places, you will divide by the parts of the hours of that day of the degree in which the significator was placed: and what you get from this division, will be the "hours of the length from the angle".

And if it is between the Ascendant and the fourth house, you will subtract the ascensions of the degree of the significator by the right circle, from the ascensions of the degree of the fourth house. However, if the significator is between the fourth and the seventh, you will subtract the ascensions of the degree of the fourth house, from the ascension of the significator, (by the right circle). And you will divide what remains from each of these places, by the parts of hours of the night of the degree in which the significator is placed - and this is if the significators are in one quarter of the circle and not in diverse quarters.

And if the significator is in the middle of the eastern circle (which is from the tenth up to the fourth, from those which succeed the Ascendant), subtract the ascensions of the degree in which the significator is from the ascensions of the degree to which you want to direct (by the right circle), and what remains will be the *"significator of the right circle"* - keep this. After this, subtract the ascensions of the degree in which the significator is placed (by the ascensions of the region) from the ascensions of the degree to which you want to direct him (by the ascensions of the region), and what this is, will be the "significator of the region". After this you will examine the remainder which is between the *"significator of the direct circle"* and the "significator of the region", and you will take one-sixth of the remainder, and you will multiply it by the *"hours of the length from the angle"*; and

what you get will be the "equation". That is, if the length is one hour, you will take one sixth; and if it is more, you will take more sixths: so that you will take one sixth for every hour. And if the *"significator of the right circle"* is less than the *"significator of the region"*, you will add the *"equation"* on to "the significator of the right circle". And if it is greater, you will subtract the *"equation"* from him; and what remains will be the degree of the direction.

And if the significator is in the middle of the western circle, you will do it at length, as Alchabitius says, who gives the method of directing in full.

# GUIDO BONATTI'S

## BOOK OF ASTRONOMY

## PART SIX

### On Rains And The Mutations Of The Air, And The Things Which Pertain To This

#### Preface

Since it seems to me that I have satisfactorily kept the promises (which I promulgated in the beginning of this work) in what has preceded, lest you might say that you were deceived in something, I think it would be to make mention of (as eloquently as I can) the mutation of the air in this Tractate, and of those things of these mutations that fall together with them, and what will result from this coinciding, and of those things which we can perceive from thence, and to which the human mind is able to attain.

And even if the action of rains, and of the other things which fall together with the mutations of the air, are very particular, and more particular than the rest of the particular things, nevertheless, those things which can be said of them, and known of them, do not seem to me to be omitted; and according to the sayings of our wise predecessors, and according to those things besides this which will be possible to be seen, and would seem to be useful, and according to the truth of it, just as it is possible to discuss more certainly;, and not deviating from their opinions, according to how it seemed to our reverend predecessors, Jafar, Lencuo, Ptolemy, and others who strove to light the way for us. To discuss this briefly, therefore, so we can more quickly arrive at the main topics desired, without a great introduction to the beginning of this matter; nor do I intended to weigh you down with a lengthy discussion, but to more quickly arrive at those things which will lead you to the desired matter, and faithfully apply my mind and intention on them.

#### What Is To Be Set Out In This Work

Amongst those things which pertain to this work are all the planets, and the lunar mansions (even if certain other things are considered at first, as is necessary). And as has already been said, it is necessary to consider the Moon before the other things, and it is necessary that her conjunction with the Sun be considered, and their opposition, and also their square; and then to their aspects of the others, and their corporeal conjunctions, and even the increase of the light of that luminary, and its decrease, and the slowness and fastness of her course, and her rising, ascent and descent, and likewise her setting, and also those things which seem to make for generation and corruption from her motions: since in the aforementioned times the effects of the mutations of the air, and their fallings, are apprehended more, just as will be extensively shown in the following chapters, God willing.

And Jafar said that also her similar departure and return into the south and the north, and the application of the same, and whatever things happens to the figure, the same thing will be introduced, all of which actions are easily distinguished, and her efficacy, the power of the Moon by means of begetting animals, and of the earth - which things sense perceives, and vision discerns.

# Tractate X

## I

### On The Knowledge To Be Had Of The Benefics And Malefics, And Of All Temperate Or Changing Things

If it is intended to attain a fuller knowledge of the mutation of the air, it must be known first which planets are benefic, which are malefic; and likewise you ought to know first which are now for fortune, and which are now for misfortune. For as the ancient sages unanimously confessed, and as is the truth, Jupiter and Venus are naturally benefics, and workers of fortune. Indeed, Saturn and Mars are naturally malefics, and of their own nature they bring misfortune, just as the same sages affirmed, and just as appears from the most manifest test of truth. Indeed, they said that the Sun, Mercury, and the Moon are common and temperate: namely that the Sun is sometimes benefic and sometimes malefic; but Mercury and the Moon are convertible, so that they are converted to the nature of those planets to which they apply (whether they are benefics or malefics).

## II

### To Know When Coming Rains Will Be Signified, And When Not

To have knowledge of future rains, it is necessary for you to consider the conjunction of the Sun and the Moon (as was touched on above), and to consider if one of the planets is joined with them at that time, or aspects them by any aspect. Since if Jupiter, or even Venus is corporeally joined to them, or if Jupiter aspects them from a trine or sextile aspect, and none of the malefics are placed with them, nor project their rays to them; or if Jupiter aspects the Moon after her separation from the Sun, it will undoubtedly deny future rains. However, if Jupiter aspects the luminaries from a square or opposition, without the mixture of malefics, as I said, it will signify that there will be light rain, or almost none. But if one of the malefics aspects without the aspect of a benefic, or if the Moon joins one of them first, by conjunction or opposition, after the conjunction, you will be able to announce future rains without a doubt.

For the peculiar nature of the benefics is to make the air thin, and to purify it of thick vapours, and likewise to resist the malice of malefics, and to the contrary, the malefics strive to resist the goodness of the benefics. And since the nature of their heaviness and impurity concords with the thick vapours gathered in the air, they generate heavinesses which bring a disturbance into the lower parts of the air, on account of the heaviness and the impurity of the air, and likewise they bring powerful rains descending into the thickness.

Even though Venus is one of the fortunate stars: nevertheless, since her nature inclines in a certain manner to the side of moisture, if she is mixed with one of the malefics, and one of the benefics does not assist her, she will allow rains to move: yet not very harmful rains, unless she is exceedingly weak, and strong malefics are found, so that she could shatter their malice, nevertheless she will always alleviate it to some extent.

## III

### On The Forecast Of Rains In General

However in the forecast of rains, it is necessary to apply discretion, and to consider the places, situations [in a geographical sense], seasons, climes, regions, and similar things which occur to you to be considered. For the mutations of the air are usually are diversified in diverse ways: for it usually rains (and likewise snows) more often and more strongly, in the Alps than it does in flat places, on account of the thickness of the air and the assailing of the vapours; more in the seventh clime (on account of the aforementioned reasons) than in the sixth; more in the sixth than in the fifth; more in the fifth than in the fourth; more in the fourth than in the third; more in the third than in the second; and you will understand this for each and every clime, and for each and every region according to its own nature, and according to its situation.

## IV

## Which Lunar Mansions Are Wet, Which Are Dry, And Which Are Common

You will also consider in which, and from which lunar mansions the aforementioned conjunctions and the aforementioned aspects are made. Since certain of these mansions are wet, certain are dry, and certain are common, certain are lucky or fortunate, certain are unlucky or unfortunate, just as I will explain to you in what follows.

For indeed, there are 28 of the aforementioned mansions:

The first of which is called Albarain

The second: Altamaser

The third: Aldebaran

The fourth: Albachia

The fifth: Alvata

The sixth: Alziraa

The seventh: Albiathia

The eighth: Altarfin

The ninth: Algetua

The tenth: Alaracen

The eleventh: Alzarfa

The twelfth: Alafraze

The thirteenth: Alzamee

The fourteenth: Alchafre

The fifteenth: Alzebene

The sixteenth: Aliachil

The seventeenth: Alchabin

The eighteenth: Astialia

The nineteenth: Abuaarca

The twentieth: Abelaca

The twenty-first: Azea

The twenty-second: Bolah

The twenty-third: Zacazad

The twenty-fourth: Alasboa

The twenty-fifth: Alhumadez

The twenty-sixth: Almaiehe

The twenty-seventh: Alahut

The twenty-eighth: Anathe

And each one of the mentioned mansions contains 13 degrees and 20 minutes; to which another 28 secondary mansions are subordinated (that is, enclosed in them): namely

The first is Alazelazlazenet first

The second: Agasie

The third: Azulierie

The fourth: Alchil

The fifth: Alchali

The sixth: Alzula

The seventh: Almara

The eighth: Albeldie

The ninth: Alzabel

The tenth: Alialciz

The eleventh: Zaudazaa

The twelfth: Zaudolabia

The thirteenth: Alsuganfaboel

The fourteenth: Alsurgalabet

The fifteenth: Racamavide

The sixteenth: Alnatha

The seventeenth: Albucan

The eighteenth: Alciraze

The nineteenth: Aldabaran

The twentieth: Alchada

# Tractate X

The twenty first: Aluzana

The twenty second: Alamoha

The twenty third: Alirazma

The twenty fourth: Alcaubua

The twenty fifth: Alcebira

The twenty sixth: Alararen

The twenty seventh: Alzaut

The twenty eighth: Alaacen

: just as these names are found in the translation of John.

And the secondary ones are subordinated to the aforementioned primary ones in this manner. For:

Alazelazenet is subordinated to Albaraya

Agasie is subordinated to Altamazer

Azulierie is subordinated to Aldebaran

Alchil is subordinated to Albachie

Alchali is subordinated to Alvata

Alzula is subordinated to Alziraa

Almara is subordinated to Albiathia

Albeldie is subordinated to Altharfin

Alzabel is subordinated to Algetua

Alialcim is subordinated to Alaracen

Zaudazaa is subordinated to Alzarfa

Zandolabia is subordinated to Alafraze

Alfuganfaboel is subordinated to Alzamee

Alsurgalabet is subordinated to Achafre

Racamavide is subordinated to Alzubene

Alnatha is subordinated to Aliachil

Albucan is subordinated to Alchabin

Alciraze is subordinated to Astrala

Aldabatan is subordinated to Abuaarca

Alchada is subordinated to Albelaca

Aluzana is subordinated to Bolah

Alamoha is subordinated to Azea

Alirazma is subordinated to Zacazad

Alcabua is subordinated to Alasboa

Alcebira is subordinated to Alhumadez

Alararen is subordinated to Almaiehe

Alzaut is subordinated to Alahut

Alacen is subordinated to Anathe

Twenty-Seven of which Twenty-Eight mansions with their subordinates, are counted in their effects. The twenty-eighth, namely the one in which the conjunction of the Sun and Moon happens, is not counted (even if it does operate something almost imperceptibly), but the virtue which the Moon has in that mansion, is left to the Sun, and likewise the strength of the mansion itself. Nevertheless, the Moon gives the Sun the virtue which she acquires for herself (which belongs to a planet when she is joined to him).

Of which mansions, six are dry, namely: Alzarfa, Alafraze, Alzamee, Alchabin, Alasboa, Albelaca. Of which six mansions, four are lucky and fortunate, namely: Alzarfa, Alzamee, Alchabin, and Alasboa. Indeed, the other two, namely Alafraze and Albelaca, are unlucky and unfortunate.

Indeed, nine of them are wet, namely: Altamazer, Aldebaran, Albachia, Alziraa, Albiathia, Abuaarca, Bolah, Alhumadez, and Alahut. Seven of which are lucky and fortunate, namely: Albachia, Alziraa, Albiathia, Bolah, Abuaarca, Alhumadez, Alahut. However, two are unlucky and unfortunate, namely Altamazer and Aldebaran.

Indeed, the remaining thirteen are temperate or common, which are: Albarain, Alvata, Altarfin, Algetua, Alaracen, Achafre, Aliachil, Astiala, Azea, Alzebene, Zazacad, Almaiehe, and Anathe. Out of which thirteen, six incline more to the side of fortune than misfortune, namely: Altarfin, Algetua, Alaracaren, Astiala, Azea, Zacazad. Indeed, five incline more to the side of misfortune than fortune, namely: Alvata, Achafre, Aliachil, Almaihe, Anathe. Indeed, the other two, namely

Albarain and Alzubene, remain in their own quality, not inclining more to the side of fortune or misfortune

Having considered all of these individually, you will examine in which of the aforementioned mansions both of the luminaries come together, and in what sign, and in what place of the circle, and which of the planets regard her, and to whom the Moon is first joined by body or aspect after her separation from the Sun, and in which of the mansions that planet to whom she then joins is placed. For if the conjunction of the luminaries is in a wet mansion, and in a wet sign, without the aspect or corporeal conjunction of some benefic, and the mentioned planet is in a wet sign or a wet mansion, you will be able to announce that without a doubt there will be an abundance of future rains. Nor could you resist that in any judgement; and this more greatly so if the aspect is from square or opposition, and the planet to whom she is joined is a malefic. But if it is a benefic it will mitigate the malice in a certain way. However, if the conjunction of the luminaries is as I said, and the planet to whom the Moon is joined is in a dry mansion, even if it is in a wet sign, even if he is a malefic, the rains will be somewhat more reduced; and indeed, if it is a benefic, it will be more greatly reduced. If the mansion is dry, and the sign is dry, the rains will be more greatly alleviated. But if the aforementioned conjunctions, and the aforementioned aspects are in dry signs, and dry mansions, the rains will cease entirely, whether the planet to whom the Moon joins, or who she aspects, is a benefic or a malefic, unless the planet whose dignity this mansion is, operates to the contrary. For if it is the dignity of Venus, since her nature inclines more on the side of moisture, it will assist the rain somewhat, and will temper the dryness somewhat, even if it won't be much. And the ancient sages wanted us to note all of these things diligently.

And Jafar said that they are drawn by means of a center of lines in the circles, namely those whose arcs are referred to the tetragon, trigon, and hexagon, by means of a certain condition of blessedness of knowledge. Nevertheless, the places from which the application of each of the stars is made are also strongly configured to the place of each star; that is to say, from where they apply from (I say a masculine or feminine one), that is to say, of the nature of the places related to the four

elements; even if they apply themselves from a certain longitude and latitude.

Therefore, having understood the applications of the stars from places of this kind, the agreeing and firm reception that is had shows the effects and means. The learned ancients wanted to mark and distinguish these mansions (which they called "knots", or rather "bindings"), to note them and to attend to their effects; for they wanted us to consider all of the aforementioned, so that definite judgements could be handed down on rains and mutations of the air.

## V

## On The Mutation And Variation Of The Air, And The Knowledge Of Future Rains

For the knowledge of the mutation and variation of the air (and likewise of rain) it is necessary to examine the degree of the conjunction of the luminaries, and the degree of their opposition, and I say the last degree of the first quarter, and likewise that of the second, and the middle degree of the quadrature of any lunar month, even though these four aforementioned places are secondary; and principally the degrees of the dichotomies. Indeed, it is necessary to more principally consider the conjunction and the prevention, and also certain other things which will be discussed in their own time and place (namely that other places are subject to these aforementioned places).

And these twelve are called the waxes of the Moon, which are when the Moon stands up from the degree in which her conjunction with the Sun ought to be made, by exactly 12 degrees in front or behind; but in the prevention it does not happen as necessarily; indeed, in the angles of the dichotomies it happens more often than it usually does in the prevention.

And Mecra said that this is the reason that they principally and especially wanted to note that which is called Biabene, since the two stars fill up the sign of Libra, and its figure, in every way. And he said that the Moon is snatched in the hands of Virgo, and nowhere else. Also, in the same way, since that degree where these two stars are placed is seated in the beginning of Scorpio, and the Moon will stay there as long as she walks this path: the peculiar nature of which stars they took up an introductory discussion.

Indeed, Merca preserved all of these hidden things as far as reason goes, not as far as the operative effects. And he said that as for what things are like with the rest of the lunar mansions, and the things connected to that, this business will be pursued in the following subjects; even though there was something sad about this above when I was about to speak about the natures of the mansions; and I will adjoin the opinions of individuals which pertain to this chapter in the required places. For the greater clarity of the reader I will preserve a fitting order, and I will demonstrate it in what follows, in the manner which I ought to proceed.

Indeed, Jafar listed the names of certain of the aforementioned mansions, just as is found in another translation.

For he called the first of those which signify moisture, and which have the virtue of making rain fall Aldebaran, which is called Altamazer above.

He called the second Alzama, which was called Aldebaran.

He called the third Aliabetha, which was called Albachia.

He called the fourth Alzarfa, which was called Alziraa.

He called the fifth Alzarfa, which was called Albiachia.

He called the sixth Alichil, which was called Abuaerca.

He called the seventh Auitiam, which was called Bolah.

He called the eighth Alelelach, which was called Alhumadem.

He called the ninth Alfaraz, which was called Alahut.

Six of the aforementioned mansions signify rain more greatly than the other three; and these six are: Aldebaran, Alziraa, Alialbetha, Alzarfan, Alzafra, and Alithil. Indeed, the remaining three are less wet, and signify rain less so than the aforementioned six.

Whence, if the Moon is in one of the mansions just mentioned, and especially in one of those six which I mentioned above (and this more strongly so if she is joined with, or applied with one of the stars signifying dew), you will be able to announce without a doubt that there will be future rains; but in the other three, it will be below this; and all of these things will be according to the nature of the planet to whom she is joined, or applied to.

However, if you find her in dry mansions, you will be able to announce dryness according to the aforementioned methods.

If she is in one of them which were said to be temperate or common, you will be able to judge the coming disposition of the air according to the nature of the planet to whom the Moon is joined or applied; and likewise in the three temperate ones, namely in those which Jafar called one Alanatha, another Atumech, and the third Adalaz, which incline more to dryness than to moisture.

From whichever kind of mansion the conjunction or aspect was, the effecting of the matter will be according to its nature, whether it is wet, dry, or temperate or common: and this more strongly for rains, if the aspect is from square or opposition; however, in the prohibition of rain, if it is a trine or a sextile; always considering that the benefics add in good, and reduce in the bad.

And Jafar said that for Anathe, Atarfin, Alibee, Avuala, Alnayn, and the Belly of Pisces, take up the effect, and with the rest which follow them, as it was had in the figure of rain, and it will be something to follow. And this is a table:

| | Complexion | Complexion | Complexion |
|---|---|---|---|
| ♈ | 12°15 Temp' | 14°.23' Dry | 4° Temp |
| ♉ | 8°30' Temp | 13°.36' Wet | 9° Dry |
| ♊ | 10°17' Dry | 7°.9' Temp | 13° Wet |
| ♋ | 12°25' Temp | 13°13' Dry | 5° Wet |
| ♌ | 8°14' Wet | 13°26' Temp | 9° Wet |
| ♍ | 10°17' Wet | 7°9' Temp | 13° Temp |
| ♎ | 12°51' Wet | 13°13' Wet | 5° Wet |
| ♏ | 8°9' Wet | 13°26' Dry | 9° Wet |
| ♐ | 10°17' Wet | 7°7' Wet | 13° Temp |
| ♑ | 12°51' Wet | 13°13' Temp | 5° Temp |
| ♒ | 8°34' Temp | 12°26' Dry | 10° Dry |
| ♓ | 10°17' Dry | 7°9' Dry | 13° Temp |

## VI

### A Chapter On Rains And The Mutations Of The Air

However if you wish to forecast on rains, the mutations of the air, the clouds signifying rains or drops, or on the clouds signifying neither of them, and on future winds, and likewise at what time, and what part of the year, and what hour the aforementioned things (or any of them) will occur, and of their increase or diminution, it will be necessary for you (just as Jafar attests that he heard from the most experienced of the Indians) to examine according to the position of the circle of the signs at the hour of the conjunction and prevention of the Sun and the Moon, which immediately preceded the Suns' entrance into the first minute of Libra; and the position and disposition of all the other planets in the circle, yet principally that of the luminaries.

And it is even necessary for us to consider (after the Sun has entered the first minute of Libra), his procession up until he has ambulated the whole via combusta, and another 5 degrees of Scorpio on top of this; and this happens in the middle of the seven climes, since Libra and the first 20 degrees of Scorpio have signification over rains, winds, and mutations of the air in the whole fourth clime, and likewise in the last half of the third, and in the first half of the fifth.

And they said with the Sun and the Moon having been rectified to these two hours of the meeting (I say) and opposition, or to the aforementioned two signs, therefore it will be necessary to direct our undivided attention towards the mansions to be observed. Therefore, from this point onwards the task will be to discern the mansions in this way, since wherever the luminaries' conjunction or opposition of the luminaries is, from the beginning of Aries to the end of the signs, you will give 13 degrees and 20 minutes according to equal degrees. And when you have discovered the place of the conjunction or opposition, you will see whether that mansion is dry, wet, or temperate (or common). You will even see in which mansions the rest of the planets are found, just as you considered in the case of the Moon. When you have done this, you will examine to which planet the Moon will apply, or corporeally join, after the conjunction or prevention, since according to what her conjunction or application with a planet in the circle is like, so will be her signification over rains or no rains, or winds, or moisture, or mutations of the air.

For if the Moon is joined to Saturn, or applying to him, and she is in good condition and well disposed, and in a wet mansion, likewise without any other application, you will undoubtedly be able to announce temperate and suitable rains, and likewise that the air will be completely full of dark clouds. And if Saturn is impeded or badly disposed, it will increase the rains, winds, and the darkness of the clouds, and all the aforementioned things, to the contrary of the good; and all the significations according to the places, positions, significations of the houses, mansions, conditions, conjunctions, aspects or applications, as we said above with the complexions of the lunar mansions themselves.

And if Venus and Mercury apply their testimonies and their virtues which were mentioned, the significations will be greatly increased: and this more greatly and strongly so, if their conjunction or application is in the angles, or from angles, for then the collisions of the winds will be feared, and their fury; even the ruin of certain houses, and the breaking of trees, and even the uprooting of some of them.

## VII

### On The Hour Of Rains, Heavy Rains, And Winds

However, in order to know the hour of the aforementioned events, it is necessary for you to know the hour of the conjunction (if your consideration is conjunctional), or the hour of the prevention (if your consideration is preventional), and see how many degrees the completion of the conjunction, or the application or prevention, or tetragon, is distant from the aforementioned places. Since the effecting of rains or the mutation of the air will arrive up to as many days or hours, just as the aspects, applications, or conjunctions are from such signs.

For if they are in fixed signs, it will be days. If they are in common signs, they will signify hours. If they are in mobile signs, hours: but the mobile signs will portend things to happen more quickly than the common signs. The arrival of the aforementioned things will even be hastened by one-sixth if the Moon is fast-of-course, or even if the increase of her light is not lacking. But if only one of them is there, their arrival will be hastened somewhat less than this.

However, if you find the Moon in the opposition of the degree of the conjunction or prevention, or the tetragon, or her course is slower, it will delay the arrival of the aforementioned according to the sign or place in which she is, just as was said with regards to is hastening.

Indeed, if the Moon applies to some benefic after her meeting with the Sun, and this benefic aspects Saturn from any aspect, and receives him from some dignity of his own, or Saturn receives him; and this more greatly if both of them receive each other - the aforementioned things will be altered; yet they won't exceed measure; and they will signify delay, and their arrival will be prolonged by one-sixth of the total. However, if the Moon applies to him from a square or opposition aspect (nor should it impede any of the others in the effecting of rains), a delay will not interfere with her parts,, and especially if the two aforementioned inferiors testify to them, and offer their support, as was said, so they will meet together, and not waver, and they will not even be diminished.

## VIII

### When Saturn Prohibits Rains

Indeed if Saturn is placed in a dry mansion, and the Moon applies to him while she is in a dry mansion, and none of the others offer their support, rains will not arrive, even if constant clouds greatly disturb the air.

## IX

### On The Application Of The Moon With Jupiter

And if the Moon applies to Jupiter from the aforementioned or similar places, or is with him in the same place or mansion (one which is wet), and Venus and Mercury present their testimonies, clouds with moisture and soft rain (or practically no rain), will be signified. However, if Venus and Mercury do not present their testimony to them, the rain will cease completely. But if one of them helps them, and the other doesn't, something of the matter of rain will occur, even if it will only be a moderate amount. And if

Jupiter then applies to Saturn, it will signify a fraction of the aforementioned (but not an amount exceeding measure), is going to come.

But if the Moon applies to Mars from the aforementioned places or mansions, after her separation from the Sun, and Venus or Mercury aspects them, with the testimony of any masculine planet, and such an application is in an angle or from an angle, and in a wet mansion, or from a wet mansion, it will signify a gathering and mixture of clouds; but, it will portend little moisture, or almost none. However, it could signify thunder and flashes, and even lightning without a multitude of rain in the regions suited for this, provided that Mars is then applying to Saturn or Jupiter: since if he is then applied to them, it will indicate future rains.

And Jafar said that this even presents itself to be noted, since Mars greatly increases the signification of rain from any aspect; and the Moon and the stars to which he applies, assist the generation of rain altogether; for is a delay already, especially and principally by this. And he said that if something else happens, he will not signify this, and the same thing corrupts; however, the clouds which are produced by the Martial nature have saffron radiance from above, and are not without a dazzling whiteness.

## X

### On The Application Of The Moon With Mars

Again, if the Moon applies to Mars and Saturn at the same time after receding from her conjunction with the Sun, and she is placed in a wet mansion, and those planets are also placed in a wet mansion, it will portend immoderate future rains. That if she only approaches one of them (or both of them) and things are like so with her, and they are in temperate mansions, it will signify rains. Indeed, if she is placed in a wet mansion, and those two are placed in dry mansions, or vice versa, it will mitigate most of the future rains.

Likewise if the Moon is joined to the Sun, and is then joined to Jupiter at the same time, or is joined to him by aspect, and one or both of them are receiving her, they will prohibit the rain from remaining so that it does not overflow.

And Jafar said that if the Moon is precisely in an optimal place then, namely one of the centres, places, that is, in places dedicated to this signification, so that she is made fortunate, it would cancel her peculiar nature and overthrow her command, for as long she agrees with a benefic in some configuration. And he said that therefore these general occasions are always to be noted. And he said that even the white clouds that will be generated at that time will portend much and inconstant moisture.

## XI

## On The Application Of The Moon With The Sun

And if you find the Moon corporeally connected with the Sun, and none of the other planets are looking at them, or corporeally joined to them, it will prohibit rains from arriving. If one of the others are then applying to them, and this planet in a wet mansion (and this more so if this is in an angle), and the Sun is outside of his own dignities and his fortitudes, and he applies to Saturn and Mars at the same time (or separates from one of them, and applies to the other) it will announce strong rains to occur. However, if he only applies to one of them, and is not separating from the other, the signified rain will be one half, one-third, or at least one-quarter, less than the aforementioned; and in these aforementioned cases it will bring in dense clouds between grey, saffron, and semi-red, which are not quickly dissolved;, but after they are dissolved, they will announce the air to be slight and serene air. Indeed, if the Moon after her separation (whether they are joined by body or aspect) applies to the Sun from a triangle, it will come into act according to the nature of the houses or mansions in which their significations are. And Jafar said that in no way is the conjunction and opposition called an application.

## XII

## On The Application Of The Moon With Venus

However if the Moon applies to Venus after her separation from the Sun, and she is in a water sign, or an air sign (but air signs less so) and in wet mansions, it will announce rain to come without a doubt; and this more greatly, and certainly, and infallibly, if Mars and Saturn aspect them. But if only one of them aspects them, their signification will be something below this, nor will it be necessary for Mercury to offer any assistance in any of the aforementioned cases; but if he does offer it, he will increase the future rains. But if the aforementioned malefics do not aspect them, but Jupiter aspects them, or if she is otherwise made fortunate, without a doubt the rains will cease, nor will they come. However, if Venus applies to one of the three superiors in the same knot and if nothing else impedes Venus significations, it will portend constant (And not a moderate amount) of rain to come. And the aforementioned things will more strongly occur, if their application is from a wet mansion, or from a water sign. But if Venus is free, fortunate, and strong, and the Moon is not found joined to her in the same knot, and she is not in a water sign, or a wet mansion, or even a temperate mansion, this will signify that the aforementioned rains will not happen. For indeed, if Venus (as was said) conducts herself in this manner, and the Moon is joined to her in the same way, there will not be rain, but clouds and some moisture will appear in the air.

## XIII

## On The Application Of The Moon With Mercury

Again, you must examine if the Moon, when is joined with the Sun (or when she is separated from the Sun after the conjunction) applies to Mercury first in the same place, and in a wet mansion, without the aspect or conjunction of another planet: since it will indicate continual rain without a delay in time. If she is joined to him, you will be able to announce for certain that they will come, but not exceeding measure.

Indeed, if Mars and Saturn testify to their conjunction at the same time, it will announce without a doubt that there will be horrendous, submerging, constant, and threatening rains. But if Venus up to now is a participant in this conjunction from any of her dignities, it will be to be doubted if the rains will not exceed the measure in the aforementioned places.

However, if at the hour of the conjunction of the Moon with the Sun, Mercury applies to Venus in the same place, knot, water sign, and wet mansion, it will indicate rain exceeding measure. Indeed, if you find the aforementioned being from other signs and mansions, you will be able to announce moderate rains for certain.

And Tilcinius said that if Mercury regards Venus from water signs and wet mansions, or placed in the same knot or joining, the rain will exceed measure. However, if Jupiter or another one of the benefics (yet Jupiter more strongly), then aspects the aforementioned malefics, you will judge mediocre rains. And if Mercury alone is applying to the Moon, and he signifies moisture and rain, and Jupiter is aspecting him with reception for him from his own domicile or exaltation, or from two other dignities, Mercury will take the nature and significations of Jupiter for himself, and he would not permit the Moon to exercise her own significations; and he will bring in serene air, however, with a multitude of winds; and the quality of these winds shall be according to the nature of Jupiter or of another star, to whose nature he is applied, if you find him transformed and applying to some other planet.

However, if the Moon, after her separation from the Sun, applies to Mercury and Venus at the same time, before any of the other aforementioned places, or even to Mars and Saturn, as was said, they will overthrow the significations of the Moon, and manifest their own; unless, I say, Jupiter and the Sun operate to the contrary from whatever aforementioned aspect or conjunction this will occur: and this more strongly and infallibly, if the conjunction is with the aforementioned malefics - for the rain and moisture will be increased, and likewise the air will be made cloudy. And if the aforementioned benefics operate to the contrary, they will cancel the aforementioned moisture and rains, yet they will not be able to prohibit the clouds from being present. And you may remember, to by no means forget the aforementioned things, but always keep them in the secret places of your mind, so that you will be able to respond eagerly, and likewise to know and foresee them for your own utility.

## XIV

## On The Application Of The Moon With The Benefics Or Malefics

However if the Moon applies to one of the benefics after her separation from the Sun, it will prohibit the coming rains. If she is joined to one of the malefics, or aspects them from whatever aspect, and her application departs from this malefic up to 5 degrees or less without the aspect of one of the benefics, it will announce future rains in the same week.

I say that if the Moon is joined to one of the planets after her separation from the Sun, and this happens in a wet mansion, or even in some other one of the places of the circle, and she is not impeded, nor received by any planet, it will signify that the air will become moist, and clouds, moisture, diverse rains, and the sky to be filled with clouds; and indeed, the incitement of diverse winds, and sometimes will make the cause of flashes and lightning.

Indeed, if after this the Moon applies to some planet who makes her fortunate, or who is fortunate himself, it will amend all of the aforementioned things, and convert them to their contrary. However, if this planet is a malefic, or is made unfortunate, the aforementioned things will be increased, and will be increased to such an extent that they appear to be doubled. But if she is unfortunate, and in bad condition, and badly disposed, she will be found stronger in observing the strong promises of the malefics; nor will she torment another from this. And even though from these things which are said now, and were said in the past, it should be held more clearly, that the Moon is converted to the nature of that planet to whom she is applied (and this is true); nevertheless until now it did not appear that I should omit to tell you again, that if she is with benefics, or other stars who are applied to benefics (as was said), or if she is there without any impediments of the benefics in their dignities (as was said), it will not make the rain stay (even if it does not resist them). But if she is applying to malefics, just as was said with benefics, it will announce future rains.

And Jafar said, explaining the general influence of the Moon with individual stars (such as in Aligistivia), that is explaining the meeting, that in those things which seem necessary to have for the knowledge of this, the which things written above, I have devised in a suitable order; therefore, next it will be explained how it ought to be done in the opposition and tetragon.

## XV

## On The Four Tetragons, Or The Four Quarters, Or The Four Figures

In this matter it is necessary to principally examine seven places in the circle, namely the degree of the conjunction of the luminaries, its tetragons (which are distant from it, one in front, another behind, by 90 degrees), and the degree of its opposition, and the degrees of its quarters.

The first of which is in the beginning of the month up to seven days, and this is the first quarter.

The second is from the mentioned seven days up to another seven, and this is the second quarter, and is even the degree of the prevention.

The third is from those fourteen days up to another seven (namely twenty-one), and this is the third quarter.

The fourth is after these twenty-one days up to the following conjunction, which is the fourth quarter.

Secondarily you ought to examine another ten places outside of the aforementioned ones:

The first of which is three days before the conjunction of the Moon with the Sun.

The second is three days after it.

The third is three days before the first quarter.

The fourth is three days after it.

The fifth is three days before the prevention.

The sixth is three days after the prevention.

The seventh is three days before the second quarter.

The eight is three days after it.

The ninth is 12 degrees before the opposition

And the tenth is the same after it.

Whence, if in three days after the conjunction, around evening you see her fine and bright, and shining, without a cover of clouds, and she is not otherwise impeded by malefics, it will signify serene air for as long as she stays in that sign. That if she is fine, and her colour inclining to redness, and the parts of her which are illuminated are shining, and likewise that she almost appears to be quivering or moving, it will signify winds are going to come from that direction towards which she seems to incline.

If the Sun is then placed in Capricorn or Aquarius, and the Moon is found in Taurus or Virgo, and she has any meeting with Saturn, then the occurrence of cold winds will come, and this more strongly so if Saturn is found in Capricorn. However, if she inclines to the side of blackness, or almost greenishness, with some density, or undoubted thickness, it will indicate clouds threatening rain, and even rain. However, in the other aforementioned places, you will announce the future disposition of the air according to the signs, and according to the mansions, and according to the conjunctions or aspects of the planets with her.

## XVI

### To Know The Qualities Which Are Prolonged By More Than One Day

That if you wish to foreknow the qualities of the air which are prolonged for more than one day, as Ptolemy said, you will consider the hours of the connections of the luminaries in the figure: since for every quality of the figure which is from this hour of that figure up until the hour which follows it in the figure, it will signify for the majority. Moreover, it appeared to have seemed to Ptolemy that we ought to consider the hour and minute of the conjunction of the luminaries, and erect a figure for the Ascendant of this minute, and establish the four angles, and see which of the planets is stronger at that time over the Ascendant: since he will rule over the disposition of the air up until the Moon arrives to the next angle of the mentioned figure (namely the second one); and the air will be disposed according to how that Almutem is disposed, unless something else operates to the contrary, which will be necessary for you to consider by your own industry, by considering the things which were said above, and those things which are still to be said.

You will also consider when the Moon will enter the first minute of the mentioned angle, and you will see which one of the planets is the Almutem over the Ascendant at that time: since he will rule over the disposition of the air up until the Moon arrives to the third angle of the mentioned figure of the conjunction, which will be disposed according to the disposition of the Almutem of this Ascendant. Again, you will examine to see when the Moon will enter the first minute of the degree which will be opposite to the degree of the designated conjunction: since according to how the Almutem of this Ascendant is disposed, so will the air be well disposed or badly disposed, up until the Moon arrives to the first minute of the fourth angle of the mentioned figure (provided that nothing else operates to the contrary).

Afterwards you will consider when the Moon arrives to the minute in which the aforementioned conjunction was: since then the air will be disposed according to how the planet who is the Almutem over the Ascendant at that time is disposed, up until the Moon arrives to the minute of the following conjunction, unless something else operates to the contrary - namely that one of the malefics impedes the mentioned Almutem, or if the Almutem himself is in a mansion or sign contrary to the nature of any of the aforementioned Ascendants, and similar things: or even if the season operates to the contrary, namely adding or detracting, according to what Ptolemy testifies, just like if that lunar month is in summer, and the significators (namely signifying moisture or rain), wherefore the rain and moisture will abound less. However, if it is winter, and the significators are signifying little moisture, more rain will follow from this than appears to be signified, and vice versa.

Indeed, Hali appeared to have said that Ptolemy divided the lunar month into just four divisions, namely according to the four quarters: but if I remember correctly, what is explained above is enough.

And always make the Moon a participator with the Almutem of the Ascendant of each of the aforementioned angles, according to how you find her in the places, mansions or signs (whether dry, wet, or common).

Moreover it is necessary for you to attend to the condition of the Sun and the Moon, when the Sun enters the first minute of Libra (from this minute up until he has passed through the 20th degree of Scorpio), and see what kind of condition he has, whether with benefics or malefics; and in what kind of mansion the Moon is running through at that time, and likewise in what kind of sign, and the positions the other planets, and with which one of them the luminaries are applied, since the air will be disposed according to those significations which are at that time, up until the Suns' entrance into Aries - yet with the admixture of the significations which were met with in the connections of the luminaries up until this time.

And Jafar said that if you completely execute those things which I put down you will meet with variations or ambiguities concerning the renewal of the air.

Likewise, it is to be examined whether the Moon is running through a dry or equal mansion, and applying to Venus or Mercury; or, as Jafar attests, is placed in water signs and applying to Saturn or Mars: for she will indicate future rains. And he said that the Moon and Mercury are stars signifying moisture. Likewise he said that therefore if they are regarding the Moon from signs of this kind, or staying in them, and even if the Moon applies to them from places of this kind, it will signify rains. And he said that the Moon applying or regarding from dry or equal places, on the whole will cause mediocre rains. Likewise he said that the Moon by her own peculiar and unique nature brings forth white and thin clouds and fog.

## XVII

### On What The Circles Which Are Around The Moon And The Sun, And Likewise Around The Other Stars, Both Wandering And Non-Wandering, Bring About

However, it is necessary to attend to the circle which is made around the Moon, to see whether there is one or more. However, if there is only one, and it is thin and bright and of little durability, and it moves back step by step and goes into hiding, it will signify serene weather, and clear and pure air. Indeed, if there are more than one, they will signify winter wind. But if they are inclining to a bright red, and almost appear to be in pieces and cut off, they will indicate the disturbance of the air from wherever it comes to be, on the occasion of winds. Indeed, if they are clouded with thickness, and dark, it will portend the disturbance of the air cold, winds, and snow.

And Ptolemy said that if they incline to a black greenness, they will signify winter air which happens for both reasons (namely by winds, cold, and snows). And he said that if the circles are many, the significations will be many, according to what we said before.

And Ptolemy said that if a circle will appear around the wandering and shining non-wandering stars, it will signify by way of similarity those things by means of the colours of their circles, and of the stars which they enclose.

And he said that it is even fitting for us to observe the non-wandering stars, as are the Pleiades, Alfecta, and ones similar to these, and of the stars in which many stars approach each other; and we should look at the collections of the erratic ones, their colours, and apprehend their quantity or number. For if they appear of greater light and greater quantity appear than usual, they signify

blowing winds to come from the direction in which they are stationed. You will be able to say the same about certain other stars which are called Praesepe, and similar ones to these, which appear almost cloudy: which, if they appear while the air is serene, almost spreading, or decreased in light and thick (just as Ptolemy attests), they will indicate the disturbance of the air and a multitude of rains. But if you see them inclining to splendour and clarity, you will be able to announce strong future winds. And Ptolemy said that even the method of those of the appearances of the other signs, which happen to take place in some season is the same

## XVIII

### On Comets And Tailed Stars

Indeed the comets which are called "tailed", when they appear, will signify winds and the dryness of the air, especially if they appear almost cloudy; and the strength of their significations will be according to the multitude and scarcity of them, and their length or shortness.

## XVIV

### On Shooting Stars

With shooting stars you will examine in serene weather, to see when they are seen, and if the stars fell when they are moved: and from whichever direction they are moved and shoot from, they will announce that the blowing of winds is going to come from that direction; and by how much more and thick the shootings are, by that much more will their significations will be increased and hastened. However, if they are from different directions, they will portend disordered winds to come from here and there. But if you see such significations appear everywhere, they will portend disturbances of the air everywhere, and likewise thunder and flashes will be looked for from this, and will happen from it. You will almost be able to say the same thing if you see clouds similar to light wisps of wool.

## XXV

### On The Significations Of Diurnal And Nocturnal Qualities

In the investigation of diurnal and nocturnal qualities, it is necessary for us to consider the body of the Sun in that hour and that minute, when he begins to appear above the horizon, and to understand well and examine whether his body rises bright and shining: since if this is so, it will indicate serene weather that day. But if you see the contrary, you will be able to judge the contrary. However, when he sets, it seems that the same should be forecasted concerning the qualities of the weather of the night. If his body is of diverse colours, as Ptolemy says, or inclining to a fiery red, or the Suns' rays which proceed from him, or are around him, are red, or if the clouds which surround him incline to red on account of excessive clarity, and his rays are extended very far, and separated from each other outside of the circle, they will signify the strongest of winds, whose blowings will proceed from the angles in which those signs (which were discussed) appear in: which if they ascend to blackness, or decline to greenishness in clouds, or if there are one or two circles around him, or around they have clouds which are called "Suns" around themselves, and their rays are inclining to greenness, or black, they will indicate wintry air and rains.

## XXII

### On The Rainbow, If It Were To Appear, And In What Times, And What It Would Signify

You should even examine the rainbow, and see in what weather it will appear, and in what seasons its apparition will be. For if it appears in serene weather, and this serenity is not of a long time and great dryness (since then its signification will not be as necessary), however, it will hardly or ever be mistaken, since it will signify either wintry air or rains. And this will happen since the vapours which were thin, will begin to thicken: since most of the time, in fact always, the rainbow will not appear unless the vapours are rarefied or thickened. However, if the winter season is serene, it will demonstrate that it is going to be a serene time, since the vapours then begin to be rarefied, dried out, and annulled, as Ptolemy said.

We will generally add that for the most part, the peculiar colours which appear in the air will signify qualities similar to the accidents signified by the aforementioned colours.

## XXIII

### On The Investigation Of The Year, If There Ought To Be Much Rains

However if you care to know whether a year will be rainy, as was touched on above, you will consider the entrance of the Sun into the first minute of Libra, and what his condition is like, up until he has traversed past the twentieth degree of Scorpio. You will also examine what the condition of the Moon is like with the other stars in these times, since the signification of this year will be taken from them. Therefore, you will also examine in this entrance, to see which of the planets the Moon is first joined to corporeally or by aspect: since if this planet is oriental, just as Jafar attests, it will indicate that the end of the year, month, or week will be rainy. However, if this planet is occidental, it will declare benefit for the beginning of the aforementioned rains: yet this application (particularly when it is made with Venus or Mercury) will signify the aforementioned things. But if she is applied to them with one of them oriental, and the other occidental, from the middle, it will demonstrate common and great rains to come throughout the whole year.

And he said that the said multitude of rains particularly threaten while Venus and Mercury hasten to enter Scorpio, Capricorn, Aquarius, and Pisces, And I say this more strongly so, if their application is from wet places or mansions, with the Moon placed in them. Which if they are had in this way, they show general, yet useless, rains. And if the Moon is applying to another planet, who regards her by a noted aspect, for as long as such an application lasts, and to the completion of the application, or aspect or conjunction, the multitude of rains will cease.

## XXIV

### On The Application Of The Moon With Saturn And With The Rest Of The Planets

Ptolemy said that if the Moon is applying to Saturn, it signifies that soft and pleasant, or temperate rains are going to come, unless Mars or Mercury operate to the contrary.

For indeed, Jupiter characteristically has serene air and winds; also, he does not otherwise help the adjoinings of the rest of the stars. Should there be a community or admixture of bodies, as is said above, he will show efficacy, but even the influences and alternating colours of clouds, and variations of the air. With these things having been weighed first, it will be allowed to look through the whole year.

If the Moon is applying to Mars, it will signify clouds between saffron and red, having radiance from above; and thunder and flashes, and even lightning in seasons suitable for this: unless Jupiter operates to the contrary. But if you observe her applied to the Sun, it will indicate saffron clouds, and rains having great drops of water. However, if the Moon applies to Venus, it will generate soft and continuous rains, and much moisture, almost similar to clouds. However, if the Moon is applied with Mercury, it will demonstrate savage winds and rains, and their severity, and likewise diverse and scattered clouds, and ones similar to smoke.

## XXV

### On Certain Extraordinary Things

There are certain other extraordinary things, which I do not remember finding in the sayings of any of the philosophers, but I saw them to be often, and mostly truth-speaking, and this will especially have a place in the whole of the sixth clime, and on the edge of the fifth, and in the south of the seventh.

Namely when the Sun sets (even if in other parts the air might appear clear and the weather serene), and where his body sets there are clouds almost like a cloth [Mappa], it will signify that there will be rains or winds, or both, in the same night, or on the following day. For if this cloth is thick, and likewise dense, and in addition to this the air is clear, and the weather is serene, it will usually indicate winds. Indeed, if some small cloud, almost like *lictura* is next to the cloth, almost like the matizotius of paintings, it will indicate rains. But if he sets in serene air, and the air appears red from after his setting up to the completion of dusk, it signifies that there will be serene weather to come in the same night, and likewise in the following day.

And Christianus said that you will consider what kind of weather there is on the second day of Subat, since up until the entrance of the Sun into Aries, you will expect the contrary of the weather which is at that time.

And Gerardus said that you should see when thick and dark clouds from the direction of the north (right under the arctic pole, or inclining somewhat to the western direction) are contiguous with the horizon: since then it will rain almost immediately. But if a small mountain of clouds almost like the bed of a river, appear from the same direction, and they are separated from the horizon, they will signify the harmonising of the air. Likewise, if you see the flashings in the same direction at a late hour, it will show the disturbance of the air is near, in such a way that its arrival of this disturbance will not be easily prolonged beyond eight days, unless great dryness operates to the contrary.

And Alanus said that you will also examine if the clouds opposite to the plain, and especially opposite to the north, seek higher mountains: since it will be a sign for rain to come in the same day, or the following day at the latest. The same will usually happen when thick and dense rains surround the peaks of mountains, announcing that winds are going to come at that time. And the aforementioned things will more strongly occur, if the clouds are extended from an eastern or northern wind. However, if the clouds seek the plains from the mountains, you will announce that it is a sign of the alleviation of the air and its improvement (unless a lot of moistness operates to the contrary); and much more so if it is moved by a western wind.

And there is another accident, which often, in fact which most of the time, I have seen to speak truly: that if a rainbow appears in the morning, then it indicates rain, unless great dryness of the air operates to the contrary. However, if it appears around evening, then the weather will be made serene, unless great moisture of the air operates to the contrary. Even when a great and closely compacted thickness of stars, or the greatest thinness appears, then an alteration of the air will be signified in a short space of time. These accidents, even though they are often true, nevertheless they are not necessary.

## XXVI

### On The Accidents Whose Durations Will Be Prolonged For A Little While

In accidents whose durations will be prolonged, I think you will examine the Sun, for if you see him in the southern direction, and Venus is hidden under his rays, and the Moon is applying to them, or either of them (and especially Venus), by conjunction or aspect; you will announce rain to come on the same day, and also in the same hour, and its minute, in which such a conjunction happens in that land.. You will be able to say the same if you find Mercury in the southern direction with the application of the Moon; or if she is not applying to him by conjunction, but is joined to him diametrically opposite him: and this more strongly if the Moon is found in Scorpio at the time. You will be able to say the same if Mars and Venus are found together in Scorpio.

And moreover, Jafar said that if the Sun is in Aquarius, and the Moon is applying to him, or placed in his opposition, and Venus is in the same place, rains will be present in that hour. And in the same way he said that if Mars or Venus are applying to the Sun, and the Moon running through their opposition or square, provided that Venus is burnt, makes the judgement of rains certain. Indeed, if Venus applies to the Sun, as was said, and Mercury is conjoined to her, or at least they are joined to Venus, it will announce rains to come on the same day. Moreover, if you find the Sun in Libra, but Venus in Sagittarius, and the Moon is joined to them (and especially to Venus) minute for minute, it will indicate that there will be rains on the same day in the land where you are. But if the Sun is in Aquarius, or in his exaltation, and the Moon is placed in Leo, it will indicate that many rains are going to come on the day and hour of their conjunction or application. You will be able to judge the same about Sagittarius as I said about Leo, since according to the testimonies of the authors, the images are said to be of a river. However, Leo still causes a greater multitude of

rains than Sagittarius, and likewise makes them thicker, and the same usually happens in the first face of Taurus. However, even though Sagittarius does not make as much rain, it still makes the drops of water thicker And the aforementioned things will more strongly and certainly occur, if the Sun is in Sagittarius, or if he aspects it, and the Moon aspects Mercury, or applies to him, and he pursues Venus, and their efficacy will be made known on that same day. Similar things to the aforementioned will be generated in the domiciles of Mars and in the domiciles of Venus: large raindrops, flashes, thunder, and hailstones will appear.

And Jafar said that when the Sun is running through Pisces or Aries, and the Moon is placed in Virgo, Libra, or Sagittarius (namely in vaporous places), it will bring in an abundance of rains on that same day. Again, if Venus and Mercury are joined to the Sun in one of the aforementioned places outside of Leo, and the Moon applies to them (and this more greatly so if the application is from Leo), it will indicate flashes and thunder, even though it will be with little rain, or almost none. And this more so, if the Sun is right opposite to any of them, whether this planet is direct or retrograde (but retrograde is found more greatly joined). However, if the Sun is in Aquarius, Aries, Leo, Libra, or Scorpio, and the Moon is directly opposite to him or Venus, namely minute for minute, after the rain or raindrops it will signify luminous flashes, and likewise thunder. And this more strongly so if the Moon is exposed before her from Leo: since then, in addition to the flashes and thunder, if the air is disposed for this, it will signify generative lightning bolts.

And according to Albumashar the Thracian [or the fierce] the said things will also take place in a like manner in the regions subject to the equinoctial line in the second clime, they will be mediocre in the third and the fourth, and more relaxed in the fifth and sixth. But if you find the Sun or the Moon in Pisces, and Mars aspects them from a square or opposition without the support of any benefic, they will signify an abundance of rain, lightning, thunder, and flashes. And the Thracian said that even the Sun is in Aries or Scorpio, and the Moon in Leo in the meeting of the Sun, prefigures the same.

## XXVII

### On The Consideration Of The Places Of Rains

Even if you have understood the other aforementioned considerations, nevertheless you should not forget to consider the places of rains (which are Cancer, Leo, Capricorn, and Aquarius). Whence if you find the Moon in one of these signs, and she is applying to Venus by body or by any aspect (and especially from square or opposition), you will announce that there will be rains: and this more greatly so, if their conjunction is completed before, minute for minute, one degree or below. However, the first half of Capricorn is less unfortunate than the preceding ones: indeed, the latter half signifies more coldness than rain. However, you will consider all of these things with discernment.

## XXVIII

### On The Signs And Places Signifying Less Rain Than The Aforementioned Places And Signs

However, there are certain other places in certain signs signifying less rain than the aforementioned: and these are the last terms of Aries (and this on account of a certain moisture which is found in these terms); and Gemini, Virgo, and Libra are also places signifying fewer rains.

## XXIX

### In The Conjunction Of Which Planets Rains Are Signified

However if after the conjunction, the Moon immediately joins Mercury, Venus, and Mars, or one of them, by body or aspect, unless Jupiter speaks to the contrary, it will announce that rains are going to come. However, if she applies to Mars or Venus, it signifies that rain will happen on the same day. If she applies to Mercury it will follow the footsteps of that planet to whom Mercury adheres.

## XXX

### If You Wish To Know Whether Some Month Will Be Rainy Or Not

However if you want to forecast whether there are future rains in some month, you will erect a figure in the beginning of whichever one of them, and you will adapt the twelve cusps to it, and you will consider the hour and the minute of the meeting of the Sun and the Moon, and you will see which of planets regards them at that time, or to whom they apply, and from what places, and from what mansions that application is from. Since if they apply to stars bringing in rain, and do so from wet mansions, it will indicate wintry rain. However, if they aspect planets signifying rains from dry places, their significations will be below the aforementioned by one-third, or at least one-fourth.

You will also examine to see if Venus is joined with Saturn, and this more greatly so if Venus transfers the light of Mars, Mercury, or Jupiter: since then you will be able to announce that there will undoubtedly be future rains. And if apart from this the aforementioned planets have application with the Sun, they will indicate some kind of rains, since the nature of the Sun in this case inclines more to moisture than to dryness. You will also consider if the Sun and Venus run in the same knot, and are in s mansion of the nature of one of them, and in addition to this, one or both of them are joined to one of the stars ruling the place which they occupy, and this star is in a good place of the figure, and the star receives the planet joining it: for if this is so, without a doubt rain will be signified.

Moreover, if the Moon transits the degree of her conjunction with the Sun, and is joined to Jupiter and Mercury at the same time (or one of them), in a water or air sign; and this more greatly so if she is in the southern direction; and this more strongly so if reception intervenes between the aforementioned planets - great rains will be indicated, nor will they be contradicted in any way.

## XXVI

## On The Conjunction Of The Moon With Planets, And On The Conjunction Of The Other Planets Individually To Each Other

In the forecasting of rains you will examine to see if one of the interior planets is joined with one of the superior planets in the southern direction, and one of the inferiors is applied to by to one of the superiors, and one of the inferiors to one of the superiors: since immediately when the aforementioned inferior planet is separated from the superior, rain will be expected necessarily.

And Albumashar, who was the most experienced of the ancient astrologers, examining the places, yet taking care to attend to the names, whose discernment is as follows: as many times as the Moon goes away from Venus, the signification of rains is led back to profit.. And he said that the Moon going away from Mercury and applying to Jupiter or the Sun, or vice versa, no other judgement is at hand. And he said that these things however, are individual and made known, and certain things of the openings of the planets which are named suitably enough. And therefore he said that the opposition of those stars from the third clime to the fourth, flows with its own rains towards the southern direction, and the significations of rains happen all together from the same direction.

And again, Jafar said, that those things which were said with regards to the opposition in the signs which signify waters, the application having been made (namely in their degrees) and the meeting, or perhaps the regarding being unobserved, with the Moon in her own domicile applying to Saturn, it will bring in manifold rains.

# FINIS